Small Screen, Big Picture

Small Screen, Big Picture

Television and Lived Religion

Diane Winston
Editor

BAYLOR UNIVERSITY PRESS

Cover Design by Nicole Weaver, Zeal Design.
Cover Images: "Televisions stacked on top of one another," Photographer
Gary Cornhouse. Used by permission of Getty Images. SAVING GRACE
©2007 Twentieth Century Fox Film Corporation, All Rights Reserved.
Used by permission. John From Cincinnati is a service mark of Home Box
Office, Inc. Used by permission. "Lost" cast photo ©American Broadcasting
Companies, Inc. Used by permission.

Library of Congress Cataloging-in-Publication Data

Small screen, big picture : television and lived religion / Diane Winston,
editor.
    p. cm.
 Includes bibliographical references and index.
 ISBN 978-1-60258-185-2 (pbk. : alk. paper)
 1. Television broadcasting--Religious aspects. 2. Religion on television.
I. Winston, Diane H., date-

 PN1992.6.S58 2009
 791.45'682--dc22

                          2008029712

Printed in the United States of America on acid-free paper.

Contents

SECTION II: NEITHER MALE NOR FEMALE

SECTION III: REVELATION

Acknowledgments

Among the many colleagues deserving of thanks for this collection, three stand out: Carey Newman, Jane Iwamura, and Liza Baker. As director of Baylor University Press, Carey has been responsible for the development and production of *Small Screen, Big Picture: Television and Lived Religion.* The consummate muse, advocate, and go-to guy, he transformed an arduous process into an invigorating journey. The idea for writing about religion and television was his, and after that initial inspiration, he was generous with intellectual, emotional, and financial support. Likewise, we are indebted to Jane Iwamura who helped shape the book and gave editorial guidance for many contributors. Jane also served as a technical guru, linking us online so that the book would have greater coherence. Last but not least, Liza Baker kept us on track, monitoring deadlines, overseeing finances, and supervising technical support. In making sure we all got our jobs done, Liza took on extra work for herself.

Additional thanks go to Rene Aubuchon, Lisa Bitel, Doris Egan, Marie Feudo, Tom Fontana, Elizabeth Klaviter, Ethan Rieff, Ali Siegler, and Cyrus Voris. I also am deeply grateful to the writers and producers who graciously visited my classes to discuss the role of religion, ethics and spirituality in their work: Barbara Hall, David Milch, Nancy Miller, Ronald D. Moore, Kamran Pasha, David Shore, David Simon, and John Tinker (their lectures are available on http://uscmediareligion.org/).

I have been privileged to work with and learn from all the book's contributors: S. Elizabeth Bird, Sheila Briggs, Vincent Brook, Rudy V. Busto, Anthea Butler, Lynn Schofield Clark, Marcia Dawkins, Craig Detweiler, Lanita Jacobs-Huey, Heather Hendershot, Amir Hussain, Leonard Norman Primiano, Horace Newcomb, Adele Reinhartz, and Elijah Siegler. This interdisciplinary group, few of whom had written about religion and television before we began together, enthusiastically embraced the topic and produced pioneering essays. I also am grateful for my students in "Religion, Media, and Hollywood: Faith in TV," whose mix of gusto and insight continues to inspire me. Their delight in using television for intellectual pursuits and their openness to what constitutes religion are contagious.

The professionals at Baylor—Diane Smith, Jennifer Hannah, and Elisabeth Wolfe among them—contributed mightily to making this a smart and beautiful book. Also instrumental to the book's sense and sensibility has been Nick Street, whose editorial interventions helped the prose to sing. As always, friends and family have provided a strong baseline for support, patiently listening as I have tried to explain why I seem to watch so much television.

This book is dedicated to Chris Bugbee, my beloved companion in all things. Chris has supplemented my reading, polished my writing, and encouraged my wildest flights of fancy. He has also watched countless hours of television with me, happily discussing and debating what we have seen. I also dedicate this to my youngest daughter, Isabelle—who already sees more in *Hannah Montana* than meets the eye.

Introduction

Diane Winston

The year 2000, and more precisely the tragic events of 9/11, provide a natural starting point for examining popular discourse on religion, ethics, and spirituality. The confluence of George Bush's presidency (i.e., the candidate who named Jesus Christ as his favorite political philosopher) and the political ascendancy of the Religious Right; the coalescence and deployment of political Islam; and growing concerns about climate change begat an acute apocalyptic sensibility among true believers and a heightened sense of anxiety among everyone else.

Americans felt vulnerable: catastrophe could strike at any moment. Subsequently, moral choices blurred: Was phone-tapping justifiable? Racial profiling? Waterboarding? Questions of agency arose, too: If politicians and generals could not protect us, who would? And consider the metaphysics of death: if the worst did occur, what lay beyond the veil?

These and similar concerns have dominated public forums, town halls, classrooms, church basements, and news outlets for several years. But they also have found dramatic expression on television; coinciding with the expansion of the bandwidth—and myriad cable and premium options—the number of new series exploring issues of meaning, morality, and identity has exploded. Programs took different tacks. Some spilt a lot of blood; others focused on crime and punishment; still others fantasized about cheating death. Some were supernatural; others explored professional ethics; still others pushed the seemingly tenuous line between good and evil.

This volume looks at some of those shows. Whether or not you agree with Jack Bauer, Gregory House, or Laura Roslin that torture is justified, or science trumps religion, or humanity must be saved at any cost, the characters' problems—set within the yin and yang of personal drama and real-world dilemmas—bring ethical and religious dimensions to the day-to-day routines on *24*, *House*, and *Battlestar Galactica*. Calling television a religious text may strike readers as oxymoronic, but *Small Screen, Big Picture: Television and Lived Religion* argues to the contrary: watching television is a link in the chain of sacred storytelling, a latter-day version of Western traditions, such as hearing scriptures, "reading" stained glass windows, or absorbing a Passion Play.

Our contention is that television converts social concerns, cultural conundrums, and metaphysical questions into stories that explore and even shape notions of identity and destiny—the building blocks of religious speculation. Aptly reflecting life in a time of fear and uncertainty, many of these stories echo religious, spiritual, and ethical predicaments: Why am I here? How can I make a difference? What happens when I die? Television brings questions of ultimate meaning into the home, linking viewers through a network of oral (as opposed to print-based) "sensemaking."[1] Media scholar John Hartley describes this function as a "secularization of the medieval Catholic church" insofar as television provides identity, community, and instruction through stories.

Small Screen, Big Picture goes one step further, arguing that television has superseded church insofar as it is a virtual meeting place where Americans across racial, ethnic, economic, and religious lines can find instructive and inspirational narratives. Pulling together the work of media and religion scholars, the volume posits the centrality of television as a site for creating cultural identity as well as for the "religious" tasks of meaning making, reenchantment, and ritualization.[2]

By applying these insights to a range of television programs, and using the notion of "lived religion" to analyze plots and characters, *Small Screen, Big Picture* offers the first extended discussion of how television functions as a discursive space for constituting both individual and communal religious identity—a task notable in light of recent surveys showing that the fastest growing religious segment in the United States is "not affiliated."[3] Television provides entrée into a world of novel possibilities and new relationships as its characters and narratives are integrated into personal or group rituals: online communities around *Lost*, sorority sisters gathered for *Grey's Anatomy*, and post-9/11 viewers of *The West Wing*.

Our approach to television places storytelling front and center: television today is essential to the production of American cultural narratives that shape opinion on issues ranging from torture to sexuality.[4] At the present moment, television is the most pervasive medium in American society.[5] Ninety-nine percent of U.S. households have TV sets, and most are watched more than four hours daily.[6] On any given day, more Americans view television than listen to radio or read a newspaper.[7]

Given its almost complete penetration of the American market, television reaches more eyeballs with its stories than do films, books, and magazines. In recent years, even as the networks' share in audience has slipped, viewership has risen for cable and premium offerings.[8] The days when a few programs could dominate the cultural narrative—*Bonanza* ('60s), *M*A*S*H* ('70s), *Dallas* ('80s), and *Friends* ('90s)—have given way to a multiplicity of visions. But for every hundred flowers that bloom each broadcast season, few win critical notice or audience traction. Fewer still receive scholarly attention.

For most of its history, television studies have focused on negative effects. Almost from the outset of television's commercial debut in the 1950s, researchers probed its capacity for social control, commodification, propagandizing, and similarly troubling consequences of viewing. No surprise, then, that their conclusions about its impact ranged from worried skepticism to outright censure.[9] With the 1980s "cultural turn," academics began studying television "texts," production, and reception, frequently pursuing issues of gender, race, and class.[10] Subsequent work explored how television reinforces the status quo or, at best, gently tweaks hegemonic formations.[11] Initially, few studies focused on religion; what research there was concentrated on televangelism, occult-themed shows, and science fiction fandom.[12] Tomes on *Star Trek, X-Files,* and *Buffy the Vampire Slayer* piled high, often mixing analyses of otherness with speculation on the attractiveness of apocalyptic smackdowns between good and evil.

Small Screen, Big Picture takes a different starting point. Essays look at prime-time programs that premiered after 2000 and that forgo the explicitly religious or metaphysical elements of series such as *Buffy, Seventh Heaven,* or *The Book of Daniel.* We limited our exploration to American dramatic series not only for the sake of comparison but also because of the importance of narrative and/ or character to the particular genre. Since most television dramas are actually melodramas, they are predisposed to stories and personalities that embody the struggle of good versus evil. Additionally, this focus reflects the idea that the challenges of the new millennium, however grandly framed, are most frequently felt in choices that occur in everyday life; for example, Dr. Miranda Bailey's decision to allow a faith healer to treat her young son or the Walker family's mixed reactions when Justin is sent to serve as a medic in Iraq.[13] Subsequent choices, enacted in actions and behaviors that manifest the good, the true, and the just—or sometimes, evil, injustice, and ambivalence—constitute the "lived religion"[14] that defines our own lives as much as the characters we watch on television.

Specifically, television turns the big picture into small stories that enable audiences to see characters' growth over time. Its long arc and quotidian perspective mirror our own experience of coping with profound issues in the midst of day-to-day life.

Thus, as science stretches the realm of the possible, enabling outcomes that defy the probable, doctors on *House, ER,* and *Grey's Anatomy* confront roiling questions: Who should live, who must die, and who controls the technology that makes either possible? (And, of course, whom to date this week?) Traditional marriages decline, divorce increases, and cohabitation choices proliferate. Alternative couplings in *Big Love, Brothers and Sisters,* and *Dirty Sexy Money* confront the pain and hostility that often greet sexual subversion: Who defines normal, what constitutes family, and can love conquer all? (But don't forget: Who really is Mom's favorite?) Natural disasters claim thousands of lives, and man-made tragedies spare no corner of the globe. Flawed heroes on *24*, *Rescue Me*, and *Lost* wonder whom to trust, when to fight back, and how to safeguard loved ones. (If only significant others weren't so needy!)

Lived religion comprises the ways in which religion is practiced and experienced in everyday life—from hanging mezuzahs to devouring matzo balls—and from christenings and confirmations to weddings and wakes. In recent years, religious studies scholars have deployed lived religion as a hermeneutical tool that corrects past privileging of intellectual, institutional, and theological studies. As Robert Orsi reminds us, "Rethinking religion as a form of cultural work, the study of lived religion directs attention to institutions *and* persons, text *and* rituals, practice *and* theology, things *and* ideas—all as media of making and unmaking worlds."[15]

Lived religion in *Small Screen, Big Picture* signals the ways in which television characters express, in words and deeds, their spiritual commitments and moral dilemmas, as well as the ways that viewers structure television watching and integrate it into their daily experience and meaning making. Such transactions have been enabled by the growth of Web sites that allow viewers to interact with programs through games, forums, podcasts, and blogs as well as for writers and producers to respond to audience desires.[16] Internet traffic thus enhances the porousness of the media: writers discover what viewers want, and viewers respond positively when their needs are met.[17] (Of course, the feedback loop only works if there are sufficient viewers to ensure a program's commercial success.) In other words, buzz shapes the medium that, in turn, shapes viewers. Audiences make and unmake their media worlds, which refract their understanding of and participation in lived religion.[18]

David Morgan's work looks more closely at this interaction with his notion of the "sacred gaze."[19] If the gaze "encompasses the image, the viewer, and the act of viewing," then the sacred gaze "is the manner in which a way of seeing invests an image, a viewer, or an act of viewing with spiritual significance."[20] In the Western world, art forms—whether prose, drama, painting or music—have a longstanding connection to religious, specifically Christian, tradition, and Morgan's analysis focuses on familiar examples of visual piety—religious art and architecture.

Small Screen, Big Picture extends this framework to a contemporary secular medium that, encapsulating passion, mystery, and metaphysics, works on an emotional level to engender spiritual feeling. That the media then subvert the gaze for commercial purposes, is also part of the equation. In anticipation of *Battlestar Galactica*'s 2008 network return, *Entertainment Weekly* posed the cast in a tableau of *The Last Supper* and asked Executive Producer Ronald D. Moore to provide clues to the upcoming season.[21] That Jesus' place is held by a sexy robot in a slinky red dress, whose religious exhortations resemble Jerry Falwell's, exemplifies the interpenetration of religion, entertainment, and sexuality that composes the contemporary sacred gaze.

While much of what Americans see on television has no spiritual significance whatsoever, this collection argues that some programming—more than a casual observer might assume—can and does serve the religious function of raising questions and posing ethical concerns. By considering the image (i.e., the program itself), the viewers' perspective on it, and the social context of the viewing, these essays treat television as a discursive field that mediates contemporary issues of faith and values through character and narrative; that is, through storytelling. In other words, the experience of watching, and responding to, TV characters' moral dilemmas, crises of faith, bouts of depression, and fits of exhilaration gives expression—as well as insight and resolution—to viewers' own spiritual odysseys and ethical predicaments.

This tracks with Horace Newcomb's observation that television drama is essentially melodrama, "a nineteenth century narrative invention, [that] took on the social function previously secured by religion and religious belief—the marked distinction between good and evil and the attendant social forms of these categories."[22] Just as the rise of melodrama coincided with the decline of religious certainty, the popularity of secular art forms—such as theater, opera, and film—spread among nineteenth-century Christians who previously eschewed worldly entertainments. Throughout the twentieth century, echoes of a religiously based suspicion toward popular media, and television in particular, continued to resonate.

In *American Protestants and TV in the 1950s,* Michele Rosenthal documents mainline Protestants' ambivalence to the new medium.[23] More recently, groups like Donald Wildmon's American Family Association organized boycotts and letter-writing campaigns against television programs that allegedly denigrate Christian values.[24] But Wildmon misses the forest for the trees. The salient fact of "immoral" shows—whether the 1980s hit *Dallas* or the 2006 failed series, *Book of Daniel*—is not that television standards are lax, but rather that audiences enjoy the battle between good and evil, the classic religious narrative, and expect good to triumph.

Accordingly, for nearly five decades, network melodramas drew on conventional moral notions to valorize good and dispatch evil on Westerns, cop shows, and legal and medical ensembles. But the twenty-first century—witness to both new tragedies and new technologies—heralded complications in notions of good and evil, guilt and innocence—along with a heightened awareness of mortality. At the intersection of these trends, writer-producers who previously had pushed the boundaries of network television saw expanded possibilities on cable.

Subsequently, many successful shows tell stories addressing the moral and spiritual dilemmas of modern life, which is not to say they tackle religion head-on. In her essay "True Believers and Atheists Need Not Apply: Faith and Mainstream Television Drama," S. Elizabeth Bird explains why the direct approach frequently fails. A better tack is to confront spiritual questions obliquely, weaving familiar quandaries into plots that recapitulate the ways in which the outside world encroaches on daily life. Since 2000, many series have attended to the physical catastrophes and spiritual cataclysms of the post-9/11 era. The stuff of dark dreams, our dread and anxiety surface in a television landscape of mutilated corpses, troubled spirits, and amoral vigilantes. How else to explain the wave of shows that graphically portray death, conjure an afterlife, question life's meaning, or introduce supernatural, death-defying heroes?[25] Scholar Lynn Spigel, describing post-9/11 television culture, writes, "It is tempting to say that television's 'return to normal' transcended the events of 9/11 and that everything is as it was before. On the other hand, 9/11 haunts U.S. commercial television."[26]

Even as the subject matter of shows has shifted in the new millennium, new technologies have amplified television's capacity to reach more people with greater viewing options. Digitization expanded and enhanced offerings as cable and premium networks increased niche services for audiences hungry for a wide range of programming. Among the new options, many were riskier than standard network fare. *Weeds*' drug-dealing soccer mom, *Dexter*'s jugular justice, and *Battlestar Galactica*'s sympathetic suicide bombers would have been unimaginable when ABC, CBS, and NBC controlled the airwaves.

Equally significant has been the Internet's impact on the medium.[27] Pioneering producers developed online content, creating stand-alone shows as well as bonus episodes of broadcast series.[28] Viewers, who once bonded via fan clubs, TV nights, and chats at the watercooler, form online communities around the dissection of plotlines and character twists, the creation of sequels and prequels, the development of wikis and portals, and actual video production. This enthusiasm belies what some critics see as television's most deleterious effect: its role in maintaining a populace complacently bound to a racist, sexist, and capitalist system. Might the Internet proclaim a new turn, one in which viewers participate in the creation of alternative readings that use television texts to liberate?

This two-sided view of television, similar to critiques of religion as both liberator and oppressor, leads back to Morgan's notion of the sacred gaze, the discursive field where spiritual reflection occurs. These reflections are not the result of explicitly religious content, which tends to fall flat, but of the emotional punch of melodrama, the appeal of well-drawn characters, and viewers' response to the medium itself. Morgan's work is representative of the small but growing field of religion and media studies that explores the relationship between the two as sites for meaning making and identity construction. Anticipating this move, Stewart Hoover wrote more than a decade ago, "The ties and rituals of daily life now involve, among other things, interaction with the symbolic resources of the media sphere. That among those resources should be found texts, symbols, or ideas that may be seen to be religiously significant should no longer surprise us."[29]

Challenging the familiar social sciences-based assumption that religion, like television, is an instrument for social control and the preservation of the status quo, recent interdisciplinary research has investigated its capacity for individual and group transformation.[30] Likewise, following James Carey's twofold definition of communication as steeped in religion and ritual,[31] scholars have theorized how media might engage, encode, and intersect religious messages. For example, television may provide viewers with a time-out-of-time experience that Gregor Goethals, borrowing Victor Turner's term for "symbolic activity that resembles but is not exactly identical to the liminal," calls liminoid.[32] According to Goethals, media, as well as art and games, enable human beings to "transcend social structures to play with ideas, fantasies, word, paint, and social relationships."[33] During this time of transcendence, Robert A. White believes it is possible to participate in a "sacred space" in which the sacred and the secular engage—each serving to affirm and constitute the other.

> The media are working in "sacred space" and are a site for the dialogue of the sacred and secular in three areas: (a) the search for ultimate, consistent patterns of mythic meaning and the integration of the "unexplainable" into the commonsense cultural consensus; (b) the search for perfect community and the confrontation of community with the power structure of social practice; and (c) the search for authentic personal identity and the resolution of the conflicts between personal and social identities.[34]

In each of these areas, television dramas become a vector of lived religion, enabling viewers to negotiate between the sacred and secular. In *Lost*, for example, all three of White's domains— meaning, community, and identity—are in play. For her essay, "You Lost Me: Mystery, Fandom, and Religion in ABC's *Lost*," Lynn Schofield Clark read fan forums and bulletin boards to understand how viewers make sense of the series' mythos, characters, and island community. The very open-endedness of individual and communal plights—and the ad hoc ways in which characters cope with ethical tests and spiritual trials—may explain why the show inspires such a dedicated following. The clashes between Jack Shephard and John Locke, the man of science versus the man of faith, or between Kate Austen and Juliet Burke, the honest criminal and the duplicitous doctor, are ones that viewers recognize, prompting spirited online discussion and debate.

It is easier to show that these online debates occur than to explain why they happen. Perhaps it is a desire to rehash a good story, to explain the inexplicable, or to participate in a ritual of meaning making. Television creates an "us" by providing shared, vicarious experiences. Do participants in online discussions constitute a "we"? And what of those who never post but faithfully track fan sites, games, and videos? Is this geek culture, escapism, or the latest iteration of a sacred priesthood of all believers that extrapolates the gospel to the masses? With Talmudic precision, the threads on fan boards painstakingly parse character development and narrative thrust for clues to meaning, significance, and change. Each imagined world carries its own signification and the faithful want to know, and will argue intently, whether Dexter is good or evil, why Gregory House suffers, and when Grace Hanadarko will accept God's love.

These questions trouble writers, too; indeed, many say their shows are personal attempts to explore them. David Milch's short-lived HBO series, *John from Cincinnati*, is a case in point.[35] Wondering what would happen if God tried to intervene in our society's abysmal self-absorption, Milch placed his eponymous hero, "the spirit of the universe," among footloose and feckless Southern California surfers. Like the fictional characters with whom John interacted, viewers had no idea who he was or what he was trying to teach them. Similar to a Zen koan, the series sought to interrupt the rational mind, subverting business as usual with a metaphysical riddle. In this light, the series' failings are less significant than its very existence, a bold challenge to audience (as well as network) expectations.[36]

Milch's work on *John from Cincinnati* is unusual because its transgressive message is embodied by the series itself. Other writers use more traditional means to explore religious themes, spiritual quandaries, and ethical dilemmas. In shows such as

St. Elsewhere, Homicide and *Oz*, Tom Fontana created powerful characters whose search for redemption often occurs at society's outposts—prisons, interrogation rooms, and operating tables. Barbara Hall took on the mysteries of suffering and immanence in *Joan of Arcadia* and hoped to explore evil and expiation in *Demons*. The proposed series, about an ex-Jesuit priest-psychologist who performs exorcisms, was not picked by CBS, although shows about a vampire-detective and a postapocalyptic small town were.[37]

Ronald D. Moore, creator of the retooled 1970s series *Battlestar Galactica*, had more luck with the Sci-Fi Channel. The conflict between monotheism and polytheism, which could have been a minor aspect of the struggle between Galactica's human population and their Cylon enemies, was encouraged by network executives.[38] As a result, episodes plumbed hot-button topics—from terrorism to torture—at the intersection of religion and politics.

Other writer-producers may not publicly avow a personal interest in spirituality or religion, but ethical questions infuse their work. When David Shore, *House*'s creator, does not have his curmudgeonly doctor pushing the conflict between medicine and faith, he's testing the limits of medical ethics.[39] Trying cases ripped from the headlines, the lawyers in David Kelley's *Boston Legal* vie to see how far they can bend professional standards in service of any number of good causes.[40] In Aaron Sorkin's *West Wing*, President Jed Bartlet and his White House staffers work in morally compromised situations that pit religious beliefs against political realities. More recently, Sorkin's *Studio 60 on the Sunset Strip* featured an intriguingly complex born-again character as a star performer on a *Saturday Night Live*-type show who sought to reconcile entertainment-world conventions with the fundamentals of her faith.[41]

To be sure, other television series also address issues of meaning, ethics, and identity. *Six Feet Under* places death at the center of life, and *Heroes* speculates that anyone could develop an ability to save the world. Each survivor in *Lost* needs spiritual salvation as much as physical rescue, and *Big Love*'s polygamous families hold fast to religious values in a secular age. In shows like *Dexter*, *24*, and *The Shield*, amoral protagonists skewer every ethical norm yet follow their own moral code. In each series, lived religion—the everyday expression of ultimate commitments—is part of what compels viewers. Whether it is Jack Bauer's willingness to sacrifice himself for his country, Margene Hendrickson's befriending a potential sister-wife, or Hiro Nakamura's ultimate acceptance of his father's death, characters demonstrate grace in complex and uncomfortable situations.

———

Television's immediacy, familiarity, and even its position in the home help explain devotees' allegiance as well as critics' neglect. It also suggests why examining television as lived religion is a significant development: the medium has much to tell us about ourselves. Elijah Siegler, describing how the religious genius of television differs from film, proposes an architectural metaphor: "Movie palaces are (or were, before the rise of the megaplexes) cathedrals of the image, where we partake in shared experiences. TVs are home shrines, personalized and comfortable."[42]

The beating heart of the American home—and most often the largest and most expensive object in the family room—television is an altar where we exchange our daily struggles for visions of transcendence. The medium's conventions do not suit dramatic instances of conversion, salvation, or redemption, but its intimacy and familiarity allow characters to develop over time—raising religious issues, asking ethical questions, and experiencing spiritual insights in the course of our ongoing relationship with them. More than other media, television reflects life as we experience it. We see our own struggles and successes in the small gestures of characters who, like us, strive to do good, fall short of the mark, and try again.

The essays in *Small Screen, Big Picture* are organized into three sections that explore television's depiction of traditional religions, gender and religion, and new religious visions. Although lived religion is a primary framing device, contributors also address issues of race, class, and gender when appropriate. The array of contributors and the diversity of methodologies they apply to their analyses reflect our aim of producing a truly interdisciplinary volume: but, as always in these efforts, there remain many areas we could not investigate. We also plead guilty to organizing sections according to familiar Christian tropes. Their very familiarity makes them useful and, as Christianity is the predominant faith in the United States, its beliefs, practices, and narratives inform many of the series we examine.

Section I, "Old Wine in New Skins," examines current depictions of mainstream faiths—and the ways in which Protestantism, Roman Catholicism, Judaism, and Islam have been bent and refitted for contemporary audiences. To set the stage, S. Elizabeth Bird explains why "True Believers and Atheists Need Not Apply," when seeking successful television formulas. In "In the Beginning," Horace Newcomb considers how the body of Christ organizes *Deadwood*, and Craig Detweiler analyzes *The Wire* as a jeremiad with Roman Catholic and African Methodist Episcopal strains. Leonard Norman Primiano looks at *The West Wing* as a site for vernacular Catholicism in "For What I Have Done and What I Have Failed to Do," and Vincent Brook probes mixed marriages in "Mixed Blessing": Generational Effects of Interfaith Marriages in *Everwood* and *The O.C.*" The section ends with Amir Hussain's personal reflection, "'The Fire Next Time': *Sleeper Cell* and Muslims on Television Post 9/11."

In the exploration of gender and religion in section II, Sheila Briggs leads off with "'Elect Xena God': Religion Remixed in a (Post-)Television Culture." Briggs' feminist perspective recasts *Xena* in a gender-bending theological light. Heather Hendershot examines the changing discourse around abortion, highlighting *House* and *Battlestar Galactica* in "'You Know How It Is with Nuns . . .': Religion and Television's Sacred/Secular Fetuses." Lanita Jacobs-Huey interweaves race, gender, and disability in "Moralizing Whiteness in *Joan of Arcadia*," and Anthea Butler and Diane Winston examine the gendered nature of religious calling and its impact on spirituality, sexuality, and power in "'A Vagina Ain't a Halo': Gender and Religion in *Saving Grace* and *Battlestar Galactica*."

Essays in section III stray from mainstream analyses to explore ethical and spiritual possibilities on some of television's most imaginative programs. In "'*Chiariidaa o Sukue, Sekai o Sukue!*': Nuclear Dread and the Pokémonization of American Religion in Season One of *Heroes*," Rudy Busto charts the intersection of orientalism and postapocalypticism in the NBC series. For "You Lost

Me: Mystery, Fandom and Religion in ABC's *Lost*," Lynn Scho-field Clark reads fan forums and bulletin boards to track viewer perspectives on the island's mysteries. Marcia Dawkins draws on fantasy-theme analysis to understand the mantra, "Have a little faith," central to *Prison Break*, and Adele Reinhartz considers the fundamental questions posed by *The Sopranos*—who am I and where am I going? Ending the section, Elijah Siegler's essay, "A Television Auteur Confronts God: The Religious Imagination of Tom Fontana," brings many of these themes full circle, exploring Fontana's three-decade-long exploration of evil, redemption, and restitution in *St. Elsewhere, Homicide*, and *Oz*.

Lest readers begin with a misapprehension, let me be clear: *Small Screen, Big Picture* is not arguing that there is anything inherently sacred, spiritual, or religious, in a traditional institu-tional sense, about television. (Nor should the book be construed as arguing either for or against religion.) Rather, our central argu-ment contends that since television is the most popular medium in our increasingly mediated electronic culture, it is worth taking a second look at representations that speak to the existential issues of our time. These issues become all the more salient insofar as they play out in a media environment in which increased inte-gration will further the interplay between audience and content production as well as during a cultural moment when a growing number of religious "nones" seek direct experiences of the Divine unmediated by institutional authorities. Television provides a direct and (ironically) minimally mediated experience of the magic, fantasy, and possibility associated with the Divine. That this per-sonal encounter also can be shared among a (virtual) community whose postings, in turn, may affect the next iteration of program-ming is, indeed, changing the big picture.

SECTION I

*Old Wine
in New Skins*

True Believers and Atheists Need Not Apply
Faith and Mainstream Television Drama

S. Elizabeth Bird

Introduction

In April 2005, NBC premiered a "miniseries event," titled *Revelations*, created by David Seltzer, the force behind theatrical successes such as *The Omen*. The series was heavily promoted with "teasing" promos on the network as well as billboards and large advertisements on the sides of New York buses. Drawing from the New Testament book of Revelation, it was a thriller about the ultimate battle of good versus evil as the world approaches the end times. The main protagonists are an astrophysicist, Dr. Richard Massey (Bill Pullman), and a beautiful Roman Catholic nun, Sister Josepha Montafiore (Natascha McElhone). Massey is well known for his skeptical public stand on paranormal events (a kind of fictional Carl Sagan, apparently), and before the series opens, his twelve-year-old daughter has been kidnapped and murdered by a Satanic group led by Isaiah Haden (Michael Massee), who is now being taken into custody. Sister Josepha is a scholar of supernatural events who believes in the reality of the coming apocalypse and sets out to convince Massey that the end is indeed nigh. The series was characterized in the press as representing a response to the rise in popular religious fervor in the post-9/11 world, reflected in such media phenomena as the Left Behind book and movie series and movies like *The Da Vinci Code* and *The Passion of the Christ*. NBC planned to bring it back the following season as a dramatic series. The producers had set up the story at the end of the sixth episode, with the birth of both the antichrist and a child who was the second coming of Jesus; the series would presumably launch into stories about the end of days.

Even debuting against the Fox powerhouse *American Idol*, the first episode attracted almost sixteen million viewers, although reviews were mixed. However, the audience declined steadily with each episode, reaching a low of around six million by the end, and plans for a series were dropped. In this chapter, I will explore why this project, planned carefully to address faith after 9/11, failed. My central interest, however, is not in *Revelations* for its own sake; rather, I use its failure to lead into a discussion of the kind of religious representations that apparently succeed with audiences and those that do not. In this context, I will consider how religion is addressed in some other highly successful popular TV drama series, most notably *CSI: Crime Scene Investigation*, which in some quarters has been labeled as "antireligion," and *House M.D.*, whose "hero" is an avowed atheist. My discussion blends content analysis with audience study, adding the voices of viewers to my own consideration of textual themes.

I argue that television drama as a genre is actually very supportive of faith, although not of overt or sectarian religiosity (such as portrayed in *Revelations*) or any religious practice that is perceived as extreme, fanatical, or hypocritical. Alongside that, TV drama is demonstrably hostile to atheism, which is essentially seen as an extreme and immoral philosophy. In all these respects, I believe TV drama reflects the "lived religion" of mainstream America—a practice-based religion concerned with moral choices and personal growth rather than debates over faith and dogma. To be successful, television drama (unlike theatrical movies) must tread a fine line, offending as few people as possible, while also providing stimulating stories and characters that will bring audiences back week after week.

Revelations

Revelations was explicitly and unashamedly religious, drawing especially on Roman Catholic imagery and dogma (in the tradition of *The Exorcist, The Omen,* or *Rosemary's Baby*), but with heavy overtones of fundamentalism, treading the same path as the Left Behind phenomenon. Each segment opens with a biblical quote, sometimes from Revelation, but often also from Old Testament prophets and other books. The early episodes frequently use phrases like "in these days," and the post-9/11 context is underlined frequently; the series opens with a montage of images that include war, disaster, and the familiar horrifying clip of a man plunging from the top floors of the World Trade Center. Sister Josepha spells it out in the second episode: "When has every living thing stood so clearly on the point, the very brink of instant and simultaneous annihilation? Famine, plagues, false prophets preaching intolerance," going on to talk about suicide bombers and terrorism and explaining that all this was foretold "as the end of days." Sister Josepha is associated with a foundation that is looking for Christ on Earth, and believes in the possibility that "perhaps hope can save the world." She seeks out Massey, hoping to enlist him in her crusade.

Initially reluctant, he joins forces with her after a series of terrible events: his stepson is abducted; a young girl, brain-dead after a lightning strike, apparently begins to channel his dead daughter; and Haden, who has been converting prisoners to Satanism, leads a bloody insurrection in prison, escaping and inspiring satanic prison breakouts across the world.

Creator David Seltzer was publicly quite cagey about his specific religious beliefs and intentions in the series, although he told Christian Web site Christiananswers.net that "all of the things that signal the Bible in regards to the end of days really looks like it's in place; not just the constant war and bloodshed, but famine and plague and the fouling of the environment; technically the collapse of everything physically, socially, and politically; the distress of nations, the turbulence of the ocean roaring. We are all seeing it right now." [1] However, he argued that "We are in no way following a fundamentalist track." Executive Producer Gavin Polone was more explicit. In an interview with the *New York Times*, extensively excerpted on the same Web site article, Polone explained that "his personal interest in religion and Armageddon stems from a long-ago summer spent at an evangelical Christian youth camp, where he was encouraged to read Hal Lindsey's apocalypse-themed treatise *The Late, Great Planet Earth*." He explained that he had tried before to create television "that would be different and would speak to the faith that is held by most of the people in our country." His agenda to show the "truth" is clear: "I think the time has come, the time has been at hand many times in history of the last two thousand years, and I think it's closer now than it's ever been . . . clearly, Professor Massey isn't correct about what he's thinking; he starts off saying this is all a lot of hooey. And there's no way he can deny it by the end of the first episode."

It did seem apparent that the time was right for such a venture. The Left Behind series of books and movies (twelve books cowritten by Jerry Jenkins and Timothy LaHaye) had been extremely popular, and Hollywood was struggling to deal with how to address a seeming upsurge in religiosity. It had become a common assumption that September 11 had spurred an increase in faith; in December 2001, the Pew Research Center for the People and the Press reported that "The Sept. 11 attacks have increased the prominence of religion in the United States to an extraordinary degree. . . . Fully 78% now say religion's influence in American life is growing, up from 37% eight months ago and the highest mark on this measure in surveys dating back four decades." In 2002, a second Pew report indicated that just over half of Americans say Sept. 11 proved there is too little religion in the world." Hollywood was certainly beginning to take notice.

So what went wrong with *Revelations?* Initial viewer figures showed great interest. Mainstream reviewers were mixed, praising its good production values and well-known performers (along with Pullman and McElhone, it featured respected actor John Rhys-Davis). Although *Washington Post* critic Tom Shales called it "monotonously bombastic and overblown," a *Seattle Post-Intelligencer* reviewer wrote that "*Revelations* is sure to please the Trinity Broadcasting Network crowd, as well as viewers who enjoy their religious treatments à la *The Omen*."[2]

However, it turned out that the series essentially failed to please anyone. Evangelical Christians, who were clearly a large segment of the intended audience, hated it. Comments on Christiananswers.net point to one of the key problems: fundamentalists generally look for a literal interpretation of biblical accounts, and the series offers a version of Revelation that didn't sit well with many. Producer Polone was quoted as saying "The Book of Revelation is metaphor, and it needs to be interpreted," but for evangelicals, that is anathema.[3] The site's reviewer, Joseph Sinko, while acknowledging that the show is at times "fun," writes, "Concerning 'end times' events, there is a marked contrast between what comes out of the imagination of Hollywood and the illumination of Holy Scripture . . . I knew its purpose was not to teach correct biblical eschatology, but to tap into the spiritual-genre craze so popular in our society today. One thing is sure, if we want to know the truth about what's to unfold in mankind's future we will not find it in this miniseries." Sinko expresses his astonishment when it appears that Sister Josepha is searching for ambiguous signs that the second coming is at hand: "The Bible is clear, when Jesus returns to earth there will be no doubt. Jesus made this clear in Matthew 24 and 25, and so did the Holy Angels in Acts 1, and the Apostle Paul in Thessalonians. Jesus Christ's return to earth will not be a secret!"[4]

Viewers offered their own assessment on the site, and while a few appreciate the attempt to address biblical themes, more do not like it. A thirty-six-year-old man deems the program "offensive": "The first hour . . . held my attention but this just isn't worth the occult themes that are so strong you can't figure out if this is pro-Christianity or not. Yes, scripture and The Lord's name are thrown around a lot, but reincarnation and contacting the dead seem to be just as important as scripture to the writers." A twenty-year-old man writes that it "spiraled down fast. The first scene that really bugged me was the shadow of Christ on the cross which appeared on the mountain. I do not think he will appear again on the cross since he was freed from it and rose again. . . . The only good thing is it shows exactly how the world is today. Trying to be explained by evolution and big bang." A twenty-five-year-old woman writes, "from my Faith's viewpoint, I find it unbelievable.

This could possibly be [a] tool for Satan to use, to confuse people even more."[5] Evangelical writer Jerry Jenkins claimed that the series is "not going to appeal to evangelicals at all. . . . It's about the end times and the return of Christ, but beyond that I actually found it kind of silly." He takes issue with the idea that Christ might return as a baby: "That's not in the Bible. . . . He came back as a baby the first time. The second time he'll come back in the clouds for the Rapture, and then will come to Earth and set up an earthly kingdom—as the king, not as the baby."[6]

The fundamentalist Web site leftbehind.com also invited comments about the series, and posted 166 comments on its site, many quite long and detailed.[7] Of these, only five expressed clear enthusiasm, stating that it was "exciting" or "well done." A few others disliked it but grudgingly suggested that it might spark interest in more religious programming; but the majority expressed extreme disappointment, often after initially tuning in with high hopes. The major criticisms were of its "inaccuracies," especially the idea that Jesus may return as a baby, and the central suggestion that the inevitable apocalypse might actually be averted by human action. Says "Sharon," "It's no wonder that so many will be deceived by the antichrist." Some interpreted it as just another example of Hollywood Satanism, dressed to deceive, while others called it "ridiculous," "dangerous," and "blasphemous." "David" writes, "I was raised in a Catholic home so I immediately picked-up on the mysticism and misinterpretation of Scripture so readily offered and accepted by Catholics in general." "Constance" concludes, "It kind of looked as if it was going to be one of those Hollywood devil movies."

And it was not just evangelicals who disliked the series. While they felt offended by it, more liberal Christians believed it actually pandered to them. Viewer comments on a secular review site, imdb.com (all anonymous apart from Internet handles), were dismissive:

> I personally love these apocalyptic movies, but feel this is in so many ways a sop to the religious right, whose penetration into government is alarming. It feeds the creationist fervor, the cheap exploitive political acts behind the Schiavo carnival of fools.

If any research was actually done for this story, it was certainly only on the religious angle because Bill Pullman's astrophysicist is not only a shallow character, but a horribly generic Hollywood depiction of what science is . . . *Revelations* has discovered a new extreme to take it to by contrasting it with a well-researched religious background.

[It] regurgitated every tired bugaboo of fundamentalist Christianity, and the effect was not a good one. Do you think we should include a Satanic child murderer? What a great idea! How about something that would appeal to the Guadalupe and face-in-the-tortilla believers? Super! I know, I think we should include a sexy nun and a cute baby! Wow, that's absolutely brilliant! Hey, why don't we fan the Intelligent Design-Evolution flames a bit in the opening scene? Pure genius!

On the interdenominational and ecumenical Web site beliefnet. com, reviewer Blythe hit the nail on the head:

Christians from various backgrounds will find something to hate about *Revelations*. Liberal Christians will find the fiery "end of the world" signs at best hokey and at worst mean-spirited, playing into stereotypes that assume all Christians believe in a literal interpretation of the Book of Revelation. . . . On the other side of the Christian spectrum, biblical literalists will complain that the TV show does not stick closely to what they see as God's apocalyptic "to do" list.[8]

Salon.com reviewer Havrilesky was especially vehement:

For all its pretensions about adhering to the Bible *and* science, *Revelations* is just another slice of shadowy, fearmongering pap that will only annoy the informed—Christians and non-Christians alike—who recognize it as the emotionally manipulative, slanted fable that it is.[9]

Blythe concludes with one "larger question": "What happens when producers use religion to creep people out?"

This last comment points to another failure for the series. The show was a rather uneasy combination of biblical allusion and paranormal/religious horror motifs drawn from *The Exorcist* genre. It included scenes such as satanist Haden severing his own finger to show that he does not bleed (and later reattaching the digit), a "brain-dead" girl speaking and writing clues in the voice of Massey's previously slaughtered daughter, and a bloody sacrifice of a goat. Clearly the producers also hoped to attract the religious horror audience. In that quest, they not only turned off the evangelicals and the Catholics (offended by the strongly Catholic imagery throughout) but also horror fans, who found the series slow moving and tame.

Thus horror aficionado Johanson calls it "Apocalyptic cheese," continuing, "That's it? They're kidding, right? . . . Where was the 'satanic combat' we were promised? . . . After all this apocalyptic end-of-the-world supernatural stuff, it's just gonna [be] Bill Pullman beating the crap out of the dude? Booorrring!"[10] Fellow horror-critic Staci Wilson commented "Even though it's penned by screenwriter David *The Omen* Seltzer, the devil's in the details—and the big guy is conspicuously absent here . . . it really needed a scary or mysterious hook in the beginning and it didn't snag me."[11]

This snapshot of popular response to the series offers some idea of why it was doomed to failure. It essentially pleased no one. And now the question is, why?

Is TV Simply Antireligion?

One response to the failure of efforts like *Revelations*, as well as many short-lived overtly religious series such the *Book of Daniel* and even the relatively successful *Joan of Arcadia*, is that TV is "antireligion." Many critics have expressed this belief, often as part of a general critique of the entertainment industry as dangerously liberal and secular.[12] Gahr argues that "television remains ground zero for the culture of disbelief."[13] The Parents Television Council, an affiliate of the conservative Media Research Center, recently released a report that slams television for negative portrayals of religion, concluding that "Hollywood's 'creative' elite . . . demonstrates its contempt for religion—and for its own viewing audience—by deliberately portraying God as subject of ridicule, and followers of organized religion as oppressive, fanatical, hypocritical and hopelessly corrupt." It especially condemns "irreverent" comedies, such as *South Park*, *The Simpsons*, and *Family Guy*, but also argues that "such dramas as *Boston Legal* and *C.S.I.* viciously caricature religious individuals and beliefs and put diatribes against religion into the mouths of their lead characters."[14] As well as these more popular critiques, much academic analysis has supported the contention that television portrays religion negatively.[15] Much of this research, academic and otherwise, tends to rely on the kind of content analysis that counts instances of "negative portrayals," a crucial point to which I will return.

It is certainly clear that the TV dramatic landscape is littered with failed attempts to present religious themes in TV drama, especially after 9/11. In the 2003–2004 season, the first season fully planned after those events, many shows were launched, including *Carnivale*, *Tru Calling*, *Dead Like Me*, *Wonderfalls*, and *Joan of Arcadia*. Other attempts have included the *Book of Daniel*, as well as *Revelations*. However, I would argue that, contrary to much critical commentary, the failure of overtly religious drama is not because TV is inherently antireligion. Even Gahr, who generally condemns television, mentions a study by the conservative Media Research Center that said "depictions of religion [were] overall positive."[16] In contrast to the oft-accepted critique, I believe the default position for TV drama is an assumption of faith, although leaving vague the question of exactly in what. At the same time, it is almost impossible to create explicitly faith-based stories without offending or alienating someone, as *Revelations* and some other failures demonstrate. Let us look for a moment at one of the shows condemned by the Parents Television Council for their irreligious attitudes, *CSI: Crime Scene Investigation*, which supposedly "puts diatribes against religion into the mouths of lead characters." This characterization is somewhat mystifying. Religion rarely surfaces overtly in *CSI*, but when it does, faith is consistently represented positively. This is especially significant because the entire premise of the show rests on the efficacy of science, which in our culture is not infrequently seen as antithetic to faith. Given the critiques, one would expect *CSI* to be relentless in its championing of science over religion—but it is not. The key figure in *CSI* is lead investigator Gil Grissom (William Petersen), who clearly functions as both the scientific and moral core of the team. He does constantly hammer home the point that the answers always lie in the scientific evidence.

Nevertheless, Grissom is by no means an atheist. In a second season episode, "Alter Boy," Grissom has an exchange with a priest who has arrived at the scene:

> GRISSOM: We both have jobs that begin after the crime.
> FATHER POWELL: After the sin.
> GRISSOM: Some people would call that a career in futility.
> FATHER POWELL: Some people call it a vocation.

Grissom goes on to explain that while he is no longer a churchgoer, he believes in both God and science, while having trouble with the evils done in the name of God. The priest is not demeaned, and no direct aspersions are cast on any specific faiths. Indeed, Grissom frequently comments on the need to be respectful of all faiths, as in a 2002 episode "Felonious Monk," which involves the murder of several Buddhist monks. Crime scene investigator (CSI) Nick Stokes makes a reference to "that guy in the robe," to which Grissom responds, "guy in the robe is a monk, Nick." Later, he says to CSI Sara Sidle, "wherever you live is your temple. If you treat it like one." When Sara challenges him for his source, he answers, "Buddha." In a 2004 episode, "Harvest," Grissom confronts a man, David, who has killed his sister rather than allow her to commit suicide. She had been conceived as a bone marrow donor for him and had suffered great pain from repeated donations. The following exchange ensues:

> DAVID: Suicide isn't an option. It's an unforgivable sin in
>   the eyes of God.
> GRISSOM: But you believe your God forgives murder?

Grissom clearly does not forgive murder, and through his moral authority, we see David as a sinner who has transgressed the faith he claims to hold. Later, David acknowledges this too. He assumes that, as a scientist, Grissom is an unbeliever, but he tells him he was the only person who really cared for his sister's fate: "You know, you may not believe in God, sir, but you do his work." True faith, we learn, is about doing good for humanity, not hypocritically touting one's religion.

The one character who questions faith significantly is Sara Sidle (Jorja Fox), a CSI who became Grissom's love interest after a few seasons. In an episode titled "Double Cross" (aired 19 October 2006), the CSI team investigates the case of a woman found dead in a parish church, having been hung on a cross in a crude parody of the crucifixion. The episode offers several moments that explore faith and that gently put down the option of unbelief. The episode is especially significant because it focuses on the growing personal relationship between Grissom and Sara, who has on occasion suggested that she is agnostic. The following exchange in the lab is revealing:

> GRISSOM: Memory is a gift.
> SARA: Hmmm. *(long pause)* From whom?
> GRISSOM: Who do you think?
> SARA: Well, I wouldn't necessarily call myself an atheist, but I am not sold on the notion of a higher power. However, I used to love the stories of the Saints.
> GRISSOM: This job certainly challenges your faith.
> SARA: Yes it does. But, I have science.
> GRISSOM: I believe we need a little of both.
> SARA: Sometimes, I think we made up God just to have someone to blame for our mistakes.
>
> *(Grissom leaves the lab without replying.)*
>
> SARA: *(calling out, and sounding very unsure of herself)* It's . . . just a theory!

Later, Sara takes up the conversation:

> SARA: I didn't offend you, did I? Did I say something offensive to you as a Catholic?
> GRISSOM: I'm not really a Catholic anymore, you know. I suppose I practice a kind of secular Catholicism that involves ritualizing certain aspects of everyday life, and then viewing them with a spiritual intensity they

> might not otherwise possess. But, I don't want to put
> too fine a point on it. *(He brings out some rosary beads.)*
> SARA: And rosary beads are a part of that?
> GRISSOM: This belonged to my mother.

The significance of this exchange lies again in the moral authority that Grissom has established over the course of the series, stressing the balance between science and spirituality. As should be clear from the examples above, his is a pragmatic, situational faith, but it is faith, and it goes with his rock-solid persona as a fair, impartial scientist and human being. Sara, on the other hand, is the team member who has apparently had the most personal troubles. She is (or has been) an alcohol abuser, and there have been irrational outbursts of anger and hints of promiscuity. Clearly her uncertainty about faith is tied to this. Grissom, while he is falling in love with Sara, is also worried about her personal problems, and his homily to her about faith seems to be an attempt to show her a way to overcome them through religion. As we shall see below, lack of faith on the part of a central character is frequently a sign of a flawed or damaged personality.

But do viewers find this rather amorphous approach to faith appealing? Apparently they do: *CSI*, along with the *Law and Order* franchise, remains one of the most popular dramas on television. I would not argue that viewers tune in *because* of its take on faith— but rather that this take does not offend and indeed matches the "lived religion" of many Americans. A look at CBS' *CSI* message board reveals some discussion of the show's position on faith, after someone posted a topic about whether portrayals of religion are positive or negative. The shared position of most posters was that Grissom is indeed the heart and soul of the show and that he sets the tone.

> Grissom is of course the focal point of the show so how he
> reacts to religion can be taken as an indicator. He must have
> some beliefs to keep his mother's rosary in his desk.

> I don't think the writers have shown any prejudice against
> certain religions or religion in general.

Many commented that *CSI,* like other mainstream shows, does portray religious extremism negatively:

> Where *CSI* is negative toward religion it is about the people who pervert the teachings of Christ, Buddha, Allah, Confucius, Moses, whomever. . . . They really come down hard on the hypocrisy of people who follow the form of a particular religion but not its spirit.

> Grissom's problem with religion is that there is a lot of hypocrisy going on, like people killing in the name of religion.

> I think Grissom voices people's disconnect with *organized* religion.

Like Grissom, these viewers see science and religion as compatible:

> Science and religion seem to contradict each other, but God was the one who created science in the first place by creating the universe, planets, humans, animals etc. . . . In fact, he's the master of science and mathematics . . .

> I've known many scientists who say that science brought them closer to God. Science can answer a lot of questions about how and why not. But only faith can answer who and why. Science gives us the laws of nature. Only faith explains why, as messed up as humanity is at times, we seem to be able to rise above the laws of nature. Grissom's few words about science and religion express what many faithful scientists would say.

Others talk about the show's clear moral sense:

> I think all the characters have a somewhat universal sense of what is right and wrong. Murder is wrong. Robbery is wrong. Rape is wrong. Find me a religion that says they are. The CSI's work is bringing the guilty to justice so that they can atone for their crimes, or as some would put it, their sins.

This might be a stretch, but I would think that with all the horror they see of man's inhumanity to man, that the CSIs must have faith in some form of a loving and just God or they couldn't go on doing what they do.

Maybe another way to put it is that *CSI* portrays that doing harm to others is just plain wrong. On conduct that religions come down on, gambling, promiscuity, substance abuse etc., it seems to me that they take a neutral stance; a kind of no harm, no foul approach. It's like the moral compass that Grissom talked about . . . Hangout, party, go a bit crazy? Okay. Beating people to death for fun? Uh, not okay!

And What about Atheism?

If TV drama really were antireligious, we should expect to find nonbelievers, such as atheists and agnostics, represented sympathetically. In fact, this is not the case at all, just as atheism is rejected by most Americans. It is extremely rare to see atheism portrayed, and when it is, typically it is seen as almost a form of pathology. When occasionally featured, overt unbelievers are usually portrayed as lacking human empathy or having some psychological problem that prevents them seeing the value of faith. Often a sign of their maturity is when they realize the errors of their ways, in the same way as rational scientists frequently come around to seeing the need for faith.[17]

Indeed, research suggests that this position is in step with prevailing American attitudes. Edgell, Gerteis, and Hartmann used a national survey to show that atheists are less likely to be accepted, publicly and privately, than any other group.[18] For instance, of ten named ethnic and religious groups (including Muslims), average Americans would least like their children to marry an atheist. A recent Gallup poll revealed that of ten categories (including Mormon, woman, homosexual, or seventy-two-year-old man), fewest people (45%) would consider voting for an atheist, while 53% would never consider it.[19] (The next highest in the "would never vote for" category was 43 percent for homosexual.) Edgell, commenting on her research to the NPR segment "On the Media," noted: "It is religion, having a faith that makes people, in the

American context, seem trustworthy, like good citizens and good neighbors. So if you don't have that as a moral boundary, you're an outsider, an other, and, perhaps, a dangerous other."[20]

The same NPR segment offers examples of negative portrayal of atheists, citing frequent allusions to the cliché "there are no atheists in a foxhole," which assumes that under threat of death, atheists will recant. One example is from the now-defunct series *Dawson's Creek*, which featured Jen, a "troubled" character. Early in the series, Jen tells her incredulous grandmother: "I don't do real well with church and the Bible and this prayer stuff . . . I don't covet a religious God. Grams, I'm an atheist." In the series finale, Jen is terminally ill and tapes a farewell message to her baby daughter: "I've never really believed in God. But I hope that you are able to believe in God, because the thing that I've come to realize, Sweetheart, that it just doesn't matter if God exists or not. The important thing is for you to believe in something." Thus, the atheist is redeemed, having realized that her lack of faith was willful and destructive. We might well have expected the same redemption for agnostic Sara Sidle in *CSI*, had not the departure of Jorja Fox cut her story short. However, it seems significant that Sara's exit from the show was framed in terms of a crisis in her confidence to continue this emotionally grueling work, leaving Grissom shocked and deeply hurt.

The most prominent (perhaps only) atheist lead character is Dr. Gregory House (Hugh Laurie), on Fox's procedural medical drama, *House, M.D.* He regularly rants about religious faith, as in "House vs. God": "You know, I get it if people are just looking for ways to fill the holes. But they want the holes. They want to live in the holes. They go nuts when someone else pours dirt in their hole. Climb out of your holes, people!" In this episode, his adversary is a fifteen-year-old faith healer who is eventually diagnosed correctly as having a sexually transmitted disease. Along the way, he apparently heals a woman with cancer, although ultimately House uses medical science to refute that. In fact, the real efficacy of the faith healer is effectively disproven, although House's colleagues, who are keeping score in a battle between House and God, declare the contest a tie.

Is this a positive portrayal of atheism? I would argue that it is not and that in fact the entire series essentially presents the position that House's atheism is a symptom of his inadequacy as a human being. Throughout, he is portrayed as a hurt, damaged person who cannot interact in a normal, human way. He appears to have no social life, playing poker with acquaintances whose names he doesn't even know; he is addicted to painkillers; he is rude, overbearing, and offensive to everyone, including the few people who actually care about him, most notably his only real friend, Dr. Wilson (Sean Michael Leonard). Throughout the series, other characters function to point out to House (and us) why he lacks faith and why this is such a problem. In a first-season episode, "Damned If You Do," there is a suggestion that he protests his unbelief too much, when a nun tells him "You can't be angry with God and not believe in him at the same time. No one can. Not even you." In "House vs. God," Wilson argues that House uses unbelief as a defense mechanism:

> When it comes to being in control, Gregory House leaves our faith healer in the dust. And that's why religious belief annoys you. Because if the universe operates by abstract rules, you can learn them and you can protect yourself. If a supreme being exists, he can squash you anytime he wants.

The tie in "House vs. God" results from the fact that even though the faith healer was a liar, he has learned, repented, and repaired his faith in a more realistic way, while House has simply remained obnoxious. Wilson, rather than House, has the last word, concluding, "House? You are . . . as God made you." And because Wilson is intrinsically a much more sympathetic character, this is the message that remains. One of the most striking messages about House's belief comes in the third-season episode "One Day, One Room," in which, for rather unlikely reasons, House is forced into interacting with Eve, a rape victim who has contracted an STD and become pregnant from the rape. The fact that the young woman eventually chooses to terminate is unusual on TV; however, the attitude to House's atheism is not. Eve (a comparative religion major) and House get into some protracted discussion about the existence of God. She is questioning her faith in a God who would let things like this happen and wonders about the overall meaning of everything:

EVE: If you don't believe in eternity then what you do here
    is irrelevant.
HOUSE: Your actions here are all that matters.
EVE: Then nothing matters. There's no ultimate conse-
    quences. I couldn't live like that. . . . I need to know
    that it all means something. I need that comfort.
HOUSE: Yeah. Are you feeling comfortable? You're feeling
    good right now? You feel warm inside?
EVE: I was raped! What's your excuse?

The clear message is that loss of faith is the result of painful experiences, and later this is confirmed when House reveals that his
father abused him as a child. In the end, House emerges as a deeply
flawed human being whose atheism is a protective mechanism to
cover his pain and damaged soul. As Karnick approvingly notes in
the conservative *National Review, House* as a whole is most definitely profaith:

> [T]hough he usually wins through the sheer force of his
> great intellect, . . . the emptiness in his soul becomes increas-
> ingly clear. His doubts in his own abilities suggest that for
> this man, science is not enough . . . Dr. House . . . increasingly
> reveals a loneliness and personal despair that . . . points the
> viewer inexorably toward a spiritual explanation of his prob-
> lem: Dr. House is a lost soul who desperately needs to find
> some transcendent meaning to his life. Though he claims to
> be a strict materialist, his frequent references to Dante's Cir-
> cles of Hell suggest what is really troubling him.[21]

In contrast, all the characters who surround House are clearly
people of faith who constantly try to redeem him as a human
being. Indeed, by the beginning of the fourth season, we see signs
that House is softening and even desperately seeking faith. For
instance, in the third episode of season 4 ("97 Seconds"), House is
clearly deeply unsettled by a patient who deliberately gives himself an electric shock in order to try to regain the spiritual bliss
he achieved in an earlier near-death experience. House scoffs, but
then in a bizarre turn of events, he shocks himself unconscious
by inserting a knife into an electrical outlet, as the patient did, in

search of the "white light." While he fails to experience the light, the message is rather clear: his emptiness is so profound that he will risk death for the mere chance of a spiritual awakening. If he ever is redeemed, part of that redemption will almost certainly be an embrace of religious faith—although that would probably destroy his fascination to audiences. House clearly is a compelling character to viewers, many of whom see him as someone they "love to hate." As one poster on IMDb.com put it, at first "I just didn't 'get' Greg House's character and wondered how anyone could watch an ass like that every week," but later he learned to relish House's sarcasm and wit. Do viewers identify with House in the way they might do with beloved characters? Many find a way to do so, by referencing his emotional damage: one comments, "The sarcasm is . . . a front for his pain (I'm guessing both physical and emotional)," while another says she would like the series to explore the "untapped reasons for the fact that he pops prescription pills as if they were candy, his dependence on his inner anger and other things." Essentially, Wilson is more truly the moral center who invites viewer identification, not House himself. Interestingly, House's atheism in itself seems to cause little viewer comment because it is so much a taken-for-granted aspect of his general jaded hostility and cynicism. Why else would anyone not believe? Indeed, I would argue that it is very unlikely that TV drama will ever present an overtly atheist character who is also well-balanced, functioning, and happy in his or her choice. The significance of this brief discussion of atheist portrayals should be clear: successful TV drama consistently embraces faith, and one aspect of that embrace is its rejection of faithlessness.

Television and Movies: Two Different Sensibilities

More than thirty years ago, Raymond Williams drew attention to some fundamental differences between cinematic and televisual drama.[22] His main focus was on the difference in visual quality, lighting, and so on, but I would argue that there are broader differences that also help us understand why particular depictions of religion may be more or less successful depending on which medium presents them. In discussing television, Williams suggests that television, once it moved past merely filming plays, fundamentally altered our ways of experiencing drama. "It is clearly one of the unique characteristics of advanced industrial societies that drama as an experience is now an intrinsic part of everyday life . . . watching the dramatic simulation of a wide range of experience is now an essential part of our modern cultural pattern.[23] While today's media scene might have staggered Williams in its intensity, I doubt if it would have surprised him, as he clearly saw the direction we were headed—into "living" media in our daily lives. Today we live in a culture that is so mediated that it no longer makes sense to talk about the "effects" of media;[24] rather we need to how we all engage with, and construct, our senses of self through media.

In this mediated culture, while to some extent all messages and genres become intermingled, I believe there are differences in the way we engage with different texts. Television has become the place of familiarity, where we interact with and get to know characters on a regular basis. The rise of the Internet has intensified this process, allowing multiple ways in which viewers can interact with and within the worlds of their favorite shows (and especially, their favorite characters). Fan activities have mushroomed, including chat rooms, message boards, fan fiction, conventions, and so on.[25] As I discuss in my extended audience analysis of the series *Dr. Quinn, Medicine Woman*,[26] viewers use TV drama to discuss wide-ranging issues of good, bad, morality, and appropriateness, and simply get wrapped up in the lives of beloved characters. Clark's discussion of *Lost* fans (in this volume) is a rich exploration of how open-ended, continuing dramatic arcs allow viewers to ponder motives, speculate on coming events, and interrogate issues of morality and faith. Even viewers who are not die-hard, active "fans" still become invested in the characters and the milieu of the shows.

I believe that to be widely successful, any TV drama must be able to allow large numbers of viewers to identify with the central characters and storylines over an extended period of time—and they should not be turned off by overtly sectarian themes. Specific depictions of religious dogma, as we have seen from the range of negative reactions to *Revelations*, are a minefield for this kind of identification. This is why leading characters in major, mainstream shows are rarely seen discussing or actively practicing their faith. We may surmise that that CSI Catherine Willows is Catholic when we see her briefly lighting a candle for her dead father, but we do not expect (or want) her to launch into a discussion of why Catholicism is correct. The "safe" position for lead characters, as I suggest above, is one of rather general and unspecified faith, as Clark discusses in relation to *Lost.*

This has to be the case, otherwise large segments of the audience will be alienated. This is true not only in shows like *CSI* or *Law and Order,* which are not "about" faith, but also in successful "spiritual" shows like *Touched by an Angel,* which was resolutely nonsectarian, redeeming doubting people of all faith origins. This position was affirmed often by *Joan of Arcadia* creator Barbara Hall, whose guidelines included "God can never identify one religion as being right" and "God talks to everyone all the time in different ways."[27] If the producers of *Revelations* had understood this basic point about TV, they would never have attempted to reach a mass audience with this format.

Movies, especially those with mass appeal, are "events"—even when watched later on TV. They generally offer "one-time-only" opportunities to enjoy highly dramatic stories that rely more on plots than characters, and they generally have a clear resolution. This is not to say that movie characters cannot be emotionally engaging. They can, but they are not generally asking for an ongoing viewer commitment and so can be more extreme, more tragic, more tied to the specific dramatic events of the movie. In that context, it is much more likely that specific faith and religion can be dramatized; viewers' investment is shorter term, and often tied more to the story than to the character. The major exceptions to this would be multipart movie cycles, such as *Star Wars, Lord of the Rings,* and the Harry Potter series, all of which not only operate in a fantastical environment but also offer a resolutely nonspecific form of faith. Harry Potter's Lord Voldemort may be the epitome of evil, but he is not a Christian-defined Satan any more than Darth Vader or Sauron. These three series attract the same kind of devoted attention to character as TV dramas, and their versions of morality can engage people of all faiths. *Revelations* drew on more standard cinematic conventions, in the same way as blockbusters like *The Da Vinci Code* or *The Exorcist,* which certainly offended some Catholics, but because of its dramatic story, still offered an exciting, one-off movie experience.

Conclusion: Television and "Lived Religion"

So as we have seen, the idea that television is "antireligion" has become commonplace. There can be no denying that mainstream dramas quite frequently do present unflattering portrayals of faith. In the *Law and Order* franchise, for example, there have been several episodes that depict crazed murderers who feel they are driven to kill by God, or sanctimonious clergymen who transgress sexually. However, what is often lacking in critics' analysis is a consideration of the context of the events. As my earlier discussion of *CSI* viewers suggests, audiences may clearly see a larger message: that faith is good, but when perverted by fanaticism or hypocrisy, it should be condemned. Inevitably in these storylines, those who are guilty of such perversions are convicted (or die) and effectively "cleansed" from the faith, leaving the good faithful to carry on. Frequently, explicit comparisons are made, often by lead characters, between "real" faith and that espoused by evil-doers, a point that Clanton made effectively: in *Law and Order*, "religious faith is acceptable as long as it is 'normal' and one is rational enough to base one's behavior on commonly accepted mores and practices rather than 'odd' religious truths."[28] This theme plays out across the franchise; for example, in one *Law and Order: Special Victims Unit* episode, it is revealed that a pastor not only impregnated his son's wife, but also killed her to cover his crime—certainly a "negative" representation of faith. However, the shock and horror of his family and church, along with the condemnation of the investigators, leaves no doubt that faith in itself is not the culprit here. In an episode of *Law and Order: Criminal Intent* ("The Third Horseman"), a man claiming that he is doing the Lord's work murders a doctor who performs abortions. However, it turns out that his motive is simply revenge against the doctor who terminated his former girlfriend's pregnancy, at her request. Again, individual choice, although hypocritically framed as faith, is identified as the evil, not faith itself.

Indeed, the consistent message is that "true believers" are likely to be hypocrites or potentially dangerous or misguided individuals who will behave irrationally. An episode of *Law and Order: Criminal Intent*, called "The Healer," makes this point in a compelling way: a young woman who has made a name for herself as both a traditional nurse and a voodoo healer has been poisoning patients. When Detective Mike Logan ridicules voodoo, his partner Detective Barak defends the principle of religious freedom, saying that it is "just another kind of religion." However, once it has become apparent that the healer's follower has obeyed her blindly, the two agree that the "true believer" is the most dangerous person of all—someone who cannot think for himself, but follows dogma mindlessly.

Orsi lays out an agenda for the study of "lived religion," rather than the theological, textually driven study that has long typified religious history. Drawing on approaches that have long been standard in anthropology, he defines this as "religious practice and imagination in ongoing, dynamic relation with the realities and structures of everyday life in particular times and places."[29] He calls for "rethinking religion as a form of cultural work," which "directs attention to institutions and persons, texts and rituals, practice and theology . . . concerned with what people do with religious idioms, how they use them, what they make of themselves and their worlds with them . . . Religious practices and understandings have meaning only in relationship to other cultural forms and in relation to the life experiences and actual circumstances of the people using them. . . ."[30]

The connection to audience-based television study becomes obvious as we move between the text and the lived experience of the viewer. Orsi points, for example, to particular practices, such as praying to the Madonna "the meanings of which seem to be clear enough and discernible through Catholic theology,"[31] but which in reality are intertwined with individual circumstances and habit. It is highly probable that when people follow such practices, they are not consciously or formally engaging with theology but rather following cultural practice. I would argue that television texts also cannot be read alone or that we can assume that certain elements of those texts can be isolated and taken out of the context in which they are experienced. General, nontheological references to faith of the kind discussed in this chapter speak to people's lived religion, which is more about getting through the day than debating the finer points of faith. When Gil Grissom simply says that he keeps his rosary because it belonged to his mother (and not because of some complex theological reason), this speaks directly to audiences' own experiences. As Blythe suggests, "the theology found on television is not systematic, nor is it terribly profound."[32] I would add to this that for most Americans, systematic consideration of theology is not an important part of their everyday lives. However, concerns of morality, family, death, and survival are. That is a key reason why procedural police and medical programs are such rich sources of discourse on these issues: as Siegler points out, "the elements of everyday life are brought to the fore on the modern television cop drama; and the audience is brought in as a partner to the men and women who have to face these issues."[33]

The Parents Television Council (PTC), like much academic content analysis, reaches its conclusion about negative portrayals by identifying isolated instances. What such critics forget is the very nature of television engagement I have discussed above. Most people watch drama series in the context of their knowledge of the whole cycle of themes and characters and see particular events as contextualized. "Sound-bite" content analysis can never capture that. For instance, I note three of PTC's many examples of incidents judged derogatory to religion. I would argue that each actually speaks to the lived reality of viewers' experience in a way that is much more subtle than a simple positive/negative dichotomy would suggest.

> Members of a synagogue believe that their Chamash, a copy of the Torah used in prayer, has been saved from the Nazis and has been sacred for generations. The Chamash is desecrated and a man is murdered. When a man is about to be convicted for the killing, a rabbi comes forward and states that he has lied about the Chamash, admitting that he bought it in a used bookstore. When McCoy asks him to account for his deception, the rabbi replies: "The Bible is full of stories that may be apocryphal. Do we believe that Methuselah lived 900 years? Or that Moses parted the Red Sea?" (NBC, *Law and Order*, 7 December 2005)

In this episode, the rabbi has lied about the sacred book for complex reasons—not for personal gain but to give the congregation a focal point for community identity and to validate the importance of the Holocaust in their traditions. He questions the literal truth of the Bible, just as many others surely do as they work to reconcile sacred texts and everyday life. In the end, the rabbi has made what might be considered a poor decision, but for arguably defensible reasons. The value of Jewish faith is never questioned here; the question is about human beings wrestling with the intersection of faith and life. These questions are left open for the audience to figure out themselves.

Another "negative" example:

> An aide tells candidate Santos before a political debate, "You can't let this communion thing bother you. Most Catholics are pro-choice. How do bishops expect politicians to do what they can't even do in their own church?" (NBC, *The West Wing*, 30 October 2006)

The reality of course is that many Catholics do struggle with the church's position on abortion. The episode does not condemn or defame the church for this; it simply raises the question for its audience to consider and relate to their lives. They will do so within the context of what they know about Santos and his own struggles over faith and practice.

Perhaps less controversial is a third example:

> Maya and Darnell argue over whether to go to Darnell's Episcopal church or Maya's Baptist service. They ask young Jubari to decide. Jubari tells them to do what they always do. The family drives straight to a restaurant to arrive "before all the church folks show up." (UPN, *Girlfriends*, 12 December 2006)

Once again, this vignette is probably familiar to almost anyone who identifies with a church. Daily life necessitates compromise and sometimes involves skipping the formal trappings of religion. Does that mean that Darnell and Maya have no faith? What would the "positive" portrayal be here—that the couple chooses one church over the other?

Many more examples make the same point: without context, and without an understanding of the function of TV texts in people's daily lives, we achieve only a one-dimensional view of religious representation. Rather, we need to understand television drama as one way through which people construct their worlds, living not only their religion but also their politics, their morality, and their aspirations. The mainstream TV dramatic landscape is generally one of tolerance for difference; intolerance for cruelty, violence, hypocrisy, and extremism; assumption of faith (and intolerance for lack of it); and a pragmatic, nontheological approach to religion. This general profaith stance is apparent across the dramatic genre, even in such basically secular franchises as *CSI* and *Law and Order*, as I have suggested; these shows would not succeed if they really were antifaith or advocating atheism. Programs that acknowledge this middle-of-the-road faith without seeming sectarian, such as *Touched by an Angel* and *Highway to Heaven*, seem to do well, treading a fine line between overt preachiness and a perception of disrespect, such as the reaction that doomed efforts like the short-lived *Book of Daniel*. It seems probable that a new 2007 show, TNT's *Saving Grace*, which again features a generic "guardian angel" will be able to walk this line successfully.

This rather bland approach to faith may seem "secular" to some, but I submit that it captures the overall picture of mainstream U.S. culture today, where almost everyone professes a faith in some kind of higher being, even when they are alienated from organized religion. There will always be media that appeal to smaller segments of that culture more than others, and those media can be more explicit in their depictions of faith, politics, or anything else. But to reach large audiences, TV drama is most successful when it speaks to audiences' lived realities, in the voices of familiar characters about whom they care. When it comes to religion, it makes perfect sense that theologically based attempts like *Revelations* will fail. Conversely, hugely popular dramas like *CSI, Law and Order, House*, or *Lost*, while not overtly religious at all, actually speak very successfully to the lived religious experiences of the majority of Americans. Indeed, in the warm television landscape of faith, only the nonbeliever is left out in the cold.

In the Beginning . . . Deadwood

HORACE NEWCOMB

As is so often the case with television fictions, the title sequence of *Deadwood* informs much of what is to follow. Unlike many such sequences, however, the information is far more symbolic than iconic, ambiguous rather than specific, foreboding rather than appealing or inviting in a conventional "entertainment" manner. We are introduced not to characters and stories, but to place, tone, environment in every sense of the word.

A ground-level shot focuses on what seems to be puddled water and mud. Into the mud step well-worn boots and beside them the tip of a walking stick. Before we have time to consider this, a hoof splashes into the water and the camera shifts to a full shot of a powerful horse running through wilderness. The horse does not gallop. Rather, it runs at a lope, the steady, efficient gait that can cover much ground, long distance, without exhaustion.

The point of view shifts as images of this place come into view. Close shots follow the horse's hooves sinking and splashing in mud. Chicken carcasses hang from a pole. A man hoists a meat cleaver over the neck of a chicken. The shot is set from a low angle, tilted up, and the cleaver seems to rise over the viewer's face. Streams of blood (the chicken's?) ooze down a white background as if on a canvass, perhaps the fabric of the butcher's tent. Miners pan for gold as the horse runs through a working scene. A nude woman, viewed from the back, lowers herself into a bath tub. The horse runs in water, a flowing creek. A hand holds playing cards. The horse passes from woods and water and moves into a settlement, into what would be, in a conventional western, civilization, or at least a protocivilization. Shots of whiskey are poured into glasses. Gold dust rains from a leather sack onto a mounting pile. The horse is reflected in water standing in the streets—then the image slowly dissolves. All this takes place in a flowing montage that matches underlying music, matches the lope of the horse that disappears, still running through this single street.

In some ways, these images prepare us for—or perhaps better, condense—some of the key elements in the narrative(s) to follow. These are narratives that do rely, to a degree, on historical fact, on real persons who inhabited the Deadwood mining camp in the years before and after the region was annexed to a politically defined territory. Woven onto these facts and personages are layers of invented commentary dealing with such mundane matters as the formation of businesses, the building of houses, the establishment of educational systems, and the roles of mass communication in print and electronic form. These topics and others are presented in the context of far graver issues of politics and economics, violence and sex, race and gender. And all are constructed within specific views of human natures, behaviors, and interactions; the movements of history; and the significance of social and cultural formations—views that can well be described as theological. The factual, sensational in its own right, is a good place for beginnings.

Deadwood in History

Located in the Black Hills in what is now South Dakota, Deadwood became one of several mining camps following the discovery of gold. At the time, the region was part of the vast range belonging to Native Americans under terms of the 1868 Treaty of Fort Laramie. The gold discovery came during one of George Custer's expeditions in 1874, and prospectors invaded the protected areas, despite weak attempts by the military to keep them out. When tribal leaders rejected an offer of six million dollars for the land in 1876, Congress, under pressure from the prospectors and more and more settlers, repealed the Fort Laramie treaty. The act also required all native tribes to remain on the great Sioux Reservation. On 25 June 1876, George Custer's troops were defeated by Native Americans in the Battle of the Little Big Horn, leading to further military repression and enabling the region to be flooded with those seeking fortunes, including entrepreneurs and con men, gamblers, actors, prostitutes, and opportunists of all sorts.

Most of the characters who appear in *Deadwood*—Wild Bill Hickok, Seth Bullock, Sol Star, Charlie Utter, Al Swearengen, Calamity Jane, George Hearst, and others—did actually come to the mining camp, which grew in population to several thousand. Many of the events depicted in the television series occurred, including the smallpox epidemic of 1876, General Crook's passage through the camp in pursuit of the groups who had defeated Custer, the establishment of various businesses, and perhaps most famously, the murder of Hickok. The lawless quality captured in the television series appears to have been the rule in the actual camp, but so too was the entrepreneurial spirit and the concern for a future framed by political decisions and a sense of the settlement's relationship to society, culture, and governance.

In short, there is a strong factual basis in events, conditions, and personages underlying the television series. What emerges in the fictional version, however, takes great liberties with these raw materials, at times rearranging details and almost throughout developing characters "based on" actual individuals rather than in any way attempting to capture them as "real" figures. The writers, directors, and actors of the series, under the strong control of creator/producer David Milch, invented and embellished in order to imagine a world in the manner of all powerful fictions. The meaning and significance of that world are complex and compelling.

The *Deadwood* Narrative(s)

Much of the *Deadwood* story focuses on two major characters, Seth Bullock and Al Swearengen, but as the narrative moves forward their stories are intertwined with a large cast of characters who take on more and more significance, most notably among them,

George Hearst. The story begins, however, with Bullock. He first appears as he prepares to leave a settlement in Montana territory. There he serves as marshall, but has decided to move to the Black Hills with his partner, Sol Star, to open a hardware store in Deadwood. In the first episode ("Deadwood"), Bullock faces down a mob intent on lynching a horse thief held under his authority. Rather than allow the lynching, Bullock pulls the prisoner from his cell, places a noose around his neck, stands him on a box, and confronts the lynch mob. Holding a gun on the leader of the mob, he makes his intention clear: "I'm executin' sentence now and he's hangin' under color of law."[1] The prisoner notes that the box is too low for a "drop." Bullock says he will "help [him] with the drop." He then hears the thief's words to be relayed to his sister, who was to come the next day for the official hanging.

> CLELL: You tell my sister, if my boy turns up, raise him
> good.
> SETH: What else?
> CLELL: Tell her, give him my boots.
> SETH: What else?
> CLELL: Tell him, his . . . daddy loved him. Tell him, he asks
> God's forgiveness.
> SETH: Anything else?
> CLELL: You help me with my fuckin' fall![2]

After he steps off the box and struggles—as he expected, the drop is insufficient to kill him—Bullock grabs his feet, jerks, and breaks his neck. Sol Star has driven their wagon to the front of the jail. Bullock steps on and with guns still covering the angry crowd, Star drives the wagon out for Deadwood.

Swearengen first appears indirectly. When Bullock and Star arrive in Deadwood, they seek to rent a lot on which to begin their hardware business. Swearengen's main henchman Dan Dority negotiates, renting them a corner lot for twenty dollars a day: "In advance, every morning, to Mr. Swearengen at the Gem." The lot is only available by rent; there is to be a tent, but no building. The Gem is Swearengen's saloon, brothel, and home. When first seen, he is setting up a tab, a running account with a miner,

Ellsworth, to exchange gold for drinks and sex. Within minutes he is confronted with a problem. Trixie, one of his prostitutes, with whom he has a personal relationship, has shot a client. He had beaten her and accused her of robbing him. When he dies, Swearengen calls Trixie to his office and berates her for not calling one of the henchmen to take care of the matter. She tells him to do what he has to do, knowing he will hurt her. He yells for her not to instruct him, throws her against a wall, then onto the floor where he pushes his boot against her throat, choking her, and waits to hear her say, "I'll be good now."

By the end of this first episode Swearengen has swindled an easterner into a mining deal and instructed Dority to murder the miner who was involved. Bullock and others, including Wild Bill Hickok, have learned of a family massacred outside of Deadwood and have ridden to the scene; rescued the only surviving child; returned to the camp; confronted Ned Mason, the man who brought news of the massacre; charged him as one of the perpetrators; and outdrawn, shot, and killed the man.

We have now met Hickok and his friends Calamity Jane and Charlie Utter. We know Brom Garret the easterner and his wife Alma. At the Gem we have a crew of characters including Trixie, Dority, Johnny Burns (another of Swearengen's henchmen), and Jewel, the handicapped maid. Doc Cochran, physician to the camp, has come to the saloon to take care of the murdered "john." E. B. Farnum, proprietor of the local hotel, has established his sycophantic nature. The Reverend Smith has greeted Bullock and Star. A. W. Merrick, voluble editor of the *Pioneer*, Deadwood's newspaper, has established his attitude as the camp's (easily intimidated) progressive:

> Paradoxes. The massacre at Little Big Horn signaled the Indians' death throes, Mr. Utter. History has overtaken the treaty which gave them this land. Well, the gold we found has overtaken it. I believe within a year, Congress will rescind the Fort Laramie Treaty, Deadwood and these hills will be annexed to the Dakota Territory, and we, who have pursued our destiny outside law or statute, will be restored to the bosom of the nation. And, that's what I believe.

Merrick's comments capture two other great narratives that will swallow up the personal relations shaped by Bullock and Swearengen. The first is the narrative of the gold. Nothing in *Deadwood* is ever far from materialist concerns. But the key element in the narrative of the gold is the arrival of George Hearst (who did, in fact, make much of his fortune in a Deadwood mine). In *Deadwood*, Hearst sets out to control gold extraction in the region. Through his emissary Francis Wolcott (an invented character), he buys most of the producing mines. Alma Garret, on advice of Bullock and Ellsworth, refuses to sell, though she does make one naive proposal that Hearst rejects.

Hearst's successes result from his complicity in the other overarching historical narrative in *Deadwood*, the movement toward formal political status. Long before we see Hearst, Swearengen recognizes that some form of order is necessary, even if to allow his own criminal activities to find a proper and continuing niche. He calls meetings of camp leaders: Farnum from the hotel; Merrick from the newspaper; Tom Nuttall from the other major saloon; Cy Tolliver, the owner of a competing (and more upscale) brothel and gambling establishment; Bullock from the hardware store; and Doc Cochran, the camp physician. These men assume civic duties—fire marshall, health commissioner, and the like. They act on memories of other places and experiences, on models of civic life left behind and pointing to, even hoping for or anticipating, a substantial future.

Again, Hearst bends the narrative trajectory. Wolcott is able to purchase mines cheaply because he circulates rumors that mining claims will be invalidated when the camp is annexed into a territory. By the final episode, Hearst buys sufficient politicians and voters to see that Bullock is denied office. He forces Alma Garret to sell her claim because she wishes to remain in Deadwood. He requires Swearengen to murder a prostitute he thinks tried to kill him—though Swearengen sacrifices a completely innocent woman from his establishment instead. In short, he has manipulated the entire "world" of Deadwood to his own ends and leaves the camp triumphant, accompanied by a company of Pinkerton agents who stand ready to engage in a battle that will destroy the place if necessary.

The opening hour of *Deadwood*, then, has put into motion a set of conflicts that will be played out in thirty-five more episodes. By the end of the series, a degree of order is established, but at an expense so great as to throw doubt not on specific historical personages or events, but on history itself, and on the meaning of a nation.

Deadwood by Design

All these matters are constructed under control of producer David Milch, who has spoken and written both plainly and metaphorically about what he intended to invent. His comments establish yet another overarching *Deadwood* narrative and begin, not with the creation of the series, but in personal experience and professional history.

Milch has been open and forthcoming regarding his affections for and struggles with many forms of addictive substances, including heroin, as well as with other types of behavior such as compulsive gambling. His career as a writer has doubtless drawn on actions and events undertaken and undergone under these influences, but equally under the influence of great writers, such as Robert Penn Warren, and great scholars, such as R. W. B. Lewis, both of whom acted as guides and encouragers during his time at Yale and after. His television work began on *Hill Street Blues*, and his first script for that series (his first television script), "Trial by Fury" (1982), is one of the most famous episodes. It involves the brutal murder of a nun and the manner in which Frank Furillo, a central character in the series, engineers retribution. He went on to write or co-write twenty-seven other episodes of *Hill Street*, then created other television series, most notably, with Stephen Bochco, *NYPD Blue*. The series aired from 1993 to 2005. During that run, the central character Andy Sipowicz developed from a racist, alcoholic, amoral, violent police detective into an alcoholic police detective who struggled mightily with his racism, his violence, and his morality. He had become the conscience of the entire fictional universe in which he participated and stood as the image of a complex, compassionate, tortured, deeply humane figure. The approaches and the vision that shape such a character are those that carry over into the creation of *Deadwood*. About this, Milch has been explicit:

> I originally proposed to HBO to do a series about city cops in Rome at the time of Nero. Nero was crazy and it interested me to think about what it would be like to be a cop, an instrument of order, in a world that could invoke no ordering principle besides, "Do what an insane person tells you to." Nero would be walking down the street, and he'd say, "That man would be better with his tongue cut out and his hands hung around his neck," and the cops would have to do it. I wanted to imagine what it was like for the cop, and then for the cops to encounter a new organizing principle, which was faith. In the first episode, the head cop was going to be told to arrest Saint Paul.[3]

At the time, of course, HBO was developing *Rome*, a series quite different from that envisioned by Milch, despite its own level of requisite violence. There is no Saint Paul in *Deadwood*, nor even a specific Neroic figure. But for a world without any "ordering principle" other than something approaching insanity, Deadwood as Milch imagined it and transferred to it his own principles certainly suffices.

> I settled on a story about Deadwood, because the camp came together in the mid-1870s, deep into the Industrial Revolution, and yet it was a reenactment of the story of the founding of America, and a reenactment, too, of the story of Original Sin. I suppose I accept Hawthorne's definition of Original Sin as the violation of the sanctity of another's heart. (12)

Add to this another factor cited by Milch as fundamental to his plans for the series. "I was interested in how people improvised the structures of a society when there was no law to guide them . . . [h]ow the law developed out of the social impulse to minimize the collateral damage of the taking of revenge."[4] Elsewhere Milch points out that this description is from Oliver Wendell Holmes' discussion of the rise of common law.[5] How likely it is that Holmes' notion was influenced by his physician father, Hawthorne's contemporary. Yet Milch adds another layer to this harsh description, a layer that enables him to write of violations and revenge and the resultant damage with a compassion surpassing judgment.

> My feeling about *Deadwood* is it's a single organism and I think human society is the body of God, and in a lot of ways it's about the different parts of the body having a somewhat more confident sense of their identity over the course of time.[6]

Any attempt to examine the full "society" that is *Deadwood* will diminish the significance of many characters, many of the parts of God's body, who populate the place or any sense of its fundamental story. It is impossible to truly capture Swearengen's importance, for example, without a complete account of his relationship with the prostitute, Trixie. It is unfair to Bullock to overlook his connections to Sol Star, a man much more "normal" than Bullock himself, who falls in love with Trixie and in effect wins her away from Swearengen. It is unfair to both Swearengen and Star to leave off a full summary of Trixie's role, because in so many ways she is central to all the other narratives and supporting narratives. Similarly, without a study of Alma Garret, Bullock's relationship with her can only be noted and Hearst's motives in intimidating and threatening her can only be barely understood. Cy Tolliver becomes a link between Hearst and Swearengen, and his own relationship with another prostitute, Joanie Stubbs, leads to critical events in Hearst's designs. Joanie's descent into near-madness, her "rescue" through a relationship with Calamity Jane, Jane's connection to Wild Bill Hickok, and Doc Cochran's or E. B. Farnum's chorus-like observations on the camp at large—all these ties illuminate Milch's visions for the meaning of the series and his strategies for an overarching narrative realized on an almost epic scale. The choices, engagements, and actions of these and many other characters are far more fully realized than those of "supporting" roles in most television series.

Given that very scope of the series, however, the thirty-six hours constructed in extraordinarily dense fashion, it is impossible

to chronicle here all the ways in which Milch's designs are constructed. Still, it is perhaps possible to grasp a sense of this effort
by attending to the narrative agents driving the three central lines
summarized earlier—Swearengen's attempt to maintain a site for
his corrupt and somewhat trivial empire; Hearst's grand obsession, his battle to extract as much of "the color," the gold, as possible from the earth at large; and Bullock's desperate need to control
himself and the settlement around him, to create something of an
"ordered" life. To an extent, these figures and their narrative arcs
allow some understanding of how many violations of the sanctity
of the hearts of others occur, how often revenge is taken, how
much collateral damage is done. And though it is impossible to
give an account of the entire "society" Milch and his collaborators have created—all the variations on the construction of God's
fragile body that truly define *Deadwood*—their encounters open a
way to at least understand what is at stake.

First Words

As described in a *New Yorker* profile, "While others sat on a sofa
or chairs, Milch reclined on the floor in the center of the room, a
few feet from a microphone and a twenty-inch computer monitor,
on the other side of which was a desk where an amanuensis, seated
in front of a computer and another monitor was poised to type
whatever he dictated."[7] Other writers have received credits for
the *Deadwood* scripts far more frequently than Milch himself, but
it is highly unlikely that the diction defining the dialogue varies
significantly from his. The language has been described as Shakespearian, but as I have written elsewhere:

> As much as it is Shakespearian, then, the language of *Dead-
> wood* also draws on that other great text of the period, the
> 1611 Authorized (King James) Version of holy scripture. The
> language is biblical. In *Deadwood* a world is molded from the
> materials of history and historical research, the muck of pri-
> mal matter. It is as if the place is spoken into being, as if
> Milch's dictated pilot is a Genesis of sorts.
>
> This, of course, points to yet another literary model,
> for this world is populated with beings already far fallen

from paradise. In this regard *Deadwood* is Miltonic as well as Shakespearian. Here knowledge of good and evil is not a thing new, astonishing, and bewildering, but already sharply developed.[8]

There is a troubling aspect in this comparison. If Milch, like blind Milton, dictates this account of "the fall" that establishes original sin, he does so without constructing the paradise that is lost. In the first episode of the series, there is, perhaps, a hint at something left behind that may be better than what is to come. The wagon train with which Wild Bill Hickok, Calamity Jane, and Charlie Utter are traveling toward Deadwood is stalled behind a broken wagon. As Hickok and Utter head on toward the mining camp, Jane sees a wagon, the Metz's, headed in the opposite direction. She calls out to them.

> JANE: Do you know a back way into the camp?
> PA METZ: Whoa.
> *Metz's wife speaks to her husband in another language, then turns*
> *to Jane.*
> MA METZ: We don't go to the camp. We go home . . . back
> to Minnesota.
> JANE: You probably got the right idea.

As the wagon drives away Jane exchanges smiles with a young girl in the wagon, whom we will later come to know as Sophia Metz.

It would be pleasant, perhaps reassuring, to think of Minnesota, to think at least of "home," as paradise, a place where families live and thrive among their own. There they might speak their own language rather than the foul tongue we have already experienced as the vernacular of frontiersmen and women and the inhabitants of Deadwood. In this story, however, one Ned Mason rides into Deadwood and happens to address Bullock and Sol Star.

> NED: I seen a terrible thing tonight.
> SETH: What'd you see?
> NED: I seen white people dead and scalped and . . . man,
> woman, and children with their arms and legs hacked
> off.

SETH: Where? How many dead?
NED: Well, it was a whole family on the road to Spearfish. Oh
my God, it's them heathens, bloodthirsty savages.

Bullock and Hickok force Mason, against his wishes, to lead
them to the site. There, at the edge of the bloody scene, Sophia
Metz is found cringing inside a hollow log and returned to the
mining camp in Bullock's arms. When Calamity Jane meets them
on the road, Bullock hands the child to her. In the camp, Mason
is challenged by Bullock and Hickok as one of the true murderers
and shot dead when he attempts to draw his pistol.

Whatever drove the Metz family from their Minnesota-
Scandinavian idyll to the gold-riven gulches of Deadwood, it was
hardly worth it for anyone involved. Bullock and Star and, fate-
fully, Wild Bill Hickok are now fully engaged with Deadwood and
must come to terms with the mining camp's key figure.

Al Swearengen

"He is moved by grace even as he disavows it." (19)

Even before the events described above are fully developed, while
the riders are on their way to the scene of the massacre, word is
brought to Swearengen. Johnny Burns comes to Al in his busi-
ness/living quarters above the Gem Saloon. He tells Swearengen
that knowledge of the murders and the expedition have circulated
in the saloon. Swearengen responds with a comment that defines
whatever paradise he is intent on constructing for himself.

> How many people do you think the people he talked to have
> talked to by now? I guarantee it this minute, my entire fuckin'
> action downstairs is fucked up! Nobody's drinkin', nobody's
> gambling, nobody's chasin' tail. I have to deal with that!

This, then, is what Swearengen does—he deals with things. As we
learn later in this episode, there is a chance he himself would have
approved of the Metz murders had he been able to control the
event. And he does engineer the death of one of the murderers and
sends Dan Dority to murder Sophia Metz. When he realizes that

the child cannot recognize the second murderer, he spares her and kills the murderer on the spot. In subsequent episodes we watch as Swearengen murders others, brutally cutting their throats. He abuses women and cohorts and manipulates anyone he chooses for his own ends. His past is no different from the present we witness. There is a warrant for his arrest in Chicago, on a charge of murder, but again, he is able to "deal with" it.

As what part of the body of God does Swearengen possibly function and why does he seem somehow noble? Why do we see him on more than one occasion on his knees, scrubbing blood from the floor where he has just murdered someone by cutting a throat?

We learn in the course of the long story that Swearengen was delivered to an orphanage by his mother as she abandoned him on her way into prostitution and that he was likely abused while there. We come to know that all the prostitutes he profits from were bought from that same orphanage in order to be put under his "care." We see him suffer to the point of death with kidney stones. These qualities are again evident as he comforts Reverend Smith, who suffers seizures resulting from a brain tumor, seizures like those experienced by Swearengen's brother. When in a later episode he euthanizes the suffering Reverend Smith, the act takes on the quality of a tender mercy—but it is also used to teach Johnny Burns the correct and efficient manner in which to suffocate a victim. As Milch says,

> What Al Swearengen thinks he is doing and what he is actually doing are two absolutely opposite things. Swearengen believes he is in solitude, but in fact he is absolutely engaged with the world. He is a very good man with none of the behaviors of goodness. He's a whoremongering murderer who protects the whores he abuses. (18)

He is willing to submit to some rule of law because he knows officials can be murdered when necessary and politicians bribed. In early episodes, he exhibits a resemblance to Milton's Satan, but there is surely no paradise from which he has fallen, no epic struggle with radiance and purity. The epic battle that does ensue is with George Hearst.

Swearengen first attempts to collaborate but soon realizes his interests will not be recognized or served. In a moment of pure intimidation, Hearst's thug, Turner, holds Swearengen down as Hearst chops off part of his finger. Even then, Swearengen holds out the possibility of retaliation. As Bullock supports him on a pained walk back to the Gem Saloon and offers to go after Hearst, Swearengen stops him, saying, "I'll have mine served cold." His revenge does come later when Dan Dority beats Turner to death in a horrible street fight. But that, too, has its drawbacks. Johnny Burns reports that Dority is despondent following the fight. Puzzled, Burns points out that both Dority and Swearengen have killed before. Swearengen replies that it's "different in a fair fight. You see the light go out of their eyes." Such a sentiment would be unthinkable for Hearst. Swearengen clarifies their respective positions:

> Pain-in-the-balls Hearst. Running his holdings like a despot,
> I grant, has a fucking logic. It's the way I fucking run mine.
> It's the way I'd run my home if I fucking had one. But there's
> no practical need for him to run the fucking camp. That's out
> of scale. It's out of proportion, and it's a warped, unnatural
> impulse, this fucking cocksucker!

George Hearst

"The only price he had to pay was to treat human beings as if they were inanimate. That's a version of original sin. But original sin got us out of the garden and got us to Manhattan." (46)

In Milch's narrative, Hearst's arrival is preceded by that of his agent Francis Wolcott, an invented figure who purchases properties for Hearst. Wolcott is a sexual deviant who murders prostitutes purchased from madams fully aware of his intention. By the time of Hearst's arrival, Wolcott has become a liability in two ways: he has indulged his sexual appetite and killed three prostitutes, all in one event, and he has been unable to secure title to Alma Garret's rich holdings.

Wolcott confesses to Hearst that he has killed before and compares his motivations with Hearst's supposedly "mystical" ability to discover silver and gold. Named by Native Americans as "the boy the earth talks to" in honor of this effect, Hearst insists on distinguishing himself from his assistant.

> WOLCOTT: As when the earth talks to you particularly,
>   you never ask its reasons.
> HEARST: I don't need to know why I'm lucky!
> WOLCOTT: What if the earth talks to us to get us to arrange
>   its amusements?
> HEARST: That sounds like goddamned nonsense to me.
> WOLCOTT: Suppose to you it whispers, "You are king over
>   me. I exist to flesh your will."
> HEARST: Nonsense.
> WOLCOTT: And to me . . . "There is no sin." It happened in
>   Mexico and now it's happened here.

When Wolcott takes his own life, it is a minor event to the employer. More significant is the title to Alma Garret's mine because there his obsession is in play. His exchange with Swearengen, before their enmity fully surfaces, explains:

> HEARST: Do you know prospecting, Mr. Swearengen?
> AL: Fuckin' nothin' of it.
> HEARST: And the securing of the color once found?
> AL: Not a fuckin' thing.
> HEARST: All I really care about.
> AL: I fuckin' hope so. I'd hate to think you're this good at
>   somethin' that's only a fuckin' hobby.
> HEARST: Most often my finds are in wild places, which I
>   prefer. When that is not so, I want friendly rela-
>   tions with my predecessors so that I *can* secure the
>   color . . . undistracted.

In the interest of efficiency, Hearst threatens and intimidates all who counter him. In a scene that makes his intentions clear, he takes a sledge hammer in hand and batters a hole in the wall of his hotel rooms. It opens onto a porch roof, and he steps through to survey Deadwood's main street and all its activity. This mirrors Swearengen's own habit of standing on his own balcony, monitoring the same scenes in episode after episode. Once he stands above the camp, Hearst becomes the story's major antagonist.

Hearst arranges murders. He mutilates Swearengen's hand. He sends his man, Turner, into the street to do battle with Dan Dority and watches as Turner is beaten to death. When Bullock pulls him by the ear into jail, embarrassing him in public, he immediately plots revenge. When Alma Garret Ellsworth comes to him, naively offering to "sell" the mine so long as she owns controlling interest, he very nearly attacks her. His account of the event, expressed to Cy Tolliver, is chilling:

> But I should say too that in these rooms just this afternoon such displeasure brought me near to murdering the Sheriff and raping Mrs. Ellsworth. I have learned through time, Mr. Tolliver, and as repeatedly seem to forget, that whatever temporary comfort relieving my displeasure brings me, my long-term interests suffer. My proper traffic is with the earth. In my dealings with people, I ought solely have to do with niggers—and whites who obey me like dogs.

All interested parties in Deadwood join forces to battle Hearst. Swearengen sends for gunfighters. Trixie, the prostitute, races bare breasted, to Hearst's hotel. She pounds on the door to his rooms and, when he opens, lifts her skirts and shoots him as he stares at her body. The wound is minor, however, and she becomes yet another target for him.

Hearst wins. He has his wound patched. He rigs an election to his own ends. Alma is intimidated into selling her mine in order to remain in Deadwood. He requires that Trixie be killed. Swearengen agrees—but in one of the most poignant and telling events in the narrative, murders Jen, an innocent prostitute, Johnny Burns' girlfriend, in her place. Hearst looks at the corpse, touches the bloody neck, and accepts the ruse. In the final scenes he sits high on the stagecoach taking him from Deadwood, having accomplished his aims, scoffing at those like Seth Bullock who still offer puny challenges.

Hearst, not Swearengen, rules like an arrogant Satan in *Deadwood*. One description of that place knows it as "a hell of a place to make your fortune."

Seth Bullock

"Our desire for order comes first, and law comes afterward." (121)

In many ways, Bullock walks between Swearengen and Hearst, perhaps intended to be as close to "normal" as any inhabitant other than his partner Sol Star. He comes to Deadwood purposely to leave behind his work as a professional lawman, to join the entrepreneurial class, to settle his wife (his brother's widow) and stepson in the new world of frontier opportunity. His passionate commitment to the some semblance of order places him on the side of civilization, contrary to Swearengen's criminal dedication and Hearst's primitive drive.

Yet by the end of the first season, barely able to tolerate the lawlessness of the camp, he agrees to become sheriff. He has begun an affair with Alma Garret and beaten her sleazy father almost to death. He has, in fact, beaten an Indian warrior to death during his search for Jack McCall, Hickok's murderer. His temper erupts again in the first episode of the second season when he is offended by Swearengen, and the two battle in the muck and mud of the main street. When he looks up from the mud, he sees his wife and stepson, who have arrived by stagecoach and now look down on him, appalled at what they see. He manages to recover sufficiently to walk them to the elegant house he has built, to make mundane conversation, and then return to Alma Garret once more.

Again and again Bullock regains, then loses, control—of himself, of others, and of Deadwood. At the conclusion of the series, he has been defeated in the election for sheriff, thwarted by Hearst's machinations, and made more complicit in Swearengen's plans than he would have first thought. Still, he tries. As Hearst steps to the top of the stagecoach that will take him out of Deadwood, tipping his hat to Alma, Bullock is again angered at the arrogance.

> BULLOCK: You've looked at your last body. You're done tipping your fucking hat. Get out of here or I'll drag you out by the ear.

Unfazed, Hearst merely tells his driver to "Drive on." Charlie Utter attempts to console Bullock.

CHARLIE: You done fucking good.

BULLOCK: I did fucking nothing.

CHARLIE: That's often a tough one, in aid of the larger purpose.

BULLOCK: Which is laying head to pillow, not confusing yourself with a sucker?

CHARLIE: Far as I ever get.

BULLOCK: 'Cause that's gonna be a project tonight.

If Bullock can indeed avoid confusing himself with a sucker, if he can lay his head on a pillow in peace, he will have accomplished something, perhaps achieved some self-awareness. That doing so will still be "a project" suggests that more awareness is yet needed. Milch's comments here are central:

> Law is a fiction the members of society rely on to protect their lives and to preserve the order they have already built. Cops preserve order while pretending to be interested in the law. Seth Bullock embraces the sheriff's badge as a way of binding his inner rage to the external force of the law, which sanctions his own violence. Pitted against wrongdoers from Jack McCall to George Hearst, he succeeds in suppressing the contradictions within himself and within the life of the town, which in turn makes life in Deadwood possible. (119)

Bullock, with his aim to establish order and his barely controlled rage, exemplifies another of Milch's observations—"Civilization is a very young thing" (213). His posture, stiff and upright, seems out of place beside Swearengen's slouch and Hearst's confident raring. His clothes, as neat as possible, are often covered with muck and blood. His intention to establish a business is constantly set aside as he rushes to encounters all too violent. His belief in family is strained by his passion for Alma. Everything about Bullock is evidence of an adolescent of civilization, malleable, filled with promise, but potentially self-destructive. Still, as much as anyone in *Deadwood*, however, he enacts Milch's plans for his Rome series— "I wanted to imagine what it was like for the cop, and then for the cops to encounter a new organizing principle, which was faith." Bullock struggles to maintain a faith in something that exceeds the raw material of Deadwood. If order is all he can achieve, if the law will come later, that may be sufficient.

Lived Religion in *Deadwood*

Whatever that order might be it is unlikely to depend on any formal sense of religious organization or religiosity, but this is not to say that the Deadwood camp is without these qualities. It would have been disingenuous to present an account of this period in American history without acknowledging the role of received and institutionalized belief. Thus, one of the first citizens Bullock and Star meet as they begin their hardware business is Reverend Smith. Like most of the key characters in the narrative, he is based on a historical figure. Reverend Henry Weston Smith, a Methodist preacher and Civil War veteran, was apparently the first ordained minister in the Black Hills. Though there was no church in Deadwood, Smith preached in the streets and, as depicted in the series, worked odd jobs. Having watched the two newcomers almost sell out their wares in one day, he adds himself to their staff, yet witnesses in the same conversation.

> REV: My ah, wife and children are in Louisville, Kentucky. I'm, I'm, I'm saving to bring them out. Days I dig on the Foster's water ditch and nights I watch folks' goods like I'm going to do for you.
>
> SOL: Schedule like that, Mr. Smith, seems like you'll have 'em here in no time.
>
> REV: And then Sabbaths I preach Christ's crucified and raised from the dead.

Later in the same episode he witnesses in another way as Bullock and Hickok kill Ned Mason. As he later confirms that Mason was the first to draw his gun, he notes that "Men like Mr. Seth Bullock raise the camp up" and that Bullock has commissioned him to prepare a coffin for Mason and to conduct a funeral. It is at the funeral that we begin to see the struggle for any indication of religiosity in the camp and the depth of Reverend Smith's personal perspectives.

REV: Our Christ, as he was crucified addressed the thief who
was hanging by his side. Verily I say unto thee, this
day, shalt thou be with me in paradise. Your ways
are not our ways, oh Lord. We abide the just and the
unjust alike under your tearless eye. Tearless, not
because you do not see us, but . . . because you see
what we are so well. *(Seth raises his brow, the Reverend
shuts his eyes and looks to the sky.)* Lamb of God, who
takes away the sin of the world, send your angels to
welcome this body into paradise. Lamb of God, who
takest away the sin of the world, grant this soul eternal rest. Amen.

SOL: That's a real generous perspective, Reverend.

REV: And don't we need all the generosity we can get?

Sol Star, the Jew, remains far more sympathetic to Smith than
his partner Bullock. When Wild Bill Hickok has been murdered,
it is again Star and Bullock, with a few mourners and Merrick, the
newspaper editor, who attend the funeral to listen again to Smith's
interpretive application of Scripture.

REV: Mr. Hickok will lie beside two brothers. One he likely
killed, the other he killed for certain, and he's been
killed now in turn. So much blood. And on the battlefields of the brothers' war, I saw more blood than this.
And asked then after the purpose and did not know.
But know now to testify that, not knowing, I believe.

Saint Paul tells us, by one spirit, are we all baptized in the one body. Whether we be Jew or gentile,
bond or free. And they've all been made to drink into
one spirit. For the body is not one man, but many.
He tells us, the eye cannot say unto the hand, I have
no need of thee. Nor again, the head to the feet, I
have no need of thee. They, much more those members of the body which we think of as less honorable,
all are necessary. He . . . he says that, there should be
no schism in the body, but that the members should
have the same care, one to another. And whether one
member suffer, all the members suffer with it.

> I believe in God's purpose. Not knowing it. I ask
> him, moving in me, to allow me to see his will. I ask
> him, moving in others, to allow them to see it. Let us
> sing "How Firm a Foundation" as Mr. Hickok is laid
> to rest.

I quote here at some length for several reasons. Significantly, the choice of this passage, from the twelfth chapter of First Corinthians, strongly mirrors Milch's own oft-quoted comments regarding the "body." His focus on the connectedness of communities, societies, and even nations is reducible (or expandable) to a holy communion of bodies and souls, of all humanity. Such a communion is absent in Deadwood, and despite Smith's claim that Bullock is the sort of man who "lifts up" the community, it is Bullock who runs out of patience when Smith presses him on what his "part" of the body, the community, is. "I can't say I know what you're talkin' about, Reverend."

Equally important is that in spite of what would by others be taken as the futility of his mission, Reverend Smith is bathed in faith: "But know now to testify that not knowing, I believe." He has seen the bloody battlefields of the Civil War, and we learn later that he served there as a battlefield nurse. His belief in "God's purpose" is what adds the next layer to his character as the representative of formal religion. When smallpox strikes the camp, it is Smith who volunteers to assist Doc Cochran in caring for the sick. Calamity Jane also nurses the infected, having discovered that she is immune to the disease. But it is Smith who continues even as he discovers a more profound affliction of his own. In the same episode in which he preaches the funeral of Wild Bill Hickok, we see him suffer a seizure while sitting outside his tent—no one notices.

In the next episode he again falls with a seizure, this time in public, during a meeting of the camp's "leaders," called by Al Swearengen to discuss the smallpox attack. Doc Cochran assists, but it is Swearengen who also knows how to help. We learn here that his brother was also stricken with seizures of some sort. Smith's illness progresses, even as he comforts smallpox patients and aides Doc Cochran in the camp's "pest tent." In episode 12 Reverend Smith is unable to move or care for himself, and at this point Al Swearengen's "mercy killing" is sufficient.

Another minister does appear in the series. Andy Cramed, a con artist colleague of Cy Tolliver, brings smallpox to the camp and is removed and abandoned in the hills by Tolliver's henchmen. Saved by Calamity Jane, he later returns, having found religion, and confronts an unrepentant Tolliver. He performs the funeral when the Bullocks' son is killed in an accident and later performs the marriage for Alma Garret and Ellsworth. But at the wedding celebration he stabs Tolliver, almost killing him. Despite an "apology" in a later episode, his influence remains minor in the world of *Deadwood*.

This is not the case, however, for Doc Cochran, central throughout the series. He treats prostitutes and miners, the Chinese as well as the dominant community, drunks and gunshot victims. He battles his own demons with alcohol and rude scientific experiments in which he studies the anatomy of the dead victims of Deadwood's violence. But in one moment he reveals his deepest concerns and also expresses one of the linchpins in Milch's perception of religion in Deadwood.

When it becomes apparent to him that Reverend Smith's condition leaves no hope of cure, he cries out in prayer.

DOC: If I was a more adaptable primate or one of your regular petitioners, I suspect I wouldn't feel this pain. I guess I—I'd have a wad of cartilage covering the patella, protecting me from this—this discomfort.

Jesus Christ. Jesus Christ, just please, God. Take that Minister.

What conceivable Godly use is his protracted suffering to you? What conceivable Godly use? What conceivable Godly use was the screaming of all those men? Did you . . . did you need to hear their death agonies to know your . . . your omnipotence? Mama! Mother find my arm! Mommy! Mommy! Mommy they . . . they shot my leg off . . . it hurts so bad. It hurts so bad.

Admitting my understanding's imperfection, trusting that you have a purpose, praying that you consider it served, I beg you to relent. Thy will be done, Amen.

Doc Cochran's plea exceeds even Bullock's quest for some type of order in the world. His prayer moves from intercession for the individual, the suffering Reverend Smith, to his agonized recollection of men he tried to save during his own days on bloody Civil War battlefields. In this, one of the few references to that conflict in the entire narrative, he begs answers to the meaning, the use—any "conceivable Godly use"—of that suffering. Yet in the end, there is a humility that underscores the confusion and the anger. There, he acknowledges the impotence of reason. Like Job—"who can know"—or Paul—"through a glass darkly"—he can merely "trust" that such horrors serve some purpose. His plea for mercy is capped by his subservience to the greater "will." It is, of course, the unanswerable question, the problem of evil branded into this story of national origins and repeated in the conclusion to this epic account.

In the very last scene of the series, Al Swearengen is again on his knees, scrubbing blood from the floor, blood that flowed from the throat of the innocent woman he sacrificed in order to protect Trixie. Johnny Burns steps to the door and looks down at him.

JOHNNY: Did she suffer?
SWEARENGEN: I was gentle as I was able, and that's the
       last we'll fucking speak of it, Johnny.

As Johnny walks away, Swearengen has the last word in the series as he continues scrubbing the bloody floor.

SWEARENGEN: Wants me to tell him something pretty.

In the Beginning . . . Deadwood

Perhaps there is nothing pretty to say here, no pretty story to tell. If, as Milch avows, he "settled on a story about Deadwood, because . . . it was a reenactment of the story of the founding of America, and a reenactment, too, of the story of original sin," (11) how could there be? But a story that is not pretty is not the same as an ugly story.

There is instead a beauty in *Deadwood* that surpasses "pretty." As Milch also says, "I think the human heart yearns to be lifted up. What lifts us up with less excess weight and baggage better than anything else is a story about our brothers and sisters?" (10) Take Bullock, then, as the closest thing we can find to the best brother.

But Milch's notion is far broader. Unconditional is the word that comes to mind as he reaches out to include his whores and gamblers, his rapists and murderers. They, too, are connected into the shape of God's body. Milch again: " . . . when you trump any defect in a man's character, instead of forgiving it, then anything becomes possible. There is no longer a human proportion to your behavior" (59). While some characters in *Deadwood* seem to have exceeded human proportion, I believe Milch would forgive rather than trump them with some standard of his own. This is, after all, one primary component of original sin: that the fall was itself fortunate, forcing recognition, regret and repentance, opening the gates of grace and making forgiveness possible.

The horse that lopes through the *Deadwood* title sequence fades each time into images of the camp's main street. A wild horse running from wilderness to town could be a fine symbol for that traditional notion of "the western" as an account of our movement from savagery to civilization, to the gradual construction of school buildings and telegraph wires. But this horse is neither captured nor tamed. Although there is a school building readied by the end of *Deadwood* and although the telegraph has become crucial to the narrative, Deadwood itself remains very much on the edge—of wilderness, nature, order. Milch reminds us that for all the claims of progress and enlightenment we still have far to go, and reminds us that *Deadwood* is our story.

> None of us want to realize that we live in Deadwood, but all of us do. That is the point of the exercise. After first recoiling in horror, we come to love the place where we live, in all of its contradictions. To love not just America, but the world of which America is simply the most recent form of organization. American materialism, in all of its crassness and extravagance, is simply an expression of the fact that we have organized ourselves according to a more energizing principle than any civilization that came before us.
>
> I guess I'd paraphrase Jefferson, that with all its horrors, Deadwood is the last, best chance of all human cocksuckers. (213)

Jefferson's words paraphrased here by Milch come from the First Inaugural Address in 1801. Seeking compromise and reconciliation following a bitter contest, Jefferson asked: "But would the honest patriot, in the full tide of successful experiment, abandon a government which has so far kept us free and firm, on the theocratic and visionary fear that this government, the world's best hope, may by possibility want energy to preserve itself?" His concern, expressed six decades prior to the Civil War, already recognizes a fear of attempts to dissolve that government and acknowledges that its preservation will require energy. His images of honest patriots, successful experiments, of a citizenry kept "free and firm" by its government are so much cleaner and purer than the world experienced in subsequent historical settings and certainly more so than in the world of the *Deadwood* narrative.

By contrast, Milch's account is of an America mud covered and blood spattered, of men driven deep into the ground, eager to tear wealth from the earth's womb or fight to death to protect their holdings. It is as if much of the "energy" required to maintain the "best hope" had been funneled into avarice and lust. But this world should be understood as the truer presentation of Jefferson's necessary cultural energy, stripped of his noble language and expressed instead in the profane vernacular of the people who had to do the actual work of preserving. In choosing to paraphrase Jefferson in this manner—not only in the quoted passage but in the entire *Deadwood* narrative—Milch affirms the ideal and honors the labor it demands, even when that labor lurches toward violence and exploitation. For him, it is in the blend of the two descriptions that the true American epic is constructed. Beside Jefferson, who remains in our collective imagination as the image of elegant reason and comforting order, Milch places the Hickoks and the Swearengens, the Bullocks and the Tollivers, the prostitutes and gamblers and suffering Chinese. This is where his faith in the American experiment resides. These are the ones for whom his compassion is exercised. These are our truer progenitors.

Milch's unconditional acceptance (love?) for the people on whose names he embroiders his elaborate characters extends beyond them to his "reenactment of the story of the founding of America." It is an America riddled with violence and greed but one that must be forgiven rather than trumped. It is an America begun over and over again, in places like Deadwood, in motives as flawed as Adam's. And he thinks that in our multiple beginnings we still have a chance.

Milch is a believer. He believes all are touched by grace. He believes in the communion of all human beings. He believes in hope that the communion will someday, perhaps when civilization is older, wiser, and better, work itself into forgiveness.

The Wire
Playing the Game

CRAIG DETWEILER

The game is the game. —Brother Mouzone

Once upon a time, I cared about the inner city. Back in the 1980s, I started an urban Young Life program in my hometown, Charlotte, North Carolina. Our team of volunteer leaders joined the efforts of Progressive Baptist Church. Each afternoon, Reverend Charles Mack opened his church's doors to the teenagers from Dalton Village, the public housing project across the street. We offered tutoring, games, and occasional field trips. The teens wore out the carpet and broke a few chairs, but Reverend Mack considered that a small price to pay for offering a safe haven from the street corners.

For a wealthy city with a booming economy, Charlotte had an alarming murder rate among the black community. I crossed over the tracks to tutor teens at Progressive Baptist in an effort to put my faith into practice. I remember joining a casual game of pickup basketball in the middle of Dalton Village. Beepers lined the court, signs of the players' trade. When they were not shooting hoops, they were slinging drugs, just a beep away from their boss or a hungry client. They all seemed too young to be in business. They were flunking math in school, but practicing the economic law of supply and demand.

Yet, amid such active drug dealers, I never feared for my safety. An assault or robbery of a white male would bring inordinate attention to the drug trade in Dalton Village. But how could an after-school program combat the systemic roots of a complex problem? Did I merely serve as a conduit for white guilt, an easy way for donors to feel like they were supporting the inner city? I positioned myself as a youth minister who demonstrated a different side of "the man." The teens feared the police but welcomed me. While many in the white community considered my efforts to offer tutoring and friendship "brave," the true courage came from young men and women who dared to get up in the morning and face another day on the court of life.

The endangered species on that basketball court was the young black male, guys like James Owens, who admitted, "I don't expect to reach sixteen." The basketball players shot fast, played hard, aware that this game of hoops was only a temporary respite from a much more brutal game they were playing in Dalton Village. Reverend Mack's best efforts to shelter James proved ineffective. James never celebrated his sixteenth birthday. He may have played a prank on the wrong person, acted a bit too much of "the fool." Or James may have been guilty of nothing more than growing up in the crossfire of west Charlotte. He was the first of far too many Dalton Village teens who I befriended and Reverend Mack buried. Success proved elusive.

The Wire delves into a similar neighborhood, rooted in the experiences of white cops and Anglo reporters, who covered the streets of Baltimore in the late '80s. It is an examination of the failed war on drugs, told with passionate, prophetic rage. It offers moments of genuine humanity amid a sea of hopelessness. Religion offers scant comfort compared to the crippling effects of "the game," the drug trade that threatens to swallow cops *and* robbers. Viewers searching for signs of life must look closely amid a culture of death. Yet, the individuals treading the wire between law and order press on, despite the odds.

The Wire is dotted with religious references. Tom Waits' gospel-tinged song "Way Down in the Hole" plays over the opening credits. A cross hangs on the wall of the funeral home where

Stringer Bell teaches his drug dealers to observe Robert's Rules of Order. When Roman Catholic city councilman Tommy Carcetti needs to secure more police cars, he leans on a buddy who shared first communion with him. When Detective Michael Santangelo needs a break in a murder case, he turns to a palm reader for advice. Madame LaRue offers him a statue of Saint Anthony. Her instructions? "Bury Saint Anthony at the grave of the victim. He'll tell you who did it." At D'Angelo Barksdale's funeral, the mourners sing, "Jesus is on the mainline. Tell him what you want." The characters on *The Wire* want a little relief, a time out from the game they are all playing.

These small, finely observed moments demonstrate how religious practices bubble under *The Wire*. Amid the nefarious activities of cops and crooks, abiding faith traditions inform their daily lives. Religious roots may be distant, but they are not dead. As Baltimore struggles to survive, so do its religious institutions. Lived religion in *The Wire* operates below the surface, beyond the drug deals and crooked politicians and institutions that threaten to crush the individuals pledged to serve them. Statues of Saint Anthony are the last vestiges of hope in a rapidly decaying world. Religion rites offer small consolation compared to the deadly, totalizing lure of the game.

Time, Entertainment Weekly, the *Philadelphia Inquirer* and the *Chicago Tribune* all crowned *The Wire* as the best TV program.[1] *Variety* suggested that "When television history is written, little else will rival *The Wire*."[2] *Slate* magazine went even further, calling *The Wire* "surely the best TV show ever broadcast in America."[3] So, why did it fail to develop a broad following? Despite nearly universal critical acclaim, *The Wire* attracted comparatively few viewers and no Emmys.[4] Perhaps its vision of the American city was perceived as too angry, too negative, or too hopeless. *The Wire* explores America's shifting priorities from the costly "war on drugs" to the post-9/11 "war on terror." *The Wire* examines the collateral damage of these unwinnable wars among America's underclass, specifically within Baltimore. *The Wire* chronicles the collapse of Baltimore's ports, the rise of drug barons, the ineffectiveness of the educational system, and the complicity of the media.

Series creator David Simon spent years covering the city and its gnawing problems. Simon recalls, "When I was a reporter for

The Sun, I was covering West Baltimore when cocaine hit and just tore apart families. The factories were closing and moving to where there weren't unions. I watched the port of Maryland deteriorate."[5] Simon found a creative partner on *The Wire* who shared his passion for the city: Ed Burns. Simon recalls, "A lot of the commentary on the police department and the dysfunction of the drug war, that comes from Ed Burns, he was a police officer from '72 to '92 and deeply involved in the war on drugs."[6] Simon and his writing staff explored vexing issues of race, class, and gender. They assembled a remarkable cast that featured a plethora of African American actors. They also employed a host of nonprofessionals—former cops, dealers, and rappers—to give *The Wire* a gritty, local texture.

Yet, despite their noble efforts to empower actors and audiences, Simon and his team have been too ambitious. Critics compared the show to the finest English literature, calling *The Wire* "as complex a picaresque as one is likely to find this side of Dickens."[7] Brian Lowry of *Variety* called it "a series of such extraordinary depth and ambition that it is, perhaps inevitably, savored only by an appreciative few."[8] Was the program too smart? Were viewers unwilling to be challenged? The efforts of Simon and his staff to reveal the tangled web of inner city problems reminded (some) viewers why it is not worth wading into West Baltimore. *The Wire* is both a perpetuator of, and victim of, enlightened racism, turning audiences off of the urban underclass. Was it too complex and infuriating to be recognized with awards or Neilsen households?

The Wire suggested that despite the best efforts of politicians, ministers, educators, and police officers, individuals are merely pawns in the game, the corrosive drug trade that undermines life in the black community. Fueled by righteous anger, the producers of *The Wire* reinforced hopelessness. Where can hope be found amid such daunting circumstances? This chapter will examine the Roman Catholic roots of Baltimore's white residents and the African Methodist Episcopal churches within the black community. *The Wire*'s critique of institutions, subversion of dramatic expectations, and advocacy for the urban underclass echo the biblical prophets call for justice. Yet, dedicated reformers fail to make a difference in *The Wire*. My earnest efforts in inner city Charlotte could not alter the drug trade in Dalton Village. Still, we continued to offer tutoring for local teens. In the same way, the creators of *The Wire* (and its characters!) soldier on despite the odds. Will their hope prove to be folly? Lived religion in *The Wire* offers slight consolation amid the destructive power of the game.

America's Longest War

You can't call this a war. Wars end. —Sergeant Ellis Carver

The Wire arrived in the wake of September 11, 2001. The title alludes to our surveillance society where eavesdropping has become standard police procedure. The first episode was shot two months after the Twin Towers fell, before the subsequent war on terror commenced. Yet producer David Simon anticipated the government's shifting law-enforcement priorities. Detective Jimmy McNulty is the restless policeman who serves as the series gadfly, always pushing harder to solve a case. As expertly portrayed by Dominic West, McNulty is a vexing bundle of contradictions—prone to drunken binges, separated from his wife and kids, passionately committed to beating criminals to the punch. McNulty tries to get the FBI (and their superior wiretapping technology) involved in his unit's case against the drug-dealing Avon Barksdale gang.

But in the post-9/11 world, FBI Special Agent Terrence Fitzhugh explains the shift to McNulty: "Wrong war, brother.

Incorrigible Detective James McNulty (Dominic West) pushes the limits of the law on The Wire.

Most of the squad's been transferred to counterterrorism. This is the last drug case I got pending." McNulty is shocked: "You guys are getting out of drugs?" The FBI agent responds: "For awhile, yeah. We just don't have the manpower to see anything big. Not since those towers fell." McNulty is incredulous: "What, we don't have enough love in our hearts for two wars?" If McNulty and the unit hope to secure federal help in their local war on drugs, they must make the dealers' activities look like a national security issue. Ten episodes later, how do they get a wiretap on local drug kingpin "Stringer" Bell? The FBI inquires about "Stringer's" given name. McNulty answers, "Russell." FBI agent Fitzhugh corrects him: "For now, Akmed." Any efforts to continue the war on drugs must be couched within the post-9/11 obsessions with the war on terror.

The Wire is an extended exposé of America's forgotten front, the war on drugs. Series creator David Simon makes his aim clear: "The first season of *The Wire* was a dry, deliberate argument against the American drug prohibition—a Thirty Years' War that is among the most singular and profound failures to be found in the nation's domestic history. It is impossible to imagine pitching such a premise to a network television executive under any circumstances."[9] Yet, freed from the demands of advertisers, HBO offered Simon an opportunity to explore what Professor Steven Duke has called, "America's Longest War."[10]

"The War on Drugs" arose as a response to the rise of '60s drug culture. With American youth increasingly experimenting with marijuana, cocaine, and heroin, President Richard Nixon identified drug abuse as "public enemy number one in the United States."[11] In 1971, Nixon created the Special Action Office for Drug Abuse Prevention, with an emphasis upon treatment rather than law enforcement. The War on Poverty shifted to the War on Drugs. While the frontlines remained remarkably similar, the techniques diverged in haunting ways. The war on drugs grew in profile and intensity during President and Nancy Reagan's "Just Say No" campaign. The Anti-Drug Abuse Act of 1986 created mandatory minimum sentences for drug offenses. Efforts to capture and extradite leaders in foreign drug cartels increased. With all drug use criminalized, the American prison population exploded. Presidents George H. W. Bush and Bill Clinton increased funding for the drug war, especially via military support in Central and South America. Despite billions of dollars devoted to interdiction and prosecution, by 1996, even the conservative *National Review* concluded, "The war on drugs is lost."[12] Working as a reporter for the *Baltimore Sun*, David Simon determined, "What began as a war against illicit drugs and the damage they do has now become a war on the underclass."[13]

The first season of *The Wire* pointed out the similarities on both sides of the war on drugs. Police and dealers suffer under their supervisors' attention to statistics. Human lives are reduced to numbers, another stat waiting to be solved. By contrasting scenes of the foot soldiers' frustration with their commanding officers expectations, *The Wire* pointed out the personal, human cost of war *for both sides*. Season 2 of *The Wire* waded into the Baltimore harbor, where shipping containers become an occasion for contraband. Without overt reference to 9/11, the season suggested how much illicit activity could occur on the docks despite extensive security measures. The stevedores can always be paid to look the other way.

Season 3 returned to the streets, where control of the corners equaled a corner on the drug trade. In the first episode, "Time After Time," a dilapidated housing project is demolished, making way for urban renewal. As the project falls, ashes and smoke ripple across West Baltimore. Only a red traffic light and a church steeple peer through the haze. *The Wire* made an obvious nod to the collapse of the World Trade Center's towers. David Simon commented, "The theme of this season was reform. Not only political but social and personal reform. We were using the housing project being demolished as a metaphor for reform in a post 9/11 world."

The Wire's third season also contained eerie parallels to the war in Iraq. An insurgency grows within West Baltimore's drug trade. With Avon Barksdale still in prison, a power vacuum has arisen that Marlo Stanfield vows to fill. The Barksdale gang constructs a plan to take out Marlo. But in a lawless battlefield, the best-laid plans still go awry. Marlo evades the Barksdales' bullets. Bubbles, a drug-addicted sage declares, "Marlo's flying his own colors. The Westside is about to become Baghdad."

The police try to quell the insurgency. Major Bunny Colvin instructs his officers to move the drug trade off the corners and into a designated arrest-free drug zone. Like Amsterdam, Bunny Colvin's "Hamsterdam" is an experiment in prevention rather than incarceration. In episode 10, "Reformation," Bunny explains his philosophy to the zealous Sergeant Carver: "This drug thing, this ain't police work. If you call something a war, pretty soon everybody gonna be running around acting like warriors. Pretty soon everybody is an enemy and the neighborhood is an occupied zone. Soldiering and policing ain't the same thing. You ain't talking about protecting the neighborhood now. The worst part of this so-called drug war is that it ruined this job."[14] Bunny's frustration parallels the U.S. military's fruitless efforts to secure a safe "green zone" in Baghdad. We have incarcerated those we intended to free.

As Marlo's gang continues to undermine the Barksdales' authority, soldiers on both sides of the turf war are ready to fight irrespective of the cost. In episode 12, "Mission Accomplished," Barksdale warrior Slim Charles (indirectly) compares the beef with Marlo to the Iraq war: "Don't matter who did what to whom at this point. Fact is, we went to war and now, there ain't no going back. That's what war is. Once you in it, you in it. If it's a lie, we fight on that lie. But we gotta fight."[15] The parallels to our vexing post-9/11 situation are almost too troubling to consider. Viewers may have considered such pointed commentary as something other than entertainment. *The Wire*'s prophetic edge drove away viewers accustomed to clear answers and tidy endings.

Beyond Good and Evil

On HBO, nothing other than the stories themselves are for sale, and therefore—there is nothing to mitigate against a sad story. Or a subversive story. Or even a disturbing story. —David Simon[16]

The Wire looks like a crime drama. It follows the efforts of a police unit to gain enough evidence (primarily via wiretaps) to put criminals behind bars. Yet, viewers expecting *The Wire* to follow preestablished patterns of television drama are bound to be frustrated. Crimes are not solved within an hour. Instead, *The Wire* uncoils like a novel, with ample time devoted to character development. To enter into *The Wire*'s West Baltimore requires a profound commitment of time and effort. It requires multiple viewings just to track the extensive characters' complicated histories and inter-relationships. *The Wire* subverts the Hollywood paradigm of the individual rising above circumstances. Here, the circumstances, the game, crush people.

The Wire cannot be viewed casually. It is multidimensional and multi-institutional. Each season concentrates upon a distinct sector of the urban fabric: cops, docks, politics, education, and journalism. Cases stretch over the course of the season, with each episode offering scant clues to a resolution that will only arrive twelve or thirteen television hours later. Whole seasons hinge upon small moments. In season 2, the plot was driven by a dispute over the donation of a church window. The junior high students featured in season 4 see their lives unravel over five dollars they accept to watch out for the principal. *The Wire* makes a deal with its audience, gambling that the delayed gratification that occurs over three months of episodes will be worth the wait. Consequently, the arrests and deaths that arrive in the eleventh or twelfth episode of each season hit with a convulsive force. Viewers feel the loss of Wallace, the long final walk of Frank Sobotka, the grisly shooting of Stringer Bell, the death of the ultimate soldier, Bodie. Even Proposition Joe cannot cut a deal to save his life. *The Wire* makes us care about these people, whether dishonest union bosses or calculated drug dealers. It puts a human face on inner city life, turning mere crime drama into epic Greek tragedy.

The Wire subverts the Western myth of good and evil. Crime drama is "often seen as the most conservative genre in prime time—a world where clean-cut paragons of decency uphold social mores against deviants and evil-doers, where moral and legal standards never diverge, where disorder and ambiguity are dispatched with equal disdain."[17] Think of the moralizing exhibited by Elliot Ness on *The Untouchables* or Joe Friday on *Dragnet*. By the seventies, socially conscious law enforcers questioned "the system" and even empathized with lawbreakers. In *The Mod Squad*, the officers dressed and thought like those outside the law. In cop shows like *Baretta*, *Kojak*, and *Police Story*, Linda Lichter noted, "Police officers mixed sensitivity with moralism. They could sympathize with victims or people trapped by circumstance in a bad life, but they still despised crime and criminals."[18] Crime drama matured in the 1980s with shows like *Cagney and Lacey* and *Hill Street Blues*, in which "police officers worked in a very complex world where good and bad were not sharply delineated . . . the new realist dramas set themselves apart by creating less perfect police officers."[19] The cop show as struggle between clear-cut, Manichean forces was waning.

David Simon traces his dramatic roots to Greek tragedy rather than Shakespearean drama. The characters in *The Wire* may make ethical choices, but their fate is often predetermined. Well-intentioned characters make innocent mistakes they do not realize. Detective McNulty pushes for investigations that prove personal and costly. Casual decisions have consequences days, weeks, and many episodes later. Viewers expecting an uplifting finale are bound to be frustrated. Even when their cases are closed, the cops on *The Wire* struggle with the sense that they have not won in any traditional sense. McNulty ends up just as restless as when he began, only now he knows the depths of the evil he encountered. It is systematic, far larger than any case or any bureaucracy.

How has *The Wire* been able to flaunt television conventions? Only the artistic freedom offered by pay television (specifically HBO) has allowed Simon and company to defy dramatic expectations. Television bought and paid for by advertising must offer a certain amount of predictability and reassurance. The broadcast networks offer a gratification delivery system. Viewers essentially know what they are buying with each genre. Having been beholden to NBC and its advertisers during his earlier series, *Homicide*, Simon recognizes how rare an opportunity subscriber-funded television presents. He suggests that "until recently, all of American television has been about selling. And therefore little programming that might interfere with the mission of reassuring viewers as to their God-given status as consumers has ever been broadcast—and certainly nothing in the form of a continuing series."[20] As a premium cable series, *The Wire* is released from the burden of salesmanship. Stories do not have to conclude each week. They can drag out across a season.

Premium channels offer an alternative to network fare. But *The Wire* broke even HBO's precedents by taking on established network genre conventions. When the future of the show was in limbo, Simon wrote a gutsy letter. Simon appealed to HBO executive Chris Albrecht's desire to beat the television networks at their own genre. He wrote, "It would, I argue, be a more profound victory for HBO to take the essence of network fare and smartly turn it on its head, so that no one who sees HBO's take on the culture of crime and crime fighting can watch anything like *CSI*, or *NYPD Blue*, or *Law & Order* again without knowing that every punch was pulled on those shows."[21] Simon's blatant appeal to Albrecht's ego worked. *The Wire* was renewed. A quick listen to any of Simon's commentaries or interviews also reveals the enormous ambition (yes, even ego) energizing *The Wire*. It aspires to nothing less than redefining the television crime drama.

White (Catholic) Baltimore

"It's Baltimore, gentlemen. The gods will not save you."
—Commander Ervin Burrell

Although angry in its expression, *The Wire* loves Baltimore. Galvanized by their eyewitness experience of inner city life, Simon's team approaches the creation of *The Wire* with a religious zeal. Like the biblical prophet Jeremiah, they seek the welfare of the city, reminding us, "When it prospers, you will also prosper."[22] They mourn what Baltimore has become and offer a blistering critique of unchecked capitalism. Simon observes, "You look around the harbor and there's all this real estate development, but it's all for Washingtonians who are looking for a good investment and are willing to accept a long commute. It's artificial and it's leaving behind generations of people who once had meaning in America."[23] Simon insists that *The Wire* has been "exploring what it means to live in an American city and be beholden to the institutions that form a city."[24] Like the prophetic books of the Bible, *The Wire* is an angry letter to leaders, fueled by profound ethical concern.

Any show set in Baltimore must include a nod to its profound religious roots. Baltimore is the most Catholic city in the first Catholic state in the union, Maryland. It is home to the first Catholic diocese in America, founded in 1789.[25] Its basilica was America's first cathedral. As host to the American plenary council, the archdiocese spawned the Baltimore catechism—the traditional study method in parochial schools from 1885 until 1963.

Two-thirds of American Catholics trace their religious roots to Baltimore. Such a profound spiritual heritage is bound to inform a program like *The Wire*, so committed to its local milieu.

Detective Jimmy McNulty embodies the lived religion of Baltimore's Catholic community. At a Washington, D.C. fundraiser, McNulty heads for the bar. He asks the bartender, "Can I get a Jameson's?" The bartender asks casually, "Bushmill's all right?" McNulty scoffs, "That's Protestant whiskey." Bushmill is brewed in Protestant Northern Ireland, while McNulty's roots (shared by the Irish actor, Dominic West) are decidedly Catholic. *The Wire* offers a glimpse into McNulty's spiritual psychology to start season 2. Demoted to the harbor police, McNulty finds a body floating in the water. After hours, while sharing a drink with his old partner, Bunk, McNulty makes a vow: "I'm gonna give this one a name. I'm gonna find where her people are at." Bunk offers a cynical response: "What does that matter? This is that Catholic shit, Jimmy. This is that little altar boy guilt talking." Issues of guilt, confession, and obsession haunt McNulty inside or outside a formal ecclesiastical setting. McNulty's Catholic roots tug at him in inescapable ways.

Baltimore is also home to undercelebrated aspects of our American heritage. Francis Scott Key penned the words to our national anthem, "The Star-Spangled Banner," at Fort McHenry. The city also embodied America's melting-pot ideals. Religious freedom was granted in Maryland's Toleration Act of 1649. The ports made Baltimore the second leading immigration city throughout the eighteenth century. Pledges of toleration were put to the test. Baltimore also spawned homegrown leaders like Frederick Douglass. *The Wire* explores the growing gap between this proud heritage and a shocking present reality. It is an elegy to a once great city.

What caused the destruction of the American dream in Baltimore? White flight to the suburbs? The collapse of local industry? Season 2 focused upon the harbor and the dockworkers who supported companies like Bethlehem Steel. *The Wire* staff writer Rafael Alvarez comes from a family of stevedores. He said, "Season Two of *The Wire* was about the last days of being able to follow in your old man's footsteps to make a living if nothing better—and legitimate—came along. It was, said David Simon, a twelve-episode wake for the 'death of work.'"[26] It followed the tireless, but frustrated efforts of Frank Sobotka to revitalize the longshoreman's union and bring jobs to the docks. The entire season turns upon a dispute over competing donations of a memorial window at the local Polish Catholic church, Saint Casimir.

In "Ebb Tide," the first episode of season 2, Frank Sobotka delivers an envelope of cash to the parish priest. After kneeling before the crucifix, they both stand before an illuminated stained glass window that celebrates the heroism of dockworkers. Sobotka has spared no expense, importing the window from Germany. In exchange for his generosity toward the church, Sobotka asks the priest for a favor—some "face time" with U.S. Senator Barbara Mikulski (D-Maryland). He wants to ask about the canals, to get more jobs for his union. Yet, when the priest inquires about his last confession, Sobotka laughs and exits. He is too busy fixing things to worry about confession. In *The Wire*, religious rites battle everyday concerns and lose every time.

Police Major Stanislaus "Stan" Valchek also has his eyes on the window. He gives the church $2500 for the nave. Valchek has already commissioned a stained glass window—"To Polish police and firefighters." The major admires its craftsmanship with pride and anticipation. When he discovers that the stevedores already secured the spot, Valchek grows apoplectic. He asks the priest, "How much did the dock boys offer for this spot. Did they go higher than $4000?" Outmaneuvered for the church window, Valchek goes on a personal vendetta. He senses something amiss at the local union, "Frank Sobotka has that kind of money?" He exercises his police power to launch an investigation. Despite the priest's appeal to Valchek to "Talk to Frank, work it out. . . ," the season (and the union) unravel under Valchek's less-than-righteous grudge.

In the second episode, "Collateral Damage," Valchek threatens Sobotka: "Father Lou says 'He could take another window in the rectory on the second floor.' If you don't want my finger in your eye, you better do what's right here." Frank digs in with equal resolve, "What's right is for you to come down here to my house like a decent human being and ask a common courtesy. But that's not you. That's not your way." Valchek proceeds to reassemble the unit from season 1 with a new imperative: "I think Francis

Sobotka's into some dirt." Public resources are channeled toward a private religious dispute. For each move by Valchek and the unit, Sobotka and his union counter, even stealing a police surveillance van and shipping it around the world. They torture Valchek, mailing photos taken by the dockworkers at each port of call. Both men and both institutions (police and longshoremen) suggest, "Don't mess with us." An apparent, maybe even genuine, desire to honor God and their coworkers devolves into a deadly face-off.

As the second season plays out, the pride of both men proves costly. Sobotka's shiftless son, Ziggy, has gotten involved in the theft of cameras and cars. Ziggy murders a middleman who attempts to stiff him. Sobotka's nephew Nick has also gotten dragged into organized crime. Nick sides with the vicious crime boss, "the Greek," rather than his uncle. Sobotka's efforts to bribe politicians also unravel, with no new business secured for his beloved union. He becomes a tragic figure, longing for redemption. Actor Chris Bauer explains how he brought so much empathy to his role as Frank Sobotka. Bauer comments, "The role of Frank Sobotka was the closest I've come to playing someone who actually lived—real heartache, real suffering, real ecstasy. That's how I felt about Baltimore. I miss it."[27] With Ziggy jailed for murder, Sobotka declares, "I need to get clean." Yet, Frank does not turn to the church for absolution. The harbor policewoman, Beatrice Russell, begs him to turn himself in, but Frank resists: "I ain't turning in no union." In climactic episode 11, "Bad Dreams," Sobotka justifies his choices to Beatrice: "I knew I was wrong, but in my head I thought I was wrong for the right reasons." His efforts to free his son, protect his nephew, and preserve the union all fail.

Valchek gets the satisfaction of putting Sobotka in the back of a police car, parading the arrest before news cameras. But the "victorious" Valchek ends up haunted. He hoped Sobotka's arrest would advance the career of his son-in-law, Detective Pryzbylewski. But "Prezbo" sees through Valchek's plan. Tired of his father-in-law's badgering, Detective Pryzbylewski knocks him down in front of the unit. Valchek stumbles out of the police department, nursing his wounded jaw and punctured pride. Sobotka is eventually released on bail. But before he reaches the trial, "the Greek" murders him. Sobotka's blood essentially stains Valchek's hands. Even from the grave, Frank Sobotka sends messages to Valchek. The police major receives another Polaroid photo of the van, taken in a remote corner of the globe. Valchek's police van is lost at sea— just like Sobotka. An act of religious devotion and generosity has been twisted into a series of murders. A stained glass window intended to unite a community only brought them together for a funeral. Neither Francis Sobotka nor Stan Valchek escaped the dirt or experienced absolution. Religious practices cannot compete with corrupting power.

Black (A.M.E.) Baltimore

The king stay the king. Everyone stay what they is 'cept the pawns.
They get capped quick. They be out of the game early.
—D'Angelo Barksdale on the rules of chess

The Wire's season 3 features a neighborhood meeting in the basement of the historic Bethel A.M.E. Church. Formed in 1811, Bethel Church played the largest role in the foundation of the African Methodist Episcopal denomination. Historian C. Eric Lincoln identifies such black churches as "the only stable and coherent institutional area to emerge from slavery."[28] Churches

"God's own drug addict," Bubbles attended a narcotics anonymous meeting in a
Baltimore church basement.

like Bethel A.M.E. "became the womb of black culture." Almost two hundred years later, Bethel A.M.E. remains a beacon in West Baltimore, under the dynamic leadership of Reverend Frank Reid. A community-wide meeting was held in this same church in 1937. From the community's cries for justice came the appointment of Baltimore's first black police officer, Bethel A.M.E. member Violet Hill Whyte.[29] Season 3 of *The Wire* begins in the Bethel basement, under the banner of Jesus' Last Supper, with a policeman fielding questions. The people gathered in the fellowship hall complain, "My kids can't play outside no more." They want to know what is being done to restore order and spur economic opportunity.

The Wire's third season explores the potential for reform—from the basement up. It follows three parallel reform efforts—from the personal to the political and onto the police department. How much change can we expect to see in urban America? Are the problems of race, class, and poverty so entrenched that we should abandon hope? *The Wire* asks, "Is reformation possible?"

In West Baltimore, historic black churches like Bethel A.M.E. remain a visible vestige of hope. We see residual respect for the church in the ghetto's traditional Sunday morning code. Hardened gangsters are free to attend church without feeling threatened. Yet, when Avon Barksdale's overzealous soldiers spot freelance thief, Omar, taking his grandmother to church, Stringer Bell orders his assassins to "hit him." As Omar puts his grandma in a taxi, Barksdale's boys open fire. Bullets fly but Omar escapes. His grandmother loses her hat. Omar is outraged: "Ain't nobody in this city that lowdown to disrespect a Sunday morning! On a Sunday morning, they shot off her best church crown?!"[30] Omar vows to take it to the Barksdales. Avon Barksdale acknowledges the error: "The Sunday truce been around as long as the game itself." Sanctity has been shattered. The game roughed up old-time religion. Regrets cannot undo the blood oath Omar vows to eliminate the Barksdales.

Not only has the church code been undercut, the unwritten rules within the game are vanishing. As season 3 begins, Dennis "Cutty" Wise gets out of a jail. He was a neighborhood legend, an enforcer within the drug trade. He receives a homecoming pack-age from the Barksdales—drugs he can sell to establish a financial base for life after prison. Cutty stares at the supply. He hoped to abandon his old drug-dealing ways. But getting a job and waiting for that first paycheck can take a long time for an ex-convict. He asks a young drug dealer to sell his supply. But the brazen dealer rips him off. The ethical code, even among drug dealers, has changed while Cutty was serving time.

In episode 7, "Back Burners," Cutty turns to Bethel Church, confessing to the deacon, "It's like, I'm standing outside myself watching me do things I don't want to do, you know. Seeing me like I'm somebody else. But never being able to stop the show. I'm tired."[31] This echoes Saint Paul's self-disgust, tiring of doing the things he does not want to do. In Romans 7, Paul writes, "I do not understand what I do. For what I want to do I do not, but what I hate I do." Cutty is at war with himself. The scene ends with one of his first clear steps. He introduces himself not by his street name, "Cutty," but as "Dennis." Perhaps *Dennis* can find the personal, professional, and spiritual integration *Cutty* seeks.

For Dennis, salvation is about much more than an individualized forgiveness. He longs to give back to his community, to right some of the wrongs he has done. Cutty seeks his salvation in a broken-down boxing club. He cleans it up by himself. But when Dennis seeks permits to open a gym, the health department gives him the runaround. He asks the reverend (portrayed by Bethel A.M.E. pastor Frank Reid) for help. The reverend calls up his local politician Delegate Watkins. Church and state cooperate to give an individual a chance to carve out a life, to put his faith into practice. Dennis gets clearance to open a gym.

While Cutty cleans up his act, Major Bunny Colvin resolves to clean up the streets. He adopts a laissez faire attitude toward the war on drugs. Unable to defeat it, he decides to contain it, just like in Amsterdam. Bunny instructs his police officers to stop arresting drug dealers and instead corral them into a designated free zone. The drug slingers are skeptical—there must be a trick attached to "Hamsterdam." But Bunny has a method to his madness—to take back the corners by freeing up a single place for the drug trade to flourish. Bunny invites the deacon to see the results. As they walk the suddenly quiet streets, Bunny beams, "Those ain't touts, those are birds chirpin." But Hamsterdam is a different story. The deacon is outraged by the hellish conditions, "A great village of pain and you're the mayor. Where's your drinking water? Where's your toilets? Your heat? Your electricity? Your condom distribution? The drug treatment intake?" With his conscience tweaked by the deacon, Bunny implements social services in Hamsterdam. Drug treatment centers welcome the opportunity to distribute clean needles and condoms among the users gathered in Hamsterdam. Bunny shifts the war on drugs from policing to public health. In episode 11, "Middle Ground," the community gathers for another meeting at Bethel Church. A resident praises the changes: "When I grew up, we knew the police. I haven't seen that face-to-face policing in a long while. That is how it should be." Bunny shows Councilman Carcetti the positive results: "Have you ever seen a Westside community meeting like this one?"

Bunny's revolutionary methods reflect the real-life policies of a former mayor, Kurt Schmoke. In 1988, Schmoke's call for decriminalization generated massive controversy.[32] How could a mayor undercut national laws with his own local code? While national drug czar William Bennett escalated the war on drugs, Schmoke opposed more enforcement. Like Schmoke, Bunny's peaceful alternative to the war on drugs is not allowed to last. Despite his success, Bunny is punished by his superiors. With his retirement plans gone, Bunny regrets his bold decision: "The city is worse than when I started." The deacon assures him, "Drugs are a force of nature. You fought the good fight." Bunny can take comfort that he shares the struggle of Saint Paul. In 2 Timothy 4:7, Paul summarizes his life and work: "I have fought the good fight, I have finished the race, I have kept the faith." Bunny knew he was losing the war on drugs. His shift in strategy from incarceration to cooperation worked for a season—before the system ground down the individual and his hopes for reform.

When Bunny is marched before the city council for a public humiliation, Councilman Tommy Carcetti sees an opportunity to reverse the official story. In the final episode of season 3, Carcetti chides the police commissioners, "We can forgive Major Colvin. But what we can't forgive, what I can't forgive ever, is how all of us turned away from those streets of West Baltimore."[33] Carcetti's meteoric rise on *The Wire* parallels the real-life victory of Baltimore mayor Martin O'Malley. When two leading black politicians split the African American vote, O'Malley slipped into office. As mayor, O'Malley responded to *The Wire's* depiction of Baltimore with considerable frustration. O'Malley launched an attack: "Along with *The Corner, The Wire* has branded us in the national and metropolitan eye in a way that is very counterproductive to growth, hope, violent-crime reduction, and recovery." O'Malley cited how "Baltimore is reducing crime and overdose deaths faster than any major city in America this decade . . . [*The Wire*] has done nothing to help us in that important fight."[34] David Simon responded to the mayor with equal intensity: "Our purpose and intention in presenting this material cannot and should not be the same as that of Baltimore's civic leaders. We are not merely trying to entertain viewers, but to speak to existing problems in a meaningful way—problems that are not confined to Baltimore, but are universal."[35] Simon and company shift the spotlight from the War on Drugs, to the forgotten War on Poverty.

Baltimore serves as a stand-in for a much larger urban problem of economics. *The Wire* chronicles what Michael Harrington described as "the other America."[36] Sadly, in the almost half century since Harrington's groundbreaking report, little progress in combating poverty has been made.[37] David Simon explains, "It's not about the America or the Baltimore that is viable and that is part of the information age, where people are valued and have meaningful jobs and educational experiences and futures. It's not that Baltimore. It's not that America. It's the other America. It's the part that got left behind. And that's what the story is about. It's about the cost of doing business this way. It's about capitalism as it's actually practiced on the ground in an American city."[38] The acute poverty that plagues black, inner city Baltimore arose *after* advances in civil rights.

How did more freedom hurt black Americans? Sociologist William Julius Wilson connected the decline of America's inner cities to the mobility made possible by the Civil Rights Movement. In *The Truly Disadvantaged*, Wilson writes, "I believe that the exodus of middle- and working-class families from many ghetto neighborhoods removes an important 'social buffer' that could deflect the full impact of the kind of prolonged and increasing joblessness that plagued inner-city neighborhoods in the 1970s and early 1980s."[39] As industry relocated to the suburbs, legislation that promised opportunity irrespective of race inadvertently bankrupted the inner city. Black businesses and the middle

class moved out, leaving a depressed and angry younger generation behind. Yet, Wilson challenges the notion that an inherent
"culture of poverty" has overtaken black neighborhoods.[40] The
exodus of role models and job opportunities pushed those left in
the inner city to gravitate toward the only remaining industry—
the drug trade.

The Wire producer Ed Burns laments, "We have a culture of
violence made up of kids two generations removed from people
who worked and neighborhoods that were viable. Now, we're seeing the limits of what teachers and police can do."[41] Baltimore's
homicide rate remains six or seven times higher than New York
or Los Angeles. After several seasons of shooting on location, even
the cast has commented on the blighted conditions of Baltimore.
Wendell Pierce, who portrays homicide detective Bunk observes,
"West Baltimore is so small and the concentration of poverty and
destruction of the educational infrastructure (so intense) that it's
a mass of clinical depression just now being diagnosed."[42] Robert Wisdom, who portrays Major Bunny Colvin, also noticed the
decline. He recalls, "I grew up in Washington, and when I look at
Baltimore and see the boarded-up houses, there's a sadness. As a
black man, I can speak the language of that foreign country—the
invisible America—but I don't know the spiritual devastation."[43]

The Wire takes the particular problems of Baltimore but asks
the audience to examine their own cities. Who is prospering?
Who is suffering? As Baltimore serves as a case study for other
cities, so the characters in *The Wire* stand in for all people living
in urban settings. David Simon admits, "I think we're just using
Baltimore in an allegorical way. The vast majority of Americans
live in a metropolitan area and we are an urban people. I think the
institutions we're depicting, people can recognize as being very
similar to the institutions and problems of their own city. I think
the show feels really different than the rest of American television
because it's made by people who are not supposed to be making
television."[44] Yet for all its prophetic intensity, *The Wire* remained
a relatively obscure program. What kept viewers away?

Enlightened Racism?

Television, despite the liberal intentions of many of its writers, has pushed our culture backward. White people are not prepared to deal with the problem of racial inequality because they no longer see there is a problem.
—Sut Jally and Justin Lewis[45]

The Wire is the blackest drama on television (by far!). It offers more variety, more complexity, an invigorating mix of heroes and villains. Among the memorable black characters identified by a single name are Bunk, Daniels, Freamon, Kima, Omar, Stringer, D'Angelo, Avon, Marlo, Cheese, Cutty, Snoop, Bunny, Namond, Wallace, Bodie, and Bubbles. As a confirmed drug addict, Bubbles occupies the bottom of *The Wire's* social food chain, struggling to find money, a place to stay, and another hit of crack. Yet, Bubbles demonstrates a remarkable ability to see through daunting circumstances. At a Narcotics Anonymous meeting, he introduces himself as "God's own drug addict." While hawking t-shirts in Hamsterdam, Bubbles sings "Oh, Happy Day." As a police informant, he finds creative ways to identify dealers and remain unharmed. For a self-destructive junkie, Bubbles demonstrates considerable faith and resolve. At the conclusion of season 3, Bubbles looks upon the rubble of Hamsterdam and announces, "You don't know but there's love out there baby, cops be messing on you, hoppers be banging on you." In the end, actor Andre Royo came to see Bubbles "as someone trying to hold on to his goodness through all of it. Drugs are destroying his mind and his body and his ego, but not his good spirit."[46] Bubbles is a portrait of perseverance, an embodiment of hard-earned hope.

He is joined in the rogue's gallery by Omar, a Haitian who robs drug dealers for a living. Omar erases the gap between the white-collar crimes of lawyers and his own thuggery. Both are benefiting from the same game. The scarred face of actor Michael K. Williams makes the joy he displays as Omar that much more jarring.

Omar demonstrates remarkable courage and creativity in his brazen robberies. Yet, not everyone survives unscathed. As a gay man, Omar has lost two lovers in the crossfire of the game. Omar's passionate kiss with his boyfriend, Dante, was a shocking affront

Omar goes on the rampage when the Barksdale gang breaks the church code: shooting on Sunday.

to the homophobic aspects of hip-hop culture. No character on *The Wire* has taken more risks or triumphed through unlikely circumstances like Omar. Having survived prison, ambushes, and contract killers, Omar develops a legendary reputation as a Robin within the 'hood.

Omar finds an unlikely ally in a hired gun, Brother Mouzone. Brought from New York to uphold Avon Barksdale's corner on the drug trade, Brother Mouzone resembles Malcolm X. As a Black Muslim, Mouzone wears bifocals and a bowtie. He reads *Harper's* Magazine and *The Nation*, declaring, "Nothing is more dangerous than a nigger with a library card." His clean-cut appearance is mocked by the eastside drug dealer, Cheese, who wonders if he's selling bean pies. Brother Mouzone responds with a gunshot, securing West Baltimore for the Barksdales. Brother Mouzone walks with confidence, even facing the barrel of Omar's gun without fear, at peace with his God. The lived religion of Mouzone, Omar, and Bubbles is forged through suffering. Black theologian James H. Cone notes that "black reflections about suffering have not been removed from life but *involved* in life, that is, the struggle to affirm humanity despite the dehumanizing conditions of slavery and oppression."[47] They work out their salvation within the game.

David Simon developed these memorable characters out of fidelity to *The Wire's* setting. He admits, "I think there are probably more continuing roles for African American actors on *The Wire* than all the rest of television combined. We have 50–60 continuing roles for African Americans—can you name 50 or 60 from the rest of the network lineups? You can't. That's an embarrassment. And we're just trying to reflect Baltimore, a city that's 65 percent black. We're not trying to make a statement."[48] *The Wire* employs an arresting mix of professionals and amateurs, classically trained actors like Lance Reddick act beside real-life cops like Jay Landsman. Their performances appear so effortless that they may have been penalized. David Simon admits:

> One of the things I am a little bit resentful for is we have a remarkable cast of African American actors who are utterly unacknowledged by the industry. They are never nominated for anything. They are never regarded as having created any characterizations or achieved any sense of craft for what they are doing. It's almost as if they think we turn the camera on people, and they just were being; that's the way they are. And in fact, these are incredibly professional actors who are reading from a script.[49]

Within that impressive cast are relatively few women. *The Wire* depicts primarily a man's world. Detective Kima Greggs (portrayed by Sonja Sohn) must navigate both the streets of Baltimore and the politics of the police department. She compartmentalizes her private life, shared with her live-in lover, Cheryl. Kima is a minority in race, gender, and sexual preference. Yet, Simon and his writers work overtime to give Kima a more complete back story. When Kima is shot in a botched undercover operation, she is rushed to the hospital on life support. Cheryl arrives at the hospital eager to see her. Yet, the masculine police power structure does not know how to respond. Issues of partners' rights spring up as the policemen debate how to include Cheryl. In season 3, as Cheryl prepares to have a baby, Kima withdraws into her police work. Try as she might to stay close to home, the thrill of the chase takes Kima back to the unit. Domestic life is tough on all police officers, but the challenges for a lesbian hesitant to enter into motherhood prove insurmountable. The lone woman cop rejoins the boys, playing the game on their terms.

Opportunities for male or female black actors are rare because black dramas are rare. In their history of blacks on television, Cynthia E. Griffin and George H. Hill note that "historically, the black television shows or roles that were most popular and managed to last the longest were usually comedies or musical variety shows, not dramatic programs."[50] Not until the 1960s did "blacks began finding themselves in more meaningful dramatic series and began proving that they could win awards for acting excellence."[51] The shift in positive black images coincided with the Civil Rights Movement. Griffin and Hill observe that "blacks were seen as doctors, nurses, secretaries, law enforcement officials, entertainers, social workers and more. They were beginning to be seen as a multi-dimensional people with troubles and joys."[52] Recent scholarship has questioned how much progress was made. Darnell Hunt of UCLA suggests, "In reaction to the social movements and racial reforms of the 1960s, television moved to present 'respectable' images of blacks that more closely reflected America's newfound sense of racial morality. Thus 'assimilationist' shows like *I Spy* (NBC) and *Julia* (NBC), to borrow Herman Gray's nomenclature, introduced novel black characters whose accomplished middle-class lifestyles positioned them, unfortunately, as tokens in a white world disconnected from the realities of the rest of the black community."[53] White guilt was assuaged by a few positive portrayals of black America blending in. The underlying assumption for audiences, "Things must be getting better—just look at TV!"

Unfortunately, the same social and economic trends confirmed by William Julius Wilson found an equivalent in prime-time television. *The Cosby Show* suggested that the promises of civil rights had been fulfilled in a color-blind America where anyone can prosper like Dr. Huxtable and his kids. Their progress came at a double-edged price. While some blacks fled to a real or televised suburbia, the poorest sectors of urban America languished. The plight of the underclass was ignored by a white America mollified by the success portrayed on *The Cosby Show*.[54] Encoded to combat discrimination, *The Cosby Show* may have been decoded as "mission accomplished." Sut Jally and Justin Lewis describe the resulting indifference as "enlightened racism."

If a few high-profile, positive portraits of black America could inspire indifference, what would an array of programs targeted exclusively to black viewers produce? Upstart networks like Fox and UPN built a fan base by narrowcasting. All-black sitcoms resulted in a new segregation, with black and white audiences embracing completely different shows. Darrell Hunt wondered, "What does the apparent 'ghettoization' of prominent black representations in prime time tell us about the contemporary meaning of blackness in America?"[55] In response to increased pressure to reflect the breadth of America, the established networks (CBS, NBC, and ABC) developed more diverse casts. But simply casting "one of everything" within a network drama did not make the stories more diverse in their style or concerns. Herman Gray found that most black shows resort to the domestic issues of white dramas, self-contained problems with no connection to larger social issues.[56] The black characters blended in, supplying a homogenized, totalizing portrait of blackness. The "black guy" or the "Latina" did not bring more awareness or insight to the show. As the characters in networks dramas got along, so viewers were encouraged to move beyond issues of race, class, and power.[57] The seemingly color-blind corridors of *Law and Order* or the multicultural cast of *E.R.* reassure us that the American melting pot is simmering on low boil. Could *The Wire*, with such a wide range of black characters, from cops to criminals, provide a more authentic multicultural model?

Off the Couch

The forces that profit from the game, that allow the carnage to occur—without outrage, without fear, without shame or guilt—include us, the audience and wider public off-screen, with our own comfortable notions of justice, our own necessities, our own reasons and partial rationalizations for doing nothing to demand that it stop. —Anthony Walton[58]

The Wire's initial seasons focused upon Jimmy McNulty as the entrée point. His passion drove the investigation and put the Barksdale gang behind bars. Would McNulty become another televised white savior for inner city crime? Darrell Hunt criticizes network crime dramas that depend upon Caucasian heroes: "When hints of the 'ghetto' style surface, they do so as implicit threats to (white) order that invoke the binary and its related chains of equivalence. These threats, of course, are contained by the show's end at the hands of the (white) lead, likely feeding an enduring white ambivalence toward blackness and generating considerable audience pleasure."[59] I connected McNulty's efforts in West Baltimore to my own efforts in West Charlotte. Like McNulty, I learned a valuable lesson. Success would not come as I made a difference, but as Dalton Village developed its own leaders. Season 4 of *The Wire* focused upon the future, specifically four teenagers navigating the public school system. McNulty took a back seat, allowing the even more street savvy Bunny, Omar, and Bubbles to emerge as leads. *The Wire* resisted the temptation to resort to a white notion of progress.

David Simon and his writing staff acknowledge the tension inherent in white writers constructing a black show. But they resist any suggestion that the show's impressive grasp of street talk is improvised. Simon insists, "It's all scripted. . . . The dialogue is from the world that Ed policed, that I covered as a crime reporter in Baltimore for twelve years, that is very common to us from having spent time in West Baltimore. We are who we are. I am sure we miss things because we are a couple of white guys, but what we catch we catch because we have good ears, and we are careful and pay attention and we are patient listeners."[60] Nevertheless, George Pelecanos, staff writer for *The Wire* wrestles with his privileged position: "I make my living writing about people who, because of an accident of birth and circumstance, are less fortunate than me. In interviews I often say that my mission is to illuminate and dignify their lives to a public that rarely reads about them or recognizes their humanity in film, television, and fiction . . . What goes unsaid is the gnawing feeling that I am also exploiting them for my personal gain."[61] *The Wire* acknowledges our tendencies toward enlightened racism but pushes through old ways and habits. It leaves viewers uncomfortable rather than reassured.

The audience immediately assigns stereotypes to the adolescents featured in season 4. Namond is the gangbanger, headed for prison like his father, Wee Bay. Randy is the crafty kid, surviving in a series of foster homes with financial hustle. Dukie is the victim, destabilized by a home life that keeps him in soiled clothes. Only Michael seems capable of transcending his circumstances. He demonstrates responsibility and resolve, protecting his stepbrother, Bug, from their drug-abusing mother. Yet, as the season unfolds, we see how frayed their social net becomes. Detective Pryzbylewski has surrendered his badge and become a math teacher. He befriends the boys. Prezbo becomes the surrogate do-gooder, out to change the system, one life at a time. Veteran educators have given up. The school principal crosses herself before she opens the doors. Her prayer cannot stem the tide of junior high students with decidedly adult problems. Cutty is hired as a truant officer to sweep through the neighborhood. He fails to keep kids in school. The deacon finds Bunny Colvin a job working with researchers. Namond becomes a social science experiment, with Bunny as the facilitator.

I was snapped back to my time in Dalton Village. I knew similar teens—tough ones, weak ones, and wise ones. The young characters on *The Wire* got under my skin. I started rooting for Michael to make it. I wanted to shake Namond, to cut off his pony-tail and get him straightened out. Randy and Dukie simply needed some support—a home, a bath, and a fresh set of clothes. I related to Prezbo's sincere efforts to make a difference. I was just as white and "green." I made the same mistakes, falling for sad stories and made up crises. I once drove James and his brother to a "friend's" house—only to discover that after I dropped them off they beat up a rival, settling a score from school. While I attempted to treat everyone equally, I tended to invest in those with the most potential (as I determined it). On *The Wire*, Michael stood apart from the crowd. He had natural leadership abilities. He was not just bigger and tougher, but also smarter. Yet, when Bug's father is released from prison, Michael refuses to give up his leadership at home. He cannot turn to social workers or the police for help in removing an unwanted adult. Michael turns to the local drug dealer for help. Marlo and his soldiers offer training, a discipleship course in how to handle a gun and take out a rival. I watched Michael descend into gangbanging with disbelief. The final episode of season 4 rocked me. It felt like a punch in the gut. Why was I surprised by Michael's downfall? Had I forgotten the lessons I learned in inner-city Charlotte? What caused me to expect something other than murder? By the conclusion of the series, Omar has fallen and Michael is poised to replace him as a feared, shadowy thief. They are just pawns in an unchanging game.

What happened in the years between my experience in Charlotte circa 1987 and *The Wire*'s Baltimore in 2007? Had I been anesthetized by one too many cop shows? Did I really expect a happy ending to *The Wire*? Hadn't the death of James Owens been burned into my psyche? I needed a strong dose of *The Wire* to remind me of the forgotten War on Poverty. I was an eyewitness to suffering, but too much television had turned me into a tourist. Enlightened racism dulled my senses. Weren't inner-city problems solved each week on network television? Crimes were committed, but cases were solved within the hour. *The Wire* offered a much-needed corrective.

The final season was an elaborate ruse. McNulty cooked up a false story about a serial killer in an effort to secure more funding for legitimate police work, and a craven reporter took the bait. The fake murders made headlines, received journalistic rewards, and expanded the police department's resources. David Simon conducted a social experiment both within and beyond the show. Would self-serving journalists carp about their (mis)representation on the series or catch the subversive point? *The Wire* chides the media for resorting to sensationalistic reporting to get ahead, for ignoring the everyday struggles of the inner city. We must consider what happens when we fail to pay attention. *The Wire* reminds us that some things are more important than our careers or our entertainment.

David Simon and his writing team reminded me what matters. Anthony Walton summarizes the show's impact:

> The true achievement of *The Wire*: its subtle awareness and understated indictment of the larger game that occurs off-screen. As much as I enjoy crime drama, I am wary of shows that use urban suffering as a forum for entertainment. I constantly search for the escape, "the letting off the hook," that these shows leave the middle- and upper-middle-class audience; the ritual purgation that allows the audience—myself

included—to go on with their lives while the poor and African American body count continues to accrue in real projects.[62]

I write about *The Wire* because it reminds me of my own commitment to lived religion. It assaults my indifference. If *The Wire* is merely studied or admired, we all lose. *The Wire* gnaws at our national conscience. It gets me off the couch and back into urban America. The characters on *The Wire* may not win the game, but they are committed to playing. Am I? Are we?

"For What I Have Done and What I Have Failed to Do"

Vernacular Catholicism and The West Wing

LEONARD NORMAN PRIMIANO

My chapter looks at the first four years of the television series *The West Wing* (originally broadcast 1999–2006), written by Aaron Sorkin, and in particular one of the drama's central characters: the president of the United States, Josiah Edward "Jed" Bartlet. I argue that *The West Wing*, ostensibly a politically centered drama about the personal lives of the staffers of a presidential administration, was a provocative yet enormously appealing site for the expression of American Catholicism. Not the Catholicism of the institutional Church, with its hierarchies, structures, and various dogmatic, textual, liturgical concerns, but the practiced religion of the tradition's people—including the Church's hierarchical functionaries—a rich, vibrant, "vernacular Catholicism."

Vernacular Catholicism is the tradition of Catholicism as it is spoken about, thought about, acted upon, interpreted, negotiated, created, and recreated in the lives of all Catholics whether leaders or immigrants, whether conversant with the tradition or awed by it, and whether educated about it through a department of theology at a Catholic college or university, through Mother Angelica on cable television, through one's parents, or through structured classes at the local parish. I contend, moreover, that it was this

Catholic expression of vernacular religion in *The West Wing* that made the series particularly resonate with and appeal to viewers, both prior to and after the attacks of 9/11; in so doing, I examine how Sorkin ingeniously integrated religion into his drama, never making it the center of concern per se, but always focusing it as an important context within contemporary American life.

The Rosary in the Tomato

The political drama *The West Wing* was first seen on American television on 22 September 1999, broadcast over the National Broadcasting Company (NBC) television network. The program in its initial years highlighted a character portrayed by the actor Rob Lowe, along with an ensemble cast. Show creator, writer, and executive producer Aaron Sorkin concluded its "pilot" episode with what could best be described as an extended cameo by the character around whom all of the drama's action revolved, namely Josiah Edward "Jed" Bartlet, the president of the United States of America.[1] Indeed, *The West Wing* was an episodic series whose characters work in the administrative section of the residence of the chief executive in Washington, D.C.

Rendered by the actor Martin Sheen, President Bartlet's first significant words, and the audience's introduction to this character, take the form of a soliloquy of sorts[2] in which the chief executive of a nation, one which notably and distinctively separates church from state affairs, employs a vernacular parable to impress two important lessons upon his eager, but, at this point somewhat inexperienced, presidential staff: the necessity of constant diligence in their work and the daily recognition that their work involves the administration of a country that other human beings are courageously willing to risk their lives to enter, settle, and claim as their new homeland. The following excerpt from that episode aptly sets this stage:

> BARTLET: Seems to me we've all been taking a little break. Thinking about our personal lives or thinking about keeping our jobs. Breaks are good. It's not a bad idea taking a break every now and then. I know how hard you all work.

(Margaret, Leo's secretary, brings Leo, Bartlet's Chief of Staff, a note, which he slips to Bartlet after reading it.)

BARTLET *(Speaks while reading the note)*: There was this time
that Annie [his granddaughter] came to me with
this press clipping. Seems these theologians down
in South America were very excited because this
little girl from Chile had sliced open a tomato, and
the inside flesh of this tomato had actually formed
a perfect Rosary. The theologians commented that
they thought this was a very impressive girl. Annie
commented that she thought it was a very impressive
tomato. I don't know what made me think of that.
(Reporting the information from the slip of paper.) Naval
Intelligence reports approximately 1200 Cubans left
Havana this morning. Approximately 700 turned
back due to severe weather, some 350 are missing
and presumed dead, 137 have been taken into custody
in Miami and are seeking asylum. *(pause)* With the
clothes on their backs, they came through a storm.
And the ones that didn't die want a better life. And
they want it here. Talk about impressive. My point is
this: Break's over.[3]

With these first meaningful words, writer Aaron Sorkin identifies the president of the United States as a Roman Catholic. The
content of the president's narrative in this scene is not something
frequently heard on American series television: namely, a story
told with all seriousness by a character employing Roman Catholic themes. In this case, the story is best appreciated if one has an
understanding of the function of the Roman Catholic sacramen-
tal known as the rosary, the traditional prayer/meditation device
consisting of an assemblage of wood, stone, or precious metal
beads joined by a chain to a crucifix. Furthermore, this character
communicates his narrative without any postmodern contestative
irony about religion and especially not about Catholicism.

The parable of the tomato and the rosary highlights how oral
and material traditions about religion can color the way believers
think and speak about a tradition as insiders of that tradition, an

example of what folklorists call "the esoteric factor."[4] That is, the president tells the story with its rosary and a reference to theologians somewhat matter-of-factly, assuming that his listeners will have enough knowledge of the language and culture of Catholicism to allow him to color and then carry this parable with these Catholic references to its nondenominational, yet moral, conclusion. It is this remarkable matter-of-factness about Catholicism that highlights the unique contribution of *The West Wing* in the history of representations of Catholicism on American television.

In this television drama, religious observance/faithfulness and its intrinsic complexities are respectfully represented as a part of the fabric of life for most Americans. This broadcast took religious traditions, and the Catholic tradition in particular, quite seriously several years before the revival of popular, as well as institutional, governmental, media, and academic interests in the world's religions emerged in the aftermath of the events of 11 September 2001. Moral issues inspired by religious doctrine were not scorned or laughed away but rather were sought out as sources of reflection, if not obedience. Religious ritual did not impinge on freedom but supported individuals, families, and communities in difficult times.

The West Wing reminded its viewers of something they already recognized as Americans: namely, that religious beliefs and practices naturally influence and shape people's lives—even intelligent and successful American lives. As this series unfolded, faithful viewers witnessed another remarkable sight for American television: a character who is accomplished, well-spoken, intellectual, athletic, and thoughtful—and still an observant Catholic! *The West Wing* represented an infrequent instance on a network dramatic series of a Catholic character being allowed to speak thoughtfully and also develop as a person before the public over a course of several seasons. Viewers of this series were able to observe just such a sustained process of religious belief, if they remained faithful to the series and to the character of this fictional president over seven years and 114 episodes.

The West Wing was lauded in several religious publications and granted several awards by religious bodies during its years in production. Jim McDermott, Jesuit associate editor of the periodical *America*, for example, appreciated the drama as a Catholic of the post-Second Vatican Council generation who found the program's treatment of issues of social justice in the contemporary era exemplary. *The West Wing*, he wrote, is "a hymn to our childhood dreams of the common good, the dignity of the human being, the pursuit of justice and democracy."[5]

Beyond its awards for drama and acting, its outstanding cast and nuanced and insightful writing, McDermott extolled the program for "its combination of idealism and humanity. At the core of every episode lies a deep appreciation for our humanity, an impassioned concern for the needs of the oppressed and the fierce belief that the good, the right, and the true are things worth fighting for."[6] McDermott saw the arc of these concerns continuing for several years after the departure of series creator Sorkin at the end of its fourth season in 2003, and the inclusion of new characters running for the presidency ("Matthew Santos," another Catholic Democrat, played by actor Jimmy Smits, and "Arnold Vinick," a Republican pro-choice senator, played by Alan Alda). While essayist McDermott does not note it explicitly, the program, if not on a week-by-week basis but taken as a whole, is filled with references to Catholic tradition and the culture of American Catholicism. As fellow Jesuit Raymond A. Schroth wrote in an early *National Catholic Reporter* review, "The hints were there early on; he wore a Notre Dame sweatshirt, his daughter attended Georgetown, and he quoted Augustine when confronted with a crisis."[7]

In the pilot episode, his Communications Director, Toby Ziegler, makes it quite clear to a ministerial representative of the Christian Right that Bartlet is "a deeply religious man . . . He spent eight months traveling around the country discouraging young women from having abortions." The viewer, therefore, was aware of beliefs, formality, and idealization representative of institutional religion while watching the series, but also the reality of the "rosary in the tomato" in everyday Catholicism—that is, the "vernacular religion" of everyday life, "religion as it is lived: as human beings encounter, understand, interpret, and practice it."[8] Sorkin chose the religious life of a Catholic president as the prime vehicle for the dramatic expression of vernacular religion in the Roman Catholic context, what I have termed "vernacular Catholicism."[9]

Televised Catholicism

Surprisingly, the scholarship on the relationship of Catholicism to television is not extensive. The legacy of early television pioneer and Catholic evangelist, Archbishop Fulton J. Sheen (the prelate inspired Martin Sheen's stage name) and his enormously popular weekly religious lecture/commentary broadcast *Life Is Worth Living*, which started on the DuMont television network from 1951 to 1955 and later on ABC (1955–1957) for thirty minutes on Tuesday evenings at 8:00 p.m., is one exception.[10] Even as notable and useful a text as *The New Encyclopedia of Catholicism*—a scholarly resource supervised by the faculty of the Catholic University of America—in both its post-Vatican II editions (1967, 2003) lacks an entry on the topic of television.[11] Two pivotal areas of debate concerning the communication media's treatment of Catholicism, specifically focusing on television, are represented by Philip Jenkins' 2003 work on the presence of anti-Catholicism in contemporary America, and the discussion of the influence of Catholicism on American popular culture fueled by Fordham University scholars James Fisher and Mark Massa.

It is Jenkins' interest to identify and analyze TV productions that give "hostile treatment" to Catholicism.[12] Such "television shows all, to different degrees, raise significant issues about the public expression of prejudice, and the appropriate response."[13] He offers examples from such television genres as animated comedy (*South Park*, Fox 1997–), sketch comedy (*MADtv*, Fox 1995–), and episodic drama (*Ally McBeal*, Fox 1997–2002; *Night Sins*, CBS 1997; *The X-Files*, Fox 1993–2002). In these cases, church conspiracies, pedophilia, and clergy and church hierarchy depicted as "cynical, worldly, [and] dedicated to the suppression of any authentic spirituality," were stressed.[14]

The drama *Nothing Sacred* (ABC 1997–1998) was targeted—unjustifiably, Jenkins feels—with an intense protest and boycott by a conservative Catholic watchdog organization called "The Catholic League for Religious and Civil Rights," which succeeded in destroying the show's corporate sponsorship. Jenkins argues that "it is difficult to find a moment in the show that could be described as anti-Catholic or even anticlerical."[15]

Jenkins does not cite two relevant studies by Thomas Skill and James D. Robinson, which indicate a wider problem in the characterization of *all* Christian denominations and their leadership on American television and not merely Roman Catholics.[16] In their study of the portrayal of religion and spirituality on episodic network television, Skill and Robinson report that in an analysis of one hundred episodes of fictional television comprising 67.5 hours of prime-time commercial network programming broadcast for a five-week period from October to November, 1990, "when the appearance of religious groups are compared to the United States population statistics, all traditions with the exception of Catholics were under-represented."[17] Making use of the same sample, Skill and Robinson also analyzed in a second study how Christian leaders were portrayed on fictional prime-time television. Christian leaders in this case were defined as "a character who was portrayed as having a formal church or religious role within a Christian religious tradition (Catholic, mainline Protestant, other denominational or nondenominational Christian church)."[18] In their findings, *no* Christian leaders, whether Protestant or Roman Catholic, fared well, with Christian leaders "most likely to be presented as relatively bland and shallow—regardless of the prominence they may have in a particular program. . . . In the final analysis, we must conclude that Christian leaders in television rarely behave as Christians or exhibit a capacity for leadership."[19]

At least in the cases of this research, Roman Catholics were neither erased nor was Church hierarchy being singled out for specific criticism through weak, deceptive, or calculating characterizations because no Christian leader received a positive treatment on fictional TV drama. Granted, it is Catholic leadership, priestly functionaries and the hierarchy of the institutional Church, not the Catholic laity, that Jenkins accentuates in his assessment of Catholic representation on television.

James Fisher and Mark Massa underscore not the anti-Catholic dimension of Catholic portrayals on television, but rather the ever-present question of whether American Catholics and their culture have been formed by or themselves inform the larger sphere of popular culture in America.[20] Fisher inverts the question in their analysis, suggesting that, indeed, it is American popular culture itself which is firmly rooted in the American Catholic experience. Fisher, for example, is not surprised with the portrayal of an American president as Roman Catholic on *The West Wing* given the influence of Catholic actors like Martin Sheen and Catholic television executives such as NBC President Robert Wright.[21] Noting "the complicated history of cultural negotiations between Catholics and public culture in twentieth-century North America," Massa is fascinated by the idea of a Catholic influence on American popular culture, yet weary of the reductionistic possibilities of a Catholic culture diluted by American mass culture. He asks, "If Fisher is perhaps overly sanguine about the leadership of Catholics in mass culture during the course of the twentieth century, then I would like to pose an alternative question: Why have Catholics fairly consistently been successful as "players" in popular culture, but have left others to write the scripts and direct the action?"[22]

Massa argues that the popular culture left to Catholics to influence may not be as influential as Fisher thinks—that the broader American culture needs to be consistently challenged by Catholic principles and sensibilities—and that the outsider status of Catholics has helped form their unique spiritual, moral, aesthetic, political, prophetic voice in America as both an intentional series of local communities and as a distinctive cohesive cultural force. Massa concludes by lamenting: ". . . I . . . don't want to have my faith tradition reduced to exceedingly thin cultural props."[23]

The intricacies of their debate aside, I am especially drawn to the way that both Fisher and Massa have opened up the understanding of American Catholic culture in general to accentuate and appreciate formal, institutional, informal, and especially vernacular Catholic expressions and understandings of creativity, influence, and power. There is always the potential to leave such religious creativity out of consideration when discussing the media, as can be seen in even such a thoughtful social critic as Raymond Williams. In his book *Television: Technology and Cultural Form*, Williams notes,

> [T]here is a complicated interaction between the technology of television and the received forms of other kinds of cultural

and social activity. Many people have said that television is essentially a combination and development of earlier forms: the newspaper, the public meeting, the educational class, the theatre, the cinema, the sports stadium, the advertising columns and bill boards. . . .[24]

One obvious source that Williams leaves out of his consideration is the multitude of forms received from the religious contexts of ritualizing, prayer, testimony, and preaching of the Christian gospel. The expression and representation of Catholic practice—liturgical and personal—obviously needs to be added to any such consideration of the medium. So too does the way television subverts an already powerfully visual, material, oral, and belief culture to the point where it effaces the real, or what Jean Baudrillard conceives of as the "simulacrum."[25]

In this reversal of the relation between representation and reality, the media, according to Baudrillard, can come to constitute a (hyper)reality, a media reality which seems "more real than real."[26] In the electronic sites of the medium communicating religion, the distinction between the real and the representation collapses and dissolves away because of a misunderstanding, unwillingness, hesitancy, or even a fear to present authentic reality. This distortion of reality is especially present in contemporary television's representation of American Catholicism post-Vatican II, the reforming ecumenical council of the 1960s, as will be explored below.

When it comes to the representation of Christian religious beliefs and practices on television, filmed religious services are arguably the safest path for television networks and syndicates that seek to avoid offending any given religious viewing demographic. Indeed, in the case of dramatic television, especially weekly episodic productions of drama, great care is often taken to represent organized religion tactfully, deferentially, and inoffensively to avoid any conflicts with institutionalized churches and religious communities that may complain to, or even boycott, valued sponsors of commercial television. What this approach has meant for Roman Catholicism is that the tradition—for example, its theology, liturgical life, architecture, pastoral perspectives, life-cycle customs, clergy, religious orders, and laity—often stand frozen in time in episodic television. In other words, it is a tradition that appears in its mediated electronic versions not to have changed significantly since before the Second Vatican Council, or in some cases not since the Middle Ages.

When Catholicism *is* expressed, the images used are not of post-Vatican II sanctuaries, where the altars are centered in the ritual space and prompt a relational dynamic with the congregation, but rather continue to be (re)presented as hierarchical with high altars, altar rails, shimmering stained glass windows, a multitude of statues of saints, a plentiful supply of priests, and even habit-wearing sisters/nuns. Many churches in the United States have done away with votive candles for fear the church will burn down and cause exorbitant insurance rates, but not necessarily the churches depicted on American television. They are always ablaze with flickering votive candles, and the institutional Church and its elite functionaries remain the supreme authority on religious matters. Since Catholics believe that their Councils are influenced and inspired by the power of the Holy Spirit, the representation of an unreformed Catholicism on television is tantamount to a rejection of any revelation having occurred at the Second Vatican Council, the medium itself stripping the unified Church of its power to reflect on and transform itself.[27] One television drama that *has* worked to pierce this veil of such Catholic simulacrum, this copy of an idealized vision of what constituted Catholicism in America pre-Vatican II, is *The West Wing*.

This drama about the everyday lives of Washington insiders took care to weave religion, and especially Catholicism, into its seasonal plot lines. More specifically, this drama challenged the typical stance that television took about the representation of Catholic practice precisely because it featured a religiously observant Catholic who could be seen seriously reflecting on, reframing, negotiating, and creating a personal system of belief while remaining closely affiliated with the tradition itself. Sorkin, as the show's creator and chief writer, wisely accomplished this feat by not having the drama revolve around Catholicism, but around an American Catholic who was not a representative/functionary of the Church.

The West Wing, therefore, never encroached on the institutional Catholic Church's sensibilities. Moreover, as in the case of the president's initial story of the tomato and the rosary, this dramatic moment creatively negotiates religious metaphors to achieve both a religious and a secular point about the moral and civil responsibility of government workers to perform at the highest level for their fellow citizens. This balancing of religious and secular values not only shows Sorkin at his rhetorical best, but also serves as entrée to two especially useful focal moments in the first two years of the program. Let us turn now to two episodes that are telling, compelling, and representative of this exemplar of mediated vernacular Catholicism.

"Take This Sabbath Day"

The first season of *The West Wing* contains an amazing moment with regard to American television serial drama. At the conclusion of one particularly compelling episode ("Take This Sabbath Day," season 1, episode 14, aired 9 February 2000) centered on the death penalty, a man confesses to a friend that he has not acted to stop the execution of a prisoner, a drug dealer convicted of a capital offense. Out of the need to be pardoned for what he considers a moral failing and a sinful act, he kneels down and confesses his offense to this old friend, who is a Roman Catholic priest. The character, rosary in hand, asking for the forgiveness of God through the mediation of the Roman Catholic Church is none other than the president of the United States, Josiah Edward Bartlet. The location of the act of confession and absolution is the Oval Office in The White House in Washington, D.C. This remarkable closing represents one of any number of narrative themes in this series portraying the culture and sensibility of North American Catholicism. To reiterate, it is not the position of the Catholic hierarchy that these story lines highlight or portray, but rather the position of the lay believer and the expression of his or her vernacular Catholicism.

The West Wing was—and remains—particularly notable for the way it has presented issues of religious belief and practice without ostensibly being a drama about religion—and especially not a drama explicitly centered on Christianity, such as the weekly series *Nothing Sacred* or *The Book of Daniel* (NBC 2006), programs that had short runs due to their attempts to portray the reality of the people in religious institutions, specifically clergy. Because of his popularity among viewers, the central character of *The West Wing* gradually evolved to be President "Jed" Bartlet, a convinced Catholic with a stern Protestant father and a mother who never appears on screen, but whose Catholicism notably affected her Notre Dame graduate, Noble Prize in economics winning, Bible-quoting, presidential son.

In this episode, the president suffers greatly over his decision to allow the aforementioned prisoner to die. He knows that this act of murder is on his hands and is against the culture of life representative of the Catholic views of, for example, Pope John Paul II, though the pope's name is never invoked. Still, this decision is politically expedient: the president is also considering his popularity among the electorate. President Bartlet both makes up his mind to send the man to his death and calls for his childhood priest, old friend, and confessor, Father Thomas Cavanaugh—played by actor Karl Malden—who scolds him and accepts his act of penance as mediated by the institutional Church through the sacrament known as Reconciliation.[28]

This episode necessitates a complex reading, for it portrays the hegemonic character of the Church—along with emphasizing that the institution is mediating what is defined as sinful and what is offered as forgiveness—and at the same time emphasizes the independence of this thoughtful Catholic to act autonomously of that institution, by portraying a tradition as old as Catholicism itself: the ability of religious individuals, even within restrictive frameworks of belief, to create their own religion. Admittedly, capital punishment is not the only moral question relevant to Catholics concerning this president or other characters in the program. Other key episodes consider religious persecution, race relations, poverty, homosexuality, and war. It gradually becomes evident that, yes, Bartlet is the president of the United States and must make significant administrative decisions; but in perspective, these are the same decisions that ordinary Catholics make in their more mundane lives. Vernacular Catholicism in all its personal dramatic moments of negotiation of religious tradition—in every-day contexts of living—lies at the core of this program, a drama magnifying the everyday religious life of an individual who happens also to be a world leader.

This fourteenth episode of *The West Wing* was a multiple award winner, including the Christopher Award, the Humanitas Prize, Wilbur Award, and Emmy Award. It not only considered the Catholic view on capital punishment but also included a thoughtfully written scene between Communications Director Toby Ziegler and his rabbi, which Aaron Sorkin composed after an e-mail exchange with his own rabbi, as well as speaking with a Catholic priest, a Baptist minister, and a Quaker.[29] Martin Sheen mentions that he attempted to influence the outcome of this final scene and have the prisoner live.[30] This particular segment with all of its highly charged, yet contained, emotion is reminiscent of another powerful consideration of duties to office and duties to Church, namely the confrontation between King Philip II and the Grand Inquisitor (two bass voices) in Giuseppe Verdi's opera *Don Carlo*, itself based on a play by Schiller.

In this instance, the head of the government in sixteenth-century Spain is visited by this representative of the Church to discuss the monarch's duties as leader and the weighty decisions he needs to make, which may cost men, including his own son, their lives. The priest-inquisitor threatens and reinforces the Church's power in the face of this secular ruler, and the king reflects that he must accede to the demands of the Church. In a scene quite different in tone in terms of the Church's temporal power, but equally as serious in terms of the Church's spiritual power, lived religion, and civil outcome, President Bartlet calls his confessor to his office after his decision to not stay the execution. The priest reiterates the Church's stance. The president acknowledges his religion's position on the death penalty and concedes his personal guilt, but he still reserves the right as a secular leader, as the representative of "the office" and not Jed—"the man"—to permit the punishment of a criminal by the state. As a vernacular Catholic, he chooses to disobey his institutional Church's idealized sense of justice for a more realistic form of retribution.

Karl Malden as Father Thomas Cavanaugh hears the confession of President Jed Bartlet as played by Martin Sheen in "Take This Sabbath Day," The West Wing, *season 1, episode 14, aired 9 February 2000.*

CUT TO: INT. THE OVAL OFFICE – NIGHT
SUNDAY, 11:57 P.M.

Bartlet is standing at the window in the Oval Office. He is looking out at the falling snow and holding a rosary. Charlie comes in.

CHARLIE: Mr. President? *(beat)* Excuse me, Mr. President?
BARTLET:Yeah.
CHARLIE: Father Cavanaugh.
BARTLET:Thank you.

(He walks to the door. FATHER THOMAS CAVANAUGH enters.)

BARTLET:Tom.
FATHER CAVANAUGH: Mr. President.

(They hug.)

BARTLET: Thank you, Charlie.

(Charlie leaves.)

BARTLET: Thanks for coming all this way down.

FATHER CAVANAUGH: It was no trouble. I'm just sorry
    I couldn't get here until now.

BARTLET: Yeah, it seems like a wasted trip.

FATHER CAVANAUGH: Oh. I can see the Oval Office.

BARTLET: This is it.

(They walk farther into the room.)

FATHER CAVANAUGH: Show me around the room.

BARTLET: You're looking at the room.

FATHER CAVANAUGH: Well, uh, where's the red phone?

BARTLET: We don't use the red phone anymore.

FATHER CAVANAUGH: Well, how do you talk to the
    Kremlin?

BARTLET: I tell Mrs. Landingham I want to talk to the
    Kremlin. Would you like a drink?

FATHER CAVANAUGH: No. No thanks. *(pause)* I don't
    know how to address you. Would you prefer Jed or
    Mr. President?

BARTLET: To be honest, I prefer Mr. President.

FATHER CAVANAUGH: That's fine.

BARTLET: You understand why, right?

FATHER CAVANAUGH: Do I need to know why?

BARTLET: It's not ego.

FATHER CAVANAUGH: I didn't think it was.

BARTLET: There are certain decisions I have to make while
    I'm in this room. Do I send troops into harm's way?
    Which fatal disease gets the most research money?

FATHER CAVANAUGH: Sure.

BARTLET: It's helpful in those situations not to think of
    yourself as the man but as the office.

FATHER CAVANAUGH: Then Mr. President it is.

BARTLET: I want you to know that I had a number of peo-
    ple on my staff search for a reason the public would
    find palatable to commute the sentence. A technical-
    ity. Any evidence of racism.

FATHER CAVANAUGH: So your staff spent the weekend
    looking for a way out.

BARTLET: Yeah.

FATHER CAVANAUGH: Like the kid in right field who doesn't want the ball to get hit to him.

(They sit down.)

BARTLET: I'm the leader of a democracy, Tom. Seventy-one percent of the people support capital punishment. People have spoken. The courts have spoken.

FATHER CAVANAUGH: Did you call the Pope?

BARTLET: Yeah.

FATHER CAVANAUGH: And how do you do that?

BARTLET: *(upset)* Oh, for crying out loud, Tom. I open my mouth and say, "Somebody get me the Pope."

FATHER CAVANAUGH: No, I'm sorry, Mr. President, but I was thinking . . . You're just this kid from my parish and now you're calling the Pope.

BARTLET: Anyway. I looked for a way out, I really did.

FATHER CAVANAUGH: "'Vengeance is mine,' sayeth the Lord." You know what that means? God is the only one who gets to kill people.

BARTLET: I know.

FATHER CAVANAUGH: That was your way out.

BARTLET: I know.

FATHER CAVANAUGH: Did you pray?

BARTLET: I did, Tom. I know it's hard to believe, but I prayed for wisdom.

FATHER CAVANAUGH: And none came?

BARTLET: *(shakes his head)* It never has. And I'm a little pissed off about that.

(He looks at his watch, which says it's a few seconds before midnight. It hits him hard.)

BARTLET: *(dead serious)* I'm not kidding.

FATHER CAVANAUGH: You know, you remind me of the man that lived by the river. He heard a radio report that the river was going to rush up and flood the town. And that all the residents should evacuate their homes. But the man said, "I'm religious. I pray. God loves me. God will save me." The waters rose up. A guy in a row boat came along and he shouted, "Hey, hey you! You in there. The town is flooding. Let me take you to safety." But the man shouted back, "I'm religious. I pray. God loves me. God will save me." A helicopter was hovering overhead. And a guy with a megaphone shouted, "Hey you, you down there. The town is flooding. Let me drop this ladder and I'll take you to safety." But the man shouted back that he was religious, that he prayed, that God loved him and that God will take him to safety. Well . . . the man drowned. And standing at the gates of Saint Peter, he demanded an audience with God. "Lord," he said, "I'm a religious man, I pray. I thought you loved me. Why did this happen?" God said, "I sent you a radio report, a helicopter, and a guy in a rowboat. What the hell are you doing here?"

(He pauses. Bartlet looks very upset.)

FATHER CAVANAUGH: He sent you a priest, a rabbi, and a Quaker, Mr. President. Not to mention his son, Jesus Christ. What do you want from him?

(There is a knock on the door.)

C. J.: Excuse me.

(C. J. comes in, hands Bartlet a note, and leaves. Bartlet reads the note, and then crumples it up as he goes to lean on the desk. He looks exceedingly troubled.)

FATHER CAVANAUGH: Jed. Would you like me to hear your confession?
BARTLET: Yes, please.

(Father Cavanaugh pulls out his stole and puts it on. The president kneels beside him, over the presidential seal. He performs the sign of the cross.)

BARTLET: Bless me, Father, for I have sinned . . .
DISSOLVE TO: END CREDITS.
FADE TO BLACK.
THE END[31]

"Not the man . . . but . . . the office."

Viewed through this lens, Sorkin's creation of this episode can be seen to be challenging a medium that is afraid to represent religion as anything but hierarchical, institutionally centered, and not individually or communally creative. Here, he dramatizes the process of vernacular religion as a constant, dynamic, powerful, conflicted, dramatic force in a person's life. The president acts as a Catholic *bricoleur*, to borrow the metaphor developed by Claude Levi-Strauss, processing elements from his religious culture with its dominant system of sinfulness and guilt into a cohesive vernacular religious system of belief and action all his own that in the end contests and challenges the very tradition from which he comes and respects.

This dramatic expression of vernacular Catholicism in this character's reflection and action is not, however, what a representative of the institutional Church might characterize as another blatant example of thoughtless, self-serving, relativistic "pick and choose" or "cafeteria" Catholicism, a Catholic changing the faith to serve his or her immediate needs. Such characterizations of individual religiosity not only lack the *gravitas* of the intentionality of the decision-making process, but also fail to appreciate the gift of improvisation in reinterpreting and reusing Church teachings, as well as the transformation of religion that individuals make in their lives. Catholicism in America—like, for example, Mormonism—remains a "marked category," in the spirit of Michel Foucault's notion. That is, public figures like Sorkin's representation of this Catholic president may not be able to keep their belief systems invisible (as an evangelical Christian in office may do); nonetheless, he still needs to manage the competing value systems of being the chief executive and being Catholic.

"Two Cathedrals"

Religion is not simply an idealization of beliefs and practices, but is how individuals actually live their religious lives. Catholic Christianity can thus be viewed as a tapestry for faithful believers of standards and pressures and decisions and creativity. Even at the very start of the Mass, the central Catholic liturgy, there is the acknowledgment that within the religious life idealized behaviors and practices will be accommodated by an individual and that the institution itself has accepted this reality of lived religion. This Penetential Rite in the order of the Mass involves petitionary prayers that ask pardon from the deity for actions done to others—that is, sins of commission—as well as righteous actions that should have been enacted—that is, sins of omission. There is, thus, attention to both individual and social dimensions of sin in the words "For What I Have Done and What I Have Failed to Do." *The West Wing* surprisingly observes this tradition of interpretation in the Catholic life; this political drama in its own way publicly legitimates—in a media source—the complexity of religion, mirroring it back to a public living, practicing, and creating their own vernacular religion.

One of the building blocks of vernacular religion is the relationship that an individual has with one's own culture in the context of one's own daily life, a concept I have termed an individual's "uniculture," and through a process best described as a "system of conscious and unconscious knowledge, beliefs, behaviors, and customs particular to the individual to which he or she refers and which she or he employs as the basis of everyday living."[32] An extraordinary example of religious uniculture is found in the closing episode of *The West Wing*'s second season ("Two Cathedrals," season 2, episode 22, aired 16 May 2001), which visualizes and vocalizes a special, intimate, private moment of an individual negotiating with the reality of his God and with the power of his religious tradition. Here, the Catholic president must face the fallout from not admitting to the public that he suffers from multiple sclerosis, as well as make decisions about how to deal with the fact that the American embassy in Haiti is surrounded by violent protesters. Viewers also learn that Mrs. Landingham, President Bartlet's secretary, old friend, supporter, and moral conscience from his prep school days, has died. During the episode, Mrs. Landingham, who has just purchased a new car, is killed by a drunk driver on her first trip with the vehicle.

As Bartlet grieves, he reflects on when, as a student at the Protestant institution where his stern Protestant father was headmaster, he first met Mrs. Landingham. Jed has previously made the decision to practice Catholicism, his mother's religion; to

President Jed Bartlet, as played by actor Martin Sheen, smoking a cigarette in the Washington National Cathedral, in "Two Cathedrals," The West Wing, season 2, episode 22, aired 15 May 2001.

contest one of the school's literature teachers who has banned such writers as Henry Miller, D. H. Lawrence, and Ray Bradbury from the library; and, against his father's protest and strong rebuke, to smoke cigarettes.

In a flashback, the president relives being slapped by his father for insubordination for speaking in a way the father does not approve. In an episode filled with pathos, memories, the passion of an ardent Catholic, and the personal negotiations of a vernacular one, President Bartlet asks that the doors of the National Cathedral, the site of his secretary's funeral, be sealed so that he can speak to his God, in English and in Latin, in candor and in anger. In that sealed cathedral, he lights a cigarette, smokes it, and in spite of God and his father, he stamps out the smoldering tobacco on the spotless marble floor at the center of the edifice and ponders "the appalling strangeness of the mercy of God."

CUT TO: INT. NATIONAL CATHEDRAL—PRESENT
     DAY

(Bartlet stands alone glaring at the altar. Most of the guests have left the church. Abby, Leo, and Secret Service agents are standing at the back of the sanctuary. Leo approaches Bartlet.)
LEO: *(sighs)* It was a beautiful service I thought.
BARTLET: Yeah.

LEO: *(quietly)* I thought it was a beautiful service. *(Smiles.)* She was a real dame, old friend. A real broad.

BARTLET: *(nodding)* Yeah.

LEO: *(leans in close)* We've gotta go back to the office now, sir.

BARTLET: *(nods)* Yeah.

LEO: *(quietly)* We've got some decisions to make now.

(Bartlet looks absently for a moment.)

BARTLET: Leo, would you do me a favor?

LEO: Yeah?

BARTLET: *(motions to the agents)* Would you ask the agents to seal the cathedral for a minute?

(Leo looks at him.)

LEO: Yeah.

(Leo walks towards the agents. As Bartlet waits, we hear the sound of several heavy doors closing. Bartlet turns back towards the altar.)

BARTLET: *(tired)* You're a son of a bitch, you know that?

(He slowly walks up the center aisle.)

BARTLET: She bought her first new car and you hit her with a drunk driver. What, was that supposed to be funny? "You can't conceive, nor can I, the appalling strangeness of the mercy of God," says Graham Greene. I don't know whose ass he was kissing there 'cause I think you're just vindictive. What was Josh Lyman? A warning shot? That was my son. What did I ever do to yours but praise his glory and praise his name? There's a tropical storm that's gaining speed and power. They say we haven't had a storm this bad since you took out that tender ship of mine in the north Atlantic last year . . . 68 crew. You know what a tender ship does? Fixes the other ships. Doesn't even carry guns. Just goes around, fixes the other ships and delivers the mail. That's all it can do. *(angry)* *Gratias tibi ago, domine.* Yes, I lied. It was a sin. *(holds out arms)* I've committed many sins. Have I displeased you, you feckless thug? 3.8 million new jobs, that wasn't good? Bailed out Mexico, increased foreign trade, 30 million new acres of land for conservation, put Mendoza on the bench, we're not fighting a war, I've raised three children . . .

(He ascends the stairs to the Inner Sanctuary.)

BARTLET: *(pleading)* That's not enough to buy me out of the doghouse? *Haec credam a deo pio? A deo iusto? A deo scito?*

(He stops at the top of the stairs and extends his arms.)

BARTLET: *Cruciatus in crucem! Tuus in terra servus nuntius fui officium perfeci. (angry) Cruciatus in crucem. (waves dismissively) Eas in crucem!*

(Bartlet turns away in anger. He descends to the lower sanctuary and lights a cigarette. He takes a single puff, drops the butt to the floor, and grinds it defiantly with his shoe. He looks back at the altar.)

BARTLET: *(betrayed)* You get *(Vice President of the United States John)* Hoynes!

(Bartlet holds back tears as he walks down the aisle.)[33]

"Cruciatus in crucem. Eas in crucem!"

In this conversation with a God who does not answer back except through the stillness and beauty of the empty cathedral, we are witness to the president delivering yet another soliloquy, but not to his staff. This time the soliloquy takes the form of a personal communication between this angry Catholic and his God. The mystery of the scene is centered in the traditional language of the Church that the president uses and that Sheen so forcefully delivers. Here the creativity and sense of negotiation evident in religious uniculture is expressed in this active declaration of President Bartlet's vernacular religion: through the use of Latin, the Church's own mode of "institutional" communication, to challenge

God; through the verbal abuse of the deity; through the physical action of lighting, smoking, and extinguishing the cigarette on the floor of God's house. One loose translation of the spoken text is as follows:

> *"Gratias tibi ago, domine. Haec credam a deo pio? A deo iusto, a deo scito?*
>
> Oh, thanks a lot, Lord! Am I to believe this treatment from a caring God? From a just God? From the God I know?
>
> *Cruciatus in crucem. Tuus in terra servus, nuntius fui. Officium perfeci.*
>
> I've been tormented to the point of being on a cross! Even though I've been your servant on earth and your messenger! I've done my duty/fulfilled my office!
>
> *Cruciatus in crucem. Eas in crucem!"*
>
> Yet, I've been tormented to the point of being on a cross! You think you suffered; so go suffer![34]

Of particular poignancy here is the sarcasm and the pain this character uses to register his fury and disappointment with God. In the face of mounting pressures and disappointments, this Catholic does not threaten the Church, and he does not threaten to depart from its membership. Like a Catholic who turns a saint's statue around to face a wall when a requested favor or blessing has not been received, Bartlet directly threatens who he feels is the source, whether passively or actively, of all of his woes.

Not some quiet Job who sits and takes his abuse, Bartlet emphasizes here the action of expressing vernacular religion and in so doing highlights the authority of the individual to create his (or her) own religion, and his (or her) own relationship to God, even in the face of a lifetime of belief and connection to a religious institution. The reality of lived religion is thus seen here in both confirmation and doubt, in agreement with and contestation of a religious tradition. It is in such powerful moments—when *The West Wing* dramatizes the personal creativity found in the religious life of a person responding to life's triumphs as well as trials—that the drama intimately connects to its audience. In this vibrant segment, individuals no doubt respond because they are witness to a private conversation that they may themselves have had with their own deity on some previous occasion.[35]

The irony of this outpouring of anger, confusion, and questioning of God on an American dramatic television "entertainment" is obvious; the fact that it was broadcast four months before the attacks of September 11, 2001, makes it even more poignant in retrospect. Whether this scene contributed to the popularity of *The West Wing* may never be known, but it is an episode and scene that many viewers recall.[36] Its meaning to a Catholic could certainly be the same as its spiritual significance to any religiously thoughtful or observant person, for Aaron Sorkin cleverly uses the religious life of a Catholic to communicate the anger of loss. Moreover, he accomplishes this task within one religious tradition while not closing the experience to individuals who may belong to other belief systems.[37] In this sense, Sorkin is a master at communicating the "religious mixing" representative of America, what Catherine Albanese has characterized as the American process of contact, encounter, exchange.[38]

How is it that a Jewish writer can communicate truths to Catholics about their religious tradition?[39] Mark Massa's previously cited question about the dearth of Catholics' participation in actually crafting such creative observations and questions about life themselves may bear further scrutiny.[40] Let me offer, as but one point of reflection, my own development as a Catholic scholar of Catholic culture, one who appreciates the multiplicity of forms of the religious tradition and the diverse and pluralistic religious backgrounds that may inform our understanding of religion in America.

It was my folklife professor at the University of Pennsylvania, Don Yoder, a Methodist-born Quaker, and not a Roman Catholic or even a scholar of Roman Catholicism, who taught me to appreciate and then sensitively study the culture of my own tradition. He accomplished this task by exemplifying and modeling a respect, fascination, and curiosity for all components of Catholicism. It may not be Aaron Sorkin's intention, but his emphasis on religion as it is lived—that is, on what we have done and what we have failed to do—that may well assist Catholics to understand religious experience in general and the religious experiences of American Catholics in particular.

Conclusion

To extend the critical reflection on how the personal is political, how popular media reflects and is part of vernacular religion, I offer one final episode from my own daily life. Friends and colleagues who knew I was researching *The West Wing* have frequently remarked to me: "Oh God, if *only* he was the president," an obvious critique of the current U.S. President, George W. Bush. In a network television culture seemingly detached from authenticity and social justice, the profundity of vernacular religion infused into a weekly television series about the White House has been a timely reminder that it is possible for the man (or woman) in the Oval Office to be reflective, creative, and even to have a soul.

Mixed Blessing
Generational Effects of Interfaith Marriage
in Everwood and The O.C.

VINCENT BROOK

So Bo'az [the Israelite] took Ruth [the Moabite] and she became his wife;
and he went in to her, and the Lord gave her conception,
and she bore a son. —Ruth 4:13

The conjugal union and procreation of the Jewish Bo'az and the Gentile Ruth may not be the earliest biblical recording of the realization and consummation of interfaith marriage (the nuptials of Joseph and the Egyptian Asenat bear that distinction), but it is arguably the most significant. The interfaith aspect not only undergirds the book of Ruth's moral of crosscultural tolerance ("your people shall be my people, and your God my God"[1]); it injects the narrative's denouement with portentous genealogical implications. For no ordinary son is born to Bo'az and Ruth: he is none other than Oded, father of Jesse, father of David—of Goliath-killing, king of Israel, Star of David fame, from whose house the Messiah, in the Jewish tradition, is prophesied to come and, in the Christian tradition, already came.[2]

Postbiblical relations to interfaith marriage have been less exulted. The notion that out-marriage produces outstanding progeny was dismissed at best, vehemently opposed at worst,

125

throughout most of Western history. For ascendant Christianity, the nonconsensual wedding of Old and New Testaments reified an evolutionary hierarchy that privileged Christian over Jewish spirituality. Gospel-inspired, church-sponsored anti-Semitism, meanwhile, made actual intermarriage with Jews conscionable only in cases of (often coerced) Christian conversion. For diasporic Jews, centuries of symbolic annihilation, ghettoization, expulsion, and pogroms made intermarriage anathema from a historical and religious standpoint and its opposition imperative for Jewish survival as a distinct ethno-religious group. The legal emancipation of Jews in late eighteenth-century Europe, while it (tentatively) eased tensions and opened opportunities in mainstream society, added a new factor to the survivalist threat: assimilation. Here the assault on Jewish continuity was more de facto than de jure, as the fading of differences between middle-class Jews and Christians, while it certainly facilitated intermarriage and conversion, eroded Jewish specificity more insidiously through the shedding of personal, familial, and communal expression.

Nonetheless, due to persistent anti-Semitism among Christians and survivalist angst among Jews, intermarriage between the two groups remained the exception rather than the rule into the mid-twentieth century. Even in melting-pot America, where ethnic identity has hinged more on consent than descent, intermarriage rates for Jews were still less than 2 percent in the 1920s and hovered around 5 percent as late as the mid-1950s.[3] Jews' rapid economic, social, and cultural advancement in the post-World War II era caused a dramatic rise in intermarriage, to an estimated 20 percent in the early 1960s and 32 percent by 1970, a seismic shift that created a major survivalist crisis in a community whose portion of the U.S. population teetered at around 2 percent.[4] When the 1990 National Jewish Population Survey (NJPS) reported an intermarriage rate of 52 percent, panic ensued. Although subsequent studies reduced the rate to 42 percent, the revision was scant comfort to survivalist Jews who (rightfully) saw an ineluctable trend and who (more problematically) accused Jews who married outside the faith of perpetrating a "Silent Holocaust."[5]

It is in this complex historical and fraught contemporary context that the intermarriage aspect of two prominent recent American television dramas featuring mixed-faith couples, *Everwood*

(2002–2006) and *The O.C.* (2003–2007), must be viewed. *Everwood* centers on the family of the recently widowed celebrity neurosurgeon Andy Brown (Treat Williams), who is Christian and whose wife Julia (Brenda Strong) was Jewish; their two children are fifteen-year-old Ephram (Gregory Smith) and eight-year-old Delia (Vivien Cardone).[6] *The O.C.* features the Cohens: Jewish lawyer father Sandy (Peter Gallagher), Presbyterian real-estate-developer mother Kirsten (Kelly Rowan), and two sixteen-year-old sons— the biologically related Seth (Adam Brody) and recently adopted Ryan (Benjamin McKenzie).[7] These popular prime-time network shows (originally on the WB and Fox, respectively) are not the first TV programs, much less cultural texts, to foreground Jewish-Christian marriage. They are, however, the first dramatic (or comedy) series to deal extensively with the intermarriage theme not merely from the married couple's and their respective parents' perspective, but from that of the couples' offspring as well. The dramedy *thirtysomething* (1997–1991) confronted child-rearing concerns (baptism vs. circumcision, Christmas vs. Hanukkah), but only on the infant level. The sitcoms *Dream On* (1990–1996) and *Friends* (1994–2004) and the crime drama *The Commish* (1991–1995) dealt with intermarriage effects on teenagers or young children, but only in single episodes. Two more recent shows, the dark comedy *Weeds* (2005–) and the prime-time soap *Brothers and Sisters* (2006–), the latter coproduced by *Everwood* creator Greg Berlanti, have the diegetic potential to treat intermarriage from a generational standpoint but have, as of this writing, done so only minimally (*Brothers and Sisters*) or not at all (*Weeds*).[8]

Ultimately, how mixed marriages are manifested in their "hybridized" children is the only way to measure, from an ethno-religious standpoint, such marriages' longer-term beneficial or detrimental effects. If, on the one hand, intermarried children are raised in, or choose to identify with, one of their parent's religions, that religion has not—depending on the degree of commitment— "lost out," numerically speaking. If, on the other hand, the non-Jewish or no religion is the end result, the outmarried Jewish parent remains vulnerable to charges of finishing what Hitler started. As philosemitic Christian theologian Harvey Cox puts it, "The bottom line is the question, 'What about the children?' In short, many Jews fear that since they constitute a minority in most places in the world, every mixed marriage puts the next generation's Jewishness at risk. . . . At some level, most Jews feel very intensely that something of immeasurable importance would be lost, not just to them, but to everyone, if all Jews were to disappear from the earth."[9]

Indeed, despite aggressive conversion campaigns intended to counter the intermarriage trend, the prevailing wisdom, backed by NJPS and other surveys, is that intermarriage does, on the whole, tend to dilute, if not to extirpate, religious—especially Jewish religious—expression.[10] In one recent study, 8 percent of adults who grew up in mixed-married families identified with Judaism, 24 percent identified with Christianity, and 68 percent with another or no religion. By comparison, 90 percent of children from in-married Jewish families described themselves as Jewish by religion.[11] Some surveys have been more encouraging, such as a recent Baltimore study reporting that 62 percent of children in intermarried homes there were being raised Jewish. But the rate in a San Diego study was 21 percent, and in another nationwide study about 40 percent. In addition, just 15–20 percent of intermarried couples are synagogue members, studies show, compared with 60 percent of inmarried couples.[12] Indeed, according to sociologist Stephen M. Cohen in his polemical article "Stop Sugarcoating Intermarriage," "[O]n no measures do the intermarried outscore the inmarried."[13]

A related problem, from a Jewish survivalist standpoint, is syncretism, or the blending of religions in mixed-marriage families. The danger here, as Jewish philosopher Martin Buber warned in regard to German-Jewish syncretism in the Weimar period, was the tendency to lose "one's primordial Jewish cultural identity . . . in a syncretistic brew."[14] In the modern-day United States, the syncretistic threat to Jewish identity has been aggravated, Sylvia Barack Fishman believes, by the American melting-pot ethos generally and by popular culture specifically—preeminently television: "American mainstream television indoctrinates viewers to believe that religious syncretism is fair, highly evolved, and truly American. In these programs [featuring intimate relations between Gentiles and Jews] religious syncretism is not just tolerated—it is a desideratum."[15]

The two television texts under examination here, however, tend to challenge Buber's and Fishman's syncretistic concerns—

and even to some extent Cohen's statistical ones—regarding exogamy's generational effects.[16] While religious or even cultural Judaism is certainly not the driving force in the lives of the inter-married families in either show, neither Ephram and Delia Brown in *Everwood* nor Seth Cohen in *The O.C.*, exhibit a loss of religious identification as a result of their parents' intermarriage; if anything, their identification (and, to a certain extent, their expression) is enhanced in the process. Similarly, while Seth, via his "Chrismuk-kah" celebrations, engages in the most high-profile example of televisual syncretism on record, its detrimental implications for the furtherance of Jewish religious *principle* is very much open to question. Before analyzing in greater detail how *Everwood* and *The O.C.* address some of the controversial issues surrounding inter-marriage, it is necessary, first, to define my use of the term *religion* and, second, to contextualize the shows in relation to representa-tions of intermarriage in U.S. media as a whole.

Socio-Religious Formation

Following Robert Anthony Orsi, I differentiate between *official* and *lived* religion, with a focus on the latter. Official religion is organized around formal institutions, sacred scriptures, autho-rized agents, and prescribed rituals; its essence is abstract, eso-teric, steeped in tradition. Lived religion is realized through family life and personal expression; its emphasis is on "embodied practice and imagination."[17] Experiential and physical rather than theo-retical or verbal, lived religion shares much with what sociologist Robert Bellah considers the taproot of all religious practice: "In the deep history of religion, embodied, non-verbal (mimetic) prac-tices are fundamental. Dancing, eating and drinking, processing, kneeling, gestures . . . , have all been formative of religious life."[18] An even more inclusive, if highly personal and somewhat mysti-cal, approach to lived religion was offered by Martin Buber: "I have given up the 'religious' which is nothing but the exception, extraction, ecstasy. . . . I possess nothing but the everyday out of which I am never taken. The mystery is no longer disclosed, it has escaped or it has made its dwelling here where everything happens as it happens. . . . If that is religion, then it is just *every-thing*."[19] To achieve such a transcendent bond with the everyday, admittedly no easy task, Buber urged the nurturing of an inter-subjective "I-Thou," as opposed to an impersonal "I-it," relation-ship with the world in all its particularity and totality.[20]

As for the moral or ethical *value* of lived religion, I draw on my own understanding and experience of Judaism. For me, as for a significant number of Jews (and others), meaningful religiosity is grounded not in belief in a personal God or ritual observance but in an engaged social conscience whose basis, while reinforced by secular humanist principles associated with the Enlighten-ment, has scriptural ties to *tzedakah* (righteous charity), *gemilut hasadim* (acts of loving-kindness), *tikkun olam* (healing the world), the biblical prophets (speaking truth to power), and political mes-sianism (preparing the way for the Messiah through righteous acts).[21] Termed a "civil religion" by Neil Gillman, a "politics of meaning" by Michael Lerner, and akin to the Christian notions of good works and the social gospel, such a social justice orientation grounds my analysis of lived religion in *Everwood* and *The O.C.*[22]

Philosopher Jürgen Habermas, in "Religion in the Public Sphere" (2006), reinforces the notion of the sacral origins of pro-gressive political principles. Religious intuition, he argues, must be acknowledged as a significant basis for liberal practice and as a key resource for the creation of meaning and identity. Besides the undeniable contribution of religion "to the motivations of most social and socialist movements in both the United States and Europe," ideas of ethics and morality that are the foundation of Western civilization can be shown to have religious roots. World religions that emerged in the first millennium of the common era "achieved the cognitive leap from mythical narratives to a logos that differentiates between essence and appearance in a very similar way as did Greek philosophy. . . . Greek concepts such as 'autonomy' and 'individuality' or Roman concepts such as 'eman-cipation' and 'solidarity' have long since been shot through with meanings of a Judeo-Christian origin." Thus, while "the Golden Rule is not the Categorical Imperative," and one does not need to believe in God to be a righteous person, "both the philosophical and the theological efforts to define the relationship between faith and knowledge generate far-reaching questions as to the geneal-ogy of Modernity."[23]

Mediating Interfaith Marriage

Intermarriage-themed texts are more than a footnote to the history of mass culture in the United States. Jewish playwright Israel Zangwill's *The Melting Pot* (1908), which made the freighted romance between a Jewish woman and a Catholic man the cornerstone of the play's brief for the melting-pot ethos, did "more than any social or political theory" to shape "American discourse on immigration and ethnicity."[24] Ann Nichols' hit play *Abie's Irish Rose* (1924), featuring a Jewish husband and an Irish Catholic wife, spawned a host of imitators, including the breakthrough sound film *The Jazz Singer* (1927), and was adapted for the big screen in 1928 and again in 1946.[25] American television took on the interfaith romance theme during its first year of regular prime-time programming in 1948, and on several anthology dramas and series episodes in the 1950s and 1960s.[26]

The sitcom *Bridget Loves Bernie* (1972–1973), the first TV series to make intermarriage its prime focus, chose an inauspicious moment to take this narratological leap. Not only had the recent statistical spike in the Jewish intermarriage rate suddenly turned exogamy into a hot-button issue, but the identity politics movements of the period, combined with policy changes in the television industry, provided a ready platform for organized protest on content grounds.[27] Taking their cue from media-monitoring groups advocating increases and improvements in images of people of color, women, and gays, Jewish groups mounted an aggressive campaign against a show that blithely portrayed the lightning romance and marriage of a New York Jewish cab driver, whose parents run a delicatessen, and the daughter of a wealthy, conservative Irish Catholic family. Despite high ratings, CBS buckled to the outside pressure and canceled *Bridget Loves Bernie* after one season.[28]

Interestingly, the next high-profile show in which intermarriage played a significant role, the *Mary Tyler Moore Show* spinoff *Rhoda* (1974–1979), suffered neither the controversy nor the cancellation fate of its immediate predecessor. While intermarriage was not the raison d'etre of the show, as it had been for *Bridget Loves Bernie*, the first-season wedding of the Jewish Rhoda to a Catholic construction company owner was a major series highlight and a ratings bonanza. Yet *Rhoda* sailed through the highly touted wedding and its two-year intermarried aftermath with nary a peep from the Jewish media monitors, a discrepancy from *Bridget Loves Bernie* that can be explained largely in terms of gender. Given the traditional Jewish law of matrilineal descent, and the 1970 NJPS' claim that intermarried Jewish mothers were more likely than their Jewish-father counterparts to raise their children Jewish, the eponymous Rhoda, as compared to Bernie, if not exactly a more positive role model for Jewish continuity, posed less of a threat.[29]

Child-rearing, as it turned out, never became an issue for Rhoda, or Joe, since the TV couple divorced, without offspring, after two years. Nor did the generational effects of interfaith marriage assume any importance in the occasional episodes, miniseries, and TV movies dealing with the subject that dotted the television landscape in the 1970s and 1980s.[30] Things changed significantly in the late 1980s. Reflecting demographic reality (increased intermarriage), industrial paradigm shifts (business concentration, the rise of cable and other new media), a revitalized multiculturalism, and a younger generation of Jewish television personnel more self-confident of their position in American society, the period from the 1987 premiere of *thirtysomething* through the mid-2000s has seen an unprecedented surge in regular programming centered on interfaith relationships. I count close to thirty such interfaith shows from 1987 through 2006, compared with only two—*Bridget Loves Bernie* and *Rhoda*—in the previous forty years.[31] Five of these—*thirtysomething, The Commish, Dream On, Everwood,* and *The O.C.*—have addressed generational issues relating to intermarriage, and four—all except *thirtysomething*—have dealt with intermarriage-sired children old enough to speak for themselves.[32]

Dream On was the first series to treat intermarriage issues from the standpoint of the progeny of an exogamous union. Indeed, one of the intermarried parents, the protagonist Martin Tupper, is himself the product of the intermarriage of a Jewish mother with an Irish Catholic father.[33] Exogamy only becomes a problem, however, in relation to his teenaged son Jeremy, who, in one episode, shows a sudden interest in Christianity. At a rare Passover Seder that Martin hopes will help "convert" Jeremy to Judaism and that his wife Judith hopes will leave their son's Christian orientation in tact, Jeremy surprises both parents when he blurts, "You're both fucked! For sixteen years neither of you has given two shits about religion. I never saw either of you go to services, pray, or do anything. Do you even believe in God? You're such hypocrites! As of now I'm not Jewish. I'm not Christian. I'm a nothing!" Stung by Jeremy's jeremiad, Martin and Judith vow to become more observant, yet the religious turnaround is subverted by Marx (consumer fetishism) and Freud (sexual desire): Judith ends up going shopping instead of to church, and Martin has intercourse on the dining room table in the glow of the Sabbath candles. While this episode's ribald denouement, in keeping with cable's niche-marketing strategy, is morally ambivalent, the message from a *generational* interfaith-marriage standpoint is more heartening. For although Martin's mixed Jewish-Christian background may have had no spiritually beneficial effect on him, such an effect, like a recessive gene, has become manifest one generation later. Jeremy's youthful experimentation with religion, not as rote response to his upbringing but as an autonomous quest for meaning, indicates that the "sins" of the parents—their intermarriage—are not necessarily visited on succeeding generations but, on the contrary, can serve a *regenerative* purpose. Moreover, at least on U.S. television, such a redemptive prospect (with some caveats) appears to have become the norm for interfaith-marriage shows with generational components, as my analysis of *Everwood* and *The O.C.* indicates.

Recombinant Genres

Everwood and *The O.C.* both exhibit a form of genre hybridization associated with the postmodern cultural formation.[34] Specifically, each show features an amalgamation of adult and teen forms that further encourages an analysis centered on generational effects associated with intermarriage.

Everwood combines the edgy teen soap with the homespun family drama: *Dawson's Creek* meets *Little House on the Prairie*.[35] Its most direct antecedent is another postmodern show, *Northern Exposure* (1990–1995), a self-consciously ironic dramedy which, like *Everwood*, centers on a New York City doctor who moves to a frontier town steeped in America's rural past and surrounded by natural splendor. Both shows' protagonists undergo identity crises, undertake spiritual quests, and engage in interfaith romances. The main differences are that *Northern Exposure*'s Dr. Joel Fleischman is Jewish, remains single, and is *sent* to the backwoods burg of Cicely, Alaska, to fulfill his scholarship contract; Dr. Andy Brown is Christian, widowed with two children, and *chooses* Everwood, Colorado, to revivify himself and his family after the tragic death in a car accident of his Jewish wife Julia.

The O.C. adds another postmodern ingredient to its prime-time adult/teen-soap mix. The heightened romantic/relational conflict, multiple protagonists, interlocking narratives, and serial storylines characteristic of classical TV melodrama are leavened with "hyperconsciousness"—Jim Collins' term for media texts' hyperawareness of their status, function, and history within popular culture.[36] A few examples: a running gag on the show is a teen soap-within-the-soap called *The Valley*, to which Seth's girlfriend Summer (Rachel Bilson) is addicted;[37] a comic-book publisher winks at *The O.C.*'s metanarrative when he critiques Seth's superhero idea, asserting that "putting pretty people by the beach isn't good enough, even if they have powers";[38] Kirsten hopes her new magazine about the community's "rich and fabulous" is "an opportunity to turn Newport Beach upside down, to be subversive and irreverent";[39] Seth reflexively riffs on *The O.C.*'s melodramatic tropes, such as the obligatory endings at large gatherings—"These formal things, they seem like they're going to be boring, but usually something crazy happens, something exciting"—or the propensity for disaster—"Every time things are going too well around here, that's when doom comes a knockin' [the door bell rings] . . . or ringing";[40] Ryan's girlfriend-to-be, Taylor (Autumn Reeser), in taking a photo of the show's teen couples of the moment (Ryan/Melissa [Misha Barton] and Seth/Summer), calls them by their extratextual moniker, "the core four."[41]

(Dis)Location

As already indicated, *Everwood*'s and *The O.C.*'s eponymous settings play seminal roles in both shows—but in diametrically opposed ways, both of which relate to intermarriage and to lived religion. Everwood, Colorado, a Norman Rockwellian village nestled in the Rocky Mountains, was not picked willy-nilly by Andy Brown; it was selected because his deceased wife had remembered it, from the time she was stuck at the train station with her parents during a snow storm, as the most beautiful place she had ever seen. The change of residence thus represents a radical break from the past yet also a reconnection with it, a combination that Andy hopes will help reunite his shattered family and repair his broken soul. *Patriarchal* connections have determined the Cohen family's relocation to Newport Beach, California. Kirsten has returned there to take on a position with her father Caleb Nichol's (Alan Dale) megadevelopment firm, and her family has moved into what was once the Nichol family mansion, an incestuous mix that compounds the Cohens' individual and collective struggles to maintain their moral integrity in the face of the coastal city's class privilege, political corruption, and conspicuous consumption.

While Everwood is fictional (and was shot first in Canada and then Utah) and Newport Beach is an actual place (though filmed prominently in Malibu and Brentwood), both serve pregnant metaphorical purposes.[42] Given Everwood's televisual genesis in Julia's memory (her own, and the Brown family's of her), her (Jewish) spirit hovers over the decidedly Gentile town: "No synagogue?" Ephram asks his love-interest-to-be Amy (Emily VanKamp), in the pilot episode, as she points out Everwood's multidenominational but strictly Christian "church row." The village itself, meanwhile, introduced as it is through Rockwell-inspired opening credits and a folksy wise narration by Everwood's lone black resident, Irv (John Beasley), is *Our Town* personified—"with a bent."[43] Like Thornton Wilder's Grover's Corner, New Hampshire, archetypal Everwood is a mixed bag, its postcard-perfect exterior belying an all-too-human core. Andy Brown and family can certainly learn from Everwood's hominess and civility, but so too can the backwoods burg gain from the Browns' cosmopolitanism and civic-mindedness. As Irv avers in one of his episode-closing voice-overs, "This is the story of a man, and of a town, that lost its center and strove to regain it."[44]

The O.C. creator Josh Schwartz and coproducer Bob De Laurentis, on the DVD commentary, speak of their show's setting in frankly symbolic terms: "the story is rooted in fairy tale"; "it's a mythical idea of Orange County."[45] The myth is darker and more

ambivalent than Everwood's, for Newport Beach's outward paradise of blue waters, bronzed bodies, and gilded opulence is not
only contrasted with a noirish underbelly of corruption, hypocrisy, and deceit, but the postcard picture itself is held up to scorn.
Seth captures the cognitive dissonance in his comic-book rendering of the coastal town as one in which "demon water polo players
emerge from the toxic Pacific and attack Atomic County."[46] Or
as Trey (Logan Marshall-Green), Ryan's working-class, ex-con
brother, puts it in regard to a paradigmatic Orange County youth:
"He looked like every other kid in this town—tall, tan, and a face
you just wanna . . . flatten!"[47]

Both the Browns and the Cohens, then, are, at least initially,
gefilte fish out of water, their geo- and demographical otherness grounded in, or at least heightened by, their interfaith status. The two families bring to their new (or in Kirsten's case,
renewed) abodes an alien consciousness and an uncommon moral
code. Everyday Everwoodians are intrigued by their Jew York
City interlopers and stunned by Dr. Brown's free clinic, although
they readily line up for his services; Ephram brings a brooding
intellect and high-cultural predilection (he plays classical piano)
that are not unknown, but also not prototypical, in the provin-
cial town; Delia must travel out of town to find a rabbi who can
answer her query about God's existence.[48] The Jewish Sandy and
Jewish-identifying Seth maintain an uneasy truce with WASPish
O.C. society, expressing disgust at the shallowness and cupidity
of their unchosen digs while never rejecting its material comforts;
Kirsten, through Sandy's influence, gradually loosens the ties to
her venal father and the rapacious side of Newport Beach he represents; Ryan fights the most difficult, and least successful, battle with his own inner (psychological) and outer (O.C.-induced)
demons.[49]

One fundamental difference marks the two locations' relationship to their two "immigrant" families: Whereas Everwood eventually embraces and is embraced by the Browns, to the town's
and the family's benefit, Newport Beach remains essentially (if
ambivalently) opposed to and by the Cohens, whose moral righteousness is maintained through their steadfast, if somewhat
studied, marginality.

Lived Religion

Neither *Everwood*'s nor *The O.C.*'s main family is formally religious. Attendance at houses of worship is an anomaly, and professions of belief in God, with the exception of prepubescent Delia's, are nonexistent. The trappings of religious practice are cursorily evident: Ephram and Seth have been bar-mitzvahed (we see video clips of the latter's reception[50]), and Delia is bat-mitzvahed at the close of the Everwood series;[51] Ephram wears a yarmulke to his mother's funeral and chants the mourner's Kadish at her gravestone unveiling the following year;[52] one *O.C.* episode revolves around the lone Passover Seder the Cohens have ever held at their own home;[53] and we catch a glimpse of Seth and Summer's Jewish wedding in the series finale's coda montage.[54] Such traditional observances are significant in the context of episodic television's comparative dearth of overt religious expression in general, but they hardly qualify as indications of meaningful religiosity. Moral, ethical, and spiritual concerns, however, which I have conceptualized in relation to *lived* religion, permeate both shows.

In overall tone, theme, and narrative throughline, *Everwood* is the more pervasively religious of the two shows. Irv's sagely omniscient voice-overs establish an inspirational air that, as we suspected all along and have confirmed when Irv dies of a heart attack near the end of the series,[55] derives from the narration's emanation in some otherworldy, if not heavenly, place. Blogger Daniel J. Stasiewski affirms (and evokes) this transcendent mode in his recapitulative gloss of the show: "It was the mother who first believed in Everwood . . . not as a patriotic fanatic but as if God had made this place for people like her [and her family]."[56] As for the theme and throughline, Andy Brown's quest for personal and familial redemption in the melding of Julia's bountiful (Jewish) spirit with Everwood's majestic beauty and small-town (Christian) values puts transcendence into practice. The transformation is manifested not in religious observance or in Bible readings but in Andy's free clinic, in his selfless devotion to his patients, and in acts of social conscience.[57] For *Everwood*, while not exactly a problem-of-the-week type show, does often engage topical issues that call on Andy, as doctor and ordinary citizen, to take a moral stand.

In "Friendly Fire," for example, Andy supports his neighbor Nina (Stephanie Niznik) in her controversial decision to act as a surrogate mother for a woman in her mid-fifties. In "The Doctor Is In," he puts queer theory into practice by informing the despairing parents of a hermaphroditic child that gender identity is not an either/or thing. In "Vegetative State," he again bucks majority local opinion in advocating medical marijuana use for a suffering cancer patient. In "Episode 20," he counsels a young girl about the options for dealing with her unwanted pregnancy, including abortion, but decides not to perform the operation himself, not out of higher principle (he's staunchly pro-choice) but from personal experience: "I don't know when life begins. I don't even know if, for a scientist, that question is answerable. But I do know when it ends. And after this year, after losing Julia, I just don't think I can be the one to end it." Traveling psychotherapist Gretchen (Jane Krakowski), who makes regular visits to town in her "shrinkmobile," sums up Andy's obsessive need to do the righteous thing as an "altruism complex."[58]

The overweening cause and carrier of Andy's renewed soulfulness are his children, to whom his dedication, despite frequent setbacks, is tireless. Teenaged Ephram, deeply alienated from his long-neglectful celebrity surgeon father and resentful of the move from the Big Apple to "Nowheresville," poses the biggest parenting challenge. But Andy perseveres, gradually earning his son's respect and regaining his affection through humility, compassion, and, when called for, tough love.

Lived religion for Ephram, a piano prodigy whose musical development is initially stalled by his mother's death, is channeled largely through culture. To attribute religious value to secular cultural expression may seem counterintuitive at best, but from a postemancipation Jewish perspective the notion is less far-fetched. When Jews in the late nineteenth century were finally granted entry into European universities and public life and began participating more fully in the world of Western arts and ideas, cultural and intellectual pursuits took on for them near totemic power. Melding Kant's ethical idealism with their own deep-seated love of learning, assimilating Jews (in Germany especially) placed profound faith in culture as a quest for the good, the true, and the beautiful "that symbolized the ideal of a shared humanity."[59] This exalted view of culture not only became an integral part of Jewish identity and self-image but ultimately, as George Mosse suggests, "became detached from the individual and his struggle for self-cultivation and was transformed into a kind of religion."[60] Belief in the sacredness of culture was brought to American shores in a series of Jewish immigrant waves: first from Germany in the mid-1800s; next in the vast Eastern European influx of the late nineteenth and early twentieth centuries that contributed crucially to the development of "tin pan alley," vaudeville and legitimate theater, and the Hollywood film industry; and finally in the flight of Jewish refugees (including the cream of Continental arts and letters) from Nazi Germany. Immigrant Jews' attachment of religious significance to both high and low culture, whatever its compensatory psychological motivation, is exemplified in *The Jazz Singer* (1927), the seminal early sound film inspired by and starring vaudevillian Al Jolson. Samuel Raphaelson, the author of the play from which the film was adapted, writes of being "overwhelmed and astonished by the religious fervor of Jolson's ragtime."[61] "I hear jazz, and I am given a vision of cathedrals and temples collapsing, and silhouetted against the setting sun, a solitary figure, dancing grotesquely on the ruins. . . . Jazz is prayer."[62] Seth, in *The O.C.*, draws a similar analogy between religion and mass culture when he responds to Ryan's plea to the saints: "Jews don't believe in saints, just in really good stand-up comics."[63]

Ephram's Jewish connection to culture, in *Everwood*, is made explicit when Julia's parents, Jacob and Ruth Hoffman (Mark Rydell and Doris Belak), arrive unannounced at the Brown house with the intention of taking Ephram and Delia back with them to New York where they believe they can provide a healthier home environment.[64] Andy manages to thwart their nest-robbing efforts but he can hardly deny the Hoffmans' positive effect on Ephram, whose affinity for his grandparents, especially grandpa Jacob, is palpable. A Renaissance man who is himself a top surgeon and a virtuoso pianist, Jacob seemingly trumps his son-in-law at parenting as well when he is able to reignite Ephram's passion for the piano, both classical and pop. As Ruth observes to Andy as they watch Jacob and Ephram playing a keyboard duet together, "They have a good rhythm, Andy."[65]

Ephram and Grandpa Jacob: "They have a good rhythm."

Young Delia's developmental issues relate mainly to feelings of abandonment (by her mother) and peer rejection (by her schoolmates). Both concerns are addressed and (tentatively) resolved, in a manner commensurate with lived religion, in an episode appositely titled "Deer God."[66] The deer in the title refers to Ephram's spiritual epiphany when he realizes that his intense identification with a stray deer arises from his feelings for his mother. Delia's dilemma is of a primal nature. Prompted by her only school friend Magilla's (Brett Loehr) claim that God doesn't exist, Delia asks her grade school teacher for guidance. The cartoonish Miss Violet (Beth Grant) does more harm than good by mangling the story of Hanukkah to prove that he does: "Let's say your people believe in God because of the oil. Way back in something-something before Christ, which your people don't believe in anyway, the Hebrews were chased out of their land—again—but when they got back there was only enough oil to light their lamp for one day. They said to heck with it and used it all up. But it turned out that the oil that was just enough for one day lasted eight more days." When Andy's nurse, Edna (Debra Mooney), takes Delia to the nearest rabbi—on a military base eighty miles from town—his rigorous theological explanation, bellowed in military cadence, proves equally unsatisfactory. Lived religion comes to the rescue, however, when on the trip back from the rabbi, Edna's motorcycle manages the eighty miles on less than an adequate tank of gas—a "miracle" that Delia connects to the eight magical days in the story of Hanukkah. When Magilla dismisses this as "just a coincidence," Andy restores Delia's faith by reminding her of something her mother used to say: "Coincidence is God's way of preserving physics."[67]

Lived religion functions here on several levels. Within the diegesis, it relates to Delia's ability to adapt religious tradition to her own immediate needs, making the tradition not only resonant with her everyday life but of practical use to it. Hermeneutically, Delia's rearticulation of the Hanukkah miracle melds personal and collective meaning and postmodern and ancient myth—an admixture that reinforces *Everwood's* grounding in fable and fairy tale but also enriches spiritual faith's embodied potential. On the metanarrative level, Delia's "applied spirituality" offers a model, not for direct action in the world necessarily, but—at least for those with a touch of "the child within"—for expanded consciousness.

In *The O.C.*, acts of social conscience and more explicit religious experience divide, as in *Everwood*, along generational lines; their denominational aspects, however, are reversed. Jewish Sandy Cohen does not provide free legal service, but as a long-time public defender he is as committed as Christian Andy Brown to helping those in need ("fighting the man and sticking up for the little guy," as Seth describes it[68]). Sandy even outdoes Andy's long-distance

Delia and Nana Ruth: Making tradition (and challah) resonant with everyday life.

house calls by taking one of his clients, the then-juvenile delin-
quent Ryan, into his home and treating him like one of his own.
When he does "move up" (briefly) to a top law firm, and later to
head his deceased father-in-law's development company, in the
first instance it is to have a broader social impact, in the second
it is just a big mistake. The lapse in judgment is one Sandy fully
acknowledges in a key speech that sums up much of his own and
the show's ethical conflict: "I used to think I was better than this
place. I came from outside the bubble, so I thought I was fit to
judge it. So when it came time to run the Newport Group, I wasn't
worried at all about losing my way. But I learned that despite the
wide streets and the sunny views, you take one wrong turn in this
town and you can end up—totally lost."[69]

Unlike Andy's compassionate moral sense, which can only
partly be attributed to Julia's influence (in marriage and in memo-
riam), Sandy's clearly derives from his Jewishness. A UC Berkeley
graduate raised by a social-worker mother in the Bronx, but now
comfortably ensconced in patrician Newport Beach, Sandy is the stereotypical leftist Jew who, atypical for the upwardly mobile American, "lives like an Episcopalian but votes like a Puerto Rican."

The Chrismukkah Complex

Sandy's son Seth, even more than his father, sees himself as the
Jewish-identifying "other" in the relentlessly (if unrealistically)
Gentile O.C.[70] Yet his lived religious goals, unlike those of the
cultural Jew Ephram and the Yahweh-seeking Delia, are decidedly, indeed proactively, ecumenical. Seth's desire for spiritual
union is expressed most forcefully during the winter holiday season when he promotes, as he's been doing since he was six years
old, his own personal fusion of Christmas and Hanukkah called
"Chrismukkah." A "super-holiday drawing on the best Christianity and Judaism have to offer," the event serves admittedly
opportunistic purposes, both psychologically ("I really only know
how to handle ridicule and rejection") and materially ("eight days
of presents plus one day of many presents").[71] But it also entails
some of Delia's faith in God's magic and Seth's own belief in healing, if only momentarily, some of his own, his family's, and perhaps even the larger society's problems.

In the first Chrismukkah episode ("The Best Chrismukkah Ever"), when Sandy, confronted by interrelated occupational and marital conflicts, says "Chrismukkah is ruined," Seth will not have it: "Chrismukkah is unruinable. It has twice the resistance of a normal holiday. Don't give up on the miracle—you'll see!" And when stunning circumstances lead to the resolution of Sandy's ordeal, and an amazing coincidence allows Ryan to avert a potentially disastrous scrape with a cop, Seth draws the obvious Chrismukkah conclusion: "You had Jesus and Moses working for you . . . to give you a second chance!"[72] In the next season's "The Chrismukkah That Almost Wasn't," Seth's non-Jewish girlfriend Summer gets into the spirit of holiday hybridity by making truncated red-and-white Santa Claus caps called "yarmuclauses," which literally brings the family back together when an even worse rift than the previous year's had even Seth despairing.[73]

A paradigmatic example of syncretism, Chrismukkah's cultural convergence also resonates with Sarah Barack Fishman's notion of "coalescence." A specifically American Jewish phenomenon, coalescence describes an orientation wherein "the texts of two cultures, American and Jewish, are accessed simultaneously . . . and the resulting merged messages are perceived not as being American and Jewish values side by side but as being a unified text, which is identified as normative Judaism." Theoretical grounding for coalescence relies on "proof texts" that combine "contemporary Western ideas such as inclusiveness with ancient [Jewish]

Seth and Summer deck their heads with "yarmuclauses."

concepts," such as welcoming and loving the stranger, and "being kind to the 'righteous convert.'" This "blurring of boundaries between insider and outsider, creating the image of a biblical inclusivist utopia, reflects the fact that American Jews like to think of Judaism as a faith tradition that encourages inclusiveness."[74]

The psychological underpinnings of coalescence are self-evident, given that "American Jews yearn to think of themselves as inclusive—and included!—because so much of historical Jewish experience has been marked by exclusiveness."[75] Nor, in an American television context, can political economic factors be ignored, given that the "loading up" of audience appeals, through a coalescent agenda, is commensurate with the commercial demands of a perpetually cutthroat and increasingly convergent media environment. Whatever the theoretical, psychological, or material benefits, Chrismukkahs and yarmuclauses are not *every* American Jew's idea of constructive coalescence, much less meaningful religious expression—lived or otherwise. *O.C.* creator Schwartz and coproducer De Laurentis, in the DVD commentary, speak directly to the controversy the first two Chrismukkah episodes generated: "The rabbis were not happy. They thought we were watering down the Jewish tradition. . . . And what we were trying to do was bring people together, obviously. We come from different faiths [Schwartz is Jewish, De Laurentis is Catholic] and like the idea of religion being inclusive. . . . Especially at a time when religion is so divisive."[76] As laudable as such a sentiment may be—and it is one that I share—its evocation in the yarmuclaus episode is undermined by a blatant commercialization that characterizes *The O.C.* in general. Self-reflexivity softens the ethical compromise, but does not evacuate it.

In the third season's "The Chrismukkah That Almost Wasn't," the first season's Chrismukkah "miracle," combined with Seth's subsequent romantic (and sexual) breakthrough with Summer, goes to Seth's head. "If my sense of the cultural zeitgeist is accurate, then this year Chrismukkah sweeps the nation!" he proclaims, adding facetiously that as the holiday's founder he will of course oversee the merchandizing of mugs and T-shirts and will pen a Chrismukkah hymn set to Dead Cat's "Lack of Color." Later, however, when Summer, Ryan, and Marissa start running with the idea, Seth begins to have second thoughts: "What if it's starting—the Chrismukkah backlash? What if it's getting too big and commercial? It starts out as this really cool holiday, flying beneath the radar. Then all of a sudden it crosses over and there's too much pressure. I mean truthfully, can it really be bigger than Thanksgiving? Can it top Halloween? They'll ask me to create new holidays—Easter-over, Kwaanza-shanah!"

Schwartz and De Laurentis are quite frank, again in the DVD commentary, about how Seth's angst over Chrismukkah's potential commodification mirrored their own anxiety over *The O.C.'s* becoming not only an overnight ratings bonanza but a pop-cultural phenomenon. Calling into question Seth's self-reflexive gesture, and the showrunners' own seemingly genuine concern, however, is the fact that during the episode's original airing, multiple commercial announcements marketed yarmuclauses on *The O.C.'s* official Web site. An independent chrismukkah.com Web site, inspired by the show, has since arisen, as have other sites devoted to selling interfaith greeting cards and other paraphernalia, and two books on the subject were published in 2006.[77] *The O.C.'s* own fourth-season DVD collection includes a special feature on the Chrismukkah phenomenon—for which I, incidentally, as an outgrowth of my research for this chapter, was interviewed. One thing I pointed out was that while the mainstreaming of Chrismukkah may be a recent phenomenon, the holiday itself is not. Just as the dearth of Jews in Newport Beach is a risible myth, so is the notion that six-year-old Seth Cohen single-handedly invented Chrismukkah. The holiday's origins extend at least as far back as the late 1880s, when *Weihnukkah* (*Weihnachten* is German for "Christmas") developed among assimilated German Jews. Immigrant German Jews, including my parents, brought *Weihnukkah* to America, and my non-Jewish wife and I have continued the tradition. As for Seth's, and *The O.C* creators', desire that Chrismukkah be seen as a way "to bring people together," the late nineteenth-century German variation was similarly subtitled "the festival of the world around us."[78]

In the second-season DVD commentary, Schwartz and De Laurentis deal specifically with the marketing mania around Chrismukkah but (apparently) without a hint of irony. De Laurentis: "They [yarmuclauses] pop up in odd places, like Vegas, and Miami." Schwartz: "Well, they're big there. It's a big interfaith community." De Laurentis: "Yeah." Schwartz: "And if you can kind of smile about it [the whole Chrismukkah idea], laugh about it, come up with new merchandizing opportunities based on it, then it's a win-win for everyone."[79]

But this "win-win" is not quite for everyone, at least not for those concerned with the devolution of lived religion, a devolution that—at least partially—proceeds apace in *The O.C.*'s third Chrismukkah episode. I say partially because this episode proto-typically displays *The O.C.*'s postmodern penchant for getting it both ways. Just as the series as a whole both glamorizes and trashes Newport Beach's vapidly affluent lifestyle, the third-season epi-sode, titled "The Chrismukkah Bar Mitz-vahkkah," both devalues and redeems lived religion. The bar-mitzvah boy is none other than seventeen-year-old, non-Jewish Ryan, whose instant "con-version" and quasi-coming-of-age ceremony is concocted by Seth as a fundraiser to pay for an operation for Marissa's indigent friend Johnny (Ryan Donowho). Ryan will mutter a few hastily learned Hebrew words, make a speech, and *voila* (or is it abracadabra?), the bad boy from Chino will have entered the Jewish fold. The rit-ual's misuse, much less its delegitimacy—given that no rabbi or Torah will be on hand—does not go unnoticed, however. Sandy reminds the family (and *O.C.* viewers), in no uncertain terms: "A bar mitzvah is a sacred religious event, a tradition that marks a Jewish child's obligation to observe the Ten Commandments." Seth counters with a Lenny Bruce routine: "That's the problem with the Jews right there. They have no concept of marketing." But ultimately compromise and moral principle move Sandy to embrace the bizarre idea: the event will only be an *honorary* bar mitzvah, and the money will go for a good cause.

The event itself follows a similar sacrilege-to-redemption arc. Just as he's due to make his grand entrance, Ryan rushes off to rescue Johnny, who, renouncing charity and determining to get the operation money himself, plans to rob a mini-mart. Forced to improvise, Seth tries to tell the Hanukkah story to a Newport Beach crowd which, incredibly, is not only exclusively Gentile but also utterly ignorant of a holiday that even elementary school chil-dren in Everwood are conversant with. The nadir, from a Jewish standpoint, comes when Summer and Marissa get everyone (none of whom even knows the dreidel song!) to join them in a joyous rendition of "Deck the Halls." Then, a minor miracle! Fulfilling the episode's self-reflexive promise that *this* is going to be "the best Chrismukkah ever," Ryan not only prevents Johnny from ruining his life but returns to the event to deliver a stirring speech: "I wouldn't be here if it weren't for a mitzvah that the Cohens performed for me. You see, 'mitzvah' means any act of human kindness. Well, that's what we're really here to celebrate."

"The Chrismukkah Bar Mitz-vahkkah" points to both the limits and the potential of lived religion in its coalescent (and mainstream-mediated) form. The anything-goes approach displayed in the episode, in which a sacred rite is exploited for its brand potential and stripped of even a semblance of traditional content—"no tallis, no hallah, no tefillin," as Sandy puts it—is unquestionably a religious affront and a cultural preservationist loss. But the redirection of the event from personal fulfillment (and aggrandizement) to selfless acts of human kindness—with Ryan's "saving" of Johnny made even more noble given his jealousy of Johnny's relationship with Marissa—upholds Jewish *ethical* traditions of equal if not greater value. "If I am not for myself, who will be?" Rabbi Hillel famously asked in the Talmud, but then added, "If I am for myself only, what am I?" Ryan's honorary bar mitzvah, like Delia's motorcycle miracle, injects fresh and immediately pertinent meaning into a ritual that, like most traditional ceremonies, is prone to atrophy through mindless repetition. The bar mitzvah's transformation into a fundraiser also offers pungent satire of and a potential alternative to an event that (at least in its postmodern American variant) has degraded into a venal exercise in which personal financial gain, in the form of monetary gifts, has become the celebrant's chief goal ("Just people handing over envelopes of cash," as Seth quips).[80]

A satirical lens, in the end, is perhaps the most useful one with which to view "The Chrismukkah Bar Mitz-vahkkah" and the Chrismukkah episodes in general. For even if one takes the position that a stripped-down bar mitzvah is a dispiriting lapse of taste at best, such a deracination of religion to the point of oblivion can be seen as symptomatic of a larger moral crisis for the Cohen family, and *The O.C.*, as a whole. The show's third season also witnesses Kirsten's painful struggle with alcoholism, Sandy's ethically challenged stint as head of the Newport Group, and Seth's pot-smoking binge that leads to a delay in his entrance to Brown

University and his inadvertent torching of the Newport Group offices. Even "new man" Ryan is dragged back into a world of violence and crime that ultimately contributes to the season's, and series', biggest bummer: Marissa's death in a fiery car crash. The many faces of Chrismukkah thus demonstrate lived religion's ability to act as a catalyst and a channel for spiritual growth, but also as a barometer for moral turbulence and decline.[81]

"Foreverwood"

Delia's bat mitzvah in *Everwood* provides a telling comparison with *The O.C.*'s Chrismukkah bar mitz-vakkah. For although Delia's event also acts as a narrative catalyst and barometer, here spiritual growth, in both cases, is the order of the day. Her coming-of-age ceremony in *Everwood*'s two-part series finale is not only treated with greater reverence than Ryan's mocku-mitzvah, it is given pride of place. Titled, with fairy-tale faithfulness, "Foreverwood," the finale nonetheless features a credible bat mitzvah ritual that includes a rabbi and a cantor, part of a Torah reading, and, in a personal and moving touch, Delia's dedication of one of her ceremonial candles to Julia: "My mom and I used to talk about what this day would be like, and how the three of us would be up here together. But I feel like she's watching us right now. I hope she knows she's still a part of us, every day, and she always will be."[82] Even the material gifts Delia receives possess spiritual meaning, especially the one from her father. Fulfilling a promise he had made to her in the pilot episode ("You weren't ready four years ago, but you are now"), Andy drives Delia to Temple Ranch (no kidding!) and presents her with a horse and riding lessons.

Although it seems gratuitously sensationalistic at first, the bat mitzvah reception in the fairgrounds carnival house turns out to be strikingly apt. The circular motif established by the merry-go-round and hora dancing extends to the series' larger arc, for the event is a major turning point not only for Delia but also for the two couples whose romantic roller-coaster rides have provided *Everwood*'s melodramatic core. As the party whirls along, Amy gets drunk (on kosher wine) and realizes that Ephram is indeed her one-and-only, a sensation he comes to share as they entwine on the dance floor. Andy's new true love Nina, meanwhile, breaks up with her fiancé Jake at the train station, opening the revolving door for Andy's subsequent proposal and Nina's acceptance. The "Foreverwood" bat mitzvah thus serves a maturation function textually and metatextually, as coming-of-age for Delia and coming-full-circle for the series.

Postethnicity

David Hollinger's concept of "postethnicity" offers an additional model for assessing the representations of lived religion in *Everwood* and *The O.C.* Unlike postmodernism, postethnicity posits an extension rather than a rejection of that which it "posts"—in this case, ethnic pride and identity politics—retaining certain elements of multiculturalism and challenging others. Both a descriptive and prescriptive approach, postethnicity, in Hollinger's words, "balances an appreciation for communities of descent with a determination to make room for new communities, and promotes solidarities of wide scope that incorporate people with different ethnic and racial backgrounds. A postethnic perspective resists the grounding of knowledge and moral values in blood and history, but . . . [recognizes] that many ideas and values once taken to be universal are specific to certain cultures."[83] Moving toward a more inclusive form of multiculturalism, postethnicity favors a "rooted cosmopolitanism" that "promotes multiple identities, emphasizes the dynamic and changing character of many groups, and is responsive to the potential for creating new cultural combinations."[84]

Everwood's metaphorical significance as a place in which the most humane Jewish and Christian values imaginatively interact to produce a moral sum that is greater than the parts, and Seth's Chrismukkah concept for fusing the best that Judaism and Christianity have to offer (not only in Orange County but potentially everywhere), point to the postethnic possibilities of "new cultural combinations" that maintain yet also transcend ethno-religious difference. Together with Sandy Cohen's "Left Hand of God" activism—Michael Lerner's phrase for a spiritually based politics "that require understanding and conscience rather than obedience"[85]—the generational effects of intermarriage, at least in these two popular television programs, can be seen as fostering both religious consciousness and interfaith understanding.

Of course, when new cultural combinations cross over into gross commodification or semiotic vacuity, as in the yarmu-claus marketing campaign and, to a lesser extent, in Ryan's mocu-mitzvah, the compositing aspect of postethnicity risks getting tossed onto the compost heap. Additional concern, from a Jewish survivalist standpoint, arises from the prospect that both *Everwood's* Ephram and *The O.C.'s* Seth will eventually decrease the Jewish side of the intermarriage equation by a factor of two. If Ephram marries Amy and Seth weds Summer, as metanarrative destiny decrees in the former and actualizes in the latter, their resulting offspring would be technically one-quarter rather than one-half Jewish. More fodder for the "Silent Holocaust" crowd, no doubt—or is it, necessarily?

Ephram's and Seth's Jewish identification is beyond question. And given Ephram's deep ties to his Jewish mother, one can surely speculate that in *Everwood, the Next Generation,* his children would be raised with a strong Jewish consciousness, if not religious training. As for Seth and Summer, she has already indicated a willingness and ability to swing both ways, soulfully speaking. Besides her initial saving of Chrismukkah, in the Passover episode she bones up on the Haggadah, informs Kirsten she's reading the booklet backwards, and volunteers to read the Four Questions.[86] After Seth proposes early in the fourth season, she starts to learn Hebrew, to cook brisket, and joins Seth in preparing to construct their own hupah, under which, in the series finale's coda, they are Jewishly betrothed.[87] As for social consciousness, in the fourth season Summer turns into a radical environmentalist and puts off college, and even marrying Seth, to work for an international anti-global warming organization (facetiously named George), prompting Sandy to comment, "Who knew that of all you kids, she'd turn out to be the young Sandy Cohen?"[88] Given Summer's political awakening, her Jewish-looking plastic-surgeon father, her own dark hair and spunky personality, and her finale-proffered Jewish last name, it seems reasonable to surmise that the series' reincarnation could well be titled *The Oy C.*[89]

Speculation aside, contrary to cold statistics and conventional wisdom, *Everwood's* and *The O.C.'s* Jews certainly appear to be bucking the intermarriage trend, at least in terms of its alleged generational effects. In terms of ethical values and lived religion, the torch is not only being passed in these two hit TV shows, but raised higher. In so doing, the Brown and Cohen offspring may be swimming against the mainstream on the one hand but flowing with one of its tributaries on the other—namely, the worldwide religious revival generally and the Jewish renewal movement specifically. Further explanation, and inspiration, for the shows' "return to the fold" trajectory can be found in "Hansen's law." This 1938 thesis, formulated by Marcus Lee Hansen in 1938 and still widely held, asserts that ethnic traits tend to be rejected and reclaimed in generational cycles: "What the son wishes to forget, the grandson wishes to remember."[90]

All of this is not to overestimate the transformative potential of Seth's Chrismukkah ritual, or either show's lived religion in general, whether diegetically, intertextually, or societally. Nor can one discount the fact that 50 percent of the recent "intermarried shows with children," namely *Weeds* and *Brothers and Sisters*, in soft-pedaling or eschewing Jewish survivalist issues (at least so far), come closer to mirroring real-world American tendencies (at least statistically). By the same token, neither should *Everwood*'s and *The O.C.*'s positive potential be dismissed. Indeed, whether it is a matter of life imitating art or a historiographic blip, Joel Kotkin and Zina Klapper report an emergent tendency "for intermarried couples to raise their children in the tradition of Diaspora Jewry, retaining some traditions and at the same time assimilating others from the dominant culture."[91] And as George Lipsitz suggests, while the issues addressed in mass media run the risk of making culture "seem like a substitute for politics, a way of posing only imaginary solutions for real problems," culture also "can become a rehearsal for politics." At its best, television offers "a kind of free space of the imagination," "a place where desire does not have to be justified or explained."[92] Viewed from this perspective and in light of my comparative analysis, interfaith marriage, as represented in *Everwood* and *The O.C.*, may be a mixed blessing, but it is not a lost cause.

"The Fire Next Time"
Sleeper Cell *and Muslims on Television Post 9/11*

AMIR HUSSAIN

Introduction

Salman Rushdie's 1988 novel *The Satanic Verses* dealt with issues of being a Muslim immigrant in the West. One of the main characters, an Indian Muslim, is hospitalized in an immigration detention center in London after being assaulted by police. There, he discovers to his horror that he has begun to transform into an animal/human hybrid. He also discovers that he is not alone and is surrounded by others who have been changed into monsters. When asked how this is possible, he is told, "'They describe us,' the other whispered solemnly. 'That's all. They have the power of description, and we succumb to the pictures that they construct.'"[1] Issues of description and representation of Muslims are more crucial now than they were two decades ago when the novel was published.

In this chapter, I describe and analyze the portrayal of Muslims in the two seasons of *Sleeper Cell*, the first show on American television created to examine Muslim lives post 9/11. I deal briefly with Muslim characters on *Oz* for a look at pre-9/11 portrayals (*Oz* is examined in greater detail in Elijah Siegler's chapter) as well as *Lost* (discussed in Lynn Clark's chapter) and *24*, the other television dramas that fit the parameters of this volume. Characters in shows such as *JAG*, *NCIS*, and *The Unit* could also be studied, but they would not add further insights to my argument.

I conclude that Muslims are not recognized in American television as ordinary citizens of this country but instead are portrayed as dangerous immigrants with a religion that is both alien and evil. Moreover, their "lived religion" consists solely of expressions of violence—there seems to be no other substantive practice that embodies Islamic faith on television. As this is the only chapter to deal with Muslims, and because there are specific issues affecting the Muslim community in America post 9/11, I go into some detail about who American Muslims are and why negative media portrayals of them are so problematic.

"Here we are now, entertain us": Teaching about Muslims in America Post 9/11

It would be difficult to overstate the role of media in forming impressions of Islam and Muslims in the United States. The importance of news media, for example, became clear to me through my courses on Islam. In the years before the terrorist attacks of 9/11, I would begin with a standard historical introduction to the life of Muhammad and the beginnings of Islam.[2] I did this because my students—regardless of whether they were Muslim—often knew very little about Islam before they took my course. In the semester after 9/11, I found that this was no longer effective, as the students thought they had a great deal of knowledge about Islam and the religious lives of Muslims. Most of their "knowledge" came from the popular media, however, and was often at odds with the ways in which the majority of Muslims understand their own faith.

An August 2007 poll by the Pew Forum on Religion and Public Life indicated that while 58 percent of Americans said that they knew "not very much or nothing" about Islam, 70 percent said that Islam was very different from their own religion (up from 59 percent in 2005), and 35 percent held unfavorable opinions about Muslims (American Muslims specifically were rated unfavorably by 29 percent. The only group to rate lower than Muslims were atheists, who were "unfavorable" to 53 percent of those surveyed).[3]

There is a growing body of literature on religion and media[4] in general as well as several good studies on how Muslims use the media.[5] There are also excellent studies of how the media view and create representations of Islam.[6] Most often, news stories present negative views of Islam. For example, according to an online poll of the members of the Religion Newswriters Association, a professional association of secular journalists, the top two religion news stories in 2006 were the Muslim world's reaction to the controversial Danish cartoon depictions of Muhammad and remarks by Pope Benedict XVI that linked Islam and violence.[7]

Representations of Muslims on commercial television are no better than those in the news media. When I ask students about Muslim images on television, they are initially stumped. Often a student will name Apu from *The Simpsons*, who is actually a Hindu. Dave Chappelle is the most famous Muslim on television, yet only a few students know that, and none of the major characters on *Chappelle's Show* are Muslim.[8]

Eventually someone in the class will recall the characters of Sayid on *Lost*, Imam Kareem Said and the Black Muslims in *Oz*, or the terrorists on *24*. Others mention characters from Showtime's *Sleeper Cell*. A few cite professional wrestlers such as the Sheikh, Abdullah the Butcher ("the madman from Sudan"), the Iron Sheikh, Sabu ("homicidal, suicidal, and genocidal"), and Muhammad Hassan.

All of these characters are evil, violent men: the wrestlers are all villains ("heels"), Sayid is a former member of the Iraqi Republican Guard, Kareem Said and the Black Muslims are all prisoners, and the terrorists in *24* and *Sleeper Cell* are, well, terrorists. Only one major character, Darwyn Al-Sayeed from *Sleeper Cell*, is a good guy: an undercover FBI agent.[9] But he too is heavily involved in violence and does nothing to upend the simple dichotomy of "us/them" or "good/bad" that establishes, promotes, and sustains the cultural status quo.

Terrorists, prisoners, enemy combatants, and wrestlers—these portrayals do not reflect the realities of American Muslim life, most notably the fact that American Muslims are equal in wealth and higher educational achievement than non-Muslims. A recent *Newsweek* cover story on Islam in America highlighted another 2007 Pew survey which found that 26 percent of American

Muslims had household incomes above $75,000 (as compared to 28 percent of non-Muslims) and 24 percent of American Muslims had graduated from university or done graduate studies (as compared to 25 percent of non-Muslims).[10]

In fact, the majority of American Muslims are professionals: engineers, professors, doctors, and business owners. Geneive Abdo in her book *Mecca and Main Street* provides vignettes of this community, dispelling many of the stereotypes of Muslims as "un-American."[11] The Pew survey of American Muslims cited in the *Newsweek* article—touted as "[t]he first-ever, nationwide, random sample survey of Muslim Americans"—described them as "largely assimilated, happy with their lives, and moderate with respect to many of the issues that have divided Muslims and Westerners around the world."[12] This contentment comes despite the fact that many Muslims may be marginalized by their race as much as by their religion—and increasingly subject to post-9/11 religious profiling.

The majority of North American Muslims are "brown" or "black" (at least 25 percent African American, 35 percent South Asian, and 33 percent Middle Eastern) and so are automatically marginalized by the racism that persists in the United States. Many Muslim immigrants in North America are shaped by postcolonial cultures that still bear the imprint of imperial rule. African American and other indigenous Muslims have their own experiences of racism and discrimination. While immigrant Muslims in North America may be better off due to the privileges that come from a higher socio-economic class, as members of a religious minority, they remain marginalized relative to the mainstream of American culture and power.

Muslims on Contemporary Television Shows

Before looking at television portrayals of Muslims, I want to note that what I identify as a post-9/11 problem has been evident in films for much longer. From the beginning of the twentieth century, film depictions of Arabs and Muslims represented bloodthirsty men and exotic, oversexed women.[13] The trend only intensified after the collapse of the Soviet Union, and the standard archetype of the "bad guy" shifted from being a Communist to being an Arab.

Television drama is obviously fictional and designed to entertain; even so, it is important to consider what stereotypes are permissible and why. Those questions are key because the line between fictional entertainment and reality is increasingly blurred in television dramas, which often tout stories "ripped from today's headlines." Many television dramas "borrow" real events and individuals (e.g., the Yemeni cleric in the fourth episode of *Sleeper Cell*) as a way of tweaking in their plotlines.

Beginnings: Oz

Islam in prisons, particularly among African Americans, is often neglected in the academic study of American Muslim life. In fact, one reason that the American Muslim population is continually underestimated—the 2007 Pew survey estimated a population of 2.4 million American Muslims (or some three times smaller than scholars of American Islam estimate it to be)—is because of low counts of Muslim prisoners in particular, and African Americans in general.

The first regular Muslim character on television was the leader of a Black Muslim prison gang. Kareem Said (played by Eamonn Walker) debuted in 1997 on HBO's drama, *Oz*. Tom Fontana, the series creator, has said, "For me, there was no, 'oh I'm going to break ground here with a Muslim character.' I looked at American prisons and I said if this mosaic is going to truly reflect what is going on in American prisons right now then I have to create this character. Islam is a very compelling part of prison life; it would have been dishonest of me to ignore it. So that's where it came from, there was no nobility involved, it was story-telling."

Considering that he is a prisoner, the character of Kareem Said is portrayed fairly positively. He is an articulate man, often seen with a book in his hands (including a biography of W. E. B. Dubois in the second episode). He represents "traditional family values" insofar as he is against the use of alcohol and drugs (including cigarettes and prescription medication for himself), as well as profanity and homosexuality. In the ecology of prison life, he is more respected than he is feared by other prisoners and members of the prison staff. He is offered a pardon by the governor in the month of Ramadan (during the second season) but publicly refuses this politically motivated gesture. In the third season, he becomes romantically interested in the sister of a deceased white inmate and mentors another white inmate who becomes his cellmate. This crossing of racial lines causes friction within his group of disciples, and he is removed as their leader. Said is shot to death in the final season, and his dying words are to ask his companion not to hurt his killer.

Curiously, other Black Muslims (such as Huseini Mershah) are portrayed as violent and conniving, while those who take over the group after Said are weak leaders.

"Old Ali Baba, he's a different species"[14]: *Muslims on* Sleeper Cell

In 2005, Showtime released a promotional video titled "Know Your Enemy" for their new fall series, *Sleeper Cell.* The advertisements included the tagline: "Friends. Neighbors. Husbands. Terrorists." Concerned that this would be yet another stereotypical portrayal of Muslims, I wrote to Showtime to get more information about their series and was provided with the promo, as well as DVDs of the entire series. The promo begins with the music of Yo-Yo Ma and Alison Krauss singing "Slumber my Darling." I found this children's lullaby to be an interesting yet disturbing choice, especially since it played over children's drawings of the United States and 9/11. The message seemed clear: Our children are at risk, will we slumber through another attack? Further blurring the lines between entertainment and reality, a voice-over narration said that the show worked with the Joint Terrorism Task Force, the FBI, police technical advisors, as well as Arabic and Islamic cultural advisors.

For me, this immediately begged the question: What is "Islamic culture?" The world of Islam encompasses over a billion people with differing ethnicities, languages, socio-economic statuses, and degrees of religious observances, among other characteristics. I wondered whether the show would consider any of these differences. In a conversation between series star Michael Ealy and two of the advisors included as a bonus feature on the DVD, the issue of racial profiling was raised. It was ironic to see an African American actor talking about profiling Muslims, and troubling to hear the response that it was necessary to profile anyone who was "traditional Muslim looking." Given the diversity of the Muslim world—and the Muslim population in the United States specifically—this would involve profiling South Asians, Arabs, Iranians, African Americans, Latino/as, East Asians, and Whites. In short, there seemed to be the usual conflation of "Arab" with "Muslim." Nevertheless, despite my fears of seeing a depiction of a monolithic Islam, the series had a multiethnic Muslim cast of characters, including a Bosnian, an Arab, a French convert, an American convert, and an African American.

Ethan Reiff and Cyrus Voris, *Sleeper Cell*'s creators and executive producers, screened the pilot at my university a month before it aired on 4 December 2005. Although the experience was positive and the discussion frank, I have a deep ambivalence about the series. On the one hand, it has, for the first time, an American Muslim hero. It also deals with some of the nuances of Muslim life that are otherwise absent from the television screen. Examples include the multiethnic cast mentioned above, the ordinary scenes of celebrating a child's birthday, dietary restrictions, and the ablutions before prayer. On the other hand, it perpetuates some of the old stereotypes about Muslim violence, and suggests that any Muslim could be a terrorist.

Season 1

The title of the pilot is "Al-Fatiha," Arabic for "the opening" and the name of the first chapter of the Qur'an. The very first words heard on the pilot are *"Allahu akbar"* or "God is great," the opening lines of the call to prayer. The first image is of the Sacred Mosque in Mecca (the Masjid al-Haram). Clearly, this is a show about Islam. However, in a great visual, the camera pans back to reveal that the image we see is a photograph of the mosque, outside the bars of a prison cell, while an African American Muslim does his prayer inside the cell.

The protagonist (played by Michael Ealy), we discover, is not a prisoner but an undercover Muslim FBI agent. He is oddly named "Darwyn," which is not a traditional Islamic name but instead a creation of Voris and Reiff.[15] He meets with Israeli (more on this later) actor Oded Fehr who plays Faris al-Farik, the leader of the "sleeper cell." What follows is an interesting interchange in a synagogue about verse 5:60 of the Qur'an, in which God turns some of the People of the Book (a Qur'anic reference to Jews and Christians) into "apes and swine." This verse is often trotted out in discussions of Muslim anti-Semitism, but Darwyn puts it in the correct context of a punishment only for those who disobeyed God and worshipped Satan. In the same scene, Faris (who is wearing a yarmulke) tells Darwyn to "keep that off your head," referring to the kufi prayer cap that Darwyn wears. It is clear here that some head coverings are acceptable, but others will arouse suspicion.

Darwyn and Faris: Not all head coverings are equal.

Leaving the scene, Darwyn encounters a Sikh man on the subway who is threatened by a group of thugs who think he is a Muslim. This is a direct reference to the many hate crimes that have taken place in America in which Sikhs have been mistaken for Muslims. Darwyn saves the man and beats up the thugs, telling them that Muslims and Sikhs are as different as "Crips and Bloods" who have been "killing each other for centuries." While there is truth to this, especially during the partition of India into India and Pakistan in 1947, it ignores the much greater contemporary violence between Hindus and Sikhs.

Another reference to contemporary politics comes when we meet the Bosnian terrorist Ilija (played by Henri Lubatti), who talks about the massacres of Bosnian Muslims by Orthodox Serbs and Catholic Croats. In a moving passage, he speaks of his love for American culture, including hip-hop music, but his frustration with American foreign policy: "I loved America, but you never came, not for us."

Ilija (in mirror) telling Darwyn of his love for America.

This sentiment is crucial, as it undermines the simplistic rhetoric that terrorists "hate our freedom," instead separating the love that many have for American culture from the problems that those same people may have with American action (or inaction) in the world.

There are many references to Islamic practices throughout the episode. In a debriefing with his FBI superior, Darwyn says, "These guys have nothing to do with my faith." That line is crucial as it sets the differences between Muslim terrorists and the vast majority of Muslims who abhor violence and terrorism. Darwyn gets involved with a single mom named Gayle (played by Melissa Sagemiller), and after he expresses regret that they have had sex outside of marriage, which is a sin in Islam, she points out that it is also a sin in her Catholic faith. She then talks about all humans being conceived in sin, to which Darwyn points out that Muslims do not believe in original sin. These are wonderful lines of dialogue that give an accurate portrayal of some of the differences between Islam and Christianity and illuminate how these differences can be overcome by remembering the common humanity of Muslims and

Christians. Unfortunately, there are other, dangerous stereotypes at play, suggesting that Muslims are alien and violent.

There is the honor killing of the daughter of a Yemeni immigrant. While honor killings are a feature of life in some parts of the Muslim world, the danger is the perception that somehow it is only Muslim women who are at risk from the men in their lives. More troubling is a comment from Faris that universities should not be targets because there is "too much potential support" from them.

The rest of the first season contains an equal mix of positive and negative Muslim stereotypes. In the positive column is the fact that one of the terrorists is a White American, while another is undercover as an Israeli Jew. This gives the lie to racial profiling: should we now profile Jews and White Americans? There is also an Indonesian Muslim character, representing the most populous Muslim nation, and there are connections drawn in episode 3 between the experiences of Muslims in the United States with Latino/as in the United States and Algerians in France, to highlight shared discrimination. On the negative side, the same episode is set in a Mexican brothel that uses children as sex-trade workers. There, one of the criminals says "these aren't American kids; you can do what you want with them." This supports the idea that somehow America is pure, and evil occurs only in other places or is introduced into America only by aliens.

The fourth episode is centered around a Yemeni sheikh named Zayd Abd al-Malik, a character based on Hamoud al-Hattar, chair of Yemen's Religious Dialogue Committee, formed in August 2002 by President Saleh.[16] In November 2002, he began working with militants who were released from jail and vowed to give up extremism and violence.

In this episode, Darwyn again makes the distinction between his religious practices and those of the terrorists. And it is in this episode that one of the terrorists goes to Canada to pick up some anthrax. When Darwyn wonders to his FBI superior if they can spy on the man while he is in Canada, the agent responds, "We're Americans; we get to spy on whoever we want."

Episode 6 shows the characters Christian and Tommy beating up a Christian evangelist on a university campus where Tommy's mother is giving a talk. Here, there is a gross misrepresentation of reality: in America, it is Muslims who are victims of hate crimes, while one rarely hears of a Muslim beating a Christian. On a positive note, there is a discussion of the differences between the Nation of Islam and Sunni Muslims, and Darwyn does a wonderful job of trying to explain his religion to children. The next episode continues this sensitive portrayal by introducing a character who is an Afghani boy who has been wrongly accused of being part of the Taliban, and subsequently is serving several years in Guantanamo Bay. It is there, in prison, wrongly accused, that he learns to hate Americans. Darwyn tries to explain to him the richness of the Muslim world, introducing him to Sufi practices and gender equality.

In the concluding episode, there is a reprise of the trope that somehow Americans are different from the terrorists in that Americans do not kill civilians. This is stated by one of the characters who is held hostage by the terrorists. Of course, this notion overlooks the numerous civilian deaths at the hands of Americans in Iraq and Afghanistan. In this episode, the terrorists work with White supremacists to get explosives. While this twist is interesting, as it shows the existence of non-Muslim hate groups in the United States, it also moves the show closer to the realm of caricature through the use of another stock villain.

Another issue in the series is the negative portrayal of women. The only strong female character is FBI Agent Patrice Serxner (played by Sonya Walger), who has to deal with challenges to her authority from the men she supervises (including Darwyn). Clearly, there are interesting comparisons with the ways in which both women and Muslims are negatively portrayed in the series.

The season ends on a positive note, with the terrorist attacks being thwarted and Farik being captured. The last scene is an echo of the opening scene, with Darwyn saying his prayers in community in a mosque.

Season 2: Sleeper Cell: *American Terror*

The series was renewed for a second season in 2005. The tagline now became "Cities. Suburbs. Airports. Targets," and the first episode of the second season was called "Al-Baqara," the name of the second chapter of the Qur'an. The opening scene was the same as that of the first season, with a view of the Sacred Mosque in Mecca. This time, however, it was Farik who was saying his prayers in an interrogation cell. In this season, Farik is brutally beaten by his CIA captors and then sent back to Saudi Arabia to be tortured even more. This is an actual practice of the U.S. government, known as "rendition." Reiff and Voris are to be commended for including this, as it is a practice that contradicts the facile notion that Americans somehow play by the rules while the terrorists do not.

In the second season, Darwyn infiltrates another Los Angeles terrorist cell. This one includes a Latino convert (based according to Reiff and Voris on the real-life terrorist Jose Padilla) and a female terrorist (based on an actual terrorist Dutch convert and played by Dutch actor Thekla Reuten). In this season, the terrorists are more successful: Darwyn's FBI handler (Agent Serxner) and his love interest Gayle are both murdered, Ilija murders the woman who helped to hide him, and the Dutch terrorist Mina does a suicide bombing in a Las Vegas hotel. The violence in this season is much more brutal and graphic than in the first season, becoming pornographic with scenes of Farik's torture.

Unfortunately, the negative portrayals of women from the first season are carried over to this season. Carly, the girlfriend of the terrorist Ilija, is played as a dupe, and Faris' wife Samia is used as a dupe to lure Darwyn into a final confrontation with Faris. The meetings between Darwyn and his new handler take place not in the sex shop of the first season but in a strip club in order to present even more naked women than before.

There are some interesting developments, however, in the portrayals of the Muslim terrorists. Mina is raped by her employer, a sad reflection on the reality of female immigrants who may not be able to go to the police. Another terrorist, Salim (played by Omid Abtahi) talks about the racism he experienced in Britain. Salim also struggles with his homosexuality, which is forbidden in traditional Islam. The shaping of this character deserves special praise, as to my knowledge it is the first portrayal of a gay Muslim on American television. There is also an American Muslim chaplain, who may or may not be based on the real-life character of Chaplain James Yee.[17]

The second season ends in tragedy, with Mina murdering Gayle and then hundreds of others in a suicide bombing. Darwyn takes his revenge by going on his own (unsuccessful) suicide mission and killing Farik's wife in Qur'anically sanctioned retribution for Gayle's murder. The last scenes are of a wounded Farik being driven away by a fellow terrorist, and an injured Darwyn collapsing in a village in Yemen. Presumably, the inconclusive ending allows for the possibility of a third season.

Analysis of Both Seasons

There is much to admire in both seasons. One gets at times a very sensitive and nuanced portrayal of American and international Muslim lives, and the hard realities of life for Muslims in a post-9/11 world are raised. However, the show is also deeply problematic. There is a Muslim hero, but he too is caught up in cycles of violence and revenge. There are Muslim terrorists who unfortunately are planning their next attack on American soil, but this show somehow makes all American Muslims objects of suspicion.

In the DVD commentaries for the show, Voris and Reiff talk about the first Gulf War (Operation Desert Storm in 1991) as the key moment for Islamic radicalism. In so doing, they were off by over a decade. For many scholars of Islam, this radicalization took place in 1979 with the Iranian revolution and the Soviet invasion of Afghanistan. Ignoring the events of 1979 allows us to forget America's role in the development of radical Islam: selling weapons to both Iran and Iraq during their war and helping to gather, arm, and train the mujahideen who would become the Taliban.

Reiff talks about his own political conservatism: he is far to the right. This perspective he says is balanced by some of the directors, including Clark Johnson, who he describes as being far to the left. Both creators mentioned that they were going to show an American beheaded on the first season, but didn't because of the number of actual Americans who were beheaded in Iraq in the fall of 2004. While I approve of this, I wonder why, for example, they did not deal with the fact that many more Iraqi civilians have been killed in the Iraq war than American soldiers or private contractors. They talked about Iraq being the undercurrent for the second season and how there were Muslims exporting violence around the world. Left unsaid was the American role in exporting violence to Iraq.

In discussing the rendition of Farik, the creators talk about him being sent to Saudi Arabia to be tortured, as if he was not tortured by the CIA in America. In that episode, they have the CIA officer saying, "Americans hate this shit—it's not who we are." Unfortunately, as countless memoranda about torture in the United States show, it is unfortunately who we are.[18] And in talking about the real-life Yemeni judge who was portrayed in episode 4 of the first season, one of the creators says that "he was turning Muslims away from extremism." In fact, 'the judge was turning terrorists away from terrorism. This equation of Muslims with terrorists was quite troubling.

In his discussion at the University of Southern California, Kamran Pasha, a writer and co-producer of *Sleeper Cell*, talked about how he saw immigrants being portrayed in stages on television and film: first as objects to induce fear, then in comedy, and finally in drama. Clearly, we are still in the first stage with portrayals of Muslims in America. This happens on other shows as well, two of which I mention briefly below.

Lost

One of the most powerful anticolonial characters created in the last century is that of Kirpal (Kip) Singh, a Sikh sapper for the British army in Michael Ondaatje's brilliant novel, *The English Patient.* In the novel, Kip, who is defusing bombs while stationed in Italy at the end of the Second World War, hears of the atomic bombs dropped by the United States on the civilian populations of Japan. In his outrage, Kip speaks to the English patient:

> You and then the Americans converted us. With your missionary rules. And Indian soldiers wasted their lives as heroes so they could be *pukkah.* You had wars like cricket. How did you fool us into this? Here . . . listen to what you people have done . . .
>
> One bomb. Then another. Hiroshima. Nagasaki.
>
> . . . If he closes his eyes he sees the streets of Asia full of fire. It rolls across cities like a burst map, the hurricane of heat withering bodies as it meets them, the shadow of humans suddenly in the air. This tremor of Western wisdom.

. . . My brother told me. Never turn your back on Europe. The deal makers. The contract makers. The map drawers. Never trust Europeans, he said. Never shake hands with them. But we, oh, we were easily impressed—by speeches and medals and your ceremonies. What have I been doing these last few years? Cutting away, defusing, limbs of evil. For what? For *this* to happen?

. . . All those speeches of civilization from kings and queens and presidents . . . such voices of abstract order. Smell it. Listen to the radio and smell the celebration in it. In my country, when a father breaks justice in two, you kill the father.[19]

Recently, there has been concern over Iran, a Shi'a Muslim state developing nuclear technology that may lead to nuclear weapons. With the rumors and threats of nuclear weapons being used by terrorists, it is sobering to remember that the United States, a White Christian nation, remains the only county to have used nuclear weapons—on civilian, non-White, non-Christian populations.

In the film version of *The English Patient*, the character of Kip was played by Naveen Andrews. In 2004, Andrews took up the role of Sayid Jarrah in *Lost*. Sayid was a member of the Iraqi Republican Guard and was at first thought to be responsible for the crash that brought down the plane and began the series. It is later revealed that he became a torturer because he was asked to torture his commanding officer by American soldiers during the first Gulf War. However, he continued to torture people after the war ended. He continues to torture people on the island after the crash.

Other than his background, there is no real development of the character as a Muslim. Given his identity as a member of the Iraqi Republican Guard, however, it is clear that he also has a violent background, actively engaging with American soldiers during Desert Storm. Again, one sees a Muslim depicted primarily as a violent character.

24: Season 6

When the show premiered in November 2001, I was too busy giving talks in the aftermath of 9/11 to take notice. I became aware of the controversy surrounding the show in seasons 2 and 4, which featured Middle Eastern terrorists. Season 4 (beginning in January 2005) included several scenes of torture that in the wake of revelations of real torture taking place at Abu Ghraib created concern among viewers.[20]

There was even more torture by season 6. In fact, producers of the show met mid-season with people from West Point who mentioned that cadets were being unduly influenced by the show. In response, executive producer Joel Surinow told *TV Guide* in an interview that "Our show lives in its own world. I just don't believe that adult behavior is changed by watching a tv show."[21] While adult behavior may not be changed by watching a television show, it does speak volumes that the military was concerned about what was on television. Couple this with the fact that *24*, unlike *Sleeper Cell*, is on broadcast television and so is part of the public airwaves, and I think the concern is legitimate.

To be fair, however, one sees worse behavior than those of the terrorists among members of the White House staff on *24*, particularly among those who support Vice President Noah Daniels. Also, Bauer's family is worse than the terrorists, with Jack's father killing one of his own sons. There are also evil villains among the Chinese and the Russians (who are working with the terrorists), so it is not simply just Muslims who fill the roles assigned to villains. One of the members of the Counter Terrorist Unit (played by Carlo Rota, who also had a simultaneous role in the Canadian Broadcasting Corporation's hit sitcom *Little Mosque on the Prairie*) ends up helping the terrorists by arming their nuclear weapons.

The season was not a big hit with fans, earning the lowest ratings for any season and a promise from the creative team to reinvent things for season 7. Writing for *TV Guide*, Matt Roush noted that the show ". . . fell apart with wacky detours into Jack Bauer's twisted family tree, redundant conspiracy plots against the wooden new President Palmer and dreary dead-end intrigues in the depleted corridors of CTU."[22] Yet again, however, one dealt with the cinematic portrayal of the stock Arab Muslim terrorist, who exudes and exults in violence.

Conclusion

In 1970, at the age of four, I left Pakistan and came to Canada with my parents. At that time, there were less than 34,000 Muslims in all of Canada. By 2001, this number had grown to 579,600. While the population of Muslims grew tremendously in North America, we were almost absent from the array of characters portrayed on television. When I was a child, Hadji from reruns of the animated show *Johnny Quest* was the only Muslim I could identify on television, with the added bonus that he was also a fellow East Indian. However, I was puzzled as to how a child could have made the pilgrimage to Mecca and earned the title of "Hajji," and as someone who spoke Urdu/Hindi and Punjabi, I had no idea what his magic words "sim sim salabim" meant.[23]

There was an Arab character (Cpl. Max Klinger), played by Jamie Farr on *M*A*S*H*, but he was a Lebanese Christian, not a Muslim. He also spent much of the series in drag, trying to get out of the army. This pattern of "odd" Arab characters would continue with Tony Shalhoub's title character of Adrian Monk in *Monk*. Monk is a brilliant detective but suffers from obsessive-compulsive disorder.[24] Interestingly, most of the Arabs on television (and Casey Kasem on radio) were Christian, not Muslim.

In 1977, I stayed up to watch *Roots*, and was delighted to learn that Kunta Kinte (played by LeVar Burton) was a Muslim. I knew about African American athletes who had converted to Islam: Muhammad Ali, who came to Sunni Islam via the Nation of Islam, and Kareem Abdul-Jabbar, who came straight into Sunni Islam. And in 1978, I came to admire the character of Venus Flytrap (played by Tim Reid) in *WKRP in Cincinnati*. On one episode in the final season (1982), a detective who was about to arrest Venus asked him if he was a Muslim.[25]

Since the time of my youth, while the Muslim population in North America has increased tremendously, the number of Muslim characters on television has remained negligible. The few that exist are of alien, violent men.

In all of the shows analyzed for this chapter, there are stereotypically negative representations of Muslims. This, however, is not surprising. Very few Muslims are involved in the television industry. Kamran Pasha is one of the few. Not surprisingly, it was *Sleeper Cell* that had the most positive images of Muslims. Until Muslims become more involved in television and film, we will leave the telling of our own stories to others. As such, while we can and should protest against inaccurate descriptions, we also cannot expect others to tell our stories in the ways that we would like them to be told. James Baldwin ended a famous letter to his nephew and namesake with the following words. He was writing about race at the time, but his lines are equally applicable about religion now:

> But these men are your brothers—your lost, younger brothers. And if the word *integration* means anything, this is what it means: that we, with love, shall force our brothers to see themselves as they are, to cease fleeing from reality and begin to change it. For this is your home, my friend, do not be driven from it; great men have done great things here, and will again, and we can make America what America must become.[26]

We, as Muslims, must help in the construction of an America where our stories are told for what they are, part of the nation's fabric.

SECTION II

Neither Male nor Female

"Elect Xena God"
Religion Remixed in a (Post-)Television Culture

SHEILA BRIGGS

"Elect Xena God"—these words are painted on the walls of a temple of Aphrodite by two young vandals in the episode of *Xena Warrior Princess,* "The Quill is Mightier. . . ." Although this is a comedy and the extensive use of religious imagery and themes is restricted in the series to its more dramatic episodes, there is probably an intended irony here. In the high drama of the series, a visual narrative portrays Xena unmistakably, if not explicitly, as Christ. Xena's death and resurrection and their aftermath will overthrow the Olympian gods and usher in a thinly veiled Christian era, and Xena will travel to the ends of the earth, bringing salvation to those whom she encounters until she suffers her latest (but especially if there is a movie, not final) death in Japan.

Xena is fully human and ambiguously divine. This essay probes the space occupied by religion in contemporary society and culture and the category of "lived religion," used in this volume and by scholars of religion more generally to analyze religion as a socio-cultural phenomenon. Although the conceptual framework of lived religion is central to this essay, it has turned out to be, in large part, a meditation on the cultural significance and signification of death.

The primary reason for this is that *Xena Warrior Princess* itself was a dark narrative, with its major religious imagery being that of crucifixion. The study of lived religion, however, lends itself to such an emphasis because cultural practices surrounding death have both in the past and in the present been so strongly associated with religion. Also, in trying to address the broader volume's concern with "9/11," I needed inevitably to invoke the cultural specter of death. The underlying argument of this essay is that religion is not a stable or discrete domain of culture. A television series like *Xena Warrior Princess* can show how "lived religion" occupies a cultural space that is not intrinsically or inherently religious. *Xena Warrior Princess* takes explicitly religious imagery and themes and places them within a narrative that renders their religious character ambiguous. Religion is in the eye of the beholder, and viewers decide whether to invest what they see on the screen with religious meaning or not. The fan reception of this content runs the full gamut, from assimilating it into the story arc of traditional Christianity to appropriations that separate it from any religious interpretation.

The Fantastic and Heroic in Everyday Life

Five aspects of lived religion can be drawn from Robert Orsi's essay in *Lived Religion in America* to illuminate the interaction of *Xena Warrior Princess* with its viewers.[1] At first glance, *Xena Warrior Princess* would seem to have little to do with what is central to how lived religion is conceived: the practices of everyday life. A mythical woman warrior and her companion wander the ancient world in a sort of parallel universe where historical events and characters merge with the fantastic. Yet, as Orsi's own work on Marian devotion shows, the focal point, around which everyday practices coalesce, is often itself the miraculous and extraordinary, that which is definitely not everyday.[2] Watching television is, of course, itself an everyday practice, but cult TV shows like *Xena Warrior Princess* engage their fans in the same activities that provide the texture of everyday life in religious communities: sharing common meals, doing charitable works and acting for social justice, finding comfort in illness and support for the care of the sick, the receiving and giving of solace at times of bereavement and other serious loss.[3]

None of this is unique to *Xena Warrior Princess* and all can be found in shows where religious imagery and themes are either largely or entirely absent, such as the *Star Trek* series. This is an indication that forms of sociability, highlighted by the conceptual framework of lived religion, are not intrinsically or inherently religious, although in many historical contexts religion may be the predominant or sole idiom through which they are expressed.

Orsi stresses the materiality of religion when it is looked at through the lens of the practices of everyday life.[4] Above I have described some of the material practices of *Xena* fandom that shape and are shaped by the embodied existence of the fans. The television series itself conveys an intense materiality because its makers were deeply interested in the texture and quality of the visual narrative. I will explore in the next section their attention to the visual elements of their storytelling. Here I want to point out how they confounded on the visual level the boundaries between reality and fantasy, body and spirit. Sarah Gwenllian-Jones understands *Xena Warrior Princess* as a preeminent example of the way in which cult television seeks not only to tell a story but creates a world with its own dense history and geography.[5] As she remarks, the immersion in the virtual reality of a cult television series always seeks to fully embody a fictional world; the strongly visual narrative of *Xena Warrior Princess* enhances this sense of embodiment.

It is noteworthy that the term *Xenaverse* denotes not only the fictional universe on the television screen but also the *Xena* fandom. The fans insert their embodied material existence into the fictional world in ways reminiscent of the Catholic devotion that Robert Orsi describes. Likewise, Mary and the saints are heroes of a virtual reality in which the Catholic faithful can participate through the material practices of their everyday life.

The third aspect of lived religion that I want to discuss here explains how the practices of everyday life together with the materiality of embodied human existence can constitute such a cultural phenomenon as religion. Imagination connects our actual lives with our desires that may exceed what is possible within our sociohistorical context. This does not mean that our imagination has an unrestrained free play in how it figures our desires and their relation to the self. One of the things that Orsi believes is necessary to understand religious practice is "a sense of the range of idiomatic possibility and limitation in a culture—the limits of what can be desired, fantasized, imagined, and felt."[6] Imagination is grounded in the forms of embodied material existence of a specific historical time and culture and never can leave that ground behind. There is a tension between the miraculous and the mundane and between the heroic with the quotidian, but if this becomes sheer opposition, then the imagination has no place to work. The fully transcendent is, as Christian theology has acknowledged, inconceivable, ineffable, and unimaginable.

Even the most mystical religious practices seek not to join the participant directly to the transcendent *per se* but to its boundary, the point at which it touches material human existence. Such religious practices are always imaginative exercises, and among these one of the most important is *imitatio*. Within Christianity, the exhortation to the believer to "put on Christ" has encouraged an *imitatio Christi* that has taken on such widely diverse forms as Thomas à Kempis' mysticism and the more pragmatic practice of holding up Jeșus as a role model for the socially responsible and compassionate citizen in contemporary liberal circles. *Imitatio* is not an inherently religious practice, although in Western cultures all its expressions have been influenced by the dominant religious idioms of Christianity. Similarly, one is not compelled to conceive of the transcendent in religious terms; it can be thought of as the unknown, the realm of unconstrained possibility and therefore beyond the reach of the imagination grounded within the constraints of our actual lives.

Science and fantasy fiction with their fandoms are primary sites for secular forms of *imitatio* and ideas of transcendence. In the nineties, some television series in these genres decided to exploit the tension between ordinary human life and the fantastic and heroic. For example, In *Babylon 5* and *Farscape* as well as *Xena Warrior Princess* we find a pronounced psychological realism in the portrayal of the main characters. These are very ordinary people who do not initially adjust well to the extraordinary circumstances into which they are thrust. John Crichton of *Farscape* is a NASA scientist and astronaut who, when an experiment goes awry, finds himself in a strange and distant region of space where, in a state of confused shock, he grieves the loss of his life on Earth. John Sheridan of *Babylon 5* is a somewhat pedestrian military bureaucrat who, on a space station of the future, reluctantly discovers his role is to save earth from an antidemocratic conspiracy and military coup—and eventually to save the universe from the ancient forces that battle to control it. Xena is a village girl who, through the trauma of war, is turned morally into a monster before she becomes the redeemed redeemer.

These are ordinary people who go through a painful transformation into heroes and who in their heroic lives stubbornly cling to everyday practices that symbolize their preheroic existence: John Crichton continually makes references to twentieth-century popular culture that no one around him understands, Xena goes fishing, and John Sheridan washes his socks every night. At the same time that these heroes are endowed with the recognizable psychological characteristics of ordinary human beings—specifically ordinary Americans—in the late twentieth century, they are placed in fictional worlds that are far more fantastic than that of Superman or the Flash Gordon films. The heroic becomes the boundary between everyday life and the secular transcendent, the realm of unconstrained and therefore unimaginable possibility.

The emergence in the mid-nineties of this trope of the ordinary person transformed into a hero in a hyperfantastic world occurred at the moment when awareness of the consequences of rapidly accelerating technological advances became widespread. Our real and not very distant future is more fantastic than the imaginary futures of earlier science fiction. The limitless malleability of human bodies and material culture generates anxiety about a posthuman future that exceeds the capacity of the contemporary cultural imagination.

In popular culture, we have seen a proliferation of graphic novels, films, and television series with the theme of genetically mutated human heroes (and villains), endowed with superhuman powers. Most recently, the television series *Heroes* has combined this storyline with post-9/11 fears about an apocalyptic terrorist attack. In the finale of season 1, "How to Stop an Exploding Man," when the genetically mutated heroes have prevented the genetically mutated villain from destroying New York in a thermonuclear explosion, a narrator's voice tells us, "So much struggle for meaning, for purpose. And in the end, we find it only in each other—our shared experience of the fantastic . . . and the mundane." If we share our humanity with heroes, we can, through their example, survive the disruption of our lives by the extraordinary and unthinkable.

Babylon 5, Xena Warrior Princess, and *Farscape* became cult television because they were able to address fears about our posthuman future. Their fans are engaged in a new form of *imitatio* in which they emulate their fictional heroes' coming to terms with the eruption of the unknown, the realm of unconstrained possibility, into their everyday lives. The restrictions of everyday life may be shattered, but so also are its certainties. The imitation of the heroic preserves a boundary, albeit a permeable one, between the unknown and the everyday.

The *imitatio Xenae* is usually seen as the empowerment of women, which it is, but this takes place in a world where not only patriarchal discourses of gender are unraveling but all constructions of gender and the human as well have been destabilized. It is significant that both *Babylon 5* and *Xena* use religious idioms to describe the transformation of the ordinary into the heroic in fictional worlds that become increasingly fantastic as the series progress. John Sheridan, like Xena and Gabrielle, dies and is raised from the dead; indeed, all of these characters fulfill a preordained salvific role. Yet neither *Babylon 5* nor *Xena* can be considered religious narratives in any direct sense. They have thick but ambiguous connections to (Catholic) Christianity, and one of the reasons why fans can appropriate these stories in a thoroughly secular way is because traditional Christianity is finding it very difficult to engage the posthuman future. This inadequacy of traditional religious mediations between the everyday and the transcendent has released the cultural space that they have occupied for postreligious (and I would argue also ultimately postsecular) configurations of the relationship of the quotidian to the heroic and fantastic.

Everyday practices, materiality, and the imagination constitute the core characteristics of lived religion, and these entail two further aspects of the cultural space it inhabits and today shares with cult television. In the introduction to *Lived Religion in America*, David Hall remarks, "It is tempting to abridge, even to censure, the messiness that leaks into everyday life."[7] This is a temptation not only in the study of lived religion but also for the investigation of popular culture.

A particular instance of lived religion—or a cult television series *as* lived religion—produces multiple meanings that cannot be tidily fit into a single ideal type or interpretative framework. Yet this messiness not only complicates lived religion as an object of inquiry but also pervades the experience of those who take part in it. Orsi conceptualizes this messiness under the rubric of hybridity, which defies neat distinctions and clear boundaries.[8] Cult television's worldwide distribution makes it part of a global popular culture in which viewers combine the characters and plots of the series with their local experiences.

Xena Warrior Princess maximizes cult television's potential for hybridity by bringing together in its storylines and visual elements motifs from a wide variety of cultures. Although Xena and Gabrielle's homeland is Greece, they travel in the course of the series to Britain and Scandinavia, to North Africa and Egypt, to India, Siberia, China, and Japan. Filmed in New Zealand, the series has Xena wearing armor with Maori designs and carrying a chakram, a weapon of Persian origin, although Xena's use of it more resembles a boomerang. This pastiche extends to religion. In the show's imagined multicultural antiquity, Xena meets the Chinese woman Lao Ma, who in the Xenaverse is the founder of Tao, not Lao Tzu. Xena prays to and is given aid by the god Krishna (an episode which brought down on the producers the wrath of some Hindu fundamentalists). She learns the ways of a Siberian shaman. She has close but troubled relations with the Olympian gods, most of whom she ends up killing, and in her evil past she was the chief warrior and lover of the Norse god Odin. She saves on more than one occasion the life of Eli, a thinly veiled Jesus character, and later assumes the role of Christ herself. The dizzy array of religious cultures that Xena and Gabrielle encounter may, on one level, reflect the eclecticism of postmodern cultural consumption under the conditions of globalization. However, such hybridity has always resulted from the contact of cultures, and in this respect the multicultural Xenaverse is closer to the historical facts of the ancient world than many more sober treatments.

The older vocabulary of the history of religions would label such hybridity in the Xenaverse as "syncretism." The concept of syncretism presupposes that individual religious traditions subsist as essences that are separate from each other. In evaluative accounts of religion, religious expressions are most authentic when they are unequivocal representations of the core essence of a single religious tradition. Lived religion tends to fare badly when judged by such criteria because it is likely to be viewed as diluting the distinctive essence of a religious tradition by introducing into it content from external sources and even other religions.

It should not surprise us, then, that *Xena Warrior Princess* is especially popular in religious cultures, such as those of Latin America, that have previously been found guilty of syncretism. In Latin America, Catholicism has long been commingled with indigenous and African traditions and now with evangelical Protestantism. Alongside its traditional Catholic iconography, which is familiar in regions like Latin America, *Xena Warrior Princess* also tells its stories through the material symbols of religion that are particularly mobile between religious traditions. In the episode "Devi" from the India arc of season 4, holy water is sought to exorcize a demon; in the opening episode of season 5, "Fallen Angel," Xena and Gabrielle enter a bath of purification during their brief sojourn in heaven. Water is a ubiquitous material symbol in religious cultures and, although its valence is specific to the particular context, these meanings are easily transmitted, appropriated, and repurposed across traditions. *Xena Warrior Princess* therefore not only inhabits the same cultural space as lived religion but for some viewers, like Latin Americans, operates alongside lived religion as a site for the circulation of the material symbols of religion.

The relationship to social power is the fifth and final aspect of lived religion that is relevant to a study of *Xena Warrior Princess* and many other television series in the science fiction and fantasy genres. Orsi identifies "religious practices and imaginings" as "one of the primary sites of transgression" and links lived religion to "dissent, subversion, and resistance, rather than harmony, consensus, and social legitimation."[9]

In this vein, *Xena Warrior Princess* foregrounds traditional Catholic imagery of Christ and at the same time utterly subverts its officially authorized content. Two women who love each other undergo a process of crucifixion and resurrection that is redemptive and transforms the world. Yet Orsi cautions, "It is not enough to speak of religious subversion and resistance unless one also speaks of how these movements of opposition may be at the same time idioms of discipline."[10] The regulation of bodies and material practices by social regimes of power may never be complete, but it is also not entirely unsuccessful. Fictional bodies, no less than real bodies, are subjected to discipline, and the adoption of religious imagery brings with it the inseparable content of idioms of discipline. Furthermore, television studios as well as Christian churches are among the regimes of power that regulate sexuality in society.

Xena Warrior Princess never grew simply out of the free play of the imagination of its creators. Its producers were accountable to the studio that financed and distributed the series. Although the location of the production of the series in New Zealand obviated close scrutiny by the studio, it did not evade their overall control. The making of the series still had to conform to industry-standard practices such as the authorization of scripts by studio executives.[11] Indeed, the intersection of religious and (homo)erotic imagery in *Xena Warrior Princess* is displayed in exactly the same ways as it has been within the religious practices of Catholicism, especially Catholic visual culture: evident but never acknowledged. In both the television series and broader Catholic culture, discipline is also not simply imposed from above. The studio allowed the "lesbian subtext," but the producers were responsible for ensuring that a lesbian relationship between Xena and Gabrielle never became explicit. The creative task was to portray Xena and Gabrielle as sharing the ultimate bond of love with its undeniable sexual connotations but never to allow their sexuality to be directly thematized. Hence, the death and resurrection of Xena and Gabrielle (homo)eroticize Christ but simultaneously spiritualize, desexualize and occlude any lesbian relationship between them. The transgressive moment becomes the instance of discipline.

Seeing Xena, Seeing Christ

In this and the next section on the erotics of death, I am going to explore how *Xena Warrior Princess* fully exploits visual language to tell its story. All television programs have to pay attention to what the viewer sees on the screen, and this is especially important for the television drama. However, the weight given to the visual varies considerably among television dramas. Many are dialogue driven, and in these productions visual elements complement and reinforce what the characters are saying. *Xena Warrior Princess* was an action series but had ambitions to address moral questions and spirituality. Instead of wedging reflective dialogue in between the obligatory fight scenes, its makers decided on a different strategy. The visual became the vehicle for developing the story, and at certain critical moments in the series dialogue is suspended. Dialogue is, if not sparse, at least terse and is rarely used to fix the meanings of the visual narrative. Although Xena and Gabrielle engage in reflection and self-reflection, this dialogue is also brief, and their interiority is often explored visually. Music is used in every television drama to create mood, but *Xena Warrior Princess* relies especially heavily on music not only to indicate to the viewer the general emotional tone of the scene but also to provide a key to the inner feelings and motivations of the characters that might in other television dramas be expressed verbally.

The emphasis on the visual allows *Xena Warrior Princess* to take over without commentary the traditional imagery of Christ's crucifixion and resurrection and therefore without having to define it. Although I will refer to Xena (and Gabrielle) as "Christ," Xena and Gabrielle are never named that at any point in the series. The identification of Xena and Gabrielle with Christ occurs entirely through the visual language of the narrative. Within Christianity—and not only Catholicism—the theological location for the origins of the Christian church and Christian belief is an act of vision: seeing the risen Christ. Early Christians thought that for a brief period Jesus, raised from the dead in a glorified body, appeared to his followers and entrusted to those who saw him the leadership of the Christian community. Thus *Xena Warrior Princess* taps into a tradition of visual representation and legitimation that has deep historical roots within Christianity. These images wield visual authority, and on them the social power of Christianity has been built.

Visual authority is also located in other images, not necessarily religious ones, and can also endow those who know how to manipulate them with social and political power. The endless replay of the collapse of the Twin Towers on our television screens has shaped the political as well as visual context in which viewers watch television drama after 9/11. The filming of *Xena Warrior Princess* ended a few months before September 11, so its storylines do not reflect the chain of events that followed the destruction of the Twin Towers. Rather, the dark themes of its narrative appear as metaphors for the world in which 9/11 and the subsequent tragedy of the wars in Afghanistan and Iraq occurred. Specifically, the dominant image of Xena's destiny is the cross. Xena does not die once upon a cross but several times. In fact, of the six seasons of *Xena Warrior Princess*, there are only two in which Xena is not crucified. These are the first season—where a crucifixion would probably have gotten the show canceled—and the fifth season, which begins with the resurrection after a previous season dominated by what perhaps counts as Xena's ultimate crucifixion. The cross is ubiquitous in *Xena Warrior Princess* but it is neither unambiguously a religious symbol nor one of salvation. Behind Xena's (and Christ's) cross is a history of violence directed not only against its victims but against all those who stand in the way of those who invoke its power.

"Destiny," the second-season episode in which Xena is first crucified, does not in and of itself have any christological references. On the contrary, it reminds us of something that Christian imagery has obscured: Jesus was just one among millions who died on a cross in antiquity. Outside every city of the Roman Empire crosses were to be seen, and when the Romans encountered resistance to or rebellion against their imperial expansion they crucified by the thousands and even ten thousands. Xena, her legs broken, is crucified by Julius Caesar, but then rescued by a friend who gives her life to save Xena's. At the end of the episode, Xena says, "Tell Hades to prepare himself. A new Xena is born tonight—with a new purpose in life—death."

Xena's first death on the cross initiates what the series constantly refers to as the cycle of violence and hatred. This is the driving narrative force behind much of the series, and the visual metaphor of the cross exposes a Christian history of violence against all who oppose those who wield power in Christ's name. In the double episode "The Debt" from the third season, Xena remembers her past and relates to Gabrielle how, "With shattered legs and crippled soul, I went East to lose myself in vengeance—not against Caesar—but the entire human race." She allies herself with the warlord Borias, savagely massacring all in the path of her conquest. In the kingdom of Chin, Xena is rescued from a grisly fate by a woman, Lao Ma, the Xenaverse's founder of Taoism. Lao Ma heals Xena's legs, which is metonymic for the greater cure that Lao Ma's wisdom offers her. In "The Debt," Xena sadly remembers the crucial moment at which Lao Ma challenged her to "stop hating" and how she refused the opportunity to let go of her hatred.

The transformation of the cross from a metaphor for violence and revenge begins in the third-season musical episode "The Bitter Suite." In song lyrics featured in the episode, we find some of the longest dialogue given to Xena in the entire run of the show; indeed, music is used elsewhere in the series to give the viewer insight into Xena's interiority. "The Bitter Suite" takes place in Illusia, an alternative reality and place of torment, where Xena hangs on a cross with Gabrielle chained on an altar beneath her. The tragic events of the previous episode, "Maternal Instincts," have brought them to this fate, and they sink ever deeper into darkness after killing and trying to kill one another through much of the episode. The turning point in the episode—and it is a turning point in the whole series—comes when Xena sings from the cross a duet with Gabrielle.

> XENA: If we can turn again to love.
> GABRIELLE: If we can heal these open wounds.
> XENA: We'll leave this hatred far behind.
> GABRIELLE: So not a trace of hate remains.
> BOTH: We'll overcome our damaged past!
>   And we'll grow stronger side by side!
>   To stand together through the storms!
>   We're safe 'cause love will be our guide!

Xena is here Christ, a salvific trope that will be reinforced in the next scenes, when Xena gets down from the cross and sings her version of parts of the Lord's Prayer and Sermon on the Mount.

After the "turn to love" in "The Bitter Suite," the cross has clearly become a symbol of redemption—of Xena's redemption from her evil past and of the redemption from oppression, which she brings others. In the opening double episode of season 4, "Adventures in the Sin Trade," Xena learns of her future crucifixion after she travels to Siberia so that through shamanic ritual she might enter the Amazon land of the dead. Gabrielle (who is also an Amazon princess) has died at the end of season 3, and Xena's quest is to reunite herself with the soul of Gabrielle.

In her evil warlord days, Xena had allied with Alti, an evil shaman, who promised her that she would become the "Destroyer of Nations" in exchange for the blood of the tribal leaders of the Siberian Amazons. Xena brutally massacred the Amazon leaders, which left the Amazons easy prey to genocide. Alti used the blood of the slain Amazons to enslave the souls of dead Amazons and prevent them from entering eternity. Xena gives up her greatest desire, reunion with Gabrielle in eternity, to lead the remnant of the Amazon tribe, a small group of adolescent women, into battle against Alti. Xena and Alti fight in the spirit realm, where Alti's chief weapon is to make Xena feel the pain and anguish of her future battles and death. But Alti has seriously miscalculated the effect on Xena of seeing her death on a cross. In "Adventures in the Sin Trade" Xena has a vision not of her past crucifixion but of a future death on a cross. This second death on a cross is the culmination of the "turn to love" which began in "The Bitter Suite." At her first crucifixion, Xena defined the meaning of her life as death, but now her future crucifixion discloses that the redemptive power in her life is love.

The vision of her future death empowers Xena to defeat Alti because she sees that she will not be crucified alone but with Gabrielle who, by the end of season 3, has also become a Christ figure. It reveals to her that Gabrielle is alive and that their death on the cross will fulfill the bond of love between them. The show's opening credits since season 1 ended with the phrase, "her courage will change the world." By the beginning of season 4 and "Adventures in the Sin Trade," we know that more than Xena's courage changing the world, it will be Xena and Gabrielle's love that will redeem it. In "Adventures in the Sin Trade," the Amazon dead had found that their holy word, *courage*, had not been strong enough to break

Alti's curse and open their way to eternity. After the spiritual battle with Alti, Xena tells the young shaman she has trained, Yakut, that the new holy word is *love*. Then the scene shifts to the Amazon land of the dead, where the trapped souls exclaim of Xena, "She has released us!" Xena the Christ releases the dead not through her cross per se but by what it reveals: the power of love.

Throughout season 4, *Xena Warrior Princess* kept its viewers in suspense as to whether its makers would boldly go where no science and fantasy fiction on TV had gone before—to use explicit and traditional Christian imagery to represent their main protagonists as Christ figures. The climax of season 4 came with the episode "The Ides of March," where we see events inexorably drawing Xena and Gabrielle to their deaths on the cross. This iteration of Xena's torment, like her first crucifixion and also that of Jesus of Nazareth, occurred at the hands of the Romans. Julius Caesar, who betrays and crucifies Xena in the episode "Destiny," brings about Xena's and Gabrielle's death in "The Ides of March"—and unwittingly his own destruction. "The Ides of March" is remarkable in how the visual elements craft the drama. One of the challenges that makers of the series faced is that they were portraying perhaps the most famous death in history. It would not escape any viewer that Xena's and Gabrielle's deaths were happening analogously to that of Jesus of Nazareth. The Jesus story and its ending are so well known that the fictional retelling of it might prove to be anticlimactic. Their solution was to pair the crucifixion of Xena and Gabrielle with the second best-known death from antiquity: the murder of Julius Caesar.

In the final scenes of the episode, dialogue becomes sparse before entirely dropping away. After Xena and Gabrielle are led away to crucifixion, there is a brief dialogue between Xena and her nemesis Callisto, who, although dead, has been released from hell to destroy Xena and make Caesar a dictator. Callisto tells Xena, "You're about to die like a slave." This may be an oblique but far from obvious reference to the description in Paul's Letter to the Philippians (2:7) of Jesus' taking on the form of a slave and dying on a cross. A verbal link between Xena and Gabrielle's crucifixion and that of Jesus never gets any closer than this. After this, there is only one short exchange between Xena and Gabrielle when they have been placed on the crosses and turn to look at each other:

Xena and Gabrielle are placed on the crosses.

XENA: You're the best thing in my life, Gabrielle.
GABRIELLE: I love you, Xena.

This declaration of love was the climax of Xena's original vision of the crucifixion. The final minutes are without dialogue as the scene shifts between the crucifixion of Xena and Gabrielle on a snowy mountainside and Caesar in the senate at Rome. We see the Roman soldiers approach the crosses with hammers; we see and hear the metal of the daggers drawn from the senators' togas. Hammers are lifted to nail the women to the crosses, but the blows we see are Caesar's stabbing. Xena's and Gabrielle's death has brought about the death of its perpetrator and rid the world of an evil conqueror. Xena experiences solidarity with her friend even to the point of death; Caesar is betrayed and murdered by his friend, Brutus. This visual symmetry and opposition of the two deaths is reminiscent of the structure of the Catholic Good Friday liturgy, where human ignorance of the meaning of Jesus' death is contrasted with its salvific effect. The episode ends with a strangely romantic but enormously powerful conclusion: Xena and Gabrielle are hanging dead on their crosses but then Xena's spirit awakens and, leaving her body behind, moves toward Gabrielle. She raises Gabrielle's chin, awakening her spirit too, so that together with hands clasped they can ascend into the heavens.

Xena's vision of her future crucifixion and its fulfillment dominate season 4 of the series. It is repeated in several episodes and
becomes many things: a revelation of love, the source of hope that
Gabrielle is alive, a source of anguish when Xena is reunited with
Gabrielle and must now face her gruesome death in the future. But
Xena's and Gabrielle's death on a cross is more than their personal
fate; its christological associations confer on it a cosmic dimension. In the fourth-season episode "Between the Lines," Xena and
Gabrielle are transported into one of their future lives so that they
can capture and bring back to defeat in their present life the shaman Alti. Alti uses her powers in this instance to force Gabrielle
to experience her future crucifixion. Gabrielle's hands and feet are
pierced and bleeding, but out of this stigmata flows the power of
the universe that overcomes Alti. In season 6, in one of the very
last episodes of the series, "When Fates Collide," Xena is crucified in an alternative reality, which Gabrielle destroys in order to
restore Xena and the world along with her. When "Between the
Lines" gives flashes of Xena's future lives as she is taken to the one
in which she confronts Alti, the viewer sees a lot of crosses. The
story of Christ is inseparable from the cross, and *Xena Warrior
Princess* embraces this narrative imperative wholeheartedly.

The redemptive work of the cross never seems to be done, and
one wonders whether it is being undone by the violent history
of the cross. Can the cross be separated from violence, allowing
Xena to break the cycle of hatred and revenge? Do the historical dynamics behind 9/11 find a mythological representation in
Xena Warrior Princess? In the spring and summer of 2001, the final
episodes aired took up the themes of revenge and redemption.
In "To Helicon and Back," Bellerophon, a son of Artemis, seeks
revenge against Xena (who slew his mother in her struggle with
the Olympian gods) and against her friends, the Amazons, whom
he believes betrayed Artemis, their patron goddess. In the end,
Xena defeats Bellerophon in combat but is willing to spare him.
"Why add one more name to the ranks of the dead?" she pleads,
"End it here, Bellerophon. Make the decision to walk away from
the cycle of killing." As she turns to walk away, Bellerophon tries
to stab her in the back but she runs him through. "It didn't have
to end this way," Xena cries, to which Bellerophon replies, "Oh
yes, it did."

At the end of the final episode, "A Friend in Need," Xena chooses to remain dead so that forty thousand souls who died as a result of one of her past actions might be redeemed, since this is the only way *they* can enter a "state of grace." The coupling here of vengeance and grace place Xena in close affinity with the warrior Christ of the Middle Ages, who in the fight against sin chooses death so that the divine Father's vengeance against the human race may be satisfied. But can Xena's or Jesus' deaths, or the dead in New York or Iraq, break the cycle of hatred and violence? In "To Helicon and Back," Xena says to Gabrielle, "That's the thing about vengeance. You're never really satisfied."

The Erotics of Death

One irony of the idea of "lived religion" is that it becomes most significant for understanding human experience when people are confronted with death. Death, therefore, is the point at which television drama almost inevitably addresses religion. Through the depiction of the religious rituals of funerals or through characters' seeking spiritual solace to deal with issues of loss and bereavement, guilt and anger in the face of death, the television drama takes us to a place we all have to visit. Indeed, in Western societies with low death rates and where the once ubiquitous rituals of mourning have become increasingly rare, television drama has become a major cultural mechanism for representing and coping with our mortality.

Some of this happens in *Xena Warrior Princess*, especially in the show's treatment of the death of a child and the failure of a mother. However, the mythical setting of the show allows the viewer to experience another side of mortality: the extraordinary death that generates meaning and establishes identity not only for individuals but for whole communities. Perhaps the greatest change in the cultural signification of death in modernity is the increasingly elaborate attention given to the deaths of those whom the popular imagination consider extraordinary.[12] With television and satellite transmission, the funerals of the famous become spectacles watched, in the case of Princess Diana or Pope John Paul II, by millions or even billions.

These extraordinary deaths become the occasions for collective outpourings of grief that cross the boundaries of nation and religion and become global phenomena. Television plays a key role in these public displays of grief since it legitimizes the viewers' sense of bereavement at the death of someone to whom they have no personal connection and encourages them to take part in local mourning events, which then in turn become part of the groundswell of public grief that television reports.

One wonders whether in modern secular Western countries the mass expression of grief at the deaths of the famous is in part a substitute for earlier devotions that centered on Christ's death. Xena and Gabrielle's death on a cross fuses the traditional imagery of Christ's death with that of contemporary celebrity death. They may be fictional characters, but the television has turned them into celebrities whose death has a similar (in some cases, I suspect, the same) emotional impact on viewers as the death of the "real living" famous. On the television screen, news coverage of celebrity death and the demise of popular characters in drama series converge.

In both cases, the viewers are encouraged to experience grief for someone who is in no way part of their ordinary everyday lives—outside of the television screen. Xena and Gabrielle, therefore, enter people's lives no differently than Princess Diana, and their deaths play the same role in contemporary cultural constructions of mortality. What Xena and Gabrielle have in common with Princess Diana and Pope John Paul II is that they are "larger than life." In the case of the princess and the pope, television endowed them with personae that had a tenuous connection to their historical lives, removing the complexity and ambiguity of real lives and turning messy interactions and rancorous disagreements into the more simple, elegant, and compelling mode of dramatic tension and conflict.

So as real lives become fictionalized, fictional lives appear emotionally real, and the deaths of both can be the vehicles for myths that support individual and collective searches for meaning in ways that the ordinary deaths of our loved ones cannot. Ordinary deaths, like ordinary lives, contain the trivial and the messy; they are not stylized through media presentation. We experience loss at the death of our loved ones but rarely epiphany because these deaths are too much part of our everyday lives, too far from the boundary of the transcendent. Even an atheist could mourn the death of Pope John Paul II, not because of any lingering religious hope for a resurrection of the dead, but because of the media's construction of the pope as a hero.

Xena Warrior Princess portrays death in a way that both resonates with the contemporary viewer's experience of televised spectacles of grief and mourning and connects the viewer with older religious representations and practices that mediated meaning and identity through the contemplation of Christ's death on the cross. It makes use of its mythical setting and richly articulated system of visual symbols to present the most famous death in history in unfamiliar ways that are still recognizably connected to the iconography of Christ. More pointedly, *Xena Warrior Princess* draws heavily not only on traditional Catholic visual imagery but also on the religious practices in which they have been embedded. The Stations of the Cross are both fourteen representations of Jesus' final sufferings and death, found on the walls of Catholic churches, and the devotional practice that is focused on them. One of the stations is the deposition, when Jesus' dead body is taken down from the crosses. In the episode "Fallen Angel," Xena and Gabrielle's friends come under cover of night to remove their bodies from the cross. This is a scene with no dialogue in which the attention of the viewer is directed to the friends' reactions of anguish and horror at the visible signs of Xena and Gabrielle's suffering. The emotions of the friends in this episode are also the ones that the Catholic devotion seeks to cultivate in the faithful. The viewer can share these emotions vicariously and, like the Catholics performing the devotion, can also hope that these broken and dead bodies can be restored to a physical vitality.

The deposition of Xena and Gabrielle, like their crucifixion, underscores a feature that is prominent in the Christian visual culture and devotional life, from which they are drawn, but which remains at best marginal to the formal discourse of Christian theology: an aesthetic of death. Xena and Gabrielle have beautiful bodies that are not marred by imperfections or frailty, bodies in full possession of their sensuality. The very force of their sensuality seems capable of overcoming their physical torment and death. I mentioned earlier the curiously romantic ending of "The Ides of

March," when Xena and Gabrielle ascend into the heavens with loving glances at each other and hands clasped together. The hope of an invincible sensuality is anchored in the power of the erotic, however spiritualized that may have become in much of Christianity.

The connection between death and sexuality was explored by Freud in *Beyond the Pleasure Principle* and has remained a topic of interest for psychoanalytical theory as well as more generally in psychology. My approach here, however, is not to look into the depths of the soul but to remain on the surface of the skin. This is where the viewer's gaze rests when she is in an art gallery looking at the beautiful body of Saint Sebastian pierced by the arrows of both martyrdom and desire. Indeed, if she moves on to look at pictures of Christ's crucifixion from the sixteenth and seventeenth centuries, she will see that Jesus' body also became eroticized when confronted with death.[13] So when the viewer sits in front of her television and sees the beautiful bodies of Xena and Gabrielle nailed to a cross, she gazes on them with the erotic imagination of Western religious art since at least the Renaissance. Religious art as the purveyor of (homo)erotic desire in early modern culture was always more than religious and ambiguously religious. During this historical period, there was a tacit and semiconscious transaction between artist, patron, and viewers in which it was understood that the pleasure derived from seeing the almost naked, suffering, and dying Christ went beyond pious devotion. In sharp contrast, the contemporary viewer of Xena and Gabrielle's crucifixion can more easily acknowledge (homo)erotic desire than religious devotion. Nonetheless, the erotic and the religious are inextricably intertwined in both representations of crucified bodies.

Although the Christian imagery and themes of Christ's crucifixion are the primary sites of the erotics of death in *Xena Warrior Princess*, the series explores the connection between death and sexuality in other contexts as well. Perhaps the most powerful statement comes in the episode "Between the Lines," in which Xena and Gabrielle during their travels to India have been sent by a darshan, a human epiphany of a deity, into the future to defend their karmic cycles of life from the reincarnation of the evil shaman Alti. Captured by Alti, she orders them crucified.

The darshan had instructed Gabrielle on how to paint the signs of the Mehndi on their bodies to give them the power to return with Alti to their time and place and defeat her there.

In the Xenaverse, the Mehndi is not just body ornamentation with religious significance, it is also the force for good within the universe itself. In a scene entirely devoid of dialogue, the visual narrative and a sensuous but wordless music interweave the erotic with images of death.

The sensuality of Xena and Gabrielle is highlighted and the erotic bond between them becomes palpable as they cover each other's body with the signs of the Mehndi. The scene of the body painting is then intercut with shots of the crosses where they will die and of a funeral pyre in their own world into which the darshan, disguised as a Sati widow, is about to be cast. As Alti reenters the scene to lead them away to crucifixion, she is confronted with their bodies glowing with the power of the Mehndi. In this episode the body becomes the bearer of the universe's ultimate power, which is simultaneously spiritual and sensual, moral and erotic. In the ensuing scenes Xena and Gabrielle are mortally wounded in their contest with Alti, but through the agency of the darshan and with the power of the universe quite literally inscribed on their bodies, they defeat Alti and their bodies are restored to health and beauty. Xena and Gabrielle's painting of the Mehndi hardly qualifies as

Xena and Gabrielle unleash the power of the Mehndi.

an everyday spiritual practice; that is not the source of its appeal for the viewer. Rather its impact lies in its visual, indeed visceral, representation of the interplay of death and sexuality. The desire enunciated here is not to escape our ordinary bodies, even their sufferings and death, but to see our physicality vicariously renewed by our heroes on the boundary of the transcendent.

Between Afterlife and "Second Life": Where Television Heroes Go

In general, what fans take away from *Xena Warrior Princess* is not real possibilities for their daily lives but imaginative ones out of which they can form meaning for their everyday practices. I do not wish to offer an ethnography of *Xena* fans, since my interest here is in the fans as creative agents and in the cultural artifacts that they produce. I am therefore primarily interested not in what the fans think about the series but what they make out of *Xena Warrior Princess*, what they circulate on fan sites, and what is as much part of the Xenaverse as the televised series.

The Internet has enabled a global network for fans to present their creative work (such as fan fiction and artwork) to a large international audience. In all of these forms of fan production, questions of religion and spirituality arise and are addressed from a wide range of religious traditions, spiritual orientations, and secular commitments. In short, whether *Xena Warrior Princess* is given a religious interpretation or not and what kind of religious interpretation it is given depends entirely on the viewpoint of the fan. The makers of the series exploited the ambiguity of the visual to create a narrative that would be open to multiple meanings and would foreclose as few interpretations as possible. They succeeded, and this culture of ambiguity has been embraced by large sections of the fandom in their creative extensions of the television series. A good example of the fluid boundaries between religion and other cultural domains in *Xena* fan culture can be seen in the creation of music videos that take and recut shots from the television series and then overlay them with music, usually but not always songs from contemporary popular artists. I will explore two examples that illuminate how ambiguously religious religion is when it is refracted not only through the visual narrative of the original series but also when this medium is remixed in the cultural production of fans.

The ever-shifting boundaries between religion and other cultural domains can be exemplified in the genealogy of one particular *Xena* music video. From the last quarter of the twentieth century onward, Christian churches, especially evangelical ones, have tried to attract youth by absorbing elements of popular culture into their worship. However, this retrofit of popular music to serve the religious aims of evangelical Christianity can itself be repurposed within the secular contexts of popular music. Of course, already in the eighties Madonna had seen the artistic and commercial possibilities of a heady mix of Catholic imagery and transgressive sexuality. There remains an insatiable appetite for such acts of transgression where religion is subverted by being refilled with gendered and sexual content not authorized by traditional or official religious bodies. The desire for such transgressive displays was, after all, exploited by the original TV series and its presentation of the Xena Christ. In 2002 Groove Coverage released their single "God Is a Girl." Apart from the occasional comment about paying devotion to the female sex, the composition of "God Is a Girl" does not seem to have had a spiritual motivation.[14] Indeed, the music video in which Groove Coverage performs "God Is a Girl" seems to be a parody of evangelical Christianity as a spiritual money scam.[15]

"God is a Girl" lends itself to being transposed into *Xena* fan culture, now as "Xena God Is a Girl." This music video, posted by Martin on YouTube on 7 February 2007, is a double remix.[16] Both clips from *Xena Warrior Princess* and the Groove Coverage song are reshaped into a new cultural artifact. The element of parody, so visible in Groove Coverage's own music video, is absent from "Xena God Is a Girl." Similarly, where the original TV series relied solely on visual narrative to portray Xena as Christ, Martin uses the Groove Coverage lyrics to make explicit that Xena is divine. It would be going too far to suggest that "Xena God Is a Girl" invites personal faith in the Xena Christ, but it takes the shared musical idiom of evangelical Christianity and Groove Coverage to hold Xena up as a symbol of the divine that might provide spiritual satisfaction for the viewer. It uses the intrinsic absurdity of religious commitment to a television character to broaden the boundaries of spirituality itself. To find spiritual significance in "Xena God Is a Girl" does not require religious belief on the part of either the maker or viewer of the video. Rather, the simple juxtaposition of an image of Xena with the refrain "God is a girl, wherever you are/ Do you believe it, can you receive it?" highlights the fact that in the Christian tradition, and therefore in most of Western culture, the idea of God taking on female flesh has been largely unthinkable but today constitutes a popular transgression of traditional Christian limits throughout the broader culture of the contemporary West and beyond. One can seek spiritual emancipation from a faith one does not hold.

In portraying Xena as the Christ in its visual narrative, the original television series did not undermine Christology through irony but gave it a new location. "Xena God Is a Girl" does not undo this strategy. Instead, it accentuates this move by condensing the scenes from the several episodes that depict Xena as a savior and the relationship between Xena and Gabrielle as an embodiment of the divine love into a music video of just over three minutes. What is visually implicit in the TV series becomes fully explicit in the combination of lyrics and recut shots in the music video.

Not surprisingly the music video ends on a visual climax—the crucifixion scene of Xena and Gabrielle from the "Ides of March" episode—followed immediately by a clip of their resurrection from the episode "Fallen Angel." The traditional christological imagery of the series is not discarded but rather is presented in concentrated form as the ultimate expression of "God Is a Girl." The music video therefore follows in the footsteps of the television series in creating a compelling Christ narrative without Jesus. The new space for Christology is not a claim about historical reality or the ontological status of Jesus or Xena—Martin is not trying to convince the viewer that Xena had a historical existence in which the divine was incarnate in her. Instead, *Xena* is about the imaginative reality of Christ, a location for Christology in which the distinction between historical and fictional is not pertinent.

Neither the television series nor the music video gives us even an indirect answer to the question of whether Xena, like Jesus, is a construct of the human imagination striving for meaning or whether the Xena story like the Jesus narrative points to a Christ reality that transcends human imagination as well as history. In fact, although the music video strongly implies that imagining Xena as the Christ will enhance human well-being, it does not seek to persuade the viewer that this is a spiritual benefit. The viewer is left to decide whether the transgressive pleasure of receiving Xena as girl God constitutes a spiritual experience.

The other video to discuss here is "Beautiful (Even in Death)," posted by Mikaela Nordlund (Web name: "placebowithmeds") on YouTube on 6 October 2006.[17] Mikaela Nordlund is a Swedish fan who was voted a winner by fellow fans in the online video contest, run by the largest *Xena* fan site, the Australian Xena Information Page (ausxip.com). Nordlund takes the song "Beautiful" by the Finnish group H.I.M. and overlays it with clips from episodes in which Xena or Gabrielle or both of them die. Dying is a frequent activity of the heroes of the Xenaverse, so there are several episodes and plenty of footage to choose from when editing a short video. Unlike Martin's video, there are no religious references in the music and Nordlund could have found enough footage to make the video without taking material from any of the crucifixion episodes. Instead, three minutes of a video four and a half minutes long are taken from the crucifixion episodes "The Ides of March" and "When Fates Collide."

What seems to attract Nordlund to the Christ-like crucifixion of Xena and Gabrielle in "The Ides of March" is not the religious character of its imagery but how the visual narrative deploys it in an erotics of death. In her brief description of the video on YouTube she writes, "I think what I'm trying to portray is that their deaths are beautiful and not saddening coz they always find their way back to life—and each other." Before their execution in "The Ides of March," the wounded Xena rests in Gabrielle's arms in the pose of the Pietà. Since most depictions of the Pietà are of a handsome young man resting in the arms of a beautiful young woman, even as a religious artifact the Pietà does not foreclose erotic interpretations of lovers lying in a swoon of satisfied sexual desire. The indeterminacy of the meanings of the Pietà, which can include both death and sexuality, makes it a preeminent example of the aesthetic and erotics of death and what is visually imitated in this scene.

As Gabrielle places a kiss on Xena's forehead, Nordlund matches the video to the music's words "Just one kiss and I'm

alive. Just one kiss and I'm ready to die coz you're so beautiful."
As the words are replaced by a sensuous humming in the music,
Nordlund intercuts the lowering of the women on the crosses,
Xena and Gabrielle's final declaration of love, nails poised to be
hammered into hands, the raising of the crosses, and their lifeless
bodies hanging from the crosses. Nordlund's visual choices are
analogous to the representational decisions implicit in imagery
depicting Christ's crucifixion in traditional Christian art. Obviously, she was guided to these decisions by the choices made in
the television production, but she has appropriated this visual
material to representational purposes that are in no way discern-
ibly religious. Later in the video, Nordlund includes the footage
of Xena's spirit awakening Gabrielle's and their ascension from
the crosses into the heavens. She combines this with the repeated
refrain of the song, "And you're so beautiful!" Nordlund's belief,
though not a religious one, is that Xena and Gabrielle "always
find their way back to life—and each other." Her video's pairing of
images and music suggests that their physical bodies and beauty
endow them with an erotic power that can overcome death. Sensuality is salvation.

Conclusion

All long-running television dramas find that their storylines get
bigger and bigger. When the focal point of the storyline of *Xena*
becomes her own redemption and her salvation of others, culminating in her death on a cross and being raised from the dead, it
is not dramatically possible for Xena and Gabrielle to retire to
help Xena's mother run her inn in Amphipolis! Christian saints
confront the same expectations—Bernadette after her vision at
Lourdes could not have chosen a life of marriage and family even
though such domesticity was normative for women in her context
of nineteenth-century France. It is therefore not a religious but
a dramatic imperative that Xena and Gabrielle remain indelibly
marked as Christ figures. *Xena Warrior Princess* disrupts the traditional theological content of such imagery by giving its Christ
figures female (and, depending on the viewer's interpretation, lesbian) bodies. On the other hand, the christological shaping of the
narrative also imposes on it certain constraints. So in Xena and

Gabrielle's declaration of love on the cross we hear the possibility of transgressive sexuality being joined to redemptive love in a context where that sexuality is drastically constrained.

Xena Warrior Princess has, like other cult television, moved into the cultural space of "lived religion." Its exploitation of religious idioms did not convert it into a religious narrative per se but did forge a real, even if very ambiguous, connection to the realm of religion. It thus resituates the older symbolic resources of Christ's death and resurrection and the devotional forms surrounding them into a new context where everyday practices are watching television and going online, where the transcendent no longer has to be imagined in religious terms, and where anxiety about the technological creation of our posthuman future reigns. Moreover, in a post-9/11 world, haunted by destruction and revenge, we fear that our ordinary lives may be torn apart by the cycle of violence and hatred that has deep roots in the Western and Christian past. We look for heroes, real or fictional, ordinary people who are willing to give up their everyday existence to move to the boundary between the ordinary and the transcendent, the realm of unconstrained but also frightening possibility. Xena and Gabrielle inhabit that boundary vicariously for us, nourishing our various contemporary desires—for a dark past redeemed, for an embodied existence transformed by an erotic power that can be simultaneously physical and spiritual. What *Xena Warrior Princess* offers its viewers is a new language of transcendence.

"You Know How It Is with Nuns . . ."
Religion and Television's Sacred/Secular Fetuses

HEATHER HENDERSHOT

With the exception of overtly religious programs like *Touched by an Angel* (CBS, 1994–2003) and *Joan of Arcadia* (CBS, 2003–2005), television is widely perceived to be "secular." Yet television experiences a religious awakening the moment an unwanted pregnancy enters the picture: a pregnant woman contemplating abortion prays, talks to her pastor, or, at the very least, debates the meaning of life with friends. This now standardized formula owes a great deal to the Religious Right, which in staging its opposition to legalized abortion in the United States has fashioned a one-size-fits-all narrative to explain how women confront the possibility of terminating a pregnancy. The story goes something like this: all unmarried sex leads to pregnancy; birth control rarely works; abortion is always a traumatic experience with dark moral implications; having a baby is inevitably beautiful and fulfilling.[1]

Despite its own sense of victimization and its perennial complaint that leftists dominate the media, the Christian Right seems to have won the battle over how abortion can be represented on television. More broadly, *conservative* forces have won, for the idea that a woman's "natural" role is a procreative one is certainly not restricted to conservative born-again Christians. Indeed, though some TV characters dealing with unwanted pregnancy may see their problem as one with moral implications, others are conflicted because they feel the pull of biological destiny; to abort would be to deny their feminine nature. Here, the reproductive "ticking clock" is likely to rear its ugly head, as pregnant TV characters wonder if this is their "last chance" to have a baby.[2]

Yet the narrow spectrum of depictions of abortion on TV is more than a sign of far-reaching conservative morality. There are two very practical explanations for the situation. First, broadcasters' central objective is to sell advertising. Between ads, programmers insert what has frequently been described as "the least offensive programming." Advertisers do not want their product to become strongly associated with any particular political agenda. They are comfortable with a program that pays some lip service to a pro-choice perspective as long as no one actually gets an abortion and the program ultimately does not go out of its way to undercut conservative ideas about women's natural roles as wives and mothers. Such wishy-washy programming entertains without creating controversy; it is conservative but pretends to be either "balanced" or apolitical. Second, TV programming demands melodrama. Outside of the televisual world, some women may conceptualize abortion as a rational medical decision, but such a point of view does not make for very riveting storytelling. Even if a television program has a liberal slant and ultimately stakes a claim for "choice," the pathos-filled conservative version of the pregnancy/abortion story simply makes for great ratings. As feminist film theorist Laura Mulvey wrote some years ago, sadism demands a story. By extension, suffering does as well. Whatever pleasures melodrama may offer female viewers, those pleasures are frequently masochistic. The genre requires the infliction of pain.[3]

Thus, within the context of televisual drama, pregnancy can only be represented as joyous or as a painful moral crisis to be resolved, after much gut-wrenching debate and scenery-chewing soliloquizing, by either the decision to carry a baby to term without ambivalence or the soul-wrenching decision to abort with ambivalence. Alternatively, the conflict is resolved by either a "natural" abortion (miscarriage) or by the convenient fact that our tragic heroine was mistaken and was not pregnant after all.[4] This is what happens in a 1984 episode of *Cagney and Lacey* (CBS, 1982–

1988): "There is no mention of specific birth control technologies or how the 'mistake' might have happened. There is no mention of what Cagney would do if she were pregnant, although Lacey strongly pushes marriage. Cagney seems to be developing a relationship with the alleged baby, and abortion is never mentioned."[5] There is no room to articulate different points of view on abortion within such narrative constraints; abortion cannot be portrayed on television as traumatic for some but as liberating for others.[6] The inclusion of overtly feminist points of view on the subject is certainly beyond the pale, and even if some shows conclude that "women should have the right to choose," this pat assertion in and of itself is often not convincing as a feminist perspective.

The earliest televisual attempts to address abortion predate the 1973 *Roe v. Wade* decision; network anxiety about dealing with the controversial topic can be traced back to the 1972 *Maude* (CBS, 1972–1978) two-part abortion episode, "Maude's Dilemma." Yet anxiety about discussing abortion as a religious-political topic on TV is also strongly linked to the rise of the Reverend Jerry Falwell as a political figure in the late 1970s. His Moral Majority—along with the American Family Association led by Reverend Donald Wildmon—used boycotts and threats of boycotts to try to "clean up" TV in the 1980s, making the networks particularly gun shy about approaching abortion as a topic for entertainment programming.[7] It wasn't until thirty years after *Maude* that a prime-time character on network television would again choose to have an abortion. In effect, anxiety about protest from religious groups (Roman Catholics and especially conservative evangelical Christians—or "fundamentalists") led to a narrative blackout.

As Susan Friend Harding argues, Falwell's successful efforts to motivate evangelicals to abandon separatism and embrace political engagement make him a pivotal figure in the emergence of the New Christian Right.[8] Operating as the "Reagan Revolution" came to a head, Falwell was clearly trading on the enthusiasm for the mainstreaming of ultraconservative politics that Reagan's election symbolized. At the same time, Falwell was also fostering that enthusiasm by nurturing pro-life evangelical activism. As the right-to-life movement gained momentum, the top priorities were clinic harassment, stopping government support for abortion and other kinds of family planning, and the ongoing battle to reverse

Roe v. Wade. Fictionalized TV abortions were not the number one target of this growing political movement.

Yet TV could not be ignored. After all, in the early 1970s the networks had decided to start producing "relevant" programming, canceling comedies like *Green Acres* (CBS, 1965–1971) and *The Lawrence Welk Show* (ABC, 1955–1971), which were tremendously popular with an aging nonurban demographic group, and replacing them with Norman Lear's *All in the Family* (CBS, 1971–1979) and *Maude*, MTM's *Mary Tyler Moore Show* (CBS, 1970–1977), and other programs seeking a more affluent, young, urban demographic.[9] Feminism, civil rights, abortion, and other political issues were of interest to viewers looking for "relevant" programming. "Television executives everywhere promised to make television responsive to the political and social concerns of the youth population. 'Relevance' thus became the networks' new mission statement."[10] It turned out, however, that abortion was *too* relevant.

The networks learned quickly that abortion was too hot to handle. They were slower to figure out the role that religious activism would play in the policing of abortion and other hot-button issues. Indeed, until Falwell came along, they seemed to be only aware of Catholics as a religious group with a strong point of view on abortion. As conservative evangelical activists have increased their visibility and political power over the years, the networks have remained nervous about representing discussion of pro-life born-agains outside of the generic context of news (and occasionally on procedurals such as *Law and Order*).[11] Leaders such as James Dobson and Pat Robertson would have us believe that there is a deliberate, left-wing-produced media blackout of conservative evangelical attitudes about abortion. Yet such voices—with their conservative Catholic compatriots—ring loud and clear in print journalism, Web journalism, and television news. If fundamentalist attitudes about abortion are left unexpressed, it is only on dramatic TV programs.

On dramatic television, religiously inflected discussion about abortion is still most often associated with Catholicism. Though it would be difficult to prove definitively why this is so, I would contend that the situation can be explained in part by the industry's desire to provide "balanced" perspectives on controversial issues and by its realization that it is impossible to do this in a way that will satisfy fundamentalists (at least as they are understood by the networks, as a single, stereotypical mass). From the fundamentalist's inflexible perspective of moral rectitude, balance can only be a sham. To show the other side is to promote it. Only unbalanced, one-sided storytelling, then, can be considered fair by a viewer with a rigid, black-and-white sense of morality. Though some Catholics may share a similar sense of moral absolutism, television writers and producers are more likely to be familiar with a wider range of Catholic political perspectives. Liberal Catholicism is on the radar for TV writers and producers; liberal evangelicalism is utterly invisible to them.[12]

To show how television has represented abortion and religion, this essay will first consider the earliest appearances of abortion on TV, focusing on *Maude*. I will then turn to three contemporary programs that have addressed reproductive politics in very different manners: *Everwood* (WB, 2002–2006), *House, M.D.* (Fox, 2004–), and *Battlestar Galactica* (SciFi, 2004–2009). The right-wing melodramatic formula for narrativizing pregnancy/abortion is unwittingly sustained by *Everwood*, but it is overtly challenged by *House* and *Galactica*, programs that point to different methods television drama can use to resist dominant conservative narratives about reproductive rights. The *House* fetus is resolutely secular, conceived not as an unborn soul but as a benign or malignant parasite. The show refuses to bracket abortion as a "special issue" that demands the standard, fundamentalist-inflected traumatic narrative. In this way, the program implicitly challenges the Right's view of pregnancy, reproductive rights, and, more broadly, "normality" and "family values," but, particularly in its first two seasons, it takes a subtle approach rather than making a direct attack by overtly discussing pro-life and pro-choice politics. *Galactica* consistently grapples with religious issues and allows for the possibility that God (or gods) exist. Notwithstanding their many differences, though, both ask us to question the conservative Christian supposition that a fetus has rights and an ontological personhood superseding the rights and personhood of the woman who carries it. Only *Galactica*, though, is able to break free of the dominant TV formula whereby fervent and authentic—but not extremist or dangerous—religious belief can only be associated with Catholicism, and whereby religious sentiment is inevitably associated with conservative values.

Pushing the Boundaries of Good Taste: "It's as simple as going to the dentist"

Beginning in the 1950s, television programs were censored in much the same way that Hollywood films had been censored since the early 1930s. Network Standards and Practices employees read scripts to make sure that they did not violate norms of "good taste." Abortion, obviously, would not have been considered an appropriate topic for broadcast. As Julie D'Acci has explained, however, there were a handful of news programs that addressed abortion in the late 1960s and early 1970s. These programs strived to be balanced, not only because this was considered good journalism but also to avoid violating the Fairness Doctrine. The news programs did ultimately favor the liberalization of abortion laws, but, as D'Acci argues, they did so at the expense of excluding feminism. Showing "all sides" meant interviewing authoritative professionals—doctors and priests—not women fighting for reproductive rights. The news shows displaced the feminist perspective of abortion on demand with a more medical or technocratic discourse favoring "population control."[13]

D'Acci is concerned about how the practice of journalistic balance in TV's four pre-*Roe v. Wade* documentaries about abortion marginalized feminists, but it is clear that feminists were not the only radicals whom the networks thought it best to ignore. D'Acci notes,

> As with the 1969 [ABC documentary] *Abortion*, many letters from fundamentalist spokespeople complained that the [1973 ABC] documentary [*Population: Boom or Doom*] misled viewers by having a Catholic priest articulate the only opposing view. (While preparing the documentary, [the producer] Sanders had inquired of her bosses if having a "Protestant" spokesperson was necessary for "fairness" considerations. Obviously, she and ABC ultimately decided, as did Pendrell and the network in 1969, that it was not.)[14]

In both 1969 and 1973, Catholics were considered appropriate experts to speak on television about abortion and morality, while fundamentalists were treated as outsiders whose views should not be legitimated. This would only gradually change as conservative evangelicals would emerge from separatism and increase their political engagement. But the very first time that abortion was an issue outside of the generic confines of documentary, in 1971–1972, it was still Catholics who dominated the debate.

In 1971, a biology professor gave a speech at a Population Education Workshop in Seattle. Noting the power of the media in influencing children's attitudes, the professor praised *Sesame Street* (PBS, 1969–) and erroneously stated that the Rockefeller Foundation, which was heavily involved in promoting population control, would be collaborating with the Children's Television Workshop to influence preschoolers; a primary objective would be to picture small rather than large families on *Sesame Street.* This story was picked up by the local media and then in 1972 by a publication called *Catholic Accent.* Suddenly, the Workshop was deluged with thousands of letters, as a completely false rumor spread that the program would be promoting abortion. This first instance of non-news programming dealing with abortion never actually happened, yet the Workshop received the most mail it has in its entire history in response to the far-fetched rumor. Although a small number of letters came from people who seemed to be evangelicals, a much larger number of letters came from self-identified Catholics. As abortion had not yet emerged as a political issue of central importance to conservative evangelicals—who were still slowly pulling themselves out of their post-Scopes trial self-imposed separatism—this should not be surprising.

What is somewhat surprising, though, to a contemporary reader of these letters who is attuned to thinking of abortion as a highly charged political issue and as an issue of central concern to conservative religious groups, is that the majority of the letters did not frame their objections to abortion on *Sesame Street* in religious or political terms.[15] Instead, most of the protestors objected strongly that it would simply be in poor taste to discuss abortion on a children's show. Children were not mature enough to handle the issue, and it would be cruel and distasteful to expose them to a topic, which was, after all, not only linked to sex but also private, and implicitly shameful. It is certainly difficult to disagree that teaching three-year-olds about abortion on a TV show would have been a really bad idea, but what is more interesting is the fact that so many people who wrote to the Workshop in 1972 (and for several years thereafter) still thought of abortion as an issue much more personal than political. Those who revealed themselves as Catholics further reinforced this idea; they did not speak against abortion from the perspective of an organized movement but rather from the perspective of their own private religious beliefs.

Though resolutely secular, Norman Lear's *Maude* took a similar stance on the personal nature of abortion. In 1972, Maude had prime-time television's first abortion.[16] Or, rather, Maude learned she was pregnant and spent two episodes deciding whether or not she would have the baby; meanwhile, her husband Walter debated undergoing a vasectomy. At the end of part two, Maude decides against the baby and Walter is leaning toward vasectomy. The word "abortion" is used only toward the end of part one, but the fact that "it" has recently become legal in New York is referenced several times. Maude's feminist daughter Carol argues for the abortion and explains, "it's a simple operation now, but when you were growing up it was illegal, and it was dangerous, and it was sinister, and you've never gotten over that. . . . It's not your fault. When you were young, abortion was a dirty word. It's not anymore."

Carol also tries to allay Maude's fears by telling her that the procedure is "as simple as going to the dentist." Maude responds to this comparison not with moral indignation, as many viewers surely did, but with a punch line: "*Now* I'm scared!" A major factor in attacks on the show was that viewers found the very idea of a sitcom tackling issues such as abortion and vasectomy to be in poor taste. In fact, Kathryn C. Montgomery, who has published the most thorough account to date of the *Maude* controversy, notes that "the major complaint from viewers was that it was inappropriate to teach such a serious subject as abortion in a comedy series, especially in a show broadcast at 8:00, when many children would be watching."[17] It is certainly striking that although both Catholics and born-again Protestants attacked the show, it was ultimately complaints about poor taste that dominated the protest letters received by CBS. The sitcom was simply not an acceptable format for discussing reproductive politics according to both pro-choice and pro-life viewers. Though some of the humor does not date well, the show's best zinger occurs when Walter notes his schedule for the day, and Maude dryly retorts, "Vasectomy after golf. It sounds like a new play by Noel Coward." This kind of talk simply went too far for the *Lawrence Welk* crowd.

Prior to *Roe v. Wade*, news programs on abortion had turned to Catholics to offer negative views on abortion, and the networks demanded that Lear provide balance as well. He made only a minimal effort in this direction by including an appearance by a peripheral character, Lorraine, a fortyish woman like Maude who also finds herself unexpectedly pregnant. Her hands are already quite full with four young children, and she explains that she and her husband had planned to have only four kids. Carol asks her why she is having a fifth—in other words, why has she not considered getting an abortion? Lorraine replies, "I couldn't do that. I mean, each to his own, but I couldn't. I don't think it's right for me to make that kind of a decision." As a token gesture of evenhandedness, this response is quite interesting because it lacks a religious basis. The pro-life Catholic position had already been established by television as the appropriate way to voice antiabortion sentiment, but instead Lear opted to have someone speak not from within a religious belief system but rather from a completely individualistic perspective. Lorraine's stance is not specifically religious or pro-life at all. She simply seems to believe in a natural order of things. This might, in fact, be considered the first and last deist position on abortion expressed on television. (Further, Lorraine is not the show's token conservative, for several episodes later she teams up with Maude and other women to protest the Rockefeller Laws by showing up at a police station with a large bag of marijuana—actually oregano.)

In creating "Maude's Dilemma," Lear ignored the conservative Catholic perspective. Catholics, though, did not ignore his perspective, vociferously attacking the program for promoting not only abortion but also vasectomy. Abortion was a widely controversial issue at the time—*Roe v. Wade* would be decided only one year *after* the episodes ran, so Maude was only able to abort because she lived in one of the states where abortion was legal in 1972. Vasectomy, conversely, was not an illegal procedure or one about which most non-Catholics held a specifically religiously inflected moral stance. Including discussion of vasectomy in *Maude* was a bold feminist move because it pointed to the issue of male responsibility for impregnation and to the idea that men were not only capable of practicing birth control but also ethically obligated to do so. Although many American Protestants, Muslims, or Jews might have been unsure about vasectomy—or simply embarrassed to see it discussed on a sitcom—Catholics were the only organized group to attack the program on religious grounds for daring to promote male birth control.

Watching the "Maude's Dilemma" episodes today one is struck by several details.[18] First, there is the issue of Maude's generation dealing with the availability of legal abortion for the first time. It is clear from the beginning that Maude has no desire to have her baby, but she is afraid to have an abortion because for most of her life abortion has been illegal and, for most American women, dangerous or fatal. Second, one is struck by the episode's insistence that the decision of whether or not to abort is Maude's alone. That anyone would block her access to a legal medical procedure is unthinkable within the show's storyline. She has no apparent religious beliefs, and Walter only once mentions to a friend that he is concerned that Maude may "be fighting the idea of abortion on moral grounds." At first, Maude decides to have the baby because she assumes that Walter wants to be a father, but he tells her that he has never had any particular desire to have children. The culturally presumed "natural" desire to have children is denied in this discussion.

Ultimately, Maude admits that she really does not want to have another child, and she asks Walter to reassure her that she is doing the right thing. Walter concludes the episode by saying, "For you Maude, for me, in the privacy of our own lives, you're doing the right thing." This is not radical feminist discourse; it is the rhetoric of liberal feminism, echoing the Supreme Court's eventual ruling that abortion is linked to the right to privacy. This is also the only moment when the show implicitly acknowledges that abortion is a politically fraught issue. The final scene takes place in the couple's bedroom, not in the more public space of the living room where most of the show normally occurs and where neighbors constantly drop in unannounced. The show thus ends in the most private space of the house and insists that abortion is a private issue with no inherent moral ramifications.

Walter's conclusion is unthinkable in today's television climate, where there is simply no such thing as a woman making a completely private decision about abortion. On contemporary American TV, abortion can only be treated as a public issue, with pregnant women often functioning as ciphers for the ethical and religious crises of others.

The Incoherence of Balance: "Doing this type of thing in this type of town could get a man killed"

Thirty years elapsed between Maude's abortion and the next deliberate prime-time abortion, on *Everwood* in 2002. I say "deliberate," because, in the interim, prime-time women got pregnant and miscarried. Indeed, a writer on the now infamous *Everwood* episode remarks on the show's DVD commentary track that when his friends saw the promos for the show they called him and asked if the show's pregnant teenager falls down the stairs and miscarries at the end of the episode, since that's how the termination of pregnancy is commonly represented on prime-time U.S. television. On daytime soap operas, women also fall down the stairs at alarmingly high rates, but they are also allowed the possibility of actually going to doctors and getting abortions, though not without significant traumatic deliberation. Soaps treat abortion like *Maude* did, but according to the conventions of melodrama instead of comedy. On soaps, abortion is safe and legal and intensely personal and private.

On prime-time drama, abortion itself is, technically, safe and legal, but those who perform abortions are in great danger. Physicians and clinics are frequently attacked or bombed and abortionists are shot. Notwithstanding the difficulties, women do abort on prime-time, but they are usually extras—women (or dead bodies) to be investigated by the protagonists of procedurals like *CSI: Crime Scene Investigation* (CBS, 2000–) and *Law and Order* (NBC, 1990–). So while *Everwood* staked a claim to showing "the first abortion since *Maude*," what the program really showed was the first time prime-time network characters since Maude deliberating over whether or not to get (or perform) an abortion; then, the producers boldly allowed the character/abortionist actually to go through with the procedure rather than having the pregnant woman falling off a galloping horse or some such nonsense. There were other peripheral abortions on American TV between 1972 and 2002, but *Everwood* stands out for its "event status." The producers loudly staked a claim for the abortion episode as important and provocative. That the producers were, on some level, scared stiff is indicated by the title of the episode itself. If "Maude's Dilemma" was not a straightforward pro-choice title, it did at least point to pregnancy as a potential problem. The *Everwood* show on abortion has the disconcertingly neutral title "Episode 20."[19]

"Episode 20" stands in stark contrast to "Maude's Dilemma" on several counts. The show's lead character, Andy Brown, is a doctor, and the dilemma over whether or not to abort centers on him. The pregnant girl goes off and thinks about it on her own, but her pregnancy is his problem within the episode's narrative logic. At one point, Brown's receptionist Edna chastises him when he asks her to unpack a box of abortion supplies that has arrived in the mail. Edna gives a speech:

> Men make the mess, women clean it up. It's like this. See, a *man* got that girl pregnant. Then another man sends her in here, tells a third man what's supposed to happen to her. Now this box shows up, you don't want anything to do with it. . . . It makes you sick to your stomach to even contemplate it. This is just something *men* don't want to get close to. Who does?! The difference is, men have the luxury of walking away.

On the surface this might seem like a feminist moment, but the problems with Edna's argument are several. First of all, is "walking away" the same thing for the cad who gets a woman pregnant and then disappears as it is for the doctor who refuses to provide abortions for his patients? (Not to mention the pharmacist who refuses to dispense a woman's birth control prescription?) Men do not simply "walk away"; they have a history of standing in the way of women's access to birth control and abortion. Further, Brown acknowledges that Edna is right, explains that he is pro-choice, and then concludes (as she listens sympathetically) that he is going to refuse to provide an abortion for the girl. Suddenly, "walking away" is sanctioned by the show as a reasonable choice on this man's part. As much as I would like to tease out feminist undertones in Edna's speech, it reminds me very much of the right-wing antifeminist movement, which argued against the ERA, birth control, and abortion by expressing strong contempt for men. If women had free access to birth control and abortion, men would let their natural sexual impulses run wild, use women, and abandon them, antifeminists like Phyllis Schlafly have argued.[20]

"Episode 20" treats abortion not only as a tragic choice but also as an all-but-illegal procedure. The episode also baldly claims that patient-doctor confidentiality is impossible. Dr. Abbott, the show's conservative foil to the liberal Brown, warns Brown that if he performs the abortion everyone in their small Colorado town will know, and he and his family will be in dire danger: "Doing this type of thing in this type of town could get a man killed." Bennett advises sending the girl off to Denver for the abortion, which Brown treats as an impossible option. It is very much as if the episode took place in the 1950s and Bennett suggested sending the girl to Puerto Rico. In the episode's climactic scene, Bennett explains that the issue of abortion is "an impossible dilemma" with "no right answer." I do not deny that some people would agree with this evaluation of abortion. At the same time, though, many viewers would surely counter that the "right answer" is quite obvious: women should be allowed to decide whether or not to have children, or, conversely, fetuses have rights and must be protected from being murdered. The show's insistence that there is "no right answer" does not reflect the polarized feelings that Americans have about abortion. Instead of taking a stand, the show makes a feeble attempt to convey a balanced perspective by concluding that abortion is simply an "impossible dilemma."

In fact, *Everwood*'s abortion episode strives so hard for balance that no fervently pro-choice or pro-life viewer could possibly be satisfied by it. "Episode 20" goes so far as to show a pro-choice person acting in a pro-life manner, and vice-versa. Dr. Brown attests that "women should have the right to choose," and then he refuses to perform the abortion because a fetus is "a perfect possibility of a person," and he cannot end life. He has, he claims, no "moral sense" about the issue, and, by extension, no particular religious convictions. Conversely, Dr. Abbott, the conservative Catholic, performs the abortion, but for one reason only. His father was the town doctor before him, and he secretly performed abortions so that women would not harm or kill themselves by seeking illegal abortions. Abbott *père* has made his son promise to perform abortions as well. Thus, abortion has little specifically to do with women's reproductive rights; it is simply the lesser of two evils. Abbott explains, "I'm terrified every time I think of what could happen to my kids and to my wife," again acting as if abortion were still illegal. He concludes that, "I made an oath not to some political cause but to my father. Have her come to my office tomorrow, after business hours."

A doctor in a prime-time melodrama can only perform an abortion secretly, after hours, to fulfill a patriarchal duty? I would wager that this narrative turn of events is equally repellant to both pro-choice feminist and pro-life conservative viewers. At the end of the episode, Abbott goes to church to confess his sins, in a move that, again, seems guaranteed to offend both pro-choice and pro-life viewers. The writers and producers explain that because of the final moment of confession, they ended up getting more negative responses from the left than they did from the right, which seems to surprise them, as they saw the episode as simultaneously even-handed and, ultimately, pro-choice because the girl gets her abortion.

The show is striking for portraying Abbott's ethical beliefs as linked to his Catholicism, while Brown's ethics spring only from his personal experiences. The death of his wife makes Brown hold life more sacred, and he has a "feeling" in his gut that performing an abortion is "beyond him." The possibility that a person could have any kind of religious beliefs and also be pro-choice seems to be similarly beyond the writers' ken. And where is Protestantism in all of this? My hypothesis is that conservative evangelicalism is subtly present in this episode, symbolized by the threat of violence against abortion providers. Though Catholics have certainly been very actively involved in antiabortion activism over the years, it is conservative evangelicals who are portrayed most often in the media as pro-life activists and aligned with antiabortion evangelical Protestant politicos like Pat Robertson, Jerry Falwell, James Dobson, and Gary Bauer. Fundamentalist pro-lifers can be found shouting in crowd scenes on TV, but only Catholic pro-lifers can be presented as three-dimensional people. Abbott is *Everwood's* central conservative voice yet is also a liberal-thinking Catholic insofar as he sees abortion as a question of personal conscience. He explicitly opposes the criminalization of abortion, even if he speaks and acts as if it had never been decriminalized. Abbott serves an important token role, then, providing the much coveted balance by being religious without being an "extremist" or "fundamentalist."

A parallel picture of Catholic moderation contrasted to Protestant extremism is drawn in HBO's pro-choice 1996 made-for-TV movie *If These Walls Could Talk*. In the final section of the movie, Catholic women, rosaries in hand, camp outside a clinic and earnestly try to persuade women not to go inside. Then the men arrive. They are the radical Protestants, without rosaries, who declare that women must be submissive to men and who scream at a clinic worker, "Did you ever ask yourself if this is a good *Christian* way to make a living?!" The worker responds, "No, I don't. I'm *Jewish.*" It is the *only* televisual moment I have ever seen in which anyone besides Catholics and evangelical Christians are acknowledged to have a religiously inflected perspective on abortion. Ultimately, though, the movie subtly reinforces the rather narrow perspective that pro-life Catholics have sincere personal convictions and are not radicals, while pro-life evangelicals are basically terrorists. It is a troubling perspective, as pro-life Catholics have, of course, been very active in extremist groups such as Operation Rescue, while many evangelicals limit their pro-life activism to the act of prayer.

In any case, the greatest strength of *Walls*, and the aspect of it that sheds light on the politics of "Episode 20," is the structure of the HBO production's historical narrative. *Walls* takes place in three different years: 1952, 1974, and 1996. First, director/writer Nancy Savoca conveys the horror and desperation of abortion in the pre-*Roe v. Wade* era; the 1952 story of a pregnant widow portrays the terrifying situation that Dr. Abbott describes his father as living through, when women came to him, "cut, bruised, infected, traumatized, sterile, [and] worse." The 1996 segment of *Walls* shows how abortion is—owing to fervent pro-life activism in the years following *Roe v. Wade*—treated as if it were criminalized, even though it is technically legal. The 1996 clinic doctor wears a bulletproof vest to work, removes it before performing an abortion, and then is gunned down by a Christian protestor. It is the dire future that Abbott predicts for Brown if he performs an abortion instead of sending the girl away for the procedure. *Wall's* middle story comes from the *Maude* era, and though shot in 1996 it finely reflects the sensibility of second-wave feminism. It is only in Savoca's 1974 segment that the pregnant protagonist can think through what is best for her personally, without fear of dying from a botched abortion or being harassed by a psychotic fundamentalist. And it is only in 1974 that other women, explicitly because of the feminist movement, support the pregnant woman psychologically and emotionally; in the 1952 and 1996 segments of *Walls*, the pregnant women's closest friends reject and shame them upon learning about their predicament. The first and third eras live on via *Everwood,* but it is the middle-era of feminist consciousness that seems to have been sucked into a black hole of historical amnesia. Notably, it is only during the feminist era when the pregnant character chooses against abortion; Savoca is not saying that abortion is always the right decision but rather that it is pregnant women themselves who should be the ones to think carefully and decide what is best for them.

The 1996 segment of *Walls* is as troubling for its realist elements as the 1974 section is uplifting for its feminist elements. At the same time, the "realism" of the 1996 section of *Walls* is not unproblematic for its inclusion of the violent, murderous fundamentalist stereotype. As difficult as it is to find a nuanced feminist perspective on abortion on contemporary television, it is even more difficult to find a sympathetic—or in any way multi-layered—portrayal of a born-again Christian. It is only Catholics who can be portrayed on television as having thoughtful religious convictions bolstering antiabortion beliefs. Catholics can be passionate on television without succumbing to fanaticism.

Secularizing and Denaturalizing the Fetus: "You have a parasite"

Though the boycotts and scandal that *Everwood's* producers braced themselves for never fully materialized, American television did not rush into producing shows about abortion after the airing of "Episode 20." The burden of "balance" is an onerous one and makes it particularly difficult for TV writers with clear-cut political points of view to express themselves in a coherent manner. Though the producers of *Everwood* thought their abortion episode was a huge success, it was, as I have tried to show, a failure, because one narrative simply cannot be both pro-life and pro-choice at the same time without lapsing into incoherence.

Since the *Everwood* episode, there has been one high-profile abortion on prime-time U.S. television. A character on *Jack and Bobby* (WB, 2004–2005) terminated her pregnancy and shortly thereafter was killed in a car crash. The moral (intentional or not) was straightforward: taking life is bad, and people who do it should be killed. I refer to this as the only "high-profile" abortion because there is one show on which abortion is quite common, though no one seems to have noticed. The medical procedural *House* treats pregnancy as an ethically neutral medical condition or, more often, as a medical problem. In the first two seasons of *House,* the fetus is resolutely secular, conceived not as an unborn soul but as a benign or malignant parasite. The show subtly challenges the Christian Right's view of pregnancy and reproductive rights but does not make a direct attack by overtly discussing pro-life and pro-choice politics.

House's critique of the mythological "normal family" works precisely because the producers do not promote their attacks on the concept of normality as controversial and because they usually do not single out episodes as "special events" dealing with "special issues." It was *Everwood*'s event status, I would contend, that set the writers up to fail before they had even begun. Outside of the world of premium cable, a "very special episode" centered on any controversial political issue must cover all (usually defined as two) points of view. But if a series, like *House,* takes as its very foundation the premise that relationships and families are dysfunctional, and even pathological, there is no point in singling out any single episode on abortion or, say, the pitfalls of in-vitro fertilization as "special." So when a character is sick because she is getting fertility treatments but also surreptitiously taking birth control pills because her husband wants more children but she secretly does not, no one remarks that she is, in effect, engaged in a kind of constant self-induced abortion.

On *House*, fetus and mother rarely exist in a symbiotic relationship. Most often, the relationship is parasitic. In fact, in the episode "Maternity," Dr. House tells a clinic patient plagued by nausea and inexplicable weight gain, "You have a parasite." The panicked patient responds, "Like a tape worm or something? . . . Can you do anything about it?" House counters, "Only for about a month or so. After that it becomes illegal to remove, except in a couple of states." In a sarcastic attempt at reassurance, he adds, "Don't worry. Many women learn to embrace this parasite. They name it, dress it up in tiny clothes, arrange play dates with other parasites." It turns out that the parasite was conceived when the woman fought with her husband and then had a brief encounter with an ex-boyfriend, but House has a solution. Since the boyfriend looks much like the husband, he advises, "just have the kid. He'll never know. The most successful marriages are based on lies. You're off to a great start." House's sarcasm is relentlessly over the top, yet he is consistently proven correct in his assessments of human nature. His motto is that "everybody lies," and it is couples in relationships who lie the most.

Fetuses make women and girls sick on *House* and are usually "terminated." The word abortion is used infrequently, I think, in order to distance the program from engaging in an overt pro-life/pro-choice debate. Fetal removal is simply conceived as an effective and necessary medical procedure. This is not to say that the show is devoid of ethical deliberations. One might even say that the show is pro-life, in the most colloquial sense: House's priority is to save the lives of his patients. What is "right" on the show is what heals; what is "wrong" kills. The show works hard to distance itself from sentimental depictions of the family and maternity, and, in doing so, distances itself from the fundamentalist—and, more generally, conservative—pro-family discourse. Further, right and wrong are not absolutes on the show, beyond the terms delimited above. In certain situations, for example, it is acceptable to kill a patient so that others may live. If multiple patients (in fact babies, in one episode) suffer from the same unknown condition, and all are dying, and there are two courses of treatment that might work, two different courses of treatment will be assayed. Success can then be gauged by who lives, and the proper treatment can be applied to others. This is not the ideal way to cure one patient, but, in a dire situation, it may be the way to cure the most patients. House's staff is appalled by his logic, which seems "immoral" to them. He does not counter with an argument about morality; he simply argues for what is logical on a situation-by-situation basis. Such situational ethics are the polar opposite of the black/white morality promoted by American fundamentalist activists, politicians, and profamily groups.

House's denaturalization of the family and pregnancy goes deeper than simply showing family members lying to each other and making fetuses the cause of women's illnesses. As a medical procedural, *House* narratives often end with a bizarre twist—"It looked like lupus, but really his wife was slowly poisoning him with minute amounts of gold dust in his breakfast cereal!" One of the most interesting twists is when House discovers that the very nature of the patient he was treating was not what it appeared to be. For example, a sick teen model does not know that she is an hermaphrodite. Once her interior male sex organs are removed, she will be fine. Another patient is being destroyed by the DNA from his fetal twin; the twin was never fully created or born but lives on as a destructive trace within its "brother." A girl is the daughter of a dwarf, and appears to be a dwarf as well, but actually she has a glandular condition that can be easily cured; she has to be convinced to change her identity to become "normal." Finally, the climax of one episode is the discovery that young lovers actually share a hereditary disease; before this moment, they did not know that they were brother and sister. Birth anomalies are so common on the show that the idea of biological normality is thrown into serious doubt.

This constant questioning of the terms of normality is, I would argue, a powerful retort to the Christian Right's absolutist definitions of normality and aberration. In fact, the only thing that is so normal that it obviates commentary by the show is the existence (and banality) of same-sex couples. Such couples may lie to each other as much as heterosexual couples do, but their relationship difficulties have nothing to do with their deviation from heterosexuality. *House* does not simply celebrate difference, deviance, or dysfunction as "progressive" in and of themselves. The point is not that social rejects are consistently better or more interesting than conformists but rather that conformity is such an elusive ideal that biology itself protests it. There is no shallow nihilism here, though, for only House wallows in his own suffering. Others simply try to do their best with the cards they have been dealt. The show thus conveys a guarded humanist perspective.

House most often addresses religion by ignoring it. By focusing obsessively on deep-seated belief in logic, the program conveys its secular (or perhaps agnostic) perspective implicitly. On occasion, however, the program goes out of its way to deal directly with religious issues. Three episodes are of particular interest here. In "Damned if You Do" *House* cures a nun, Sister Augustine, who suffers from a mysterious allergy. Augustine decides that she wants to leave the hospital; God is inside her, testing her faith. When House fails to convince her to stay, he complains to his sidekick Wilson, "She has God inside her. It would have been easier to deal with a tumor." Wilson quips, "maybe she's allergic to God," which inspires House to do a full body scan to find an allergen housed within her. A cross appears on the scan monitor, and it turns out that when she was a teenager living on the streets she got pregnant and self-induced an abortion. When she was hospitalized afterward, her doctors did not see the IUD hidden in her endometrial tissue. The device is a "copper cross," a faulty technology that was pulled from the market in the 1980s; Augustine is allergic to copper. Before the cross is explained, it appears visually as a divine symbol; God really was inside of her. But what appears to be God, ultimately, has a purely rational explanation, again reinforcing the show's prioritizing of science over faith. Afterward, asked how the patient is doing, House responds, "you know how it is with nuns. You take out their IUDs, [and] they just bounce right back."

Though House is, of course, flippant throughout, "Damned if You Do" does provide a genuine opportunity to debate the meaning of faith. Asked by the nun "why is it so difficult for you to believe in God?" House responds, "What I have difficulty with is the whole concept of belief. Faith isn't based on logic and experience. . . . You can tell me that you put your faith in God to get you through the day, but when it comes time to cross the road I know you look both ways." House does not understand the nun's need for belief, yet the tone of the episode is one of respect for her perspective. Her troubles as a teenager do not imply that she is a hypocrite; her mother superior reveals her troubled history to

House only reluctantly, stating that the sisters' lives begin anew when they take their vows. For the first time on the series, House seems actually shamed to have forced the story out of the mother superior. Once again, television has proved capable of presenting Catholics as earnest and true to their beliefs. And, once again, Catholicism and abortion are linked in the episode. No one makes a ham-handed pro-life statement, but the clear implication is that the abortion is part of the nun's sinful past (her name is an obvious allusion to Saint Augustine), and that she has been fully forgiven.

Evangelicals are a different story. In "House vs. God" a teenage born-again preacher is hospitalized with a mystery disease. It turns out that his religious visions are the product of a surgically correctible abnormality in his brain, and his unrelated disease is linked to having herpes. The character's dialogue about God's will feels stilted, while Jesus, curiously, never comes up. Though the preacher is white, the episode ends inexplicably with a traditional African American hymn, and though he is a faith healer and possibly a Pentecostal, the members of his congregation are shown enraptured, yet not actually speaking in tongues. Much of the patient's dialogue is preachy and heavy handed, showing a lack of understanding of evangelicalism on the producers' part, though writer Doris Egan has stated unequivocally that the show was meant to be sympathetic to the teen preacher.[21] While the nun with the killer IUD seems like a real person, the evangelical preacher with the STD just seems like a type. His STD is not linked with abortion in any way, but it is explicitly used to show that he is a hypocrite.

Though the preacher appears to heal a terminal cancer patient, it turns out that he had spread his herpes to her with his hands, and the herpes had temporarily shrunk her tumor. Interestingly enough, when the cancer patient's doctor, Wilson, tries to talk her out of the idea that she has been divinely healed, he references Catholicism, TV's "safe"—not weird, not extremist, yet acceptably devout—religion. He tells her that the church monitors people who claim to have been miraculously healed, "but, of the thousands of cases of people who have claimed to feel better, the Catholic Church has only recognized a handful as miracles." She responds, "but they do recognize a handful," and he laughs and says, "well, they're a church. It's what they do." In other words, the minute number of miracles they do accept are phony, but Catholics are still better than evangelical faith healers because they believe in such a small number. A *little* irrationality is natural; it is what acceptable churches "do." A lot of irrationality marks one as an unfathomable Bible-thumper.

The final episode relevant to consider in relationship to *House*'s stance on religion, abortion, politics, and dominant ideas of normativity is from season 3's "One Day, One Room," in which a pregnant rape victim demands that House treat her. As far as he is concerned, the only medical treatment she needs is an abortion. She also needs counseling, he concedes, but as a cranky, depressed loner incapable of sincere conversation, he knows that he is the last person on earth who can help this girl emotionally. She instinctively insists, though, that he must talk to her and open up about his own personal history. House's coworkers, who obsessively try to heal him through a forced talking cure throughout season 3, think that this is a great idea. The season turns preachy and judgmental, an odd turn for a program that, throughout its first two years, insisted on the impossibility of any normative ideal for human interactions. Suddenly, if only House would *talk*, the show insists, he could become *normal*. The distressed pregnant girl, who rejects abortion because "every life matters to God" (no reference to a specific faith is made), becomes the potential catalyst who could crack open House and make him reveal his true feelings. At the end of the episode, he opens up, and she responds by telling the story of her rape for the first time. In an aside at the end, House mentions that the girl has "terminated" and checked out of the hospital. Having helped House by forcing him to confess some of his inner feelings, the convictions that prohibited the girl from aborting suddenly disappear. Thus, a program that has consistently taken a secular, nonjudgmental, practical stance toward abortion as a health procedure suddenly notices that abortion has moral implications for some people, only to show antiabortion beliefs ultimately to be paper thin.

House could certainly return to its radically negative roots, but, for the moment, the show has swerved from its interesting original impulse, losing sight of its critique of conventionality and its near obsessive focus on denaturalizing pregnancy and even the very core of identity. In the old *House*, your DNA could always betray you and show that you were not the person you thought you had been born as. Or your fetus could try to strike you down, and you would have to kill it before it got you first. By the time season 3 concluded, however, the show's subversive procedural plots had become fully secondary to the concern with making House into a "better," more conventional person.

Political and Religious Complexity through Allegory: "You have your pound of flesh"

In rejecting moral absolutism in favor of situational ethics, and in refusing to conceptualize the fetus as a sacred being, *House* has staged a subtle battle against fundamentalist absolutism. Though House himself is a resolute atheist, the fact that the program itself keeps asking questions about the nature of faith and belief points to a curiosity about religion; the program's outlook could be fairly characterized as agnostic. At the same time, the show is clearly limited, like so many other programs, by being largely unable to respectfully and carefully consider fervent religious beliefs that are not Catholic. *Battlestar Galactica* takes a very different approach in its insistent investigation of feminism, reproductive rights, and wide varieties of religious belief.

 Much of *Galactica's* power comes from its manipulation of the conventions of science fiction. In imagining a postapocalyptic world, a sci-fi creator makes careful choices: Will the new world duplicate the old world, or can something different be imagined? Given a chance to work with a blank slate, will characters embrace patriarchal heteronormativity? Could capitalism be kaput?[22] These are the generic concerns that animate *Galactica*—with a healthy dose of the melodrama that underpins most TV. In *Galactica's* postapocalyptic world, men and women both play powerful roles in the military. A woman is president. And she's played by an actress over 50. *Galactica* uses its alternate universe status to challenge the norms of "our" world, creating allegorical narratives that raise concerns about contemporary America and, in particular, the war in Iraq. But the show's most potent statement about contemporary politics may lie in its approach to representing reproductive choice. *Galactica* allows for the possibility of a sacred fetus/child as part of its religious mythology, but it also points to the very real dangers of sacralizing the unborn. Perhaps most importantly, it allows for the possibility of competing religious points of view without lapsing into Manichean reductionism. The show never clearly maintains that any single religion is more legitimate than another.

Galactica takes place after the world has been destroyed by Cylon terrorists. The allegorical connections to 9/11 are clear. The Cylons—robots created by humans, who look just like humans, and sometimes do not even realize that they are Cylons—are monotheists, while humans are polytheists. *Galactica* sometimes presents Cylons as bad guys and humans as good guys, but it also shows that these kinds of labels have only tenuous value. Humans are deeply flawed and frequently make the wrong decisions—torturing the enemy, for example, under the assumption that it is machine rather than human, so torture is not unethical. The first Cylon subjected to torture fights back with logic, arguing that he feels pain like a human. There is, in a nutshell, no such thing as ethical torture. The commentary on contemporary U.S. military policy is obvious.

But this is not a parable encouraging viewers simply to identify with good guys and hate bad guys; the program refuses to set up easy oppositions between well-meaning heroes and violent fundamentalist "evil-doers." It is clearly not only the terrorist enemy who behaves violently and erratically. Only the Cylons fight in the name of God specifically, but the humans are driven by their own search for the divine. Both sides struggle to interpret scripture to learn the will of God/the gods. On both sides, not everyone agrees about how literally scripture should be read or to what extent scripture should be used as a template for political action.

At the end of the three-hour miniseries that kicks off the series, William Adama, the commander of the Galactica ship, gives the few surviving humans hope by proclaiming that they are setting out to find Earth. Earth is cited in the scriptures, and no one knows where it is, but Adama reassures everyone that it is real. Afterward, he privately confesses to President Laura Roslin that, of course, Earth is just a myth. He has used religion to give people hope, but he does not actually believe in it. Roslin is not a believer herself at first, but this changes as the series progresses and delves deeper into the fulfillment of scriptural prophesy. The details are not strictly relevant here; what is important is the fact that the program shows two earnest groups of believers and skeptics (each with dissension among its ranks) fighting for survival, both guided by faith in spiritual forces and grappling with what faith really means. This is unique on television, where conflicts over faith are more often boiled down to one person believing and the other person not—with the believer typically positioned as the conservative character and the nonbeliever positioned as the liberal.

Galactica is a postapocalyptic allegory that has a better grasp on how religion and politics are intimately connected than any other more "realistic" (earthbound, as opposed to earth bound) drama on television. The show's contention that religion and politics are always interconnected is perhaps clearest when the pro-choice President Roslin reluctantly outlaws abortion to encourage population growth. In an earlier episode (one of the few that has seriously addressed the concerns of the civilian population), we have seen that in this postapocalyptic world women are increasingly turning to prostitution simply to survive. Mothers are particularly likely to be forced into sex work because it is the only way they can afford black-market necessities like antibiotics for their children. Clearly, then, the president has erred in criminalizing abortion; the only ethical way to enable population growth is to create a world worth repopulating.

Notably, Roslin tells off a Gemenian fundamentalist (polytheist, human), denying her demand to punish a young woman who had an abortion shortly before Roslin made the procedure illegal. Roslin curtly dismisses her: "You have your pound of flesh, and I suggest you take your victory and you move on." On the surface, the president is only indicating that the woman should let well enough alone, since she technically won. Yet what is more important here is the language Roslin uses. She references Shakespeare, who, of course, simply does not exist in *Galactica*'s universe of nonearthlings. This strange, completely anomalous gaffe tells us two things: we must read this exchange as directly germane to *our* world, and Roslin knows that she has erred, for there is no such thing as a pound of flesh without an ounce of blood. The population count is going to decline even faster once the coat-hanger abortions begin.

When Roslin announces her criminalization of abortion, Gaius Baltar—a human villain who is in cahoots with the Cylons, is completely self-serving, and is in large part (though unwittingly) responsible for the Cylon destruction of the home planet in the first place—announces that he is running against Roslin for president because he cannot in good conscience remain her vice president and support her new policy. As he explains it, "The Cylons have no understanding of the meaning of the word freedom. How could they? They're programmed. Machines. Every time you take away one of our freedoms, every time we restrict or curtail one of our rights we become one step closer to being like them." It is the classic phony politician's come-on, and it certainly does not spring from any feminist impulse. In fact, at the very moment Baltar says that Cylons are machines he is eyeballing a sexy Cylon, clearly indicating that he knows damn well that Cylons are flesh and bone. (Indeed, up to this point Baltar's highest priority, besides self-preservation at any cost, has been getting laid.) Like many real-world politicians, Baltar has turned pro-choice strictly to get elected. Roslin, conversely, did not bow to political pressure from the Gemenian fundamentalists when they initially demanded she criminalize abortion. She made her decision only later, upon learning that if the present low birth rates continued the entire human race would be extinct within eighteen years. She has done the wrong thing but for the right reasons. The show's cogent positioning of Roslin as a flawed heroine makes clear its feminist agenda.

On *Galactica* the control of women's bodies by others is portrayed as the worst crime imaginable. *Galactica* specifically argues against sexual torture, and the most depraved and evil act ever committed on the show is not performed by the Cylon enemies but rather by human soldiers who relentlessly rape a Cylon prisoner, reducing her to little more than a sack of barely breathing blood and bones. Rape is a common melodramatic plot point on television, typically used to reveal character psychology and framed within a therapeutic context in which (as on *House*) rape victims move toward "healing" through talking about the violence committed against them. *Galactica*'s serially raped Cylon will never be healed. She is a permanently damaged victim of the patriarchal values that underpin military ideology; the only way for her to "move on with her life" is by blowing up herself, and an enemy (human) ship, with a nuclear bomb. This may not seem to have much to do with the televisual politics of abortion, but it does.

For *Galactica* argues consistently and aggressively, and unlike any program before it on American TV, that women must be in control of their own bodies. This control is defined in terms of both sexuality and reproduction.

The point is driven home in particular by the episode "The Farm." Cylons cannot breed on their own, which is why the first human-cylon baby is of great value on the show. Indeed, this baby is treated like a Messiah, an amalgam of Moses and Jesus. In "The Farm," Cylons hook up women to machines and turn them into incubators. Discovered by their comrades, the violated women ask to be destroyed, not rescued. Also in this episode, our heroine, Starbuck, is taken captive and operated upon. In a later installment, she is informed that an egg was removed from her ovary during the surgery and that a daughter was bred without her permission, which is part of an elaborate psychological torture sequence. In sum, the show repeatedly reinforces the injustice of denying reproductive freedom. Furthermore, this is done within the context of the "masculine" generic conventions of science fiction and action-adventure. Though melodrama is never far away, on *Galactica* the personal is always framed within an explicitly political context.

Conclusion

After a long period of silence, abortion is gradually beginning to appear more often on television. Are we entering a new era of "relevance"? Have TV producers suddenly realized that they should get more political? It is certainly true that some television writers are deliberately conveying their own frustration with the current political situation. With a conservative evangelical having occupied the White House for eight years, a shift in the balance of the Supreme Court, and an ongoing war in Iraq, it is not surprising that some people in the media business would be completely fed up—or that others, like Joel Surnow, the famously conservative creator of *24*, would advance a pro-war, pro-torture line. *24* may promote a reactionary agenda, and *Galactica* a much more progressive one, but the fact remains that most television still strives for least-objectionable-programming status.

Thus, if we are seeing abortion on television more than we have in the past, it is not simply because of competing right-left political agendas. The explanation is, I think, much less dramatic. In the continuously expanding postnetwork environment, every channel competes for ever smaller numbers of eyeballs. Viewers are conceptualized in increasingly narrow interest and demographic groups—suburban gardeners, Latino teens, foodies, animal lovers, urban Generation X-ers. For years it was dangerous to represent abortion because the Christian Right would immediately be on your back, pushing for a boycott or deluging the network with angry letters. This was when the Big Three ruled. In 1979–1980, ABC, CBS, and NBC captured together a ninety percent share of U.S. households. Thanks to cable and VCRs, by 1991 the share had dropped below sixty, and it continued to decline thereafter.[23] In the postnetwork era, it is increasingly difficult to successfully market a show as "event TV." There is just too much noise for anyone to make much of a splash, outside of a few blockbuster shows such as *American Idol* (FOX, 2002–) and perennial special events such as the Super Bowl. In other words, for a religious group to protest your show, they have to find it first, and this is increasingly difficult.

Everwood deliberately marketed "Episode 20" as an important, potentially controversial episode. It got some press attention and infuriated groups like Brent Bozell's Parents Television Council, but there was no nationwide scandal because it was just one episode in a giant sea of television. (And also, perhaps, because it bent over backward to achieve its own disturbing version of balance.) Also, it was not on ABC, NBC, CBS, or FOX. It was on the WB, a medium-size cable channel targeting mostly teens and not known for having blockbuster ratings. Shows survived on the now defunct WB—they sold ads—but they did not achieve top ratings status, and they virtually never won Emmys.

That no one has noticed the presence of abortion on *House*, on the other hand, is perplexing insofar as it is a very highly rated show. Throughout its first two seasons, *House* succeeded in avoiding the standard conservative approaches to narrativizing abortion, and the show effectively undercuts any idea that "family values" are natural. At the same time, the show's challenge to normativity may be a victim of its own subtlety. The show gets away with frequent "termination" of pregnancies because nobody notices and cries "abortion!" But if nobody notices, is the show too subtle for its own good? Ultimately, the relatively large number of terminations on *House* may slide beneath the cultural radar in part because it is a procedural, with shifting characters each week. No recurring character on *House* has admitted to having an abortion. Also, House himself is deliberately provocative—a quirky, anti-politically correct figure. Thus, if he advocates amoral courses of action, this is balanced by the raised eyebrows of the more-conventional characters. In fact, in a season 3 episode House is shown as wrong for advocating a late-term abortion, and one of the "normal" characters, carried away by her own maternal instinct, fights against him to keep the fetus alive. The episode ultimately takes a pro-life stance, going so far as to show the fetus' hand grabbing House's hand while he operates on it in vitro.

Of the three contemporary programs examined in this essay, *Battlestar Galactica* is clearly the most challenging in terms of its approach to reproductive issues, religion, and politics in general. The show is antiwar, pro-choice, and, insofar as it refuses to cave into moral absolutism, antifundamentalist. Still, no conservative religious groups have stepped forward to criticize the show. Like *Everwood, Galactica* is not on one of the big four networks. In fact, *Galactica* is on the SciFi channel; it would be quite an understatement to even describe this as an underdog channel. *Galactica* has struggled with poor ratings in its first three seasons and has remained on the air in large part because it is critically acclaimed and has won a Peabody Award. SciFi cannot afford to sacrifice its "Tiffany programming." Thus, *Galactica* has been a loss leader for the network. Clearly, it has avoided a conservative backlash simply because so few people are aware of it. Also, science fiction is a genre stereotypically associated with young male nerds. Evangelicals took the time to acknowledge their disgust with *Everwood*, which was at least on the WB targeting impressionable young minds. But the SciFi channel targets a small audience of viewers that many non-science fiction fans would simply dismiss as losers. Indeed, if someone told James Dobson that a show on the SciFi channel was feminist, pro-stem cell research, antirape, and pro-choice, he would probably respond not with his usual moral indignation but by incredulously exclaiming, "The SciFi channel?!"

Clearly, *Galactica* is able to be aggressively political in large part because it is on a small cable channel with relatively low advertising revenue. The little media attention the show has garnered peaked in the fall of 2006, when *Galactica* showed the humans trying to survive on New Caprica, a planet they had recently discovered. The Cylons invaded and became an occupying force, and the humans organized a resistance movement and turned to suicide bombings. New Caprica became a stand-in for Iraq, and this was picked up as a story by a few major newspapers. What has gone unremarked about the show, though, and what may be its most important innovation, is its representation of religion. Creator Ronald D. Moore has envisioned a world in which both "good guys" and "bad guys" are strongly religious. Indeed, both sides are strongly invested in interpreting holy texts and applying them to both daily life and to long-reaching political decisions.[24] There is a sense, then, in which both sides are fundamentalist, though the Cylons are more uniformly so, while the humans have numerous religious sects, some of which are closer to the fundamentalist paradigm than others. Where *Galactica* has succeeded is in showing the possibility of fervent belief separate from conservativism, "extremism," or Catholicism, which for so long has been TV's "safe" (noncontroversial) religion. On *Galactica*, characters can be very religious without being politically conservative, a situation extremely rare on American television.

Further, Moore references a variety of religious belief systems without clearly pinning down any single "real world" equivalent to the beliefs of his science fiction characters. Thus, the polytheist humans have New Age, Jewish, and Catholic elements all mixed together in their religion. The Cylons' religion is closer to evangelical Christianity—on one episode a Cylon goes so far as to implore Gaius to have a "personal relationship with God," and the Cylons are clearly looking for a savior figure—yet, though they are the show's putative villains, they do not devolve into caricatures of the American Religious Right. Both sides make horrible ethical errors, and no one side is held up as having the *true* religion. The show's radical pluralism and refusal of simplistic black-and-white morality mark it as one of the most politically and religiously complex programs ever on U.S. television. Meanwhile, on the bigger networks where the advertising stakes are higher, fervent belief remains largely restricted to Catholics and an occasional crazy fundamentalist abortion-clinic bomber. Though Maude was able to resolve her dilemma some thirty years ago, television clearly remains highly conflicted about how to resolve the dilemma of representing religious belief and reproductive politics without offending advertisers or courting controversy.

Moralizing Whiteness in Joan of Arcadia

LANITA JACOBS-HUEY

Introduction

Last April, I ducked under my desk with a pillow, a pen, and some notepads to screen CBS' much too short-lived series, *Joan of Arcadia* (*JOA*). When I finished, I sat quietly for a spell and mourned. I already missed Joan Girardi, a modern-day Joan of Arc and self-described "sub-defective" at her cliquish high school. Her daily conversations with a tangible, chameleon-ish God spanning various ages, genders, professions, ethnicities, and even sexual orientations resonated with me. I, too, was once an angst-riddled teenager who found solace in faith. So I cried real tears as Joan faced traumatic losses and amazing breakthroughs, all while being comforted by a compassionate, witty, and ever-questioning God.

But it was Joan's brother, Kevin, played by Jason Ritter, who intrigued me the most. Kevin's high school athletic career is cut short after a car accident renders him a paraplegic. Kevin's attempts to reconcile his old and new selves were especially vivid and renewed my appreciation for the tremendous work of recovery. I knew from personal experience (my twin sister suffered a traumatic brain injury in 1994) and my collaborative research on African American families raising children with disabilities that much of this work was physically and emotionally grueling.[1] But scenes devoted to Kevin's struggles reminded me that a significant part of this labor is moral; that is, trauma victims often work very hard not to succumb to incapacitating grief or resentment about their fate.

JOA creator/writer Barbara Hall, her collaborators, and actor Jason Ritter deserve much of the credit for this insightful spin on the classic story arc of the hero. The series resonated widely because it did not simply offer miracles, quick fixes, or easy resolutions in response to the challenges faced by the characters at the heart of the story. Nor did it present a singular or monolithic religious perspective; rather the show raised profound questions about the nature of good and evil, Western spirituality and—surprisingly—science.[2]

Kevin was thus allowed to develop richly across many episodes, and his rehabilitation was depicted as long and arduous, spurred occasionally by instances of goodwill and hope. Ritter also plays Kevin with such a subtle and artistic hand that he manages to transform what could otherwise be saccharine TV moments into thought-provoking meditations on the nature of disability and loss. Ironically, his character's existential probing served to foreground morality in ways that his mother's rigid faith and his other family members' more explicit concern with good versus evil simply could not. Beset by disability and a litany of bad breaks, Kevin embodies hope and ethical responsibility in the series. It was actually Kevin then, as opposed to Joan, who helped to crystallize my thoughts as I prepared to write this chapter.

Formulating these thoughts, though, has been a challenge. Initially, I wrote at length about Kevin as an analogue to the Old Testament character Noah who, in toiling over a boat in the basement of his family's comfortable abode, exemplifies the moral work of recovery and ushers in a new world of ethical possibilities for himself and his family. As a humor scholar, I was struck, too, by Kevin's use of humor to cope with his disability. So I set to work describing how Kevin's humor evolves from caustic self-pity toward healthier self-deprecation by the show's end. But my editors, bless their hearts, saw these disparate threads for what they were: meandering commentaries that lacked the originality and passion of my current critique of the series.

Indeed, my most impassioned remarks lay in the margins of these drafts and concerned the way Kevin, his father (and Arcadia police chief) "Will" (played by Joe Mantegna), and Joan (played by Amber Tamblyn) were incessantly framed as "good" Whites within racially charged plotlines, including non-White supporting cast members that seemed to occupy scenes only to highlight the Girardis' good intentions. Thus the key concern for me in critiquing the show became fairness and accountability—in essence, the beating heart of *JOA*'s morality tale—concerning matters of race.

Chapter Focus

This chapter owes a lot to theoretical insights from recent scholarship on Whiteness that illuminate the rhetorical and cinematic conventions (e.g., silencing, hyperpoliteness, insipid color-blindness) through which White privilege is brokered and secured.[3] In the pages that follow, I reflect on the not-so-fleeting moments of disappointment I felt while screening *Joan of Arcadia*—moments where the show's complicated storylines concerning race, disability, and morality appear promising and, in the case of disability, succeed, but ultimately fail on the matter of race and Whiteness.

Developing this critique also entails reconciling *Joan of Arcadia*'s tone-deafness around race-related themes with the show's many other virtues (e.g., superb writing, a truly exceptional cast whose synergy practically leaps off the TV screen, ambitious and well-executed stories inspired by local and national headlines, well-paced character development). It also means critiquing a show that does attempt to offer ambitious and laudatory narrative arcs concerning race and disability. I say "ambitious" because too few prime-time TV shows wrestle with such provocative questions so explicitly. I offer "laudatory" because in pursuing racially charged topics such as police brutality, racism in the Arcadia Police Department, and Kevin and Joan's White privilege, *Joan of Arcadia* endeavors to treat race seriously instead of simply peppering its cast with assimilationist Black characters who resemble White characters in every way save skin color.[4]

Another reason I initially shied away from this analysis is the difficulty of discussing Whiteness, more generally. Frank discussion about race, and Whiteness in particular, is challenging not merely because Whiteness thrives by virtue of remaining unnamed but also because the work can be emotionally difficult.[5] Dreama Moon notes that White women who violate bourgeois notions of respectability by critiquing Whiteness can undermine their status as "good (white) girls" and thereby risk being branded as race-traitors by other Whites.[6] Conversely, African Americans (like myself) and other ethnic minorities who critique or identify Whiteness can be dismissed as hostile or engaged in a relentless hunt for racism, which subjects their intentions to a kind of scrutiny seldom faced by White social critics. Kendall adds, in this regard, that White privilege affords European Americans the option to speak up about racism without being seen as self-serving. She states, "In fact, we [Whites] can even see ourselves as *good* at standing up for others and mentally pat ourselves on the back."[7]

Unfortunately, *Joan of Arcadia* too often relies on this very rhetorical device, along with others, to shore up the "goodness" inherent to the relentless suffering and good intentions of its White protagonists. Thus, although the Whiteness of several characters is explicitly problematized, the moral dilemmas and potential lessons that surround these moments are systematically deflated and then lost. The manner in which Whiteness is left unscathed, or rescued and rehabilitated through race-related plots and Black characters, warrants careful consideration and critique.

Moralizing Whiteness in *Joan of Arcadia*

As noted earlier, Kevin's disability literally "re-groups" him— away from his family and some of his White able-bodied friends, which acquaints him with other characters who help to shift his views of the world and himself in poignant ways. These characters include Barry "The Bear" Caldwell (played by Mitch Longley), a paraplegic and leader of a wheelchair basketball league, who mentors Kevin through the emotional, logistical, and intimate entailments of his disability. Another significant character is Rebecca Askew (played by Sydney Tamiia Poitier), an African American woman who serves as Kevin's editor and boss at the *Arcadia Herald*, as well as his short-lived romantic interest.

Rebecca is among the show's most important figures in storylines that touch on race and morality, not merely because of her racial identity, but also because of the pivotal role she plays in Kevin's emotional and professional maturation. Rebecca is one of the first individuals outside of Kevin's immediate family who successfully shakes him out of his funk and complacency with respect to his future. ("The Bear" is another.) She is also the first person outside of his family to see him out of his wheelchair. An attractive woman, Rebecca invigorates Kevin's sexual libido, while also challenging him to acknowledge and harness his talents as a writer. In many ways, she makes it possible for him to imagine a life that includes romance as well as a thriving career in journalism.

Rebecca offers a window into one of the show's unexpected gifts around racial privilege and racism. Specifically, she is a catalyst that prompts the Girardi men (Kevin and his father Will) to wrestle with the morality of race, Whiteness, and racism. These scenes merit careful attention given Kevin's status as a moral compass—along with Joan—in the family's relentless efforts to be "good." Several episodes likewise home in on Rebecca's and Kevin's attempts to negotiate ethical questions around these issues. Plot-wise, they are a mixed bag. For while Kevin's onscreen interactions with Rebecca manage to disrupt and expand canonical representations of race and disability on prime-time TV,[8] the character of Rebecca is ultimately circumscribed within the simplistic trappings of the stock BBF (Best Black Friend) character.

Nuancing and Moralizing White Characters through BBFs (Best Black Friends)

Los Angeles Times writer Greg Braxton describes BBFs in a clever play on grade-school BFFs (Best Friends Forever).[9] BBFs are often played by a gorgeous, independent, successful, and loyal African American actress whose character's primary function is to support the heroine—often with sass, attitude, and a salty but wise insight into relationships and life. Often this character helps to humanize and nuance White (often female or gay male) characters to the detriment of her fuller development.

Admittedly, Rebecca's romantic involvement with Kevin means that her character is not entirely commensurate with this archetype. Kevin is a heterosexual man and Rebecca becomes much more than a friend to Kevin over the course of their relationship. Nevertheless, by the time she exits the show in the first season, Rebecca is less a character in her own right than a point of reference that helps to define Kevin's and Will's moral evolution.

The use of secondary Black characters to nurture the growth of Whites at the center of prime-time television dramas is one of the more subtle conventions shaping the representation of race in popular culture. Televised depictions of friendly interaction between Blacks and Whites might appear to be taking risks in the ongoing national conversation about race, but when the roundness of Black characters is diminished across subsequent episodes, the result is a reiteration of the two-dimensional portrait of Blacks offered by the myth of White normativity.

Accordingly, although Rebecca is not a stock BBF, her character's complexity and promise are squandered over several episodes. At best, she becomes a "positive" foil for Kevin and Will insofar as she shores up their goodness and morality and serves to bring his family closer together, much like Kevin's accident did, as they corroborate some of her more positive assessments of Will.

A similar BBF dynamic plays out in scenes involving other African American female protagonists: Lt. Toni Williams (Will's partner)[10] and an African American homeless teenager named Casper. Lt. Williams is a recurring cast member, and Casper was a one-time supporting role. Like Rebecca, Lt. Williams helps to nurture Will's "good" intentions and fairness as chief of the Arcadia Police Department (APD) by endorsing crime policies that have been shown to disproportionately penalize Blacks and Latinos. Similarly, Casper enables Joan to confront, albeit in a fleeting way, her own racial and class privilege.[11] I will say more about how this gets done later, but for now will focus on Kevin and Rebecca's partnership and the lessons it yields about race.

Rebecca as Kevin's Moral Compass around Race and Responsibility

Rebecca enters Kevin's world at a critical stage in his life. Episodes early in season 1 such as "Pilot," "The Fire and the Wood," and "The Boat," as well as later episodes (e.g., "Saint Joan"), underscore the far-reaching emotional toll inflicted by Kevin's accident. He loses out on a football scholarship to Arizona University. His already troubled relationship with his high school sweetheart, Beth, fizzles after his injury. His relationship with his family is particularly strained; when they try to help in their own fractured and imperfect ways, he rebuffs them with self-pitying humor and hurtful dismissals. To add insult to injury, Kevin's best friend, Andy Baker (played by Riley Smith)—whose drunken driving caused the accident that paralyzed Kevin—sues Kevin's family! It comes as no surprise, then, that Kevin spends most of his time brooding. He wryly admits to Joan one day: "Pityville is my hometown."

Rebecca's appearance on screen is a timely gift that arrives just after Kevin's darkest period. In the episode "Just Say No," Kevin has finally ventured out of his family's homey abode to search for a job. When he returns home from a day of submitting job applications, he interrupts his father's interview with Rebecca, an editor at the *Arcadia Herald*. After introductions and some small talk, Rebecca learns that Kevin is looking for a job and encourages him to apply for the fact-checker position at the paper.

In a subtle confirmation of the New Testament edict "faith without works is dead" (James 2:20), Kevin readily accepts. When Will cautions Rebecca against viewing Kevin as an "inside" contact to him (recall that Will is chief of police), she reassures him that she is an "ethical journalist." Rebecca's ethics will be tested in episodes to come—in ways that routinely affirm and trouble the presumed ethics of the White male protagonists.

A Catalytic Moment? Rebecca Squares Kevin's Disability against Race

JOA's rigor is exemplified by the fact that even Rebecca's "blessed" bestowal of a job is not without complications for Kevin. These complications serve to bring matters of race, disability, and relative privilege to center stage. During Kevin's first day at work, he goes in search of Rebecca and overhears her in the break room talking with Andy Rees (played by Andrew Abelson), the newspaper's obnoxious style editor. Their conversation concerns Kevin's hiring and his perceived limitations as a fact checker. It is not flattering.

Andy complains, "The boy doesn't know a hoodie from a poncho. He asked me the other day if muumuu was Chinese food. I said, 'Oh, sure. You get it from a restaurant run by [famous women's shoe designer] Jimmy Choo.' He believed me!"

Rebecca says, "I don't get that joke."

"Yeah, well, you're not fact-checking my articles, are you?" Andy replies.

Then, in the first of many disturbing insinuations that Rebecca hired Kevin because he was both attractive and disabled, Andy (who is gay) adds, "Look, he may be cuter than Tickle Me Elmo, but he's on your team, so I get no benefits from browsing."

"That is not why I hired him," Rebecca replies.

"Oh, please, Rebecca, I know you," says Andy. "You make Dick Cheney look apolitical. You hired him for the gimp points."

Rebecca tries to refute this assertion, but then, after some thought, concedes.

"Okay," she says. "It is partly true. We get a break from the government on him, and I figure where else are we gonna find a young, smart guy who is cheap and willing to sit at a desk all day."

Andy's final comment adds further offense: "All of which would make perfect sense if he could only spell his name." Kevin rolls away from the conversation undetected, but clearly offended. He lets Rebecca know his feelings in short order.

Later that day, when Rebecca encourages him to call it quits for the night, Kevin says he wants to finish because he is not coming back on Monday. When she asks why, he coyly responds, "It's a gimp thing."

In her attempt to explain the conversation she realizes Kevin overheard, Rebecca faults Andy. She says, "Andy is a pissy queen."

Kevin sighs and says, "Oh good, we've all got nicknames. What's yours?"

Kevin's retort attempts to trouble Rebecca's politically incorrect description of Andy and likely her failure to take responsibility for her insensitive remark about him "sitting in a chair all day." (Here, *JOA* reminds us of the limits of shared marginalization as a basis for allegiance against oppression. Rebecca and Andy both hail from marginal positions as an African American woman and gay White male, respectively, but this marginalization has its limits, as Kevin so clearly lets her know.)

Despite Kevin's challenge, Rebecca has a response at the ready that outs Kevin's privilege as a White male. She replies, "Me? I'm an affirmative action figure. When I first started as copy editor, I heard it in the hallways. I cried every night. But in here, I was all business and I made sure I was indispensable."

Nonplussed, Kevin says, "What a heart-warming story. I'll be sure to tell all my crip pals."

Rebecca's response undermines Kevin's attempt to foreground his disability to diminish the force of her powerful racially charged narrative. She says, "You know what your problem is? . . . You still identify with the guy you used to be: able-bodied, handsome White man in America. Everything was coming your way. Well now it's going to be a bit of a struggle. You're gonna have to pick your battles."

"Go to hell!" Kevin says angrily.

His outburst shocks Rebecca, but it is she who has the last word.

"One day," she says, regaining her composure, "you're gonna remember me as maybe the first person who refused to pity you!"

This scene gripped me. Did they just attempt to square disability with racial marginalization?! Did Rebecca just confront Kevin's sense of privilege as a White male despite his disability?! Further, did Kevin just resist her attempts in this regard?! Here, *JOA* offers a rare but welcome glimpse into issues of disability, race, and White privilege. This exchange establishes race and disability as potential points of both alignment and misalignment between Kevin and Rebecca. Whereas Kevin perceives his disability as a barrier that both marginalizes him in the workplace and alienates him from Rebecca, she suggests that her ethnic minority status affords her an empathetic window into his newfound marginalization *and* his White male privilege. Specifically, Rebecca will not let Kevin believe that his marginalization as a disabled person erases his privilege as a White (attractive and smart) man. But she also offers him an opportunity to navigate these new struggles without self-pity or self-congratulatory liberalism—which he firmly rejects!

This is a bold interventionist move on the part of the show's writers. Whereas Whiteness persists by remaining unstated and unmarked, the writers create a narrative circumstance that shines a light on Kevin's Whiteness. This scene is one of several instances that push the boundaries of how race is discussed in prime-time TV. This scene goes one step further by placing disability on the table as well. Race is pitted against disability by two equally impassioned young people—Kevin and Rebecca—in ways that ultimately sidestep concerns about who has suffered the most to center on several richer and morally laden questions: How will I be known, both now and in the future? What kind of person will I be? How will I respond to cruelty and simplifying generalizations based on race, disability, and/or gender, and so forth? In posing these questions as prerequisites for their learning to relate to one another, Rebecca has undertaken her first act as Kevin's moral compass.

While it is certainly important to remember that Whiteness is complex and crisscrossed by other identifications that can change its meaning(s),[12] Kevin's inability to see his White male privilege by virtue of his disability and suffering makes him intolerant and even hostile to Rebecca's intervention. Kendall notes that this is typical of many (even liberal) Whites, especially if they perceive themselves to be marginalized in some way: "For those of us who are white, and are also disabled, gay, lesbian or straight women, our experiences of being excluded from the mainstream hides from us . . . the fact that we still benefit from our skin color. By seeing ourselves as removed in some way from the privileged group, we may be all the more deaf to our silencing of people of color."[13] White privilege, Kendall adds, enables many European Americans not to see race in themselves and to be angry (like Kevin) at those who do.

If Rebecca has the last word in this conversation, Kevin exacts the figurative last word near the episode's end. He interrupts a conversation between Rebecca and Andy to deliver an eloquent and pithy exposition on the difference between a hoodie and a poncho. Some reviewers (e.g., "Deborah" from Television without Pity and an anonymous reviewer from TWIZTV[14]) suggested that Kevin's comment served as a rejoinder to both Andy and Rebecca;

they surmised that he had justifiably thumbed his nose at Andy for calling him an inept fact checker and at Rebecca, too, for her insensitive reference to his wheelchair dependency.

But I am not entirely convinced that Kevin meant for his speechifying to be taken that way, or that Rebecca, in particular, received it as such. First, Kevin directs his commentary to Andy, in particular. Secondly, if one looks closely at Rebecca and Andy's faces in this scene, one will notice that Andy's expression reflects slight embarrassment and (perhaps rightful) shame, whereas Rebecca wears a smirk of acknowledgment and pride. She is impressed that Kevin has taken her advice to heart—he has thickened his skin and begun to work toward becoming "indispensable." Her tough

Rebecca and Andy respond to Kevin's thick-skinned retort.

love has made an impression on him. Kevin's ability to rise to the challenge by figuring out what he did not know before endears him to Rebecca (and to countless fans). I make this point because it also bears on the deeper lessons around White privilege that are happening here—the fact that the show's astute reviewers focused on the richness of Kevin's last lines in this episode—even as they, too, mourned Rebecca's early departure from the show—is key.

I identified deeply with Rebecca's gaze (and its antecedents) and saw in it a moment of tremendous possibility—both for primetime TV and everyday life. First, she outs Kevin's White privilege—that elusive "everything and nothing" quality of Whiteness that pervades media depictions and everyday culture[15]—without apology. Then, after he delivers his retort, she does not acquiesce through an apology or inflated gratitude. Instead, she looks at him and appreciates the part of him that is accountable to (and for) the lessons of their prior exchange. In my mind, she beckons viewers to extrapolate similar lessons in accountability concerning Whiteness.

What does Kevin ultimately take from this pivotal conversation? He deduces that Rebecca would not pity him and he reminds her of this in future episodes. But as the show progresses, Kevin displays far less enduring appreciation for Rebecca's insights into his privilege as a White male. The latter lesson is not one he seems to retain. Rebecca, in turn, displays heightened sensitivity to Kevin's struggle with his disability but seems to forget the racialized aspect of their relationship as the sexual tension increases between them in subsequent episodes.

In fact, Rebecca begins to assume more of a caretaking role, shielding Kevin from reporters' cynical remarks about his father (Chief Girardi) and nurturing his natural talents as a writer. Rebecca is especially protective of Kevin and his father in a highly charged episode about race and police brutality titled "Death Be Not Whatever." The episode begins provocatively: As the Girardi family gets situated in the den for movie night, they witness footage on the TV news that is eerily reminiscent of the videotaped police beating of Rodney King on March 3, 1991. The footage is deeply disturbing since the Black victim appears defenseless against the baton blows of two White officers from the Arcadia Police Department.

Will promptly responds to the video by issuing a public statement promising a full investigation and "swift and draconian measures" should his officers be found at fault. The next day, a reporter named Dave extracts a copy of Chief Girardi's statement from the fax machine at the newspaper and decides to read it aloud to Kevin and Rebecca. As he does, his voice drips with sarcasm, causing them both to cringe noticeably. Dave's summary shows him to be a skeptic: "Black guy gets the holy hell beaten out of him," Dave says. "White Chief of Police says he backs his guys."

Rebecca interjects, "That's not all he said."

Dave retorts, "Oh come on. Nothing's going to happen to these cops."

Rebecca tries to tell Dave that Kevin is the chief's son, but Kevin cuts her off. "I'm just a fact checker," he says. "I got no politics."

Later, when Kevin and Rebecca are alone, he tells her, "I've been a cop's kid my whole life. You don't have to worry about me. Besides, aren't you the one I'm going to remember for not cutting me any breaks?" He also vouches for his father's fairness, telling her, "Well, if it's any consolation, my dad's a fair guy. He's not a racist. He'll do the right thing."

Rebecca asks, "Did I imply something else?"

"No, I just . . . " Kevin replies uncomfortably. "It felt implied somewhere in there."

Rebecca coopts his words and adds a dose of cheeky irony. "I've had this complexion ma [sic] whole life. You don't need to worry about me," she says with a subtle neck roll.

Rebecca's comments echo the tenor of her race-marking commentary from their prior conversation. This time, however, her exchange with Kevin is conciliatory rather than oppositional. Still, it bears noting that Rebecca is doing generous but risky work in this scene. She publicly extends Chief Girardi the benefit of the doubt and, riskier still, encourages other journalists under her watch to do the same. She also tries to "out" Kevin as the chief's son as a way of protecting him from hurtful comments from other reporters.

Arguably, her efforts are a testament to her fairness as a journalist and her mounting concern for Kevin's sense of well-being at work. Nevertheless, they remain risky interventions that jeopardize not just Kevin (who knows better than to identify himself as the chief's son) but also her own moral standing. Specifically, her comments to another reporter in the wake of the beating could jeopardize her own hard-won status as an ethical news editor who does not tolerate favoritism or respond lightly to police brutality against unarmed African Americans.

One important consequence of Rebecca's intervention is that she is no longer challenging Kevin. Instead, she is protecting and comforting him in the midst of a racially charged situation that is in some ways more challenging than their initial exchange. Kevin's attempt to frame his father as antiracist and intent on "doing the right thing" resembles a form of antiracist rhetoric known as *apologia*, or what Marty calls the speech of self-defense.[16] Citing

Ware and Linkugel,[17] Marty persuasively demonstrates how such speech enables rhetors to defend their moral character against accusation and attack as they deflect any recognition of wrongdoing or of the need for accountability. White people in particular can employ elements of apologia to ward off racist accusations, thereby rejecting responsibility for racism and reasserting their good moral standing.[18] The very process of establishing their antiracist ethos also serves to render the question of White racial privilege moot.

Given Rebecca's tough love and encouragement that Kevin develop thicker skin, a more interesting option in this episode would have been to let Kevin tolerate hearing his Dad get dissed and to allow Rebecca to feel the hurt and rage that a racial beating must kindle in her. Rebecca could still be composed and respectful of her friendship with Kevin but not so concerned about his feelings that she seems to have none of her own. Her rush to protect him essentially frees him from the moral obligation to think and act responsibly around matters of race (versus circumvent it through defensive and dismissive rhetoric). Worse, her intervention weakens the focus on White privilege that she established in their prior conversation.

Rebecca's Complexity Wanes in the Wake of Mounting Sexual Desire

Rebecca's continued interventions on behalf of Kevin and Will eventually undermine her hard-won reputation as a fair and objective journalist. A perfect case in point occurs when she, Kevin, and other reporters view a subsequent televised statement by Chief Girardi; Rebecca continues to take the chief's fairness and goodness at face value. After Chief Girardi announces that the officers involved in the beating will be indicted and apologizes to the victim's family, Dave, the skeptical reporter from the earlier scene, turns the television off and scoffs, "Okay, we'll see if it happens."

Rebecca then ventures not one but two caveats that are meant to trouble Dave's read. "He just said they're indicting the guys," she observes. When Dave retorts, "Yeah, so a white jury can exonerate them," she adds, "That's not up to the Chief of Police."

Incredulous, Dave asks, "Since when do you defend the cops?" When Rebecca struggles to form a coherent response, he cuts her off by saying, "Maybe you're just hot for his son." The newsroom clears on that awkward and, as it turns out, truthful note, leaving Rebecca and Kevin to sort through the aftermath. What is troubling for me about Dave's remark is that it points toward the fact that at this point in the series, race and matters of fairness have been displaced by a focus on the sexual tension between Rebecca and Kevin.

These issues do not fall away entirely, however. Indeed, they receive some attention from Kevin and Rebecca, but more as fleeting acknowledgments than subjects for serious consideration. Toward the end of their fractured courtship, other complicating factors will emerge that attest to the writers' attempts to complicate their relationship. These factors include Rebecca's status as Kevin's boss, what Kevin calls Rebecca's "big honkin' education," their age differences, Kevin's disability, Kevin's concern that he was hired because of his relation to the police chief, and—ultimately—Kevin's insecurities around intimacy. These factors emerge as necessary and even welcome complications in the budding romance between the two characters. Yet most of them are dismissed as irrelevant, since what really scares Kevin is coming to terms with his sexual identity following his accident. Sexual desire—or, more precisely, fears about sexual dysfunction—will trump all other factors in his relationship with Rebecca.

Shoring Up Rebecca's Complexity as a Racial Character

If Rebecca appears to shirk her responsibilities as an "objective" reporter when her sexual feelings for Kevin enter the mix, she at least partially redeems herself in a subsequent episode titled "Drive He Said," which explores the aftermath of the police brutality case. We learn that relations between the Arcadia Police Department and African American communities were strained long before Will moved his family to Arcadia. Rebecca reenters this politically fraught context by writing an editorial in which she claims, "Chief Girardi's zero tolerance for graffiti misdemeanors and moving violations is nothing more than institutionalized racism targeting the young African American male."

As a fact-checker, Kevin has a hand in her critique, having gathered the data that Rebecca uses to substantiate her claim. Rebecca's essay does not endear her to Will, who is especially distressed to learn of Kevin's role in the editorial. "Thank your boss for the great editorial," Will snaps at breakfast the morning after the editorial appears. Kevin challenges his father's read, arguing that the "facts checked out" and "facts don't lie." This generates tension between Will—who cannot believe his son thinks he is a racist—and Kevin, who claims that Will's policies as chief of police are racist, though he believes Will is not.

Will's BBF: Lieutenant Toni Williams

The remainder of this episode explores the fallout from Rebecca's editorial. A resolution is brokered, in part, through two female African American characters whose collective silencing serve to affirm the Girardi men's fairness with respect to race. This work begins with Chief Girardi's African American partner, Lt. Toni Williams (played by April Grace). When Will complains about his conversation with Kevin, Lt. Williams eases his mind by vouching for the merits of the zero-tolerance policy. How she does this is particularly revealing of how the BBF dynamic works—she is not a cop's collegial, humorous, and, in some cases, more dominant Black male sidekick (although see Colombe for a critique of the use of "magical" Black male characters in cinema[19]).

"Chief," she says, "this is a good policy. Not that you asked." Her comment resounds as a cost-free endorsement of Will's ethics as a nonracist member of a corrupt police department. Then, to clear up any factual or moral ambiguity around her assertion, she says, "Tagging leads to gang wars, gang wars mean drive-bys, which definitely count as moving violations" (see Figure 3).

What is disturbing about this exchange is the absence of any hint of racial awareness on the part of Lt. Williams concerning the racial fairness of this policy. Her silence does not diminish the power of validation procured by her race; the mere fact that the actress is Black validates her character's assessment of this racial matter and, by extension, Will's goodness. Will's response is also telling, since it reveals his reluctance to figure Lt. Williams' race as relevant to her comments. "Can I ask you something," he asks.

Lt. Williams reassures Chief Will Girardi that APD policy is fair.

"As an African American?" Lt. Williams replies. "As a cop," Will says. "Is that article going to stop my guys on the street from doing their job?" Lt. Williams says, "All they need to know is that zero tolerance is zero tolerance, no matter what color the perp behind the wheel." Then jokingly she adds, "Tell you what. I will personally bust a rich white guy today."

Lt. Williams' quip is interesting on several levels. First, it illustrates another racially laden comment that exploits the unspoken power of race; she gets away with this politically incorrect quip because of her marginal positionality as an African American woman. Secondly, her humor provides a jovial (and nicely resolved) coda to their delicate yet unsettling discussion about race. The similarities between Lt. Williams' contributions and Rebecca's pay-it-no-mind reassurance to Kevin in the newsroom after the police beating airs are noteworthy. In essence, both Black women use humorous deflections to unburden White men of the moral task of asking potentially different (and self-directed) questions about race, accountability, and APD policies.

Arguably, the circumstances of this narrative could have been deepened had Will, who is Lt. Williams' boss, instead asked her, "Am I racist?" One of the marks of White privilege is that Whites tend to think they know the answer to that question without ever having to check it out with someone who is not White. This is especially true for Kevin and Will, both of whom have attested to

Will's antiracist ethos but have been reticent to probe this question more deeply within themselves.

Significantly, the nature of Will and Lt. Williams' conversation is remarkably different from a conversation concerning police brutality that they had in an earlier episode. In "Death Be Not Whatever," Will asked Lt. Williams to be candid about her impressions of the White officers who were eventually indicted in the police brutality case involving an unarmed African American man. After some hesitation (and reassurances of anonymity from Will), she described the officers as racists. In this conversation, Lt. Williams' race was powerfully relevant—so much so that Will did not have to draw attention to the fact. But in their conversation about the merits of the zero-tolerance policy, Will considers Lt. Williams' race irrelevant to the issue; he's only interested in her opinion "as a cop." This is one of the ways in which the race of a Black actor is used to establish that a White character is at once color-blind and color-conscious, when a fully developed Black character would not likely be so quick to reassure.

Lt. Williams' race is likewise exploited toward multiple ends in both of these exchanges. Either way, Will emerges as a "good" guy, first for appreciating that her race is relevant to claims about racist cops and second by ignoring her race in favor of her status as a cop in weighing the merits of a policy that disproportionately affects Blacks and other minorities. Lt. Williams thus gets to be explicitly African American when the benefits go to Will. When polishing Will's image is better served by de-racing Lt. Williams, she becomes nothing more than a cop who happens to be Black. This is not meant to suggest any nefarious intent on the part of the writers at *JOA*; rather, it points toward how deeply the privileging of Whiteness penetrates our cultural consciousness.

Too often, the morality of White characters rests on faulty color-blind stances that belie the messiness of interracial relations. Accordingly, Moon notes that hyperpolite rhetoric inherent to color-blindness shores up both White evasion and White solipsism by requiring that White people not "see" race, which then allows them to deny their own racial situatedness.[20] Similarly, the Whiteness and morality of Kevin and Will is recuperated in this and other scenes by putting words in the mouths of Black female protagonists (i.e., Rebecca, Lt. Williams, and, as will be shown, Casper) in ways that serve, ironically, to silence them.

Returning yet again to Lt. Williams' joke about ticketing a rich White guy, we find fodder for yet another case of silencing. Lt. Williams' joke turns out to be prophetic for Will, who decides to stop a White driver. His decision (while on his way to a speaking engagement no less) is rather befuddling, since it seems to belie his conviction that the policy is fair and also suggests that he had something to prove to his son and perhaps even himself. Not surprisingly, Will's decision proves unfortunate.

In an ironic turn of events (informed by stereotypical thinking and faulty motives), Will ends up getting kidnapped by a White working-class driver who has stolen the car. It is here that the show's original plot arc shifts from interrogating the merits of the APD's zero-tolerance policy to focus instead on the safety and emotional stability of the Girardi family. And this plot shift away from issues of racial awareness begets another form of silencing by setting aside the tension that Kevin's role in the inflammatory editorial had sparked between him and his father. Hereafter, Will's safety and the reconstitution of the White family become the main focus of the storytelling. Even the eventual resolution of Will and Kevin's dispute over the editorial only serves to affirm Will's rectitude because it instantiates the chief's fairness and validates Kevin's earlier assurances to Rebecca that his father was not "racist." The moral implications are significant insofar as this resolution deems the prospect of White privilege and institutionalized racism in the APD irrelevant and negligible.

Double-Silences and Good White Men

As Will fights for his freedom, a twist in the drama is keeping things lively at the *Arcadia Herald.* Kevin has uncovered "facts" that Rebecca conveniently ignored in preparing her editorial and decides to call her on it at the precise moment she approaches him to inform him of Will's abduction. "Tell me some more fairy tales about 'objective,'" he begins. Rebecca tries to interject, but this time it is Kevin who is on a roll. He continues, "I went to the stacks to find the statistics you didn't use." As he becomes increasingly shrill, Rebecca tells him, "You have to go home." But Kevin is so angry that he does not hear her. "You said there was nothing to support the police chief's policies," he says. "What are these? You chose not to see them so you could smear my father?" Rebecca finally gets his attention by telling him his father has gone missing. Kevin then goes home to attend to his worry-stricken mother. Plotwise, this sequence of events makes sense affectively, but I sensed something disturbingly familiar in this unfolding: Rebecca's silencing.

As a Black woman in a position of authority, Rebecca is accused of unethical behavior by her frustrated (White) lover and subordinate. Strikingly, Rebecca neither reproves nor bristles. Instead, she looks at him with concern. Rebecca's silence is disconcerting since it represents a radical departure from her outspokenness in prior scenes. (E.g., recall her and Kevin's early newsroom engagements, when even her silence spoke volumes!)

Kevin's remarks carry considerable weight in shaping future conflicts between him and Rebecca, especially since she does not get the opportunity in this or future episodes to respond to his allegations directly. In this sense, Rebecca fares worse than Williams in this case of silencing. Whereas Lt. Williams, as a subordinate to Chief Girardi, serves to illuminate Will's virtue, Rebecca is actually portrayed as morally corrupt and an abuser of power.

The remainder of the show concerns the restoration of the White middle-class family whose (already threatened) foundation has been further rocked by Will's kidnapping. Will appeals to the kidnapper for empathy on this basis: "I got three kids," he says. "My oldest boy's in a wheelchair. My wife's a good woman. She doesn't deserve any more tragedy in her life." The fact that he foregrounds their suffering and his wife's morality further underscores how "goodness" and "suffering" are posed as requisites for grace and mercy for (well-meaning) White characters.

Will eventually makes it out alive (the kidnapper dies), but what is interesting about these plot twists is how they serve to tidily resolve difficult questions about racism and sanction a thematic shift to the Girardi family's safety and stability—a shift that relies on centrality of the White figurative head of a household even as it disavows Whiteness as relevant to the issues that have most deeply challenged Will and Kevin in their relationships out-side the family.

Rebecca Becomes an Ambassador of Will's Goodwill

In "Jump," Rebecca uses her pulpit as editor to reframe Will in ways that seem to belie her earlier claims that the department's zero-tolerance policy was racist. In fact, her comments serve to burnish the image of Will as someone who is good and fair on mat-ters of race. After he is freed from his captor, she writes another editorial that lauds Chief Girardi as a "hero" in the kidnapping incident and another high-profile incident involving Joan and a student with a gun. Naturally, Will's family endorses Rebecca's read. Helen exclaims, "She got it right this time. You are a hero." Will modestly refuses to claim the title, which only adds luster to his righteous sheen.

Rebecca's newly positive assessment of Chief Girardi is further amplified in the same episode when Will exposes a web of corrup-tion that implicates officers in the APD and other city officials. In another newsroom scene, Rebecca tells Kevin (whom everyone now knows is Will Girardi's son), "Your old man just brought down a city!" The police chief's feat is so remarkable that even Andy, the style editor, is impressed. "Very impressive . . . for a man who only wears off-the-rack suits," he says begrudgingly.

Kevin's prior confrontation with Rebecca concerning her edi-torial sets the stage for what happens next. In the newsroom, she and Kevin argue about whether he would be willing to get a quote from Will's father. Their bickering occasions further snickers from the staff. Scenes like this play up the specter of sexual desire between them; in fact, viewers begin to wonder why everyone else can see their mutual attraction but them. Yet again, race and dis-ability fall away as concerns.

Moral Backslides and Romantic Breaks

In "Recreation," Rebecca shifts to a mentoring role. The sexual tension between them is palpable and well executed, and they have finally acknowledged its existence in an earlier episode. You begin to root for them, especially when she says things like, "Whatever you and I have going on is a matter for the universe to handle" and when she responds to his insecurities with comments like "This is not about you being in that chair" and "Neither one of us can stop thinking about [our first kiss]." But the work of mentoring Kevin and bringing him out sexually is constantly complicated by his self-defeating determination to undermine Rebecca's attempts to be close to him.

In "Night without Stars," Kevin and Rebecca have sex. Things seem promising: they have resolved the one thing that stood between them—the thing that seemed to trump all the other mitigating factors, including race, disability, differences in their ages and professional status, and fears about exploitation. Then, in "Double Dutch," the show's worst attempt to deal with race, Whiteness, and privilege, Rebecca assigns Kevin a project to interview a sexy violinist, Michelle Turner, who has an autistic brother.

Perhaps in his youth Kevin cannot see the foolishness of his actions; in any event, he ends up sleeping with Michelle Turner (played by Meredith Monroe) after she comes on to him. The best thing about the subsequent sequence of events is Rebecca's response to Kevin when he admits that he blew off a date with Rebecca to have sex with Michelle. Rebecca covers her head with her hands and says in exasperation, "Do you think that I want to hear this? I'm not your pal or your sister!" (Her anger here is welcome since it struck me as long overdue.)

Kevin wheels after her, saying, "I feel like . . . a regular nineteen-year-old kid again. I never thought I'd feel like that, so . . . it didn't mean anything." "It did to me!" Rebecca says. When Kevin insists on making light of the incident, she says, "You know, maybe this is all my fault . . . for getting involved with a regular nineteen-year-old kid."

In a subsequent episode, "Requiem for a Third Grade Ashtray," Kevin further infuriates Rebecca when he withholds one of his essays from the newspaper to exact revenge against Andy Rees, who has written an unflattering portrayal of his mother's art exhibit. Afterward, their relationship comes to a halt with little explanation, save this exchange between Kevin and his brother Luke one day: "Did you and Rebecca go out?" Luke asks. "That's kind of on hold," Kevin replies.

Kevin goes on to find new adventures: medical tests that offer the promise of miracles, romantic encounters with old and new girlfriends (all White), and a new job as a TV reporter. Rebecca remains a faint memory—a good one at least. The last mention of Rebecca occurs in episode 20 ("Anonymous") of the first season. When Joan asks Kevin how he knew writing was his calling, he replies, "Actually I didn't know. Rebecca had to strong-arm me into it." Kevin's response confirms Rebecca's role as his moral compass and professional mentor.

Joan's BBF: "Casper"

In another episode ("Double Dutch") that relies on an African American female character to corroborate a central White character's moral uprightness with respect to race, even God is enlisted to endorse the Girardis' virtue with respect to race and class privilege. God has a helper in Casper, a homeless Black teenager (played by Erica Hubbard) who inspires Joan to consider her privilege as a White middle-class teenager and the daughter of the chief of police. But Casper disappears before Joan can sufficiently redeem this young lost soul and fully acknowledge her own privileged positionality.

At the beginning of the show and in subsequent episodes, Joan bemoans her and her peers' vulnerability as "sub-defectives" (i.e., less popular kids). This lament recedes for a moment as Joan gets to know Casper. They become so close that Joan invites Casper to her house for dinner and steals her parents' phone bill to broker Casper's enrollment in Arcadia High. Several scenes establish a basis for their hard-won connection. Early scenes show Casper and her African American friends rebuffing Joan's good-natured attempts to jump rope with them. In a subsequent scene that establishes their unity and double-dutch skills, Casper and Joan "dutch" together in gym class. Their orchestrated jumping becomes a spectacle of racial harmony. Joan's largely White classmates root them on (and even applaud) against a melodic backbeat or, more precisely, a (rather cheesy) rap ditty that proclaims Joan and Casper's "sameness."

However, this vision of racial harmony is disrupted when Mr. Gavin Price, the "evil" vice-principal of Arcadia High (played by

Patrick Fabian), discovers Casper's lack of residency and forces her to leave the school. Mr. Price's lack of compassion for Casper stands in stark (moral) contrast to Joan's; he likewise becomes a "bad" White in opposition to Joan's status as a "good" White in this scenario. Another reason Joan's intervention falls short is because Casper, true to her name, disappears, reputedly to look for her father.

Despite these failings, Joan emerges as a more enlightened and moral character—with a little help from God (herself). When Joan laments Casper's unexplained departure, God appears in the form of an even younger (and cuter) Black double-dutch partner and says, "You did what you're supposed to do. Connections are not gone just because she left. You can't fix everything. Sometimes, you can only plant a seed and see what happens." Despite that divine seal of approval, Casper's appearance in Joan's life feels just as insubstantial as Rebecca's intervention with Kevin concerning his racial privilege; the lesson fades in importance next to the White characters' purported fairness and accountability around matters of race and White privilege. Furthermore, God's embodiment as an adorable African American girl is yet another instance in which images of Blackness and femininity are used to stand in for actual demonstrations of compassion and racial sensitivity.

Conclusion

It bears reiterating that *JOA* is to be commended for actively pursuing racially charged plotlines and integrating diverse characters. The show was also largely successful in its depiction of disabled characters and disability's impact on families.[21] Yet, the series' racial arcs remain flawed in ways that plague prime-time TV more broadly.

JOA exploits a widely used convention in popular culture that distinguishes "good" White characters from "bad" White characters. But, as Shome rightly warns, this dichotomization is problematic and insidious because it locates the problem of Whiteness at an individual (versus systematic) level. Shome adds, "[this] rhetoric of deflection and evasiveness is a manifestation of the very problem of . . . how whiteness refuses to name itself, how it always likes to remain "hidden," and how it defers from acknowledging the larger issue of how everyday organization of social and cultural relations function to confer benefits and systematic advantages to whites."[22] Moreover, this rhetoric implies that as long as some "bad Whites" can be fixed and brought to task, everything—and especially the "good" White character who enacts this justice—will be all right.[23]

These dangers plague *JOA*. The Girardis' incessant "goodness" is not only brokered through an alliance with BBFs who routinely establish their "good" intentions but also in opposition to "bad" Whites who, Shome explains, have gone bad (e.g., White car thieves) or constitute the site of abuse and dominance (e.g., racist APD cops and corrupt city and school officials).[24]

Kevin and his family's constant struggle to cope with loss represents another device whereby this privileged middle-class White family is humanized and made empathetic. Indeed, their relentless struggle to be "good"—along with their occasional failures—seems like a good thing. But this unswerving commitment to the essential goodness of the White family makes it too easy to forget their relative privilege and to align them with the disadvantaged Black characters that pass through their lives. Kendall sums up the faults of such posturing, whether depicted onscreen or played out in real life: "Presenting ourselves as well-meaning is a classic way of playing our white race card . . . But meaning well doesn't equal doing well."[25]

My expectations of *JOA* mirror my yearnings for popular culture more broadly: I want to see and analyze complex shows with a diverse and equally complex cast. I want to watch shows that probe and challenge our moral outlook concerning matters of race and disability without evading the inherent messiness or moral ambiguity of this work. When that messiness is resolved or explained away by the BBFs or other rhetorical strategies that recuperate Whiteness, then promising characters such as Rebecca Askew are consigned to burdensome roles; they become the sole beacon for racial issues[26] or, worse, apologists for White privilege.

Am I expecting too much of prime-time TV? Perhaps—but for me, my expectations of *JOA* are not unlike my expectations of my students in discussions about race and privilege. When I discuss these issues with them, it helps if I acknowledge that the work is difficult for me as an African American, lest my White students confuse my comments as a Black rant and other non White students become resistant to the task of examining their relative privileges. It is especially helpful, too, if my comments are as sincere and unambiguous as Rebecca's initial intervention with Kevin. If my students meet me halfway in this vulnerable exercise, I must return to them a gaze like hers: one that is neither apologetic nor overly gracious, but instead appreciative. If I have any hope for influencing the way they think and behave, I must love them that much.

My appreciation for *JOA* and its cast lingers still, amid this critical testament. Kevin and Rebecca's relationship reveals television's considerable promise, as well as its incessant limitations, in telling stories about race, Whiteness, and disability. It also reminds us that we must nurture not just faith but accountability when representing these messy and moral issues.

"A Vagina Ain't a Halo"
Gender and Religion in Saving Grace and Battlestar Galactica

ANTHEA D. BUTLER AND DIANE WINSTON

Smoking, drinking, and buck-naked fornicating, Detective Grace Hanadarko's 2007 television debut ripped through the summer rerun blahs with a potty-mouth character far removed from traditional female leads. Following TNT's Monday night hit *The Closer*, *Saving Grace* similarly featured a sexy blonde cop with a thick Southern accent.[1] But unlike Brenda Johnson—or any other television law enforcement officer—Grace Hanadarko (Holly Hunter) has a "last chance" angel named Earl, a redneck redeemer who literally sweeps her off her feet, alighting on a remote mountaintop where his spiritual zingers melt into thin air. Although reviewers nixed the supernatural twist, viewers related to Grace's dark night of the soul. That dark night deepened when, in the last scene of the first season, Grace pointed her gun at the priest who had repeatedly molested her as a child.

Coincidentally, *Saving Grace* debuted several weeks after Kara Thrace (Katee Sackhoff), another small screen "bad girl," had died, been resurrected, and then gone on an extended hiatus with the rest of the Sci-Fi Channel's *Battlestar Galactica* crew. Like Grace, Kara (also known by her pilot call sign, Starbuck) is a blonde spitfire with more machismo than most of her male colleagues.

She drinks heavily, smokes cigars, and enjoys casual sex. Unlike Grace, Kara does not have a guardian angel. But she does have an avatar that, appearing both in flesh and in dreams, avows her "special destiny."[2] Kara, the best fighter pilot in *Galactica*'s fleet, runs from this destiny until, depressed and delusional, she embraces her fate and flies into a maelstrom. Her craft explodes, but in the last seconds of the season finale, she reappears with the good news that she can lead the fleet to Earth.[3]

This essay explores how television can augment, supplement, and supersede paradigmatic constructions of religious (i.e., Western and Christian) womanhood. For the past two millennia, women's religious options have been strictly defined. Until the twentieth century, excepting sporadic outbreaks of revival or enthusiasm, Christian women could serve as teachers and leaders only to other women and children. Women were rarely depicted as religious authority figures nor did they wield much spiritual clout. Neither bishops nor popes, rarely prophets or preachers, women occasionally became saints, typically after gory, gruesome martyrdoms.

Gender roles are among the most ingrained aspects of religion, establishing women's (and men's) relationship to spirituality, sexuality, and power—shaping, in these arenas, what they can say, what they may do, and how they define themselves. Within Western Christianity, gender roles have been set by defining archetypes, and since the formation of the Biblical canon, there have been two preeminent classifications for women: Madonna and whore. Even today, when women have entered into the innermost circles of religious power, these deep-rooted typologies— harkening back to both the Hebrew Bible's stories of Eve and the matriarchs (Sarah, Rebecca, Leah, and Rachel) and the New Testament's portrayals of the Virgin and the Magdalene[4]—are culturally pervasive, reducing women to bodies for recreation or procreation.

Kara's and Grace's lives and the narrative theology that flows from them offer an alternative. Rather than accept traditional prescriptions of the holy woman's role, the strength of these characters, despite their brokenness and rambunctious behavior, is that their stories are redemptive. They also stand as counterpoints to their female friends and colleagues who follow a more conventional path to salvation—and they hold out hope for (and elicit empathy from) viewers hungry for new perspectives on both women and religion. In this essay, we explore Kara's and Grace's "callings," their religious worlds, and the ways in which their spirituality is refracted through gender. We are particularly interested in how the embodiment and performance of religious calling on television resonates with understandings of spirituality, sexuality, and power in "real" life. Accordingly, after reading the texts themselves, we turn to fans' response to characters and plots in order to illustrate how, in Robert Orsi's formulation of lived religion, viewers use the series to "unmake and remake"[5] their own worlds.

We also will look at Grace's and Kara's alter egos because, in addition to their blond machisma and special destinies, both have female colleagues/friends with strong, if more traditional, religious callings. Grace's best friend, Rhetta Rodriguez (Laura San Giacomo), is an Oklahoma City Police Department criminalist whose Roman Catholic faith sustains her through personal and professional challenges. Kara's civilian boss is President Laura Roslin (Mary McDonnell), political leader of *Galactica*'s fleet as well as its reigning prophet. Like Grace and Kara, Laura and Rhetta share physical, behavioral, and professional traits. Handsome brunettes, their competence and conscientiousness bespeak an emotional maturity that is absent in Grace and Kara. Despite working full time, they also serve as mothers. Rhetta has two young children, and Laura functions as matriarch for the post-nuclear holocaust remnants of a human civilization. Both are comforting, nurturing presences whose efficacious applications of dry humor mitigate their rigorous standards of right and wrong.

The women of *Battlestar Galactica* and *Saving Grace* were conceived within a postfeminist world where women's sexuality is openly discussed, although rarely in an empowering manner. Rather, women who are publicly sexual (as opposed to sexy) are subject to exploitation, marginalization, and/or shame. When sexuality does appear to make a woman strong, it is usually because she uses it to coerce and manipulate. Conversely, strong women— women in positions of power—are not sexual. Thus, although the depictions appear to fit classic categories of "Madonna" (Laura and Rhetta) and "whore" (Kara and Grace), the characters also subvert traditional religious stereotypes for women. Stand-ins for contemporary uncertainties surrounding changing gender norms, these representations—abetted by new media technologies that enable the discussion, dissection, and rearrangement of characters and plots—encourage viewers to overlay old patterns with new realities. As a result, even the most hackneyed plot lines—Grace and her fellow cops solving a kidnapping or Laura's supporters stealing an election—can reflect the contested interplay of gender with ethics, agency, and authority.

How does a faithful woman behave? What is her responsibility to others? Which of her various personas is her real and true self? Where does sexuality fit into her public personas? Kara, Laura, Rhetta, and Grace hold a mirror to our deepest hopes and darkest fears, reflecting the challenge of being strong, sexual, spiritual women.

"The players change, the story remains the same"
—Leoben Conoy, "Flesh and Bone"

At the heart of both Kara's and Grace's stories is an unsought and unwanted religious calling. A calling—the perception that a supernatural power has a special plan for one's life—is a staple of Western religious literature. Yet there is no general agreement about what a call is, how it occurs, where and when it happens, and how to judge its authenticity. Given the uncertainty among real-life practitioners, how then to understand a fictional rendering? One possibility is to contextualize the phenomenon within religious traditions; three of which—Judaism, Roman Catholicism, and Protestantism—are most familiar to television viewers as well as to the series' writers.

Judaism begins with a call: God tells Abram to leave his home for a new land where he and his descendents will prosper (Gen 12:1). Abram obeys and receives additional instructions for the establishment of a covenanted community (he also receives a new name, Abraham). When God calls Abraham to the ultimate test, the sacrifice of his son Isaac, the Hebrew patriarch answers, "*Hineni*," or "Here I am" (Gen 22:1-2) and readies Isaac for slaughter. This unqualified acceptance of God's command became a touchstone for discussions of what to do when God's call seems counterintuitive. Generations of rabbis have argued whether or not blind obedience is always the correct response. Fortunately for Hebrew patriarchs and prophets, subsequent calls did not demand a similarly profound surrender. More often they expounded a vision or a set of activities aimed at collective repentance. Those who heard the call recognized it as divine, whether it came as a still, small voice, from a burning bush, or in a whirlwind. Moreover, resistance was futile. Jonah ran away, but God pursued him until he accepted his mission.

In early medieval Europe, the Roman Catholic Church developed a different notion of calling. It entailed the discernment of a religious vocation that took one out of the everyday world and into a cloistered, celibate community. (Even though the earliest communities were both single sex and mixed, chastity was a fundamental requirement.) Those who remained in the world also were expected, as Paul wrote to the Ephesians, to be "as God has called you, live up to your calling: Be humble always and gentle, and patient, too" (Eph 4:1-2). This notion of calling, more privatized and personalized than the mandates received by the Hebrew prophets and patriarchs, reflected both historical circumstance (the differences between a desert people and the medieval Church) and theology.

The idea of calling evolved further after the Protestant Reformation. Both Luther and Calvin saw it as a deeper commitment to life in this world. Among the ramifications of the doctrine of the priesthood of all believers was the conviction that all work could be a calling if performed with the right intentions. Instead of viewing membership in celibate communities as the best and highest expression of the divine will, the new religious movements taught that believers could follow God's mandate and remain in the world. As in Roman Catholicism, however, the ability to discern divine promptings (as opposed to one's own wishes or the devil's whisperings) was a serious concern. Much subsequent Protestant theology, and concomitant differences among denominations, grew out of disagreements over how to recognize and act on God's word.

Religious calling on *Battlestar Galactica* is a hybrid, reflecting a polytheistic faith that borrows from Greco-Roman myths, Christianity, Egyptian religion, and the Church of Jesus Christ of Latter-day Saints.[6] The series tracks the Colonials, human beings whose civilization, the Twelve Colonies of Kobol, has been destroyed in a nuclear holocaust by the Cylons, a race of robotic servants turned into rebels. The survivors of the holocaust seek Earth, which they believe is home to the lost Thirteenth Colony. Cruising through galaxies, perhaps light years before or after our own time, the Colonials seem just like us: they box, jog, and brush their teeth before bed. But the resemblance ends at religion. The Colonials worship a pantheon of Olympian gods and goddesses.[7] Many of the characters are atheists, but others pray to idols and visit oracles. In the 2003 miniseries, the Colonials are the victims of a religious war. Their opponents, the Cylons, have evolved from machines into human form and are guided by a militant monotheism that provides justification for the nuclear attack that drove human survivors into exile.

Laura Roslin's calling comes from within the Colonials' religious tradition: she is the fulfillment of their sacred scriptures' prophecy.[8] Initially, she is a secular figure, the Colonies' secretary of education. Traveling off world when the Cylons attack, Laura is the highest-ranking government survivor and, following protocol, assumes the presidency. In this role, she becomes the civilian counterforce to Commander William Adama, the *Galactica*'s chief officer.[9] (In season 2, Adama becomes an admiral.) Laura's calling manifests after she takes chamalla, a medicinal plant that reduces the pain of her terminal breast cancer.[10] Among the drug's side effects are hallucinations, which for Laura begin as dreams. In the episode "Flesh and Bone,"[11] she encounters a Cylon whose fate she had foreseen in a dream. In "The Hand of God," she "sees" twelve writhing snakes during a press conference.[12] When she tells the priestess Elosha about the vision, the other woman assumes it is a put-on:

ELOSHA: You're kidding me, right? You read Pythia and
      now you're having me on.
ROSLIN: No, who is Pythia?
ELOSHA: One of the oracles, in the sacred scrolls. Thirty-
      six-hundred years ago, Pythia wrote about the exile
      and the rebirth of a human race: "And the lords
      anointed a leader to guide the caravan of the heavens
      to their new homeland and unto the leader they gave

a vision of serpents, numbering two and ten as a sign
of things to come."
ROSLIN: Pythia wrote that?
ELOSHA: She also wrote that the leader suffered a wasting
disease and would not live to enter the new land. But
you're not dying . . . are you?[13]

Laura is dying, and that fact changes everything. Says Elosha,
"You made a true believer out of me . . . I know that you are the
one to lead us to our salvation."[14] Later on, when the two women
look at an aerial map of an unidentified planet that *Galactica* is sur-
veying, Elosha sees ruins on the planet's surface. Laura, however,
sees buildings that match descriptions of Kobol, a planet where
men and gods lived together until a terrible cataclysm forced the
humans into exile.[15] Accepting that her gift is genuine, Laura has
a come-to-Jesus moment—"It's real, the scriptures, the myths, the
prophecies, they're all real"[16]—and informs Adama that the mystery planet is actually Kobol. She tells him that an artifact on their
nuked home planet will enable them to find a map to Earth that is
hidden on Kobol.

ROSLIN: So according to the scriptures, if we had the Arrow
of Apollo we could take it down to Kobol and we
could use it to open the tomb of Athena and find our
way to Earth.
ADAMA: I didn't know you were that religious.
ROSLIN: Neither did I. Something wrong with that?[17]

The interchange prefigures the conflict that arises after Laura
recruits Kara, against Adama's orders, to retrieve the Arrow of
Apollo. Adama charges Laura with treason and jails her. Despite
her failing health, she is sustained by support from civilians, as
well as some members of the *Galactica* crew, who believe she is
indeed the prophesied leader. Imprisoned and physically broken
by her illness, the once-reluctant seer has embraced her calling. In
fact, she sees her roles as president and prophet as complementary.
That, at least, is her justification for sending Kara, a member of
the military, on a secret mission to retrieve the Arrow of Apollo.
Despite the "pagan" sources for Laura's revelation (chamalla and

the "sacred scrolls"), the trajectory of her journey from skeptic to convert and the archetype for her leadership, the wounded healer, have Christian resonance. Similarly, the indisputability of the call, as well as its summons to lead Twelve Colonies (tribes) to Earth (the Promised Land), have Jewish antecedents.

Laura's gender is significant to her role as a political and spiritual leader insofar as she subverts traditional expectations of womanly behavior. Her soft, conciliatory manner is belied by a ruthless realpolitik, and opponents consistently underestimate her toughness. When the safety and survival of the fleet is at stake, Laura frequently takes a harder line than Adama. In "Resurrection Ship, Part I," she urges him to assassinate the amoral admiral of another battlestar lest the other leader kill Adama first. Then in "The Captain's Hand," Laura outlaws abortion, a position counter to her previous stance but one which she now deems necessary given the fleet's dwindling population. Although the religious leadership supports the ban, Laura's decision has nothing to do with spirituality or ethics. It is based on her concern for humanity's survival and sets in motion the narrative arc that culminates in her electoral defeat.[18]

Laura's performance of gender is delimited by circumstance and volition: she is not a wife, lover, or mother, and her political style runs from dispassionate to ruthless. She frequently bests opponents by deploying a seemingly uncharacteristic (for women) lack of sentiment and sympathy. Laura appears to loosen up and engage in a mild flirtation with Adama during the early days on New Caprica, a planet where the Colonials settle at the end of season 2.[19] Cuddling under the stars, the two imagine what their lives might be like in a peaceful and secure world. Later, when the Colonials have escaped from the Cylon occupation of New Caprica and reassembled the fleet, Laura and Adama continue to share an emotional intimacy. Embellishing the bond between the two, and otherwise seeking to sexualize the Madonna, scores of online fans have created videos, stories, and blogs devoted to Laura's love life. Most frequently paired with Adama, Laura also has been partnered with his son, Lee; Kara; and other *Galactica* (as well as made-up) characters.[20]

The circumstances surrounding Kara's call are very different than Laura's, as is her acceptance of it and the gendered nature of her evolution as a person with a divine destiny. However, like Laura, Kara's first intimations of a calling come in the episode "Flesh and Bone," and its harbinger is Leoben Conoy, the same Cylon that Laura saw in her dream. When Leoben is found hiding on one of the fleet's ships, Kara is sent to question him. Intuitive rather than intellectual, Kara is chosen for the task because Adama assumes that she will not be vulnerable to the mix of half-truths and lies that this Cylon model uses to confuse humans. To Kara, Leoben is a "toaster," the pejorative human term for Cylons, and she is disgusted to see that he sweats, bleeds, and seems to suffer physical pain.

Facing-off in a dank interrogation room, the two talk at cross-purposes. Kara wants to know about a nuclear device that Leoben claims to have planted in the fleet. But his answers are metaphysical musings about the river of life and the cycle of time. After several rounds, Kara decides that waterboarding would be an appropriate next step:

> LEOBEN: I know that god loved you more than all other living creatures and you repaid his divine love with sin, with hate, corruption, evil. So then he decided to create the Cylons.
> STARBUCK: The gods had nothing to do with it. We created you . . . us. It was a stupid fraked [sic] up decision and we have paid for it. You slaughtered my entire civilization? That is sin. That is evil, and you are evil.
> LEOBEN: Am I? I see the truths that float past you in the stream.
> STARBUCK: You got a real thing about rivers and streams, don't you? I think we should indulge you in your obsession.[21]

Torturing Leoben does not enable Kara to extract the information she wants. Rather, it binds them emotionally: she chooses to inflict pain, and he chooses to acquiesce to it. After immersing Leoben for a third and prolonged dunking, Kara accuses him of "enjoying" the situation. He tells her that the players change but the game remains the same. This time she wins, but he has a "gift" for her: the abuse she suffered as a child, and the attendant pain that drives her reckless behavior, is part of her special destiny.

> LEOBEN: Each of us plays a role, each time a different role. The last time, I was the interrogator and you were the prisoner. The players change, the story remains the same. And this time . . . this time, you're wrong. You have to deliver my soul unto God. Do it for me, it's your destiny, and mine. And I told you I had a surprise for you. Are you ready? You're going to find Kobol, birthplace of us all. Kobol will lead you to Earth. This is my gift to you, Kara.[22]

For most of the next two seasons, Kara denies her special destiny, but it laps at the edges of her consciousness: sometimes inspiring her to do the right thing, more often compelling her to self-destructive behavior. But the undeniable implications of this call emerge when a bulls-eye design that Kara painted before the Cylon attack reappears as a temple drawing by the Thirteenth Tribe (the humans who long ago left Kobol for Earth) and later in the pattern of a star gone nova.[23] In "Maelstrom," Kara sees the design everywhere: as dripping wax, a planetary storm, her doodles. Discomfited by visions and a growing sense of inevitability, she becomes increasingly withdrawn and unstable. During a flight exercise, she pursues an enemy ship that is invisible to other pilots. During one engagement, she blacks out and awakens in her old apartment. Leoben is there and takes her to her mother's deathbed. In the "real" world, Kara shunned her abusive mother when she lay dying. Now, Kara realizes that her mother loved her as best she could. With the healing of this deep emotional wound and the realization that she need not fear death, Kara reawakens in her ship. She sees the bulls-eye design and flies straight into it, a decision that looks suicidal to the *Galactica* crew, who watch her ship explode.

Unlike Laura's call, which is authenticated by sacred texts, Kara's call is heterodox. Leoben, a Cylon, first announces her special destiny, which is reiterated in "Maelstrom" by an oracle. After taking Kara to her dying mother, the Leoben figure (he denies being a Cylon) says he wants her "to discover what hovers in the space between life and death."[24] He also indicates that Kara's mother, aware of her daughter's destiny, prepared her as best she could. Flying into the maelstrom, Kara accepts her fate—this time allowing Leoben to deliver her soul to God. (In "Flesh and Bone," she prayed to her special gods, Aphrodite and Artemis, to look after his soul.) When Kara reappears in the final episode and says that she can take the Colonials to Earth, her call seems fulfilled. But in *Razor*, a made-for-television movie that aired between seasons 3 and 4 of *Battlestar Galactica*, the meaning of Kara's destiny is thrown into question. Another oracle figure announces that Kara Thrace is "the herald of the Apocalypse" who "will lead the human race to its end."[25] The warning, issued as the oracle and his listener are about to die, hangs in the air.

Similar to Laura, Kara's calling echoes Jewish and Christian themes within a pagan setting. Kara dies and returns to life; that she comes back fully human provokes speculation, which may be resolved in future seasons, whether she is a Cylon, a god, or a very lucky person. (One possible interpretation is that she is the embodiment of Aurora, a goddess to whom Kara was drawn during her visit to the oracle.[26]) Fused with the Jesus motif is a Moses image: Kara returns to lead the fleet to the promised land. But the *Razor* revelation overlays a Gnostic gloss on the mission. In the cycle of time, where unknown beings oversee what has gone before and will occur again, Kara may represent a demiurge whose role, unbeknownst even to her, is malevolent.

Kara's potential malevolence is not altogether unexpected, as her sexuality has always held a dangerous edge. In acting on it, she wounds others emotionally as she herself has been physically wounded. In flashbacks and conversations, viewers learn that her daredevil persona masks the physical and emotional suffering she endured as a child. Her mother beat her, broke her fingers, and cracked her skull. Socrata Thrace wanted her daughter to be angry, not afraid; but in "Maelstrom," the oracle says Kara confused "the message with the messenger." Thus, even when her customary sangfroid is undercut by glimpses of vulnerability, those moments quickly fade into self-mocking sarcasm. The result, a volatile mix of male swagger and female sexuality, is combustible. Few men can resist Kara even though she has none of the trappings of a traditional femme fatale.

Usually dressed in baggy fatigues, Kara's hair seems to be her sole nod to gender conventions. On active duty, she wears it short or shorter. But during the year that the Colonials spend on New Caprica, her hair grows long. During this interlude, Leoben imprisoned Kara. He locks her in an apartment, where they live as man and wife. Although she repeatedly kills him,[27] he keeps coming back, assuring her that she will learn to love him. When he brings her a child whom he says is their daughter, Kara's initial indifference to the little girl gives way to strong maternal bond.[28] Kara's acceptance of motherhood, echoed when she accepts her own mother's love in "Maelstrom," is a pivotal development. Up to this point, Kara rejected both maternal and romantic love; unable to make either connection, she behaves as an unruly woman flaunting sexual, violent, and reckless behavior.[29] Accepting and acknowledging mother love enables her to overcome her deepest fears. In the course of three seasons, Kara has embraced her brokenness (represented by her unstable appropriation of gender) and accepted her destiny.

"I'm just FedEx delivering the message"
—Earl, *Saving Grace*, Pilot Episode

A similar narrative of rebellion and redemption characterizes calling on *Saving Grace*. Grace Hanadarko, like Kara Thrace, has psychic scars that help explain her unruly persona. During her prepubescent years, Grace was raped and repeatedly molested by a priest she calls Father Patrick "Satan" Murphy. Later, as a young woman, she was victimized again when a one-night stand went bad and the man slashed her. Her own pain, and the lack of resolution in her life, drives Grace to mete out justice as an Oklahoma City detective. Her personal life and career play out within the context of a close-knit Roman Catholic family that lost a sister (and daughter) in the 1995 bombing of the Alfred P. Murrah Federal Building. Grace's only real familial connection is with her young nephew, Clay, whose mother was the family member killed in the bombing. Grace's brother Johnny, a priest who appears to be the "called" person of the family, predictably questions Grace's wild life and atheism. Her younger sister Paige is less charitable in her disapproval of Grace's excesses, and the other siblings are amused by Grace's antics. Only Rhetta, who is not a member of the family, knows about the sexual abuse Grace endured and understands the toll it exacted.

Life as Grace knows it ends when, after a hard night of drinking, she drives her Porsche into a pedestrian. Trying desperately to revive him, Grace whispers, "Dear God, help me."[30] When a scruffy, white-haired man appears and announces that God has sent him to help, Grace assumes he is crazy. But when he unfurls a set of great white wings to prove that he, Earl, is indeed an angel, Grace fears that it is she who has come undone. In this initial response and in subsequent encounters, Grace makes it known that Earl's appearance is anything but the annunciation of the traditional Christian "good news." Rather, it is the beginning of ongoing resistance as Grace, like many before her, rebels against the call of faith. That first night, when Grace questions whether Earl is the "real deal," she finds herself transported to the Grand Canyon. There, Earl tells her she is going to hell unless she turns her life over to God. When Grace refuses to admit she needs divine help, Earl stirs up a tremendous storm. Fearing for her life, she takes his hand, and he wraps her in his wings. There she feels the power of faith (which by her face looks a lot like great sex), and Earl explains that he, like FedEx, is just delivering the message.

So begins a narrative arc of resistance and discovery. Throughout the first season, Grace struggles over what she must give up in order to turn over her life to God: Sleeping with her partner? Lying to her friends? Taking the Lord's name in vain? All of Grace's bad behaviors are up for scrutiny, but Earl is no *deus ex machina*, and Grace's path to salvation is anything but conventional. Soon after Earl appears, Grace asks Rhetta, a forensics specialist, to help her decipher clues to Earl's identity and purpose. Rhetta, the believer to Grace's skeptic, accepts the reality of signs, mysteries, and miracles. She also represents the Catholic world to which Grace, despite her estrangement, still belongs. In the series pilot, Rhetta and Grace debate the evidence of miracles after Grace survives a shooting.

> GRACE: Look, I know you go to mass every Sunday, and believe, but I don't. And even Saint Johnny said it didn't happen.

RHETTA: He didn't know about the blood on your shirt.
GRACE: Did you test it?
RHETTA: It's not yours.
GRACE: Is it human blood?
RHETTA: As opposed to divine. . .
GRACE: I dunno?
RHETTA: Yes, it was normal human blood.
GRACE: You gotta test the dust right?
RHETTA: Why can't you believe it just happened? Miracles
      happen all the time; you just have to believe.
GRACE: If there was a God, why would he save my ass last
      night?
RHETTA: But not in fourth grade from Father Satan Pat-
      rick Murphy?[31]

For Rhetta, Earl's existence opens up a realm of questions that she longs to ask: What about the Virgin Birth, the Trinity, heaven? Rhetta believes in mysteries that transcend everyday reality and in a God that "speaks" through daily life. Accordingly, when she examines "clues" gathered by Grace (a feather from Earl's wings, a carved duck, a half-eaten taco), she interprets them scientifically (What is Earl's DNA?) and spiritually (What is Earl's message for Grace?). Her role is that of a divine interpreter, providing Grace with a picture of what Earl is trying to tell her.[32] She also acts as a moral sounding board; even if she does not condemn Grace, Rhetta informs her friend when she is out of bounds.

Grace's issues are played out through her cases and interactions with Earl. But unlike many calling narratives, in which the message of God is clear, Grace is admonished only to accept God's help. Instead of announcing God's purpose, Earl plants clues in Grace's personal and professional lives. One major hint is that the man she thought she killed on the night Earl appeared is actually alive. The man, Leon Cooley, is a prisoner on death row. He killed a woman while driving drunk and subsequently murdered a prison guard. Earl is also Leon's "last chance" angel, and Leon dreamt that Grace hit him with her car. When Earl's clues lead Grace to Leon, she is horrified to find herself yoked to a death row inmate. She cannot accept that he holds a key to her divine visitation.

From a religious standpoint, Grace Hanadarko is anything but a meek and mild Martha awaiting God's will. Wild and rebellious, she is unwillingly drawn into a relationship with Earl, in part because he presents a puzzle to her. Not surprisingly, she puts together the pieces in an irreverent manner. Nevertheless, over the course of the first season, viewers see incremental change as Grace becomes more truthful and self-accepting. She tries to stop lying; she is more rigorous in her professional conduct, and she will not let herself be compromised by others' opinions. When a sleazy lawyer seeks to shake the detectives' commitment to a case by revealing hidden and embarrassing facts about their own lives, he parades a long line of Grace's lovers through their office. But Grace will not be shamed. Rather, she quips: "Well, that was just summer. If we're going to bring fall and winter in here, we're going to need another building."[33]

The characters of Grace and Rhetta mirror the Madonna/whore archetypes but with a twist. It is not the Madonna figure that sees the angel, or is called by God, but rather the whore. Moreover, Rhetta has no trouble believing that Grace, with all of her faults, is visited by the divine. It is in and through this apparent contradiction that the two characters work together. Even so, the Madonna/whore distinction is not always clear-cut, since Grace also has a mother's heart. She has a special love for her nephew and a passion for cases involving children. In "In the Beginning," Grace finds a young girl who has been abducted by a teenage boy. Throughout the episode, Grace is caring and maternal, albeit in her own way and with unexpected results. She tries to be open and understanding with the kidnapper, only to have him jump to his death from the top level of the high school stadium stands. She rescues the missing child and promises to take her to her mother, only to have the little girl bite her.

Saving Grace further complicates the gendered role of whore by providing explanations for Grace's behavior. Enjoying stereotypical male activities such as hunting, heavy drinking, and casual sex, Grace appears slutty. But akin to Kara Thrace, Grace's hard living masks emotional pain. The pain flares up at inopportune times, set off by inadvertent triggers. For example, when Grace is looking for clues to the missing child, she finds a DVD, "Loving

Little Girls." Flying into a rage, she is sent home by her supervisor, who tells her she needs sleep. But instead of resting, Grace reviews clues from the case. Her own pain presses her forward to a solution because she is compelled to save others from the fate she herself experienced.

Grace's calling can be understood, then, as a means to be saved from her own past. That past and its experience of pain led Grace to a profession that allows her to save others. But the evidence of her personal life—lying, cheating, fornicating—demonstrates that she cannot save herself. And despite continual efforts to worm out of her "calling," Grace is called back to accountability by Earl's persistence. In a scene reminiscent of Jacob wrestling with an angel of God (Gen 32:1-33), Grace challenges Earl to a wrestling match.[34] She pins Earl by cheating, and he "cheats" to subdue her.[35] But she learns a lesson: much like Jacob, Grace comes to understand that she can choose to rely on God's power rather than her own strength.

For Grace, and for Rhetta, the entrance of Earl into their world of "deciphering crime" places their friendship and their path of spiritual awakening into a subversion and reapplication of gender. Their gender roles are mediated through a macho profession in which they frequently assert nurturing and compassionate behavior (as in "In the Beginning"). When their boss is shot, the new commander is woman. Although the expected trope would be to have Grace and the new chief grate on each other, the two turn out to be old and dear friends. Their relationship yields new information about Grace; given all the male attention she seeks and receives, one might assume she has difficulties bonding with other women. But as Rhetta tells her, "You are the kind of person who loves everyone more than you love yourself."[36] Unfortunately, her ways of loving others often underscore how little she loves herself. When a colleague loses his cat, Grace does not just commiserate with him, she seduces him.[37] No matter how hard she may try, sex—the act that has caused her so much anguish—is the only way she can communicate with men.

"Your pain is my entertainment"
—Lee Adama, "Six Degrees of Separation"

Tight-bodied and small-busted, both Kara Thrace and Grace Hanardarko have more in common with prepubescent girls or young males than their curvy Madonna counterpoints. Likewise, both have complicated relationships with their own sexuality. Functioning on multiple levels, sex serves as a shield, weapon, and white flag. It can shield feelings of pain, hurt, or even love; conquer loneliness and self-doubt; and signal affection and need. But the subtext of these emotional skirmishes suggests a problematic message about sexuality and spirituality that prevents the characters from fully engaging either.

Kara Thrace's on-again, off-again relationship with Lee Adama, which throughout the series has interfered with her calling, takes an unexpected turn in "Unfinished Business."[38] In a series of flashbacks, viewers see Kara and Lee hook up at a party when Sam Anders, Kara's "official" love interest, drinks himself into a stupor. The two steal away and tryst together under the stars. Lee, overcome with emotion, proclaims his love aloud for Kara and asks her to do the same. When she does, albeit reluctantly, he assumes they will live happily ever after. But the next morning, Kara is gone. Not only has she left him, but she married Sam immediately upon leaving Lee's side. Seeking to mask his pain, Lee proposes to his patient (and long-suffering) girlfriend. When the show returns to the present, Lee is watching his father go down in a boxing match. Kara, with whom he has had little interaction since their night together, baits him into the ring. They pummel each other mercilessly, with their respective spouses grimly watching. Kara fights unfairly, and the match becomes distasteful to observers, who begin to leave. Blood flying, sweat dripping, chests heaving, they fall into each others arms, and Kara whispers, "I missed you."

The intensity with which Kara and Lee consummate their relationship and, subsequently, fight each other says much about Kara's relationship to sexuality and love. Performing gender through a male persona, Kara tried to mediate her sexuality by displaying a tough, devil-may-care attitude toward Lee's declaration of love. Sex is not tender but vigorous, athletic, tinged with hostility, violence, and regret. Love is equated with pain, as if the boxing match is flagellation for her weakness in loving Lee and her inability to deal with his emotions. Outwardly, the fight reads "male sexuality," but Kara uses aggression to mask her vulnerability and the feelings that she believes make her weak. Only in her pain can she finally show how deeply she cares for Lee.

Kara's emotional immaturity, coupled with her unbridled sexuality, renders her spiritually empty—incapable of a real connection with another human being. Sex is penitential, a punishment that serves to remind her of her past failings as a daughter and her current unwillingness to accept her "destiny." Her inability to enter into a committed, loving relationship suggests that within the *Battlestar Galactica* universe, for all of its sexual openness, a "whore" cannot truly enjoy sex. Women who are called, whether whore/Kara or Madonna/Laura, cannot be in fulfilled physical relationships because of their duty as spiritual figures.

Grace, similarly, has avoided marriage, and her sexual partners serve as dramatic (and sometimes comic) foils to her forceful personally. She wears her blonde hair long and flowing, yet strides like a man and strips off her clothes at a moment's notice. Her whip-strong body is slightly boyish in its leanness; no spare ounce of flesh finds comfort on her belly, buttocks, or hips. Sex for Grace, with its beginnings in the crucible of a painful experience of abuse, seems to be about subversion. She engages in light bondage with Ham, her married work partner, signaling her issues with control by tying him up and doing body shots of tequila off his stomach and chest.[39] She is not averse to switching positions however, and in "A Language of Angels," is handcuffed to the bed, sprawled backside up in a position reminiscent of a crucifixion. Ham, finding Grace with another man's name scrawled in lipstick on her backside, refuses to free her. Earl comes along next and he, too, leaves her bound, asking, "What do you want to talk about? I finally have you for a change." Although staged for fun, the bondage theme holds an element of "punishment" that hearkens back to Grace's Catholic past and how her sexuality was formed in a situation that immobilized her.

Grace's sexual encounters often allude to themes of blood and atonement. Grace and Ham go deer hunting, and she shoots a buck/doe with her handgun.[40] Recounting how, at age twelve, she made her first kill, Grace tells Ham about a dream in which a deer with sparkly hooves trampled on her entire family. (Later in the season, viewers learn that Father Patrick "Satan" Murphy stopped molesting Grace when, at age twelve, she began menstruating.) Ham, having no knowledge of this history, suddenly feels aroused and, in a strikingly primal scene, begins foreplay with Grace alongside the dead deer on the ground. When he touches a drop of blood to her face, the scene foreshadows the subsequent shooting of the detectives' squad leader, whose blood spatters all over Grace. At the end of the show, Ham gets into the shower with Grace to help wash the blood off her body.

The theme of blood and water closely mirrors the Christian themes of suffering, death, and redemption. Viewers may wonder whether redemption will come through Ham's human love or through Earl's ritual cleansing, but Grace behaves as if her sexuality is its own path to salvation. Grace tries to purge the memory of the past by fully immersing herself in the intensity of physical, vigorous sex. Sex replaces, or at least allows her to control, the pain and shame of the earlier violations. But it is in the "orgasmatron" of Earl's embrace that Grace feels something overwhelming or, as she puts it, "better than sex."[41]

For Grace and Kara, their sexuality and gender-bending role-play hints at a conundrum: is the archetype of whore mediated through male sexual behavior? In Grace's and Kara's worlds, masculine and feminine aspects are like sheaths, to be worn or discarded depending on the situation. Their behavior with men is fraught with one-upmanship, but with female friends, they become softer, more open, and less apt to push back. Moreover, blonde as they are, neither Kara nor Grace fits the "bombshell" stereotype. More Artemis than Aphrodite, their bodies hold the pain they experienced through rejection, rape, and physical abuse. For Kara, whether boxing with Lee or enduring bodily pain, strength is rooted in brute physicality. In "Six Degrees of Separation," Kara is mending slowly from a knee injury. She is weaker than normal, and Lee does not know how to respond to this new softness in her. Thus, he goads her as she would him: a man-to-man call to buck up.

LEE: Come on Starbuck, you can do it.

(Kara winces as she puts her feet down on the ground.)

LEE: Ah, that smarts . . . that smarts, but I don't care . . .
STARBUCK: You don't care?
LEE: I don't care, because your pain is my entertainment.

(He hands her her crutches, which he has been playing with.)

LEE: Your crutches of death, sir. Use them wisely.
STARBUCK: Shut up.[42]

Kara responds to physical pain not with tears but stoic endurance. She resists showing weakness, but Lee, seeing her suffer, finds her vulnerability endearing. Grace is similarly resistant to exposing any flaws. In the episode "Everything's Got a Shelf Life" a bullet hits her chest, momentarily stopping her heart. Despite wearing a Kevlar vest, Grace "dies" and sees a white light. When she awakens in a hospital room, her colleagues and friends, clearly shaken by Grace's brush with death, are at her bedside. But Grace herself refuses to take her condition seriously or to give in to the discomfort she clearly feels. Only when she is alone does she look at the huge bruise, marking the spot where the bullet hit her. Both Grace's and Kara's bodies carry scars that mirror their emotional wounds. Even when they will themselves to be impervious to pain, their bodies manifest telltale signs of their weakness. Their relationship to sex symbolizes the dilemma: what seem to be male-coded acts of casual and aggressive coupling can also be read as a feminine call for help.

"The pain I feel for her makes me want to pull her in my arms" —fans 1228

What then, do viewers make of these whores and Madonnas, female characters whose religious callings, sexual appetites, and career choices (politician, fighter pilot, criminalist, and detective) seem to render them gender renegades? Kara and Laura are beloved, Rhetta is liked and Grace evokes passionate discord. Viewers either love her or loathe her. Those in the latter category hate her skanky hair, potty mouth, and bony body. Initially, the TNT

forum was flooded with Christians offended by the show's depiction of drinking, smoking, nudity, and adultery (Grace's partner
Ham is married). But others criticize the "Christian" response as
misguided. "I was ready to complain to the network but I listened
and watched and figured out what was truly going on," wrote Della
on a beliefnet.com blog. "That is why we as Christians should not
be judgmental. I am still having a problem with an angel that
drinks and curses but I understand why Grace is like she is. She is
not a Christian and what we are seeing is the life that someone not
of faith would live."[43] This perspective, echoed elsewhere online,
treats the series as a morality tale that captures God's point of
view. As one posting on tv.com noted, "God thinks she is worth
saving so who wants to argue that point?"[44]

Other viewers, less concerned with the divine perspective, are
pleased to see a very human character on television. "For those
of us who once lived life in the fast lane, that needed to be helped
. . . we love you Grace."[45] Female cops feel special empathy: "We
cuss, we drink, we make stupid, risky sexual decisions. We find it
impossible to commit because we find it impossible to trust. We
doubt God is actually up there but so would you if you saw what
we see." In closing, the post notes, "A vagina ain't a halo,"[46] a sentiment subversive of religious gender norms and shared by viewers
who decry a double standard that condemns Grace for behaviors
that would be acceptable for men. "I've been wondering about the
equality question for a long time. Why is Grace 'slutty' but there
are few comments about Butch or Ham, or any of the other men
she has slept with?"[47] Some viewers welcome a sexually active
woman at the center of a show: "GRACE is every woman. A part
of her character exists in each of us. We all want to be loved. We
all have felt desperate and alone at one time or another"[48] Others
underscore Grace's ability to care: "I think Mary Frances saw in
Grace what I see in Grace—someone who loves the people around
her more than she loves herself."[49]

Many responses, which can be as raw as the show itself, are
from viewers who themselves were sexually abused. In a TNT
thread titled "Salvation and Forgiveness," Phillip164 relates
Grace's experience to his own, "I can and have forgiven myself
because I have and can accepted God's forgiveness. . . . I have
forgiven those who have hurt me. That said, I am not sure what

I would do in Grace's position. The desire to pull the trigger would be oh so strong."[50] The thread, following the season finale, includes nine pages on sexual abuse, forgiveness, parenting, marriage, finding God, the Bible, and mental illness. Grace's journey has become a starting point for viewers' confessions about their own experiences of abuse and its aftermath. For these viewers, Grace is an iconic figure who embodies strength as well as pain. "Grace is a beautiful angel which fell from the heavens," fans1228 writes. "The pain I feel for her makes me want to pull her in my arms."[51] Deborah195 posts, "Grace is weak/strong and powerful/tender. A living oxymoron."[52]

Not surprisingly, online viewer response reflects conflicted attitudes toward female sexuality, especially acted out within a religious context. But leaving aside negative "Christian" posts, most treat Grace sympathetically, if not empathetically. Her sexuality is accepted either as an understandable response to past abuse or as an expression of physical desire that would be appropriate (or at least less inappropriate) if she were a man. Moreover, most posts detach Grace's sexuality from her spiritual journey; her behavior is problematic because it is self-destructive rather than sinful. Accordingly, once her soul is "saved," her sexuality also will be redeemed (though there is little speculation what that would look like). Grace seems to be the patron saint for those who live life in the fast lane. Her narrative speaks to women (and men) who have been abused, whose lives are out of control and who have seen too much. Her story seeks to overcome the radical divide between Madonnas and whores as well as men and women; she breaks gender boundaries by asking viewers to bring their own experience to bear on a model for redemptive personhood.

Just as online postings "make and unmake" the unruly character of Grace Hanadarko into a spiritually seeking, sexual woman, comments on Laura Roslin and Kara Thrace show viewers making and unmaking the sexuality of a "religious" character (Laura) and the spirituality of a sexual one (Kara). Despite parallels between Grace's and Kara's past abuse and subsequent self-destructive behaviors, fans identify much more personally with the detective than the fighter pilot. Viewers feel Grace's pain; they are entertained by Kara's. The difference may be in the series' set-ups: one is a conventional cop show, and the other is sci-fi saga. Grace feels real, whereas Kara is obviously fictional. God is working on Grace; viewers are not sure who is watching over Kara.

Much of the online discussion about Kara has centered on her fate. Since the first season, when Kara learned about her special destiny, viewers have debated whether she is a Cylon, a god, or an entirely new entity. The speculation increased when she returned in the final episode, "Crossroads, Part II" after what seemed to be certain death in "Maelstrom." In Television Without Pity's BSG thread, akennedy says Kara could be a Greek hero: "She's already got the Hero's journey going for her, so it would be perfect if she were half immortal, like Achilles or Aeneas."[53] Romantique sought a more human resolution: "Kara at the end of CRII [season finale] seemed calmer and composed (especially since she's found Earth and the way there), but still seemed to be her same impish self so that gives me hope we are going to see an evolved Kara . . . still angry and arrogant but less with that chip-on-the-shoulder aggravation. After all, she has a big responsibility now as the Moses for the RTFF."[54] Still others decided she was a Cylon: "Kara Thrace is a Cylon sleeper agent, similar to Boomer [a Cylon model who believed she was human and served in the *Galactica* fleet until she shot Adama]. The difference is her Cylon programming never quite engaged and she remained convinced of her humanity up until her death. This explains her schizoid personality, her superhuman stamina, incomparable piloting skills, and instinctive ability to hot wire a dead Cylon raider and fly it back home to *Galactica*."[55]

"The Cult of Kara," a SciFi Channel forum, continues the debate on who and what Kara is, fetishizing the character and Katee Sackhoff, the actress who plays her, in series stills, celebrity photos, and fan-made video montages that accompany postings.[56] The initial post sets the tone: "come out and proclaim your allegiance to Aurora/Pythia/FifthCylon/hybrid/special destiny or whoever you think Starbuck is destined to become. . . . Show your love for that hard drinkin', Baltar dumping (. . .), Lee-lusting, Sam-marrying, viper-flying, fun-loving woman who will lead the fleet to earth."[57] The post, juxtaposing Kara's special destiny with her sexuality, sees no conflict between the two. If anything, her personal excesses are testimony to the super-human role she must assume to lead the fleet to Earth.

Starbuck fan site.

Likewise running through the seventy-plus pages of Television Without Pity's Kara forum, and similar sites on MediaBlvd and BuddyTV.com, are paeans to Kara's complexity, vitality, and charisma. For many viewers, she is the best reason to watch the series. "The thing about Starbuck is that, more than just about any other character, she makes people feel."[58] Many of those feelings are elicited by the tough-but-tender persona that creates a love/hate dynamic. Thus for every viewer ready for change—"I was ready to say good-bye to the Starbuck aspect of Kara, just not to Kara herself. Starbuck, the side of Kara that was the hotshot pilot, just wasn't working for Kara any longer"[59]—another is content with the way things were—"There is a certain comfort we all get from Kara's behavior in the past . . . it's like a lot of us can relate to certain struggles . . . She has issues with the deaths of friends, issues with her upbringing, issues with her mother, issues with god, issues with her friends and lovers and, most of all, issues with self-control."[60] As with Grace, viewers are drawn to Kara because of her flaws; her internalization of past abuse and its manifestation in her macho behavior, including her sexuality, is central to her strength. Unlike Grace, and because she is a "fictional, non-Christian" character, Kara's special destiny is less fraught. Viewers are caught up in speculation of who or what she is, but they are not debating or relating to the steps to her salvation.

Of the three characters, Laura Roslin is the most paradigmatic. Hillary Clinton, in her historic run for the White House, could have learned a thing or two from the Colonials' female president. On two key counts—gender and religion, Laura has turned potential liabilities into great strengths by embodying a pragmatic maternalism with a whiff of sexuality. She also has the advantage of being seen within a sci-fi tradition of strong women leaders. Posts on Television Without Pity may compare her to Winston Churchill, but she is still situated among fictional peers: "The idea of Roslin being female never really struck me as particularly important because I cut my teeth on sci-fi where Janeway commanded, Scully saved the day and Xena kicked everyone's butt. Roslin just seemed to me to be a conglomeration of every successful and admirable leader I'd ever read about, with a dash more compassion."[61] For many viewers, Roslin anchors the series: "She has the most qualities that you or I would ideally like to have. She's capable of growth under circumstances that might crush most people, is empathetic, strong, vulnerable, warm, can be ruthless when necessary, is practical but has a strong spiritual bent."[62]

According to viewers, Roslin's spirituality, unlike Kara's special destiny, is worn lightly. She is a believable prophet, but the role does not define her. Writes bluedevilblue, "She was deeply uncomfortable with the blessing stuff and used religion in a very calculated way to get what she needed. . . . Scripture or no,

Laura Roslin fan site.

however, Laura clearly sees her purpose as saving humanity."[63] Says tenblade: "Even with her prophet status, her attitude is, 'This is real, this will happen, there's no changing destiny,' . . . She's not running around saying, 'Worship me!'"[64] But if viewers have little trouble reconciling Laura's presidential and prophetic roles (and appreciating how well she handles both), they seem worried about her underutilized sexuality. In December 2006, bluedevilblue posted: "I'm going to be very upset if the female president goes this entire series without having a lover because—for a show that likes to pat itself on the back for how progressive it is in terms of gender—the sexless powerful woman is quite the stereotype."[65]

But in the absence of just such a storyline—other than low-key cuddling with Adama[66]—Laura has not had a serious romance in any of the three seasons, and viewers have taken matters into their own hands. On forums, message boards, and designated Web sites, posts offer a range of possibilities, including hook-ups with Adama, his son Lee, Tom Zarek (Laura's one-time nemesis), Gaius Baltar (who won the presidency from her at the end of season 2), and Kara Thrace. These speculations and others come to fruition in online stories that detail Laura's sexual adventures. Survival Instinct, a site for William Adama and Laura Roslin fan fiction, has more than eight-hundred stories by almost two-hundred authors. Ranging from action and angst to parody, romance, and smut, many offerings are crossover, as is the "drablet" (very short story) "Call Back in an Hour." Humorous and smutty, the story starts when a phone call interrupts serious business between the president and the admiral:

> Bill buried his face in Laura's sweaty hair as it curled around
> her neck and inhaled her scent as they moved together.
> "Gods, Bill . . ."
> Laura's breathy encouragements were interrupted by the
> shrill ring of the phone.[67]

Likewise, at Chamalla Dreams,[68] fans post fictional encounters for Laura, and at Chilipland, a sole author imagines Laura's romantic liaisons during the Colonials' stay on New Caprica. "Just an ordinary woman, a schoolteacher once again, separated from her Admiral, this tale is based on my imaginings of what Laura's

year on New Caprica was really like."[69] At Laurelleaves, supporters of a Laura/Lee Adama coupling spin fantasies,[70] and at Laura
Roslin Fanfic, the president gets to have her way with Lee or any
other character except Admiral Adama.[71] The online *Battlestar
Galactica* world is ripe with games, fan fiction, and videos of all
sorts, but the breadth and depth of offerings on Laura's couplings
are noteworthy. Viewers want her to have a sex life; they want
her to be fully human. Her status as a political leader and a religious prophet do not square the circle for a character who is so
obviously gendered female. (Many posts on SciFi.com's Cult of
Laura[72] thread reference the physical appeal of Mary McDonnell,
the actress who plays Laura Roslin. This is a Madonna whose fans
want a bit more whore.)

As for Rhetta, the other designated Madonna, there are far
fewer posts than for the other three. Fans like her, but she has
not stirred the same strong passion. Perhaps her persona is too
balanced: she is a happily married woman with an interesting
career. She herself is not called but gladly helps Grace discover
her mission. Unlike the others, Rhetta does not need to overcome
the dichotomies of spirituality and sexuality nor does she have to
account to a higher calling. But if postings are an indicator, the
conclusion to be reached is that this most fully realized character
generates the least heat.

"Your Calling Is Calling . . ." —Monster.com

Kara, Laura, Grace, and Rhetta resonate with viewers because their
struggles mirror problems real women face every day. Kara and
Grace prove that blondes do not have more fun: their pain, loneliness, and self-destructiveness belie the cliché. Laura and Rhetta
are responsible grown-ups immersed in nurturing relationships,
but their lives look a little boring. The archetypes of Madonna
and whore inscribed upon these characters suggest that, whether
in space or on Earth, women may seem to transcend some gender
roles—as pilots, presidents, prophets, or seers—but other stereotypes are hard to shake. Nevertheless, on *Battlestar Galactica* and
Saving Grace, one stereotype has been subverted: women who are
sexual, physical, and broken are "called" for a special purpose. For
Kara, it is to lead the fleet to Earth; for Grace, it is to heal herself.

In Grace and Kara's worlds, faithfulness does not come from purity or selflessness but through struggle. Only in the muck and mire of their messy lives are their purposes revealed and their spiritual callings affirmed. When they lose their way, their Madonna counterparts, Laura and Rhetta, provide the foundation, confirmation, and direction for their calling. For all four women, spiritual partnerships benefit not only one another but all those around them.

What then do these series and viewers' responses say about cultural attitudes regarding strong women characters on post-9/11 American television? We believe that Kara, Laura, Grace, and Rhetta allow both men and women to identify with gender traits that can transcend traditional binaries, opening a new space for what it means to be a spiritual person. If in the past religion inscribed many sorts of gender constraints, *Battlestar Galactica* and *Saving Grace* pull some of these apart, inverting traditional roles and turning the whore into a spiritual woman. Read into today's world, these fictional women argue that their real-life counterparts can protect and defend, shoot and kill, preach and prophesy, copulate and kick butt as well as any man. However, some stereotypes still need overhauling. In the next iteration of these series, perhaps, women will not need to be whores in order to become saviors.

SECTION III

Revelation

11

"チアリーダーを救え、世界を救え!"
"Chiariidaa o Sukue, Sekai o Sukue!"
Nuclear Dread and the Pokémonization of
American Religion in Season One of Heroes

Rudy V. Busto

*I'm not sure we fully grasp the devastating, world changing impact of a
nuclear attack. . . . If a ten-kiloton nuclear device goes off in mid-town
Manhattan on a typical work-day, it could kill more than half a million
people. Beyond the immediate deaths and the lives that would be shortened
by radioactive fallout, the casualty list would also include civil liberties,
privacy, and the world economy.*
–Senator Sam Nunn, on the scenario of nuclear detonation
in New York City.[1]

In post-9/11 America we again fear the bomb. We are worried
about a dirty bomb at the hands of a homegrown Al-Qaida oper-
ative, threatened by a foreign madman president who probably
has the bomb, and anxious about an Islamic nation's plutonium
enrichment program. We see our annihilation again and again in
the imagined worlds of television and cinema. The trailer for CBS'
Jericho begins with the ominous but silent mushroom cloud in the
distant prairie on a cold spring day in Kansas. *Terminator: The
Sarah Connor Chronicles* hits us with both the cloud and the shock
wave at the end of its pilot episode. Fox's hit show *24* has been
mostly successful at diverting our destruction from the bomb. Jack
Bauer, America's *übermensch* hero, forestalls the blast in season 2

(2002) only to have the California city of Valencia flattened in season 6 (2007). When a plot by Russian and Arab extremists to detonate five more explosives is uncovered, Bauer ferrets out the bad guys, finds the hidden bombs, and gets the girl all in the course of his day at the office. Our most recent TV nuclear scare we relive on the wildly popular *Heroes*, where the bomb is a human being with the will and power to nuke Manhattan.

This chapter examines how the post-9/11 telefantasy *Heroes* links the fear of the bomb to current trends in American culture and spirituality. First, as a televised expression of "secular apocalypticism" *Heroes* preaches the spiritual authority of the individual, displacing the need for transcendent agents or institutions for empowerment and species salvation. Second, as science fiction *Heroes* addresses public anxieties over race and immigration by encoding race/nationality differences in the extraordinary characterizations of otherwise "ordinary" people. The diverse cast and plot of *Heroes* work to revisualize the myth of prescriptive multiculturalism by displacing the fear of the other onto the threat of species extinction by nuclear detonation. Third, *Heroes* promotes a diffuse orientalist fascination with Asian cultures and spiritualities consonant with the "new spirituality" as a strategy to cope with national anxieties over nuclear power. The show's production and deployment of "oriental" cues serve as reminders of the healing powers of Asian religions. These palliative functions *Heroes* accomplishes through the viewers' expectations attached to the Asian actors/characters in the show, the American fetish for things oriental, and in the juxtaposition of American television tropes with Japanese popular cultural import forms and their instantiations (*Pokémonization*) in the United States.

Save the Cheerleader, Save the Ratings?

I was thinking about how crazy the world is right now, and how everybody has a collective feeling that something's got to give. And that steered me toward the idea of superheroes. But I was interested in their actual lives—how, if you actually woke up and could fly or something, you wouldn't suddenly don a spandex suit and go around fighting crime.
—Tim Kring, creator of *Heroes*[2]

"Yatta!" Hiro Nakamura raises his hands in utter joy and triumph. He is standing in the middle of Times Square when a split second before he was riding a crowded train in Tokyo. Hiro's newly discovered ability to leave and enter the space/time continuum, and the ability by other ordinary human beings to perform extraordinary feats is the hook for NBC's Monday night prime-time hit, *Heroes.* Capturing 13.3 million viewers for its time slot and winning the attention of its key demographic target (adults 18–49) in its first three weeks in 2006, *Heroes* "posted the highest rating for any NBC drama premiere in five years."[3] At a time when prime time is littered with the wreckage of reality competitions and formula sitcoms, the success of *Heroes* speaks to the continuing power of science fiction on the television screen.

With its haunting voice-over reminiscent of Rod Serling's cagey introductions to the *Twilight Zone,* or the ominous takeover of our television sets by the mysterious "we" in the *Outer Limits, Heroes* is a link for the upper end of its target audience back to the golden age of TV science fiction. The sneaking suspicion that the writers of *Heroes* are not telling us everything connects us, within more recent memory, to the 1990s' brainy and sensuous *X-Files.* And like the *X-Files* the show's characters and mysteries have spawned an Internet galaxy of Web sites that dissect with excruciating detail the minutiae of each episode, each character, the objects on the sets, and theorize over what is yet to be revealed. The impressive, if somewhat obsessive, Wiki Heroes Web site attests to the seduction and power of a television drama about a group of unlikely and unwilling superheroes. *Heroes* is a masterfully engineered multilayered drama that, like all good science fiction, builds upon the successes of its predecessors in print, film, and television—in this instance numerous tie-ins to *Star Trek,* comic books, *X-Men,* and role-playing games—allowing us to see ourselves from a distance and comment on our deepest fears and fantasies.

Driven by a complicated interconnected set of plots, the main story of *Heroes* is the threat of New York City's destruction by a suicide nuclear bomber. We are introduced to the extraordinary abilities of ordinary people engaged in their everyday routines: a Japanese salaryman at his desk tries mentally to make his desk clock turn backward; a high-school cheerleader gets her friend to video her suicide attempts, and at each instance makes a full recovery; a policeman begins to hear other people's thoughts; a drugged-out artist paints the future; a congressional candidate can fly; an online sex worker sees her alter ego in reflected surfaces. Trying to find these individuals possessing mysterious powers is Dr. Mohinder Suresh, the Indian geneticist in search of the how and why origins of the others' extraordinary abilities. What we learn along with Mohinder is that these individuals with superpowers represent the tiniest percentage of human beings at the tipping point of evolution.[4] Mohinder's philosophical voice-overs in each episode ponder with us the moral consequences of humanity's inevitable biological evolution. What can it mean to humanity that some of us can do what the gods do? Eventually the characters' predicaments intersect as they try to understand their powers and work together to avoid a nuclear blast by one of their own.

Of course there are sinister figures introduced early in the show, some of whom do not claim extraordinary abilities but know more than they let on: the man with the horn-rimmed glasses (or "HRG," reminiscent of "Cigarette Smoking Man" in the *X-Files*); the mute Haitian with the power to erase your memory; the young female shapeshifter; the billionaire mobster; the girl next door whose voice commands are irresistible. In episode 8 ("Six Months Ago"), we meet the watchmaker, Gabriel Gray, with the gift of "intuitive aptitude" that allows him to understand how things and systems work. After he is transformed into the villain Sylar, his power leads him on a murderous quest to absorb other characters' super abilities by taking their brains. The combined effort of the other characters to keep Claire Bennet, the cheerleader with the power of cell regeneration, safe from Sylar provides the show's popular catchphrase, "Save the cheerleader, save the world!"

Heroes season 1 is compelling TV because each week's episode generates more questions than can be answered in an hour and initiates the buzz about the show in the intervening days between episodes. In the era after the fall of the World Trade Center towers and the hijacking of Flight 93 we want to identify with these heroes, see them win and catch the bad guys. That we have to wait for each weekly installment only builds hope and suspense. Those of us who cannot wait can replay episodes on NBC's Web site, browse and contribute to the fan sites (seventy-six listed on the Wiki Heroes site alone at the time of this writing), or download podcasts and interviews with cast members and production staff. But unlike the masked and costumed comic book and Saturday morning heroes, or the wannabe superheroes on the reality show *Who Wants to Be a Superhero?* Hiro Nakamura and the other "evolved humans" on the show eschew the mask and cape; refusing the anonymity imposed by them or the rebirth of their identities suggested by bodies hidden underneath the spandex. They are just like us—or almost like we ordinary people, most without the desire to be a superhero but tantalized by the prospect.

Ground Zero/Patient Zero: Prime-Time Apocalypse

And if we could mark that single moment in time—that first hint of the prophecy of approaching danger. . . if we had done anything differently, could it have been stopped? Or was the die long ago cast? And if we could go back, alter its course, stop it from happening, would we?
—Mohinder Suresh voice-over ("Six Months Ago")

. . . we hear a clock saying tick-tock, tick being a beginning and tock an ending, so constituting a tiny genesis and a tiny apocalypse.[5]
—Frank Kermode

Boom! —Sylar ("Landslide")

When Isaac Mendez, the "pre-cognition" artist, reveals New York City's destruction in a painting on the floor of his studio we are drawn into nuclear dread. When Hiro transports us forward to 8 November 2006, the day of the bomb blast, the billowing clouds of Manhattan's destruction rush towards us. When Sylar discovers he has acquired the power to emit radiation, his plot to find and kill the other evolved humans takes on epic dimensions. As post-9/11 viewers, we inhabit the apocalyptic fear expressed in these scenes through a familiar discomfort.

Our anxiety is elevated as we time travel with Hiro five years past the bomb's destruction to find installed a repressive government. President Petrelli's administration has successfully passed the Linderman Act in the wake of the blast, creating an apartheid and genocidal pogrom against evolved citizens who are blamed for the catastrophe. If we know that a eugenist, security-obsessed government awaits us, this glimpse into dystopic postbomb America adds urgency to our desire to know that our heroes can and will thwart apocalypse. As with other cinematic and televised apocalypses, *Heroes* responds to a gnawing unease over catastrophes real (Three Mile Island, Chernobyl, 9/11, Katrina), imagined (tsunami, asteroid, Y2K, anthrax), and likely (earthquake, global warming, nuclear detonation).

In his examination of fin-de-siécle apocalyptic films, Conrad Ostwalt argues that these catastrophe narratives have been formed by and then transformed within a secularized context, removing any role for God in determining the outcome. Left to our own devices—or usually because of them—human beings both create and avert cataclysmic doom.[6] "Secular apocalypses" snatch us away from the comfort of traditional Christian understandings and expectations that God will save us from sinister powers and principalities beyond our control. Without the guiding principles of traditional faith or hope of redemption for the chosen, it is only through cooperation, moral fortitude, and if we are lucky, the heroes among us with extraordinary powers that can save us. *Heroes* is such a post-Christian secular apocalypse.

The traditional Christian apocalypse is scheduled at the end of a linear timeline, and we are the timekeepers. Christian time marches us inexorably toward apocalypse and the drawing close of history. We participate in winding this preset eschatological alarm clock through our ordering, scale, and routines of seconds, minutes, and hours as part of how we make sense of the world and control chaos. Literary critic Frank Kermode has described this human temporal imposition as "a tick-tock organization upon the constant tick-tock sound a clock makes. This tick-tock becomes a concord of time even though the time interval between the tock and the tick is the same as that between the tick and the tock."[7] The apocalyptic drama, Kermode argues, requires "sense-making paradigms, relative to time," into "concords," that is, the harmonious pattern of regularity that is reliable, anticipated, and perhaps even comforting. On the other hand, secular apocalypses are not preordained to the regular tick-tock countdown to the *dies irae*, and science fiction films and TV dramas about them are free from the constraints of coherent chronological narratives.[8]

This battle over temporal coherence we see in *Heroes'* opposing conceptions of time. When we first meet Gabriel Gray/Sylar, he is assembling a watch at his workbench. With fixed concentration and steady hand, he skillfully installs the gears and springs which jump into action when all of the pieces are properly configured. The steady, regular tick-tock of time symbolizes Gabriel's obsession with perfection and setting things in proper order, a mania that is also the source of his resentment over the natural progression of the "watchmaker's son—tick!—becoming a watchmaker." Sylar's comment, of course, references the theologically impotent deist watchmaker god, who creates and sets the natural universe in motion and then withdraws from the affairs of humanity. When he learns of the special abilities manifesting among the evolved humans, he concludes that they are like broken watches, he must "fix." Gabriel's slavishness to precise time and order is clarified when he chooses a watch brand name to fit his new purpose and identity: Sylar. We hear the regular tick-tock of the clock in the soundtrack that accompanies his scenes, and like the watches he repairs, Sylar methodically removes the tops of his victims' heads with the precision of the watchmaker's steady hand.[9] "That sound in your heart," Dale Smither, with the power of enhanced hearing, asks Sylar. "What is it?" "Murder."

Countering this regular, murderous measuring of time is Hiro Nakamura's time bending that disrupts the narrative flow of the drama. Hiro travels five weeks into the future only to witness the horror of the nuclear explosion that destroys Manhattan (cue the 9/11 billowing clouds of destruction and paper through the canyoned streets; the disoriented pedestrians running and covered in dust). He then has to travel backward to try and change the course of events. We are initially thrown off balance when we learn that Hiro has not only jumped from Tokyo to New York City, but he has also leapt from October 2 to November 8. Worse, Hiro cannot always control when and where he is transported, effectively removing any semblance of human control in the post-9/11 era of suicide bombers, car bombs, and homegrown terrorist cells. That is, even if we can replay history, there is no guarantee we can change it. Hiro's time travel strategy to save his girlfriend Charlie from being murdered does nothing to alter the fact of her death from a blood clot in her brain in any alternate future. As viewers, we have to wait until halfway into the season to be transported back six months to learn the histories of the other characters and the contexts for the rapidly overlapping miniplots.

If the human ordering of time assists in creating meaning out of chaos and forging coherence in having beginnings, middles, and endings, then *Heroes*—with its competing versions of time (and thus competing versions of possible futures)—exposes a world without confidence and open to catastrophe.[10] We see the struggle between Sylar's deadly "tick-tock" order and Hiro's freewheeling in the first instance of Hiro's time bending: it is the second hand on an analog desk clock that he turns back; while Sylar is never able to acquire Hiro's time travel ability. As "patient zero" on Chandra Suresh's list of identified evolved humans, Sylar is the "template" and "key" to the evolutionary singularity, the time event that flings humanity into an uncertain and morally ambiguous new species being driven by an amoral biology. "I'm a natural progression of the species," quips Sylar to Mohinder Suresh ("Parasite"). And later, "I had a reason—to take what others didn't deserve. It was natural selection" ("The Hard Part").

The disjunctive time element in *Heroes* also supports science fiction's nostalgia function.[11] Observe, for example, that the show does not offer us any fancy or futuristic technology, features we expect in science fiction. In a sense, the characters with their superpowers are the technology (for instance, Nathan Petrelli's "rocket" flying that includes the cartoonish puff of smoke), and much of the viewer's pleasure comes from the "hidden" technology of the computer-generated effects and television editing. Instead of high-tech, nostalgia is built into *Heroes* to teleport viewers back to a less dangerous pre-9/11 era and thus promote one of the show's attractions: as we travel into the past with the heroes, maybe we can avert (the 9/11) catastrophe. Science fiction author and critic, Adam Roberts tells us that "S[cience] F[iction] does not project us into the future; it relates to us stories about our present, and more importantly about the past that has led to this present. Counter-intuitively, S[cience] F[iction] is a historiographic mode, a means of symbolically writing about history."[12] As such, *Heroes* provides us with plenty of visual reminders of our recent past through semianachronisms such as the analog clock on Hiro's desk, Chandra Suresh's old fashioned Panasonic answering machine, cassette tapes, Jessica's 1966 Cadillac,[13] a 1970s Gremlin, horn-rimmed glasses, the small-town setting of Odessa, the high school homecoming event, the visualizing of 1980s Japanese corporate "salaryman" culture, references to *Star Trek*, spot songs in the soundtrack (e.g., Roxy Music's 1982 "Avalon"), and so forth. We enjoy *Heroes* partly for its cumulative recall of the things we used to own, do, and hear before the morning of September 11, 2001.

Another science fiction writer and critic, Thomas Disch, observes that science fiction since the 1940s has effectively "defused the bomb" by rendering nuclear dread entertaining, tolerable, and ambiguous politically.[14] If cinematic treatments of secular apocalypse are, in the end, forms of therapy to work out and soothe our collective anxieties about epic catastrophe, then the popularity of *Heroes* can be easily passed off as adept and entertaining dramatic manipulation. Despite the numerous twists and turns in the storyline, Sylar's defeat is never a surprise. The collective efforts of the ordinary-yet-extraordinary heroes result in victory, and both the cheerleader and the world are saved. This is television entertainment doing what it does best. And because science fiction is assumed to be adolescent entertainment, the medium and its messages are therefore disposable and without deep commitments or critiques.

Yet, science fiction remains a prime medium for metaphorizing or symbolizing the human experience. Its limitless possibilities offer one of the only modes available to the general public (aside from religion) for exploring the answers to simple but profound questions about the meaning and future of humanity.[15] Science fiction allows us not only to talk and think (safely and guiltlessly) about the nuclear dread embodied variously by Ted Sprague, Sylar, and Peter Petrelli (we are never sure who exactly will blow up Manhattan until the very end of the last episode), but also to comment on our discomforts about science/technology, race and immigration, and the future—interconnected themes in *Heroes*.

Science Fiction, Race, and "Hiroic" Power

I'm just a Japanese immigrant living the American dream and living
vicariously through Heroes. —Masi Oka[16]

Like all good science fiction, the power of *Heroes* is its ability to create a fantastic world in the existing, logical, and scientific universe.
What keeps the extraordinary flying ability of the Petrelli brothers distinct from the broomstick-straddling quidditch players in the
Harry Potter stories (i.e., fantasy) is that something "scientific" or
"natural" accounts for it. Verisimilitude in *Heroes* relies upon what
we already know about the Human Genome Project and the scientific culture that supports it. We can accept that Nathan Petrelli
can fly or that Claire Bennet can regenerate because we believe in,
or at least neutrally accept the optimism and progress embedded
in modern science and technology. Hiro Nakamura and the rest of
the evolved humans are changed through a natural process few of
us question and science has recently unlocked. The possibilities for
human improvement reside just on the other side of knowledge, and
the credibility door only has to be cracked open for the impossible
to be rendered possible. "They say that man uses only a tenth of
his brain power," Mohinder Suresh says to his students. "Another
percent, and we might actually be worthy of God's image. Unless,
of course, that day has already arrived" ("Genesis").

This "cognitive estrangement," is also responsible for the way
science fiction codes, screens, or "makes strange" that which is
familiar.[17] As *Heroes* capitalizes on the very ordinariness of its
characters, science fiction encodes their differences, especially
racial ones. Adam Roberts argues that the continuing success of
the genre as an almost exclusively American phenomenon has to
do with the way science fiction reflects race issues in the United
States. Typically, he notes, science fiction codes for race and other
types of alterity through the "novum" (specific innovation) of the
alien or robot. *Star Trek*, alien abduction narratives, and the film
Men in Black, as classic examples, deal with blackness in ways that
reflect the obsession, guilt, and anxiety over American race relations. Roberts' analysis of Klingon representation across the *Star
Trek* generations, for example, shows that "the shift from villain
status to hero status is marked by a revealing shift in the cultural
sensibilities," that "involves an internalization of the cultural sig-

nifier 'Klingon' into a North American cultural [and racial] logic, albeit one that still marks their separation."

> What I mean is by this is that, from being coded as "Japanese" (and therefore un-American), the Klingons became coded as African American (almost all Klingon characters are now played by African American actors), and more specifically as Native American (the "warrior culture" integral to Klingon life became less samurai and more Sioux: so that, for instance, the Klingon war-cry "Today is a good day to die!" is drawn from Sioux traditions). Whilst neither African American nor Native-American represent the dominant cultural strand in current constructions of "American-ness," they are both potent and significant narratives within that overall ideology. Villain (equal to "un-American") had been made American as part of the process of recreating the Klingons as heroic.[18]

Taking our cue from Roberts, we see Hiro Nakamura's transformation from his immigrant Japanese "foreignness" to the "American" Future Hiro he becomes five years later as reinscribing the American mythology of immigrant success. In his case, Future Hiro's evolution comes with the signifiers of American and Japanese youth cool: a ponytail, soul patch, samurai sword (*katana*), and of course, time travel. Future Hiro's deep masculine voice and flawless English contribute to the narrative of the immigrant's assimilation. Within the racialized discourse and anxiety over immigration in the United States, our hope in Hiro's success reassures us that even the most "unmeltable" ethnic can, over time and with hard work, become an American hero. Still, the multiracial/multinational cast and their eventual triumph over Sylar speaks to the banal plotlines of American television while also emphasizing the empty, optimistic prescription of a multiracial America.

The TV version of Hiro's Americanization is only a part of how assimilation is promoted within the myth of civil religion. This American immigrant success story is completed off the *Heroes* set, transferred to another popular entertainment venue: the celebrity profile and interview. Profiles of Masi Oka, who plays Hiro on the show, have appeared in the national press, and he has been a guest on most of the major daytime and late-night talk shows. Interviews with Oka invariably highlight the Asian American "model minority" stereotypes of his computer programming special effects skills for George Lucas' Industrial Light & Magic (blowing up asteroids for *Star Wars*, Episode 2), his Ivy League education (Brown University, computer science and mathematics majors), and his image as a twelve-year old on *Time's* notorious 1987 "Those Asian-American Whiz Kids!" cover.

On the show, as Hiro develops from the geeky, squeaky-voiced cubicle worker to the fluid, confident samurai swordsman hero of the future, we also hear the transition from his comedic, halting English to smooth American English.[19] Hiro's progression from F.O.B. (Fresh Off the Boat) Asian immigrant to cool pony-tailed Asian American superhero reenacts an immigrant success story that predicts the positive resolution of the season's crisis. We watch with confidence that good will triumph because we know through flashbacks and flashforwards that Hiro's English improves. In the flashback he is tutored by Charlie, an all-American diner waitress; in the flashforward we witness the proof of his hard work as he commands power and oozes sexuality. The power of the immigrant and model minority myths in the show, and in the crossover into Oka's public reception, are seamlessly promoted through their veiling in science fiction's ability to reveal ideological content beneath the fantastic, balancing their true and fictive qualities. But there is more.

Oriental Monks for the Twenty-first Century

What's your system? Huh, Pal? Ancient oriental voodoo?
—Ernie the Weasel to Ando ("Better Halves")

Just remember Hiro-kun: Fear leads to anger, anger leads to hate, hate leads to suffering. —Fan comment posted by "Sarah" on Hiro's Blog, advising him to abide by Yoda's wisdom[20]

A helpful way to explain the success of *Heroes* is to consider how and why Hiro Nakamura is the show's most popular character. Clearly Hiro is doing important ideological work for the audience that is simultaneous with and connected to his comedy-relief function. According to the canons of comic book superheroes, even as the idea of the comic superhero has become more complex and ambivalent since the 1990s, Hiro Nakamura—Asian, without a steady love interest, stocky, and so forth—is anything but the traditional ideal hero.[21]

Jane Iwamura has shown, nevertheless, how the lone Asian male figure in popular film and TV has been regarded as a type of religious specialist, the "oriental monk." Iwamura accounts for the power and long-lasting thematic function of the oriental monk image/idea as originating at the intersection of orientalist notions of Eastern spiritual heritages and Western disillusionment and desire. These forces are configured to demonstrate the specific nature of America's engagement with "Eastern," non-Christian traditions, and the oriental monk figure is employed to express, manage, and work through our troubled spiritual sense of self. Hence, the oriental monk as pop-cultural icon tells us a great deal about the religious ethos of twenty-first-century America: he addresses the fears, hopes, and desires of a society in spiritual turmoil and in search of meaning.[22]

We find these exact qualities in how Hiro Nakamura is portrayed in *Heroes*. As he pieces together the clues that will lead to the final defeat of Sylar, along the way he serves to alleviate the fears and confusions of the other characters/viewers through the modeling of innocence, pureness of heart, loyalty, friendship, sacrifice, and perseverance. In particular, his "cuteness" (*kawaii* in Japanese), an essential feature of Japanese pop culture, fosters care, intimacy, and companionship.[23] Whether in the form of Hello Kitty or the recurrent infestation of Tamagotchi portable pets, Japanese popular culture cuteness works in *Heroes* to subvert the emotionally distant, troubled, and rugged exaggerated masculinity of the American heroic figure. "You're cute," Charlie quips to Hiro as he tries to figure out how to save her life. These values and psychological balms, or "ideological caregiving," Hiro offers to viewers are core traits of the oriental monk, as Iwamura points out is true for previous incarnations in American popular culture (Mr. Miyagi, Kwai Chang Caine, the Dalai Lama, the Teenage Mutant Ninja Turtles, and so forth).[24]

When we are introduced to Future Hiro, the oriental monk's logical evolution is revealed. Having been given the immigrant success narrative, the viewer is now prepared to witness Hiro's transformation. As his English improves, so do his "oriental" skills with his *katana* under the training of his father (*Star Trek*'s George Takei) in one lesson (such is the narrative power of the combined TV, science fiction, and comic mechanisms!).[25] The cliffhanger at the end of the season finds Hiro plopped into seventeenth-century Japan, where he finds himself between two samurai armies about to charge into battle. The leader of one of the armies, Hiro realizes, is Takezo Kensei, the original owner of the sword Hiro had only a second ago used to kill Sylar in 2006. As if to emphasize the orientalism already established, this cliffhanger literalizes the show's connection to the actual "Orient" and the mysteries and intrigues of medieval martial arts in East Asia—the chronotope par excellence for such science fiction, comic, and video game franchises as *Star Wars*, the *Matrix*, *Naruto*, *Avatar*, and the immensely popular spin-offs of Akira Toriyama's original *Dragon Ball manga* series. This direct link to the samurai film genre at the end of season 1 is the exclamation point to the show's orientalist framework.[26] If Tom Cruise was the "last" samurai in the historic opening of Japan to the West, Hiro Nakamura reinvests the samurai trope with its racial origins in the age of globalization and deterritorialized cultures.

While Hiro's place and function in Iwamura's oriental monk typology are front and center, Mohinder Suresh as an oriental monk is less obvious. Hiro and Mohinder function in parallel, but from opposite sides of the science/magic dichotomy. Hiro's powers are "magical" in the sense that they are unavailable to other people. Mohinder's powers—science, research, deductive reasoning—provide another sort of "magic" related to the everyday seeming impossibility of wireless phones, virtual reality, modern medicine, and the Human Genome Project (thus confirming Arthur C. Clarke's Third Law, which states that "any sufficiently advanced technology is indistinguishable from magic").[27] Mohinder also represents another immigrant success story, as he makes his way from India to the United States and helps to defeat Sylar, not with the extraordinary powers of the other main characters but through higher education and perseverance.

We are not, however, the least bit surprised that the show's creators cast a South Asian to play the part of the science sleuth. Racial assignment in the United States has directed South Asians to the media roles of medical and science professionals as a legacy of the 1965 Immigration and Reform Act's recruitment strategy that targeted such professionals from India and Pakistan. Introduced to the American public this way, South Asians in their television depictions were destined to remain medical professionals. That is, if South Asian characters are not immigrant taxi drivers or the bumbling Quick-E-Mart clerk, Apu of *The Simpsons*, the American public insists they must be doctors.[28]

Television viewers have, in fact, already seen this version of the healing oriental monk in South Asian characters beginning with Kavi Raz's role as Dr. Vijay Kochar in the 1980s TV drama, *St. Elsewhere*. Recent examples of the South Asian science/medical whiz include Navi Rawat on *NUMB3RS* (as the mathematician graduate student, Amita Ramanujan), Parminder Nagra on *ER* (as Dr. Neela Rasgotra), Aasiv Mandvi (Dr. Kenchy Dhuwalia) on *Jericho*, and especially the roles portrayed by Ravi Kapoor as Dr. Siddhartha "Sid" Shandar on the short-lived series *Gideon's Crossing* (2000–2001) and as the lovable but unlucky in love sleuthing medical examiner Dr. Mahesh "Bug" Vijayaraghavensatanaryana-murthy in *Crossing Jordan* (also created by *Heroes'* Tim Kring); most recently, one notes the addition of Kal Penn as Dr. Lawrence Kuttner to the cast of *House*.[29] On "real" TV, Dr. Sanjay Gupta fills this nurturing role as CNN's medical correspondent, as did Deepak Chopra, whose 1990s appearances on Public Television enticed viewers with ancient Ayurvedic teachings cloaked in Western medical science.

Here the oriental monk legacy reinforces the presumption that these South Asians on TV, by virtue of their ancestry, are stereotypically Hindu. That they are also science professionals, usually medical doctors, blends the magical powers of "oriental" religions and Western science for the benefit, health, and survival of the West. In a revealing editing mishap ("Collision"), we see Dr. Chandra Suresh on the book jacket of *Activating Evolution* sporting a turban when otherwise he is always dressed in Western clothing; a visual marker of his dual affiliations to religion and science. As these South Asian TV doctors wield their awesome powers in American popular consciousness, they constitute the latest sect of oriental monks, supplementing the inscrutable, aphorism-quipping East Asian monk figure through direct, scientific language and worldview. The powerful *siddha,* or yoga master, now serves as companion to the benevolent wisdom-dispensing, martial arts ace East Asian oriental monk.

But while none of our TV doctors fly or regenerate body parts, they possess the knowledge for why these miracles are possible and are therefore agents of such transformative powers for others. They move between religion and science, linking them to provide the full spiritual value of the former in the container of the latter. Thus, "If the soul exists," Dr. Chandra Suresh says to Gabriel Gray, "scientifically speaking, it exists in the brain." Drs. Chandra Suresh and his son Mohinder dispense their caregiving in the usual New Age venue—the book (*Activating Evolution*)—and the traditional science fiction TV mechanism—the omniscient voice-over. The double dosage prescription of alternative oriental metaphysical therapy here promises that the heroes win because we already expect the monk/doctors to save the day. Monk and doctor, religion and science, these characters possess the hallmarks of New Age spirituality.[30]

Assisting the therapies offered by the oriental monks in *Heroes* is a pervasive "Hinduism" just below the surface. While Hinduism as a world religion has a long history as a foreign tradition in the United States, "Hindu" ideas and practices are nevertheless now a part of American culture. Gandhian strategies of *satyagraha* (civil disobedience), *ahimsa* (nonviolence), and *upavasa* (fasting) have been standard tactics among political activists for more than half a century. More recently, yoga, both as exercise and as spiritual practice, has become so mainstream among Americans that even evangelical Christians now claim the physical practices of breathing, concentration, and poses as Christian.[31]

If "Americans encounter religion constantly through popular culture that confronts them daily" in films and television, then it should not be difficult to detect the pervasive Hinduism in *Heroes.*[32] In addition to the doctor-monks in the show, the production of *Heroes* actively promotes its orientalism through its music, appeals to Asian history, geography, material culture (e.g., samurai culture), and Mohinder Suresh's narrations. This "condensing" of disparate Asian cultures and spiritualities enlarges the scope of the orientalist mystique, increasing the show's potency. The orientalist allusions in the show can be subtle, but they are unmistakable: Ted Sprague practices deadly *mudras* (sacred hand gestures), emitting radiation from his hands seated in the lotus position ("Company Man"). Perhaps the most effective veiled (i.e., nondiegetic) example of *Heroes'* pervasive Hinduism is the Sanskrit chanting in the soundtrack at the beginning of episode 2 ("Don't Look Back") and end of episode 6 ("Better Halves"). Neither the language nor the content are identified; rather, it is the audial, fetishistic sense of oriental religious chanting that carries meaning here. It does not matter to the plot that the text is the Ashtanga Yoga invocation chanted ritually by thousands of Americans daily before moving into their Downward Dog *asana.* A Sanskrit purification text is chanted at the funeral rites for Chandra Suresh, and we see the exotic Devanagari script of the "Great Mantra" blockprinted on the child dream-guide's shirt.[33] Similarly, in episode 2 Hiro runs through the streets of Times Square clutching his nicked *9th Wonders* comic with the *bhangra* "king of beats" Panjabi MC's "Jatt Ho Giya Sharabee" (cleverly sampling the *Magnum P.I.* theme) in the background.[34] We hear the unmistakable South Indian *konnakol* (*solfège* singing), the *tabla*, and *ghatam* in episode 7 ("Nothing to Hide"). The show's credits also identify the South Asian jazz/New Age musician Shenkar, who was chosen to create the "magical, mystical presence" in the music score with his haunting vocalizations.[35]

These oblique references to Indian culture and spirituality in *Heroes* resonate with the American viewer because they connect to an expanding interest in Asian religions and philosophies that began in the latter half of the twentieth century. Popular and academic publishing in Asian religious traditions, practices, and their appropriations reflect consumers/viewers searching for "oriental" wisdom and personal enlightenment. As essential resources, Buddhism, Hindu traditions, Taoism, and their American derivatives pervade and inform the eclectic spiritual beliefs and practices across the American population.

This phenomenon, which sociologists of religion call the "new spirituality," is a democratic form of religious authorizing such that the individual and her tastes, intuitions, and borrowing from diverse religious beliefs and practices take precedence over traditional, institutional and hierarchical models of being religious. Some would add that the new spirituality is the perfect reflection of American individualism and the capitalism that supports it, namely an entrepreneurial, enlightened individual, his commodified practices, and the accompanying accessories and product lines. As a result, we are no longer subject to the discipline of and obligations to the guru or master when we learn yoga, Buddhist meditation, or Feng Shui. We can learn Downward Dog at our convenience from a DVD in the comfort of our living room or sign up for a course of lessons from a menu of custom-made, consumer-driven yoga paths (yoga for pregnant mothers, yoga for surfers, yoga for golfers, and so forth). Aside from the strictly yoga-for-flexibility angle, there has always hovered around Asian spiritualities an expectation—or at least rhetorical hints—of extraordinary, perhaps magical abilities, including healing with energy, levitation, or other superhuman feats. "The yogis in India and the Aborigines in Australia," Hiro reminds Ando, "both can bend time and space. As I develop my powers, I'll learn to bend time and space" ("Genesis"). Under traditional religion humans turn to the gods as sources for power; in the new spiritual America we are the agents of our own power, and Asian religions more often than not provide the templates, practices, and vocabulary for calling forth our supernatural improved selves.

Catherine Albanese observes that the "distinct repertoire of beliefs and practices that acquired the New Age label [has] tumbled over boundaries . . . to become more or less public property. In the early twenty-first century, arguably, a renewed and far more encompassing metaphysical spirituality was abroad in the land."[36] If we understand Albanese in light of *Heroes*, the pleasures we take imagining extraordinary abilities by ordinary people is consistent with her assessment. Casting such beliefs and practices within the medium of television science fiction and the effects of the comic book genre's caricatures, the verisimilitude in *Heroes* is not as much of a stretch as it might otherwise be for realist medical and detective dramas.

In the 1990s, two competing but related TV dramas reminded us that we were not alone in the universe. *Touched by an Angel* offered us the hope and assurance that God's agents would intercede in our most desperate hour of need, while the *X-Files* kept us guessing about who these other beings were and what they wanted. September 11 changed our relationships to these extraterrestrial agents. Because we can no longer trust the gods to come to our aid, we are discovering, along with the characters in *Heroes*, that we are the benevolent angels and sinister aliens.[37] More recently, shows like *The 4400* on the USA Network emphasize the ambiguous nature of human agency in the revelation that the supposed aliens (responsible for abducting 4400 humans who return with extraordinary powers) are in fact humans from the future sent back in time to avert a genetic catastrophe. Similarly, such radical humanism in *Heroes* is bolstered by its appeal to the awe and respect the public holds for doctors and their abilities to manipulate science for performing miracles on the human body. In this sense, *Heroes* connects to the medical drama, another popular form in post-9/11 television. In his assessment of *ER* and the history of the medical drama genre, Mark Scalese notes that the emergency room crisis is an appropriate metaphor for the chaos of the world, where "everyone is in the same situation: Doctors, staff, and patients all inhabit an environment of 'permanent crisis' . . . *ER*'s doctors and nurses, and staff practice heroism on a diminished, human scale. As we look with uncertainty at a brave new millennium," Scalese concludes, "this may be as salvific as prime-time television is likely to get . . ."[38] That is, of course, until the debut of *Heroes*.

J-Pop and the Pokémonization of American Religion

Of course, American kids have long enjoyed dollops of Japanese pop culture: AstroBoy, Speed Racer, Ultraman, Transformers, and the grand-daddy of them all, Godzilla. But the Power Rangers craze dwarfs these fandoms. The tykes currently addicted to the show may end up opening up a mass market for more mature and vital Japanese popular arts now restricted to America's hipster subculture (anime and manga, principally). But they're also the grand-children of the men who dropped the atomic bomb that contributed heavily to the anxieties that fuel Japanese monster media in the first place. Not to mention that they're almost certainly watching their heroes on Japanese TVs. Nothing is innocent here.
—Erik Davis[39]

There is no longer a boundary between orient and occident. "America is more Asian than ever," writes Jeff Yang, editor of a

guide to Asian influences in the United States. It is "a place where
. . . Sonic and Super Mario duke it out on our home video screens,
and John Woo and Jackie Chan reign supreme in Hollywood . . .
the twain of East and West have not only met—they've mingled,
mated, and produced myriad offspring, inhabitants of one world,
without borders or boundaries, but with plenty of style, hype, and
attitude."[40]

My last discussion considers how *Heroes* functions similarly
to Japanese cultural productions after the nuclear destruction of
Hiroshima and Nagasaki brought World War II to an end and forever transformed global culture. By analogizing the psychological
trauma of the 9/11 attacks on the United States to the devastation
of Japan in 1945, *Heroes* reiterates Japanese cultural reactions and
forms that have since become embedded in the United States. It is,
of course, well known that Godzilla emerges out of the Japanese
reaction to the annihilating power of atomic fission. The image
of the giant, mutant, radiation-blowing dinosaur trashing Tokyo
is part of the planet's visual history, and in 1998 Hollywood produced a miniature version that stalked New York City.[41] Anne
Allison's description of the postbomb Japan that conjured Godzilla could very well have been written about the United States
after the September 11, 2001 attacks:

> Thus, the dismembering of the nation—physically, psycho-
> logically, socially—in wartime and the postwar years helped
> propel a particular fantasy construction I am referring to
> here as one of polymorphous perversity: of unstable and
> shifting worlds where characters, monstrously wounded by
> violence and collapse of authority, reemerge with reconsti-
> tuted selves.[42]

Allison's comment about "characters, monstrously wounded by
violence and collapse of authority, [who] reemerge with recon-
stituted selves" is uncannily apt for describing not only the cast of
Heroes, but also the viewers who identify with them. But I think
there is more to Allison's description that goes beyond the simi-
larity of national post-trauma cultural reaction.

To extend the orientalist fascination in *Heroes* that is both obvious (Hiro and Mohinder as types of the oriental monk) and sug-

gestive (the pervasive and fetishistic "Hinduism"), there is another visualization of "Asia" operating here. The impact and influence of Japanese popular culture in the United States, particularly in television, film, comic, and toy commodities is cleverly written into and visualized in *Heroes*. As historians and interpreters of Japanese popular culture—or "J-Pop"—note, such cultural productions over the past half century have evolved in ways that combine Japanese religion and cultures with American popular forms (the comic "superhero" for example) to reveal the fantasies, anxieties, and aspirations of national culture. As the title of a recently published book on the subject announces, *Japanamerica* suggests the infiltration and in many instances the mainstreaming of Japanese popular culture in the United States, even as American popular cultural forms like the comic book and metal toy infiltrated and became mainstream in Japanese culture after World War II.[43]

In the United States J-Pop's all-American status is, arguably, best exemplified by the *Pokémon* phenomenon. This multiplatform, mixed-media children's game involves collecting and battling almost five hundred pokémon ("pocket monsters") through trading cards or video game platforms. Players roam the landscape capturing their pokémon and gaining status as "trainers" through competition with others. Beyond the game aspect, the *Pokémon* universe also includes a television series, several movies, and accompanying toy and clothing merchandise. Anne Allison's exploration of what she calls Japanese "millennial monsters," including pokémon, argues that the explosion of Japanese popular cultural forms in the United States reflects the "recognizable signs of modernity (dislocation, separation, and materialism) reenchanted with spirits" and, I would add, other agents both nostalgic and comforting.[44]

In addition to *Pokémon*, Allison notes that children's programs such as the *Power Rangers* and the short-lived *Sailor Moon* have invited Japanese culture into every living room over the past twenty years. The genius of *Pokémon*, *Power Rangers*, *Sailor Moon*, and to a lesser extent *Digimon*, *Yu-Gi-Oh!* and *Dragonball Z* is the lack of a specific Japan (read: "foreign") referent, due in large part to conscious marketing decisions by Japanese toy and media companies.[45] But the recent flood of J-Pop into the United States runs deeper than these obvious imports. For example, the copyright controversy over Disney's *Lion King*—allegedly plagiarized from Osamu Tezuka's *Janguru Taitei* ("Jungle Emperor" or, in the United States, *Kimba the White Lion*)—took a sly twist when Disney countered the accusation by pointing out that Tezuka's earliest cartoons in the 1950s were drawn directly from Disney. Yet when "Kurosawa Productions complained that Disney's *A Bug's Life* looked a lot like *The Magnificent Seven* (and thus was based upon Akira Kurosawa's samurai film *Seven Samurai*), they did so publicly. And Disney immediately sent a top executive to Japan to deliver a gift and apologize."[46]

So the confusion continues between what is specifically Japanese (or broadly, "Asian") or American in the cultural economy. *Heroes* continues the infusion of J-Pop in American popular and mass cultures—not only in its direct link to the team-hero format (think *Power Rangers*), the erotic suggestiveness of the otherwise wholesome teenage cheerleader costume (think *Sailor Moon*), or even the competition between Mohinder and Sylar to locate evolved humans (think *Pokémon*)—but also in the ways Masi Oka's character is portrayed to evoke the power of traditional and recent Japan and its superheroes.

For viewers whose parents let them stay up past 9 p.m. on Mondays, Hiro Nakamura is clearly the avatar of *Pokémon*'s cute but powerful mascot Pikachu (whose name is a formation of the Japanese for "lightning/bomb" and "kiss"). But Hiro's form and function can be traced back through J-Pop's other "cute" heroes: AstroBoy (note the spiky hair), Speed Racer, and even further back to the innocent but powerful ogre-defeating "peach" boy of folklore, Momotaro, and the plump superboy, Kintaro.[47] As an East-West bridging action figure, Hiro is also the sword-wielding, time-traveling heir-to-a-corporation *Dragonball Z* character "Future Trunks," as well as the master katana-wielding, mixed Korean-Black samurai "Hiro Protagonist" from Neal Stephenson's cyberpunk novel *Snow Crash*—all three characters with alternate/future/virtual doubles. Masi Oka's career as a computer animator for George Lucas' Industrial Light & Magic dovetails with Stephenson's "Hiro" whose real, or "first," life as a computer hacker gives way to the heroic virtual samurai persona with the similar goal of deterring a nuclear bomb-wielding nemesis.

In addition to Masi Oka's character possessing Pikachu's cuteness and superpowers, there are other pokémonizations in *Heroes*. The most obvious tie-in occurs during Sylar's visit to his mother, one of show's most psychologically powerful and revealing scenes ("The Hard Part"). Arriving at her door, Sylar brings her a snow globe souvenir from Odessa, Texas, where he has recently killed the cheerleader he thought was Claire Bennet. In the course of their strained visit, Sylar seeks his mother's approval, asking her to affirm his career as a watchmaker. Believing that her son can be more than what he is, she suggests he could become an investment banker or even president of the United States—someone truly "special." To prove that he is already special, Sylar grabs the sink hose and with his powers freezes the water stream into snow, transforming the kitchen into a giant snow globe. Telekinetically he begins to spin his mother's snow globes around the room, one of which accidentally strikes and cuts her. Frightened at what her son has become, she flees and locks herself in the bedroom. Frustrated and distraught, Sylar attempts to reason with his mother but ends up killing her by accident.

Bringing a snow globe for his mother's collection is a direct reference to how *Pokémon* trainers catch and collect the various pocket monsters used to battle other players. As pokémon are captured, they are kept in "Poké Balls" the size of a souvenir snow globe. By collecting an assortment of pokémon, players can select specific creatures according to their particular powers to challenge other players who have similarly chosen. Players learn about each pokémon, its powers, the other forms the creature evolves into, and other assorted data through trading cards, an in-game device called the "Pokédex," and in catalogs. As Sylar "collects" his victims, he captures their powers, which he then uses to battle the evolved heroes. When Sylar's mother raises one of her snow globes and we see a picture of Gabriel as a young boy embedded inside, the *Pokémon* reference to the evolution of "Gabriel" (the young boy) to "Sylar" (the evolved villain) is obvious to any gamer paying attention. Like the information cards and catalogs in the *Pokémon* game, the list of evolved humans Sylar attempts to steal from Mohinder classifies and orders the powers of his victims.[48] Collecting and possessing these other extraordinary people not only proves

Sylar's mastery and control over them but allows him to confirm through them that he is an "absolutely singular being."[49] Jessica's tattoo of the symbol that marks the show's central mystery, and the double "tracking" scars other characters share on their necks, further bring to mind the game's practice of "branding" pokémon by players to show ownership. As Gabriel Gray takes on the name Sylar, he evolves into a more powerful and dangerous form. He is transformed into a game character, effectively escaping his tragic family life and unfulfilling career. And so the race between Sylar, Mohinder, and the Corporation to locate and "capture" the evolved humans becomes a deadly game of *Pokémon*. "You collect special people," Sylar says to Noah Bennet of the Corporation. "So do I!" ("Fallout"). *Pokémon*'s advertising slogan for the American market is chillingly apropos here: "Gotta Catch 'Em All!"[50]

Erik Davis' cranky warning about the infiltration of Japanese popular culture in the United States has for the most part come true. The circle initiated by the horrors of Hiroshima and Nagasaki closes and winds around again in shows like *Heroes*, with its orientalist allusions and J-Pop mechanisms. Hiro Nakamura, whose name the show's writers derived from "Hiroshima," is burdened by an excess of meaning; a cipher for viewers for whom telefantasy re-enchants their daily lives. Sylar is our post-9/11 Godzilla, who, as Anne Allison describes, is an ambivalent monster: "He is pitied for being a victim, feared for being inhumanly fierce, and envied for being technologically empowered."[51] Substitute the word *evolutionarily* for *technologically* here, and the comparison is irresistible. Sylar, a one-man WMD may have a bad case of *thanatos*, but deep down inside we can identify with his repressed rage, fear, and lack of intimacy in the modern world. To address this cultural anomie, Tim Craig argues, J-Pop offers Americans a complementarity and added value to Western popular cultures: "complex story and character development; frank portrayals of human nature; dreams and romantic optimism; kids' perspectives; a focus on human relations, work, and mental strength—are scarcer in Western pop culture. Western consumers find that Japan pop enriches their pop culture diet, giving them a fuller range of forms, themes and viewpoints to enjoy, and perhaps to be influenced by."[52]

The integration of Japanese and American pop cultures is so effortless in *Heroes* that the "Parasite" episode begins with the customary voice-over "Previously on *Heroes*" but this time by Hiro, accompanied by the screen text in Japanese. It would have been unimaginable a decade ago for a successful prime-time drama to have its main characters speak Japanese for extended periods as *Heroes* does. Beyond its authenticity capital, and as a mechanism to narratively track Hiro's assimilation into English, the use of Japanese on the show (along with the Sanskrit chanting), serves to further legitimate our access to the complementarities and mysteries of Japanese (and by extension, Asian) culture. The Japanese dialogue gives us insider connections to all of those Asian programs on other networks we bypass as we channel surf. Whereas the written Japanese codes for us the "cool" of J-Pop *manga* and *anime* worlds.[53]

Through the *Heroes* catalog of ordinary but extraordinary people, we the viewers take up the magical powers offered to us by the shamanism of television's production and sociological centrality in American culture. The possibilities of superhuman powers—regeneration, flight, invisibility, super hearing, telekinesis, etc.—are no longer merely science fiction or rumored experiments attributed to the machinations of external agents and authorities (aliens? secret government scientists? shadow corporations?). Hiro Nakamura will bend time and space not through the intervention of angels or aliens, but because of the steady and silent accumulation of microscopic tics in human DNA. So will we. Chandra Suresh in *Activating Evolution* argues that "tiny variations in our species' genetic code are taking place at an increasingly rapid rate."

> This should come as no surprise. So-called evolution is just that—evolving. It is an ongoing process with no beginning and no end. As the world around us changes due to technology, shifts in environmental patterns, overcrowded living conditions, war, disease, and hundreds of other seen and unseen factors, mankind reacts and mankind changes. We evolve.[54]

Science fiction's warning that progress in science and technology invite catastrophe is clear here.[55] But the potential or averted catastrophe evolves within each one of us, forcing us to make moral choices about how to use our emergent powers.

In post-9/11 America we are only too well aware of the changing world around us, and especially our inability to control change.
In *Heroes*, science and the superenchantment of everyday life operate in tandem to save our species. Hiro Nakamura and Mohinder
Suresh, our latest oriental monks, not only offer us images of "good"
minorities/immigrants (in contrast to the two menacing black men
in the show), they also provide meaning and succor for us in ways
that leak beyond Monday night. We can interact on Hiro's blog
(which disappeared when he traveled back in time, only to reap-
pear when he returned); watch video interviews with real genetic
specialists on Mohinder's Web site; read the accompanying graphic
novels; participate in the real-time polls during the show; or enjoy
and/or create one of the numerous fanvids on YouTube, which
sync popular music to clips of the show. We can visit a character's
MySpace page, share thoughts with other fans on the show's message board, and supply our own theories about the show on the
enormous *Heroes* Wiki site (which at this writing contains 1,525
pages of fan-created content related to season 1).

This interactivity with the show's production staff, the
actors/characters, and others in the *Heroes* fandom constitutes a
community in mixed media whose common interests and devotion to the show are tantamount to a virtual, secular spirituality.
Indeed, Sara Gwenllian-Jones points out that such "exuberant use
of intertextual, intratextual, and self-reflexive references" in cult
television has as a goal "to erode the boundary between spectator
and the text, saturating or replacing the material world with the
visual and aural signs of the textual world and thereby facilitat-
ing a perceptual substitution of virtuality for reality.[56] This flex-
ible, boundary-crossing experience between the show and the
fans and the melding of perceptions across interactions is akin to
the integrative, Maslovian "peak experience" Sylar claims when
learning about his powers. "A single moment that takes you out
of yourself, makes you feel . . . one with life, or nature, or God.
Like seeing all the pieces of the puzzle fit together," he explains to
Mohinder ("Run")—in other words, a religious experience. This
ability to make believers out of television viewers explains why,
for example, the short-lived Heaven's Gate religious movement
drew heavily from *Star Trek*'s cosmology to construct its theology
and eventually justify its mass suicide (earning them the sobriquet

"the most dysfunctional Trekkies to have ever walked the planet" from media scholar Jeffrey Sconce).[57]

For the viewer/consumer/fan, the pleasures and meanings derived from the endless possibilities of powers and interactions with *Heroes* (a *Pokémon* game trait), is what Allison, borrowing from Freud, means by the "polymorphous perversity" of multiple play options and scenarios: multiplying the distractions from nuclear and other catastrophic dread, and our anxieties and alienation over them.[58] As *Heroes* fans participate in the polymorphously perverse pleasures and mythmaking in the show's universe, they find meaning, intimacy, and maybe even something that counts as transcendence. As Jolyon Thomas has argued, viewers of popular film (and I would add television) are not passive observers but active creators of religious cultures out of the experience of visual media.[59] That is, the *Heroes* fandom is part of the eclectic, supermarket sampling of religions and metaphysical innovations in the new spirituality. And like many other religious seekers, "nightstand Buddhists" and dharma browsers, *Heroes* fans find that their path toward personal transformation and enlightenment meanders through Asia. As pokémon and the cast of superheroes proliferate, evolve, and are thrown into new predicaments each week and season, so also do the interactions and expanding mixed-media options for fans proliferate and evolve. These are the mechanics for the Pokémonization of American religion.

Conclusion: The Power That's Inside

> *Do you ever get the feeling like you were meant to do something extraordinary?* —Peter Petrelli ("Don't Look Back")

> *I will travel across the land, searching far and wide;*
> *Teach Pokémon to understand the power that's inside.*
> *Pokémon! Gotta catch 'em all!*
> *It's you and me. I know it's my destiny. Pokémon!*
> —*Pokémon* Theme Song

This chapter has argued that *Heroes* helps us make sense of post-9/11 America by confronting the fantasies, fears, and desires held by its viewers in palatable and entertaining weekly installments. We have seen how Hiro Nakamura/Masi Oka and Mohinder

Suresh/Sendhil Ramamurthy as racial-spiritual-scientific monk-doctors soothe the viewing public's anxiety about race and immigration and the fear of the future as exteriorized by the bomb and its aftereffects. However, following in the American tradition of made-for-TV dramas about the nuclear bomb, *Heroes* avoids graphic visuals about the effects of nuclear radiation on human bodies or the ensuing social breakdown, effectively saving (deceiving?) us from the reality and enormity of atomic holocaust.[60] Nevertheless, the images of the Twin Towers in smoke and flames saturate our national consciousness, and the show reminds us of this horror with televised footage of the ground-zero cleanup ("Five Years Gone"). Five years after 9/11, the year *Heroes* debuted, we have yet to recover all of our civil liberties and we found ourselves governed by a regime scripted from the comics, replete with scandalously inept politicians and caricatured agencies with names like the Department of Homeland Security. The brave and heroic passengers of Flight 93 require us to imagine extraordinary feats by ordinary people in similar crises, as *Heroes* does. Transformed into comic book superhumans, Claire, Peter, Hiro, Matt, Niki, D. L., Micah and the others draw us in, but not for any philosophical or cultural studies musings about "posthuman" futures (tempting as these lenses are given *Heroes'* spectacular display of superhuman feats).[61]

Heroes, I argue, provides an imagined community through TV, blogs, fan fiction, and post-episode water cooler speculation. The show lets us express and dissipate nuclear dread by drawing upon the resources of orientalism, the oriental monk, the screening functions of science fiction, and the (re)enchanted worlds of J-Pop. Television in this instance confirms visual media's ambiguous place in American religion in its affirmation of dominant values and cultures, while also critiquing those values and cultures by offering alternative ways of being religious. There is no doubt, for example, that *Heroes'* success is in large measure because one of its subtexts affirms conservative, status quo, and traditional family values through its nostalgia and heroic "all-American" characters. The blond cheerleader, the successful (Asian) immigrant, the cop, the tireless scientist, the altruistic nurse, and the struggling but triumphant nuclear family all work together to keep New York from blowing up, and so preserve our sense of order and security.

In contrast, the drug-abusing Latino artist, the morally ambivalent politician, and the two black women whose roles are outside cultural stereotypes are all violently dispatched; the "undocumented" evolved humans (code: Mexicans) are rounded up and removed by Homeland Security.[62]

Heroes affirms the healing, soothing functions of orientalist spirituality for the individual viewer, but it does so in the service of American civil religious values of individualism, optimism, multiculturalism, and now, victory over terrorists. Finally, the show offers us an alternative to normative religious beliefs and practices as it draws fans from across the world into television's ability to "give back to humanity that capacity for experience which technological production threatens to take away."[63] In post-9/11 America we again fear the bomb, but this time we are accompanied by the heroes we believe in—the ones on Monday night and the hero within, an unbeatable team for overcoming the Sylars of our uncertain futures.[64]

You Lost Me
Mystery, Fandom, and Religion in ABC's Lost

Lynn Schofield Clark

"This show is seriously losing me," one *Lost* viewer wrote mid-way into the second season of the series. "Enough with the flippin background character stuff already! Where the hell is the actual story? I am beginning to think they don't have one." "I'll admit that I get annoyed sometimes at the lack of forward movement in the plot," another blogger replied. "But I understand the quandary the writers face. They don't know how long the show is going to run, so they have to be judicious in how much of the story they mete out. They can't go and shoot their whole wad all at once or there won't be any show left."[1]

And that, of course, is a classic problem in television drama: how can a series continue to add enough new and mysterious elements to keep up the interest of the most committed fans while not adding so many as to confuse and frustrate the more casual viewer? In this chapter, I will explore this issue, considering the religious referents in the ABC television program *Lost* and the way in which viewer discussions of its mysteries have shaped the series as it has continued to air. I will focus specifically on the themes of science, faith, and religious tradition as they have taken shape in the text, through the writings of critics, and in the various online message boards, blogs, and fan wikis devoted to discussion of the text among fans. I will argue that as message boards, fanzines, and other forms of expression have become a forum for thoughtful discussions about religion and science that cross faith commitments, Internet-based discussions of television programs contribute to evolving understandings of post-9/11 religion while also providing insights into the new relationships emerging between fans, storytelling, and the television industry.

From its earliest days, *Lost* was seemingly destined to become a veritable popular culture phenomenon in the United States. More than fifteen million people tuned in to the pilot episode on September 22, 2004, with ratings soaring to twenty-two million at its highest point in the first season. The series was that rare mix in television drama: a critics' darling and an audience favorite, a combination that landed the show's cast on the covers of *Entertainment Weekly, Variety, Time, TV Guide,* and *Newsweek,* led to appearances on *Saturday Night Live,* and garnered Emmys and People's Choice awards for several of its cast members. It was parodied on NBC's *SNL,* Fox's *MADtv,* and in numerous YouTube entries. It was highlighted in the most widely read media studies introductory textbook as a series that makes its audience think.[2] By the end of 2006, the series had spawned its own magazine, a series of novelizations, a board game, a wall calendar, and a few thousand-piece puzzles. Moreover, with its numerous blogs, online chat forums, and online-only content from the program's producers, *Lost* was proclaimed as the triumph of the Internet age: the first television program to capitalize on the depth storytelling and fan interactions made possible through the Internet and its related technologies. Each of the first three seasons saw strong sales and rentals when the program was released on DVD, and *Lost* was frequently in the top of the iTunes downloads, illustrating an even larger audience for the program than the strong numbers the Nielsen company reported.

As the series wore on, however, troubles seemed to mount. The storylines were confusing to all but the most committed viewers. Comparisons with the ill-fated *Twin Peaks* became more numerous. And the long stretch between the first and second half of the third season further contributed to reports of a viewer exodus.[3] Could the series' penchant for complex serialization survive the ratings decline? Should the producers begin to plan for an end date so as to establish a framework in which all mysteries would be resolved satisfactorily—or would the network pull the plug before the series had an opportunity to play out its many themes and threads? In May of 2007, just before the end of the third season, ABC made the highly unusual announcement that *Lost* would indeed have a specified end date of 2010. After the third season, its fourth, fifth, and sixth years would consist of shortened seasons of sixteen episodes each. And two of the original creators of the series, Damon Lindelof and Carleton Cruse, signed on to work exclusively on *Lost* for the program's duration.

The Back Story to *Lost* (or Why study television, anyway?)

"Television provides a constantly updated chart of what mainstream America thinks," as one entertainment journalist claimed.[4] Like the society itself, television is filled with contradictory messages that reflect the multifaceted nature of contemporary life. An important reason for the study of television programs, therefore, is to better understand how these media resonate with the contemporary hopes and concerns of their audiences, even as they also reflect the often-unspoken contradictions of U.S. culture. This approach is founded on the belief that, as Raymond Williams wrote, the purpose of cultural analysis should be the "clarification of the meanings and values implicit and explicit in a particular way of life, a particular culture."[5] This "particular way of life" constitutes what Williams termed the "structure of feeling" and is defined by the values and ideologies under which a certain group of people operate, both consciously and unconsciously, within a specific time period and under specific material conditions.

Myth is one word that might be employed to suggest the great themes found in media stories that express a period's "structure of feeling." In its most general definition, myth is related to the overarching themes that emerge within stories, offering emotional resolution to life's challenging or unanswerable questions.

Those who draw comparisons between contemporary entertainment media and ancient myths often note that the television and film industries at times consciously look to older stories and myths for inspiration; older myths become a source of content for newer stories of popular media.[6] Yet the very fact that the popular media draw upon the stories and myths of established religions makes some people uncomfortable. A common argument among scholars who wish to distinguish the authenticity of religious stories from the popular myths of television is that religious myths were more organic in their earlier composition than they are today, as the origins of ancient myths were presumably based in a particular tribe or group of people, while mediated myths arise from vast profit-making industries and their interests.[7] It is important to remember, however, that in order to gain acceptance, myths have always had to incorporate elements that made them appealing for certain audiences and at particular times in history; they have never been free of the interests and needs of the culture in which they were repeated.[8]

Both myths and contemporary mediated stories therefore have two important and complementary dimensions, according to television theorist Roger Silverstone: they are collective, and they are constraining.[9] They are collective in the sense that the stories must be consensually accepted and hence must reinforce the views that are most central to at least a large segment of a viewing community. They are constraining because in their need to conform to the community's expectations, their codes tend to reinforce the inevitable hierarchy within social relationships.[10]

In order to garner the ratings necessary to survive on the prime-time schedule, television must operate polysemically; in other words, a series must be constructed in a way that leaves certain aspects of its interpretation open for the widest possible audience. In the case of *Lost*, for instance, viewers may have differing levels of awareness of the various mythologies and religious traditions referenced in its mysteries, or they may be primarily interested in the characters and their relationships developed in the series. There is no singular audience to the television series, therefore, but an alliance of differing audiences who may or may not agree on what is central to the narrative of *Lost*. In a similar way, there is no singular group of "fans" for the television series *Lost*. Viewers of the television series may engage in differing levels of fandom, and indeed may experience different kinds of rewards, in the practices related to their viewing of the program. As fandom scholar Cornel Sandvoss notes, "fandom is not an articulation of inner needs or drives, but is itself constitutive of the self. Being a fan in this sense reflects and constructs the self . . . [but at the same time is] interlinked to the industrial and technological context of the production of their object of fandom."[11] But it is not only the self that is constructed in these conversations about programs, as visual scholar David Morgan has argued. The study of visual culture "concentrates on the cultural work that images do in constructing and maintaining (as well as challenging, destroying, and replacing) a sense of order in a particular place and time . . . [thus the] underlying question for visual culturalists is: how do images participate in the social construction of reality?"[12] Exploring what fans from various levels of commitment to the series say when conversing about the program, therefore, can highlight both the common beliefs and ideological commitments within certain "imagined communities" as well as the constraints to interpretation that exist as a result of differing levels of interest and the differing knowledge bases viewers bring to the program. Thus, this chapter reviews mentions of religion and faith within numerous blogs and Web sites devoted to the television series *Lost*, from the large forums such as the ones at the ABC.com *Lost* site, lost.com, lost-tv.com, lostpedia.com, losttv-forum.com, oceanicflight815. com, and the forums at beliefnet.org and Internet infidels (iidb. org), to the smaller online discussion groups, individual blogs, and fan Web sites.

So what was it about *Lost* that was so appealing to so many different people in the United States in the post-9/11 world? Critics, bloggers, and even some television researchers credited its popularity to its character-driven storylines and, most importantly, to the fact that no one could easily explain the answers to the many questions the program raised. From the very beginning, it seemed that the crash on the island was not an accident. Perhaps the island drew them there, as character John Locke believed, for some higher purpose: redemption, perhaps—or maybe purgatory. Maybe there was a more sinister reason: they could have been brought there as a part of some inscrutable science experiment with religious overtones. Or maybe they were each banished to the island as a result of one individual's inescapable curse, resulting from Hurley's fateful decision to take the numbers incessantly repeated by a fellow mental health patient and play them on the lotto. Critics suggested that perhaps the entire *Lost* escapade was actually taking place in the mind of one person (as in the film *Identity*, starring John Cusack), or was taking place within a video game or virtual reality of sorts (perhaps echoing *The Matrix*), or was a sadistic psychological test that specialized in manipulation.

Every television program has its obvious precedents, and these film comparisons are part of the context that shaped viewer experiences with *Lost*. So are similarly mystical, thought-provoking series such as *The X-Files* and *Twin Peaks*. Lloyd Braun, a former ABC executive, reportedly came up with the idea of a fictional program similar to *Survivor* when he was visiting Hawaii. Producing team J. J. Abrams (*Felicity, Alias*), Carlton Cruse, and Damon Lindelof added the inexplicable and mysterious elements within the narrative. Yet *Lost* differed from previous television programs in interesting ways, in part because of the mysteries at its core. It was not a television program that provided a singular, comforting cosmology with fairly predictable outcomes, as did other successful programs in the same time period such as the *CSI* franchise and *Law and Order*. It was not a television program that followed the search for meaning of an individual or a set of individuals in the midst of amoral actions, as *The Sopranos* and *The Shield* did, or made fun of the inanity of any such search for meaning as *The Office* did. And although it followed the interactions of characters on a day-to-day basis similar to *24*'s fast-paced seasonal romp through a single day, *Lost*'s most committed fans seemed to enjoy the fact that the program made them work hard. In many ways, the series was more like the video game *Myst* than any television program, and its appeal worked in similar ways. Whereas one could get a basic idea of the storyline by watching the program, fans with a deeper interest in the program could troll through and contribute to online forums, read a book supposedly written by one of Flight 815's survivors, write a segment for the official *Lost* wiki, and participate in the online *Lost Experience* that took place between seasons 2 and 3. This kind of participatory fandom may have been an important antidote to generations of twenty-, thirty-, and forty-somethings who grew up with a relatively stable worldview of U.S. dominance that was irrevocably shaken in the context following 9/11. *Lost* echoed the sense of vertigo that many people in the United States experienced in the reeling moments following that catastrophe. It also articulated key concerns of the moment: in the midst of unspeakable tragedy, who could be a leader, and what, indeed, does leadership look like? How could a society be prepared for events that had previously seemed so utterly impossible? What do we do when worldviews of science and faith seem to clash so completely and incontrovertibly? How do we learn to identify clues to the new meanings in our world as they emerge? How are we to live together in a diverse society even as we come to recognize that the beliefs of some members hold the potential for violence and the beliefs of others can result in surprising and sometimes quite positive alliances? And how can we tell the "good guys" from the "bad guys," especially when the more we learn about the "good guys," the more their actions raise questions about their loyalties, their commitments, and even their measure of personal character?

Indeed, most *Lost* episodes focused on a particular character, interweaving events on the island with flashbacks from the character's pre-island life. This weekly back story gave the audience a framework for understanding the character's current actions and dilemmas and provided a secondary set of references for the audience that was not available to the characters. Gradually, the audience came to learn that each character came to the island with some kind of "baggage": a broken father/son or mother/daughter relationship (Jack, John Locke, Kate), a misunderstood crime of vengeance (Kate), a past as a con artist (Sawyer), a struggle with drug addiction or drug smuggling (Charlie, Eko), a career as a torturer or killer for hire (Sayid, Jin). The audience also learned that several of the characters had relationships with one another that were unbeknownst to them (Jack and Claire have the same father; Kate befriended a woman that Sawyer had conned; Sawyer met Jack's father; the same psychic that got Claire on the plane also played a role in the Nigerian priest Eko's presence there as well).

Lost's creators J. J. Abrams, Carlton Cruse, and Damon Lindelof envisioned the program as one of metaphors and mysteries that would unfold and develop in meaning as the series continued. "This show is about people who are metaphorically lost in their lives, who get on an airplane and crash on an island and become physically lost on the planet Earth," Lindelof explained in 2005.[13]

"And once they are able to metaphorically find themselves again, they will be able to physically find themselves in the world again. When you look at the entire show, that's what it's always been about."

Almost everyone can identify with the sense of being "lost" in one's own life, and all of us have wished for a "do-over" at one time or another. But how we interpret these experiences and the desire for change that accompanies them can be framed with reference to the ways in which religious traditions have explored questions of meaning, individual purpose, and redemption. And these frameworks emerged both in the program itself and in the various online forums and blogs about the program.

Religion in the Theories of *Lost*

"Redemption Island"

In the early days of the program, Christian bloggers quickly picked up on the references to their faith embedded in *Lost*. Within a month of its premiere, HollywoodJesus.com had posted a review of the series, with its author noting, "The mysterious creature on the island reminds me of the Bible passage 'Be self-controlled and alert. Your enemy the devil prowls around like a roaring lion looking for someone to devour' (I Peter 5:8). This time on the island represents their chance at redemption—if they want it," the reviewer states.[14]

The chance for redemption continued to emerge as a theme within the program. As early as October of 2004, one blogger observed, "I'd call it more Redemption Island than the Island of Second Chances . . . cause second chances suggests people regret something and have the opportunity to make it right. Boone and Shannon for example, don't seem to really care about getting their second chance the way Locke does—but their characters may be redeemed from being on the island."[15]

As the first season progressed, episodes featuring Charlie (Dominic Monaghan) were particularly noteworthy in this regard. In one flashback scene, Charlie enters a confessional to consult with a priest, who tells him, "We all have our temptations, but giving in to them, that's your choice. As we live our lives it's really nothing but a series of choices, isn't it?" Charlie responds, "Well, then, I've made my choice. I have to quit the band" ("The Moth"). Monaghan's character Charlie, who on the island struggles with life after addiction to heroin, provided the voice-over for a televised series promotion in early 2005: "How long will it take for redemption? Like the chance to put the past behind me. To start over. Maybe that's what this is. A second chance. An opportunity to earn forgiveness. They say that everything happens for a reason. I wish I could believe that."[16]

Just before the premiere of the second season, Christian film and television critic David Buckna penned what became a widely circulated quiz of twenty questions that highlighted the Christian references in the program's first season. The quiz noted that the last name of central character Jack is Shephard, and in his explanation of the connection to Christianity Buckna continues, "One of the recurring numbers on the show is twenty-three. Psalm 23 begins 'The Lord is my shepherd . . .' Jack and his fellow passengers board Oceanic Airlines Flight 815 (8 + 15 = 23) at gate 23, and (he) was assigned seat 23B." It also included a reference to the fact that one early episode ended with Joe Purdy's song "Wash Away," with the lyrics, " And I have sins, Lord, but not today/'cause they're gonna wash away, they're gonna wash away" ("Tabula Rasa"). The quiz also included more dubious connections, such as an alleged link between Claire's necklace with its Chinese symbol "ai" (love) and a scriptural reference Buckna offered to 1 John 4:8: "whoever does not love does not know God, because God is love." Two questions highlighted the fact that Evangeline Lilly, the actress who plays Kate, has a name and a background with Christian ties: clearly a coincidence rather than a part of the series narrative. Buckna also highlighted the Christian understandings associated with the term *lost*, referencing the Gospel of Luke, with its parables of the lost sheep, the lost coin, and the lost son. Buckna concluded his discussion of Christian themes of being lost with the biblical reference, "For the Son of Man came to seek and to save what was lost" (Luke 19:10).

Buckna's quiz was well-circulated on the web, facilitated by the fact that Buckna himself posted it to many forums and blogs referencing *Lost*.[17] Christian ministers such as Jollyblogger and rhettsmith uncritically posted the quiz on their blogs, and Buckna later updated the quiz to sixty-seven questions in April of 2006. By the premiere of the third season, Buckna's quiz had been expanded to 101 questions in order to include new Christian references in the second season. When (Los Angeles) *Daily News* television critic David Kronke received a copy of the expanded quiz, he reposted it on his blog with the comment, "If you get a passing grade on this quiz (without cheating), you should seriously consider getting psychiatric attention."[18] About.com's Bonnie Covel also highlighted the expanded version.[19]

The Christian referents in the series did indeed become particularly overt in the second season. Charlie's shot at redemption seemed to encounter greater challenges when a downed plane on the island was discovered to hold a very enigmatic set of objects: statues of the Virgin Mary that contained heroin. The statues, we learn, were part of an ingenious plan hatched by priest-*poseur* former drug smuggler Eko—who, upon landing on the island, begins to assume the role rather than merely the costume of a priest ("Fire + Water"). In this episode, Charlie has a dream featuring his mother and Claire dressed as angels, reproducing the Andrea del Verrochio painting, *The Baptism of Christ.*[20] They demand that he must "save the baby." Eko interprets this dream in relation to a Christian framework, leading to his baptism of Claire and her baby Aaron.

By the second season, the theme of redemption, and the links made to Christianity, had gained even greater resonance for fans and critics. In a "real life" interview published in late 2005, Matthew Fox, the actor who plays central character Jack, echoed this theme of redemption, putting it in rather therapeutic terms: "Based on what's happened so far, *Lost* is about us finding redemption so we can move on emotionally, individually, and spiritually to a better place."[21] "Redemption Island?," asked a *TV Guide* reporter in February of 2006.[22] Soon after came the release of Lynette Porter and David Lavery's book, *Unlocking the Meaning of Lost*, which included two chapters devoted to spirituality and the subject of redemption in the series.[23] As they wrote, "The Christian concept of being born again, or 'saved,' even affects characters who do not seek redemption and most likely doubt that they are spiritually saved. When self-proclaimed sinner Sawyer awakens from delirium to find himself in a bunk bed inside the Hatch, he believes the castaways have been rescued. Kate assures him that they are still on the island and finally takes him outside to prove it. 'We're not saved?,' Sawyer mournfully asks. 'Not yet,' Kate replies. Although the two outlaws have not yet sought redemption, *Lost*'s writers imply that spiritual rebirth—being saved—is possible even for those who so far have not embraced their second chance for a new life."[24]

Perhaps because of the self-advertised role of redemption in the series and its obvious references to Catholicism (the confessional, the Virgin Mary statues), a related speculation about the island had emerged by the end of the first season: that the island represented a form of purgatory. Several blogs debated the possibility of this theory. "I feel the purgatory theory may be correct," one blogger noted in agreement with an earlier posting, "as for the 10th episode in the second series, it shows u the black cloud, it kinda gives u the idea of the devil, or a bad force trying to take the religious coloured guy, but it cannot succeed as he has done to much good in his life to go to 'hell' so to speak."[25] The blogger continued, "MY view . . . They crash, the ones that already died have met they're match, hell or heaven, now they are in purgatory, as their fate has not yet been decided, and on the island, all the 'good' people die in a way that doesn't include the smoke, and all the people that have commited unforgivable sins, or whateva shit will b taken away by the black mist . . ." (misspellings in original).

But by the second season, some viewers were quite frustrated with the idea that all of the mysteries of *Lost* might be explained within a Christian framework. As one self-described non-Christian blogger wrote in response to Buckna's third season update, "I'm sorry, but if this show turns out to revolve around one particular religious belief, I may have to stop watching. I might have to stop corrosponding [sic] with you David if this is going to ruin *Lost* for me . . . If it's all about sin and redemption, it was a long road to nowhere, IMO. . . ."[26]

Others expressed frustration at the attempt to read *Lost* as a Christian allegory. When Christian Piatt's book *Lost: A Search for Meaning* was released early in the third season, one Amazon.com reviewer deemed it "a preachy bore," calling the Christian reading "nebulous" and accusing Piatt of committing a diehard fan's unforgivable sin: he got many of the series' facts wrong.[27] Yet not all references to Christian allegory were treated so harshly. Late in the third season on one fansite, a self-avowed "newbie" who confesses that her knowledge of Christianity is primarily informed by *Jesus Christ Superstar* and *The Da Vinci Code*, puts forward the theory that the island may be an allegory for the New Testament, with Jack cast as Jesus, Kate as Mary Magdelene, Ben as Pontius Pilate, and so forth. A first responder writes generously, "Although I think that theory is really interesting, I highly doubt that is where the show is going," noting the many threads in the program that seem unrelated to Christianity: the listening station with men speaking Portuguese, the utopian society, the possibility of genetic mutation.[28] Another agreed, noting that "you can easily integrate many religious or cultural beliefs into Lost, that's what has made this a great show." This example illustrates that it is not simply the possibility of Christian referents that were a problem, but the way in which such referents could be interpreted with a specific agenda in mind.

Perhaps the greatest skepticism about the program's nod to Christianity appeared, not surprisingly, on the atheist site Internet Infidels (infidels.org), which proclaims itself to be the "Secular Web: A Drop of Reason in a Pool of Confusion." By the middle of the second season, a whole forum on this site was devoted to the topic, "Anyone else mildly pissed off at the overemphasis of religion in *Lost*?"[29] This thread began shortly after the airing of the episode that featured both Charlie's dream of angels and Claire and Aaron's baptism. In reply to one blogger's question, "Why did religion have to creep in and screw this show up???" another replied diplomatically, "Eh, didn't bother me. A lot of people are Christian, it would make sense that you'd have at least a few Christians who would want the baby baptized on the island. Besides, consider that the Christian who did the baptism was a murderer and drug runner . . . I have no doubt plenty of Christians were pissed off about how their religion was portrayed in *Lost*."[30] Another blogger added, "I was fine with Rose being religious, and Eko being religious . . . but "converting" Claire rubs me the wrong way."[31] This prompted another measured response: "I'm waiting to see where they go with it before I decide whether or not to get annoyed. It's true that they've had much in the way of Biblical allusions and religious symbolism so far, but that doesn't automatically mean that the show is promoting religion. Remember, the baptism thing was Eko's interpretation of Charlie's vision. Eko is a religious guy, so he took the 'save my baby' to mean save in the religious sense, i.e. the cleansing of sin and eternal salvation. Charlie was raised in the Catholic faith, so it's not surprising his vision would be cloaked in religious imagery." Another blogger agreed: "The religious stuff doesn't bother me as long as it's interesting. It's a fictional show. If it gets boring then we have a problem." Another agreed: "I don't feel any fundie overtones from the show. There are none of the standard fundie themes that I would normally pick up on."

The Internet infidels site was one of the few places in which a blogger observed and seemed troubled by the racial stereotyping on the island in relation to religion: "We just finished watching Disc 3 of the 1st season and I was annoyed by Charlie's change from one addiction to another. That Rose is your stereotypical black Christian woman is also disappointing in that *Lost* seems to generally do a good job of avoiding stereotypes."[32]

In a different forum related to lost.com, bloggers were frustrated that some fans seemed to want to dismiss the Christian dimensions of the series: not because they themselves were believers, but because they felt that Christian imagery played such an obvious role in the series. Late in the second season, one blogger wrote, "Absolutely equal to the scientific portion of the show is the faith aspect. No ones saying you have to believe in religion, just understand how it may correlate to the scientific principals being shown and just like Jack said, 'we have to work together to figure things out' and remember he represents the man of science on the show. Before I get bombarded with the personal question

Claire is baptized on ABC's Lost.

of 'am I religous?' Thats not my F@#king point or problem with the people who don't. I wish to allow a concept simply for a better understanding of this show. If you can read you've already figured out that answer anyway! Sorry for being so hostile, but the messeges written by some people lately have been so condescending to believers that I think it's time to fire back in a new post" (misspellings in original).[33] Another blogger responded in agreement: "There's no way religion or its baby brother psychotherapy aren't important here . . . What we need is a clear-minded discussion of the role of religion in *Lost* . . . In the special episode last night [26 April 2006, nearing the end of the second season] it said a lot about the faith of the passengers and the ability to live on faith. If one were to not recognize the religious importance in the series then they would be missing out on a great part of it all. That's part of the beauty of the show, and the reason it sucks the more intelligent of us in."

Those fans who blogged did seem to enjoy self-identifying as "intelligent." Few of these fans, however, seemed to notice the lack of Jews in the program, at least until Lilit Marcus posted an article on beliefnet.com to that effect early in the third season.[34] "I'm not asking for a whole subgroup (on the island)—just some representation," she wrote, adding, tongue-in-cheek, "Slap a Chai necklace on someone. Give one of the background characters a yarmulke and make sure the audience notices. By the end of the episode, there will be at least eight websites devoted to what the yarmulke might mean and what role it plays in the mythology of the show," she mused. During the midseason break in year three, one blogger started a thread in the "lostaways" forum of lost.tv titled, "Nu, such a mechaiyeh! (aka The Nice Jewish Thread)."[35] Rather than mentioning Marcus' article or main point, however, the vast majority of the more than one hundred posts in the thread were devoted to humorous trading of Yiddish expressions. Jewish fans of *Lost* had apparently found one another online, if not in the series itself.

Beliefnet contributor Lilit Marcus made an online observation about Sayid, *Lost*'s Muslim Iraqi, a few months further into season 3. She wrote, "For one episode, (Sayid) got a semblance of peace because he was compassionate and fair. He showed mercy where none was deserved, which is significant for a guy who has spent far too many scenes getting shot and torturing others. It just goes to show that he really should be in charge."[36] In season 1, Sayid, a former expert in military torture, had prayed in a mosque as a means of infiltrating a former friend's terrorist cell. He is also pictured praying during that season.

Dharma, Karma, and Enlightenment

Notwithstanding the lack of Jews and the singular Muslim, by the end of the second season it was clear that another religion had gained prominence in the mythology of *Lost*: Buddhism. Viewers first saw the number "108" in the first episode of the second season, painted on the wall on the inside of the hatch ("Man of Science, Man of Faith"). The logo for the DHARMA Initiative is then introduced in the following episode, first in the hatch and then on the food supply that Kate finds when locked in a pantry ("Adrift"). Those in the hatch watch the orientation film for the DHARMA Initiative—Swan station, and learn that the hatch is part of a psychological experiment (and a "utopian social — " but here the film cuts off). The Asian doctor featured in the orientation film ends with the Indian greeting *Namaste*, a phrase with religious overtones that means "I recognize the divinity in you."

According to lost.about.com, *Dharma* comes from a Sanskrit word meaning "to hold," and the word refers to holding a person to his or her purpose or moral duty. Hinduism's use of the word refers to one's obligation with respect to caste, custom, or law, whereas in Buddhism Dharma refers to the duty to undertake a pattern of conduct advocated by the Buddha in order to reach enlightenment. It also refers to "The Path of the Teaching," or "the journey of the student that ends ultimately in the alleviation of suffering and/or the undoing of karma."[37] The DHARMA Initiative's logos, which appear in several episodes in seasons 2 and 3, feature a wheel of destiny from the I-Ching.

By midway through the second season, critics had begun to pick up on the references to Buddhism within *Lost*. Writing for the Buddhist magazine *Tricycle*, Dean Sluyter penned an article on the subject that noted the many symbolic references to the process of awakening within the series, including the dilating pupils in the opening shots of seasons 1 and 2, and the references to light and dark and to ancient wisdom. He also highlighted the "perspective-busting" developments such as the polar bear in the jungle and the spontaneous healing of John Locke (who needed a wheelchair when on the airplane but could walk after the plane crash). "What's going on here?" he wrote. "Is mainstream TV really making a meaningful foray into the Buddhist world? Or is it merely rummaging through the thrift shop of Buddhist terminology for the odd hat or trinket in which to play dress-up?"[38] He then pointed out that the significance of the number 108 (the hatch's computer requires that someone reset the timer every 108 minutes to prevent doomsday): "maintaining mindfulness in increments of 108 being a familiar activity, of course, to anyone who has used a standard 108-bead mala to count off repetitions of mantra." He also argued that the character John Locke is represented as a Buddha of sorts: he teaches young Walt that the seeming struggle of dark and light is a mere game of changing perspectives, he notes that other survivors need to relinquish efforts at control, and he sits cross-legged in peace and total acceptance at the prospect of changing weather. As we learn of his pre-plane-crash background as a frustrated office worker and his embrace of new life on the island, Sluyter pointed out, we see that "Yes, even schmendricks like us may rise to be bodhisattvas." The very idea of being lost, Sluyter argued, is central to the Buddhist concept of Enlightenment: "we must be willing to get lost, to cast off the moorings of what we know or think we know," and in the sense that the series continues to lead its audience into its mysteries, it "has provided

A Sanskrit greeting common in India and Nepal among Hindus, Jains, and Buddhists greets visitors to the Dharma Initiative on the Lost *Island.*

a kind of mass-audience quasi-meditative experience" for its viewers, he argued.

Chicago Tribune writer Maureen Ryan highlighted Sluyter's article shortly after its initial publication.[39] Unlike the tongue-in-cheek "where are the Jews?" article published nearly four months earlier, "The Buddhism of *Lost*" article was not only republished on beliefnet.org but also quickly made the rounds on the Web, with more than twenty *Lost*-related bloggers linking to it to their sites in the two months that followed the *Tribune* article.[40]

Despite the article, and unlike the overt Christian references in the television program, it seemed to take more time for the English-language bloggers to sort through the Buddhist references in *Lost*. "Several of the sayings seem to have a Buddhist flavor (didn't one say something like 'we cause all our own problems?'),'" one blogger observed midway through the third season on a blog called, *Completely 'Lost.'* [41] Around the same time on another blog, a viewer made a similar observation: "The Buddhist references in this show permeate everything." He supported his argument with the fact that several of the crash survivors seemed to be interconnected, mentioning also the prominence of the number 108, the DHARMA Initiative, illusions, desire, and reincarnation. "Locke, the Bald Buddhist Monk in the group, repeats instructions to 'Let Go' and goes with the flow of things. And one thing that Buddhism is huge on . . . Karma from your past life having a direct effect on suffering in your present circumstances (i.e. Fate) until you rectify your misdeeds. Every character in this show has some dark past . . . except for Locke, who's [sic] only really significant struggle is with forgiveness," this blogger noted.[42]

On a different blog related to lost.com, toward the end of the third season a viewer wrote that he had become curious about "the Dharma thing" and had looked it up. He then pasted in some information on Buddhism that he had located on a Web site. The excerpted material noted that "Dharma" was the method of eliminating ignorance by practicing the Buddha's teachings. "If we integrate Buddha's teaching into our daily life, we will be able to solve all our inner problems and attain a truly peaceful mind."[43] Unfortunately, this blogger did not elaborate on how he believed that this material related specifically to *Lost*.

Another blogger noted late in the third season that she was beginning to see the benefits to the theory that the island was "some sort of Buddhist Shangri-La."[44] Yet whereas many seemed to find the Buddhist references interesting, some were skeptical that this philosophy held the key to the overall *Lost* mystery. As one blogger wrote on the abc.com forum:

> When a mystery or puzzle is presented in popular culture, the authors have to present a solution that can be understood by the audience once it's revealed, something they can relate to, something they can go back and see how "that makes sense now" or "Sure, I should have seen that!" Basing a TV show puzzle on esoteric Buddhist or Hindu arcane probably doesn't fill the bill. Interesting how these things fit, sure; but I can't believe ABC would be asking its viewers to piece together something absolutely none of them have a snowball's chance in hell of piecing together.[45]

It is interesting to note that this last blog contribution commented not only on the Buddhist references within the series but also on the implausibility of the idea that a television network would employ Buddhist references as key aspects to the solving of its puzzles. And indeed, fan awareness of their roles as fans, along with their awareness of the structure of the television industry behind their beloved series, seemed to be a major theme in blog contributions that appeared in the third season.

Fan Self-Awareness, Intertextuality, and the Structure of the Entertainment Industry

By its third season, *Lost* had seen a ratings decline of 14 percent. That precipitous drop in ratings led some television critics and fans to speculate that the program's many unresolved threads had become confusing and had diminished the program's appeal for its vast initial audience.

"I'm bored with *Lost*," wrote one blogger who had been an avid fan during the first two seasons. He continued, "I thought *Lost* had a coherent story line but we just didn't know what it was yet. I thought *Lost* was going somewhere. Now, I'm not so sure.

Are they making it up as they go along? They've thrown a dozen lines in the water but haven't reeled any in. Every episode leaves us with more questions. What do you think? Anyone else feel this way?"[46]

One fan commented on the pressure this would put on ABC, and what might come about as a result: "judging by the drop in the fan base there's no assurance that the show will last that long, leaving the producers and the network into a *Babylon 5* corner of forcing most of its action into seasons 3 and 4 for fear of not making a fifth season. . . ." This writer went on to draw comparisons between *Lost's* predicament and that of *The X-Files*, which in his view was "a show that went too long and didn't give us any answers." He also compared it to "cult hit" *Twin Peaks*, which, in his view, failed when it strayed from its initial premise ("who killed Laura Palmer?"). Another blogger, responding to this post, agreed that it would be a shame to see *Lost* become "another *X-Files*, but argued from a position of financial incentive that "if ABC wants money from *Lost* they should let it end great, then all the fans of the show will be so happy that the writers answered all the questions and buy all the DVDs."

Clearly, fans like these are not viewing this program with a focus solely on the text. Part of the entertainment in blogging about a program, and indeed in considering oneself a fan of a program like *Lost*, comes in understanding some aspects of the network pressures that contribute to a program's successes or failures. These bloggers, writing as they were on the ABC.com Web site, might very well have hoped to influence network decisions through their writings. In blogs like this, viewers of the program *Lost* therefore analyzed both the textual elements as well as the extratextual elements that go into the creation and sustainability of their favored program as a means of performing the role of a fan.

What is interesting in these conversations is the awareness among fans that the challenge for the program's creators is to figure out a way to connect the dots. Many viewers were aware that these producers did not have a complete cosmology in mind when they started this program; indeed, that is not the way the television business "works." Rather, when a production studio gets a "green light" to produce a pilot and then a further "green light" to produce a series, they are charged anew each time with the creation of a product that entertains and satisfies, yet leaves the audience wanting more. This is quite different from a film or a novel, in which the creator would be expected to have a set end in mind. Perhaps, as another blogger noted, "we have been given the tools to write the show ourselves," and indeed those who write in online forums are doing so through their debates of the various theories of what the program ultimately "means."

Conclusions

What is the "meaning" of *Lost?* Clearly, there is no single narrative, no singular intent on the part of its producers, and no single fan community to construct that meaning. As the series' producers struggled to maintain audience share by providing online incentives to their most committed fans, as they sought through the program's episodes to offer seeming resolutions to questions that troubled its more casual viewers, the meaning continued to emerge. The most committed and expressive fans of the program found one another in various online forums, increasingly aware that the program's producers monitored their contributions. As "networked publics," these geographically dispersed groups of people acted, sometimes in concert, to articulate their understandings (and indeed, sometimes their incomprehension) of the narrative's finer points.[47] In doing so, they participated in what Henry Jenkins has called "convergence culture," a phrase that describes the way in which audiences, producers, and content creators can interact as never before due to the online environment, giving fans an active way to participate in the creation and direction of future media products.

As this chapter has primarily explored the ways in which religion was discussed in relation to the series, a few observations about these discussions can be made: first, it is evident that many of the English-speaking fans brought some understanding of Christianity to the series (even if it was from *Jesus Christ Superstar*), and this informed their ability to decipher at least the more overt Christian references in the early seasons. Second, surprisingly few seemed to comment on the fact that Sayid, the series' sole Muslim, practiced his faith even when its practice was what made it possible for him to carry out the more despicable of his duties (and led him to participate in actions he regretted, such as when his friend was killed in relation to terrorist activity). Third, few commented on the lack of Jews, or on the fact that the religiosity of the cast seemed to echo the casting trends of reality programs such as *The Real World* (the Catholic former rock star, the Muslim former torturer, the African American spiritual leaders, the materialist scientist/doctor, the nonreligious majority).

Fourth, it is interesting to note that Buddhism's entrance into the series occurred not through a character, but in relation to the ongoing mysteries of the island itself, suggesting that perhaps there was a religious/philosophical reason for the DHARMA experiments and perhaps even for the lostaways' state on the island. The fact that Buddhism seemed to be only vaguely recognized and understood by the series' fans may have served to heighten the program's mysterious, exotic appeal, thus reinforcing the sense in which Buddhism is an emergent and important "Other" in the context of U.S. faith and philosophical traditions.

So whose "lived religion" is represented in the stories and mysteries of *Lost*? This chapter has analyzed the ways in which online fans debate the series' meanings, and in doing so, how they contribute to the construction of the series itself. In order to continue to appeal to both its devoted fan base and its wider collection of less-invested viewers, the creators of *Lost* must employ religious and philosophical references in ways that reflect but do not challenge viewers' core assumptions. In reviewing the online conversations of religious representation, therefore, this chapter provides insights into what those core assumptions might be. Christianity, while a recognizable source of imagery and symbolism for many in the audience, is not embraced unequivocally by all viewers, as seen in the reservations offered regarding online evangelical quizzes and other attempts to interpret the program as a Christian allegory. On the other hand, dismissals of the program's allusions to Christianity were met with equally passionate concern. Fan consensus seemed to suggest that Christianity could be a source of allusions within the series as long as those allusions did not support a narrow viewpoint: namely, that of evangelical Christianity and its penchant for conversion or its claims to unequivocal truth.

It is interesting to note that some representations of Christianity seemed to go unquestioned in the series, such as Desmond's stint in a monastery, Charlie's visit to a confessional, and Eko's decision to assume his brother's role as a priest. On the other hand, online fans seemed disgruntled about what they interpreted as Claire's "conversion" and the positive portrayal of Aaron's baptism as a resolution to Charlie's perceived problem. Fans also expressed mixed feelings about representations of Rose as a spiritually expressive African American woman. This reveals that whereas there is some awareness of and ability to recognize allusions to Christian symbolism, certain representations are more consensually accepted than others, providing insight into the contours of how people view the role of Christianity within U.S. culture, for better or worse.

In contrast to the heightened awareness that many viewers seemed to bring to the Christian imagery in the program, fewer online discussions centered on representations of Sayid as a Muslim or the lack of Jews on the island, even among fans who self-identified as Jewish or Muslim. And when Buddhism and Eastern philosophical traditions emerged in the third season, online fans seemed intrigued but largely perplexed. Buddhism itself functioned in the series as yet another aspect to the program's "treasure hunt" appeals, with dedicated fans delving into its philosophies in a way that suggested Buddhism's continued appeal as an exotic "Other" within mainstream U.S. culture. As one fan suggested, however, the lack of familiarity with Buddhism among the U.S. population in effect relegated Buddhism to a side interest. The series stood to lose too many of its casual viewers if its central mysteries involved references to a philosophical system that was remote to the majority.

Reviewing online reactions to the religious references in *Lost*, therefore, reveals not only insights into how the program was received but insights into what is possible in the religious imagination of the U.S. public in the post-9/11 world. The program succeeded among its fans as it represented our fascination with the mystic and mystical, and as it provided representations of Christianity (and Islam, more controversially) that fell within certain parameters. Fans and viewers do not directly construct the narratives of a television series like *Lost*—but increasingly, it may be that their desire to invest in online joint interpretation strategies may help to dictate the direction and level of complexity a serial like *Lost* can embrace. As is clear in the online discussions reviewed above, message boards, fanzines, and other forms of expression have become a forum for thoughtful discussions about religion that cross faith commitments in the common quest to understand and (perhaps more importantly) enjoy the narratives of prime-time television. In this way, Internet-based discussions of television programs contribute to evolving understandings of post-9/11 religion, and analyses of such discussions provide insights into the new relationships emerging between fans, storytelling, and the television industry.

"Have a Little Faith"
Religious Vision in Fox's Prison Break

MARCIA ALESAN DAWKINS

Through acts of faith, they toppled kingdoms,
made justice work, and turned disadvantage to advantage, won battles.
There were those who, under torture, refused to give in . . . [making] their
lives of faith not complete apart from ours.[1]

Introduction

Regardless of whether the walls are visible, everyone is enclosed
in a prison. Or so it would seem, judging from the religious visions
presented in Fox Television's highly-rated and globally distributed television drama *Prison Break.*[2] At first glance, the series is
an updated combination of themes from *Oz, The Great Escape, The
Fugitive,* and *American Idol.*[3] Anchored by a story of brotherly
love, *Prison Break* tells the tale of Michael Scofield, an engineer
with first-hand access to the structural design of the penitentiary
where his elder brother, Lincoln Burrows, is consigned after he is
wrongly convicted of the murder of the vice president's brother.
After he has exhausted all legal measures to try to secure Lincoln's freedom, Michael installs himself in the prison in order to
mastermind and execute the ultimate escape. But a second look at

the broader themes in the series reveals something more—that society itself is a set of walls behind walls and that freedom is either one of two things: an illusion or a matter of having some faith. In this chapter, I will look at *Prison Break* in order to figure out the difference between these two possibilities.

Based on the premise of *The Great Escape* and calling to mind the setting of *Oz*, *Prison Break* goes beyond quasi-realistic portrayals of either incarceration or freedom by focusing on both in a way that emphasizes fantasy and faith. At the same time, the series' ensemble cast evokes the survival motif of *The Fugitive* and ethics of risk, calamity, and victory inherent in *American Idol.* These thematic qualities make *Prison Break* a ripe candidate for fantasy theme analysis, which will be used to uncover how themes such as faith, hope, grace, guilt, salvation, loyalty, safety, and redemption are encoded, imprinted, and translated into the religious visions that shape the characters' lives.

Method: Fantasy Theme Analysis

The theoretical perspective grounding fantasy theme analysis is Ernest Bormann's *Symbolic Convergence Theory,* which describes the ways in which people learn to transcend mundane events and affairs in order to generate meaning for themselves and their communities. Informed by this theory, fantasy theme analysis is a tool for evaluating communication messages or concepts rather than the speakers, characters, audiences, or historical-cultural scenes implicated in a text.

It is important to note several assumptions that underlie this analytical perspective. First, a fantasy theme perspective suggests that "through conversations, speeches and messages, people build a shared view of reality that, while not necessarily objective, is created symbolically."[4] It is presumed that an individual shares his or her fantasy or "story about people, real or fictitious, in a dramatic situation, in a setting other than the here-and-now communication of the group."[5] This disclosure serves as a catalyst for others to tell their stories until the group arrives at a shared meaning and communicates its worldview.

Second, once a group arrives at a common worldview, it is best communicated and understood "through a rhetorical concept called a fantasy theme."[6] The fantasy theme uses symbolism to shape individual experiences and, ultimately, to create a shared dream that becomes reality. In general, fantasy themes are expressed as short catchphrases called "symbolic cues" (e.g., "have a little faith" or "I pledge allegiance to the flag"). Consequently, interpretations, emotions, and motives for action are located in this message, providing a link between each character's fantasy themes and visions and his or her behavior.

Third, as characters share and extend fantasy explanations for the situations they encounter, they construct explanations of reality replete with "heroes, villains, plotlines, scenic description and sanctioning agents" for preserving the vision.[7] These explanations "chain out" within small groups and, "in turn, spread out across larger publics, serve to sustain the members' sense of community, to impel them strongly to action (which raises the question of motivation), and to provide them with a [populated] social reality."[8] Fantasy themes construct complex dramas that captivate and convert the multitudes in a symbolic reality. These dramas are rhetorical visions that create community, solidarity, and induce action.

Of course, it should also be noted that rhetorical visions compete with fantasy themes. Those who espouse divergent worldviews will react to the same situations differently, accepting information that is consistent with their theme and disregarding or devalorizing other information. For example, in *Prison Break*, the characters encounter opposing assertions about the inmates' guilt and innocence and of the role of the U.S. government and its representatives as protectors or oppressors. These fantasy themes connect to the larger visions of Christian faith and American civil religion that are dramatized when characters emphasize "social, pragmatic and righteous" descriptions of their realities.[9]

Critical elements in any fantasy theme or rhetorical vision include *dramatis personae*, storyline, sanctioning agent, and master analogue. *Dramatis personae* are "the characters depicted in messages that give life to a rhetorical vision."[10] A storyline, or plotline, consists of the historical-cultural setting and action. A sanctioning agent is a spokesperson who authorizes the vision. A sanctioning agent often takes the form of a higher power (e.g., God; a well-constructed and reasonable plan) or a political-moral framework (e.g., the U.S. Constitution). Master analogues may be righteous (justice/injustice and hierarchy), social (human relationships), or pragmatic (results, acumen, and practicality). Together, these elements unveil fantasy themes or rhetorical visions, providing a space in which ethical issues and questions of ultimate meaning are played out.

The search for religious rhetorical visions and fantasy themes in *Prison Break* leads to the pair of critical questions that will be addressed in the section that follows: How is faith defined and presented both spiritually and civilly within the context of *Prison Break*? How do these presentations construct fantasy themes that unfold in the plot, setting, and religious visions for the characters' lives?

Visions of Faith in *Prison Break*
Religious and Civil Perspectives

Faith, according to the Epistle to the Hebrews attributed to Paul, is "the substance of things hoped for, the evidence of things not seen."[11] Christian history explains that this principle was revealed to Saint Paul while he was incarcerated, which means that Paul's words are part of the great stream of prison literature. This principle of faith, born under conditions of profound un-freedom, consists of four main components—knowledge, belief, confidence, and dependence—which testify to the idea that what we see is created by what we do not see.[12] It is, therefore, the cornerstone of the Christian religious vision:

> In making the unfamiliar appear in the familiar, in making it accessible as what is inaccessible, religion formulates and practices the worldly situation of a social system that knows itself to be surrounded by the unknown in space and time.[13]

That being the case, religion can be defined as more than "words about God."[14] More than this, it can be defined as words about God that are dramatized in array of symbolic forms, beliefs, and social behaviors that tell the story of the human condition across various historical, cultural, and geographical settings. Religious visions, therefore, become the medium of faith itself by questioning the very definition of freedom and confinement, hinting that even if our bodies are free, our minds and souls may not necessarily escape confinement.

Outside the prison walls, Saint Paul warns us, invisible prisons exist. These take many forms: doubt, secrecy, selfishness, self-loathing, ethical and religious standards, legal controls, government and corporate greed, as well as the unwritten rules of racism, sexism, and classism as well as homophobia, addiction, and prejudice against the physically or mentally disabled. Since we may not be able to see these prisons without a religious vision— Christian or otherwise—it can be argued that we may not be able to escape them; we will remain prisoners of our intolerances and limited perceptions. The fantasy themes in *Prison Break* constitute a faithful attribution of these qualities of the human condition, suggesting that "the Lord appears" to rescue us from these prisons, provided we accept that we "are in need of forgiveness."[15]

On the one hand, this means that faith deals with reality— the way things actually are. This is reflected in Fox River Penitentiary, the setting of *Prison Break*'s first season. The setting is evidence of the unseen hierarchy of shame and blame that leads to imprisonment. This is because faith reminds us that we are imperfect, that "all have sinned and fall short of the glory of God" and that this condition is hereditary and contagious.[16]

On the other hand, faith is expectant. It asks questions: Can we ever know "the truth of nature, the world, the universe, *reality*" or the reality of any human setting?[17] Is the reality in which we live the only one that exists? What I am getting at here is that faith confirms that things are not the way they ought to be and serves to motivate the prisoners' plans for escape. It defies the limitations of visible settings, troubling the ground on which reality apparently rests. Moreover, faith "comes by hearing" and must be present in order for the prisoner to envision his escape.[18] The reflexive relationship between faith and shared religious visions in *Prison Break* is profound—religious vision is the key to faith, which is the fantasy theme that builds new religious visions and allows characters to exercise a deeper and broader faith.

Brief descriptions of the intricate tattoo that covers half of Michael's body and the plot against Lincoln clarify this point. Michael's tattoo is the key element of the storyline; it is literally a roadmap to freedom. The tattoo, which no one except Michael can decipher, contains blueprint plans for the prison, which he helped design. The tattoo makes Michael's plan both literal and metaphorical—a living symbol or text that evolves as his knowledge and character grow and transform.[19] Michael's master plan reflects a respect for discipline, detail, and perfection. It also accounts for every contingency except for free will. As such, Michael's tattoo/plan is a literal manifestation of his faith. Convinced that he can pull off the impossible, he has only to glance at the tattoo to artfully remind himself of his mission, no matter what his changing circumstances, interactions, and emotions bring.[20]

Michael's fate.

In many respects Michael, a nonreligious but ardently focused individual, is the only possible escape route for the motley crew of disciples he assembles. His twin identities as prisoner and savior support the Christian theme of faith, suggesting that a paradoxical freedom is earned in prison through self-sacrifice. This theme underscores the importance of faith in oneself, one's plan, the justice of one's cause, and in the redemptive power of faith to break through prison walls.

This reliance on faith is reflected in an exchange between Michael and his cellmate Sucre. Michael asks Sucre, "You believe in God don't you?"

"You know I do," Sucre replies.

"Then He'll protect you from him," retorts Michael.[21]

The "him" Michael refers to is an image of Satan, whose diabolical power is encoded in an inverted cross or "X" marking the spot where they drill into the wall. When another prisoner named

John sees the same image on the wall, he tells Sucre, "You should never underestimate a wall. Sometimes, no matter how much you try it just won't give in." The metaphor of the wall as enemy highlights the fact that one of the primary functions of a prison is to remove a person's ability to create fantasy themes of liberation that transcend space, time, and institutional authority.

Like the prison walls that receive so much attention from Michael and other inmates, the U.S. government's case against Lincoln Burrows contains many holes. This is confirmed by an expert witness who explains, "Maybe what we're looking for is what's not there. People who do this are ghosts . . . the guy behind the guy behind the guy. It's laced, ingrained. Eyes play tricks on you but ears don't lie."[22]

This element of the plotline also evokes an often unseen religious dimension in American public life: "While some have argued that Christianity is the national faith . . . few have realized that there actually exists alongside . . . the churches an elaborate and well-institutionalized civil religion in America."[23] In fact, the very name "Lincoln" is suggestive of the American civil-religious vision and its fantasy theme of faith that suffuses the series.

Civil religion, like the traditional religions with which most audiences may be familiar, is about unification. According to sociologist Robert Bellah, this process involves both a merger and a partition, that is, who is American? What actions are fundamentally American? These questions can be answered by examining the beliefs, symbols, and rituals of a group. Described in terms of civil religion, Americans can be identified by their speech and symbols—reverence for the flag, the Constitution, the holiday calendar, the invocation of God in political speeches and public monuments; the veneration of past political leaders and military veterans; and founding myths and similar religious or semireligious practices. Americans can also be identified by the ideals they uphold—freedom, individualism, and self-reliance.

Bellah identifies the American Revolution, the Civil War, and the Civil Rights Movement as three decisive historical events that have influenced the vision of civil religion in the United States. I would argue that the plot against Lincoln Burrows in *Prison Break* constitutes another, albeit fictional, event—involving a web of conspiracy that stretches from the prison to far corners of the globe and involves familial responsibility, political power, and leg-islative corruption.

Since Lincoln is paying for the sins of others he, like President Lincoln, can be seen as a type of savior or martyr. In many respects Lincoln is the "sacred cow" of the narrative, one of the toughest and most destructive men in the prison population and, because of his innocence, a redeemable person. As such, he struggles to reconcile a sense of hope with a resignation to death. His unjust imprison-ment suggests that he—a white male—is the primary victim of the series because he has been cast into a "debased" black and brown environment. In this way, his identity reflects Michael's: a heroic man of faith surrounded by those who lack faith.

The plot against Lincoln also reflects the labyrinthine struc-ture of the prison tattooed on Michael's skin. These parallel worlds are reflected in the messages, attitudes, and actions of the protag-onists and by the audiences who might identify with Lincoln and Michael as "normal" (i.e., white male) subjects, envisioning them as embodiments of their own perceived victimization.

Prisoners are identified by the particular behaviors that, we are told, justify their incarceration (i.e., lack of freedom).[24] In this sense, prisoner identity is itself a fantasy theme useful for the study of minority positions or discourses of otherness in U.S. culture. Thus prisoner identity illuminates cultural institutions such as the criminal justice system, politics, and the visual media wherein criminals are represented as "the other" in terms of race, sexuality, and moral standing (e.g., *Cops, Oz, Law and Order, America's Most Wanted*). These narratives often propagate stereotypic construc-tions of raced and gendered criminal identities. Aspects of *Prison Break*'s fantasy themes occasionally counter such constructions by critiquing the racial, sexual, and class prejudices that dominate mainstream representations of prison culture.[25] In this manner the themes of faith in *Prison Break* engage popular culture and reshape the vision of prison life that underlies the audience's reactions to those who are incarcerated.

Prison Break accomplishes this social engagement and critique by showing how people on either side of the prison walls can coex-ist even if their lives are radically separate; they are only able to meet through the bars imposed on them by others and themselves.

This interpretation of imprisonment as a pervasive existential condition is represented symbolically by nearly every window or partition on the show, in which both interior and exterior spaces are often viewed from behind bars or other obstacles. This aesthetic strategy foregrounds the characters' frustrated dreams of escape to an "outside," which may not even exist. It also implies a moral separation as well. The tension created by this separation sets the stage for dramatic reversals of fortune, which allow the series to pose important and interesting questions pertaining to faith, civil religion, and the study of television drama in a post-9/11 context.

These questions include: How do Christianity and U.S. civil religious fantasy themes present religious visions as means of imprisonment and escape? How do religious visions cause crises of faith that lead characters to change direction? What happens when someone "lays down his life for his friend?"[26] How do religious visions and the plans they catalyze attract "the unconverted" who have not yet realized that escape is possible? In the discussion that follows, I will describe the competing worldviews that prompt these questions and examine the ways in which key characters grapple with them as they fantasize about making it to freedom. I then describe how the plotlines in the first two seasons of *Prison Break* conjoin Christian and civil-religious visions by showing that the world inside the prison walls is simply a condensed, stripped-down reflection of the "free" world on the other side of the bars.[27]

This argument is extended through analysis of the prisoners' exodus, highlighting the faithful ideals that relate to characters' moral values—guilt, redemption, grace, patriotism, freedom, and hope. I argue that *Prison Break*'s ideological fixation on having "a little faith" emphasizes that confidence, intelligence, adaptability, and an ability to see beyond what is immediately visible accounts for the characters' ability to survive. I conclude by linking these fantasy themes with what I call the show's post-9/11 "perpetual prisoner perspective." This perspective suggests that the primary cultural tools for understanding events are not simply words, but interpretations of the powerful spiritual and civil-religious visions we remember, inherit, create, and encounter.

Season 1: The Look and Language of Faith

Despite dropping crime rates in the United States, the number of people in American prisons has increased by more than 450 percent since 1980.[28] "In other words, one out of every 133 U.S. residents is behind bars."[29] Depending on one's perspective, this population explosion is the outcome of political, legal, social, and economic successes or failures. From the vantage point of popular culture, the prison population boom has become a site of both cultural invention and resistance, which is reflected in music, literature, styles of speech and dress, and in televised practices and descriptions of prison life.

An informal *Google* search yields thousands of titles based on this theme, ranging from Martin Luther King's *Letter From a Birmingham Jail* and Paul Bunyan's *Pilgrim's Progress*, to *Oz*, *The Great Escape*, *The Shawshank Redemption*, *Short Eyes*, and *American History X*. These mediated representations depict prison as a product of, and a metaphor for, the forces of exclusion at work in the various physical, social, and spiritual worlds that Americans inhabit. Once inside the walls, everyone is a prisoner. In *Prison Break*, even the corrections officers, who are perceived differently only because of the symbolic authority conveyed by the badges they wear, are held captive. This fragile social construction foreshadows a reversal of roles and circumstances: Michael will assume the identity of a guard in order to secure the safest escape route, and corrections officers will eventually become inmates.

Although warden Henry Pope ("The Pope") is in charge, Michael is warned that prison is a world in which the Ten Commandments do not exist. Instead there are only two prison commandments: "You got nothin' comin'. The second one is see commandment number one."[30] The brutal realities of prison life such as rape, suicide, murder, jealousy, betrayal, and mutilation cause prisoners to undergo a personal process of breaking down and rebuilding. In this regard the relationships and rules that prisoners develop through personal encounters with (human or divine) others provide insight that influences future choices. This process is described by Michael's cellmate Sucre as a kind of initiation: "Welcome to Prisneyland."[31]

Religious fantasy themes are often juxtaposed with these "realistic" depictions of the prison setting as evidence that no human system or identity is inevitable, innate, or unchanging. For this reason, religious visions promise inclusion, acceptance, and escape in the spiritual world beyond the walls. The prisoner's ability to identify and cross over to this other world hinges on whether he "has a little faith."

As mentioned earlier, *Prison Break* can be seen as a series rife with faithful attributions, which apply definitions of faith to the setting, action, and characters' stories. Accordingly, the program represents the competing logics of faith articulated by both Saint Paul and Robert Bellah. *Prison Break* is set between a pair of conflicting worldviews that compete for control of the human soul—the physical world of the prison and the spiritual world of redemption, an earthly hell and heaven. In a superficial sense, prison is a model for all modern social organizations. It is an institution made up of many compartments whose borders are maintained by constant observation and identification. In other words, it should come as no surprise that this theme emerges in mass media entertainment. This is confirmed in *Prison Break* when inmates describe the jail as a map of the United States. The cell is "New York City," the "infirmary/escape hatch is California," and the underground pipes connecting the two are "Route 66, our ticket outta here."[32]

The allusion to escaping the United States and crossing the border into freedom is congruous with the observation of a real-life prisoner who wrote, "most Americans remain ignorant . . . that they live in a country that holds hostage behind bars another populous country of their fellow citizens."[33] The prisoners' invisibility and alienation from mainstream society are the markers of an underclass, a group from which audiences are willfully segregated in real life. This segregation accounts for representations of prison life as a minority position and a kind of afterlife in the series. Prison is the hellish place to which lost souls are banished as they serve time for their evil deeds, rarely to be seen or heard from again.

On a deeper level, however, the first season of *Prison Break* describes this hell in terms of faithful language and symbols—particularly beneath the shadow of the crucifix, signaling the powers of redemption, sacrifice, pain, freedom, and light. The show begins during Lent, a time during which faithful Christians give up something they value for forty days in order to identify with Christ's experience in the wilderness. In this vein, Michael relinquishes his freedom in order to save his brother and finds true freedom in self-sacrifice. He enters the prison approximately forty days before Easter, and his plan to free Lincoln crystallizes at Easter, the most significant event in the Christian religious tradition. Not only is Easter a time of endings, it is also a time of new beginnings made available through salvation and redemption. Its foremost symbol is the cross, a facsimile of which is visible in virtually every scene of every episode.

As the most frequently displayed symbol of faith in the drama, the cross is found multiple times on Michael's tattoo, on Sucre's chain, in the chapel, on Bible covers and crucifixes and everywhere there are fences, bars, windows, shadows, and lights. It is even used as the symbol that pinpoints locations when the inmates are tracked by radar technology.

The brothers are reunited for the first time during the first season in the prison chapel under the cross, where the minister preaches that judgment day is coming. This Armageddon is both spiritual and physical, as a race riot in the prison pits Michael against both white and black inmates. While being courted by both sides Michael explains to his brother that his relationship with a black inmate, Benjamin Franklin (a.k.a., C-Note), "tran-

The brothers meet under the cross' shadow.

scends race." To which Lincoln replies, "nothing transcends race in here."[34]

Later, Brad Bellick, a hateful white prison guard, asks Michael which side he will choose. He replies "neither." This constitutes an ironic exegetic moment because the actor who plays Michael (Wentworth Miller) is multiracial. In keeping with the religious vision of faith, however, this exchange is reminiscent of the biblical encounter between Joshua and Michael the archangel:

> Once when Joshua was near Jericho, he looked up and saw a man standing before him with a drawn sword in his hand. Joshua went to him and said to him, "Are you one of us, or one of our adversaries?" He replied, "neither; but as commander of the army of the Lord I have now come."[35]

Michael Scofield is true to the character his name represents, as an interpreter of Christ's message, because he understands that he is waging a different kind of war. His war is for freedom from, rather than for control of, the prison. Like the battle of Jericho, this battle will end when the walls come tumbling down.

In order to win this war, Michael will enlist the services of a select yet diverse group of inmates and civilians who, in many respects, can be considered his twelve disciples. In addition to his brother, he recruits his cellmate Sucre, bank robber D. B. Cooper, and mob boss John Abruzzi. As the escape plan proceeds, it is discovered by T-Bag, C-Note, Tweener, Haywire, and Sucre's cousin Manche. The final main players are two women: Michael's wife Nika—a Czechoslovakian exotic dancer who marries him for citizenship in exchange for her participation in the plan—and Michael's doctor at the prison, Sara Tancredi, who is the governor's daughter, a recovering heroin addict, and his eventual love interest. These women are allusions to women of faith—Mary Magdalene and Abraham's wife Sara.

Each of these characters is confronted with past transgressions and crises of faith that have polluted their lives and landed them in prison. Their struggles for redemption and atonement fall in line with the fantasy theme of guilt-redemption inherent in the religious vision. Within this vision, each person's level of guilt corresponds to the level of spiritual pollution he or she experiences. When this pollution reaches a critical mass, the individual is plagued by guilt. Guilt plays out in one of two ways: "victimage"—assigning guilt to the other—or "mortification," in which case the person assigns guilt to himself or herself.[36] This culture of blame harkens back to the idea of "original sin."[37]

Blaming the other is the psychological mechanism that keeps prisoners from paradise and encloses them in prisons. As a consequence, no one can be set free without taking responsibility for his or her transgressions. The guilt-redemption theme in *Prison Break* requires characters either to prove that blame truly belongs to another party or to take responsibility for their actions, confess, do penance, and seek absolution. As we see in this season, absolution is found through self-sacrifice, enduring scapegoating, or undergoing conversion, and accepting grace through faith.

Lincoln's freedom is the vehicle for his redemption, as well as Michael's, because Lincoln is the primary scapegoat. According to the religious fantasy theme, Lincoln must be freed because he is serving time for a crime he did not commit. And since Lincoln's degree of guilt is in no way commensurate with his punishment, he is part of a hierarchy of victimage in which he is forced to pay for the crimes of others.

Juxtaposed with this Christian theme are the American civil religion fantasy themes of nationalism and universality, which take shape in individual lives as the virtues of unswerving loyalty and deep patriotism. In these terms, it can be argued that Lincoln has been "kept on reserve for [a] state occasion when some ritual sacrifice was deemed necessary."[38] The events that unfold in the first season reveal that sacrifice is necessary because Vice President Caroline Reynolds is running for the presidency in an upcoming election. Reynolds' brother, corporate executive Terrence Stedman, had committed multiple Enron-style crimes for which he was about to be arrested, which meant that for his sister to ascend, he had to be "eliminated."

Though Stedman is not dead, Lincoln was framed for killing him through an elaborate web of false testimony engineered by "the Company." As a consequence, Caroline Reynolds' allegiance is to this group of powerful and unseen corporate gods, which communicates with her through an intermediary who shows her little respect. Though individuals employed by various divisions of the government describe themselves as public servants, it becomes clear that each person who is affiliated with the state is a predator, intent only on ensuring his or her own survival without regard to the welfare of anyone else.

Within this corrupt political hierarchy, justice is perverted in order to frame Lincoln and cover up underlying social, economic, political, and familial arrangements that support the dysfunctional system. "Looking back on it," Lincoln says to Michael, "I was set up. And whoever it was that set me up wants me in the ground as quickly as possible."[39]

Lincoln is correct, but what he does not know is the real target of the Company's machinations was Aldo, the father of Lincoln and Michael, a former Company agent who threatened to expose the widespread corruption in which his former employers were involved. This is why Aldo appears whenever an attempt is made on Lincoln's life. "We have a cause," Aldo informs Lincoln, "wars averted, millions of lives saved."

"And you were willing to sacrifice me, your son?" asks Lincoln, invoking the biblical story of Abraham, who is willing to sacrifice his son, Isaac, when God commands it.[40] Like Abraham, Aldo is granted a reprieve when he passes this test of loyalty to his higher ideals, and events unfold that allow Aldo to take his son's place in the witness stand, thereby sparing Lincoln, for a time, from the Company's wrath.

Michael, Lincoln's brother, knows none of this; in fact, it was he who was sacrificed by Aldo. Michael was abused and later abandoned by his father—a form of trauma that figures into the histories of many of his fellow inmates, especially T-Bag.[41] As a consequence of this experience and because of his belief in the fantasy themes of guilt, self-sacrifice, and redemption, Michael has little sense of self-worth and feels that he deserves to be in the hell of prison. But instead of perpetuating the cycle of violence, Michael resolves to become a rescuer rather than an abuser, acting on his belief that he caused his brother's suffering because his education and opportunities were financed by Lincoln's shady business activities. This vision, coupled with his fear of abandonment, is the primary motivator for his actions.

As the storyline unfolds, the brothers' worldviews begin to converge. They realize that their family's yearning for freedom and justice is intertwined with the yearnings of all the other prisoners. As they discover and begin to expose the widespread injustice perpetrated by the Company, the righteousness of their newfound cause soon looms larger than the original goal of exonerating Lincoln.

In this way, the fantasy themes of Pauline faith and American civil religion merge into a larger religious vision, one that incorporates an understanding of distinctly American ways of life with a biblical understanding of liberation through faith. This vision "is a project of common moral purpose, one which places upon citizens a responsibility for the welfare of their fellows and for the common good."[42] In the end, shared suffering becomes a call to arms, a perspective consistent with both the Judeo-Christian vision of redeemed believers as God's coworkers in the creation of a more just society and the civil-religious vision of Americans as "an almost chosen people" whose light illuminates that world.[43]

In order to expose injustices and create a better society, Michael and Lincoln must escape. Each of the other inmates has his own particular motives for escape—love, family, revenge, greed, or a desire to be reborn. But to breach the walls that hold them captive, they must put aside their differences and disagreements and act as one body. Their collective situation is, as John tells Michael, no longer "a me versus you thing—it is an us thing."[44] In each subsequent episode, the prison environment tests their devotion with its scientific and technological controls. As C-Note informs Michael, only the fittest survive because "Darwin wins inside prison. Not Einstein."[45] In other words, competition and empirical knowledge, not imagination, ensure survival within prison walls.

This social Darwinist theme recurs throughout the series; indeed, C-Note's comment illustrates the fact that few texts other than the Bible have a greater influence on human relations than Darwin's *On the Origin of Species*. And C-Note's utterance of the symbolic cue "survival of the fittest" is also important. First, it "espouses a physicalist view of reality, according to which everything that exists is either physical or else it depends necessarily on the physical for its emergence and continued existence."[46] This theme is consistent within a prison context insofar as it draws our attentions to the fact that there is little that prisoners can see beyond the prison walls. Second, this theme erases the distinctions—most notably the capacity for transcendence—between humans and animals.

"Survival of the fittest" not only invites a comparison between prisoners and animals but also between superior and inferior types of human beings; efforts to justify prejudices such as racism, sexism, and homophobia are examples of this impulse. For this reason, it is important and troubling to note that the Darwinian symbolic cue is articulated by an African American man whom a racist might see as more naturally adapted for the prison environment than Michael and other white inmates.[47]

C-Note's cue also assumes an ideological argument for a world in which God does not exist. Insofar as a social Darwinist fantasy theme can be applied to human relations outside of prison (as it was by Marx), it allows for the existence of no being with greater authority than the state.[48] So, while this theme does account for the struggles inherent in human existence and the apparent progress in human development, it does so by privileging the epistemological vision of science over the unpredictability of faith and imagination.

The virtues associated with this perspective are independence, strength, and contempt for vulnerability. These are illustrated by the technological ability to organize and communicate knowledge, which creates power for the public servants—the presidential administration, the Secret Service, and the prison officers whose livelihoods depend on the effectiveness of the prison as a container for disruptive influence—intent on preventing the prisoners' escape. As the story reaches its climax in the first season, the energy devoted to preserving and amplifying power seems to transform all of society into prison under constant surveillance.[49] In the words of David Hale, a Secret Service agent attempting to murder Lincoln's son, "I swear to God, it just gets deeper and deeper."[50]

"I swear to God" is another symbolic cue that is important to the religious vision of *Prison Break*. This oath, also taken by Reynolds when she becomes president, suggests that God is a higher moral, social, and/or political authority than humanity or any human organization. It also indicates that someone or something exists beyond what is visible. Thus, for everyone who is somehow imprisoned—but especially for the prisoners at the center of the story in *Prison Break*—faith is the answer.

Their faith is based on knowledge (allowing them to evade the authority of the state), adaptability (to do what is unexpected in the eyes of those around them), and an ability to see beyond what is immediately visible (which affords them a kind of insight into the world beyond the prison walls and the nations beyond the United States). These gifts of faith enable the prisoners to see the light and break out.[51] Though every day appears to be a lost cause, they fight and persevere because of the faith that strengthens their resolve. They know that they will escape even though they often do not know how they will do it. This fantasy theme is the inspiration for several of the visions dramatized by the escaping prisoners.

For instance, in an episode titled "Sleight of Hand," John has a revelation. He sees his first religious vision in the rust stains on the wall in his cell. He sees the face of Christ on the cross because he is plagued by guilt over murdering T-Bag's four-year-old nephew. According to John's ethical code, killing a child is unforgivable. It is for this reason that he is plagued by nightmares in which the child rises from the dead to haunt him under a crucifix. These dreams lead him to the conclusion that Christ appeared to him because he is in need of forgiveness.

He seeks counsel from the reverend. "Behold," reads the reverend, "I stand at the door and knock; if anyone hears my voice and opens the door, I will come in to him, and will dine with him and he with me."[52] John has heard the Lord's voice and accepts him as Savior because he wants to be a better man. When John extends the same choice to T-Bag, asking him to redeem himself for his offenses by backing out of the escape plan, he is violently rejected. T-Bag slashes John's throat, intending to kill him but ultimately providing the means for John to be born again.

When John returns to the prison several episodes later, he and Michael have a conversation that explains his transformation. While clutching his cross, John says that "the old sinner was confined to these walls. He's dead. The new soul deserves to be free." Michael, in a skeptical tone, replies, "The old sinner was going to have a jet ready for us." John replies, "Noah had his ark. Did he not? Let us pray."[53] John's evil actions outside the prison reveal that the old sinner was hard to kill; not surprisingly, his feuds with T-Bag and other foes resume. His inauthentic faith is responsible for his eventual demise, confirming the biblical principle that "the very moment you separate . . . faith and works . . . you get . . . a corpse."[54]

Religious visions also inform the episode titled "End of the Tunnel," when the prisoners decide to attempt escape even though Michael tells them that "the way is not finished" and Lincoln is trapped in solitary confinement awaiting the electric chair. In order to secure Lincoln's release, Michael "puts it in God's hands."[55] In an act that brings to mind a key line from the Eucharist ("This is my body—take, eat"), Michael slices open the cross on his tattoo with a razor blade, extracts a pill intended for Lincoln from deep within his flesh, and hides it in Sucre's crucifix. He then asks for the reverend and prays Psalm 23, emphasizing the fourth verse: "Yea, though I walk through the valley of the shadow of death, I will fear no evil: for thou art with me; thy rod and thy staff they comfort me."[56]

After their shared devotional, the reverend assures Michael, "He does hear our prayers." The reverend continues to comfort Michael by agreeing to take the crucifix to Lincoln and by reinforcing the religious vision at play in the scene, telling him, "If [Lincoln] accepts the Lord, he'll be free forever. This cage can't bind him."[57] In other words, by swallowing the pill, Lincoln ingests Michael's blood and body, accepting them as sacrifices for his freedom.

The pill makes Lincoln ill and he is transferred to the infirmary, where Michael and the other inmates plan to meet him and escape. The escape is thwarted when they discover that the hole that Michael created to get to the infirmary has been filled. Michael chooses to view this obstacle as a temporary setback, reminding those around him, "Preparation can only take you so far. After that you have to take some leaps of faith."[58]

In keeping with a religious vision centered on the idea that God fathers us toward spiritual maturity, Michael remains the leader of his team but begins to trust them to make and execute decisions on their own for the common good. As Michael shows faith in his fellow prisoners, they rise to the challenge, working together to keep the plan in motion. Instead of being helplessly dependent upon Michael, they grow in wisdom as their faith in the possibility of freedom deepens. For example, Sucre, Manche, and

Lincoln devise a plan to get Michael out of solitary confinement; Michael pushes Haywire to remember and draw a piece of his tattoo (an image that Michael calls "a pathway to heaven") after it has been burned away; Sara plays a "key" role when she leaves the door to the infirmary unlocked so that Michael can escape; Cooper, C-Note, and T-Bag work together to bribe a corrections officer; Nika helps Michael win Sara's affections; and Abruzzi arranges their transportation.

The escape plan begins to unravel when Tweener betrays Michael by revealing the plan to a crooked corrections officer. As a consequence of this betrayal, the prisoners are forced to leave three days ahead of schedule, and Michael attacks the Pope in order to ensure Lincoln's escape. The downward spiral continues as soon as the escapees are over the wall, when they begin to turn on one another. The rules of the invisible prison in each of their hearts are more subtle and deadly than those of the visible prison they left behind.

Season 2: Ideals of Faith

While there is no doubt that "The Fox River Eight" taste a bit of the freedom they long for after they scale the walls of the penitentiary, their escape presents a paradox. It seems that they escape a visible cage only to be trapped in invisible ones—the collective social prison of the United States and the individual prisons of their pasts. The change of venue in the second season of *Prison Break* allows for the development of a fantasy theme of freedom as a goal that the escapees must continue to pursue. What they fail to account for initially is that lives on the run are hardly different from lives in the penitentiary. "For in freeing oneself *perpetually*, one would in a sense remain perpetually a prisoner, since one would never have perpetually escaped."[59] Lincoln describes his experience of his status as a perpetual prisoner with the lamentation, "This is never gonna stop. They're gonna keep coming after us."[60] As each prisoner progresses toward the realization of his vision, he remains faithful to a plan and seeks the redemptive power symbolized by the cross. And despite the fact that trust is in short supply for people whose lives have been shaped by betrayal, the escapees learn that faith in a vision leads to faith in others.

The defining vision of faith in this season is consistent with, and more complex than, the vision of season 1, proving that "there is a time for everything, and a season for every activity."[61] Season 2 continues to elaborate on themes that equate suffering with redemption and that present a choice to surrender confidence in visible reality in order to place trust in the unseen other who points toward an unknown future path. But the vision of season 2 is distinct because it is now framed as a manhunt that requires the Company to search for the escapees and vice versa—a metaphor for the search for the body of Christ after his escape/resurrection.

The central characters must keep running forward in faith even as everything around them is reversed—identity, position, time, direction, belief, and fortune. Unable to completely trust themselves, one another, their enemies, or the evidence they unearth, they begin to see the invisible prisons in which they are enclosed and look to God for answers. "No character is sacred" or safe.[62] More to the point, each character undergoes his or her own redemption in order to reverse the process by which he or she became a prisoner. Their journeys end when they recognize and accept that they are redeemed and that, for that reason, they no longer need to run.

In this sense, the second season trades on the Christian notion that freedom begins at the moment when sinners are pardoned because they accept grace.[63] Like the Israelites in the Old Testament and Americans as they are configured in the Puritan myth of a chosen people, the escapees do not immediately find themselves in the promised land. Now that they are on the outside, the focus shifts from the construction and execution of Michael's escape plan to how the company can protect itself from exposure and defeat. Thus, before escaping the social prison of the United States, the protagonists have to confront the powers that be, decode and dismantle the plots against their families, grapple with their consciences, and endure an extended period of wandering in hostile territory.

In the spiritual world, the focus shifts from the characters' learning to place faith in fellow travelers to their learning to trust the other who cannot be seen. In the remainder of this section, I will concentrate on the faithful ideals associated with Michael, Sara, and Secret Service/Company agent Paul Kellerman to illustrate how *Prison Break*'s primary religious imperative—"have a little faith"—plays out against the ever-changing landscape of the social and political prison into which the characters have escaped.

In an episode titled "Bolshoi Booze," Michael cracks under the pressure of his inner turmoil. He begins to doubt his cause and question who he has become. After stealing a GPS system from a kind elderly storekeeper, he sinks into a depression and mulls over the pain he has inflicted on others in pursuit of his goal. Then, suddenly, he falls to his knees and turns his eyes to an image of the cross. He is riveted by it, though he has encountered and ignored the same image over the course of the day—indeed, throughout his life. But this cross catches his eye and sparks an out-of-body experience. There is nothing in the cross itself that makes it look different from any of the other crosses he has seen; it is simply that now he is seeing the image through the eyes of faith.

This experience allows Michael to feel God's presence, and the promised land seems within his grasp. But Michael is also suddenly aware of his impending judgment day. This unsettles him to the point that he enters a church to speak his truth and search for answers. His doubt and pain are the consequences of his seeing the suffering he has caused through the eyes of his victims. His symbolic convergence with their perspectives causes him to confess.

MICHAEL: Bless me father, for I have sinned.
PRIEST: How long has it been since your last confession?
MICHAEL: This is my first time, in a long time.
PRIEST: And what is the nature of your sins?

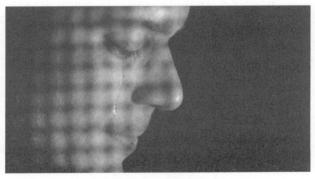

Michael's tearful confession.

MICHAEL: The nature? I'm not really sure.

PRIEST: Deep down inside your heart you know.

MICHAEL: Righteousness, maybe? Believing the ends justify the means?

PRIEST: And what are those ends?

MICHAEL: Saving someone's life.

PRIEST: And the means?

MICHAEL: I've broken just about every law you can name. But it's not just what I've done. It's what others have done. Because I let them. Because I was doing what I thought was right. I should've known better this time.

PRIEST: This time?

MICHAEL: When I was a kid, I watched a man bleed out and die. But I was glad. Because he deserved it.

PRIEST: Life is only for God to give and take, my son.

MICHAEL: Suddenly, there was this dark space inside of me. And I knew it was wrong. But here I am.

MICHAEL: There is a way to stop this. Surrender your will to God.

MICHAEL: If I surrender now, I'll lose everything I love.

PRIEST: But do you lose your soul in the process?

MICHAEL: Well, we all have our crosses to bear.

This exchange is the most direct expression of *Prison Break*'s religious vision in that it reveals the prisoner's intense desire to be free (in this case free of sin), the means that allow him to achieve this freedom, and his own definition of the concept. It also reveals that Michael fails to see his most egregious offense: the refusal to forgive. If he continues to believe that he can atone for his sins by his own efforts, he does not accept the grace that comes through faith (in other words, through the sinner's surrendering his will to God).

Michael finds himself at a crossroads, grappling with the age-old religious question posed by Jesus himself:

If anyone wants to be My follower, he must forget about himself. He must take up his cross and follow Me. If anyone wants to keep his life safe, he will lose it. If anyone gives up his life because of Me, he will save it. For what does a man have if he gets all the world and loses his own soul? What can a man give to buy back his soul?[64]

Michael is divided—trying to work out whether the will of God is a power that can carry him or a burden that he must forever carry. Because of the tension between his low self-esteem and steely resolve, Michael feels that the answer to all his problems is further self-recrimination. He manages to move beyond this impasse to see that there is no other righteousness except the righteousness that comes by grace through faith. The priest reminds Michael that if he is righteous at all it is only because he places his trust in God.

After his confession, Michael is reunited with Sucre, Lincoln, and Aldo, who tell him everything they have discovered. Namely, that Lincoln and Michael have been crucified and can be resurrected by the media and that Aldo did not abuse Michael but saved Michael from abuse and killed his abuser. Aldo goes on to explain that because the sins of the father are visited upon his children, he has returned to set things right. Michael accepts this information and incorporates it into his worldview, and Aldo and Michael are able to make peace with the past and forgive one another an instant before the Company arrives. Aldo is shot while protecting Michael and Lincoln as they make yet another dramatic escape. He dies in Michael's arms, and Michael realizes that he is loved because his father sacrificed himself for his children.

This experience reinforces the Christian fantasy theme of God as a father who protects his children regardless of whether they acknowledge him or not and who knows what they need and has plans for their lives. This vision of a Father/God sustains the brothers, and they are able to move forward after they bury Aldo and mark his grave with a cross. Aldo's death restores Michael's faith because he now has a direct and personal relationship with his father. That relationship revealed his father's true identity and gave Michael a genealogy and a purpose. As his faith grows, his hope stirs and his vision clears. He rises up, armed with "the shield of faith," and is ready to stand and fight, proclaiming, "Liberty to the [physical and spiritual] captives and the opening of the prison and of the eyes to those who are bound."[65]

Michael and Lincoln's tenacity offers the possibility of redemption to Secret Service agent Paul Kellerman when he begins to doubt the civil-religious vision to which he has devoted his life for the past fifteen years. He especially questions his service to Vice President Reynolds (who is now president because Paul murdered the sitting president), her family, and the United States. He engaged in murder, torture, kidnapping, bearing false witness, and other forms of deceit to sustain this vision.

The offense he most regrets is posing as a gay addict to earn and then betray Sara's trust. In what he believes is the interest of national security, Paul insinuates himself into Sara's life in the hope that she will lead him to Michael. When she is of no further use to him, he is instructed to kill her, and for the first time he does not want to kill. He is moved by Sara's devotion to Michael, despite the fact that her loyalty has cost her everything. He pleads with Sara to surrender the information he seeks, telling her, "Don't make me do this." She responds by telling him to "go to hell."[66]

And that is exactly what happens. After Sara escapes his custody for the second time, Paul is "terminated" by the Company. The scales fall from his eyes, and he realizes that he has pledged his life to people who do not care about him or the values they profess. The man that was Agent Kellerman no longer exists. Wracked with guilt, he finds himself with no one to turn to but God, and he begins his own redemptive process by helping Michael, Lincoln, and Sara with theirs.

It is for this reason that Paul first comes to Michael and Lincoln's aid. When the brothers are captured and transported from a local prison to a state penitentiary, Paul provides them with the opportunity once again to choose freedom. He arranges for their escape and helps them spread "the message."[67] He protects them not only so that they can reveal their story but also to advise them how to deliver it for the desired impact. "Whatever you say with your mouths, you need to be saying something different with your bodies and your eyes," he reminds them.[68]

Armed with this inside information, Lincoln and Michael testify to all they have seen and discovered—the existence and purpose of the Company, the ways in which the U.S. government "which is meant to protect and serve us" has betrayed us all, and to Sara and Lincoln's innocence.[69] Their message destroys the hierarchy constructed in the first season by assigning blame to the deserving parties and removing blame from the scapegoats. The Company responds by denying, distorting, and then burying the message. Lincoln and Paul are discouraged, calling their efforts a "Hail Mary."[70] Michael is hopeful, though another character confirms the larger religious vision that a life built on hope is "for those who live without grace." Hope keeps the prisoners running, but accepting grace through faith sets them free.

Meanwhile, Paul's newfound faith is challenged, and he is tempted to return to his old ways and turn the brothers in. He ultimately continues to help them after he finally abandons his belief in the justice of his old cause. Still, Paul is not relieved of his doubt until he finds himself willing to give up his life for his new friends—Lincoln, Michael, and Sara. Unfortunately, Sara is unable to forgive him for his earlier betrayal and, along with the brothers, she abandons him. In this moment, Paul experiences what mystics call "the dark night of the soul."

In a desperate cry for help, he visits his estranged sister and then attempts to take his own life. When he is unable to pull the trigger, he realizes that there is another way out—surrender. This is when Paul begins to have a little faith. Like his Christian namesake, Paul had served the dominant authorities as a proud and patriotic law-keeper. And his transformation bears some striking similarities to the spiritual confession of his biblical counterpart:

> I used to think I should work hard against the followers of the Way. I did that . . . I put many of the followers in prison. The head leaders gave me the right and the power to do it. Then when the followers were killed, I said it was all right. I beat them and tried to make them speak against [each other]. In my fight against them, I kept going after them. . . .[71]

And like Saint Paul the Apostle on the road to Damascus, Paul the former Secret Service agent undergoes a conversion experience and is reborn. His subsequent testimony opens the eyes of the justice system and the media, transforming them from instruments of darkness into instruments of light. In the process, Paul's sins are forgiven. He accepts grace and is "called home," taking his place in the promised land along with all those who are set apart by having a little faith.

Sara, on the other hand, has a longer road to redemption. She questions the authority of any higher power, including the state, because the Company murdered her father, who was the governor of Illinois. As a recovering addict and self-proclaimed realist, she searches for redemption but finds it difficult to accept grace. This is because she is filled with doubt and longs for her former freer life. When she confesses these things to Michael, he tells her that he sympathizes but that he prefers a different perspective: "I choose to have faith. Without it I have nothing. It's the only thing that is keeping me going."[72]

This conversation is significant because it reinforces Sara's otherness as the one of little faith, as the only woman and a damsel in distress. She is powerless to free herself because she exists only in relation to the men to whom she is tied: Michael as her lover, Paul Kellerman as her nemesis, and to her late father as a disappointment and a burden. These features of Sara's character illuminate an inequity perpetrated by the Judeo-Christian religious vision: "Humanity is male and man defines woman not in herself but as relative to him . . . He is the Subject, he is the Absolute— she is the Other."[73] This "expression of a duality . . . of the Self and the Other" extends to all aspects of Sara's experience.[74] Since Sara does not exist for her own benefit, she is the bridge between the men's imprisonment and freedom. She is referred to as "the key" and the conduit to Michael's freedom. Not only does she unlock the door through which he and all the male inmates escape from prison, she also holds the key to evidence that could exonerate his family. Finally, she surrenders herself to the authorities so that Michael can escape to Panama. In taking on this role of servitude, Sara becomes a prisoner of love.

Sara's storyline invites a gendered critique of the fantasy themes and visions at work in *Prison Break*, suggesting that "rather than looking at men as prisoners we . . . look at prisoners as men."[75] Moreover, Sara is true to the faithful attribution associated with her character as an obedient woman of weak faith. She is motivated only by her love for Michael, not by faith in any unseen higher power or in the power of the state (or even in herself). In pledging her love to Michael, she loses her individual identity to him: internalizing his concerns, pledging to defend him against his enemies, and making all of her resources available to him. In so doing she ironically finds the kind of love that she could only experience by giving up her freedom for his. In this way her actions are consistent with the religious vision of Christ on a cross, putting love on the line. Though understated, the character is surely deeply resonant with *Prison Break*'s audience, which is largely female.

Not surprisingly, Sara's sacrifice initially goes unrewarded. Although her physical and invisible shackles (i.e., drug addition) are removed, like Michael, she remains imprisoned because she does not recognize the person she has become. Still, she is ultimately rewarded for her many sacrifices when Paul testifies on her behalf in court. Yet her freedom is short-lived. When she is released and reunites with Michael in Panama, she shoots a Company agent to save Michael's life. This retriggers the guilt-redemption theme, causing Michael to take the blame for her actions because he knows that her love for him placed her in another dangerous situation.

Then Michael finds himself in a concrete prison again, only this time the prison resembles the deep layers of hell in Dante's *Inferno*. It is darker, scarier, and more tempestuous than any environment he has experienced before. Escape will thus require a stronger display of his faith as he faces his next opportunity for redemption.

Conclusion

The melodramatic finale of season 2 is consistent with Christian and American civil-religious visions and definitions of faith within a post-9/11 context. First, the ending illustrates the ways in which we are all held captive by our beliefs and the ways in which they can be expressed through symbols and rituals. Second, it reveals the consequences and benefits of acting on these beliefs—sinfulness and redemption, curses and blessings. Third, the ending provides an invitation to the characters, the audience, and the One who "stands at the door and knocks" to continue to participate in the story.[76] Whoever accepts that invitation can have a hand in shaping the meaning of the word "prisoner" in American culture after 9/11. Fourth, the ending highlights the suffering of others as an appeal to the audience to identify with people in pain, especially those who have been and are victims of terrorism, conspiracy, and abuse. In this way, *Prison Break* asks the audience to wrestle with the issue of religiously inspired violence. The storyline also illustrates that people of faith can transform tragedy into opportunity and accomplish what many prisons fail to do: rehabilitate.

The particular liberation narrative in *Prison Break* is not without its problems. In a sense, the show's audience is held captive to old narratives of subjugation and white privilege insofar as they are asked to identify most closely the suffering of white male characters like Michael and Lincoln. *Prison Break* also insulates viewers from the actual social conditions of the real-life prison population, which is predominantly black and brown and also largely female.

In this way, the technology of television works against its own redemptive potential. Television dramas like *Prison Break* become venues where audiences find mirroring for their feelings—of victimization, virtue, suffering, or faith—in the experiences of fictional characters rather than with their friends, neighbors, and fellow citizens, thus preventing social change. The consequence of this phenomenon is that actual spiritual journeys and notions of country and community are lived out primarily in the realms of mediated fantasy themes. Thus the religious vision empowering us to "have a little faith" is once again positioned as an intermediary between two worlds: the world inside the television and the world outside the box.

On the other hand, "there can be little doubt that . . . television . . . has markedly broadened the forms of public argument and discussion."[77] Televised depictions of faith and civil-religious vision can attract "the unconverted" by urging them to confront the possibility that there are cultural and religious worlds beyond the sphere that individual audience members inhabit. This kind of vision creates discourse communities that do important cultural work by influencing the public agenda through the "mediation of representation."[78]

As forms of mediation, *Prison Break*'s faithful attributions, symbols, language, ideals, and visions argue both for and against the civil-religious worldview that links the justice of God with the justice of government—an evenhandedness that can cause audiences either to question their faith in their government or to more closely examine their cynicism. Still, there is a strong element of paternalism in the show, insofar as the audience is not encouraged to challenge the assumption that the only version of faith that effects social change is the faith that is shaped by the issues and perspectives that are important to people who live in the United States. That said, an alternative reading might be that audiences are encouraged to associate the prisoners' unwillingness to accept grace with the fatal sin of arrogance, which invariably invites dire consequences.

This second reading translates into a powerful religious vision for day-to-day life. Such a vision reveals that clarity, certainty, and confidence are enhanced by faith, imagination, and the suspension of (dis)belief. The ways in which we identify ourselves and others—as prisoners or freed persons, as guilty or redeemed—are constantly called into question. Identities are no longer considered unalterable norms but are instead simply reflections of the social, political, and spiritual contexts in which they appear.

Thus our differences—of race, gender, sexuality, nationality, class, disability, or religious practice—serve not as fixed data of human experience but as fantasy types or mediated representations. In this case, the need for empirical knowledge is replaced with a need for the communication of confident faith. This means that when there is a discrepancy between the way things are and the way things ought to be, the most important differences are not found in plain sight. They are hiding behind prison walls. Television drama crashed through these walls when it brought the problems of conflicting faith and religious vision into our homes on September 11, 2001. I, for one, have a little faith that television drama can be part of the solution to those problems.

"Who Am I? Where Am I Going?"
Life, Death, and Religion in The Sopranos

ADELE REINHARTZ

For eighty-six episodes, spanning six seasons, Anthony Soprano allowed us into his world, his family, and his mind. We drove with him from New York to North Caldwell, New Jersey, followed him into bed with his wife and "goomahs," and eavesdropped on his psychotherapy sessions. We watched as he whacked those who stood in his way and protected himself and his family from being whacked in turn. During the last few moments of the final episode, we sat with Tony in Holsten's Restaurant as he waited for his family, scanned the room for potential danger, leafed through the menu, and selected a song on the tabletop juke box. And then . . . the camera cut to black, and a few seconds later the final credits began to roll. Life with Tony was over.

In the aftermath, the question on every viewer's mind was: What happened to Tony?[1] The real question, however, was what happened to us? In the pages that follow, we shall argue that over the course of eighty-six episodes viewers took a wild journey through the mental and emotional landscape of a "fat fuckin' crook from New Jersey" (season 4, episode 11 [4.11]).[2] As we hung on for dear life, we encountered most if not all of the big issues of our time: morality and violence, homosexuality and racism, popular culture and the changing American family. Amid all this, we also reflected on the fundamental existential questions: Who are we, and where are we going?

The constant awareness of impending doom is what gives *The Sopranos* its edge.[3] In season 6, Tony's wife Carmela confides:

> I worry, Tony, I do. You already got shot. Now you won't even go down and get the paper. Who is out there? What is it? What are the million other possibilities? The FBI waiting to take you away? You eat and you play and you pretend that there's not a giant piano hanging by a rope just over the top of your head every minute of every day. (6.16)

Although most of us do not fear a knock on the door, we too live our lives under a giant piano. As human beings, we must accept what Tony's psychiatrist, Jennifer Melfi, refers to as "the mystery of God or whatever you want to call it. . . . the questionable gift of knowing that we're going to die" (1.3). The awareness of death not only affects the mood and tone of the series, but also opens the way for exploring the nature of human existence itself.

The Questions

In the first episode of season 6, Tony is shot in the stomach by his clinically paranoid Uncle Junior. Shocking as this is, the event is not without irony. Tony certainly accepts the risk of being shot in the line of duty. As he tells Dr. Melfi, "We're in a situation where everybody involved knows the stakes" (2.9). But this gunshot catches him in a rare selfless moment: caring for his uncle and cooking him dinner.

Because this is the first episode of an entire season, we do not really expect Tony to die. Yet matters are touch and go. As episode 6.2 opens, Tony is lying in a coma, close to death. If his body is still, however, his brain is in overdrive; throughout episodes 6.2 and 6.3 Tony has a lengthy coma dream to which we viewers are privy.[4] In this dream, Tony is a much younger man and has lost the heavy New Jersey accent. This Tony is in the business of precision optical equipment, not "waste management." At the moment, he is in Costa Mesa, California, for a sales convention. When he approaches the convention desk to pick up his name badge, how-ever, he discovers that the wallet and briefcase that he is carrying are not his own but belong to a man named Kevin Finnerty. This discovery causes him significant distress ("my whole life was in that briefcase"),[5] to say nothing of inconvenience, as without ID he can neither attend the convention nor return home. The switch also prods some existential angst, and over dinner, he ponders aloud, "Who am I? Where am I going?"

These questions are natural within the context of a dream of mistaken identity. Since he cannot prove that he is Tony, perhaps he is indeed Kevin Finnerty. Since he cannot go home, where will he go and how will he get there?

Even in "real life," Tony is not always certain who he is. True, he does not question his identity as an Italian-American, middle-aged man. But beyond that demographic fact, who else is he? A caring father (6.19) and responsible manager (2.4), as he some-times tells Dr. Melfi? A subhuman monster, a Frankenstein, as a business associate once told him (1.3)? Or merely an overweight New Jersey gangster (4.11)?

As for where he is going, Tony has narrowed down the alternatives to two. "My estimate historically? Eighty percent of us end up in the can like Johnny Sac. Or the embalming table at Cozzarelli''s" (Tony, to his brother-in-law Bobby Baccalieri, 6.13). But the question "Where am I going?" pertains not only—or even primarily—to his life in the present, but, more pointedly, to his postmortem destiny. Most important, at least to Tony, is the con-nection between the two questions: Does who he is, that is, how he lives his life now, determine where he is going when he dies?

Within the framework of Italian-American identity, the answer to this question should be obvious: Tony is a sinner who breaks just about all of the Ten Commandments on a regular basis, and he will go to hell. This is the judgment that Carmela, furious at Tony's repeated adulteries, hands down in the pilot episode (1.1) just as Tony is about to undergo an MRI scan. "What's different between you and me," she tells him, "is you're going to hell when you die."[6]

But nothing is straightforward in this series, which offers us not one but several often contradictory answers to the existential questions that Tony poses in his coma dream. We begin by look-ing at the answers articulated by various characters within the series. These answers fall into two categories: religion, or, more precisely, answers that imply the existence of a God who sits in judgment; and science, or, rather, theories of human existence from which God is absent. We will then turn to the answers that Tony fashions for himself. Finally, we will consider what impact, if any, the series' exploration of these existential issues might have on us as viewers and as participants in the same cultural space that provides the broader context for Tony Soprano, and for *The Sopranos* as a whole.

Religion

Catholicism

Given the primarily Italian-American context inhabited by the Sopranos, it is not surprising that most of the characters at least give lip service to belief in divine postmortem judgment that consigns human souls to heaven, hell, or purgatory based on a complicated assessment of people's sinfulness during their lifetime. Of these three options, it is naturally hell that receives the most attention.

Christopher Moltisanti, Tony's "nephew" (in fact, Carmela's first cousin once removed) gives us a preview of what hell, Sopranos style, might look like. In episode 2.9, Christopher is hospitalized after being shot by two associates. His condition is grave; in fact, he is clinically dead for a full minute. Afterward he is very distressed and calls for Tony and Paulie (Tony's close associate):

> I'm going to hell, T . . . I crossed over to the other side
> . . . I saw the tunnel and the white light . . . And I saw my
> father in hell. . . . And the bouncer said that I'd be there too
> when my time comes. . . . "The Emerald Piper," that's our
> hell. It's an Irish bar where it's Saint Patrick's Day every
> day forever. Mikey Palmice and Brendan Filone were there
> too. . . . And then Mikey gave me a message for both of you.
> . . . he said . . . "Tell Tony and Paulie, 3:00."

Christopher thus believes that he has traveled to the place where they and their enemies alike will end up: hell in the form of an Irish pub (a hint that Irish pubs must indeed be hell to Italian gangsters). Tony brushes off both the dream and the warning ("Hey . . . That was a dream. Forget about it, okay?"), but Paulie becomes obsessed to the point where he wakes himself up every night at 3 a.m. to check that he is still alive.

Later, Tony describes Christopher's experience to Dr. Melfi. She asks the logical question, "Do you think he'll go to hell?" Tony is adamant that Christopher will not to go hell. Hell is reserved for others: "The worst people. The twisted and demented psychos who kill people for pleasure. The cannibals, the degenerate bastards that molest and torture little kids. They kill babies. The Hitlers, the Pol Pots. Those are the evil fucks that deserve to die. Not my nephew." Dr. Melfi then asks Tony about himself. Tony fumes: "What? Hell? You been listening to me? No . . . For the same reasons. We're soldiers. Soldiers don't go to hell. It's war. Soldiers, they kill other soldiers. We're in a situation where everybody involved knows the stakes. And if you're gonna accept those stakes . . . You gotta do certain things. It's business, we're soldiers. We follow codes . . . orders."

Uncharacteristically for Dr. Melfi, she tries to press the point, to get him to admit that, however he might justify his actions to himself, his behavior is immoral and therefore deserving of divine punishment. But Tony does not relent. Whether he has an alternate ethical system or is merely dissembling here, he nonetheless refuses to accept that who he is now (in this case, a New Jersey crook) means that he will go to hell later.

Tony is not the only one who expresses this optimism. Paulie, plagued by the three o'clock prophecy, returns to the hospital to interrogate Christopher on the details of his dream. "That bouncer that sent you back, did he have horns on his head? . . . Did anybody there have horns or buds for horns, those goat bumps?"

Christopher knows what Paulie is up to: "Paulie, it was fucking hell, okay? My father said he loses every hand of cards he plays. And every night at midnight they whack him the same way he was whacked in life and it's painful, night after night. Does that sound like fucking heaven to you?"

But Paulie does not give up: "Was it hot? . . . The heat would've been the first thing you noticed. Hell is hot. That's never been disputed by anybody. You didn't go to hell. You went to purgatory, my friend." Christopher cheers up: "I forgot all about purgatory. . . . How long you think we gotta stay there?"

Paulie has it all figured out:

> That's different for everybody. You add up all your mortal sins, multiply that number by 50, then you add up all your venial sins and multiply that by 25. You add them together, and that's your sentence. I figure I'm gonna have to do about 6,000 years before I get accepted into heaven. And 6,000 years is nothing in eternity terms. I could do that standing on my head. It's like a couple of days here.

Unlike Tony, who rejects any notion that his behavior will be found wanting, Chris and Paulie do acknowledge that they have sinned, but they, or at least Paulie, firmly believes that they will make it to heaven, no problem.

For the family left behind by the "soldiers" who have been killed "in action," Catholic ritual provides some sort of solace. During their visit to Paris, Carm and her friend Rosalie Aprile visit the beautiful church of Saint Eustache (6.11). Ro lights two candles, one for her late husband Jackie, who had been acting boss of the family, and one for her son Jackie Jr., who had been murdered on Tony's orders (3.13). Over dinner, Carm asks how Ro deals with the death of her son. Ro does not welcome the question: "Why would you bring New Jersey here?" But she does respond: "He's dead, he's gone. What can I do about it? Light a candle. I picture him with his dad, and with his grandma who he loved, and with Jesus."

Carmela, however, is convinced that unless some changes are made, there is no chance that her friends and relations will end up in heaven with Jesus. While Christopher was in surgery, she went into an empty hospital room and prayed:

> Gentle and merciful Lord Jesus, I want to speak to you now with an open heart, with an honest heart. Tonight I ask you to take my sins and the sins of my family into your merciful heart. We have chosen this life in full awareness of the consequences of our sins.

She asks God to spare Christopher's life, in order to give him a chance to redeem himself through repentance and faith. When Christopher does survive, she feels that God has answered her prayer, and now Christopher must do his part: "You have to look at this experience as an opportunity to repent . . . To change your heart . . . To start to walk in the light of the Lord. You were blessed by this, Christopher. You were blessed with a second chance." Carmela recognizes that she and her family live a life of sin.

Presumably the exhortation to repent also covers atonement for sin. But concretely, Carmela does not at all suggest that Christopher leave "the life," but only that he pray: "Will you pray? You just have to follow me. In the name of the Father, the Son, and the Holy Spirit. . ." Christopher drifts off to sleep, clutching his morphine drip in a loving embrace.

Evangelical Christianity

Carmela is not the only one who thinks that Christ is the answer for the Soprano family. During his recuperation in the hospital, Tony receives a visitor: Pastor Bob, a clean-cut and enthusiastic evangelical Protestant preacher. Bob is simply brimming with religious conviction and missionary zeal. Tony brushes off him: "I got all this covered with my parish priest."[7]

But Bob is not put off so easily. He returns in episode 6.4, bringing Tony a book called *Born Again*, by Charles Colson.[8] Richard Nixon's chief counsel, Colson was jailed on charges pertaining to the Watergate scandal. In prison he became "born again" and wrote this book in order to convince others to do the same. As Bob tells Tony, Colson "became a different man" when he found Jesus. Of course, Tony also became a different man—Kevin Finnerty— not by being born again but by nearly dying. But Pastor Bob does not know that, and Tony barely remembers.

Bob wants Tony to understand that he must seize the second chance that God has given him: "Salvation isn't just about being saved from hell after you die, it is about being saved from yourself while you're still alive." Tony's polite response ("It must be nice to have something to hold on to") intimates the absence of a similar anchor in Tony's own life. Bob does not address Tony's moral status; his goal is to get Tony to come to the Church of the Open Door of the Redeemer. Dream on, Pastor.

Judaism

Another approach to the relationship between identity and post-mortem destiny is illustrated in great detail in episode 1.3. The episode depicts Tony's business relationship with a Hasidic motel owner, Shlomo Teitelman, who seeks Tony's assistance in securing a divorce for his daughter. Tony's associate, Silvio Dante, is the go-between and gives Tony the background during a hospital visit to their friend Jackie Aprile, who has terminal cancer. Silvio asks, "Tony, you know that guy Teitelman? Owns all that property. The motel down the street from the club." Tony shakes his head no. "The Jew, you know, with the black clothes and the curls and everything. . . . He wants [to get] a divorce for his daughter."

Why trouble outsiders about a matter that can and should be handled within the family? Silvio explains, "Teitelman's son-in-law will not give his daughter the consent unless Teitelman gives him 50 percent of his motel." Paulie has a simple solution: "Why don't he just . . . ?" (He holds his right hand in trigger position). Silvio shakes his head: "It's taboo for their religion." (As if murder, for divorce or any other reason, is not also taboo for the Sopranos' religion!)

Tony meets the Teitelmans.

Tony and Teitelman—the latter in full Hasidic dress—meet at Satriale's Pork Store. To ensure that we viewers notice the delicious irony of this encounter, the camera lingers on the giant pig that decorates the roof of the store and the pork advertisements on its windows. Given that pork is utterly forbidden to religious Jews, nothing could signal more strongly the transgressive nature of what Teitelman has come to propose. The two men quickly come to agreement: Tony will exercise his persuasive talents on the son-in-law in return for a 25 percent share in the motel. Teitelman's son Hillel, who is present at the meeting, visibly disapproves of the way that his father is handling the situation. In Yiddish, he castigates his father for creating a Golem, a monster to do his dirty work: "He'll destroy you!"

The problem in Teitelman's family is by no means unique. Viewers familiar with Judaism will know that Jewish law requires the husband to grant the woman a divorce and they may even be aware of the highly fraught issue of *agunah*, that is, cases in which husbands refuse to grant the "get" at all, or refuse unless some financial or other conditions are met.[9] For Tony, however, this is strictly a business deal.

Tony assigns to Silvio and Paulie the job of knocking some sense into Ariel, the son-in-law. They seek him out at the motel.

Paulie rings the bell on the counter at the reservation desk.

ARIEL: Yes, may I help you?
PAULIE: ?That depends. Are you Ariel?
ARIEL: *(responds quickly)* That also depends. Are you a bill
    collector?
PAULIE: What is this, the Catskills? We want to talk to you
    about your father-in-law.

The repartee places Ariel at the same level as Paulie: he is not easily intimidated, and he has his principles. For Ariel, as for his father-in-law, the divorce is more about business than about marriage. He tells Paulie and Sil, "I sweated blood into this place and he owes me. And I intend to get what's mine."

Paulie roughs him up, but Ariel refuses to budge. A more aggressive approach is required. At night, Paulie and Silvio bundle Ariel into the trunk of their car and take him off to Satriale's, where they pound the daylights out of him. But Ariel remains steadfast, his principled resolve unshaken. Not only has he worked hard for Shlomo's business, but, he insists, he has always treated his wife well. Did he not pay for plastic surgery and trips to Israel?

Annoyed as they are, Tony's men admire Ariel's guts and perseverance. Silvio tells Paulie, "If we don't kill this prick, we should put him to work." But they have a job to do. Either they must kill Ariel—which, as we have already learned, is "taboo" in his religion—or they must find some other tactic.

Time to call in the boss. Tony arrives in bathrobe and slippers, not too happy at being called away from his "goomah." His appearance contrasts with Ariel's formal attire and also comes into play in the ensuing scene.

Silvio greets Tony with a ham sandwich, no doubt enjoying not only the taste but also the opportunity to remind Ariel of his grossly unkosher surroundings. Silvio fills Tony in.

> SILVIO: I tried explaining the realities here. This guy is stubborn as a fucking mule. He says it's principle. I think we gotta—you know. That's why we called you.
> TONY: I promised the father-in-law I wouldn't.
> SILVIO: I don't know what else to do.

> *[This exchange is carried out in Ariel's hearing, clearly intended to intimidate him as much as to arrive at a new course of action.]*

> TONY: *(to Ariel)* You're a stupid motherfucker, you know that?
> ARIEL: I've heard it said.
> TONY: What are you, proud of it?
> ARIEL: You kill me and a dark cloud goes over Shlomo's house. Either way there'll be no "get" unless restitution is made.
> TONY: You really would let me kill you, you sick fuck.
> ARIEL: You ever heard of the Masada? For two years, 900 Jews held their own against 15,000 Roman soldiers. They chose death before enslavement. And the Romans, where are they now?[10]

Tony utters the punch line: "You're looking at 'em, asshole." It is only now that we notice that in his calf-length white bathrobe and slippers, Tony presents a degraded but still recognizable image of the great Roman emperors,[11] filtered through Hollywood films such as *Ben-Hur* (1959), *Spartacus* (1960), and *Gladiator* (2000).[12]

Ariel is fully prepared to be killed rather than grant the "get" without financial compensation. As he awaits his death, he intones the first few lines of Psalm 23, with the sanctimonious air of a longsuffering martyr: "Yea though I walk through the valley of the shadow of death, I fear no evil for thou art with me."

Tony interrupts unceremoniously: "Hold that thought." He phones his associate Hesh Rabkin, his authority on matters Jewish: "Yeah. I'm here with my non-shellfish-eating friend. I gotta tell you something, I'm tapped out. This guy won't listen to reason. . . . He's leaving me no options. This guy's willing to go down with the ship like no man I've ever seen."

> HESH: Here's a thought . . . Maybe he's willing to go to the world to come, but if he's stuck here on this earth, I know one thing that no man wants to go through life without.

It takes Tony a moment to catch on, but then he calls up to Paulie. "Get the bolt cutters from out of the trunk" and announces to Ariel: "We're going to plan B." In his New Jersey accent, "bolt-cutters" sounds very much like "ball cutters," which is surely how Ariel heard it.

Luckily we are spared the scene of Ariel's capitulation. But the saga is not yet over. The next morning, Tony is summoned to the motel. Paulie, irate, announces that Teitelman is backing out of the business deal. The Hasid explains to Tony that, though Ariel gave the "get," Tony does not get the credit. "You scared him, threatened him with castration. But it was business that brought him around. . . . it worked out." Tony is furious and starts shoving Teitelman around: "Now you listen to me. . . . we got you your 'get,' you get us our 25 percent. Got it?" This time it is Tony who is propelled by righteous indignation. A deal is a deal.[13]

Shlomo gives in but delivers a parting blow: "My son was right. . . . You're mud. Godless—I created a living Golem."

TONY: What the fuck is a Golem?

SHLOMO: It's a monster, Frankenstein!

According to Jewish legend, the Golem was a figure created and brought to life by Rabbi Judah Loew the Maharal of Prague in the sixteenth century. The Golem was to protect the Prague ghetto from anti-Semitic attacks. The Golem was made of clay and brought to life by the Hebrew word "EMET," meaning truth, written on its forehead. But the Golem grew to be a violent giant, killing Gentiles and even turning on its own creator. The emperor then begged Rabbi Judah to destroy the Golem, in exchange for an end to persecution of the Jews. The rabbi did so by erasing the first "E" from "EMET", thereby creating the Hebrew word "MET," meaning "dead."[14]

References and allusions to Jewish religious concepts and laws, the use of Yiddish, their mode of dress, the wife's connection to Israel, and the complex workings of the family all testify to the power of cultural elements associated with religious Judaism, though certainly not exclusively with Hasidism.[15] Furthermore, the references to the Golem legend and the events at Masada show that these Jews view their own lives in continuity with Jewish myth and narrative. Most important, however, are the spiritual elements, which are here seen as providing Ariel with the courage to face death (though not castration) in his firm belief that he is right. Conspicuous by their absence, however, are the Jewish ethical principles that condemn violence and extortion.

Tony and his associates grudgingly admire these Hasidim for their resolve in the face of death. The Catholic religion, to which Tony nominally adheres, has many parallels to Hasidism; Catholicism also takes a stand with regard to divorce, and it certainly has the legends and cultural capital available for use in understanding one's place in the world, as well as an ancient tradition of martyrdom that rivals that of Masada.[16] Yet Tony and his associates have neither internalized these religious elements nor integrated them fundamentally into their lives.[17]

The contrast between the Sopranos and the Hasidim in this regard is made even clearer in the concluding scenes of the episode.[18] As Tony listens with pride to Meadow sing a solo in her Catholic school choir concert, Uncle Junior's men set out to retaliate against Christopher and his friend Brendan for a stunt they had pulled in the previous episode (see episode 1.2). Brendan is expendable; he is shot at point-blank range as he soaks in the tub. Christopher is to be spared, but not before he is subjected to a mock execution. As he walks away from an ice-cream truck and prepares to enjoy his ice cream, he is assaulted by two men. They pull out their guns and point them at his head. Christopher melts with fear: "What the fuck?! Let me go, let me go! Listen. . . . I didn't mean it, I am sorry. Listen to me! I was trying to save her! Listen to me, you speak English! Don't shoot me, don't shoot!" One gunman pulls the trigger but it is a blank. He then crosses himself and they walk off, leaving Christopher prostrate on the ground.

Unlike Ariel, who accepts the possibility of death with principled stoicism and stubborn dignity, Christopher collapses in a pathetic, sniveling heap. He confesses to a misdeed that is entirely unrelated to the reason for the assault. For us viewers, the scene affirms the contrast between the stalwart Ariel, sustained by self-righteousness and his faith, and the weak-kneed Christopher, motivated only by money and some measure of loyalty to his boss. Ariel's resistance inspires respect; Christopher's sniveling, only derision. Tony and the Teitelmans have much in common: they achieve their goals by illicit means and do not allow their religious convictions to interrogate their moral status. But the comparison between Tony's nephew and Shlomo's son-in-law suggests the superiority of the Hasidim in confronting death.

Later, Tony has another therapy session.

> TONY: Somebody called me a Frankenstein today.[19] . . . This hasid I'm doing business with. These hasids, they're out there but—they got their beliefs, you know. They're not afraid of death. At least this one guy wasn't.
>
> MELFI: Maybe they have the belief because they are afraid.
>
> TONY: I'm not afraid of death. Not if it's—for something. You know, a war, something like that. A reason. But, Jackie. To see this—this strong, beautiful man . . . Just wither away to nothing. He can't do nothing about it. You can't fight it.
>
> MELFI: Do you envy the hasids and their beliefs?

> TONY: *(rejecting the notion)* All this shit's for nothing? And if all this shit's for nothing why do I got to think about it?
>
> MELFI: That's the mystery, isn't it? The mystery of God or whatever you want to call it. Why we're given the questionable gift of knowing that we're going to die. Do you feel like Frankenstein? A thing? Lacking humanity? Lacking human feelings?

Tony does not respond.

Although it predates Tony's coma by six seasons and eight years, this episode touches on many themes that pertain to the two questions with which he is struggling. The question of personal identity ("Who am I?") is raised in the face-off between Ariel and Tony: each appeals to the long and noble history of their people, and each presents himself in continuity with that history. Ariel compares himself to the courageous martyrs of Masada, and Tony depicts himself as the heir of the imperial Romans in their nobility and in the power of life and death they held over their subjects. More important, however, Tony sees that Ariel is willing to die for his principles, misplaced as they may be, and this willingness implies that he expects to be rewarded in the world to come for not betraying his beliefs. Christopher has no such principles and therefore also lacks courage in the face of death.

The Teitelman family, Pastor Bob, Rosalie, Paulie, Christopher, and Carmela do not by any means provide a full, balanced, and theologically sophisticated description of their respective religious traditions or of Christian and Jewish views on faith, ethics, divine judgment, and the afterlife. They do however illustrate the integral relationship that each faith presupposes between who we are in the present and where we are going after we die. While they have much to say about God, presumably it is God who pronounces judgment on whether one is destined for reward or for punishment in the world to come.

Science

Tony may give lip service to the existence of heaven and hell and may admire the courage that the young Hasid displayed in the face of death, but he is fundamentally uninterested in the faith-based answers to the most basic questions of human existence. Of far greater appeal is science. While in the hospital recuperating from his gunshot wounds, Tony becomes friendly with another patient, John Schwinn, who is a scientist at Bell Labs. Schwinn gives an impromptu lesson in quantum physics to Tony, Paulie, and others as they watch boxing on television (6.4).

In a rare philosophical moment, Paulie perceives the boxing match as a metaphor: "We're each and every one of us alone in the ring fighting for our lives." But Schwinn sees things differently.

> It's actually an illusion those two boxers are separate entities. . . . Separate entities is simply the way we choose to perceive them. . . . It's Physics . . . Schrödinger's Equation. The boxers, you and me, we're all part of the same quantum field. . . . Think of the two boxers as ocean waves, or currents of air, two tornadoes, say, they appear to be two things, right? Two separate things? But they're not. The tornadoes are just wind, wind stirred up in different directions. The fact is, nothing is separate, everything is connected. . . . The universe is just a big soup of molecules bumping up against one another. The shapes we see are only in our own consciousness.[20]

Tony finds Schwinn's comments compatible with an Ojibwa proverb that had mysteriously found its way onto the bulletin board in his hospital room. He tells Schwinn: "You know what the Indians say about the wind? . . . They say that sometimes we go around feeling pity for ourselves but behind our back a great wind is carrying us." Schwinn agrees: "We don't see we're a part of a much bigger reality." And Tony comments: "Then we die."

Schwinn wonders why Tony is so interested in all this. Tony describes the feeling he had before he woke up from the coma: "I felt like I was being pulled towards something and I don't wanna go back. Then my wife told me I woke up at some point and I said, 'Who am I? Where am I going?' It all makes you wonder, about heaven and hell." Schwinn does not hold by heaven and hell at all. "That presupposes a duality of good and evil. It gets us back to the idea of separate opposing entities."

Schwinn's answers to Tony's questions differ radically from those that emphasize ethics and faith. Scientific theory has convinced him that individuality is illusory, a function of perception rather than reality. If there is no personal identity, then the concepts of heaven and hell, the opposing duality of good and evil, and, by implication, all ethical systems, are also meaningless. If "the universe is just a big soup of molecules bumping up against one another," and individual identity is an illusion, then presumably death makes no difference at all. No wonder, then, that Schwinn is not overly distressed by his own cancer diagnosis, and that he is neither put off by, nor judgmental of the crook from New Jersey, despite the obvious difference in their professions, lifestyles, and levels of formal education.

Tony has come across similar views before, in his coma dream, though he seems not to remember. In the dream, Tony, or rather Kevin Finnerty, is pursued by two Buddhist monks, who are furious with Finnerty for selling them a faulty heating system. Tony responds to a summons to the monastery because he hopes that the monks will help him locate Finnerty. To Tony's probing they respond, "One day we will all die, and then we will be the same as that tree. No me, no you" (6.3). That is, individuality ceases upon death, so that the questions "Who am I? Where am I going?" have no ultimate meaning. But that is all the monks have to say; whatever it is that happens after death, their immediate need is for a heating system that works, and in this regard they are determined to get satisfaction from Finnerty.

Schwinn's commentary, and perhaps also the perfunctory words of the Buddhist monks in Tony's dream, imply specific answers to the existential questions that Tony pondered. The answer to "Who am I?" is that "I" am just a group of molecules whom others perceive as bundled together into an entity we call "human being." The answer to "Where am I going?" is that I am headed to a reunion of the molecules I see as part of my individual self with the undifferentiated universe of molecules from whence I came.

It is not surprising that Tony is attracted to Schwinn's explanations and builds them into his own repertoire. If there is no heaven and hell and no duality between good and evil, then even a crook like him may be off the hook.

A corollary of Schwinn's theory is the ultimate insignificance of each human being in the grand scheme of things. This too appeals to Tony. During one of Christopher's hospital visits, Tony shares something that he has read in a book about dinosaurs: "Get this, it says here that if the history of the planet was represented by the Empire State Building, the time that human beings have been on earth would only be a postage stamp at the very top. You realize how insignificant that makes us?" Christopher rejects this notion immediately: "I don't feel that way."

Tony even passes some advice along to Paulie, for whom the "Who am I?" question has suddenly become acute: it turns out that the woman he knew as his mother was in fact his biological aunt and his aunt—a nun in a convent—his biological mother. Needless to say, Paulie does not keep his distress to himself. Finally Tony tells him, "You gotta get beyond this petty bullshit, Paulie, you're part of something bigger; when are you going to learn that?"

Tony does not expound on his new perception of reality to Carmela. But she independently arrives at views very similar to his. During their trip to Paris (6.11), Carm tells Ro:

> The city is so old. You think about all the people who've lived here. Generation after generation, hundreds and hundreds of years, all those lives. God, it's so sad. Maybe it's not sad, it just makes you think, it makes you look at yourself differently. There was this one night in the hospital when it was very touch and go with Tony. He came out of the coma for a minute and he said, "Who am I? Where am I going?" And at the time I didn't know what he meant. Coming here, I feel the same way. Isn't that odd?

In Paris, Carm can put her dread of the giant piano into a broader context: "We worry so much, sometimes it feels like that's all we do. In the end, it just gets washed away. All of it just gets washed away."

On their final night in the city, her reflections, like Schwinn's musings, touch on the relationship between perception and reality.

You know what's strange, Ro, when you go to a place you've never been before, it's like all the people were imaginary 'til you got there. It's like until you saw them, they never existed. And you never existed to them. . . . It's the same as when you die. Life goes on without you, like it does in Paris when we're not here.

Tony and Carmela find some comfort in the insignificance of their own individual existence. In the grand scheme of things, their worries and their very existence—and therefore their sins and shortcomings—do not much matter.

Schwinn has helped Tony to articulate the inchoate impressions and feelings that remained with him from his coma dream, in which, as he told the scientist, "I felt like I was being pulled towards something and I don't wanna go back."

Tony is here referring to the climax of the coma dream, which takes place at the very moment that the real Tony, lying comatose in the ICU, suddenly slides into extreme tachycardia (extraordinarily rapid beating of the heart; 6.3). In the dream, Tony, aka Kevin Finnerty, finds himself driving toward a big and brightly lit country estate. From within can be heard the sounds of laughter, the clinking of wine glasses, and Italian opera. Guests stroll in a leisurely manner from the grounds into the house. Tony is greeted outside the house by his cousin Tony Blundetto, whom he had murdered in episode 5.13. Tony does not recognize him, however. He inquires politely, "Excuse me, is this the Finnerty reunion?" A strange, Kafkaesque exchange then ensues.

BLUNDETTO: (*moves to usher Tony into the house*) Hello there, they're waiting for you.
TONY: Me?
BLUNDETTO: Of course!
TONY (*uncertain and unnerved*): Has Kevin Finnerty arrived?
BLUNDETTO: We don't talk like that here.
TONY: What do you mean?
BLUNDETTO: Your family's inside.
TONY: What family?

(*Tony steps closer to the house but is still hesitant.*)

BLUNDETTO: They're here to welcome you.
TONY: I don't understand.
BLUNDETTO: *(nodding reassuringly)* You're going home.
TONY: *(hopefully but still hesitant and even incredulous)* I am?

Blundetto just nods.

Tony approaches the Finnerty reunion.

Tony approaches the house slowly. He sees a woman watching him from the entrance. From this distance we cannot identify her, but she reminds us of Tony's mother Livia, who died in episode 3.2. Tony looks up into the entrance and stares at the orange wreath hanging on the wall, as in a funeral home.

Blundetto encourages him to enter: "Everyone's in there." But first, Blundetto insists, Tony must hand over the briefcase he has been carrying throughout the dream ("Looks like it weighs a ton," says Blundetto, an obvious allusion to Tony's own girth). Tony refuses, indeed, he hangs on to this briefcase for dear life. Though it is not really *his* own lost briefcase ("my whole life was in it"), it is all he has. Blundetto tries to wrest it from Tony's hand. As they struggle, Tony hears a childish voice through the rustle of trees in the woods behind him. The sound draws his attention away from Blundetto and the beckoning but almost sinister house. The voice calls: "Daddy? . . . Don't go Daddy. . . . We love you Daddy. Don't leave us!"

Tony admits to being scared. Blundetto, still trying to grab the briefcase, reassures him: "There's nothing to be scared of. You can let it go. Just come say hello." As Tony wavers, the voice calls out again, "Daddy?" Suddenly the screen turns bright white, and we hear the adult Meadow's voice: "Please don't leave us, Daddy, we love you!" We squint through Tony's surprised eyes as Carmela and Meadow's gaunt and terrified faces come into view. Tony has returned.

Within the narrative of the coma dream, Tony's invitation to the Finnerty reunion is the culmination of a process that began when Tony discovered that he was carrying Finnerty's briefcase and wallet instead of his own. Initially, Tony attributed this switch to inattention, the sort of mistake that can happen when people in a bar are distracted by alcohol and their surroundings and hence do not keep their eyes on their possessions. But as time goes on, and others, namely, the Buddhist monks, mistake him for Finnerty, he begins to wonder whether it is he who is mistaken. Perhaps he really is Finnerty.

If we view these events, however, from the perspective offered by Schwinn, perhaps it is only in his coma dream that Tony truly begins to understand that differentiated personal identity is an illusion, a matter of (mis)perception, not reality. If so, then Tony's loss of the briefcase that contained his whole life was a letting go of personal identity and the beginning of his merging with the rest of the universe, the "infinity" that Kevin Finnerty's name evokes so clearly. The next step is his move into a different hotel, the appropriately named Omni, which means "the everything." The final step in the dissolution of his personal identity—the absorbing of his individual self into the all-encompassing universe—would have been entry into the house where the "Finnerty Reunion" was being held. This reunion, in other words, may well have been the reunion of the molecules packaged in the Tony Soprano (brief) case with all the other molecules from which he had come, in the first instance, his family, but ultimately, the entire universe.

This interpretation makes sense of two of the strangest aspects of this very odd sequence. One is the fact that of all the people in the scene, only Blundetto is clearly recognizable, to us, if not to Tony, aka Finnerty. We may explain this by the fact that Blundetto himself is still outside the house. We may conjecture that once someone enters, individuality is erased, hence our inability to identify the Livia-like woman who briefly stands in the doorway looking at Tony.

The second strange element is the tussle over the briefcase. Even if this was no longer Tony's briefcase, that is, the case that held his Tony life, the briefcase represented Tony's last vestige of individual existence. Letting go of the case would have meant letting go of life and permitting the merging of self with the rest of the universe (remember Blundetto's words: *"Everyone's* in there").

Ultimately it is love that calls Tony back from the brink of dissolution. The voice of the young child (whose voice sounds something like but is not identical to Meadow's) beckons to him to resume his personal identity, to resist the temptation to go into the house, to "Just come say hello," as Blundetto had urged. At the moment that Tony/Finnerty listens to the voice beckoning him away from the big house, Tony Soprano emerges from his coma to look straight into the eyes of those to whom he as an individual matters the most: Carmela and Meadow. It may be true that we are all part of the universe and that in the larger scheme of things individual identity is irrelevant, but at the core of our own small lives, what gives us meaning and purpose is that very perception of individuality, and the attachment that other individuated beings show to our own selves.

Initially, it seems that Tony's awakening has triggered a spiritual rebirth. As he says to his sister Janice, "I'm supposed to be dead. Now I'm alive. I'm the luckiest guy in the whole world. So after this, from now on, every day is a gift." Tony's sense of rebirth initially seems to promise moral regeneration as well. He even seems poised to set aside his bitter rivalry with Phil Leotardo, assuring him of his good will as they work out a business arrangement: "There's enough garbage for everybody." As the final season spirals downward to its abrupt conclusion, however, he gradually reverts to form, indeed to an even more brutal and unfeeling version of his former self, as his cold-blooded murder of Christopher attests. And despite his sworn intentions, and his gratitude to Carmela for her steadfast care and love throughout his illness, he cannot in the end keep away from other women. As he tells Dr. Melfi in 6.9, "Every day is a gift, but does it have to be a pair of socks?"

Tony's Answer

Where does this spiritual and moral reversion, or perhaps even regression, leave Tony with regard to his existential questions? He has long ago rejected the answers offered by religion, whether Catholicism or some other religion; he believes that God is dead, or, at least, he behaves as if he does. Even the scientific theories expounded by Schwinn do not sustain him in the long run. The coma dream had been the narrative equivalent of Schwinn's scientific explanation, for it had shown him that what awaited him in his grave illness was the dissolution of his own identity into the infinity. Attractive as that view (and the big dream house that symbolized it) was, Tony ultimately resisted when he followed the young voice away from the house and returned to consciousness, where his "Tony Soprano" briefcase, with his whole life in it, was waiting for him. Perhaps everything has changed, or perhaps nothing. We can, however, point to three elements that persist as the building blocks of Tony's stance toward the existential questions that troubled him in the dream and in its wake.

The first is the absence, or irrelevance, of God. Tony's Catholicism is an important part of his identity as an Italian American, but it does not shape his view of who he is and where he is going. Despite his insistence that his son Anthony Junior undergo confirmation in the Church (2.7), he is sympathetic to the argument that A. J. throws back at him: if God is dead, as the philosopher "Nitch" (Nietzsche) has said, then what's the point of being confirmed in the faith?[21] Dr. Melfi attempts to explain away A. J.'s rejection of God and religion on psychological grounds:

> When some people first realize that they're solely responsible for their decisions, actions, and beliefs, and that death lies at the end of every road, they can be overcome with intense dread. . . . a dull, aching anger that leads them to conclude that the only absolute truth is death.

Tony, who has his own share of anger, sympathizes with A. J.: "I think the kid's onto something."

The second is that, the absence of God, and hence of judgment, heaven, and hell notwithstanding, "this is not all there is." Death may be absolute, but somewhere, somehow, there is another existential dimension. A peyote-induced experience has shown him the truth:

> All I can say is that . . . everything we see and experience is not all there is. . . . I saw at one point that our mothers are bus drivers. They are the bus, you see, they are the vehicle that gets us here. They drop us off and go on their journey. They continue on their journey. Problem is we keep trying to get back on the bus instead of letting it go. (Tony to Dr. Melfi; 6.19)

What counts, then, is arriving in this world, getting off the bus, and letting it go on without us. Tony's own answer to the question "Where am I going" is "Nowhere."

The third, then, is the absolute value attached to being "here." "Here" is all that counts. Peyote has simply confirmed what Tony has already learned upon returning from his coma. As he comes to life in the hospital, his eyes squinting in the bright light like a newborn baby, Meadow exclaims: "Dad look, Here you are!" Tony motions to Carmela and whispers hoarsely, "I'm dead, right?" Carm answers, "No, you're in the hospital with all of us, in Newark." Later, while recuperating at home, he expresses his love and appreciation for Carmela: "Hey blondie, it's all you, you know, the reason I'm back here" (6.4).

It is not only "here"—that is, with Tony's return to New Jersey and the bosom of his family—that we find an emphasis on the spatial, this-worldly element. In the very first scene of season 6 (6.1), Carmela dreams that she was with Adriana, Christopher Moltisanti's fiancée, in the unfinished "spec house" that Carmela and her father were building. Adriana looks around the house and then asks, "Who is going to live here?"

In the context of the dream, Adriana is simply wondering about who will buy and occupy the house when it is finished. She may also be expressing Carmela's guilty conscience. Carmela and her father have used inferior building materials, cut numerous corners, and exploited Tony's influence with the building inspectors in order to the complete the house cheaply and bring it to market.

Now Carm is worried that the house may not be sturdy enough to ensure the safety of people living in it, though she takes no steps to remedy the situation and is content to pocket the profit when it is bought by a relative.

But there is another level of meaning, for Adriana is dead (cf. 5.12), a fact that the viewers know but Carmela does not (though she has her suspicions). In this context, her question has a broader and more existential meaning: She (Adriana) is no longer among those who live "here," but who will be? We are left with the same question by the end of the episode, which leaves Tony Soprano bleeding on the floor of Junior's house. And if Tony does survive physically, is his stance in the world such that he is really alive, or is he truly, as Teitelman shouts in 1.3, a golem, a Frankenstein, a monster who is already dead even as he continues to walk, talk, eat, and breathe?

Conclusion

So what has happened to Tony? Nothing. Who is he? The same New Jersey crook he always was, the one with the giant piano hanging overhead. He eats, watches TV, manages his crew, enjoys his goomah, fights with his wife, frets about his children, and does the same drive from New York to New Jersey that we have come to know so well. Where is he going? Nowhere at all, unless we count Miami and Vegas, which in this series are basically the same as New Jersey but sunnier. What about us, who have traveled with Tony through the landscape of New Jersey and the dream world in his head? And what about our early twenty-first century society, in which *The Sopranos*, with its violence, cursing, irony, and humor, can flourish?

It would be tempting to follow the lead of many other critics and commentators and expound upon the greatness of *The Sopranos* and its role as a commentary on contemporary American society. The Directors' Guild of America concluded that "HBO's *The Sopranos* has quite literally reshaped television."[22] Maureen Ryan dubbed *The Sopranos* "the most influential television drama ever."[23]

In *The Times*, Ben Macintyre wrote:

The Sopranos is not Shakespeare. (Even Shakespeare's claim to be Shakespeare is disputed by some.) But as television drama, it came closer to the sweep and heft of Shakespeare than anything before it, with its tragicomic themes of loyalty and betrayal, religion and violence, manhood and ageing.

. . . *The Sopranos* marked the moment when pop-culture television entertainment became high culture. It showed that the narrative strength of television can be harnessed to the central dilemmas of existence, and it did so not with ponderous self-consciousness, but with humour. Here was a genre ever ready to undermine and mock itself.[24]

In the *New York Times*, Alessandra Stanley declared that "The decline and fall of the Sopranos—Tony; his wife, Carmela; and the rest—served as a parable of America in decline" though it was also "just a gangsters' tale, with lots of graphic sex, gruesome violence and most of all a sense of humor."[25]

So perhaps our study of Tony's existential angst can tell us the following: that America is in existential crisis; that faith and ethics have fallen by the wayside not only in practice but in theory as well; that we ignore death at the same time as we are obsessively anxious about it; that God is a delusion. Certainly there are those who would say all of the above, about themselves and about American society in the twenty-first century.[26]

Now, I was (and remain) as besotted with *The Sopranos* as the next person. As the present analysis no doubt demonstrates, I find much to enjoy and plenty to analyze. Indeed, what is striking about this series is its cinematic (including cinematographic) quality; its denseness, subtlety, and playfulness; its educated allusions to literature, art, music, and film; and the ways in which it draws the viewer into collusion with Tony Soprano and his entourage. Nevertheless, as George Anastasia reminds us, "This is television."[27] Let's not get carried away.

Whatever else it might say, *The Sopranos* may also be read as a cautionary tale about the need to maintain the boundaries between the visual media and real life. Tony, his son, and his associates watch endless hours of television. Tony relaxes in front of the History Channel, bowl of ice cream resting on his ample stomach. His son A. J. divides his time between the computer and the television. Television newscasts and documentaries provoke considerable discussion in the back office at Satriale's, never more than when the mob is in the news or the subject of so-called expert commentary. In these cases, the Sopranos are well aware of the gap between television and reality. As for the rest of what they see and hear, as Paulie says dismissively, "I gotta watch TV to figure out the world?" (3.1). When Carmela is outraged at how much the protagonist of Christopher's film *Cleaver* looks like Tony, her husband admonishes her, "It's a movie, it's fiction" (6.14).

The series acknowledges that we do tend to see our lives in terms of television and film.[28] The voice-over at the beginning of season 6 (6.1) informs us that "The ancient Egyptians postulated seven souls."

> The top soul, and the first to leave at the moment of death, is Ren, the Secret Name. This corresponds to my Director. He directs the film of your life from conception to death. The Secret Name is the title of your film. When you die, that's where Ren came in.

Nevertheless, things go terribly wrong as soon as characters blur the lines between entertainment and real life. Despite his words to Carmela, Tony himself becomes convinced that Christopher modelled *Cleaver*'s slovenly and violent main character after him. Who is to say how much Tony's mistrust of Christopher stems from that conviction? Not only Tony but his son Anthony Jr. gets sidetracked by a film. After his father gets shot, A .J. decides that he, as the son, must kill Junior in order to avenge his father. When Tony foils his attempt and takes him to task for even trying to hurt his uncle, A. J. lashes out: "Watching *The Godfather*, when Michael Corleone shoots guys in the restaurant, who tried to kill his dad, you sit there with your fuckin' bowl of ice cream and you say it is your favorite scene of all time." Tony becomes tender: "Jesus Christ, A. J., you make me want to cry. It's a movie."

At moments, the show even layers unreality upon unreality. During his coma dream, Tony stumbles upon a large television in the lobby of the Omni Hotel. On the screen is displayed a question that seems to reflect exactly what he is thinking and feeling at the moment: "Are Sin, Disease and Death Real?" A large cross super-

"Are Sin, Disease, and Death Real?"

imposed on the image of a waterfall follows. On the surface level of the dream narrative, the crucifix shows that the question is rhetorical: the screen is merely an advertisement for a televangelist. Within the dream world through which Tony's mind is moving, the question is pertinent, as he is in the process of losing his personal identity through disease (the sepsis that set into the gunshot wound), a situation that, at least indirectly, is caused by his sin (his lifestyle and that of his family members ensures that there are always plenty of loaded guns around) and may shortly lead to his death. In the context of Schwinn's scientific exposition, none of these may be real, but in Tony's "real" life, the life to which he returns, they are perhaps more real than any other reality. Surely David Chase is having us on, or else entrapping us in the circles of hell in which Tony himself may be traveling.

   In the final analysis, what I have learned in my travels with Tony can best be summed up by the poem that Meadow reads aloud while her father is still in the coma. The poem is called "Pater Noster" ("Our Father"), by the French poet Jacques Prévert: "Our father who art in heaven/stay there/And we shall stay on earth/Which is sometimes so pretty."[29] Or, in Tony's own words, "I'm not saying there's nothing out there, Paulie, but to not live your life? What the fuck you gonna do?" (6.19).

A Television Auteur Confronts God
The Religious Imagination of Tom Fontana

ELIJAH SIEGLER

Writer-Executive Producer as Auteur

If we can accept the premise of this volume, namely that the TV drama is an art form that can express religious ideas, it follows that a creative individual who works mostly in TV can be considered a religious artist. If the artist and poet William Blake, the dancer Martha Graham, and the film director Ingmar Bergman can all be seriously considered as religious artists, why not an artist whose medium is the small screen? Scholars and critics, of religion or otherwise, rarely give attention to TV artists. There are several reasons for this inattention above and beyond the generally low regard that TV is held, as discussed above. First, because TV is so commercialized, TV artists are seen as inherently compromised by their relationships to TV networks, which are in turn motivated to achieve high ratings and to please sponsors. Thus, the argument goes, the TV artist has no venue to produce works of religious truth.

But the premise of this argument is flawed. Granted, the television industry is the most centralized and commercialized of all the culture industries. Even the pop music and film industries find a space for "independent," "art," and "experimental" films or music. But almost all art everywhere has always been beholden to money and power. The spiritually gifted painters of Christian icons whom Margaret Miles valorized as she did needed funding from royalty, the church, or guilds. All artists have patrons who attempt to control the content. Financial considerations do not make a piece of art trivial, as the works of Shakespeare, Mozart, and Rembrandt attest.[1]

A second reason for the lack of attention paid to the TV auteur is that TV is considered such a collaborative medium that it is often difficult to pinpoint who are the artists responsible. Film, too, is a collaborative medium, but since the rise of *auteur* theory in the 1940s, the director has been seen as film's primary creative artist. The great French film theorist Andre Bazin, and his journal *Cahiers du Cinema*, first saw Hollywood directors such as Howard Hawks and John Ford as true artists imprinting each of their films with their unique thematic concerns. To today's audience, the idea of the auteur is built into the way films are made, marketed, and reviewed. That we say, "I want to go see the new Wang Kar-Wai film," or "If the Coen Brothers made it, it must be good," is largely thanks to Bazin and *Cahiers*. In other words, whether an art form is deemed to be "individual" or "collaborative" depends to some degree on its critical and theoretical reception. The TV drama is surely mature enough for critics and theorists to recognize that television has *auteurs.* But who are they? Is TV a director's medium, as film is taken to be? No, TV directors are hired hands, working on an episode-by-episode basis. Is the creator of the TV series, the one who comes up with the show's characters and premise and pitches it to a network, its *auteur?* Often this is the case, but other times the creator is not involved with the show's day-to-day operation. I would argue that TV's *auteur* is the writer-executive producer who is responsible for the overall development of the story and character arcs and for the "feel" of a TV series. He or she may or may not be credited as the show's creator, but he or she generally is informally known as the "showrunner." Most of the series analyzed in the collection, from *Battlestar Galactica* to *The Sopranos* can be seen as the primary work of a single writer-producer.[2]

The rest of the paper will look at religious themes in one writer-executive producer's work and argue these themes are consistent enough throughout to call him one of the best examples of a TV auteur, and certainly the best example of one who is also a serious religious artist. The writer-producer is Tom Fontana, and this chapter will focus on the three TV dramas for which Fontana is best known (and to which he refers as his "trilogy"), namely *St. Elsewhere* (NBC, 1982–1988), *Homicide: Life on the Street* (NBC, 1993–1999), and *Oz* (HBO, 1997–2003).[3]

I believe the best way to consider Fontana's theological vision is to examine themes and characters from the run of an entire series and not to focus in great detail on any given episode. (This may also be the best way to analyze TV drama in general.) I also feel that the best person to comment on the religious themes in Fontana's work is Fontana himself. Thus I have made extensive use of a personal phone conversation and several published interviews.

Tom Fontana was born in 1951 and raised in Buffalo, New York, in a middle-class Italian-Polish Catholic family. In the late 1970s and early 1980s, Fontana was a struggling playwright in New York City. In 1982, he was working at the Williamstown Theater Festival where he met TV producer Bruce Paltrow and his wife, actress Blythe Danner. Paltrow hired him to write a script for a new medical drama on NBC he was producing. Since then, Fontana has been one of TV's most acclaimed writer-producers. He is best known for having "pushed the envelope of traditional drama and challenged audiences to follow him into new territory" through unusually complex, literate scripts, including formal twists, intertextual in-jokes, and, since *Oz*, the use of graphic sex and violence.[4] I will argue that it is his unique and consistent religious vision that should constitute his lasting contribution to TV.

Tom Fontana's Lived Religion

To understand how Fontana's work is religious, it is important to see the ways in which it is not. As a Catholic, Tom Fontana might be expected to mine the rich Catholic visual vocabulary (ermine robes, saints in stained glass, Christ's bleeding wounds, and so forth) to add sensational imagery to his scripts. In fact, he is on the whole uninterested in exploiting the sheer visual thrill of the religious. When necessary, of course, Fontana's scripts (especially in the latter seasons of *Oz*) contain religious imagery, but he has written no shootouts in underlit churches with flickering candles, or any other mainstays of religious kitsch so prevalent in film and TV genres (especially the supernatural drama) eager to convey "meaning" via "symbols."

If Fontana does not use religion as a source of flashy visuals, neither does he use it as a source of topical "hot-button" issues. Dealing as he does with crime, punishment, death, and the extremes of human behavior, Fontana could easily have been tempted to write about pedophile priests, suicide cults, or Muslim terrorists. But he has resisted this temptation, allowing the "ripped from the headlines" religious storylines to remain the purview of the *Law and Order* franchise.

Finally, Fontana is not a religious writer if "religious" is taken to mean "moralistic." His scripts are deeply concerned with ethics and justice but they do not have a "moral to the story." In an article pointing out existentialist themes in *Homicide*, Philip J. Lane compared that show to earlier cop dramas, such as *Dragnet*: "Questions of right and wrong, good and evil, do not boil down to 'just the facts ma'am' but to the rules of the game and how it is played."[5] Or as Fontana himself put it, "I think it's my job to ask questions. I don't think it's my job to pretend like I know everything. I only sort of know some things."[6] In fact, Fontana has some specific criticism of TV shows that do presume to provide answers to life's moral questions: "They deal with huge issues in forty-five minutes and they expect me to sit there and go, 'oh wow, I'm glad that person saw the light in forty-five minutes; they've changed forever. They'll never be a bad person again.'" In another interview, though, Fontana recognizes the place of moralistic shows like *Touched by an Angel* and *Dr. Quinn, Medicine Women*, saying, "that isn't to say a good simple morality play isn't as effective as an hour of *Homicide*."[7] As he told me, "You need parables as well as gospels."

So, in Tom Fontana's scripts, if religion manifests neither as compelling visuals, "hot button" issues, nor as moral fables, how is Fontana a religious writer? One answer comes from his own contrasting of *Angel*, *Quinn*, and the like as parables (easily decodable, moralistic, narratively "closed") with his own work as gospels (complex, narratively "open," polyvalent). Like the Gospels and many other religious texts, Fontana's scripts are interested in theological issues as they are played out in people's lived experiences. These issues have remained remarkably consistent in Fontana's scripts over two and a half decades; foremost among them are the search for redemption (whether explicitly religious or not), the nature of forgiveness, and the question of evil. Fontana's scripts are not final pronouncements on these issues but tentative explorations. These are the issues that remain unresolved and perhaps unresolvable in Fontana's own life. As he stated, "I constantly write about forgiveness because it's the hardest thing I can do. I write about it because I need to know how it works. It constantly eludes me."[8] When an interviewer from *Corrections Today* asked Fontana whether he "believes in inherent evil," Fontana replied, "it's interesting you ask that question because it's a question that I constantly ask in my writing. And I don't have an idea. I think that I probably do believe in evil, but the idea scares the shit out of me."[9]

"I don't like things that preach. I like things that ask questions and maybe suggest answers," Fontana said, and one of the strengths of his scripts is that they do exactly that. Although Fontana is certainly not a moralistic writer, he is indubitably a moral one. His characters are called upon to make moral choices constrained from "below" by their base instincts for selfishness and vindictiveness but also constrained from "above" by institutional bureaucracies. Each series in Fontana's trilogy, though very different in tone and setting, deal with how people should and do behave under the constraints of deeply flawed institutions. This basic existential dilemma—the possibility of action in a world we have not made—undergirds the ethical, theological, and social dimensions that Fontana brings to his work. Fontana never takes the glib position that individuals are basically good and institutions basically corrupting. His institutions (the hospital, the police department, the prison) are imperfect but necessary. By the same token, institutionalized religion, although never the main concern of an entire series, is always treated as something important and worthy of respect. Catholic clergy are never depicted as malevolent or buffoonish, as they seem to be so often in popular media, but nor are they overly saintly. Fontana generally portrays them sympathetically, as committed to the spiritual life and engaged in real religious work. In *St. Elsewhere*, Father Joseph McCabe was the hard-working founder of St. Eligius. There are several sympathetic nun guest characters in *Homicide*, and, as we will see, in *Oz* two major characters are Catholic clergy.

By contrast, Fontana's least sympathetic characters are spiritual hypocrites who undergo dubious religious conversions. *St. Elsewhere's* Dr. Seth Griffin converted to evangelical Protestantism after his promiscuous lifestyle resulted in his contracting AIDS. On a more exaggerated level, *Oz's* Timmy Kirk, an Irish Catholic inmate, converted because of the persuasions of a fellow inmate, an evangelical minister; but then, in a power grab, Kirk attempted to murder his spiritual leader by bricking him up in a wall. On a more nuanced level, *Homicide's* Tim Bayliss' conversion to Buddhism is portrayed in a less than positive manner, as we will see.

So who are the characters with whom Fontana asks us to spiritually identify? Who are the characters that best represent Fontana's own religious values? Clearly, not the ones who undergo sudden conversion. But neither are Fontana's moral heroes generically "spiritual" who receive inspiration from an unspecified higher power: his heroes come out of specific faith traditions and have particular relationships with those traditions. Fontana's most interesting characters are on some kind of journey of faith, but the journey is rooted in particular institutions and circumstances. One might say Tom Fontana's best characters reveal to us their lived religion.[10]

Fontana's own religious background helps us understand how he depicts religion in his series. As Fontana describes it: "We come from a relatively traditional 50s, 60s, Catholic, Italian-Polish family. Religion was not beat into our heads by our parents. They were certainly Catholics but it's not like they were obsessively observant. We went to Catholic grade school and I went to a Jesuit high school [because] that was a better education." Fontana may be downplaying Catholicism's influence on himself and his siblings, all of whom seem to possess various kinds of religious vocation: his brother was a seminarian who dropped out before being ordained and currently teaches in a Catholic high school in the South Bronx. His sister is a nun who has occasionally worked in the prison system.

Fontana recalls that Vatican II deeply influenced him in his formative years, opening him up to more dynamic and engaged conceptions of faith. Vatican II must have offered a creative young person such as Fontana in the late 1960s a way to feel connected to his Catholic heritage's traditions, and energized by its vision of social and spiritual action, without feeling bound by its dogma. (Interestingly, a recent profile of Rudy Giuliani, seven years Fontana's senior and from a comparable background, makes a similar case as to the influence of Vatican II on the Catholic politician.[11])

As a Catholic artist too, he is squarely post-Vatican: he focuses less on ethnic assimilation, guilt, sexual repression, and other themes (or perhaps "clichés" is a better word) common in American Catholic artists whose consciousness was formed pre-Vatican II, such as Flannery O'Connor or Martin Scorsese, to give two very different examples. Today Fontana describes himself thus: "I'm not a very good Catholic in my practice but I am a Catholic in my heritage and I am a seeker of—whatever God wants to let me know about. I am open to discovery."[12]

St. Elsewhere: The Apprenticeship of Tom Fontana

This medical drama, along with Stephen Bochco's *Hill Street Blues*, which debuted a year earlier, pioneered a new format for dramatic TV: a large cast of regular, semiregular, and guest characters weave in and out of the many intertwining story lines that combine the personal and professional, the serious and the comic. Some story lines end after one episode, others last a few episodes, still others continue for a year or more.

St. Elsewhere, centering on a hospital in a working-class neighborhood of South Boston, was the perfect show for Fontana to develop as a TV writer. He wrote for characters created by more experienced writers (those responsible for creating one of the important TV dramas of the 1970s, *The White Shadow*) and played by talented actors (such as David Morse, Denzel Washington, and William Daniels), and most importantly, Fontana inherited a setting conducive to his own concerns: the flawed institution of St. Eligius Hospital, nicknamed St. Elsewhere, a financially troubled Catholic hospital committed to its teaching mission in a decaying part of town. All of these attributes became foregrounded during the show's six years.

Another reason that working for *St. Elsewhere* served as a valuable apprenticeship was that its low ratings forced Fontana to write for any contingency. As he said, "*St. Elsewhere* was never really a ratings hit—always 10 minutes from being cancelled. You had to do this weird dance: I want to get the character to a certain place by the time the story ends but I don't know if this is going to end this year or in five years. I was trying to kind of guess."

Fontana's first TV script was the third episode of *St. Elsewhere*, "Down's Syndrome" (16 November 1984), focusing on a couple debating whether to abort a fetus that tested positive for Down's syndrome. Unlike some of the conventional "abortion stories" that Heather Hendershot treats in this volume, the script ended with the woman's decision to have an abortion, thus demonstrating his concern for moral questions with no easy answers, a concern that would only become more pronounced over time.[13] One of subplots in "Down's Syndrome," an arc lasting several episodes, centers on an arrogant adolescent from a privileged family injured when he blows up a bank (played by a young Tim Robbins). Here we see an early portrait of moral hypocrisy and spiritual bankruptcy that informs Fontana's later writing.

St. Elsewhere's creators, Joshua Brand and John Falsey, left the show after the first season. Executive producer Bruce Paltrow then put Fontana, John Masius (who later created the TV series *Providence*), and John Tinker (who later wrote for many other shows, including *Judging Amy*) in charge of writing *St. Elsewhere*, with Fontana as story editor. (As Fontana put it "Paltrow said, 'here's the ball kids, come up with something great' and we examined all the levels of the characters.") Thus, beginning with the second season, characters' story arcs become longer and more focused on moral and religious trajectories. The three principal writers saw themselves as digging deeply into the main characters, discovering more about them "through their jobs as doctors and nurses and by what God was throwing them on a weekly basis of patients and family members that were coming into the hospital." Fontana has remarked that the religious differences between the three principal writers (he was Catholic, Masius was Jewish, and Tinker a born-again Protestant) generated interesting discussions that in turn made possible scripts suffused with religious and theological issues.

Indeed, the second season offered several multiepisode narrative arcs, most notably the story of a masked serial rapist who terrorized female doctors and nurses. Fontana's recurrent themes of the possibility of forgiveness and the nature of evil were brought to the fore when the culprit was revealed to be a series regular, Dr. Peter White. A handsome and charming young resident, White embodies what in Fontana's scripts is the cardinal sin: lack of personal responsibility. From the first season, White blamed others for his mistakes and manipulated his friends. His self-pity and callousness were taken to violent and criminal extremes in the second season.

Under Fontana, Masius, and Tinker, long character arcs became the hallmark of *St. Elsewhere*. Perhaps the most notable arc was that of the chief of surgery, Dr. Mark Craig. In the first season, Craig was a supporting character who functioned as a stereotype of the pompous and abrasive surgeon, "a caricature" as Fontana put it. The actor William Daniels' nuanced performance suggested there could be more to Craig than that, and the writers allowed Daniels' talent to flourish by making Craig more and more of a central character. Craig's arc manifested as a series of crises of faith—not necessarily religious faith, for Dr. Craig was never particularly pious to begin with, but faith in all that made him what he was. He lost faith in his son, his mentor, his own medical career, his marriage, and—in one of the culminating moments of Craig's "loss-of-faith journey"—in the memory of his father, a renowned surgeon on whom Craig modeled his life. This final season episode, "Weigh In, Way Out" (2 December 1987), was unusually structured by the standards of series TV: it is made up of four self-contained ten-minute dramas about life-cycle transitions—one segment each on birth, adulthood, old age, and death. The old-age segment featured Craig returning, with harmful consequences, to the boxing gym where he used to spar as a young man. We find out for the first time that his father had committed suicide; Craig is now older than his father ever was. As Fontana put it, Craig "was acknowledging the enormous amount of hurt, confusion and loss that he experienced when his father committed suicide; he felt adrift, he was no longer so self-assured." Thus, we saw Craig "having a crisis of faith because he had put his faith in medicine and in his father's understanding of the universe."

Craig's acknowledgment of his father's failings not only enlarged our understanding of Craig's character but also echoed Craig's relationships with others in the series, including his "father figure," surgical mentor Dr. Domidian, as well as his actual son and his "son figure," the regular character Dr. Ehrlich. The careful viewer will notice that these relationships parallel other paternal relationships throughout the series, including that of Dr. Westphall's with his autistic son Tommy, and the comedically played relationships between several male residents (Drs. Fiscus, Axelrod, and Ehrlich) and their respective visiting fathers. (The show was "always about fathers and sons," as John Masius put it.[14])

Fontana's "auteurship" and his religious concerns can be seen not just in *St. Elsewhere*'s story or character arcs but also in its individual episodes. The well-remembered third-season closer, "Cheers" (27 March 1985), is best known for its crossover with the NBC sitcom (senior doctors from the eponymous hospital visit the eponymous bar), but the main story found younger doctors seeking spiritual solace in religious ceremonies outside their own faith tradition: the Gentile Dr. Ehrlich (Ed Begley Jr.) at a Passover Seder, and the Jewish Dr. Fiscus (Howie Mandel) at an Easter service.

Another well-known "stand-alone" episode, "After Life" (26 November 1986) also featured religion prominently. Fiscus is shot in the ER and, while on the operating table, travels to heaven, hell and limbo. In each region, he meets deceased characters from previous seasons. Fontana has remarked that his cowriters, not being Catholic, were not familiar with the term *limbo*. Fontana imagined it as a place of "mediocre spirituality" inhabited by referees and by two former patients of Fiscus who, when alive, deliberately removed themselves from both the pain and joy of life. In hell, Fiscus meets his old friend, the rapist Peter White, who had been shot by one of his victims. White is now trapped forever alone in a rowboat on an endless sea able to hear heaven above (which is depicted as a rollicking garden party) even as he rails against God for putting him in hell, not admitting to any moral culpability. The sequence not only nicely concludes White's story arc from two seasons prior by showing Fiscus finally acknowledging his friend's guilt, but also highlights one of Fontana's principal theological concerns: the Augustinian notion of evil as an estrange-ment from God and as a lack of personal responsibility.

Homicide: Speaking for the Dead

Fontana would get the chance to explore the nature of evil on a weekly basis with his next major TV show, *Homicide: Life on the Street* (1993–1999) based on the lives of Baltimore police detec-tives. As in *St. Elsewhere*, Fontana was not the creator. Unlike *St. Elsewhere*, he was the producer-writer and "showrunner" (and therefore, *Homicide*'s auteur) right from the beginning. Thus, *Homicide* was unashamedly theological from the first episode, ask-ing probing questions about evil and forgiveness and seeing the role of homicide detective as a religious one.[15] The show revealed its theological agenda from the first line of dialogue of the first episode: when newly promoted detective Tim Bayliss, in his first day in the squad room, meets the veteran Detective Kay Howard, she says "Welcome to Homicide. We work for God" ("Gone for Goode," 31 January 1993).

Homicide set out to be a different, more cerebral kind of police drama: it featured no car chases, gun battles, or other staples of the TV cop show (at least for its first few seasons). It focused on long character arcs and literate dialogue. It explored the partnership between detectives at their desks or driving to the crime scene in white Chevy Cavaliers. *Homicide* was a true ensemble show, with at least eight well-developed characters played by talented actors featured in any given season. Their story arcs touched on moral and theological themes; as Fontana has stated publicly sev-eral times, all the characters on *Homicide* were on some kind of faith journey. Nonetheless, two characters wound up with most of the screen time and, in the process, their relationship became the moral center of the show. Detectives Tim Bayliss and Frank Pem-bleton, at first glance, embodied a stereotypical "buddy cop movie" relationship—the naive rookie and the cynical veteran, respec-tively. But, as I have argued elsewhere, the real tension in their relationship came from their opposing religious backgrounds.[16]

Bayliss, whose first day in Homicide is also the audience's, is eager to learn and to please. He is haunted for seven seasons by his very first case, the unsolved murder of Adena Watson, a ten-year-old girl with "the face of an angel." His function, I would argue, is to be the audience stand-in. His partner, Pembleton, is a lapsed Catholic who attributes his strong work ethic, his erudition, and his moral clarity to his Jesuit education. As brilliantly played by the Emmy-award-winning Andre Braugher (who, as it happens, also went to a Jesuit high school), Pembleton is a headstrong, dedicated master of his chosen craft. Pembleton's self-persona resembles nobody so much as Tom Fontana; though this resemblance may be coincidence, one cannot help think Pembleton is Fontana's deliberate self-projection.

Fontana sees Bayliss and Pembleton's theological dialogues as being more central to the series than the mechanics of crime solving. As he said, "those scenes in the cars, going to and from the murder, for me it was the heart of the show." In these scenes, our detectives discuss the nature of evil, and, obviously, come to no definite conclusions. The actual plot of any given episode might seem written to reflect their discussions: we meet murderers who are sadistic, egotistic, barely conscious of their crime, psychopathic, or just plain stupid.

For Pembleton, though, it is not the murderer that matters but the victim; he believes the role of the homicide detective is to speak for the dead. Pembleton takes Howard's joke literally: he feels he works for God. He expresses the idea of the priestly function of his vocation in several episodes. One notable example is the episode "Stakeout" (15 March 1996), in which Bayliss is thinking about leaving Homicide in part because his colleagues do not feel like family to him: they do not engage in group activities or invite each other to their homes. Pembleton replies, "the work itself is the most important thing. What we do is important. We speak for those who can no longer speak for themselves." Needless to say, Bayliss stays.

Pembleton's righteous attitude toward his chosen career is subtly linked to his Catholicism. The religious heritages of the main characters are not generally marked. Several other detectives are identified as Catholic, one (John Munch played by Richard Belzer) is identified as Jewish, and some others are identified as Protestant, but these tags are rarely a motivational factor. Many episodes may go by without a mention of Pembleton's Catholicism, despite his being the spiritual center of *Homicide*. But Pembleton makes enough references to "what the Jesuits taught me" to inform the attentive viewer that his Catholicism is a primary shaper of his identity. This impression is confirmed in the episode "Work Related" (17 May 1996) when, after Frank suffers a stroke, a montage sequence—presumably of visions in his blood-deprived brain—includes images of his coworkers, wife, and baby, but most prominently of the Virgin Mary and Christ on the cross.

Fontana has said that Bayliss and Pembleton's parallel yet contrasting spiritual character arcs had been decided since the beginning of *Homicide.* Fontana described Bayliss as "the inno-cent, [who] came into the situation with a faith in the system. Over the course of the show, that was systematically dismantled. So he was the cynical one." Pembleton began the show with little faith in institutions: early episodes show Pembleton's superiors at the Baltimore Police Department using him for political ends and promoting incompetent racists. We know Pembleton has left his church. His faith comes from the certitude of the morality of his vocation as homicide cop. When, in the episode "Fallen Heroes, Part 2" (8 May 1998), Pembleton starts to question this morality after he fails to protect Bayliss and is asked by his lieutenant to engage in a departmental cover-up, he resigns.

The final, Pembleton-less season of *Homicide* seemed by some to have declined in quality. The decline may be attribut-able to newer, less-compelling characters, an emphasis on inter-office romance, or Fontana's preoccupation with his new series, *Oz.* From our perspective of *Homicide* as a theological drama, the reason for the decline was that when Andre Braugher left, so did the series' moral center. Fontana argues that this lack actually helped Bayliss' arc come to its logical conclusion. "As hard as it was once Andre left the show, it actually helped the Bayliss char-acter because he was without his confessor," said Fontana.

The last season of *Homicide* proved to be a time of experimen-tation for Tim Bayliss. His bisexual urges, introduced in the previ-ous season, became more prominent. The near fatal shooting that Pembleton could not prevent led to Bayliss' embrace of Buddhism. In Fontana's theological imagination, this experimentation is seen as "a failure." His dabbling in Buddhism and bisexuality was a sign of a lack of spiritual identity. According to Fontana, Bayliss "was trying to say: there's a spiritual path, no, there's a sexual path."

Bayliss' essential failure as a character is brought home in the series finale. A sadistic serial killer, freed on a technicality after a series of judicial mishaps, taunts Bayliss with his plan to move to another city to continue his killings. Bayliss murders him— undermining everything the police stand for and everything that Pembleton taught him. As Fontana put it, "In the first episode, [Bayliss] is yelling that you're not going by the book. By the end, he not only stops going by the book, he burns the book."

Bayliss' unforgivable act aside, *Homicide*'s last episode, "Forgive Us Our Trespasses" (21 May 1999) focused "not on murder, detection, or even the problem of evil, but on forgiveness. Scenes of regulars coming to terms with each other for past wrongs were underscored by a subplot: a nun forgives her brother-in-law for murdering her sister."[17] With its title taken from the Lord's Prayer, this episode, the first since the season opener for which Fontana received sole writing credit, recapitulates many of Fontana's religious themes.

In the two-hour *Homicide: The Movie* (13 February 2000), nine months after the series went off the air, every single regular and recurring character from the series returned to investigate the shooting of Lieutenant Giardello. But for Fontana, the movie was a chance to resolve the Bayliss/Pembleton relationship. Fontana, who no longer had to be concerned about being renewed by the network, elaborated his theology even more explicitly than usual:

PEMBLETON: You know why I left Homicide? Because I
    couldn't hear one more confession. I got sick of hear-
    ing people confess to me. Like some Jesuit, I would sit
    there in "the box," listening to a man not just admit
    that he'd killed someone, but cop to all the crap in
    his life, over the course of his life, that had led him to
    that moment.

BAYLISS: The merit of a whole life can be undone in a single
    moment.

PEMBLETON: Who said that?

BAYLISS: The Buddha.

PEMBLETON: The Buddha. Huh. Well, he was right,
    exactly. But unlike a priest, I could never give the

"Three Men and Adena," an episode of Homicide *about guilt and confession.*

man what he really needed—absolution. I could only
give him prison time.
BAYLISS: You'd've made a great Jesuit, Frank.

Later, Bayliss confesses the murder he committed last year to
Pembleton. And, as cultural critic John Leonard put it, "It is fit-
ting, then, that *Homicide: The Movie* should conclude with Pembleton, the Roman Catholic who believes in black and white and good
and evil, refusing absolution to Bayliss, the Zen fisherman turned
Dostoevsky Jesus freak."[18] Thus resolving a remarkable seven-
year double character arc.

Many of *Homicide*'s most memorable scenes take place in the
pale-yellow police interrogation room known as "the box." Fontana has proved himself master of writing for the box (in part
because of his background as a playwright, perhaps) as evinced by
the first *Homicide* script he received solo writing credit for, "Three
Men and Adena" (aired 3 March 1993). Set almost entirely in the
box, the episode revolves around Bayliss and Pembleton's attempt
to extract a confession from a street peddler suspected of raping

and murdering ten-year-old Adena Watson. John Leonard, who as a book reviewer wrote about the best of contemporary literature, pays this episode the highest possible compliment when he writes "in a single hour that March, for which Tom Fontana eventually won the Emmy he deserved, I learned more about the behavior of fearful men in small rooms than I had from any number of better-known movies and serious plays and modern highbrow novels by the likes of Don DeLillo, Mary McCarthy, Alberto Moravia, Nadine Gordimer, Heinrich Boll, and Doris Lessing."[19]

The box, of course, is more than a place to demonstrate virtuoso writing. In a previous article, I wrote of the box as the most sacred site in the police drama television genre, using *NYPD Blue* and especially *Homicide* as examples.[20] In this windowless, clockless room, normal rules of time and space are suspended, and the drama is compressed and intensified. Both the police and the suspects engage in ritual performance. Police use a variety of techniques to extract a confession without "crossing the line" into brutality. Suspects begin by lying, but in the end generally offer a public confession, if only to "free" the conscience even as the confession leads to a bodily imprisonment. (Michel Foucault famously theorized that confession was not a liberation at all but a "ritual of discourse" that is produced by "a power that constrains us."[21]) On the other side of the one-way mirror, other police, other suspects, witnesses, or victims watch unobserved, adding another dimension to this drama of surveillance and control. In his next TV series Fontana would enlarge "the box" metaphorically and literally.

Oz: Retribution and Redemption

In *Homicide*'s fifth season, "Prison Riot" (18 October 1996) was the first time that *Homicide* (and perhaps any cop show) was set primarily inside a prison. The victim, the suspects, and the witnesses were convicted killers from previous episodes. The episode grew out of Fontana's curiosity about the transformations convicts go through in prison. In many ways, "Prison Riot" was the seed that grew into *Oz*.[22] As one online review perceptively put it, "Many of the ideas in 'Prison Riot' would appear in the show [*Oz*]—the oppressiveness of the prison, the separation of felons into cliques based on race and creed, the homosexuality that occurs when straight men are locked in a building with straight men for the rest of their lives, the long circle of endless death to avenge one crime after the other."[23] More to the point, one can see that "Prison Riot" and *Oz* share not only their setting and character types in common, but also their theological concerns with retribution and redemption. In "Prison Riot," these concerns concentrate in the figure of Elijah Sanborn, a lifer who Bayliss believes may be willing to reveal the identity of the murderer because he is "looking for redemption." Fontana's message here seems to be that rehabilitation can only occur in spite of, not because of, incarceration. Finding redemption while imprisoned is possible, as Sanborn learns, through a combination of selfless acts, inner struggle, and individual soul-searching. *Oz* explosively extends Fontana's redemptive argument.

For a show with dozens of characters and story arcs in each episode, *Oz*'s setting is deliberately monochrome: a concrete and glass experimental cellblock, nicknamed "Em City" (the brainchild of liberal prison administrator Tim McManus), within Oswald State Correctional Facility (nicknamed "Oz"). I would argue that this cellblock is the functional equivalent of "the box" in *Homicide*. Its glass-walled cells and spacious common areas invite surveillance from prison administrators and guards (as well as the audience). Em City is an enclosed, ritualized arena where normal rules of time and space are suspended. Its setting makes *Oz* into more of a sacred drama than almost anything else on TV. This "sacred" quality is both the strength and weakness of this unusual series.

Oz became known for being HBO's first hour-long original drama, and thus featuring unprecedented nudity, violence, and profanity (though its status as "groundbreaking HBO series" seemed to become overshadowed by *The Sopranos*, which debuted eighteen months later). But its true uniqueness may have been its theological themes.

"The show was always about redemption versus retribution," Fontana told me. I thought I had some kind of privileged access to the secret "true meaning" of the show until I realized that, like *Homicide*, *Oz* announced its theological position in the first episode's first lines of dialogue. In "The Routine" (12 July 1997), Augustus Hill, the wheelchair-bound prisoner who serves as on-screen narrator, introduces us to Em City with these words:

"The guards are with us twenty-four hours a day. There is no privacy. Eyes everywhere. McManus' eyes. You see in Em City retribution gives way to redemption. Timmy Boy thinks he can save every one of us—from each other, from ourselves, from the system that dumped us in here. The only thing he don't get is: you gotta want to be saved." Here is Elijah Sanborn's dilemma writ large.

Although *Oz*'s run was much shorter than Fontana's two previous successful series—54 episodes compared to *St. Elsewhere*'s 137 and *Homicide*'s 122, *Oz* has so many more characters, plot twists, and story arcs than its predecessors that it seems foolish to describe a single character's arc throughout the series, and even any given episode is too complicated to relate given the space limitations of this chapter. Suffice it to say that every major character undergoes a crisis of faith at some point.

Oz's dense layering of mininarratives may be key to understanding its essential religiousness. Cultural critic Joe Wlodarz wrote that "the series defies the closure and redemption that typically anchor prison cinema."[24] In other words, *Oz* avoids the redemptive cliché of prison dramas (the most obvious modern example being *The Shawshank Redemption*) through its soap-operatic seriality. I would argue instead that *Oz* engages in what might be called serial redemption: any given episode will contain several mini-arcs lasting around five minutes, each concerned with forgiveness, retribution, or redemption. So despite Wlodarz's assertion that "*Oz* resists redemptive narrative closure,"[25] each episode may contain as many as a dozen miniature redemptive closures and just as many "re-openings" through moral blindness and backsliding: a penal lived religion, as it were. This argument seems to conform to Fontana's overall perspective on faith, which he characterizes as "something, like democracy, you're on guard for. You can't get lazy. You have to be vigilant."

Oz's first episode implies that God—or at least "the Unseen God"—is a major presence in Oz in several ways.[26] As Fontana put it, "if you can find God in a prison then he must exist. It's easy to go to a cathedral or a mosque or a synagogue, that's the easy part; if you go to a place as brutal as a prison and you can find a piece of God there, then he must exist." In an obvious but narratively marginal arc, Bob Rebadow, the longest-serving inmate, hears messages from God. Later episodes imply that these messages may in fact be divine communication. The role of God is more subtly announced in the arrival of three new prisoners, whom we see processed and introduced into life at Em City.

One of these three major characters is Tobias Beecher, a middle-class lawyer who was convicted of running over and killing a girl while he was driving drunk. Beecher is innocent of prison life and thus functions as the audience stand-in, much as Bayliss did during the first few seasons of *Homicide*. In his overall arc, Beecher is first horrified by the brutality of Oz, then fascinated by it, then participates in it, and at last transcends it. This arc is also recapitulated in individual episodes. Thus, to some extent, Beecher is in fact redeemed by Oz, though not through conventional "rehabilitation."

The second major character that sees Oz for the first time at the same time we do is Ryan O'Reilly, a charming Irish American sociopath. Watching him put his schemes into motion gives the audience theatrical pleasure in the same way that watching Iago's "motiveless malignancy" does. Fontana must have had O'Reilly's manipulations in mind when he said "some of the writing in *Oz* was just fun to do." O'Reilly has been called the "safest figure of identification for straight white male viewers" (Beecher's torrid love affair with fellow inmate Christopher Keller disqualifies

Eamonn Walker as Muslim inmate Kareem Said, the moral center of Oz.

him).[27] He is a lapsed Catholic and the author of many of Oz's plots and schemes. Is O'Reilly the stand-in for *Oz*'s actual author?

I would argue it is the third newly arrived inmate, Kareem Said, who most clearly operates as Fontana's stand-in. Like Frank Pembleton, Said possesses moral clarity, a spiritually motivated thirst for justice, and a righteousness verging on arrogance. *Oz*'s most groundbreaking innovation, I would argue, was not its infamously graphic use of full frontal male nudity but that its most sympathetic and intelligent character—and the one whose faith journey compelled the audience most—was an angry African American Muslim leader. Although a convicted arsonist (not a murderer, significantly), Said represents a good and true man, as rather obviously indicated by his birth name, Goodson Truman. As Fontana put it, "this man who came from the same place as these gangsters has found God, and it has clarified his view of life. It hasn't stifled his anger or his actions." Said is consistently the most honorable character in *Oz*. When the cynical state governor, in a bid to win the Muslim vote, pardons Said during the month of Ramadan, Said refuses.

But Said is no more a cardboard saint than was Pembleton; he undergoes as many narrative reversals as any other character on *Oz*. In later episodes, perhaps inevitably, Said questions his faith, realizing his own addiction to power and his own violent tendencies. When Said attacks another prisoner, he is sent to the "hole"— naked, solitary confinement in a dark cell. Said refuses to leave the hole when his time is up—the only character to do so. For him, the punishment is a form of wandering in the spiritual desert.

Said's story arc includes struggles for the leadership of the Muslim prisoners (who are mostly, but not exclusively, African American). They are the most obviously religious group of all of Oz's "prison gangs" but they are not the only one. In one episode of *Oz* ("Ancient Tribes," 20 July 1998), the gangs are characterized as "the ten tribes" (an allusion to the ten lost tribes of Israel?). Three of them are culturally Catholics—the Latinos, the Italians, and the Irish. One "tribe" is quasi-religious, the Aryans, whose ideology of racial purity and white supremacy motivates many important narratives. The "Christians" play a background role until an evangelical preacher arrives as an inmate in the fourth season. At its worst, the Muslim "tribe" is no better than any other tribe: involved in leadership struggles, shifting alliances, and wars with other tribes. At their best, the Muslims are the moral center of *Oz*. They avoid the drug trade and brutality that are the *raison d'etre* of most other tribes. Their commitment to prayer and spiritual reflection is genuine.

Oz is the first of Fontana's series to feature Catholic clergy as series regulars, perhaps because Fontana created *Oz* from scratch. He cast the venerable stage and screen actress Rita Moreno as Sister Peter Marie, a psychiatrist and McManus' ally in his progressive methods. (One source for this character was Fontana's sister, a nun who had worked in a prison where one of her tasks was to arrange conjugal visits.) Fontana cast Asian American actor B. D. Wong as Father Mukada who, we learn, was once considered his diocese's "great yellow hope" but "has run afoul of his superiors and been sent to *Oz* instead of continuing his studies."[28] Sister Pete and Father Ray appeared in most episodes, though they were rarely central to either the narrative or the religious themes. As an investigator into portrayals of Catholic clergy in American media wrote, "While Father Ray and Sister Pete are key characters, they certainly don't have the spiritual lock on *Oz*."[29] (One might say theirs were not the principal spiritual journeys.) Sister Pete functions as a sounding board for Oz's inmates and staff, providing generally sound, confidential advice. Father Ray is seen praying, performing mass, and giving sacraments. These activities are not marked as exotic and mystical or as silly, but rather as part of the lived experience of this character and some of the inmates in this prison.

If *Oz* is about the tension between redemption and retribution, this tension is expressed in several registers: most obviously, as an ongoing argument in the field of criminal justice as to whether imprisonment should be a vehicle for reform (a secularized redemption) or for punishment (retribution). In *Oz*, the former position is represented by McManus, the architect of Em City, with support from Sister Pete. They believe that even the worst prisoners can be rehabilitated by giving them a measure of freedom within Oz, and that teaching them real-world skills will reduce recidivism. The opposing view is expressed by Governor Devlin and some of the more long-serving prison guards who have a "lock them up and throw away the key" philosophy. The warden of Oz, Leo Glynn, is the pragmatist in the middle. It is easy to see where Fontana's sympathies lie. McManus and Sister Pete are sincere and well meaning if naive. Governor Devlin is as amoral and vindictive as any inmate; many of the guards are corrupt and violent.[30]

However, the second register that expresses the tension between redemption versus retribution is more of a consistent theme throughout the series, as well as providing more narrative excitement than a debate on prison reform. This register represents redemption versus retribution as the characters' internal struggle that in turn implicates the audience. Prisoners do horrible things to each other every week. Main characters regularly rape, brutalize, and murder other main characters. The audience despises these actions, while forgiving the perpetrator at the same time. When a prisoner is murdered, we can safely relish his death (in that it satisfies our urge for retribution) while at the same time regret it (as our emotional investment in these characters is abruptly terminated), and finally perhaps we hope their death brought about a kind of redemption.

The Morality of Diversity

We can see now that the hallmark of all three of Fontana's major series is multiseason, complex, character arcs. Fontana's commitment to writing long arcs is in itself a kind of moral stance that he shares with the neorealist auteurs whom Bazin valorized. Neorealists (De Sica, Rosselini) avoided tidy closures in favor of messy complexities. Like Fontana, they felt an ethical obligation to the viewers to avoid the easy answer. As Fontana put it, "If you watch somebody who's got a problem on a television show get over it in forty-five minutes then I think you would sit back in your own home and go—'wow I have this problem and I can't shake it. He could shake it. What's wrong with me?'"

Fontana's refusal to write neat, easily resolved parables comes out of his theology: "I do believe that each of us individually has to find God however we find him. And so when I feel like I'm being lectured to I have a negative reaction to that. So what I've tried to do in my writing is never to do that."

Fontana's commitment to creating interesting characters includes reflecting the racial, ethnic, and religious diversity that exists in the institutions featured on his shows. Kavi Raz as the anesthesiologist Dr. V. J. Kochar in the opening two seasons of *St. Elsewhere* was the first South Asian to be featured as a regular character on network TV. The last two seasons of *St. Elsewhere* featured France Nuyen as Dr. Paulette Kiem, a surgeon of Vietnamese ancestry. Although Fontana modestly claims these casting decisions merely "reflected who worked in a hospital and what jobs they had," in fact the presence of Drs. Kochar and Kiem speak to Fontana's ethical stance to create complex TV characters.

Neither Kochar nor Kiem received many primary story lines. And in fact, neither did *St. Elsewhere*'s major African American character, Dr. Philip Chandler, played by megastar-to-be Denzel Washington. On *Homicide*, on the other hand, "minority" characters often received the majority of screentime. *Homicide* featured African Americans as victims, criminals, and police. Differences in class and religion were noted: Detective Pembleton was Catholic, middle class, and from New York. Another African American detective, Meldrick Lewis, was brought up in the Baltimore projects and raised Baptist. The very dark-skinned actor Yaphet Kotto played their superior, Lieutenant Al Giardello, with characteristically Italian expressions and hand gestures as befits his character's Sicilian American father. Cultural theorist Thomas J. Ferraro applauded Giardello and the auteur behind him when he wrote, "Fontana committed himself to getting the ethno-racial admixture of Baltimore, and that began—hallelujah!—with the creation of Captain Al Giardello, an Afro-Sicilian who 'is more old world than old school.'"[31] Higher-ups in the Baltimore Police Department, including the browbeating Colonel Barnfather and the double-dealing Commissioner Harris were also played by African American actors. Again, Fontana attributed his casting to authenticity: "The cast make-up reflected the city of Baltimore. It's not like we were saying 'Oh let's have more black characters than anybody else.'"

Oz, as we have seen, featured Kareem Said (played by Eamonn Walker, a British actor of Afro-Caribbean descent), who may have been the first regular Muslim character on TV. The series also featured many secondary Muslim characters and background extras (some of whom were in fact Muslims). As with *St. Elsewhere* and *Homicide*, Fontana's motive for this unique casting decision was narrative and not political: "For me there was no, 'oh I'm going to break ground here with a Muslim character' . . . I looked at American prisons and I said if this mosaic is going to truly reflect what is going on in American prisons right now then I have to create this character. Islam is a very compelling part of prison life; it would have been dishonest of me to ignore it. So that's where it came from; there was no nobility involved, it was story-telling."

Limits and Excesses of TV Auteurship

Although religion has been the focus of this essay, a critical analysis of Fontana's work could focus with as much justification about race, masculinity, or social institutions. Fontana speaks with a distinct authorial voice on each of these topics. If there are TV auteurs, he is one.

Clearly, Fontana appreciates his position as TV auteur and realizes he would be giving up creative freedom if we were to work for the feature film industry. As he put it, "being a writer/executive producer, I'm used to conceiving and casting and being on the set and doing the final edit. It would be hard for me to go from that to being the least important person on the set. Feature screenwriters don't get the respect they deserve."[32]

But even TV auteurship has its limits. As I argued earlier, all art forms have institutional and economics constraints. Network TV series depend on the availability and quality of actors. Andre Braugher leaving *Homicide* for its seventh season and William Daniels emerging as a superb actor on *St. Elsewhere* both had an impact on the overall arcs of their respective shows. Fontana's series also have depended on the continued support of TV executives—and its flipside, the fear of cancellation. Dr. Craig's arc shows remarkable consistency, but Fontana said he would be "lying" if he said this was "planned from the second season." Pembleton and Bayliss' arcs have a satisfying structure, but Fontana said of *Homicide*, "we were always in danger of being cancelled. I consider myself very lucky I got to get to that point with both characters."

Above all, TV is a collaborative medium. Joshua Brand and John Falsey created *St. Elsewhere*. *Homicide* was based on David Simon's nonfiction book about the Baltimore Homicide Unit and was developed by Paul Attanasio (who wrote the screenplay for

Quiz Show and is currently a producer on *House*). Fontana inherited his characters and situations. In fact, these limitations may translate into strengths. With *Oz*, Fontana created the characters, wrote or cowrote every episode, and took full advantage of HBO's tolerance for sex and violence.

If ever a show could demonstrate that the writer-executive producer was TV's auteur, it was *Oz*. An excess of auteurship may have been *Oz*'s weakness. As I argued earlier, *Oz*'s prison setting allowed Fontana to write the same kind of heightened, character-based scenes he excelled at writing for *Homicide*'s interrogation room. But a whole series set inside "the box" is not necessarily a good idea. Particularly in later seasons, Fontana tended toward baroque plotting and Grand Guignol drama, making *Oz* resemble a brutal soap opera (albeit an always entertaining one). Certainly realism was not a concern: with its constant murder and mayhem, McManus' experimental unit would have been closed long ago. Was *Oz*'s lack of realism and narrative excesses perhaps a deliberate strategy to intensify the redemptive dramas? As William Blake said, "The road of excess leads to the palace of wisdom."

Fontana may be the paradigmatic TV auteur, but he is not the only one. Recent writing on television, in light of the quality dramas of the 1990s and 2000s, regularly use the auteur concept. It is perhaps time now to look more closely at the use of the term itself. As Wlodarz notes: "Fontana is almost exclusively singled out as *Oz*'s primary creative source in both the mainstream press and in fan discussion of the series [. . .] Producers like Fontana (and Joss Whedon, David Chase, Aaron Sorkin, Dick Wolf, David Kelley, etc.) serve a certain auteur function in both the critical and the fan discourse surrounding television texts that demands closer examination."[33]

As if to confirm Wlodarz's call to examine the TV auteur discourse, in a recent article about David Chase and the end of *The Sopranos*, Emily Nussbaum writes, "there are many breeds of TV auteurs: the great mythologizers, *Buffy*'s Joss Whedon, *Lost*'s J. J. Abrams, and *The X-Files*' Chris Carter; the quirky dialogists, like *Gilmore Girls*' Amy Sherman-Palladino and the maddening David E. Kelley; deadpan craftsmen like Dick Wolf and *sadomasochistic visionaries like Tom Fontana* and California dreamers like Alan Ball. There are the utopian solipsists (okay, just Aaron Sorkin)."[34]

Nussbaum, by singling out Fontana as a "visionary," seems to share my judgment that he is unique among TV auteurs for his theological concerns. But sadomasochistic? Nussbaum is mistaking the form that Fontana's depiction of redemptive dramas takes, on *Oz* at least, for the underlying concerns, which are primarily religious.

Epilogue

Diane Winston

Initially trained as a journalist, I am ever mindful of the "so what" standard. That is why after perusing thousands of words, readers of this book are, I trust, clear on *Small Screen, Big Picture: Television and Lived Religion*'s argument and significance. Lest any questions remain, I offer a summary of the book's thesis, a discussion of its relevance, and recommendations for future research.

Small Screen, Big Picture expands the universe of religion and media studies. More specifically, it pioneers the application of "lived religion" to television studies. Robert Orsi writes that lived religion is concerned with "what people do with religious idioms, how they use them, what they make of themselves and their worlds with them."[1] In other words, not only are our tastes in, and habits of, television watching emblematic of what is fundamentally important to us, but the ways we watch—alone, with friends and family, as part of a virtual community—and what we do with the stories we see (forget them, file them away, discuss them with friends, augment them online) affect how we shape and are shaped by worlds of meaning.

Just as lived religion has opened up the study of practices, power relationships, and embodiment within the field of religious studies, applying it to entertainment media enables us to reconsider seemingly ephemeral narratives as part of the cultural material that helps us to make sense of our lives, our relationships, and our search for meaning. Moreover, these entertainment narratives gain salience given the pervasive role of media in contemporary society as well as the growing numbers of Americans who categorize themselves as religious "nones" or "others." Whether Buddhists or Brights,[2] we remain symbolizing creatures, and electronic media environments will become increasingly important spaces to discover, generate, and share meaning.

These insights into the dynamism between religion and media are not just relevant for religious studies, they also suggest new directions for television studies. Whether in investigations of effects or of texts, reception or production, the notion that there is a religious dimension to the experience of electronic entertainment has not received adequate attention from media scholars. This collection of essays is a descriptive examination of lived religion on television that focuses on texts, with some perspectives on reception and production. Its methodology is, by and large, qualitative and anecdotal; whether its conclusions would be borne out by quantitative studies is surely germane. Deeper, more extensive and systematic probing of the intersection of religion with the enactment of political and economic power in these spheres would be welcome.

However, despite its preliminary status, the volume's underlying message is imperative. Becoming intentional about media consumption is a critical skill for citizens of the twenty-first century. The ability to reflect on what we read, see, and hear—and to bring to the surface the assumptions at work in those experiences enables media consumers to adapt and use information rather than simply to be influenced or controlled by it.

For example, being intentional about media consumption adds new dimensions to the debate over the place of religion in public life. National discussions have focused on church/state issues in classrooms, courtrooms, legislatures, and public spaces. Yet this roster of meaning-making sites overlooks the ways in which religious and ethical ideas infuse the private experience of public media space. This is not to argue that religious perspectives should be absent from the media. Rather, it is to suggest that since religious assumptions are explicitly or implicitly integral to the ways in which we think about public and private life, they are mediated daily through newspapers, magazines, radio, television, and the Internet, among other sources. As a result, media consumers are often unaware of how reading, listening, and watching affects their opinions on contested questions.

Would we feel differently about Bible reading in public school if Denny Crane, *Boston Legal*'s idiosyncratic attorney, defended an evangelical student who wanted to start class with Scripture? Have we become inured to torture after watching *24*'s Jack Bauer do "whatever it takes" to stop bad guys? Might we feel reconciled to gay clergy after developing respect for the virtuous Reverend Jason McAllister on *Brothers and Sisters*? Most of us intuit a message or form a perception from watching television (or from partaking in other forms of media) without thinking about it. By increasing our intentionality, we can better exercise our autonomy—a useful capacity in the ever-expanding media marketplace.

I have tracked this phenomenon through observing students in my course, "Religion, Media and Hollywood: Faith in TV." Some students enroll in the class because it fits a requirement, others because they are interested in religion, still others because they like the idea of getting college credit for watching television. Few, if any, start out seeing the relationship between television and religion, but within several weeks, they can connect the dots. My first task is to challenge their understanding of religion by describing its historical progressions (reading Talal Asad is a good introduction),[3] and the second step is to expand their definition of faith by foregrounding practices (the notion of "lived religion"). To help them become more reflective about how they watch television, I invite guest speakers—television writers, producers, and showrunners who discuss their own interest in ethics, religion, and spirituality and how it manifests in their work.[4]

Over the course of the semester, students identify their own television rituals (weekly gatherings to watch *Grey's Anatomy* or *Scrubs*), their experiences of reenchantment (*Lost* for some, *Heroes* for others, and *Friday Night Lights* for a vocal minority) and their deployment of the "sacred gaze," frequently described as seeing the interplay between the religious and the secular in shows ranging from *House* to *Sex in the City* to *Nip/Tuck*. They also learn what it means to participate in "convergence culture" through tracking online sites and discussing their utility with industry professionals. And, by the time the course ends, their awareness of religion on television has come to encompass issues of race, ethnicity, and gender. Thus, the notion of the oriental monk not only informs an analysis of *Heroes* (as Rudy Busto's chapter describes) but also illuminates the use of Buddhism in *Lost*. The role of the BBF (black best friend) that Lanita Jacobs-Huey explores in *Joan of Arcadia* adds insight to the character of Dr. Miranda Bailey in *Grey's Anatomy*. And theories of gender, elaborated in screenings of *Saving Grace* or *Nip/Tuck*, have augmented students' understanding of *Sex and the City* (particularly Charlotte's conversion to Judaism and Carrie's ambivalence about marriage).

Unfortunately, we cannot cover all apt programs either in class or in *Small Screen, Big Picture*. (What about religion in *Rescue Me, Medium,* or *CSI*?) That we selected some of the very best post-9/11 series may make our choices appear anomalous. Several have been hailed as the finest television has to offer, and these— *The Sopranos, Deadwood, The Wire,* and *Battlestar Galactica*—have either ended or soon will be over. They remain available, however, and like favorite films can be watched again and again. These television series will become classics, speaking both to and beyond a historical moment. *The Wire*'s elegy to urban dysfunction, *Deadwood*'s saga of societal formation, and *Battlestar Galactica*'s allegory of religious warfare have resulted in characters, themes, and stories that will resonate with similarly compelling print and celluloid creations. The power of these series, like all examples of transcendent art, resides in the questions they provoke and the speculation they elicit. Evocative of our deepest wishes and darkest fears, they are latter-day counterparts of the legends and myths our ancestors parsed for meaning. Interpretations shift over time, redolent of the interplay between historical change and the ongoing quest for understanding.

Even in our own compressed span of viewing, we see the process at work. When *24* debuted in November 2001, it seemed to crystallize American paranoia. Over the next several seasons, Jack Bauer's no-holds-barred approach to saving the world appeared an apt response to terrorist threats. But as the series' bad guys were revealed as "us" (specifically American governmental and business leaders and, in season 6, Jack's own family), the easy assumption of a cataclysmic clash of civilizations—and a concomitant acceptance of a do-anything-it-takes ethic—seemed as problematic as Jack's casual brutality.

At the start of Season 6, when Jack is released from a Chinese prison, we learn he remained unbroken; he never spoke and so kept his country's secrets. But the state of his soul is another matter. Torture works in various ways, and the valence it initially had, for Jack and for us, as a means to an end is problematized by its implication in the irremediable crime of soul-robbing. What once seemed to be a vindication of George W. Bush's worldview and politics now appears to be a devastating critique.

Just as old shows may take on new meanings, new shows will continue to address old questions. Insofar as television narratives help us make sense of our lives, basic existential themes—Why am I here? What is the right thing to do? How do I find meaning in life?—will continue to light up the small screen. In the year after we began this project, a spate of supernaturally inflected shows[5] debuted, many of which address anxieties about salvation and redemption, not to mention fears of death, evil, and the apocalypse. Reporters speculated on the "woo-woo" trend, but the point is not that this season or next tackles these issues; rather, the point is that these concerns have been paramount for millennia. Why did David steal Bathsheba from her husband? What made Aaron forge a golden calf? Is Gaius Baltar a prophet or charlatan? Media evolve, characters change, but the stories remain the same.

Or do they? The contributors to *Small Screen, Big Picture* ask more questions than they answer. Among those questions, as noted previously, is how our assumptions will fare when submitted to quantitative analysis. Also research worthy would be investigating other television genres. Do the same kinds of stories, replete with religious and ethical dimensions, suffuse comedy, reality shows, and news programs? If they are different, can we assemble typologies? Our aim has been to raise possibilities for ongoing explorations of religion and media and, most of all, to demonstrate that small screens can indeed reflect the big picture.

Notes

Introduction

1   John Hartley, "Television as Transmodern Teaching," in *Television: The Critical View*, ed. Horace Newcomb (New York: Oxford University Press, 2006), 595.

2   E.g., see Robert A. White, "Religion and Media in the Construction of Culture"; Graham Murdoch, "The Re-enchantment of the World: Religion and the Transformation of Modernity"; Jesus Martin-Barbero, "Mass Media as a Site of Resacralization of Contemporary Cultures"; and Gregor Goethals, "Escape from Time: Ritual Dimensions of Popular Culture," in *Rethinking Media, Religion, and Culture*, ed. Stewart Hoover and Knut Lundby (Thousand Oaks, Calif.: SAGE, 1997), 37–64, 85–132. See also Myles Breen and Farrell Corcoran, "Myth in the Television Discourse," *Communication Monographs* 49, no. 2 (1982): 127–36.

3   "U.S. Religious Landscape Survey," 2008, http://religions.pewforum.org/reports.

4   E.g., see Rebecca Dana, "Reinventing *24*," *Wall Street Journal*, 2 February 2008, http://online.wsj.com/public/article_print/SB120189888101136151.html; and Patty Mattern, "U Research Shows *Will & Grace* Lessened Prejudice toward Gay Men," *UMN News*, 17 May 2006, http://www1.umn.edu/umnnews/Feature_Stories/Will_and_Grace_.html.

5   John Eggerton, "TV Shines in TVB Study," *Broadcasting and Cable*, 20 April 2006, http://www.broadcastingcable.com/article/CA6326694. html?display=Breaking+News.

6   Norman Herr, "Television and Health," Internet Resources to Accompany the Sourcebook for Teaching Science, http://www.csun.edu/ science/health/docs/tv&health.html; and Eggerton, "TV Shines in TVB Study."

7   "Audience Penetration." Media Info Center, http://www.mediainfo center.org/compare/penetration.

8   National Cable and Telecommunications Association, "Statistics," http: //www.ncta.com/Statistic/Statistic/Statistics.aspx.

9   Ironically, some of these same criticisms and conclusions were leveled at religion. So with the rise of the cultural turn in the 1980s, it should not have been a great leap from considering television as an "opiate" to analyzing it as a religion phenomenon.

10   For example: Charlotte Brunsdon, Julie D'Acci, and Lynn Spigel, eds. *Feminist Television Criticism: A Reader* (Oxford: Oxford University Press, 1990); Bonnie Dow, *Prime-Time Feminism: Television, Media Culture, and the Women's Movement Since 1970* (Philadelphia: University of Pennsylvania Press, 1996); Herman Gray, *Watching Race: Television and the Struggle for Blackness*, (Minneapolis: University of Minnesota Press, 1995); Sasha Torres, ed. *Living Color: Race and Television in the United States* (Durham: Duke University Press, 1998); Shaun Moores, *Interpreting Audiences: The Ethnography of Media Consumption* (Thousand Oaks, Calif.: SAGE, 1993).

11   For example: Julie D'Acci, *Defining Women: Television and the Case of Cagney and Lacey* (Chapel Hill: University of North Carolina Press, 1994); Darnell Hunt, ed. *Channeling Blackness: Studies on Television and Race in America* (New York: Oxford University Press, 2004); Merri Lisa Johnson, ed. *Third-Wave Feminism and Television: Jane Puts It in a Box* (London: I. B. Tauris, 2007); Amanda D. Lotz, *Redesigning Women: Television after the Network Era* (Urbana: University of Illinois Press, 2006); Crystal Brent Zook, *Color by Fox: The Fox Network and the Revolution on Black Television* (New York: Oxford University Press, 1999).

12   For example: Bobby Alexander, *Televangelism Reconsidered: Ritual in the Search for Human Community* (Atlanta: Scholars Press, 1994); Steven Bruce, *Pray TV: Televangelism in America* (New York: Routledge, 1990); Ross Shepard Kraemer, William Cassidy, and Susan Schwartz, *Religions of Star Trek* (Boulder: Westview, 2001); Jennifer Porter and Darcee Mclaren, eds. Star Trek *and Sacred Ground: Explorations of* Star Trek, *Religion, and American Culture* (Albany: State University of New York Press, 2000); Rhonda V. Wilcox, *Why Buffy Matters: The Art of Buffy the Vampire Slayer* (London: I. B. Tauris, 2005).

13   *Grey's Anatomy*, season 4, episode 11, "Lay Your Hands on Me" and Brothers and Sisters, season 1, episode 23, "Matriarchy."

14   See Robert Orsi, *The Madonna of 115th Street: Faith and Community in Italian Harlem, 1880–1950,* 2nd ed. (New Haven: Yale University Press, 2002), ix–xxxviii.

15   Orsi, *Madonna of 115th Street,* xix (emphasis in original).

16   Louisa Ha and Sylvia M. Chan-Olmstead, "Cross-Media Use in Electronic Media: The Role of Cable Television Web Sites in Cable Television Network Branding and Viewership," *Journal of Broadcasting and Electronic Media* (December 2004), http://goliath.ecnext.com/coms2/gi_0199-3626626/Cross-media-use-in-electronic.html.

17   See, e.g., Bill Keveney, "Lost in *Lost,*" *USA Today,* 10 May 2005, http://www.usatoday.com/life/television/news/2006-05-09-lost_x.htm; Henry Jenkins, "Getting Lost," Confessions of an Aca-Fan, 25 August 2006, http://www.henryjenkins.org/2006/08/getting_lost.html; and Matt Hoey, "All Who Wander Are Not Lost," Written By, September 2006, http://www.wga.org/writtenby/writtenbysub.aspx? id=2195.

18   This is a relatively new argument and needs further research to see how it bears out within the power economy of the entertainment industry.

19   David Morgan, *The Sacred Gaze: Religious Visual Culture in Theory and Practice* (Berkeley: University of California Press, 2005).

20   Morgan, *The Sacred Gaze,* 3.

21   "*Battlestar Galactica*: Season 4 Preview!" *Entertainment Weekly,* 7 January 2008, http://www.ew.com/ew/article/0,,20169703,00.html.

22   Horace Newcomb, "'This Is Not Al Dente': *The Sopranos* and the New Meaning of Television," in Newcomb (2006), 561–78.

23   Michele Rosenthal, *American Protestants and TV in the 1950s: Responses to a New Medium* (Hampshire, UK: Palgrave Macmillan, 2007).

24   http://www.afa.net/about.asp.

25   For example: *Dead Like Me, Tru Calling, Medium, Ghost Whisperer, New Amsterdam, Pushing Daisies, Moonlight, The Dead Zone, Terminator: The Sarah Connor Chronicles, The Dresden Files, Carnevale, Jericho, Supernatural, Reaper, Rescue Me,* and *Mad Men.*

26   Lynn Spigel, " Entertainment Wars: Television Culture after 9/11," in Newcomb (2006), 645.

27   E.g., Paul DiMaggio, Eszter Hargittai, W. Russell Neuman, and John P. Robinson, "Social Implications of the Internet," *Annual Review of Sociology* 27 (2001): 307–36, doi:10.1146/annurev.soc.27.1.307, http://arjournals.annualreviews.org/doi/abs/10.1146/annurev.soc.27.1.307?journalCode=soc.

28   E.g., *Quarterlife, Battlestar Galactica,* and *Heroes.*

29   Stewart Hoover, "Media and the Religious Public Sphere," in Hoover and Lundby, *Rethinking Media,* 295.

30   Ram Cnaan, *The Other Philadelphia Story: How Local Congregations Support the Quality of Life in Urban America* (Philadelphia: University of Pennsylvania Press, 2006); Mark Warner, *Dry Bones Rattling:*

Community Building to Revitalize American Democracy (Princeton: Princeton University Press, 2001); Richard Wood, *Faith in Action: Religion, Race, and Democratic Organizing in the United States* (Chicago: University of Chicago Press, 2002); Robert Wuthnow, *Saving America? Faith-Based Social Services and the Future of Civil Society* (Princeton: Princeton University Press, 2004).

31   James Carey, *Communication as Culture: Essays on Media and Society* (New York: Routledge, 1992).

32   Gregor Goethals, "Ritual Dimensions of Popular Culture," in Hoover and Lundby, *Rethinking Media,* 124.

33   Goethals, "Ritual Dimensions of Popular Culture," 124.

34   Robert A. White, "Religion and Media in the Construction of Culture" in Hoover and Lundby, *Rethinking Media,* 47.

35   For David Milch interview, see http://uscmediareligion.org/?the Classroom.

36   For example: Nancy Franklin, "Dead in the Water," On Television, *New Yorker,* 25 June 2007, http://www.newyorker.com/arts/critics/television/2007/06/25/070625crte_television_franklin; Cynthia Littleton, "*John from Cincinnati*: David Milch Speaks," On the Air, *Variety,* 25 August 2007, http://weblogs.variety.com/on_the_air/2007/08/john-from-cin-2.html.

37   *Moonlight* and *Jericho,* which fans brought back from cancellation.

38   For Ronald D. Moore interview, see http://uscmediareligion.org/?the Classroom.

39   For David Shore on House's atheism and religion in hospitals, see Brooke Gladstone, "God No!" *On the Media,* National Public Radio, 15 December 2006, http://www.onthemedia.org/transcripts/2006/12/15/01.

40   Eamon McNiff and Cliff Cuomo, "David E. Kelley Likes Stirring the Pot," *Good Morning America,* 3 November 2006, http://abcnews.go.com/GMA/story?id=2625856&page=1.

41   http://blog.beliefnet.com/idolchatter/2006/10/studio-60-and-evangelicals-unawares.html.

42   Siegler, "A Television Auteur Confronts God: The Religious Imagination of Tom Fontana," 2007 draft, 2.

Chapter 1

1   Chris Monroe, "*Revelations*: Personal interview with creator/writer David Seltzer ('The Omen') and Executive Producer Gavin Polone," 2005, http://www.christiananswers.net/spotlight/movies/2005/revelations2005-interview.html.

2   Tom Shales, "NBC's 'Revelations': It's a Long Way to Armageddon," *Washington Post,* 13 April 2005, http://www.washingtonpost.com/wp-dyn/articles/A48351-2005Apr12.html; Melanie McFarland, "NBC's New Thriller 'Revelations' Joins the Push for More Christianity on

the Tube," *Seattle Post-Intelligencer*, 12 April 2005, http://seattlepi. nwsource.com/tv/ 219675_tv12.html.

3   Stu Johnson, "Rapturous Ratings," 2005, http://www.leftbehind.com/ channelendtimes.asp?pageid=1135&channelID=71. The original site from which this comment was retrieved is no longer active. However, the comment from Polone cited here is also now included in a JCTV discussion forum: http://www.jctv.org/forum/post.php?replayTO=49394.

4   Joseph Sinko, review of *Revelations*, 2005, http://www.christiananswers.net/spotlight/movies/2005/revelations2005.html.

5   Viewer comments can be found below Sinko's article at http://www.christiananswers.net/spotlight/movies/2005/revelations2005.html.

6   Johnson, "Rapturous Ratings."

7   leftbehind.com, The Official Left Behind Series Site, http://www.leftbehind.com/channelinteract.asp?pageid=1156&channelID=184. The original forum from which ths comment was retrieved is no longer active, and there is no alternative source available. The site was accessed in 2006 and 2007.

8   Teresa Blythe, "The Divine Ick Factor: How Creepy Religion Heightens Television Dramas," 2005, http://www.beliefnet.com/story/164/ story_16467_1.html.

9   Heather Havrilesky, "Must-Repent TV," Salon, 2005, http://dir.salon. com/story/ent/tv/review/2005/04/13/revelations/index.html.

10   MaryAnn Johanson, "A Dan Brown Christ-mess" Review of *Revelations*, 19 May 2005, http://www.flickfilosopher.com/flickfilos/ archive/2005/revelations.shtml.

11   Staci Wilson, review of *Revelations*, 2005, http://horror.about.com/ od/tv/gr/tv_revelone.htm. The original site from which this comment was retrieved is no longer active, and there is no alternative source available. The site was accessed in 2006 and 2007.

12   E.g., Michael Medved, *Hollywood versus America* (New York: Harper, 1993).

13   Evan Gahr, "Religion on TV Doesn't Have a Prayer," *American Enterprise* 8 (1997): 58.

14   Christopher Gildemeister, "Faith in a Box: Entertainment Television and Religion," parentstv.org, http://www.parentstv.org/PTC/publ ications/reports/religionstudy06/main.asp.

15   E.g., Skill and Robinson 1994; Skill, Robinson, Lyons, and Larson, 1994. For an overview of analyses of religious representation, see Scott H. Clarke, "Created in Whose Image? Religious Characters on Network Television," *Journal of Media and Religion* 4, no. 3 (2005): 137–53.

16   Gahr underplays this conclusion, stressing that while overall depictions may be positive, this is not sufficient because there are not enough explicit considerations of religion; and he argues that when they do appear, they are in extreme situations such as blaspheming priests or criminals who kill in the name of religion.

17   A classic example of the conversion of the skeptic over time was seen
     in *The X-Files*, in which the rationalist Dana Scully eventually seems
     to buy into a very Catholic understanding of paranormal phenomena.
     When the series began, its take on the paranormal was quite secu-
     lar, even on the part of the "believer," Fox Mulder, with the emphasis
     on UFOs and aliens. However, the series took on more overtly reli-
     gious overtones as it progressed (see Paul C. Peterson, "Religion in the
     X-Files," *Journal of Media and Religion* 1, no. 3 [2002]: 181–96). Could
     this have contributed to its decline?

18   Penny Edgell, Joseph Gerteis, and Douglas Hartmann, "Atheists as
     'Other': Moral Boundaries and Cultural Membership in American
     Society," *American Sociological Review* 71, no. 2 (2006): 211–34.

19   Jeffrey M. Jones, "Some Americans Reluctant to Vote for Mormon,
     72-year-old Presidential Candidates," 20 February 2007, http://www.
     gallup.com/poll/26611/Some-Americans-Reluctant-Vote-Mormon-
     72YearOld-Presidential-Candidates.aspx.

20   Brooke Gladstone, "God No!". *On the Media*, National Public Radio,
     15 December 2006, http://www.onthemedia.org/transcripts/2006/
     12/15/01.

21   S. J. Karnick, "Must-Believe TV: Christianity Gets a Fair Shake,"
     National Review, 21 December 2004, http://www.nationalreview.com/
     karnick/karnick200412210835.asp.

22   Raymond Williams, *Television: Technology and Cultural Form* (London:
     Fontana, 1974; repr. Hanover, N.H.: Wesleyan University Press, 1992;
     2nd ed., London: Routledge Classics, 2003).

23   Williams, *Television*, 53.

24   S. Elizabeth Bird, *The Audience in Everyday Life* (New York: Rout-
     ledge, 2003); T. Gitlin, *Media Unlimited: How the Torrent of Images and
     Sounds Overwhelms Our Lives* (New York: Metropolitan, 2001); Stew-
     art Hoover, Lynn S. Clark, and D. F. Alters, *Media, Home, and Family*
     (New York: Routledge, 2004); Thomas De Zengotita, *Mediated: How
     the Media Shapes Your World and the Way You Live in It* (New York:
     Bloomsbury, 2006).

25   See, e.g., Matthew Hills, *Fan Cultures* (London: Routledge, 2002); Jon-
     athan Gray, Cornel Sandvoss, and C. Lee Harrington, eds., *Fandom:
     Identities and Communities in a Mediated World* (New York: New York
     University Press, 2007).

26   Bird, *Audience in Everyday Life*.

27   Michael E. Hill, "God Speaks, Viewers Watch," *The Washington Post*, 9
     November 2003.

28   Dan W. Clanton Jr., "These Are Their Stories: Views of Religion in
     Law & Order," *Journal of Religion and Popular Culture* 4 (2003), http://
     www.usask.ca/relst/jrpc/art4-lawandorder-print.html.

29   Robert Anthony Orsi, *The Madonna of 115th Street: Faith and Commu-
     nity in Italian Harlem, 1880–1950*, 2nd ed. (New Haven: Yale University
     Press, 2002), xiii.

30   Orsi, *Madonna of 115th Street*, xix–xx.

31   Orsi, *Madonna of 115th Street*, xx.

32   Teresa Blythe, "Working Hard for the Money: A Faith-Based Media Literacy Analysis of the Top Television Dramas of 2000–2001," *Journal of Media and Religion* 1, no. 3 (2002): 146.

33   Elijah Siegler, "God in the Box: Religion in Contemporary Television Cop Shows," in *God in the Details: American Religion in Popular Culture*, ed. Eric Mazur and Kate McCarthy, 199–216 (New York: Routledge, 2001), 214.

Chapter 2

1   Preparation of this essay was greatly facilitated by a Web site containing transcripts of the entire Deadwood series, thirty-five episodes. Although these are transcripts prepared by a viewer rather than actual scripts, my comparison while viewing indicates a high degree of accuracy. Most of the transcripts were prepared by Cristi H. Brockway (who occasionally inserts caustic and entertaining commentary). The transcripts can be found at http://members.aol.com/chatarama, or by searching for "Deadwood transcripts."

2   As frequently noted, the language in *Deadwood*'s dialogue has been defined as among the most obscene and profane in all media fictions. Although I have no intention of offending the reader, to discuss the series without quotation would be to do it a grave disservice. For more on this topic, see "The Language of Men," in David Milch, *Deadwood: Stories of the Black Hills* (Bloomsbury, N.Y.: Melcher Media, 2006). There he explains his choices and argues from a deeply philosophical perspective for the necessity of profanity and blasphemy as key elements in *Deadwood*.

3   Milch, *Deadwood*, 11. Subsequent references to this work will be indicated in the text by page number.

4   Mark Singer, "The Misfit." *The New Yorker*, 23 February 2005.

5   Heather Havrilesky, "The Man behind Deadwood," *Salon*, 5 March 2005, http://dir.salon.com/story/ent/feature/2005/03/05/milch/index.html.

6   Havrilesky, "Man behind Deadwood."

7   Singer, "Misfit."

8   Horace Newcomb, "Deadwood," in Edgerton and Jones, *The Essential HBO Reader*, 92–102.

Chapter 3

1   James Poniewozik, "The Best Television 2002," *Time*, http://www.time.com/time/bestandworst/2002/tv.html; Robert Abele, "Child in Time: *The Wire*," *LA Weekly*, 13 September 2006; Gillian Flynn, "TV: Best and Worst," *Entertainment Weekly*, 17 December 2004; and Steve

Johnson, "Why *The Wire* is the best show on TV," *The Chicago Tribune*, 1 June 2003.

2   Brian Lowry, "*The Wire*," *Variety*, 7 September 2006.

3   Jacob Weisberg, "The Wire on Fire: Analyzing the Best Show on Television," *Slate*, 13 September 2006. http://www.slate.com/id/2149566.

4   The aggregate critics' score for season 4 of *The Wire* was an unparalleled 98 out of 100 ("*The Wire*: Season 4," *Metacritic*, http://www.metacritic.com/tv/shows/wireseason4?q=the%20wire).

5   Eric Ducker, "The Left Behind: Inside *The Wire's* World of Alienation and Asshole Gods," *Fader Magazine*, 8 December 2006.

6   Ducker, "Left Behind."

7   Tony Norman, "TV Review: 'Wire' Carries Power," *Pittsburgh Post-Gazette*, 10 September 2006.

8   Lowry, "The Wire."

9   David Simon, *Introduction to* The Wire: *Truth Be Told*, by Rafael Alvarez (New York: Pocket Books, 2004), 12.

10   Steven B. Duke and Albert C. Gross, *America's Longest War: Rethinking Our Tragic Crusade against Drugs* (Los Angeles: J. P. Tarcher, 1994).

11   "Thirty Years of America's Drug War: A Chronology," PBS *Frontline*, http://www.pbs.org/wgbh/pages/frontline/shows/drugs/cron.

12   "The War on Drugs Is Lost," *National Review*, 12 February 1996.

13   David Simon, Episode 1 DVD Commentary, *The Wire:* The Complete First Season (New York: HBO Video, 2004).

14   Ed Burns, teleplay; David Simon and Ed Burns, story, "Reformation," *The Wire:* The Complete Third Season (New York: HBO Video, 2006).

15   David Simon, teleplay; David Simon and Ed Burns, story, "Mission Accomplished," *The Wire:* The Complete Third Season.

16   Simon, Introduction to *Truth Be Told*, 11.

17   Linda S. Lichter, S. Robert Lichter, and Stanley Rothman, *Watching America* (New York: Prentice Hall, 1991), 206.

18   Lichter et al., *Watching America*, 211.

19   Lichter et al., *Watching America*, 213–14.

20   David Simon, Introduction to *Truth Be Told*, 11.

21   David Simon, Introduction to *Truth Be Told*, 37.

22   Jeremiah 29:7.

23   Eric Ducker, "Left Behind."

24   David Simon, "The Target," DVD Commentary, *The Wire:* The Complete First Season.

25   Baltimore Basilica, "Our History," www.baltimorebasilica.org/history.

26   Rafael Alvarez, *Truth Be Told*, 127.

27   Alvarez, *Truth Be Told*, 137.

28   C. Eric Lincoln and Lawrence H. Mamiya, *The Black Church in the African American Experience* (Durham: Duke University Press, 1990), 17.

29   Bethel African Methodist Episcopal Church, "Bethel History," http://www.bethel1.org/history.htm.

30   David Simon, teleplay; David Simon and George Pelecanos, story, "Slapstick," *The Wire: The Complete Third Season.*

31   The deacon is portrayed by Melvin Williams, a legendary Baltimore drug dealer who inspired the character of Avon Barksdale. Williams is now a real-life deacon at Bethel Church.

32   Joshua Wolf Shenk, "An Old City Seeks a New Model," *The Nation*, 20 September 1999.

33   Simon and Burns, "Mission Accomplished."

34   Rafael Alvarez, "Mayor to The Wire: Drop Dead," *Truth be Told*, 229.

35   Alvarez, *Truth Be Told*, 231–32.

36   Michael Harrington, *The Other America: Poverty in the United States* (New York: Scribner's, repr. 1997).

37   William Finnegan, *Cold New World: Growing Up in Harder Country* (New York: Modern Library Edition, 1999).

38   Eric Goldman, "IGN Exclusive Interview: *The Wire*'s David Simon," 27 October 2006, http://tv.ign.com/articles/742/742350p1.html.

39   William Julius Wilson, *The Truly Disadvantaged: The Inner City, the Underclass, and Public Policy* (Chicago: University of Chicago Press, 1987), 56.

40   Wilson, *Truly Disadvantaged*, 61.

41   Alvarez, *Truth Be Told*, 51.

42   Alvarez, *Truth Be Told*, 72.

43   Alvarez, *Truth Be Told*, 227.

44   Ducker, "Left Behind."

45   Sut Jally and Justin Lewis, *Enlightened Racism:* The Cosby Show, *Audiences, and the Myth of the American Dream* (Boulder: Westview, 1992), 136.

46   Alvarez, *Truth Be Told*, 98.

47   James H. Cone, *God of the Oppressed* (San Francisco: Harper & Row, 1975), 183.

48   Sam Rosenfeld, "Five Minutes with: David Simon," 6 November 2006, http://www.campusprogress.org/features/1273/five-minutes-with-david-simon.

49   Bob Andelman, "David Simon, *The Wire* Creator," Mr. Media Interviews by Bob Andelman, 15 February 2007, http://www.mrmedia.com/2007/02/fridays-with-mr-media-david-simonthe.html.

50   Cynthia E. Griffin and George H. Hill, "History of Blacks on Television," in *Blacks on Television: A Selectively Annotated Bibliography*, by George H. Hill and Sylvia Saverson Hill (Metuchen, N.J.: The Scarecrow Press, 1985). See also J. Fred MacDonald, *Blacks in White TV* (Chicago: Nelson-Hall), 1983.

51   Griffin and Hill, "Blacks on Television," 3.

52   Griffin and Hill, "Blacks on Television," 6–7.

53 Darnell Hunt, "Black Content, White Control" in *Channeling Blackness: Studies on Television and Race in America*, ed. Darnell Hunt (New York: Oxford University Press, 2004), 270.

54 Jally and Lewis, *Enlightened Racism*, 60.

55 Hunt, "Black Content, White Control," 275.

56 Herman Gray, "The Politics of Representation in Network Television," in *Television: The Critical View*, 6th edition, ed. Horace Newcomb (New York: Oxford University Press, 2000).

57 Hunt, "Black Content, White Control," 300.

58 Anthony Walton, "The Rules of the Game," in Alvarez, *Truth Be Told*, 220–21.

59 Hunt, "Black Content, White Control," 299.

60 Andelman, "David Simon, *The Wire* Creator."

61 George Pelecanos, "The Writer's Ambition," in Alvarez, *Truth Be Told*, 234.

62 Anthony Walton, "The Rules of the Game," in Alvarez, *Truth Be Told*, 220.

Chapter 4

This research was supported by a Faculty Development Grant from Cabrini College. It was first presented as a paper at the 2007 meeting of the American Folklore Society. I am grateful to Daniel Wojcik for the organization of that panel. Diane Winston suggested the topic to me and was a tremendous support throughout the preparation of the essay. I wish to thank Deborah Ann Bailey; Father Michael Bielecki, O.S.A.; Lourdes Barretto; Shaun Butler; John DiMucci; Tracy Fessenden; Raymond A. Harris; Kathleen M. Joyce; Elizabeth McAlister; Charlie McCormick; Kathy McCrea; Lisa A. Ratmansky; Abel Rodriguez; and Gary Rupacz; as well as Dianna McKellar, Corey Salazar, and Anne Schwelm of Cabrini College's Holy Spirit Library for their reference assistance. I am especially grateful to Katie Reing for her technical advice, Nicholas Rademacher and Joseph Sciorra for their comments, and especially Nancy L. Watterson, who generously read drafts of the article.

1   Aaron Sorkin, in the oral commentary to the pilot episode contained in the DVD set of the series, notes that the character of the president in his original conception was not to be as central a character as he became under the acting ability of Martin Sheen. Sheen himself recalled: "I was never supposed to do this series. . . . It was originally only about the staff at the White House. The president was just a minor character. But after I did the pilot, they looked it over and saw what a great set the Oval Office was. Well, Aaron Sorkin, the creator of the show, came back to me and asked if I wanted to do the series" (Greg Heffernan, "Martin Sheen: Catholic President on Prime Time," *St. Anthony*

Messenger, May 2000, http://www.americancatholic.org/messenger/ May2000/feature1.asp).

2   A notable dramatic element of Sorkin's writing style for stage drama, cinema, or television, each episode contains such soliloquies by at least two of the characters. Anna Deavere Smith, a playwright and actor, who appeared in *The West Wing* described Sorkin as "a writer who anticipates the actor and the actor's intelligence . . . . There's more language and more character than we're used to. That's one of the things he brought to TV from theater" (Bruce Weber, "Prodigal Returns, Bearing Dialogue," *The New York Times*, 4 November 2007, http:// nytimes.com/2007/11/04/theater/04webe.html?_r=1&oref=slogin).

3   *The West Wing* and all its characters are properties of Aaron Sorkin, John Wells Production, Warner Brothers Television, and NBC. No copyright infringement is intended. Quotation can be found at http:// www.westwingtranscripts.com/search.php?flag=getTranscript&id=1 &keyword=Pilot.

4   Wm. Hugh Jansen, "The Esoteric–Exoteric Factor in Folklore," in *The Study of Folklore*, ed. Alan Dundes, 43–51 (Englewood Cliffs, N.J.: Prentice-Hall, 1965).

5   Jim McDermott, "American Dreams: *The West Wing* and *Commander in Chief*," *America* 194 (2006): 21.

6   McDermott, "American Dreams," 22.

7   Raymond A. Schroth, "*The West Wing*—A Liberal Catholic White House?" review of *The West Wing*. *National Catholic Reporter*, 22 October 1999, http://natcath.org/NCR_Online/archives2/1999d/102299/ 102299m.htm.

8   Leonard Norman Primiano, "Vernacular Religion and the Search for Method in Religious Folklife," *Western Folklore* 54 (1995): 44.

9   Leonard Norman Primiano, "What Is Vernacular Catholicism? The 'Dignity' Example," *Acta Ethnographica Hungarica* 46, nos. 1–2 (2001): 51–58.

10   See, e.g., Peter G. Horsfield, *Religious Television: The American Experience* (New York: Longman, 1984), 7–8; D. P. Noonan, *The Passion of Fulton Sheen* (New York: Dodd, Mead, 1972); John Tracy Ellis, *Catholic Bishops: A Memoir* (Collegeville, Minn.: Liturgical Press, 1983); Kathleen Riley Fields, "Bishop Fulton J. Sheen: An American Catholic Response to the Twentieth Century" (Ph.D. diss., University of Notre Dame, 1988); Peter W. Williams, "Fulton J. Sheen," in *Twentieth-Century Shapers of American Popular Religion*, ed. Charles H. Lippy (Westport, Conn.: Greenwood, 1989), 387–93; Christopher Owen Lynch, *Selling Catholicism: Bishop Sheen and the Power of Television* (Lexington: University Press of Kentucky, 1998); Thomas C. Reeves, *America's Bishop: The Life and Times of Fulton J. Sheen* (San Francisco: Encounter, 2001). I might add that the dramatic series *The Sopranos* (HBO 1999–2007) has had a number of scholars consider the significance of its religious content.

See Carla Gardina Pestana, "Catholicism, Identity, and Ethics," in *A Sit Down with the* Sopranos: *Watching Italian-American Culture on TV's Most Talked-About Series*, ed. Regina Barreca, 129–48 (New York: Palgrave, 2002); Peter H. Hare, "What Kind of God Does This . . . ?" in The Sopranos *and Philosophy: I Kill Therefore I Am*, ed. Richard Greene and Peter Vernezzi, 195–206 (Chicago: Open Court, 2004); Peter Vernezze, "Tony Soprano in Hell: Chase's Mob in Dante's *Inferno*," in Green and Vernezze, Sopranos *and Philosophy*, 185–94.

11   It is somewhat amusing to report that the 2003 edition misses this opportunity, but does include a two-page entry on "telepathy." Of course, it is also significant to note the omission of an article or even many references to Catholicism in the 2002 *Encyclopedia of Communication and Information*, ed. Jorge Reina Schement (New York: Gale Group, 2002).

12   Philip Jenkins, *The New Anti-Catholicism: The Last Acceptable Prejudice* (New York: Oxford University Press, 2003), 157.

13   Jenkins, *New Anti-Catholicism*, 174.

14   Jenkins, *New Anti-Catholicism*, 173.

15   Jenkins, *New Anti-Catholicism*, 163.

16   Skill and Robinson, 1994.

17   Skill, Robinson, Lyons, and Larson, 265.

18   Skill and Robinson, 1994, 76.

19   Skill and Robinson, 1994, 83.

20   James T. Fisher, "Catholicism as American Popular Culture," in *American Catholics, American Culture: Tradition and Resistance*, vol. 2: *American Catholics in the Public Square*, ed. Margaret O'Brien Steinfels, 101–11 (Lanham, Md.: Rowman and Littlefield, 2004); Mark Massa, "'As If in Prayer': A Response to 'Catholicism in American Popular Culture,'" in Steinfels, *American Catholics, American Culture*, 112–18.

21   Fisher, "Catholicism as American Popular Culture," 105–6.

22   Massa, "'As If in Prayer,'" 113–14.

23   Massa, "'As If in Prayer,'" 118.

24   Williams, *Television*, 38.

25   Jean Baudrillard, "The Precession of Simulacra," in *Art after Modernism: Rethinking Representation*, ed. Brian Wallis, 253–81 (New York: New Museum of Contemporary Art, 1984).

26   Steven Best and Douglas Kellner, *Postmodern Theory* (New York: The Guilford Press, 1991), 119.

27   What is additionally fascinating about this treatment of post-Vatican II Catholicism on television is the fact that the growth of the medium, in terms of it literally finding a place in every American home as well as the gradual expansion of network news divisions to cover national and international affairs, coincides so nearly with the years of the development, actual meeting, implementation, and aftermath of the Second Vatican Council.

28   In the DVD commentary on the program, a nice intertextual touch about this scene is noted by Aaron Sorkin: the small Bible held by Karl Malden's clerical character is the same Bible that he used as Father Barry in the classic film *On the Waterfront* (1954), where he also essayed the role of moral conscience—on this occasion for ex-prize fighter turned longshoreman Terry Malloy (played by Marlon Brando).

29   Nancy Haught, "A True Believer in *The West Wing*," *Atlanta Journal-Constitution*, 31 March 2001, http://b4a.healthyinterest.net/news/archives/2001/03/a_true_believer.html.

30   Frazier Moore, "Hail to the Chief of 'The West Wing,'" *Associated Press*, 8 May 2000, http://www.westwingepguide.com/S1/Episodes/14_TTSD.html. *Washington Post* writer Sharon Waxman reports, "That episode—the brainchild of two writers on the show, one a former aid to Senator Daniel Patrick Moynihan—also sparked heated debates on the set, especially among producer Aaron Sorkin, director Tommy Schlamme, and Sheen. The actor desperately wanted the episode to end with the president commuting the execution; Sorkin and Schlamme were adamant that he see it through. They won . . ." ("Hollywood Pleads Its Case" *Washington Post*, 7 May 2000, http://www.westwingepguide.com/S1/Episodes/14_TTSD.html). In an interview with Sheen, Frazier Moore quotes the actor: "'He [Bartlet] had the chance to save a guy's life,' says [Martin] Sheen almost accusingly. 'He knew it was sinful—to kill anyone is sinful—and out of political expedience, he chose not to save him. . . . Our president on *The West Wing* is not Catholic by accident,' says Sheen. 'We added that (element) so that he would have a moral frame of reference and take personal responsibility for sin'" (Moore, "Hail to the Chief"). In an interview later in the year, Sheen recalled: "My only input was that I insisted the character of Bartlet be Catholic and that he would have a degree from Notre Dame. . . . And I got both of those things. I'm a Catholic, and I wanted this president to have to deal in the moral frame of reference of these issues. I'm personally opposed to the death penalty, but as the president in the show, at least on one occasion, I had to allow a man to die. So I knelt on this presidential seal and asked for forgiveness. If the president wasn't Catholic, he couldn't do that" (Andrew Ryan, "Corridors of Power," *The Globe and Mail*, 16 December 2000, http://www.westwingepguide.com/S1/Episodes/14_TTSD.html). In a 2000 interview in the Catholic periodical *St. Anthony Messenger*, Sheen describes the character of his President Bartlet: "It's me. . . . But no matter who this president is, an actor wants to know what makes the character tick. And that's what Aaron told me: 'He's you, Martin. Make him you'" (Heffernan, "Martin Sheen: Catholic President.").

    Martin Sheen, who is a radical Catholic and ardent pacifist in the tradition of Dorothy Day, was (according to a May 2001 interview on *Charlie Rose* [PBS 1993–] with Sorkin, Sheen, and other cast members)

Sorkin's first choice for the role of the president. Sorkin would also check various religious details with the Catholic Sheen. Of course, that spirit of creativity extended only so far for the actor. I was told by co-executive producer, Lew Wells, in a June 2007 conversation that Martin Sheen never improvised his scenes adding religious content; he acted only the lines that were given to him, especially in the show's early years when they were penned by Sorkin. This information was gathered listening to Lew Wells, cast members Bradley Whitford and Melissa Fitzgerald, as well as a writer in its later seasons, Josh Singer, at the event, "The Making of *The West Wing*: Art Imitating Politics," sponsored by the World Affairs Council of Philadelphia, and held in Radnor, Pennsylvania, on 7 June 2007. NiCole Robinson, another actor from the program who played Margaret Hooper, Chief of Staff Leo McGarry's secretary, was also present at this event and told me that there was little doubt of Sheen's Catholicity. When she was first introduced to Sheen, he was holding a rosary; and after a Saturday night in Las Vegas in which the cast and crew celebrated someone's birthday at Sheen's expense, he prompted as many of the partygoers as possible to attend Mass with him on Sunday morning. I wish to thank Regina Black Lennox and Ed Satell for their invitation to this occasion.

31   http://www.westwingtranscripts.com/search.php?flag=getTranscript&id=14&keyword=Take%20This%20Sabbath%20Day.

32   Primiano, "Vernacular Religion," 49–50.

33   http://www.westwingtranscripts.com/search.php?flag=getTranscript&id=44&keyword=Two%20Cathedrals.

34   I thank E. Ann Matter, Neal Hébert, and J. Melvin for their skill and time in assisting me with this translation of the Latin text. The translation included with *The West Wing* shooting script is as follows: "Am I really to believe that these are the acts of a loving God? A just God? A wise God?" Bartlet exclaims. "To hell with your punishments. I was your servant here on Earth. And I spread your word and I did your work. To hell with your punishments. To hell with you" (Lynn Elber, "*West Wing* Ends Season Powerfully," *Associated Press*, 17 May 2001, http://www.westwingepguide.com/S2/Episodes/44_TC.html).

35   Admittedly, a Catholic speaking Latin seems to be a turn back to a pre-Vatican II characterization of Catholicism, though few lay Catholics would have been proficient in spoken or written Latin even at that time. Given the educational background of President Bartlet and his personality as revealed in various episodes, it does seem to be in his character that he would have both the ability and the desire to communicate to his Catholic God in Latin.

36   This is a point that was noted during the June 2007 forum.

37   Aaron Sorkin, the creator of *The West Wing* is easily identified as a Los Angeles screenwriter, playwright, director, and producer of thoughtful television dramas, but he has never been given any public credit for

another sensitivity and sensibility, namely as a folklorist. While not a professional folklorist, Sorkin possesses the uncanny ability to make folklore content the central driving force of a plot that he is conceiving. The first such identifiable example can be found in his 1992 play and film, *A Few Good Men*, which as a film starred Tom Cruise and Jack Nicholson. This murder mystery, courtroom drama, military saga, and coming-of-age morality tale could not exist were it not for the Marine oral tradition of a "Code Red" for disciplining a soldier falling behind in his or her duties, as well as Sorkin's keen recognition and appreciation of how oral folklore and folk traditions exist as an unwritten, orally transmitted, traditional, community-held practice within the military. A second, more subtle but equally powerful, example of folklore in use in Hollywood creations is observed in how Sorkin employs what I have been identifying as vernacular Catholicism to drive the character of President Bartlet.

38   Catherine L. Albanese, "Exchanging Selves, Exchanging Souls Contact, Combination, and American Religious History," in *Retelling U.S. Religious History*, ed. Thomas A. Tweed, 200–26 (Berkeley: University of California Press, 1997), 223.

39   Sorkin identifies himself as Jewish in a 2001 article: "I'm Jewish, but I never went to Hebrew school." Journalist Nancy Haught adds that "while he spent the seventh grade attending friends' bar mitzvahs, he didn't have his own." Sorkin, who does not describe himself as a deeply religious man, clarifies: "Growing up, it was very easy for me to think, as it is very easy for a lot of people to think, that religion—that most often one should be suspicious of it. That most often it's an instrument of hypocrisy or, worse yet, of bullying. 'You're not living your life the way I would have you live it, the way God would have you live it. Therefore, God is going to punish you; you are somehow less in God's eyes.' Obviously, that kind of thing is insidious and terrible, and I point to that often on *The West Wing*." Sorkin says, "But what I want to make sure to point to just as often is the way in which faith can be magnificent, an enormous comfort and an incredible road map" (Nancy Haught, "A True Believer").

40   Massa, "'As If in Prayer,'" 114–15.

Chapter 5

The author wishes to thank the creators and production staffs of *Everwood* and *The O.C.* for their generous cooperation in the writing of this essay.

1   Book of Ruth, *The Holy Bible* (Philadelphia: National, 2005), 1:15. Some scholars believe that the sympathetic view of intermarriage posited in the book of Ruth was inserted into the Scriptures to counter the vehement opposition to intermarriage put forth in the book of Ezra, which

urges Jews to cast off their non-Jewish wives and any offspring of these marriages (Susan Weidman Schneider, *Intermarriage: The Challenge of Living with Differences between Christians and Jews* [New York: Free Press, 1989], 13). Biblical injunctions against intermarriage also appear in Genesis 24:3, Numbers 25:1–9, and Nehemiah 10:30.

2   Said to be born of a Jewish mother and a Holy Ghost "father," Jesus can be regarded as the direct progeny of intermarriage. The Messiah's purported hereditary bond to David appears in Isaiah 11:1–4, 9–10.

3   Werner Sollers, *Beyond Ethnicity: Consent and Descent in American Culture* (New York: Oxford University Press, 1986); Karen Brodkin, *How the Jews Became White Folks . . . and What That Says about Race in America* (New Brunswick, N.J.: Rutgers University Press, 1998), 86.

4   Chaim Waxman, *America's Jews in Transition* (Philadelphia: Temple University Press, 1983), 174; Ellen Jaffe McClain, *Embracing the Stranger: Intermarriage and the Future of the American Jewish Community* (New York: Basic, 1995), 126. The NJPS's more statistically sound reporting, in 2000, of a 47 percent intermarriage rate in 2000 hardly assuaged Jewish survivalist concerns.

5   J. J. Goldberg, *Jewish Power: Inside the American Jewish Establishment* (Reading, Mass.: Addison-Wesley, 1996), 68; McClain, *Embracing the Stranger*, 11.

6   Julia dies in "Pilot" (season 1, episode 1). She appears in flashback sequences in several first-season episodes thereafter.

7   Liane Pritikin points out that the use of the name Cohen in an intermarriage context can be taken as offensive from an Orthodox perspective. Cohenim, in the Torah, were priests descended from the tribe of Levi who were not allowed to marry a divorcee, a convert, or a Jewish woman who has slept with a Gentile. Kirsten, meanwhile, is a familial name for Christianity. From a dramatic standpoint, of course, the religious associations of the two names serve to highlight the interfaith nature of the marriage.

8   In one episode of *Brothers and Sisters*, one of the intermarried couple's grandchildren, upon learning about Hanukkah in school, indicates that she wants to identify as Jewish. Her grandmother, a politically progressive secular Jew (played by Sally Field!) who has raised her children areligiously, suggests a similar approach for her grandchild. As for *Weeds*, although protagonist Nancy Botwin (Mary-Louise Parker) remarries (briefly) in the second season, her two sons (one around ten, the other in high school) are the progeny of her first marriage to a Jewish man who died just prior to the start of the series and whose father is played by Albert Brooks. Another regular family on the show, the Hodeses, features a Jewish-Christian couple with a ten-year-old daughter. Thus far, however, the main tension around religious issues concerns Nancy's lascivious brother-in-law Andy, whose seeming attempt

to tap his Jewish roots, such as by enrolling in rabbinical school, is motivated largely by a desire to "shtup" Jewish women.

9   Harvey Cox, *Common Prayers: Faith, Family, and a Christian's Journey through the Jewish Year* (New York: Houghton Mifflin, 1999), 250–51.

10   For views and statistics on the effects of Jewish intermarriage, see Sylvia Barack Fishman, *Double or Nothing: Jewish Families and Mixed Marriage* (Hanover: Brandeis University Press, 2004); Schneider, *Intermarriage*; McClain, *Embracing the Stranger*; Kerri Steinberg, "Photography, Philanthropy, and the Politics of American Jewish Identity" (Ph.D. diss., University of California, Los Angeles, 1995), 34–35; Julie Wiener, "Intermarriage: The Contest," *Los Angeles Jewish Journal*, 9 May 2003, 7; Julie Gruenbaum Fax, "Married to It," *Los Angeles Jewish Journal*, 19 December 2003, 12, 14–15.

11   Bruce Phillips, "Children of Intermarriage: How Jewish?" in *Studies in Contemporary Jewry* 14 (1998): 86.

12   Stephen M. Cohen, "Stop Sugarcoating Intermarriage," *Jewish Journal* 9 (2007): 12.

13   Cohen, "Stop Sugarcoating Intermarriage," 63.

14   See Paul Mendes-Flohr, *German Jews: A Dual Identity* (New Haven: Yale University Press, 1999), 93.

15   Fishman, *Double or Nothing*, 156.

16   While there are no in-married couples to compare them with, the four recent shows featuring intermarried couples with children split fifty-fifty in survivalist terms, with *Everwood* and *The O.C.* maintaining a Jewish connection and *Brothers and Sisters* and *Weeds* (so far) tending to let it slide.

17   Robert Orsi, *The Madonna of 115th Street: Faith and Community in Italian Harlem, 1880–1950*, 2nd ed. (New Haven: Yale University Press, 2002), xix–xxiv.

18   Robert Bellah, "Finding Meaning in Human Experience," *Chronicle of Higher Education*, 1 December 2006, B10.

19   Martin Buber, "Dialogue," Chapter 1 in *Between Man and Man* (1929), trans. Ronald Gregor-Smith (London: Routledge, 2002), 17.

20   Martin Buber, *I and Thou* (1936), trans. Walter Kaufmann (New York: Scribner, 1970).

21   Eliezer Schweid, in "Jewish Messianism: Metamorphosis of an Idea," *Jerusalem Quarterly* 36 (1985), points out that secularism itself, in its Jewish messianic form that emerged from the Enlightenment, "used religious elements and ways of thinking in its war with religion."

22   Neil Gillman, *Sacred Fragments: Recovering Theology for the Modern Jew* (Philadelphia: Jewish Publication Society, 1990), 56; Michael Lerner, *The Politics of Meaning* (New York: Unger, 1996). Speaking from a Catholic perspective, Senator John Kerry proposed in a 2006 speech to college students "that fighting poverty and global warming and reducing the number of abortions were 'godly tasks' and of critical

importance to people of faith" (Maria L. La Ganga, "Mixing Religion and Politics," *Los Angeles Times*, 27 October 2006, E16).

23　Jürgen Habermas, "Religion in the Public Sphere," *European Journal of Philosophy* 14, no. 1 (2006): 1–25, 6–7, 17, 11, 19. Habermas' descriptive analysis of the links between several progressive principles in religion and secularism is made prescriptive in his concept of "post-metaphysical thought," which posits "an agnostic but non-reductionist philosophical position in regard to religion. It refrains on the one hand from passing judgments on religious truth while insisting (in a non-polemical fashion) on drawing a strict line between faith and knowledge. It rejects on the other a scientistically limited perception of reason and the exclusion of religious doctrines from the genealogy of reason." It proposes more than simple tolerance of religion by secularism, and vice versa, but a "complementary learning process" in which both sides acknowledge their shared humanistic and spiritual elements" ("Religion," 16, 4).

24　Sollers, *Beyond Ethnicity*, 66. Zangwill was British, but *The Melting Pot* is set in the United States.

25　*The Jazz Singer* also was remade several times, as theatrical films in 1953 and 1980, and as a TV anthology drama in 1959.

26　For a detailed overview of intermarriage-themed television episodes and shows, see Jonathan Pearl and Judith Pearl, *The Chosen Image: Television's Portrayal of Jewish Themes and Characters* (Jefferson, N.C.: McFarland, 1999), 195–227.

27　For more on the WLBT case that opened the door to monitoring American television, and on media monitoring in general, see Kathryn Montgomery, *Target: Prime Time: Advocacy Groups and the Struggle over Entertainment Television* (New York: Oxford University Press, 1989).

28　See Montgomery, *Target: Prime Time*; Vincent Brook, *Something Ain't Kosher Here: The Rise of the "Jewish" Sitcom* (New Brunswick, N.J.: Rutgers University Press, 2003), 48–54. *Bridget Loves Bernie* was rated fifth overall for the season.

29　Peter F. Langman, *Jewish Issues in Multiculturalism: A Handbook for Educators and Clinicians* (Northvale, N.J.: Jason Aronson, 1999), 313. While the comparatively small Reconstructionist movement accepted patrilineal descent as equally valid in 1968, the largest reform movement officially affirmed it only in 1983, while the two other sizeable denominations, Orthodox and Conservative, remain steadfastly matrilinealist (see McClain, *Embracing the Stranger*).

30　Pearl and Pearl, *Chosen Image*, 195–227.

31　The post-1987 interfaith shows include (besides the already mentioned *thirtysomething, The Commish, Dream On, Everwood, The O.C.*, and *Weeds*) *Chicken Soup, Anything But Love, The Marshall Chronicles, George and Leo, Brooklyn Bridge, Flying Blind, Love and War, Mad About You, The Nanny, Ned and Stacey, Dharma and Greg, You're the One, Rude Awakening, Will and Grace, Relativity, Bette, Curb Your Enthusiasm, Friends, Three Sisters,*

Inside Schwartz, and *Lucky Louis*. In addition, shows over this period whose main or secondary characters meaningfully engaged interfaith issues to some extent include *Cheers, LA Law, Murphy Brown, Suddenly Susan, Seventh Heaven, Beverly Hills 90210, Sisters, A Year in the Life, Buck James, I'll Fly Away, The Days and Nights of Molly Dodd, Our House, Homefront, Caroline in the City, Sex and the City, Studio 60 on the Sunset Strip*, and *The Nine*.

32   *Cheers* is not counted here because, despite the aforementioned circumcision storyline concerning Frasier and Lilith, the show itself was not centered on an interfaith relationship.

33   Half-Jewish characters had appeared on earlier shows, Juan Epstein in *Welcome Back, Kotter* (1975–1979) and Doris Schwartz in *Fame* (1982–1987), but their intermarried origins played little if any role in the narrative.

34   Jim Collins, "Postmodernism and Television," in *Channels of Discourse, Reassembled*, 2nd ed., ed. Robert C. Allen (Chapel Hill: University of North Carolina Press, 1992), 327–53.

35   *Everwood*'s creator, Greg Berlanti, wrote for *Dawson's Creek* and refers to the two shows' kinship in the DVD commentary for the pilot episode. Berlanti has gone on to create *Jack and Bobby* (2004–2005) and co-produce *Brothers and Sisters* (2006–). He was raised Catholic but has been "exploring other religions for interest," he explained in an e-mail (received 26 February 2007). As for the rest of the writing staff, "it was an across-the-board mix—Jewish, Protestant, Catholic, Christian."

36   Collins, "Postmodernism and Television," 335.

37   In the series finale, "The End's Not Near, It's Here" (season 4, episode 16), when Taylor acts surprised that *The Valley* is still on TV, Summer facetiously references *The O.C.*'s own somewhat abrupt cancellation in exclaiming, "It just got picked up for five more seasons! You know these teen dramas, they just run forever."

38   "Lonely Hearts Club" (season 2, episode 12). *The O.C.* was far from the first show to comment on itself in this manner. Among the more prominent antecedents: *The Simpsons* (1989–) featured the *Itchy and Scratchy* cartoons within the cartoon; *Twin Peaks* (1991–1992) had the *Invitation to Love* soap within the soap; and Seinfeld, the "show about nothing" within the "show about nothing."

39   "The Blaze of Glory" (season 2, episode 16).

40   "The Risky Business" (season 2, episode 18); "Safe Harbor" (season 3, episode 11).

41   "Party Favor" (season 3, episode 23).

42   The shooting locations are identified in the shows' DVD commentaries.

43   Greg Berlanti, *Everwood*, DVD commentary: "Pilot" (season 1, episode 1). The Rockwell-style credits are gone by the third season, as is, with rare exceptions, Irv's narration.

44 "Home" (season 1, episode 23).

45 *The O.C.*, DVD commentaries: "Pilot" (season 1, episode 1); "The Chrismukkah That Almost Wasn't" (season 2, episode 6).

46 "Lonely Hearts Club."

47 "O.C. Confidential" (season 2, episode 20).

48 "Deer God" (season 1, episode 5).

49 The Cohens' sense of being outsiders in Newport Beach is metatextually affirmed by Sandy and Kirsten's return, in the series finale, to Berkeley, the place where they had met in college and, as they had reminded us throughout the series, had spent the happiest years of their lives.

50 "The Chrismukkah Bar Mitz-vahkkah" (season 3, episode 10).

51 "Foreverwood" (season 4, episode 21).

52 "Pilot"; "The Unveiling" (season 1, episode 18).

53 "The Nana" (season 1, episode 23).

54 "The End's Not Near, It's Here" (season 4, episode 16).

55 "The Reckoning" (season 4, episode 19).

56 Daniel J. Staziewski, "On *Everwood*," http://thefilmchair.com/comment061006.html, accessed October 2006 [link no longer active].

57 In "Till Death Do us Part" (season 1, episode 8), Andy does go to a church to pray for renewed faith and a reason to go on living.

58 "Friendly Fire" is the title of season 1, episode 3; "The Doctor Is In" of season 1, episode 6; "Vegetative State" of season 1, episode 12; "Episode 20" of season 1, episode 21; Gretchen's "altruism complex" comment is from "The Doctor Is In."

59 Mendes-Flohr, *German Jews*, 26. The assimilationist aspect of Jews' religious devotion to education and culture is aptly captured in the popular quip that Jews were "Germans by the grace of Goethe" (Mendes-Flohr, *German Jews*, 5).

60 Quoted in Mendes-Flohr, *German Jews*, 27. A recent National Endowment of the Arts study, the first to measure the connection between the arts and civic engagement, affirms a link between culture and ethics. People who participate in the arts, even if only reading literature, the study concluded, are twice as likely to be socially committed and to volunteer in their communities as those who do not (http://www.arts.gov/pub/CivicEngagement.pdf).

61 J. Hoberman, "On *The Jazz Singer*," in *Entertaining America: Jews, Movies, and Broadcasting*, ed. J. Hoberman and Jeffrey Shandler (Princeton: Princeton University Press, 2003), 77.

62 Samuel Raphaelson, "Preface to *The Jazz Singer*" (New York: Brentano's, 1925), 9. For more on the attractions of Jews and other immigrant groups to black entertainment forms, especially blackface minstrelsy, see Michael Rogin, *Blackface, White Noise: Jewish Immigrants in the Hollywood Melting Pot* (Berkeley: University of California Press, 1996); Eric Lott, *Love and Theft: Blackface Minstrelsy and the American Working*

Class (New York: Oxford University Press, 1993); Louis Chute-Sokei, *The Last "Darky": Bert Williams, Black-on-Black Minstrelsy, and the African Diaspora* (Durham: Duke University Press, 2006).

63 "The Chrismukkah Bar Mitz-vahkkah."

64 "Turf Wars" (season 1, episode 9).

65 The Hoffmans appear in two episodes, "Turf Wars," and "Is There a Doctor in the House" (season 1, episode 10). Ruth's quote is from the latter.

66 "Deer God."

67 An added irony, of course, is that Magilla, while associated with the popular cartoon character Magilla Gorilla, is also the name for the Jewish scroll on which the Purim story is written—a story in which intermarriage, of the Jewish Queen Esther to the Babylonian King Ahasuerus, plays a crucial part.

68 "Fight Club" (season 4, episode 1).

69 "Man of the Year" (season 3, episode 24).

70 That Seth would have trouble finding Jews in Orange County, as he asserts in "The Chrismukkah That Almost Wasn't" (season 2, episode 6), is one of the show's most outrageous poetic liberties. Neighboring Los Angeles County has more than half-a-million Jews; Josh Schwartz, in his DVD commentary for this episode, refers to a local publication called *Orange County Jewish Life*. And, most damningly, a student of mine who hails from Newport Beach and grew up in a mixed-marriage family—and whose name happens to be Ashley Cohen!—decries in a class paper concerning the show, "the absurdity of the portrayal of the lack of a Jewish community in the city of Newport. As a private-school student, I found myself surrounded by Jewish families throughout my life. The Jewish community's prevalence . . . is difficult to ignore with the multiple synagogues, state-of-the-art Jewish community center, and a very successful Jewish day school."

71 "The Best Chrismukkah Ever" (season 1, episode 13).

72 "Best Chrismukkah Ever."

73 "The Chrismukkah That Almost Wasn't."

74 Fishman, *Double or Nothing*, 131–32.

75 Fishman, *Double or Nothing*, 132.

76 DVD commentary for "The Chrismukkah That Almost Wasn't." The quote is a composite of Schwartz's and De Laurentis's statements.

77 Chrismukkah.com's creator Ron Gompertz acknowledged in a phone interview that while the idea for the Web site preceded *The O.C.*'s first Chrismukkah episode, the formation of the site was spurred by the show. The two books on the subject include Gompertz's own *Chrismukkah: Everything You Need to Know to Celebrate the Hybrid Holiday* (New York: Stewart, Tabori & Chang, 2006), and Gersh Kuntzman, *Chrismukkah: The Official Guide to the World's Most Beloved Holiday* (Seattle: Sasquatch Books, 2006).

78   Gompertz, *Chrismukkah*, 20.

79   I was unable to determine whether Schwarz and De Laurentis' comments about the online marketing of yarmuclauses were meant tongue-in-cheek, because neither of them responded to repeated e-mail communications.

80   The sitcom *It's Like, You Know* . . . (1997–1998) skewered the venal aspects of religious ritual with its focus on a *Pay per Jew* television network formed to give Jews the opportunity to enjoy the High Holiday services in the comfort of their homes and for a cheaper price.

81   The fourth season's "Chrismuk-huh?" (episode 7), as the title suggests, continues the show's downward moral(e) slide, mirroring a dip in the show's ratings. The holiday celebration makes only a cursory, last-second appearance here, playing second fiddle to Ryan's and Taylor's coma-induced nightmares in which the Cohen family has completely fallen apart. Sandy seems to reference the show's metanarrative (and ratings?) crisis when, in explaining the sorry state of affairs in Ryan's bad dream, he says, "After Marissa died, everybody got stuck."

82   Although Delia's candle dedication is rendered in loving detail, the bat mitzvah ritual is also slighted through its incorporation into a musical montage with a nondiegetic vocal drowning out Delia's Hebrew recitation.

83   David Hollinger, *Postethnic America: Beyond Multiculturalism* (New York: Basic, 1995), 3.

84   Hollinger, *Postethnic America*, 3–4.

85   Lerner, *The Politics of Meaning*. The quote is from Dan Levine, "Daniel Dennett's Theory of Religion," *Tikkun* (November–December 2006), 51–53, 77–79, 52.

86   "The Nana."

87   "My Two Dads" (season 4, episode 9); "The End's Not Near, It's Here."

88   Summer's going to work for George is in "The End's Not Near, It's Here." Sandy's quote is from "Thanksgiving" (season 4, episode 3).

89   Given the elder Cohens' move to Berkeley in the season finale, perhaps *Boikley* would be a more apt title. As for Summer's dark hair, another unrealistic anomaly of the show's Newport Beach setting is its blondness. Summer, Seth, and Sandy seem about the only dark-haired people *in* Aryan Orange County.

90   Marcus Lee Hanson, "The Third Generation in America" (originally titled "The Problem of the Third-Generation Immigrant," 1938), *Commentary* 14 (1952): 495. This syndrome was represented even more forcefully in the *Dream On* episode described above.

91   Joel Kotkin and Zina Klapper, "Diaspora Shifts, But Isn't Going Away Anytime Soon," *Jewish Journal*, 10 November 2006, 20, 22.

92   George Lipsitz, *Time Passages: Collective Memory and American Popular Culture* (Minneapolis: University of Minnesota Press, 1990), 16, 9.

Chapter 6

This chapter is dedicated to the blessed memory of James Baldwin, on the twentieth anniversary of his death. He taught us all a great deal about images and representation. My thanks to Liza Baker, Jane Iwamura, and Diane Winston for allowing me to be a part of this project. I am thankful as well to helpful editorial suggestions by Jane and Diane, as well as Remi Aubuchon, Omid Safi, and Kathryn Sorrells.

1   Salman Rushdie, *The Satanic Verses* (London: Penguin, 1988), 168.

2   F. E. Peters, *Muhammad and the Origins of Islam* (Albany: State University of New York Press, 1994).

3   For complete details of the poll, see http://pewforum.org/surveys/religionviews07/.

4   See, e.g., Stewart Hoover, *Religion in the News: Faith and Journalism in American Public Discourse* (Thousand Oaks, Calif.: SAGE, 1998); Judith Buddenbaum and Debra Mason, eds., *Readings on Religion as News* (Ames: Iowa State University Press, 2000); Stewart Hoover and Lynn Clark, eds., *Practicing Religion in the Age of Media: Explorations in Media, Religion, and Culture* (New York: Columbia University Press, 2002); John Giggie and Diane Winston, eds., *Faith in the Market: Religion and the Rise of Urban Commercial Culture* (New Brunswick, N.J.: Rutgers University Press, 2002); Claire Badaracco, ed., *Quoting God: How Media Shape Ideas about Religion* (Waco, Tex.: Baylor University Press, 2005); Stewart Hoover, *Religion in the Media Age* (London: Routledge, 2006).

5   See, e.g., Dale Eickelman and Jon Anderson, eds., *New Media in the Muslim World: The Emerging Public Sphere*, 2nd ed. (Bloomington: Indiana University Press, 2003); or Miriam Cooke and Bruce Lawrence, eds., *Muslim Networks: From Hajj to Hip Hop* (Chapel Hill: University of North Carolina Press, 2005).

6   See, e.g., Jack Shaheen, *The TV Arab* (Bowling Green, Ky.: Bowling Green State University Press, 1984); Edward Said, *Covering Islam: How the Media and the Experts Determine How We See the Rest of the World*, updated ed. (New York: Vintage, 1997); or Karim Karim, *Islamic Peril: Media and Global Violence*, updated ed. (Montreal: Black Rose, 2003).

7   As noted in "Religion Newswriters Identify Year's Top Ten Religion Stories," *Religious Studies News* 22, no. 3 (2007): 11.

8   As of this writing, there was news that Chappelle would produce a film of Muslim comics from the "Allah Made Me Funny" comedy tour.

9   It is interesting to note that all three characters are named some variant of sayyid, a title given to a descendent of the Prophet Muhammad.

10   "Islam in America," special report in *Newsweek*, 30 July 2007, 27.

11   Geneive Abdo, *Mecca and Main Street: Muslim Life in America after 9/11* (New York: Oxford University Press, 2006).

12   Survey available from the Pew Forum on Religion and Public Life, "Muslim Americans: Middle Class and Mostly Mainstream," 22 May 2007, http://pewforum.org/surveys/muslim-american.

13   The classic study of Arabs in Hollywood films is Jack Shaheen, *Reel Bad Arabs: How Hollywood Vilifies a People* (Brooklyn: Interlink, 2001). In the book, Shaheen describes more than nine hundred films in which Arabs are portrayed. He describes Hollywood's portrayal of Arabs as the ". . . systematic, pervasive, and unapologetic degradation and dehumanization of a people" (1).

14   The quote comes from "Dad's Gonna Kill Me," a song from Richard Thompson's 2007 CD, Sweet Warrior. The "Dad" of the song's title is U.S. soldier slang for Baghdad. Thompson is a Muslim and has spoken in an interview about the song being explicitly political about his opposition to the Iraq war: "Sometimes you want your political songs for the sake of impact to be more subtle, to be couched in metaphors. At other times, you have to stand up and be counted. You have to name names. . . . There are times for songs like that, and this song is somewhere in between" (From an AP story by Nekesa Mumbi Moody, 13 March 2007).

15   Kamran Pasha, a Muslim producer for the show, said in a presentation at the University of Southern California (7 March 2007) that he had no knowledge about the character's name.

16   For information on this story, see Greg Johnson, "In Yemen, a Benevolent Alternative to Osama Bin Laden," Pacific News Service, 20 January 2004, http://news.ncmonline.com/news/view_article.html?article_id=be013890b8c48cf458e54f95b8708629.

17   Yee wrote about his experiences as a Muslim chaplain at Guantanamo Bay in his book *For God and Country: Faith and Patriotism under Fire* (New York: PublicAffairs, 2005).

18   For a comprehensive look at this, see Karen J. Greenberg and Joshua L. Dratel, eds., *The Torture Papers: The Road to Abu Ghraib* (New York: Cambridge University Press, 2005).

19   Michael Ondaatje, *The English Patient* (Toronto: McClelland & Stewart, 1992), 283–85.

20   Here, I must confess to watching only the last season (season six) due to seeing a promo for my favorite hockey team, the Montreal Canadiens, featuring Kiefer Sutherland (who plays series star Jack Bauer) in a *24* parody.

21   *TV Guide*, 26 February to 4 March 2007, 11.

22   *TV Guide*, 23 April 2007, 24.

23   In the 1990s version of the show, the character became Hadji Singh, which confused me to no end. Perhaps he was meant to be pan-Indian, with a Muslim title as a first name and a Sikh surname.

24   And this is not to demean transvestites or people with OCD. It is just that it might be nice for an Arab actor to have a character who was not outside the mainstream.

25   "Circumstantial Evidence," season 4, episode 16, original air date 24 February 1982.

26   James Baldwin, *The Fire Next Time* (New York: Vintage, 1993), 9–10.

Chapter 7

1   Robert Orsi, "Everyday Miracles: The Study of Lived Religion," in *Lived Religion in America: Toward a History of Practice*, ed. David D. Hall (Princeton: Princeton University Press, 1997), 3–21.

2   Robert Orsi, *The Madonna of 115th Street: Faith and Community in Italian Harlem, 1880–1950*, 2nd ed. (New Haven: Yale University Press, 2002).

3   Local fans continue to meet for potluck meals and to watch in common Xena episodes on videotape and now DVD. Raising money for charity is a frequent activity, and the large Internet sites of Xena fandom, such as ausxip.com (the Australian Xena Information Page), regularly hold or coordinate charity auctions. At the March for Women's Lives in May 2004 in Washington D.C., there was a group walking behind the banner "Xenites for Choice." In my conversations with Xena fans from several countries, I have often heard fans report that they began to watch the show or watch it more fervently in times of illness or when they have been caring for a sick or dying loved one.

4   Orsi, "Everyday Miracles," 6–8.

5   Sara Gwenllian-Jones, "Virtual Reality and Cult Television," in *Cult Television*, ed. Sara Gwenllian-Jones and Roberta E. Pearson (Minneapolis: University of Minnesota Press, 2004), 83–97. "This is the Xenaverse" she writes, "a fictional cosmology mapped onto the real New Zealand landscape where XWP was filmed. . . . Its extensive use of characters, events, and places from history, mythology, and popular culture blurs the boundaries between fictional and actual worlds so that the Xenaverse continually opens out onto and interconnects with wider narrative possibilities" (88).

6   Orsi, "Everyday Miracles," 7.

7   David D. Hall, *Lived Religion in America: Toward a History of Practice*, ed. David D. Hall (Princeton: Princeton University Press, 1997), x.

8   Orsi, "Everyday Miracles," 11. "The key words here are *tensile, hybridity, ambivalence, irony*; the central methodological commitment is to avoid conclusions that impose univocality on practices that are multifarious."

9   Orsi, "Everyday Miracles," 13–15.

10   Orsi, "Everyday Miracles," 15.

11   See Donald E. Biederman, *Law and Business of the Entertainment Industries* (Westport, Conn.: Praeger, 2001), 663–65. An executive producer who ignores the input of the studio puts the budget and continuation of the series at risk, although the makers of successful shows with high ratings are more immune to the intervention of studios.

12   For the roots of contemporary celebrity death in nineteenth-century Britain, see John Wolffe, *Great Deaths: Grieving, Religion, and Nationhood in Victorian and Edwardian Britain*, British Academy Postdoctoral Fellowship Monograph. (Oxford: Published for the British Academy by Oxford University Press, 2000).

13   For a broader discussion of this phenomenon, see Leo Steinberg, *The Sexuality of Christ in Renaissance Art and in Modern Oblivion* (Chicago: University of Chicago Press, 1996), 18–24, 81–106, 135–39, 146–47; and Margaret R. Miles, *Carnal Knowing: Female Nakedness and Religious Meaning in the Christian West* (Boston: Beacon, 1989), 141–43, 156.

14   The group member D. J. Novus used the phrase in an interview with the German online music magizine, musicbeat.de (July 18, 2004). At the time of publication musicbeat.de was being reorganized and their Web site with this interview was no longer accessible. See http://www.musicbeat.de/starbeat/interviews/04/groovecoverage.php, last accessed 27 February 2008.

15   Groove Coverage, "God Is a Girl," Music video, http://youtube.Com/watch?V=u-nBeOOuEgE. This video is no longer available due to a copyright claim by Viacom International, Inc.

16   "Martin," "Xena God Is a Girl," music video, http://www.youtube.com/watch?v=CHg4MoHkx8k, last accessed 17 October 2008.

17   Mikaela Nordlund (placebowithmeds), "Beautiful (Even in Death)," music video, http://youtube.com/watch?v=Rfm46lWc7RE, accessed 17 October 2008.

Chapter 8

1   See Emily Bazelon, "Is There a Post-Abortion Syndrome?" in *New York Times Magazine*, 21 January 2007.

2   This is Miranda's quandary in the "Coulda Woulda Shoulda" episode of *Sex and the City*, season four (HBO, 1998–2004).

3   I focus on melodrama because this is virtually the only context—outside of documentary or news programming—in which abortion can be addressed on television.

4   A character on *Grey's Anatomy* (ABC, 2005–) considered abortion, but it turned out she had an ectopic pregnancy. Thus, the show had its cake and ate it too, showing a character taking a pro-choice position, but not actually representing a non-medically necessary abortion.

5   Julie D'Acci, "Defining Women: The Case of *Cagney and Lacey*," in *Private Screenings: Television and the Female Consumer*, ed. Lynn Spigel and Denise Mann, 169–200 (Minneapolis: University of Minnesota Press, 1992), 190.

6   In *If These Walls Could Talk*, Sissy Spacek's character considers abortion and asks her best friend if she has ever felt guilty about her own abortion. Her friend says that she has not and that her main feeling

was one of relief. This perspective on abortion is only possible on HBO, not on network television or nonpremium cable. HBO's *Sex and the City* also goes out on a limb by revealing that Carrie had an abortion in the past and by maintaining that this was the right decision for her to make. *Six Feet Under* (HBO, 2001–2005) allows a character to abort, with little fanfare, only to punish her later.

7   On Wildmon and Falwell, see Kathryn Montgomery, *Target: Prime Time* (New York: Oxford University Press, 1989). On censorship in the 1970s and debates over the family viewing hour, see Geoffrey Cowan, *See No Evil: The Backstage Battle over Sex and Violence in Television* (New York: Simon & Schuster, 1978). On both liberal and conservative TV activism, see Heather Hendershot, *Saturday Morning Censors: Television Regulation before the V-Chip* (Durham: Duke University Press, 1998).

8   Susan Friend Harding, *The Book of Jerry Falwell: Fundamentalist Language and Politics* (Princeton: Princeton University Press, 2000).

9   After being cancelled by ABC, Welk created his own production company and successfully continued the show in syndication until 1982.

10   Kirsten Marthe Lentz, "*Quality* versus *Relevance*: Feminism, Race, and the Politics of the Sign in 1970s Television," *Camera Obscura* 43 (2000): 61.

11   Procedurals introduce nonrecurring characters each week. In this context, born-agains, abortion providers, women who have had abortions, and other "controversial" characters can appear because they will be gone by the following week. It is quite another thing for a recurrent character to provoke controversy and scare advertisers by aborting. Also, abortion can function less controversially as a plot point on a procedural rather than on a traditional drama because procedurals center most often on medical and legal professionals who deal with health clinic bombings, self-induced abortions, and so forth, as a matter-of-fact aspect of their working lives. In this context, an episode in which abortion plays a role will not stand out as high-profile "event TV" (to be targeted by conservative activists) the way it would on a drama centered on people's personal rather than professional lives. Thanks to Allison McCracken for her many insights on procedurals and comments on earlier drafts of this essay.

12   On liberal evangelicalism, see Jim Wallis, *God's Politics: Why the Right Gets It Wrong and the Left Doesn't Get It* (San Francisco: Harper, 2006). Wallis feels that conservatives have hijacked evangelicalism, draining away much of Jesus's progressive social message. While he favors legal access to abortion, his perspective is not strongly feminist. Randall Balmer also critiques right-wing abuse of the gospel in *Thy Kingdom Come: How the Religious Right Distorts the Faith and Threatens America: An Evangelical's Lament* (New York: Basic, 2006).

13   Julie D'Acci, "Leading Up to *Roe v. Wade*: Television Documentaries in the Abortion Debate," in *Television, History, and American Culture:*

Feminist Critical Essays, ed. Mary Beth Haralovich and Lauren Rabino-vitz, 120–43 (Durham: Duke University Press, 1999).

14   D'Acci, "Leading Up," 134.

15   The letters are housed in the Sesame Street collection at the National Public Broadcasting Archives, University of Maryland, College Park.

16   And shortly after *Roe v. Wade,* Erica Kane on *All My Children* (ABC, 1970–) had an abortion. Daytime drama continues to be the place where the possibility of abortion appears most frequently, though these abortion storylines do not usually make national news or raise the ire of conservative religious organizations, presumably because daytime television is widely dismissed as inconsequential. On daytime televi-sion's willingness to engage in "the post-sexual revolution society with a degree of complexity and ambiguity difficult to come by in the more high-profile world of prime time," see Elana Levine's *Wallowing in Sex: The New Sexual Culture of 1970s American Television* (Durham: Duke University Press, 2007; quotation from p. 251). Notably, and to the dismay of many viewers, Kane's abortion was "reversed" in 2006, with the implausible revelation that Erica's abortionist had implanted her fetus in his own wife.

17   Montgomery, *Target: Prime Time,* 34.

18   *Maude* was released on DVD in March of 2007. The abortion episodes were aired during the 1972–1973 season but omitted from the summer 1973 rerun schedule. It seems unlikely that the episodes were included in syndication packages later. The episodes basically disappeared until 2007.

19   On the commentary track, lead writer Vanessa Taylor explains obtusely: "I guess I didn't think I was really up to coming up with a name that would express what I felt about the episode, so 'Episode 20' seemed to suffice."

20   Barbara Ehrenreich, *The Hearts of Men: American Dreams and the Flight from Commitment* (New York: Doubleday, 1984).

21   Egan was a visitor when the contributors met as a seminar to discuss this volume in September 2006. The authors watched "House vs. God" together and discussed the show with Egan.

22   Heather Hendershot, "Lessons from the Undead: How Film and TV Zombies Teach Us about War," *Flow: An On-line Journal of Television and Media Studies* 3, no. 10 (2006), http://flowtv.org/?p=214.

23   Janet Staiger, *Blockbuster TV: Must-See Sitcoms in the Network Era* (New York: New York University Press, 2000), 171.

24   Here, Moore is clearly building on the ideas he first developed as exec-utive producer on *Star Trek: Deep Space Nine* (UPN, 1993–1999).

Chapter 9

1   Cheryl Mattingly, Mary Lawlor, and Lanita Jacobs-Huey, "Narrat-ing September 11: Race, Gender, and the Play of Cultural Identities," *American Anthropologist* 104 (2002): 743–53.

2   Hall notes (30 January 2008, University of Southern California guest lecture) that the show was cancelled before they could incorporate references to Eastern and other religions.

3   Richard Dyer, "White," *Screen* 29, no. 4 (1988): 44–65; Richard Dyer, *White* (New York: Routledge, 1997); Noel Ignatiev and John Garvey, eds., *Race Traitor* (New York: Routledge, 1996); George Lipsitz, *The Possessive Investment of Whiteness: How White People Profit from Identity Politics* (Philadelphia: Temple University Press, 1998); Raka Shome, "Outing Whiteness," *Critical Studies in Mass Communication* 17, no. 3 (2000): 366–71.

4   Gray, *Watching Race.*

5   Shome, "Outing Whiteness"; Lipsitz, *Possessive Investment*; Ruth Frankenberg, *White Women, Race Matters: The Social Construction of Whiteness* (Minneapolis: University of Minnesota Press, 1993); Frances E. Kendall, "Understanding White Privilege" (2001a), http://www.cws workshop.org/pdfs/WIWP2/4Underst_White_Priv.PDF; Frances E. Kendall, *Understanding White Privilege: Creating Pathways to Authentic Relations across Race* (London: Routledge, 2001b).

6   Dreama Moon, "White Enculturation and Bourgeois Ideology: The Discursive Production of 'Good (White) Girls,'" in Nakayama and Martin, *Whiteness*, 177–97. See also Kendall, *Understanding White Privilege.*

7   Kendall, "Understanding White Privilege," 11.

8   Gary L. Albrecht, "Disability Humor: What's in a Joke," *Body & Society* 5, no. 4 (1999): 67–74.

9   Braxton, Greg. "Hollywood Loves BBFs 4-Ever," *Los Angeles Times*, 29 August 2006.

10   The character Lt. Toni Williams is also referred to as Detective Williams and Sergeant Williams in *JOA* episodes and scripts.

11   See also Patricia J. Williams, "My Best White Friend: Cinderella Revisited," *Callaloo* 19 (1996): 809–13.

12   Thomas K. Nakayama and Robert L. Krizek, "White: A Strategic Rhetoric," *Quarterly Journal of Speech* 81, no. 3 (1995); Sarah Projansky and Kent A. Ono, "Strategic Whiteness as Cinematic Racial Politics," in Nakayama and Martin, *Whiteness*, 149–74.

13   Kendall, "Understanding White Privilege," 6–7.

14   The author benefited greatly from the nuanced and impassioned episode reviews of "Deborah" on www.televisionwithoutpity.com and show transcripts posted by an anonymous reviewer from www.TWIZTV. com.

15   Dyer, "White"; Dyer, *White*; Shome, "Outing Whiteness."

16   Debian Marty, "White Antiracist Rhetoric as Apologia: Wendell Berry's Hidden Word," in Nakayama and Martin, *Whiteness*, 51–68, here 52.

17   B. L. Ware, and Wil A. Linkugel, "They Spoke in Defense of Themselves: On the General Criticism of Apologia," *Quarterly Journal of Speech* 59 (1973): 273–83.

18   Marsha Houston, "Why the Dialogues Are Difficult, or Fifteen Ways a Black Woman Knows a White Woman's Not Listening," in *Overcoming Racism and Sexism*, ed. L. A. Bell and D. Blumenfeld, 52–55 (Lanham, Md.: Rowman & Littlefield, 1995); Teun Andrianus van Dijk, "Discourse and the Denial of Racism," *Discourse and Society 3*, no. 1 (1992): 87–118.

19   Audrey Colombe, "White Hollywood's New Black Boogeyman," *Jump Cut* 45 (2002), 1–12.

20   Moon, "White Enculturation," in Nakayama and Martin, *Whiteness*, 177–97, here 194.

21   Nonetheless, some fans indicate that Kevin, unrealistically, spent the first half of season 1 in a wheelchair with armrests.

22   Shome, "Outing Whiteness," 367.

23   Shome, "Outing Whiteness," 369.

24   Shome, "Outing Whiteness."

25   Kendall, *Understanding White Privilege*, 97.

26   See Kendall, *Understanding White Privilege*.

Chapter 10

1   *Saving Grace* creator Nancy Miller previously wrote for *The Closer*.

2   *Battlestar Galactica*, season 1, episode 108, "Flesh and Bone."

3   *Battlestar Galactica*, season 3, episode 320, "Crossroads, Part 11."

4   The conflation of Marys became official in the sixth century.

5   See Robert Orsi, *The Madonna of 115th Street: Faith and Community in Italian Harlem, 1880–1950*, 2nd ed. (New Haven: Yale University Press, 2002), xix.

6   James E. Ford, "*Battlestar Galactica* and Mormon Theology," *Journal of Popular Culture* (Fall 1983): 83–87.

7   "Religion in the Twelve Colonies (RDM)," Battlestar Wiki, http://en.battlestarwiki.org/wiki/Religion_in_the_Twelve_Colonies_%28RDM%29.

8   "Sacred Scrolls," Battlestar Wiki. http://en.battlestarwiki.org/wiki/Sacred_Scrolls.

9   *Battlestar Galactica* miniseries. Adama is referred to by his last name in keeping with the way he is addressed in the series.

10   "Chamalla," Battlestar Wiki, http://en.battlestarwiki.org/wiki/Chamalla.

11   *Battlestar Galactica*, season 1, episode 108, "Flesh and Bone."

12   *Battlestar Galactica*, season 1, episode 110, "The Hand of God."

13   twiztv.com, Free TV Scripts Database, http://www.twiztv.com/scripts/battlestar/season1/galactica-110.htm.

14   twiztv.com, Free TV Scripts Database, http://www.twiztv.com/scripts/battlestar/season1/galactica-112.htm.

15   For more on Kobol, see "Kobol (RDM)," Battlestar Wiki, http://

en.battlestarwiki.org/wiki/Kobol_%28RDM%29. Kobal, which also was integral to the original Battlestar Galactica series (1978–1979) was thought to be a play on the name Kolob, a star nearest to God in Mormon scripture. Glen Larson, the creator of the series was a member of the Church of Jesus Christ of Latter-day Saints.

16 twiztv.com, Free TV Scripts Database, http://www.twiztv.com/scripts/battlestar/season1/galactica-112.htm.

17 twiztv.com, Free TV Scripts Database, http://www.twiztv.com/scripts/battlestar/season1/galactica-112.htm.

18 Laura does have moral limits. In "Lay Down Your Burdens, Part II," she discovers that her supporters have stolen the election. She concedes because she does not want to subvert the democratic process.

19 The Colonials, tired of running from the Cylons, settle on New Caprica—an uninhabited and hard-to-find planet—at the end of season 2. Laura is no longer president; she has been defeated by Gaius Baltar, who supported the colonization plan. At the start of season 3, the Cylons occupy New Caprica.

20 E.g., Survival Instinct: William Adama and Laura Roslin Fanfiction, http://mujaji.net/adamaroslin/index.php; and "Psyphilosopher," Hold This, Will You? personal blog, http://psyphilosopher.livejournal.com.

21 twiztv.com, Free TV Scripts Database, http://www.twiztv.com/scripts/battlestar/season1/galactica-108.htm.

22 twiztv.com, Free TV Scripts Database, http://www.twiztv.com/scripts/battlestar/season1/galactica-108.htm.

23 *Battlestar Galactica*, season 3, episode 311, "The Eye of Jupiter" and episode 312 "Rapture."

24 twiztv.com, Free TV Scripts Database, http://www.twiztv.com/scripts/battlestar/season3/galactica-317.htm.

25 twiztv.com, Free TV Scripts Database, http://www.twiztv.com/scripts/battlestar/season4/galactica-401.htm.

26 "The Destiny," Battlestar Wiki, http://en.battlestarwiki.org/wiki/The_Destiny#The_Aurora_Connection.

27 If a Cylon body is destroyed, its consciousness can be downloaded into a duplicate model. See "Resurrection (RDM)," Battlestar Wiki, http://en.battlestarwiki.org/wiki/Resurrection_%28RDM%29.

28 Leoben tells her the child, Kasey, was created with an ovary that the Cylons had removed from Kara in "The Farm" (season 2, episode 205). When Kara learns that Kasey is a human child that Leoben has stolen from its mother, her grief precipitates the downward spiral that culminates in "Maelstrom." However, just as learning how much her own mother loved her, Kara's ability to love Kasey is crucial to the character's development.

29 On the unruly woman, see Natalie Zemon Davis, *Society and Culture in Early Modern France* (Stanford: Stanford University Press, 1975), 124–51.

30   *Saving Grace*, season 1, episode 101, pilot.

31   *Saving Grace* pilot.

32   *Saving Grace*, season 1, episode 113, "Taco, Tulips, Duck, and Spices."

33   *Saving Grace*, season 1, episode 100, pilot 111, "This Is Way Too Normal for You."

34   *Saving Grace*, season 1, episode 112, "Is There a Scarlet Letter on My Breast?"

35   *Saving Grace*, season 1, episode 102, "Bring It On, Earl."

36   "Bring It On, Earl."

37   *Saving Grace*, season 1, episode 106, "And You Wonder Why I Lie."

38   *Battlestar Galactica*, season 3, episode 309, "Unfinished Business."

39   *Saving Grace*, season 1, episode 105, "Would You Want Me to Tell You."

40   "Bring It On, Earl."

41   *Saving Grace* pilot.

42   twiztv.com, Free TV Scripts Database, http://www.twiztv.com/scripts/battlestar/season1/galactica-107.htm.

43   "Della," comment on "'Saving Grace,' If She'll Save Herself" by Paul O'Donnell, Idol Chatter, Beliefnet, 3 December 2007, http://blog.beliefnet.com/idolchatter/2007/12/saving-grace-if-shell-save-her.html.

44   "How 'Bout That Saving Grace?" online discussion board thread, TV.com, http://www.tv.com/saving-grace/show/72393/how-bout-that-saving-grace/topic/85990-845475/msgs.html?tag=board_topics;title;7.

45   "How 'Bout That Saving Grace?" online discussion board thread, TV.com, http://www.tv.com/saving-grace/show/72393/how-bout-that-saving-grace/topic/85990-845475/msgs.html?page=1.

46   "TenNinetySix," "It's About Time," online discussion board comment, TNT, 13 August 2007, http://forums.tnt.tv/jive/tnt/thread.jspa?messageID=22223&#22223.

47   "TXJetSet," "Re: The Character," Online discussion board comment, TNT, 30 November 2007, http://forums.tnt.tv/jive/tnt/thread.jspa?messageID=46415&#46415.

48   "FalconT," "The Best Show Ever," online discussion board comment, TNT, 7 September 2007, http://forums.tnt.tv/jive/tnt/thread.jspa?messageID=31548&#31548.

49   "A Shot at Redemption," MySpace, http://www.myspace.com/savinggracereport.

50   "Philip164," "Salvation and Forgiveness," online discussion board comment, TNT, 19 December 2007, http://forums.tnt.tv/jive/tnt/thread.jspa?threadID=13642&start=0&tstart=0.

51   "Fans1228," "Grace Is a Beautifull Angel Which Fell from the Heaven," Online discussion board comment, TNT, 16 February 2008, http://forums.tnt.tv/jive/tnt/thread.jspa?threadID=15642&tstart=0.

52   Deborah 195, Grace is a Beautifull Angel." http:"forums.tnt.tv/jive/tnt/thread.jspathreadID=15642&tstart=0.

53   "akennedy," "Capt. Kara 'Starbuck' Thrace," online discussion board comment, Television without Pity, http://forums.televisionwithout pity.com/index.php?showtopic=3122148&st=1035.

54   "Romantique," "Capt. Kara 'Starbuck' Thrace," online discussion board comment, Television without Pity, http://forums.televisionwithout pity.com/index.php?showtopic=3122148&st=1020.

55   "Lish," "Capt. Kara 'Starbuck' Thrace," online discussion board comment, Television without Pity, http://forums.televisionwithoutpity. com/index.php?showtopic=3122148&st=1020.

56   "The Cult of Starbuck, Kara Thrace Anders (Whoever's Next) Lovers, OUR Time Has Come!" online discussion board thread, Sci-Fi Forums, http://forums.scifi.com/index.php?showtopic=2278169&st=0.

57   "The Cult of Starbuck, Kara Thrace Anders (Whoever's Next) Lovers." "Vipers" are the ships that Galactica pilots fly.

58   Online discussion board comment, Television without Pity, http:// forums.televisionwithoutpity.com/index.php?act=Search&CODE =show&searchid=5d5b545ffa1594d21d784b53c4dcb513&search_ in=posts&result_type=posts&highlite=%2Bmakes+people+feel. No longer available.

59   Online discussion board comment, Television without Pity, http:// forums.televisionwithoutpity.com/index.php?act=Search&COD E=show&searchid=7609e1922212eb9d9890351e1a313355&searc h_in=posts&result_type=posts&highlite=hotshot+pilot. No longer available.

60   "Aprilrayne," "Re: How Kara Looked," online discussion board comment, Sci-Fi Forums, April 2007, http://forums.scifi.com/index. php?showtopic=2271179&hl=Kara.

61   "celticleod," "President Laura Roslin," online discussion board comment, Television without Pity, 6 February 2006, http://forums.tele visionwithoutpity.com/index.php?showtopic=3122147&st=150&p=4 473709&#entry4473709.

62   Aubrey, "President Laura Roslin," online discussion board comment, Television without Pity, 31 December 2005, http://forums.television withoutpity.com/index.php?showtopic=3122147&st=105.

63   "bluedevilblue," "President Laura Roslin," online discussion board comment, Television without Pity, 16 January 2006, http://forums. televisionwithoutpity.com/index.php?showtopic=3122147&st=105.

64   "tenblade," President Laura Roslin," online discussion board comment, Television without Pity, 12 August 2005, http://forums.television withoutpity.com/index.php?showtopic=3122147&st=90&p=3393355 &#entry3393355.

65   "bluedevilblue," "President Laura Roslin," online discussion board comment, Television without Pity, 7 December 2006, http://forums. televisionwithoutpity.com/index.php?showtopic=3122147&st=300& p=6782963&#entry6782963.

66   Season 3, episode 9.

67   "Call Back in an Hour," Survival Instinct (http://mujaji.net/adama roslin/index.php), http://mujaji.net/adamaroslin/viewstory.php?sid= 1020&chapter=1 (site registration required).

68   Chamalla Dreams: A Laura Roslin Fan Community, http://comm unity.livejournal.com/chamalla_dreams.

69   Chilipip and Associates, "The Missing Year," fan fiction, Chilipipland: Laura Roslin Fiction by Chilipip & Associates, http://chilipip.word press.com/welcome-2.

70   Laurel Leaves: A Laura Roslin and Lee Adama Website, http://laurel leaves.net/lauralee/index.html.

71   Laura Roslin Fanfic, http://lauraroslin.biggiantspaceship.com/index. php.

72   "The Cult of Laura, The Cult of Laura/The Cult of Mary," online discussion board thread, Sci-Fi Forums, http://forums.scifi.com/index.p hp?s=496da303b0037c53f859ac0740e1f455&showtopic=2278335.

Chapter 11

1   Japanese for "Save the Cheerleader, Save the World!" "9th Wonders Board," posted by Coin-Operated Boy (13 December 2006, 12:24 a.m.), HeroesWiki.com, http://boards.9thwonders.com/lofiversion/index. php/t34922.html. Sam Nunn quoted in Richard Rhodes, "Living with the Bomb," *National Geographic*, 208, no. 2 (2005): 113.

2   "Tim Kring Biography," TV.com, http://www.tv.com/tim-kring/per son/22510/biography.html, 14 July 2007.

3   *"Heroes* Continues to Dominate Mondays with High Ratings" Variety. com (10 October 2006); www.heroestheseries.com (2 July 2007); "*Heroes* premiere delivers NBC's highest 18–49 rating for any fall drama debut in five years," AZCentral.com (26 September 2006; no longer available online).

4   The show studiously avoids the use of the term *mutant* preferring instead *evolved* and most often the neutral euphemism *special*. *Mutant* is too much of a concession to the show's obvious debt to *X-Men*, although Hiro likens his powers to the X-Men's in the first episode. The charge that *Heroes* is a poor version of *X-Men* misses the point that a large segment of the American public is receptive to narratives about the evolutionary transformation of humanity.

5   Frank Kermode, "Waiting for the End," in *Apocalypse Theory and the Ends of the World*, ed. Malcolm Bull (Cambridge, Mass.: Blackwell, 1995), 250.

6   See also Conrad E. Ostwalt Jr., "Vision of the End: Secular Apocalypse in Recent Hollywood Film," *Journal of Religion and Film* 2, no. 1 (1998), www.unomaha.edu/jrf/OstwaltC.htm (20 July 2007).

7   Quoted in Conrad E. Oswalt Jr., "Hollywood and Armageddon: Apoc-

alyptic Themes in Recent Cinematic Presentation," in *Screening the Sacred: Religion, Myth, and Ideology in Popular American Film*, ed. Joel W. Martin and Conrad E. Ostwalt Jr. (Boulder: Westview, 1995), 61–62.

8 This shift away from traditional Christian apocalyptic formulas toward secular apocalypticism, particularly after 9/11, may help explain the radical decline of television dramas in which people are assisted by traditional supernatural agents or shows with specifically Christian themes like *Touched by an Angel* (1994–2003), its spinoff *Promised Land* (1996–1999); *Christy* (1994–1995), and *7th Heaven* (1996–2007). On the other hand, recent shows like USA's *4400* (2004–), *Dead Zone* (2007), *Psych* (2007–); NBC's *Medium* (2005–), short-lived *Raines* (2007); CBS' *Ghost Whisperer* (2005–); and possibly ABC's *Kyle XY* (2006–) all deal with human beings with extraordinary abilities. The 2007 summer lineup, however, aired one show, *Saving Grace* (TNT) featuring an "unconventional" angel.

9 In the five-year memorial service to the victims of the bomb blast that destroyed New York City, President Petrelli (Sylar in disguise) slyly mocks the event by commemorating each anniversary year with the regular ringing of "five bells for the five years of sorrow" ("Five Years Gone").

10 Ostwalt, "Hollywood and Armageddon," 62.

11 I am following Adam Roberts' discussion in *Science Fiction* (New York: Routledge, 2000), 30–36.

12 Roberts, *Science Fiction*, 35–36.

13 The exact model of Cadillac is in question. Note the obsessive detail involved in the *Heroes* Wiki page dedicated to the car: "According to the registration, Niki's car is a 1966 Cadillac convertible with a V-8. The tail fins do not match the stock versions of either the DeVille or the Eldorado, the only two series offered in a convertible that year. In reality, the car is a 1959, not a 1966. (Don't Look Back)," "Jessica's Cadillac," HeroesWiki.com, http://heroeswiki.com/Jessica%27s_Cadillac, 5 September 2007.

14 Thomas M. Disch, *The Dreams Our Stuff Is Made of: How Science Fiction Conquered the World* (New York: Touchstone/Simon & Schuster, 1998), 78–96.

15 ". . . 'what is the meaning of life?' or 'what is the destiny of man?'—is a question raised by almost no one these days apart from theologians and s[cience] f[iction] writers" (Edward James, "Utopias and Anti-Utopias," in *The Cambridge Companion to Science Fiction*, ed. Edward James and Farah Mendlesohn [Cambridge: Cambridge University Press, 2003], 228).

16 Masi Oka, winning the outstanding television actor award at the AZN Asian Excellence Awards, May 2007. Wendy Leung, "'Excellence' Airs Memorial Day," AsianWeek.com (25 May 2007), http://www.asianweek.com/2007/05/25/'excellence'-airs-memorial-day.

17   Science-fiction theorist Darko Suvin refers to science fiction's ability to "make strange" or defamiliarize the familiar as "the presence and inter-action of estrangement and cognition, and whose main formal device is an imaginative framework alternative to the author's empirical envi-ronment" (Darko Suvin, *Metamorphoses of Science Fiction: On the Poetics and History of a Literary Genre* [New Haven: Yale University Press, 1979], 8–9).

18   Roberts, *Science Fiction*, 131.

19   In a strange parallel with the drama's immigrant narrative, Masi Oka's introduction by Tavis Smiley included the *Time* "Whiz Kids" cover with the twelve-year old Oka and the *Wired* magazine cover (May 2007) with the suave Future Hiro (although in "reverse" order). Tavis Smiley, PBS interview with Masi Oka, 27 April 2007, http://www.pbs.org/kcet/tavissmiley/archive/200704/20070427_oka.html.

20   "Hiro's Blog," NBC.com, http://blog.nbc.com/hiro_blog/2006/09/kitty_pride.php, 23 August 2007.

21   Mila Bongco, *Reading Comics: Language, Culture, and the Concept of the Superhero in Comic Books* (New York: Garland, 2000), 118.

22   Jane Iwamura, "The Oriental Monk in American Popular Culture," in *Religion and Popular Culture in America*, rev. ed., ed. Bruce David Forbes and Jeffrey Mahan (Berkeley: University of California Press, 2005), 25–43.

23   Anne Allison, *Millennial Monsters: Japanese Toys and the Global Imagina-tion* (Berkeley: University of California Press, 2006), 16–18.

24   Jane Iwamura, "Oriental Monk," 37.

25   His training by George Takei connects the show to the lineage of tele-vision's most successful science-fiction franchise. Adam Roberts notes that this "legacy" function of SF is one of the genre's hallmarks (Rob-erts, *Science Fiction*, 50–51).

26   In season 1, the orientalism is also bolstered by the scenes in India. Tim Kring notes that the studio backlot in Los Angeles was unmistakably "India" with the CGI imposition of two "thousand year old" temples in the background (Tim Kring, "Commentary to Unaired Pilot," *Heroes* season 1 DVD, directed by David Semel [New York: NBC Universal Television, 2007]).

27   Arthur C. Clarke, *Profiles of the Future: An Inquiry into the Limits of the Possible*, rev. ed (New York: Harper & Row, 1973), 39.

28   Rey Chow refers to this forced role playing of racialized others as "coer-cive mimeticism." The expectations for the Asian American actors on the show insist that both Oka and Ramamurthy play "Asian" charac-ters marked by accented English and are understood to originate from Asia. In other words, their characters would not make any sense to the viewer as Asian Americans. Rey Chow, *The Protestant Ethnic and the Spirit of Capitalism* (New York: Columbia University Press, 2002), 95–127.

29   Bill Keveney, "Stars of South Asian Descent are on the Ascent," USA TODAY.com, http://www.usatoday.com/life/people/2007-04-08-south-asian-actors_N.htm, 20 July 2007. Note how Kapoor's impossibly long South Indian surname on *Crossing Jordan* contributes to the incomprehensibility and exotic nature of the oriental monk's origins. The depiction of South Asian oriental science monks is linked to the public's general confusion between South Asians (particularly Sikhs) and Arabs in post-9/11 America. The benevolent and rational South Asian Hindu professional foils the potential *religious* confusion between Arab Muslims and South Asian non-Muslims. The original unaired pilot of *Heroes* included a plot by Muslim extremists (who are responsible for the train fire in Odessa), but the network decided it was too inflammatory for the public. Note that Amid Helebi, "The Engineer" and "twentieth terrorist" for the 9/11 attacks in the unaired pilot is described as "a Saudi national with a Ph.D." Viewers would see Helebi's Arab origin as the marker of his essential evil, while Mohinder Suresh (also with a Ph.D.) is received through the lens of orientalist ideas about India. (Tim Kring, "Commentary to Unaired Pilot").

30   Thanks to Mimi Khuc who reminded me of this essential fact. Personal communication, 5 August 2007.

31   Brooke Boon, author of *Holy Yoga*, e.g., does theological yoga in defense of the practice for evangelicals: "Our use of the postures of Hatha Yoga together with the spiritual intent—although thoroughly Christian— of Bhakti Yoga are what make our practice of yoga truly holy" (*Holy Yoga: Exercise for the Christian Body and Soul* [New York: FaithWords, 2007], 8. See also Susan Bordenkircher, *Yoga for Christians: A Christ-Centered Approach to Physical and Spiritual Health through Yoga* (Nashville: Thomas Nelson, 2006).

32   Conrad E. Ostwalt Jr., "Conclusion: Religion, Film, and Cultural Analysis," in Martin and Ostwalt, *Screening the Sacred*, 153.

33   The text for Chandra Suresh's funeral begins "Hiranya shringam varunam prapadye. . . ." The origin of the text eludes identification. My thanks to Barbara Holdrege for assistance with possible text identification (personal communication, 31 August 2007). The written text is the "Mahamantra" or "Great Mantra" familiar to Americans as the International Society for Krishna Consciousness' ubiquitous chant: Hare Krishna, Hare Krishna, Krishna Krishna, Hare Hare / Hare Rama, Hare Rama, and so on.

34   In addition, Panjabi MC's most famous hit, "Mundian To Bach Ke" is heard in the "Homecoming" episode.

35   Wendy Melvoin and Lisa Coleman, the score's composers say they sought Shenkar "when we began to see and fold in the more magical, mystical presence [in the show] . . . a lot of it ended up being Shenkar. Lisa and I are Shenkar fans because he goes back to the days of a band called Shakti. And it was sort of in the heyday of spiritual art rock, kind

of like the Mahavishnu Orchestra kind of school, where it was like a lot of Indian music put in with a lot of jazz, and a lot of experimental jazz." Melvoin notes that Shenkar's haunting voice has marked the show's identity (Wendy Melvoin and Lisa Coleman, "Special Feature: Score" *Heroes* DVD).

36   Catherine L. Albanese, *Republic of Mind and Spirit: A Cultural History of American Metaphysical Religion* (New Haven: Yale University Press, 2007), 511.

37   E.g., note how the frequent abduction or sequestration of characters, and other events associated with close encounters of the third kind— lost time, medical procedure, telepathy—redirects the *X-Files* preoccupation with aliens back to human agents.

38   Marc Scalese, "ER and Medical Dramas: Moments of Grace in the Midst of Chaos," in *Watching What We Watch: Prime-Time Television through the Lens of Faith*, ed. Walter T. Davis Jr., Teresa Blythe, Gary Drebelbis, Mark Scalese, S.J., Elizabeth Winans Winslea, and Donald L. Ashburn (Louisville, Ky.: Geneva, 2001), 154.

39   Erik Davis, "Half Japanese: The Mighty Morphin Power Rangers," *The Village Voice*, 21 June 1994, http://www.techgnosis.com/chunkshow-single.php?chunk=chunkfrom-2005-10-15-1627-0.txt, 9 July 2007.

40   Jeff Yang, Introduction to *Eastern Standard Time: A Guide to Asian Influence on American Culture from Astro Boy to Zen Buddhism*, ed. Jeff Yang, Dina Gin, et al. (Boston: Houghton Mifflin, 1997), vii.

41   *Godzilla*, directed by Roland Emmerich (New York: TriStar Pictures, 1998).

42   Allison, *Millennial Monsters*, 12. My discussion of J-Pop's influence and the *Pokémon* mechanisms draws heavily and shamelessly from Allison's brilliant analysis. Her use of the term Pokémonization refers more to the capitalist economic and attendant cultural infiltrations of Japanese forms than my borrowing of its mechanisms for describing how *Heroes* fans as *believers* interact with the show.

43   Allison, *Millennial Monsters*, 234–70, 35–50; D. P. Martinez, ed., *The Worlds of Japanese Popular Culture: Gender, Shifting Boundaries and Global Cultures* (Cambridge: Cambridge University Press, 1998), 9–15; Roland Kelts, *Japanamerica: How Japanese Pop Culture Has Invaded the U.S.* (New York: Palgrave Macmillan, 2006).

44   Allison, *Millennial Monsters*, 8–9.

45   Allison, *Millennial Monsters*, 243–49. I am indebted to Maria Feudo for sharing her first-hand experience playing *Pokémon* and explaining the nuances of the game.

46   Kelts, *Japanamerica*, 192–93.

47   Tom Gill, "Transformational Magic: Some Japanese Super-Heroes and Monsters," in Martinez, *Japanese Popular Culture*, 49–50. Roland Kelts informs us that "The Japanese word for the [World War II] bomb . . . we called 'Little Boy' the Japanese called pika-don, an ono-

matopoetic term. Pika is a sudden extremely bright light, such as lightning, and don is a thunderous blast, like fireworks exploding, or something heavy falling to the floor. It is the same pika that appears in Pikachu—the Pokémon with the power to unleash lightening bolts from his tail. Chu is Japanese onomatopoeia for the sound of a kiss" (Kelts, *Japanamerica*, 39).

48   The *Heroes* Wiki pages replicate this classificatory feature in the "score cards" that appear on each character's entry complete with picture, sex, superpower, and so forth. Similarly, in the *Pokémon* origin story, the creatures are researched by a professor who then creates a cataloguing device, the Pokédex, similar to Professor Chandra Suresh's computerized list of evolved humans.

49   Jean Baudrillard on collecting: "The particular value of the object, its exchange value, is a matter of cultural and social domain. Its absolute singularity, on the other hand, arises from the fact of being possessed by me, in turn to recognize myself in the object as an absolutely singular being" (quoted in Neil Badmington, *Alien Chic: Posthumanism and the Other Within* [New York: Routledge, 2004], 96).

50   A fanvid posting on YouTube by goaliejedi35 cleverly matches the *Pokémon* theme song to clips of Sylar attacking his victims: "Sylar Pokemon," YouTube.com, available at http://www.youtube.com/watch?v=2ACW-ovub-E.

51   Allison, *Millennial Monsters*, 46.

52   Timothy J. Craig, Introduction to *Japan Pop! Inside the World of Japanese Popular Culture*, ed. Timothy J. Craig (Armonk, N.Y.: M. E. Sharpe, 2000), 17.

53   Allison, *Millennial Monsters*, 257.

54   Chandra Suresh, *Activating Evolution* (n.p., 1993), x, http://www.activatingevolution.org/book_p2.shtml, 9 August 2007.

55   Suvin, *Metamorphoses of Science Fiction*, 10.

56   Sara Gwenllian-Jones, "Virtual Reality and Cult Television," in *Cult Television*, ed. Sara Gwenllian-Jones and Roberta E. Pearson (Minneapolis: University of Minnesota Press, 2004), 85. See John Storey on the influence of TV dramas in viewers' everyday lives in his *Cultural Studies and the Study of Popular Culture*, 2nd ed. (Athens: University of Georgia Press, 2003), 18–25.

57   Jeffrey Sconce, "*Star Trek*, Heaven's Gate, and Textual Transcendence," in Gwenllian-Jones and Pearson, *Cult Television*, 219.

58   Allison writes that these entertainment distractions and the anxieties mirror our place in a capitalist framework where *Pokémon* "players become addicted to the rush of transformation, and this itself feeds a capitalist imagination, one dressed in commodities of limitless play and possibility. But, true to the principles of capitalism, the desire to expand further (by acquiring more powers, more pokémon, more wins in battle) eludes ultimate closure or satisfaction (there is always more—of whatever—to obtain/attain)" (*Millennial Monsters*, 26).

59   Jolyon Baraka Thomas, "Shûkyô Asobi and Miyazaki Hayao's Anime," *Nova Religio: The Journal of Alternative and Emergent Religions* 10, no. 3 (2006): 73–95.

60   James M. Welsh, "Nuclear Consciousness on Television," and Eric Barnouw, "The Case of the A-Bomb Footage," in *Transmission: Theory and Practice for a New Television Aesthetics*, ed. Peter D'Agostino (New York: Tanam, 1985), 186, 189–98.

61   There is also a critique of nonevolved humans in the show signaled by Sandra Bennet's dog/daemon, Mr. Muggles, a reference to the "non-magic folk" in the Harry Potter series.

62   This critique is similar to Lucius Shepard's view that the *X-Men* mutants are emblems of reactionary and Orwellian ideologies (Lucius Shepard, "XcreMENt," *Projections: Science Fiction in Literature and Film*, ed. Lou Anders [Austin, Tex.: MonkeyBrain, 2004], 243).

63   Walter Benjamin quoted in Allison, *Millennial Monsters*: "It is in this way that technological *re*production gives back to humanity that capacity for experience which technological *production* threatens to take away" (190).

64   Ostwalt, "Visions of the End."

Chapter 12

1   Online discussion posted 15 January 2006, http://www.iidb.org/vbb/archive/index.php/t-152179. No longer available.

2   See Richard Campbell, Christopher Martin, and Bettina Fabos, *Media and Culture: An Introduction to Mass Communication*, 7th ed. (Boston: Bedford/St. Martin's), 2007.

3   A number of prominent television scholars challenged the journalistic reports of a viewer exodus. Jonathan Gray (2007) has pointed out that during this supposed exodus, *Lost* often led iTunes and ABC downloads. Sales for the DVDs of the program also did very well, suggesting that some viewers might prefer to wait for the season's conclusion to watch the entire third season in sequence. Gray also notes that with its appeal among a higher income audience, Lost is ideal for recording and playing at a later time with TiVo and DVR (digital video recording), both of which are not registered on audience-measurement systems. The reports of a viewer exodus, therefore, may be overstated.

4   Caryn James, "To Get the Best View of Television, Try Using a Wide Lens," *The New York Times*, 1 October 2000, 46.

5   Raymond Williams, *The Long Revolution* (London: Chatto & Windus, 1961), 57.

6   Myles Breen and Farrel Corcoran, "Myth in Television Discourse," *Communication Monographs* 49, no. 2 (1982): 127–36; Robert White, "New Perspectives on Media and Culture," *Communication Research Trends* 8, no. 2 (1987).

7   Ernst Cassirer, *An Essay on Man: An Introduction to the Philosophy of Human Culture* (New Haven: Yale University Press), 1925; Mircea Eliade, *Myth and Reality* (New York: Harper & Row), 1963; Claude Levi-Strauss, *Myth and Meaning* (New York Schocken), 1979.

8   This subject has been of interest in recent decades in the field of history and memory. For instance, historians such as Ed Linenthal and Tom Engelhardt detail the controversy surrounding the Smithsonian's installation of the *Enola Gay*, the remains of the plane that dropped the first atomic bomb on Hiroshima. They note that while some saw the bomb's creation as the beginning of an era of destruction and fear wrought by technology, others saw it as a symbol of victory and world peace. Depending on who you were, therefore, the "myth" of the bomb either meant societal harmony achieved through the triumph of Western science or the continuing strife resulting from the belief that some societies have the right and the means to destroy others. See Tom Engelhardt and Edward Linenthal, *History Wars: The Enola Gay and Other Battles of the American Past* (New York: Henry Holt), 2001.

9   Roger Silverstone, *The Message of Television* (London: Heinemann Educational), 1981.

10   Ron Grimes has conducted an analysis of the cultural conflicts surrounding the rituals of the Fiesta de Santa Fe with similar results. Grimes notes that the myths of that city's formation and history are not as consensually accepted as the celebrated ritual would lead a visitor to believe. See Ronald Grimes, *Symbol and Conquest: Public Ritual and Drama in Santa Fe, New Mexico* (Ithaca: Cornell University Press), 1976. Similarly, in her groundbreaking work on the myths of the American West, Patricia Limerick has demonstrated that these stories of the frontier were far more destructive and controversial than the romanticized Anglo perspective has suggested. See Patricia Limerick, *The Legacy of Conquest: The Unbroken Past of the American West* (New York: W. W. Norton), 1987. Current controversies over definitions of history itself suggest that myths must be understood in relation to the context in which they are seen to be meaningful to their audiences.

11   Cornel Sandvoss, *Fans: The Mirror of Consumption* (Cambridge, UK: Polity, 2005), 48.

12   David Morgan, *The Lure of Images: A History of Religion and Visual Media in America* (New York: Routledge, 2007).

13   Bridget Byrne, "Lost Plots Endgame," E! Online, 15 January 2007 http://www.eonline.com/uberblog/b54173__amp_lt_i_amp_gt_Lost_amp_lt__i_amp_gt__Plots_Endgame.html.

14   Maurice Broaddus, "*Lost*—The TV Show," Hollywood Jesus, 10 December 2004, http://www.hollywoodjesus.com/comments/maurice/2004/ 12/lost-tv-show.html.

15   "Amberlita21," "Re: In Which I Obsess about 'LOST,'" online discussion

board comment, Rotten Tomatoes, October 2004, http://www.rotten tomatoes.com/vine/printthread.php?t=367316& page=25&pp=30.

16   Quoted in David Buckna's quiz, "Can the Lost be Found?: The Pop Gospel," online quiz, 19 September 2005, http://www.dickstaub.com/culturewatch.php?record_id=916.

17   Of the two hundred or so blogs that reference the quiz, almost half are nonsequitur mentions from Buckna himself in the blog's comments section. Somehow, he seems to have located nearly all of the twenty- and thirty-something white Christian young men who blogged about *Lost.* He also circulated his quizzes by e-mail; I received two copies in 2006 with a tailored e-mail message based on my interest in *Lost.*

18   David Kronke, "'Lost' Souls," The Mayor of Television, 27 September 2006, http://www.insidesocal.com/tv/2006/09/lost_souls.html.

19   Bonnie Covel, *Lost.* About.com, http://lost.about.com/ad/lostquizzes/Quiz_Yourself_on_LOST.htm.

20   This reference is mentioned in the 2006 revised version of David Buckna's quiz, "Can the Lost Be Found?": The Pop Gospel.

21   *Honolulu Star-Bulletin,* 22 August 2005.

22   Nerina Rammairone, "Redemption Island?" *TV Guide* (USA) 54, no. 6 (2006), 9.

23   Lynette Porter and David Lavery, *Unlocking the Meaning of* Lost*: An Unauthorized Guide,* 2nd ed. (Naperville, Ill.: Sourcebooks, 2006).

24   Porter and Lavery, *Unlocking the Meaning of* Lost.

25   "kimmy," comment David Wayne's Jolly Blogger online blog, 3 November 2004 post, http://jollyblogger.typepad.com/jollyblogger/2004/11/lost_tv_show_ab.html.

26   Anonymous poster, 2006.

27   Valerim9, 9 February 2007, http://www.amazon.com/Lost-Search-Meaning-Christian-Piatt/dp/082722138X/ref=sr_1_1/102-8387725-8858507?ie=UTF8&s=books&qid=1178032292&sr=1-1.

28   DepecheSinner87, reply to "The Rapture?" online discussion board comment, 22 February 2007, http://forum1.aimoo.com/LOST1/LOST-Theories/The-Rapture-1-531094.html.

29   http://www.iidb.org/vbb/archive/index.php/t-152179.html. [No longer available.]

30   http://www.iidb.org/vbb/archive/index.php/t-152179.html. [No longer available.]

31   http://www.iidb.org/vbb/archive/index.php/t-152179.html. [No longer available.]

32   http://www.iidb.org/vbb/archive/index.php/t-152179.html. [No longer available.]

33   "Religion Stays!!!" Online discussion board thread, April 2006, http://forum1.aimoo.com/LOST1/LOST-Theories/RELIGION-STAYS-1-407488.html.

34   Lilit Marcus, "The 'Lost' Tribe," beliefnet.com, http://www.belief

net.com/story/211/story_21132_1.html. Article appeared first in the *Yeshiva University Commentator*, 23 October 2006.

35 "Nu, Such a Mechaiyeh! (aka The Nice Jewish Thread)," online discussion board thread, started 30 November 2006, http://www.losttv-forum.com/forum/showthread.php?t=28611&page=12.

36 Lilit Marcus, "Sayid: The Real Leader of Lost," Idol Chatter, beliefnet. com, 8 March 2007, http://blog.beliefnet.com/idolchatter/2007/03/sayid-real-leader-of-lost.html.

37 "Dharma Logos," About.com, http://lost.about.com/gi/dynamic/offsite.htm?zi=1/XJ/Ya&sdn=lost&cdn=entertainment&tm=14&f=00&tt=14&bt=1&bts=1&zu=http%3A//www.lostpedia.com/wiki/DHARMA_logos.

38 Dean Sluyter, "Are You Willing to Get Lost?" *Tricycle* (2007). Reposted at beliefnet.com, http://www.beliefnet.com/story/186/story_18617_1.html.

39 Maureen Ryan, "The Buddhism of 'Lost.'" *Chicago Tribune*, 16 February 2006. http://www.buddhistchannel.tv/index.php?id=12,2333,0,0,1,0.

40 Google.com search results, http://www.google.com/search?hl=en&q=%22the+buddhism+of+lost%22&btnG=Google+Search.

41 "Barry," "The Bus Stops Here," Completely "Lost," 8 February 2007, http://njmg.typepad.com/lost/2007/02/the_bus_stops_h.html, referencing the episode "Not in Portland."

42 ABC.com, *Lost* forums, http://losttvfans.com/thread/412658/Buddhist+references.

43 "Amariea," "Poll: Found Out What the Meaning of 'Dharma' Is> Very 'Coincidental,'" 12 April 2007, http://forum1.aimoo.com/LOST1/LOST-Theories/Poll-Found-out-what-the-meanin-1-672614.html.

44 http://noscope.com/journal/2007/03/lost.

45 JimCub3d, "A Flag Tells Our Theory," online discussion thread, Lost Theories, ABC.com, 5 March 2007, http://forums.abc.com/n/pfx/forum. aspx?nav=messagelist&webtag=lost&tid=479.

46 Blogger Ashley Langford is a thirty-one-year-old Texas wedding photographer who self-avows as a Christian. This comment on *Lost* is posted at http://blog.ashleylangford.com/archives/2006/11/lost_me.html#more.

47 Mimi Ito, "Networked Publics: An Introduction," in *Networked Publics*, ed. Kazys Varnelis (Cambridge: MIT Press, 2008).

Chapter 13

1 Hebrews 11:32-38 (The Message Version).

2 According to Wikipedia.com, http://en.wikipedia.org/wiki/Prison_Break, season 1 ranked number fifty-five in the United States, with 9.5 million viewers in the eighteen to forty-nine demographic. In Canada, *Prison Break* was the only new television series to be positioned in the

top twenty television shows of 2005–2006; averaged 876,000 in the key demographic of eighteen to forty-nine and 1.4 million viewers nationally for its first season. It has consistently retained the highest number of viewers in its time slot. In Australia, the show premiered with an average audience of 1.94 million and peaked at 2.09 million viewers. The second season premiered with 1.226 million viewers (47% share). In France, the show premiered with 5.5 million viewers (25.8% share), and rapper Faf Larage's song "Pas le Temps" is used to replace the show's original music in the title sequence, which generated publicity and helped to localize the show. Season 2 premiered with an average number of 7.5 million viewers (29.0% share), making it one of the most watched programs for the 2006 year in the U.S. In Poland, it premiered to 7 million viewers (38% share), making it the highest-rated episode of any foreign series in Polsat history. *Prison Break* was also the highest-rated show in sixteen to forty-nine demographic of the week in which it premiered (46% share). Not only is it very popular in Thailand and Singapore, but a three-day *Prison Break* convention ran from 18–21 May 2007 in England. Although these ratings are important and impressive, 20th Century Fox Television executives are more concerned with the show's "ancillary distribution" potential. Based on that potential, they have faith that *Prison Break* will be a "long-term player." This is due to the show's narrative strategy of keeping the caper plot progressing in serialized fashion.

3   These programs, specifically *The Great Escape* and *American Idol*, are cited by the show's creator Paul Scheuring as inspirations (see Diane Kristine, "After the Break: An Interview with *Prison Break* Creator Paul Scheuring," 4 June 2006, http://unifiedtheorynothingmuch.blog-spot.com/2006/06/after-break-interview-with-prison.html).

4   Donald C. Shields and C. Thomas Preston Jr., "Fantasy Theme Analysis in Competitive Rhetorical Criticism," *National Forensic Journal* 3 (1985): 102.

5   Ernest G. Bormann, "Fantasy Theme and Analysis and Rhetorical Theory," in *The Rhetoric of Western Thought*, ed. James L. Golden, Goodwin F. Berquit, and Wiliam E. Coleman (Dubuque, Iowa: Kendall/Hunt, 1993), 365.

6   Shields and Preston Jr., "Fantasy Theme Analysis," 103.

7   Shields and Preston Jr., "Fantasy Theme Analysis," 104.

8   Ernest G. Bormann, "Fantasy and Rhetorical Vision: The Rhetorical Criticism of Social Reality," *Quarterly Journal of Speech* 58 (1972): 398.

9   J. F. Cragan and D. C. Shields, *Symbolic Theories in Applied Communication Research: Bormann, Burke, and Fisher* (Cresskill, N.J.: Hampton, 1995).

10   Cragan and Shields, *Symbolic Theories*, 40.

11   Hebrews 11:1 (New International Version).

12   Rafael Matos, "El Razón y La Fe," sermon, Bellerose Baptist Church, Bellerose, N.Y., 24 June 1984.

13   Niklas Luhmann, "Morality and Religion," in *Religion and Media (Culture Memory in the Present)*, ed. Hent de Fries and Samuel Weber (Stanford: Stanford University Press, 2001), 556.

14   Kenneth Burke, *The Rhetoric of Religion: Studies in Logology* (Berkeley: University of California Press, 1970), 2.

15   "Sleight of Hand," *Prison Break* season 1 DVD, directed by Dwight H. Little (2005, Beverly Hills: 20th Century Fox Entertainment, 2005–2006).

16   Romans 3:23 (New International Version).

17   Julia D'Acci. "Television, Representation, and Gender," in *The Television Studies Reader*, ed. Robert C. Allen and Annette Hill (London: Routledge, 2003), 374.

18   Romans 10:17 (New International Version).

19   In a book review of Marwan Draidy's *Hybridity, or the Cultural Logic of Globalization* (Philadelphia: Temple University Press, 2005) titled "No Halvsies!" Tavia Nyong'o explains that "the full-torso tattoo covering Miller's hybrid body is both the disguised map to the prison he helped design and the alibi for our fetishistic attachment to his frequent on-screen nakedness, a nakedness that is itself a disguise insofar as the body anxiously posed as 'white' is crossed literally and metaphorically by a not-so-secret 'black' ink" (*American Quarterly* 59, no. 1 [2007]: 460).

20   C. S. Lewis, *Mere Christianity: The Case for Christianity, Christian Behaviour and Beyond Personality* (Westwood, N.J.: Barbour, 1952), 117–27.

21   "English, Fitz or Percy," *Prison Break* season 1 DVD, directed by Randall Zisk (2005).

22   "English, Fitz or Percy."

23   Robert N. Bellah, "Civil Religion in America," *Journal of the American Academy of Arts and Sciences* 96, no. 1 (1967): 1–21 (http://www.robert-bellah.com/articles_5.htm).

24   This civil-religious fantasy theme of Americans as free and as protectors and arbiters of freedom is also profound in a post-9/11 environment because it extends beyond the prison and is used to justify U.S. international relations and policies (i.e., bringing freedom to the Middle East, battling "terror").

25   According to Amaury Nolasco, the actor who portrays Fernando Sucre, Sucre is not a stereotypical Latino thug. Although he is a street kid who fell through the cracks, he is a nice and sensitive man at heart ("Prison Break Featurettes," *Prison Break* season 1 DVD, directed by Brett Ratner [2005]).

26   John 15:13 (New International Version).

27   Kristine, "After the Break."

28   Ruth Wilson Gilmore, *Golden Gulag: Prisons, Surplus, Crisis, and Opposition in Globalizing California* (Berkeley: University of California Press, 2007).

29   Pierre Thomas, Jason Ryan, Jack Date, and Theresa Cook, "U.S. Prison Population at All-Time High," *ABC News*, 27 June 2007, www.abcnews.go.com/print?id=3321586.

30   "Pilot," *Prison Break* season 1 DVD, directed by Brett Ratner (2005).

31   "Pilot," *Prison Break* season 1 DVD.

32   "End of the Tunnel," *Prison Break* season 1 DVD, directed by Sanford Bookstaver (2005).

33   Jimmy Santiago Baca, "Past, Present" *Prison Writings in Twentieth-Century America* (New York: Penguin, 1998), 63; quoted in Lorna A. Rhodes, "Toward an Anthropology of Prisons," *Annual Review of Anthropology* 30 (2001): 72.

34   "Allen," *Prison Break* season 1 DVD, directed by Michael W. Watkins (2005).

35   Joshua 5:13-15 (New Revised Standard Version).

36   Kenneth Burke, *Permanence and Change: An Anatomy of Purpose*, 3rd ed. (Berkeley: University of California Press, 1984).

37   Christian theology explains that original sin is a fallen state of humanity, committed when Adam and Eve fell to the serpent's temptation in the garden of Eden (Genesis 3). Consequently, Christianity regards it as the general condition of sinfulness into which all subsequent human beings are born, distinct from any actual sins that they may later commit. Original sin is also used to explain physical and spiritual death, the spiritual death being the loss of the grace of God. While some theologians cite references to original sin in the Old Testament (e.g., Psalm 51), the doctrine is not found in Jewish theology.

38   Burke, *The Rhetoric of Religion*, 217.

39   "Pilot," *Prison Break* season 1 DVD.

40   "The Key," *Prison Break* season 1 DVD, directed by Sergio Mimica-Gezzan (2005).

41   According to Donald Miller and John MacMurray in *To Own a Dragon: Growing Up without a Father* (Colorado Springs: Navpress, 2006), 85 percent of prisoners grew up without fathers and another 10 percent had abusive or neglectful fathers. They stress the importance of the religious vision of God as Father because he does what many human fathers are unable to do: bring their children to states of maturity and wholeness. Additionally, in the second season, we learn that T-Bag was the product of incest and abuse. This upbringing has debilitated his character and his faith. For T-Bag, an "equal opportunity abuser," people are meat and useful only for his own animalistic gratification.

42   Robert N. Bellah, Richard Madsen, William M. Sullivan, Ann Swidler, and Steve M. Tipton, *Habits of the Heart: Individualism and Commitment in America* (Berkeley: University of California Press, 1996), ix.

43   Bellah, "Civil Religion in America," 1–21.

44   "Sleight of Hand."

45   "Sleight of Hand."

46   J. P. Moreland, *Kingdom Triangle: Recover the Christian Mind, Renovate the Soul, Restore the Spirit's Power* (Grand Rapids: Zondervan, 2007), 40.

47   Recent reports reveal that "more than 11 percent of black men between the ages of 25 and 29 are behind bars, and that, considering all ages, approximately 4.8 percent of all black males in the general U.S. population were in prison or jail, contrasted with 1.9 percent of Hispanic males and 0.7 percent of white males. The trends also held true for black women, who are incarcerated at four times the rate of white women and more than double the rate of female Hispanics" (Thomas et al., "U.S. Prison Population"). Those who would advance a social Darwinist position might use this data to support the racist claim that African Americans are inferior to other racial and ethnic groups regardless of gender. Their overrepresentation in the general prison population can more logically be explained by macro-level social/institutional variables such as discrimination, racial profiling, and uneven sentencing.

48   Karl Marx, *Das Kapital*, Gateway edition (Washington D.C.: Regnery, 2000).

49   Michel Foucault. *Discipline and Punish: The Birth of the Prison*, trans. Alan Sheridan (New York: Random House, 1977).

50   "Sleight of Hand." This quote is from Secret Service Agent David Hale, who has a crisis of faith after murdering women and children. He could no longer turn his back on murder and injustice. In order to redeem himself, he agrees to act as an informant for Lincoln's defense attorneys. Unfortunately, he is killed before he can divulge the plan in its entirety.

51   According to Albert Einstein's general theory of relativity, light reaches all objects from all directions at the same speed, regardless of their motion. Faith is neither a respecter of persons nor a static and inescapable prison. It is, for the prisoners, the path to freedom.

52   Revelation 3:20 (New American Standard Bible).

53   "The Key."

54   James 2:26 (The Message Version).

55   "End of the Tunnel," *Prison Break* season 1 DVD, directed by Sanford Bookstaver (2005).

56   Psalm 23:4 (King James Version).

57   "End of the Tunnel."

58   "By the Skin and the Teeth," *Prison Break* season 1 DVD, directed by Fred Gerber (2006).

59   Kenneth Burke, *Grammar of Motives* (Berkeley: University of California Press, 1969), 36.

60   "Bolshoi Booze" *Prison Break* season 2 DVD, directed by Greg Yaitaines (2007; Beverly Hills: 20th Century Fox Entertainment, 2006–2007).

61   Ecclesiastes 3:1 (New International Version).

62   Kristine, "After the Break."

63   In Judaic tradition, that moment in time is called Pesach, the going out of Egypt. http://www.chiefrabbi.org/ft-index.html.

64   Matthew 16:24–26 (New Life Version).

65   Ephesians 6:16 (New International Version); Isaiah 61:1 (Amplified Version).

66   "Bolshoi Booze."

67   "The Message," *Prison Break* season 2 DVD, directed by Bobby Roth (2007).

68   "The Message."

69   "The Message."

70   "Bolshoi Booze." "Hail Mary" is a Catholic prayer and the name of a football play. The denotative reading, in a Christian religious context, alludes to godly grace: "Hail Mary, full of grace, the Lord is with thee. Blessed art thou among women, and blessed is the fruit of thy womb, Jesus. Holy Mary, Mother of God, pray for us sinners now and at the hour of death. Amen." According to the *Catholic Catechism 2675*, "beginning with Mary's unique cooperation with the working of the Holy Spirit, the Churches developed their prayer to the holy Mother of God, centering it on the Person of Christ manifested in His mysteries. In countless hymns and antiphons expressing this prayer, two movements usually alternate with one another: the first 'magnifies' the Lord for the 'great things' He did for His lowly servant and through her for all human beings. The second entrusts the supplications and praises of the children of God to the Mother of Jesus, because she now knows the humanity which, in her, the Son of God espoused" (http://www.ewtn.com/Devotionals/prayers/mary3.htm). A connotative reading, in terms of attack strategy, is "an offensive play where the quarterback throws the ball up in the air without really targeting any particular receiver, hoping someone on his team catches it. A Hail Mary is generally used on the last play of the half or end of the game when a team is out of field-goal range and has just enough time for one play" (James Alder, "About Football Glossary—Hail Mary," http://football.about.com/cs/football101/g/gl_hailmary.htm). Such is the case for Michael, Lincoln, and Paul at this point in the storyline.

71   Acts 26:9–11 (New Life Version). This quote is taken from Saint Paul's testimony before the head of state, King Agrippa, as recorded biblically by Luke. It is cited here because it is the template for Paul Kellerman's final testimony before the grand jury at Sara's trial in "Fin Del Camino" (*Prison Break* season 2 DVD, directed by Bobby Roth [2007]).

72   "Chicago," *Prison Break* season 2 DVD, directed by Jesse Bocho (2007).

73   Simone de Beauvoir, *The Second Sex* (New York: Alfred A. Knopf, 1989), xxii.

74   Beauvoir, *Second Sex.*

75   Joe Sim, "Tougher Than the Rest? Men in Prison," in *Just Boys Doing Business: Men, Masculinities, and Crime*, ed. Tim Newburn and Elizabeth A. Stanko (New York: Routledge, 1994): 110. This one-dimensional representation of prisoners as male is not true to reality since, as of June 2006, "the number of female inmates rose at a faster rate than male inmates—an increase of 4.8 percent, to a total of more than 111,000." This statistic was reported in the article by Thomas et al., "U.S. Prison Population."

76   Revelation 3:20 (New American Standard Translation).

77   Raymond Williams, *Television: Technology and Cultural Form* (Hanover, N.H.: Routledge, 2003), 43.

78   Williams, *Television.*

Chapter 14

1   In the period before the last episodes of season 6 were aired, it seemed that every journalist, film critic, and blogger was predicting the ending. Within moments of the now famous cut to black at the end of the final episode, the Internet was filled with analysis and emotion. Due to sheer volume, all of the commentaries cannot be listed, but here are some interesting commentaries: Paul Levinson, "*The Sopranos* End and the Closure-Junkies," 12 June 2007, http://paullevinson.blog spot.com/2007_06_01_archive.html; Marisa Carroll, "*The Sopranos.*" http://www.popmatters.com/pm/tv/reviews/42792/the-sopranos-series-finale; Associated Press, "Debate Rages over 'Sopranos' Existential Ending," http://www.msnbc.msn.com/id/19176918. My own theory is that David Chase is having a good laugh and at the same time ensuring that his audience will continue to talk about Tony and *The Sopranos* for many years to come. There are enough hints in the series to support several contradictory theories, including the position that Tony is dead, that Meadow is dead, or that they all survived. I would only point out that the several seconds of black before the final credits roll at the end of the final episode correspond to the several seconds of black that we experience after the opening sequence of the very first episode, before we find ourselves with Tony as he waits for his first appointment with Dr. Melfi. Normally, each episode begins immediately after the opening sequence, as Tony emerges from his car, and the camera cuts to the stylized *Sopranos* trademark. It may or may not be coincidental that the key question that Dr. Melfi asks Tony that day is "Any thoughts at all on why you blacked out?" Just as we have been parachuted into the midst of a complicated life, so are we parachuted out when its creator—Chase, not God—has had enough.

2   Episodes will be identified in parenthesis as follows: (season number. episode number).

3   On the ways in which the series resembles *film noir*, see influences on the series, Kevin L. Stoehr, "'It's All a Big Nothing:' The Nihilistic Vision of *The Sopranos*," in The Sopranos *and Philosophy: I Kill Therefore I Am*, ed. Richard Greene and Peter Vernezze (Peru, Ill.: Open Court, 2004), 37–47.

4   Some viewers were annoyed by the dream sequences. In their defense, the device succeeded in taking us into the consciousness of the characters, particularly Tony and Carmela, and gave the analysts among us something to do. See Heather Havrilesky's answer to the burning question "Should you waste your time analyzing Tony Soprano's dreams or fearing for Donna Moss' life?" "I Like to Watch: Dreamscape Architecture," Salon, 24 May 2004, http://dir.salon.com/story/ent/tv/review/2004/05/24/i_like/index.html.

5   It would not be surprising to learn that David Chase or another individual involved with *The Sopranos* was aware of Alex Garland's novel *The Coma*, which appeared in 2004 (New York: Penguin). The novel is about a man who is beaten up in a subway and falls into a long and complicated coma dream. Here, too, music and a lost briefcase feature prominently as keys to the injured man's identity. The man has amnesia and has no recollection of his name, family status, or work. Initially, he believes that listening to familiar music will cause him to wake from his coma; when this proves ineffective, he focuses his energies on regaining his lost briefcase, which will reveal to him who he really is. Throughout, we realize that at least some of what we are reading is his dream, but the boundary between his dream life and his "real" life are unclear.

6   Later, however, Carmela regrets these words. Some bloggers, however, agree with her. See the Patton Dodd's article "Tony Soprano Is Going to Hell," http://www.beliefnet.com/story/219/story_21982_1.html.

7   In fact, Tony has almost nothing covered with his parish priest; Tony has not gone to confession or taken Communion for the eight years that we have known him. It must be said, however, that his parish priest does not exactly reach out to him either. While he makes an appearance to comfort Carmela during Tony's coma, he does not visit Tony after he wakes up. In the final scene of the series, Tony, Carmela, and Anthony Jr. share an order of onion rings. Each one places the entire the ring on their tongues and eats it whole, calling to mind the Eucharist in which the wafer (symbolizing or representing the body of Christ) is eaten in much the same way. Some bloggers have used this point to argue that the family dies at the end (hidden by the cut to black), but this explanation fails to take Chase's playfulness into account.

8   Charles W. Colson, *Born Again* (Old Tappan, N.J.: Chosen Books, 1976.).

9   As in numerous episodes, the series acknowledges a real, and very serious social problem, in this case, the problem of the agunah within Jewish religious law, namely the situation of a woman whose husband

refuses to grant a divorce. For background, see B. S. Jackson, "Agunah and the Problem of Authority: Directions for Future Research," *Melilah* 1 (2004): 1–78; and Tzvi Gartner, "Problems of a Forced Get," *Journal of Halakhah and Contemporary Society* 9 (1985): 118–42.

10   Masada is a first-century palace built by King Herod the Great on an isolated plateau on the edge of the Judean desert overlooking the Dead Sea. During the Jewish revolt against Rome in 66–70 C.E., the Roman forces laid siege to the fortress and, according to legend, the besieged residents of Masada committed suicide en masse rather than be defeated by Rome. The story is told in Josephus, *The Jewish War*, book 7, paragraphs 304–406. See Josephus, *The Jewish War*, newly translated with extensive commentary and archaeological background illustrations, ed. Gaalya Cornfeld et al. (Grand Rapids: Zondervan, 1982). See also Nachman Ben-Yehuda, *The Masada Myth: Collective Memory and Mythmaking in Israel* (Madison: University of Wisconsin Press, 1995); Yigael Yadin, *Masada: Herod's Fortress and the Zealots' Last Stand* (London: Weidenfeld & Nicolson, 1966).

11   Robert Viscusi sees this scene as an example of the "buried Caesar" motif, which allusively draws on the imperial history of Rome in its characterization of *The Sopranos*. It is not coincidental that David Chase's "real" name is De Cesare. Viscusi notes that "In Mafia stereotyping, the Italian name is the sign that transformed the body to something terrible, something to be wasted. In *The Sopranos*, the process is returned to the roots of language: *the name itself* is the thing that has been wasted. There is no *De Cesare*. The name having been wasted, it haunts the story. Caesar reappears everywhere. The family Caesar is continually dying and being buried all over again in this series." Robert Viscusi, *Buried Caesars, and Other Secrets of Italian-American Writing* (State University of New York Series in Italian/American Culture; Albany: State University of New York Press, 2006), 212.

12   For analyses of films about the Roman Empire, see Sandra R. Joshel, Margaret Malamud, and Donald T. McGuire Jr., eds., *Imperial Projections: Ancient Rome in Modern Popular Culture* (Baltimore: The Johns Hopkins University Press, 2001); Maria Wyke, *Projecting the Past: Ancient Rome, Cinema, and History* (London: Routledge, 1997); Jon Solomon, *The Ancient World in the Cinema* (South Brunswick, N.J.: A. S. Barnes, 1978).

13   See Ronald M. Green, "'I Dunno about Morals, but I Do Got Rules': Tony Soprano as Ethical Manager," in Greene and Venezze, *The Sopranos and Philosophy*, 59–71.

14   For a discussion of the Golem legend, see Hillel J. Kieval, "Pursuing the Golem of Prague: Jewish Culture and the Invention of a Tradition," *Modern Judaism* 17, no. 1 (1997): 1–20. The Golem appears frequently in popular culture, including fiction (e.g., Michael Chabon, *The Amazing Adventures of Kavalier and Clay* [2000]; Umberto Eco,

Foucault's Pendulum [1990]), animation (a 1970s issue of Marvel Comics *The Hulk*, the ancient legend is capsulized, and the story then segues into the Hulk taking on the Golem's role to protect people living under a dictatorship), television (in *The Simpsons Treehouse of Horror XVII*, *The X-Files* episode "Kaddish," in which a young Hasidic woman creates a Golem who avenges her husband's murder by neo-Nazis), and film (*Stranger than Fiction*, 2006; Professor Jules Hilbert [Dustin Hoffman] asks Harold Crick [Will Ferrell] "Aren't you relieved to know you're not a Golem?" To which Harold sarcastically replies "Yes . . . I am relieved to know that I'm not a Golem.").

15   It is interesting to note that while the episode portrays Hasidim, the views associated with Teitelman and family are not distinctive to this branch of Judaism, and the views that are specific to this group are not at all mentioned. The majority of observant Jews, who would also for example be concerned about the laws of divorce and would know about the martyrdom at Masada, do not look significantly different from others in mainstream American society. Portraying Hasidim in their distinctive appearance allows the contrast between Tony and Teitelman (and Ariel) to be drawn more easily. The episode also alludes several times to the tension among different groups of Jews, which is evident in the distrust that Tony's Jewish associate, Hesh Rabkin, who is a secular but knowledgeable Jew, displays toward the Teitelmans and other Hasidim.

16   See the article "Martyr," http://www.newadvent.org/cathen/09736b.htm. Of particular interest is early Christian martyrdom at the hands of imperial Rome, beginning in the late first century C.E. and continuing until the conversion of Constantine in the early fourth century. The martyrs of Masada, whom Ariel sees as his ancestors, and the earliest Christians, who are spiritual ancestors of the Catholic Church, were therefore facing a common persecutor, the Roman Empire, with which Tony identifies, at least in this scene.

17   Arguably, the women in the series, most notably Carmela, have integrated Catholicism more fully and more sincerely than Tony and his associates, though one can point to numerous instances of hypocrisy in their behavior, such as Carmela's cost-cutting measures in building her "spec" house.

18   This final sequence borrows a page from the ending of *The Godfather* by cutting quickly back and forth between an uplifting family event (a baptism, in the case of *The Godfather*, and a Christmas concert, in the case of *The Sopranos*) and the vicious acts that are an inevitable part of "family" life.

19   While Teitelman refers to Tony as "a Frankenstein," meaning "monster," it is worth noting that in the original book and films, Frankenstein is the name of the scientist who created the monster, not the monster itself.

20   On Schrödinger's equation, a foundation of quantum mechanics, see David J. Griffiths, *Introduction to Quantum Mechanics*, 2nd ed. (New York: Prentice Hall, 2004).

21   A fascinating analysis of nihilism in the series can be found in Stoehr, "It's All a Big Nothing."

22   Sopranos Invitation, Directors Guild of America, dga.org, http://www.dga.org/news/v29_1/images/dgaevnts_may04/sopranos-invite.html.

23   Maureen Ryan, "*The Sopranos* Is the Most Influential Television Drama Ever," *PopMatters*, 23 April 2007, http://www.popmatters.com/pm/features/article/32795/the-sopranos-is-the-most-influential-television-drama-ever.

24   Ben Macintyre, "*The Sopranos*: Every Inch a Shakespearean Drama," *The Times* (London), 15 June 2007, http://www.timesonline.co.uk/tol/comment/columnists/ben_macintyre/article1934775.ece.

25   Alessandra Stanley, "One Last Family Gathering: You Eat, You Talk, It's Over," *The New York Times*, 11 June 2007, http://www.nytimes.com/2007/06/11/arts/television/11sopr.html?_r=1&oref=slogin.

26   Cf. Richard Dawkins, *The God Delusion* (Boston: Houghton Mifflin, 2006) and Christopher Hitchens, *God Is Not Great: How Religion Poisons Everything* (Toronto: Macmillan & Stewart, 2007).

27   George Anastasia, "If Shakespeare Were Alive Today, He'd Be Writing for *The Sopranos*," in Barreca, *Sit Down with the Sopranos*, 151.

28   For a detailed argument demonstrating this point, see Neal Gabler, *Life the Movie: How Entertainment Conquered Reality* (New York: Alfred A. Knopf, 1998).

29   The original poem, written in French, is titled "Pater Noster" by Jacques Prévert and can be found in a collection called *Paroles* (Paris: Éditions Gallimard, 1949), 58–59. The next few lines, though not read aloud by Meadow, also align quite closely with plot elements within the series: With its mysteries of New York/And its mysteries of Paris/At least as good as that of the Trinity.

Chapter 15

1   In her essay "Image" in Mark C. Taylor, ed. *Critical Terms for Religious Studies* (Chicago: University of Chicago Press, 1998), Miles contrasts "fifteenth-century Christians [who had] long instruction and practice in the devotional use of vision. It required training, exercise, and concentration" with "twentieth-century Americans [for whom] media images usually require little engagement of the imagination; the possibility of watching them passively, with little investment of imaginative embellishment, is greater" (168–69).

2   Ronald D. Moore and David Chase in the shows above.

3   Two of his less successful shows deserve mention: *The Jury* ran for ten

episodes during the summer of 2004 on Fox. A longer run might have allowed Fontana to use this variation on *Twelve Angry Men* to explore the justice system. Eight episodes of *The Bedford Diaries*—a collaboration between Fontana and *Homicide* writer Julie Martin—aired in the spring of 2006. Its premise—college students record video diaries of their sex lives as homework—stirred controversy before the show even aired. The series might have directed Fontana's moral concerns toward sexual and social behavior. Alas, *Diaries* was not picked up and became best known for being criticized by various conservative media watchdog groups, an attack Fontana thought misplaced: "Fundamentalists attacked us because we were doing a show about sex—what was ironic was that the intention of the show was to talk about sexual responsibility. It was not to say, 'let's get laid.' It was about taking an action and taking responsibility for that action. I thought it ironic that their impulse was to slam us and yet if they had watched the show they might have applauded."

4   James L. Longworth, *TV Creators: Conversations with America's Top Producers of Television Drama* (Syracuse, N.Y: Syracuse University Press, 2000), 38.

5   Philip J. Lane, "The Existential Condition of Television Crime Drama," *Journal of Popular Culture* 34, no. 4 (2001): 137–52.

6   Tom Fontana, telephone interview with the author, 8 March 2007. All subsequent quotes from Fontana, not otherwise identified, are from this interview.

7   Longworth, *TV Creators*, 45.

8   "An Evening with Tom Fontana," Makor Center, New York, 26 September 2005, author's personal transcription.

9   Gabrielle DeGroot and Gabriella Daley, "An Interview with Tom Fontana," *Corrections Today* 60, no. 1 (1998): 50–53.

10   The term "lived religion" became popular in the academic study of religion in North America about a decade ago. See, in particular, David D. Hall, ed. *Lived Religion in America: Toward a History of Practice* (Princeton: Princeton University Press, 1997).

11   One Giuliani quote from this profile that could easily have been uttered by Fontana: "The way to understand me as a Catholic is, it's my religion. I have learned a lot from it. I am informed by it. But I am not directed by it" (Peter J. Boyer, "Mayberry Man," *New Yorker*, 20 August 2007, 57).

12   Fontana's status as a Catholic artist is cemented when one considers the television movies he wrote for Paulist Productions, a Catholic media company. In 1985, very early in his career, Fontana wrote *The Fourth Wiseman*, based on a classic 1895 story by Presbyterian theologian Henry Van Dyke. His second film for Paulist, *Judas*, was filmed in 2001 but shelved by ABC only to be aired in March 2004 to coincide with the release of Mel Gibson's *The Passion of the Christ*.

Obviously these films do not develop long character arcs of faith and doubt, nor do they probe the theological nature of evil. Rather they offer various perspectives on the life of Jesus, in a fairly mainstream, Church-approved, family-friendly manner. What these films do have in common with Fontana's "trilogy" is a desire to depict lived religion: ordinary lives intersecting with the possibility of the divine—albeit in this case during New Testament times. He is currently writing, for Paulist, a new script about Nicodemus, a member of the Sanhedrin mentioned in Gospel of John. As Fontana describes it, "Nicodemus does not convert to Christianity, he maintains his Jewish faith and Jewish heritage, but he looks at the story of Jesus and comes to it with a new understanding for us." Besides the Nicodemus script, Fontana's other works in progress (as of 2007) show his continued engagement with the Catholic tradition. He is writing a novel for HarperCollins about the papacy in the tenth century (sometimes known as the "pornocracy" or government by whores) which Fontana describes as "a lot of really really bad popes." The novel, he says, is "about faith and the meaning of faith."

13   Fontana posted the entire script online on his Web site, http://www.tomfontana.com/scripts.

14   Longworth, *TV Creators*, 109.

15   This is the main argument I make about *Homicide* in my chapter "God in the Box: Religion in Contemporary Television Cop Shows" (in *God in the Details: American Religion in Popular Culture*, ed. Eric Mazur and Kate McCarthy [New York: Routledge, 2001], 199–215), where I compare the religious themes in *Homicide* to the very different religious themes in two other high-quality cop shows on during the same years (*Law and Order* and *NYPD Blue*).

16   "Pembleton, the premodern—however facetiously—sees religion as divine warfare. Bayliss, the modern, sees religion as a convenience to be changed or discarded as needed" (Siegler, "God in the Box," 209).

17   Siegler, "God in the Box," 214.

18   John Leonard, "Ancient Histories," *New York*, 14 February 2000, http://nymag.com/nymetro/arts/tv/reviews/1927.

19   John Leonard, *Smoke and Mirrors* (New York: Free Press, 1997), 6–7.

20   Siegler, "God in the Box," 211–13.

21   Michel Foucault, *The History of Sexuality: An Introduction*, vol. 1 (New York: Vintage, 1980), 60–61.

22   One could argue that the roots of *Oz* go back even further, to "Cheek to Cheek" (12 March 1986), an episode of *St. Elsewhere* in which Dr. Morrison, volunteering at a prison infirmary, is raped by an inmate during a riot.

23   DavidB266Morris, "Adventurous," review of *Prison Riot*, TV.com, http://www.tv.com/homicide-life-on-the-street/prison-riot/episode/36517/reviews.html.

24   Joe Wlodarz, "Maximum Insecurity: Genre Trouble and Closet Erotics in and out of HBO's Oz," *Camera Obscura* 58, no. 20 (2005): 58–105.

25   Wlodarz, "Maximum Insecurity," 62.

26   *The Hidden God* is the title of a recent book on religion and film, describing in particular the role of God in Robert Bresson's films and films in general. The phrase refers to Blaise Pascal's description of God as "absent but present to those who seek him." See Mary Lea Bandy and Antonio Monda, eds., *The Hidden God: Film and Faith* (New York: Museum of Modern Art, 2003), 10.

27   Joe Wlodarz, "Maximum Insecurity," 74.

28   Joyce Smith, "The Media Diary of an American Priest: Christian Ministry in Popular and News Media," presentation given at the annual meeting of the Society for the Scientific Study of Religion, Houston, Texas, October 2000, 7.

29   Smith, "Media Diary," 7.

30   For Fontana's view on the characters of Governor Devlin and the guards, see DeGroot and Daily, "Interview with Tom Fontana."

31   Thomas J. Ferraro, *Feeling Italian: The Art of Ethnicity in America* (New York: New York University Press, 2005), 173.

32   Interview with Alex Epstein (Crafty TV), blog post, Complications Ensue, 6 June 2006, http://complicationsensue.blogspot.com/2006/06/tom-fontana-part-six.html.

33   Wlodarz, "Maximum Insecurity," 101.

34   Emily Nussbaum, "The Long Con," *New York*, 25 June 2007, http://nymag.com/news/features/33517 (emphasis added).

Epilogue

1   See Robert Orsi, *The Madonna of 115th Street: Faith and Community in Italian Harlem, 1880–1950*, 2nd ed. (New Haven: Yale University Press, 2002), xix.

2   Brights believe in a naturalistic universe. Coined in 2003, the term was intended as a positive alternative to descriptives including *atheist, agnostic, skeptic,* and *humanist.*

3   Talad Asad, *Genealogies of Religion: Discipline and Reasons of Power in Christianity and Islam* (Baltimore: The Johns Hopkins University Press, 1993).

4   An interesting measure for "quality television" might be the spiritual issues and ethical concerns embedded in the stories.

5   For example: *Pushing Daisies, Moonlight, New Amsterdam, Terminator: The Sarah Connor Chronicles, Reaper, Saving Grace,* and *Eli Stone.*

Bibliography

Abdo, Geneive. *Mecca and Main Street: Muslim Life in America after 9/11.* New York: Oxford University Press, 2006.

Abele, Robert. "Child in Time: *The Wire.*" *LA Weekly,* 13 September 2006.

Albanese, Catherine L. "Exchanging Selves, Exchanging Souls Contact, Combination, and American Religious History." In *Retelling U.S. Religious History,* edited by Thomas A. Tweed, 200–26. Berkeley: University of California Press, 1997.

———. *Republic of Mind and Spirit: A Cultural History of American Metaphysical Religion.* New Haven: Yale University Press, 2007.

Albrecht, Gary L. "Disability Humor: What's in a Joke." *Body & Society* 5, no. 4 (1999): 67–74.

Alexander, Bobby. *Televangelism Reconsidered: Ritual in the Search for Human Community.* Atlanta: Scholars Press, 1994.

Allison, Anne. *Millennial Monsters: Japanese Toys and the Global Imagination.* Berkeley: University of California Press, 2006.

Alvarez, Rafael. The Wire: *Truth Be Told.* New York: Pocket, 2004.

American Family Association. "General Information." AFA Online. http://www.afa.net/about.asp.

Anastasia, George. "If Shakespeare Were Alive Today, He'd Be Writing for The Sopranos." In *A Sitdown with the Sopranos: Watching Italian American Culture on TV's Most Talked-about Series,* edited by Regina Barreca, 149–66. New York: Palgrave Macmillan, 2002.

Andelman, Bob. "David Simon, *The Wire* Creator." Mr. Media Interviews by Bob Andelman, 15 February 2007. http://www.mrmedia.com/2007/02/fridays-with-mr-media-david-simonthe.html.

Arkoun, Mohammed. *Rethinking Islam: Common Questions, Uncommon Answers*. Translated by Robert D. Lee. Boulder: Westview, 1994.

Asad, Talad. *Genealogies of Religion: Discipline and Reasons of Power in Christianity and Islam*. Baltimore: The Johns Hopkins University Press, 1993.

Asmussen, Joen. "Do We Like Being Lost?" NoScope, 12 March 2007. http://noscope.com/journal/2007/03/lost.

Associated Press. "Debate Rages over 'Sopranos' Existential Ending," 12 June 2007. http://www.msnbc.msn.com/id/19176918.

"Audience Penetration." Media Info Center. http://www.mediainfocenter.org/compare/penetration.

Baca, Jimmy Santiago. "Past Present." In *Prison Writings in Twentieth-Century America*, edited by H. Bruce Franklin, 358–62. New York: Penguin, 1998.

Badaracco, Claire, ed. *Quoting God: How Media Shape Ideas about Religion*. Waco, Tex.: Baylor University Press, 2005.

Badmington, Neil. *Alien Chic: Posthumanism and the Other Within*. New York: Routledge, 2004.

Baldwin, James. *The Fire Next Time*. New York: Vintage, 1993.

Balmer, Randall. *Thy Kingdom Come: How the Religious Right Distorts the Faith and Threatens America: An Evangelical's Lament*. New York: Basic, 2006.

Baltimore Basilica. "Our History." http://www.baltimorebasilica.org.

Bandy, Mary Lea, and Antonio Monda, eds. *The Hidden God: Film and Faith*. New York: Museum of Modern Art, 2003.

"Battlestar Galactica: Season 4 Preview!" *Entertainment Weekly*, 7 January 2008. http://www.ew.com/ew/article/0,,20169703,00.html.

Baudrillard, Jean. "The Precession of Simulacra." In *Art after Modernism: Rethinking Representation*, edited by Brian Wallis, 253–81. New York: New Museum of Contemporary Art, 1984.

Bazelon, Emily. "Is There a Post-Abortion Syndrome?" *New York Times Magazine*, 21 January 2007.

Beauvoir, Simone de. *The Second Sex*. New York: Alfred A. Knopf, 1989.

Bellah, Robert N. "Civil Religion in America." *Journal of the American Academy of Arts and Sciences* 96, no. 1 (1967): 1–21. http://www.robertbellah.com/articles_5.htm.

———. "Finding Meaning in Human Experience." *Chronicle of Higher Education* (1 December 2006): B10.

Bellah, Robert N., Richard Madsen, William M. Sullivan, Ann Swidler, and Steve M. Tipton. *Habits of the Heart: Individualism and Commitment in America*. Berkeley: University of California Press, 1996.

Ben-Yehuda, Nachman. *The Masada Myth: Collective Memory and Myth-making in Israel.* Madison: University of Wisconsin Press, 1995.

Best, Steven, and Douglas Kellner. *Postmodern Theory.* New York: The Guilford Press, 1991.

Biederman, Donald E. *Law and Business of the Entertainment Industries.* Westport, Conn.: Praeger, 2001.

Bird, S. Elizabeth. *The Audience in Everyday Life.* New York: Routledge, 2003.

Blythe, Teresa. "The Divine Ick Factor: How Creepy Religion Heightens Television Dramas," 2005. http://www.beliefnet.com/story/164/story_16467_1.html.

———. "Working Hard for the Money: A Faith-Based Media Literacy Analysis of the Top Television Dramas of 2000–2001." *Journal of Media and Religion* 1, no. 3 (2002): 139–51.

Bongco, Mila. *Reading Comics: Language, Culture, and the Concept of the Superhero in Comic Books.* New York: Garland, 2000.

Boon, Brooke. *Holy Yoga: Exercise for the Christian Body and Soul.* New York: FaithWords, 2007.

Bordenkircher, Susan. *Yoga for Christians: A Christ-Centered Approach to Physical and Spiritual Health through Yoga.* Nashville: Thomas Nelson, 2006.

Bormann, Ernest G. "Fantasy and Rhetorical Vision: The Rhetorical Criticism of Social Reality." *Quarterly Journal of Speech* 58 (1972): 396–407.

———. "Fantasy Theme and Analysis and Rhetorical Theory." In *The Rhetoric of Western Thought,* edited by James L. Golden, Goodwin F. Berquit, and Wiliam E. Coleman. Iowa: Kendall/Hunt, 1993.

Boyer, Peter J. "Mayberry Man." *The New Yorker,* 20 August 2007, 57.

Braxton, Greg. "Hollywood Loves BBFs 4-Ever." *Los Angeles Times,* 29 August 2006.

Breen, Myles, and Farrel Corcoran. "Myth in Television Discourse." *Communication Monographs* 49, no. 2 (1982): 127–36.

Broaddus, Maurice. "Lost—The TV Show." Hollywood Jesus, 10 December 2004. http://www.hollywoodjesus.com/comments/maurice/2004/12/lost-tv-show.html.

Brodkin, Karen. *How the Jews Became White Folks . . . and What That Says About Race in America.* New Brunswick, N.J.: Rutgers University Press, 1998.

Brook, Vincent. *Something Ain't Kosher Here: The Rise of the "Jewish" Sitcom.* New Brunswick, N.J.: Rutgers University Press, 2003.

Bruce, Steven. *Pray TV: Televangelism in America.* New York: Routledge, 1990.

Brunsdon, Charlotte, Julie D'Acci, and Lynn Spigel, eds. *Feminist Television Criticism: A Reader.* Oxford: Oxford University Press, 1990.

Buber, Martin. "Dialogue." Chapter 1 in *Between Man and Man* (1929). Translated by Ronald Gregor-Smith. London: Routledge, 2002.

———. *I and Thou.* 1936. Translated by Walter Kaufmann. New York: Scribner, 1970.

Buddenbaum, Judith, and Debra Mason, eds. *Readings on Religion as News.* Ames: Iowa State University Press, 2000.

Burke, Kenneth. *Grammar of Motives.* Berkeley: University of California Press, 1969.

———. *Permanence and Change: An Anatomy of Purpose.* 3rd ed. Berkeley: University of California Press, 1984.

———. *The Rhetoric of Religion: Studies in Logology.* Berkeley: University of California Press, 1970.

Byrne, Bridget. "Lost Plots Endgame." E! Online, 15 January 2007. http://www.eonline.com/uberblog/b54173__amp_lt_i_amp_gt_Lost_amp_lt__i_amp_gt__Plots_Endgame.html.

Campbell, Richard, Christopher Martin, and Bettina Fabos. *Media and Culture: An Introduction to Mass Communication.* 7th ed. Boston: Bedford/St. Martin's, 2007.

Carey, James. *Communication as Culture: Essays on Media and Society.* New York: Routledge, 1992.

Carroll, Marisa. Review of *The Sopranos,* 19 June 2007. http://www.popmatters.com/pm/tv/reviews/42792/ the-sopranos-series-finale.

Cassirer, Ernst. *An Essay on Man: An Introduction to the Philosophy of Human Culture.* New Haven: Yale University Press, 1925.

Catholic University of America. *The New Catholic Encyclopedia.* New York: McGraw-Hill, 1967.

———. *The New Catholic Encyclopedia.* 2nd ed. Detroit: ThomsonGale, 2003.

Chabon, Michael. *The Amazing Adventures of Kavalier and Clay.* New York: Random House, 2000.

Chow, Rey. *The Protestant Ethnic and the Spirit of Capitalism.* New York: Columbia University Press, 2002.

Chute-Sokei, Louis. *The Last "Darky": Bert Williams, Black-on-Black Minstrelsy, and the African Diaspora.* Durham: Duke University Press, 2006.

Clanton, Dan W., Jr. "These Are Their Stories: Views of Religion in *Law & Order*." *Journal of Religion and Popular Culture* 4 (2003). http://www.usask.ca/relst/jrpc/art4-lawandorder-print.html.

Clarke, Arthur C. *Profiles of the Future: An Inquiry into the Limits of the Possible.* Rev. ed. New York: Harper & Row, 1973.

Clarke, Scott H. "Created in Whose Image? Religious Characters on Network Television." *Journal of Media and Religion* 4, no. 3 (2005): 137–53.

Cnaan, Ram. *The Other Philadelphia Story: How Local Congregations Support the Quality of Life in Urban America*. Philadelphia: University of Pennsylvania Press, 2006.

Cohen, Stephen M. "Stop Sugarcoating Intermarriage." *Jewish Journal* (9 March 2007): 12.

Collins, Jim. "Postmodernism and Television." In *Channels of Discourse, Reassembled*, 2nd ed., edited by Robert C. Allen, 327–53. Chapel Hill: University of North Carolina Press, 1992.

Colombe, Audrey. "White Hollywood's New Black Boogeyman." *Jump Cut* 45 (2002): 1–7.

Colson, Charles W. *Born Again*. Old Tappan, N.J.: Chosen Books, 1976.

Cone, James H. *God of the Oppressed*. San Francisco: Harper & Row, 1975.

Cooke, Miriam, and Bruce Lawrence, eds. *Muslim Networks: From Hajj to Hip-Hop*. Chapel Hill: University of North Carolina Press, 2005.

Covel, Bonnie. *Lost*. About.com. http://lost.about.com.

Cowan, Geoffrey. *See No Evil: The Backstage Battle over Sex and Violence in Television*. New York: Simon & Schuster, 1978.

Cox, Harvey. *Common Prayers: Faith, Family, and a Christian's Journey through the Jewish Year*. New York: Houghton Mifflin, 1999.

Cragan, J. F., and D. C. Shields. *Symbolic Theories in Applied Communication Research: Bormann, Burke, and Fisher*. Cresskill, N.J.: Hampton, 1995.

Craig, Timothy J., ed. *Japan Pop! Inside the World of Japanese Popular Culture*. Armonk, N.Y.: M. E. Sharpe, 2000.

D'Acci, Julie. *Defining Women: Television and the Case of* Cagney and Lacey. Chapel Hill: University of North Carolina Press, 1994.

———. "Defining Women: The Case of *Cagney and Lacey*." In *Private Screenings: Television and the Female Consumer*, edited by Lynn Spigel and Denise Mann, 169–200. Minneapolis: University of Minnesota Press, 1992.

———. "Leading Up to *Roe v. Wade*: Television Documentaries in the Abortion Debate." In *Television, History, and American Culture: Feminist Critical Essays*, edited by Mary Beth Haralovich and Lauren Rabinovitz, 120–43. Durham: Duke University Press, 1999.

———. "Television, Representation, and Gender." In *The Television Studies Reader*, edited by Robert C. Allen and Annette Hill, 373–88. London: Routledge, 2003.

D'Agostino, Peter, ed. *Transmission: Theory and Practice for a New Television Aesthetics*. New York: Tanam, 1985.

Dana, Rebecca. "Reinventing *24*." *Wall Street Journal*, 2 February 2008. http://online.wsj.com/public/article_print/SB120189888101136151.html.

Davis, Erik. "Half Japanese: The Mighty Morphin Power Rangers."

The Village Voice, 21 June 1994. http://www.techgnosis.com/chunkshow-single.php?chunk=chunkfrom-2005-10-15-1627-0.txt.

Davis, Natalie Zemon. *Society and Culture in Early Modern France*. Stanford: Stanford University Press, 1975.

Dawkins, Richard. *The God Delusion*. Boston: Houghton Mifflin, 2006.

DeGroot, Gabrielle, and Gabriella Daley. "An Interview with Tom Fontana." *Corrections Today* 60, no. 1 (1998): 50–53.

De Zengotita, Thomas. *Mediated: How the Media Shapes Your World and the Way You Live in It*. New York: Bloomsbury, 2006.

DiMaggio, Paul, Eszter Hargittai, W. Russell Neuman, and John P. Robinson. "Social Implications of the Internet." *Annual Review of Sociology* 27 (2001): 307–36. doi:10.1146/annurev.soc.27.1.307. http://arjournals.annualreviews.org/doi/abs/10.1146/annurev.soc.27.1.307?journalCode=soc.

Disch, Thomas M. *The Dreams Our Stuff Is Made of: How Science Fiction Conquered the World*. New York: Touchstone/Simon & Schuster, 1998.

Dodd, Paton. "Tony Soprano Is Going to Hell." Beliefnet. http://www.beliefnet.com/story/219/story_21982_1.html.

Dow, Bonnie. *Prime-Time Feminism: Television, Media Culture, and the Women's Movement Since 1970*. Philadelphia: University of Pennsylvania Press, 1996.

Ducker, Eric. "The Left Behind: Inside *The Wire*'s World of Alienation and Asshole Gods." *Fader Magazine*, 8 December 2006.

Duke, Steven B., and Albert C. Gross. *America's Longest War: Rethinking Our Tragic Crusade against Drugs*. Los Angeles: J. P. Tarcher, 1994.

Dyer, Richard. "White." *Screen* 29, no. 4 (1988): 44–65.

———. *White*. New York: Routledge, 1997.

Eco, Umberto. *Foucault's Pendulum*. Translated by William Weaver. Orlando: Harcourt Brace Jovanovich, 1989.

Edgell, Penny, Joseph Gerteis, and Douglas Hartmann. "Atheists as 'Other': Moral Boundaries and Cultural Membership in American Society." *American Sociological Review* 71, no. 2 (2006): 211–34.

Edgerton, Gary, and Jeffrey P. Jones, eds. *The Essential HBO Reader*. Lexington: University Press of Kentucky, 2008.

Eggerton, John. "TV Shines in TVB Study." *Broadcasting and Cable*, 20 April 2006. http://www.broadcastingcable.com/article/CA63 26694.html?display=Breaking+News.

Ehrenreich, Barbara. *The Hearts of Men: American Dreams and the Flight from Commitment*. New York: Doubleday, 1984.

Eickelman, Dale, and Jon Anderson, eds. *New Media in the Muslim World: The Emerging Public Sphere*. 2nd ed. Bloomington: Indiana University Press, 2003.

Elber, Lynn. "'West Wing' Ends Season Powerfully." *Associated Press*, 17 May 2001. http://www.westwingepguide.com/S2/Episodes/44_ TC. html.

Eliade, Mircea. *Myth and Reality*. New York: Harper & Row, 1963.

Ellis, John Tracy. *Catholic Bishops: A Memoir*. Collegeville, Minn.: Liturgical Press, 1983.

Engelhardt, Tom, and Edward Linenthal. *History Wars: The* Enola Gay *and Other Battles of the American Past*. New York: Henry Holt, 2001.

Everwood: The Complete First Season. Warner, 2004.

Fax, Julie Gruenbaum. "Married to It." *Los Angeles Jewish Journal*, 19 December 2003.

Ferraro, Thomas J. *Feeling Italian: The Art of Ethnicity in America*. New York: New York University Press, 2005.

Fields, Kathleen Riley. "Bishop Fulton J. Sheen: An American Catholic Response to the Twentieth Century." Ph.D. diss., University of Notre Dame, 1988.

Finnegan, William. *Cold New World: Growing Up in Harder Country*. New York: Modern Library Edition, 1999.

Fisher, James T. "Catholicism as American Popular Culture." In *American Catholics, American Culture: Tradition and Resistance*. Vol. 2: *American Catholics in the Public Square*, edited by Margaret O'Brien Steinfels, 101–11. Lanham, Md.: Rowman & Littlefield, 2004.

Fishman, Sylvia Barack. *Double or Nothing: Jewish Families and Mixed Marriage*. Hanover, N.H.: Brandeis University Press, 2004.

Flynn, Gillian. "TV: Best and Worst." *Entertainment Weekly*, 17 December 2004.

Fontana, Tom. "Down's Syndrome." *St. Elsewhere*. Aired 16 November 1984. Screenplay. http://www.tomfontana.com/scripts/.

———. "An Evening with Tom Fontana." Makor Center, New York, 26 September 2005.

———. Interview with Alex Epstein (Crafty TV). Blog post. Complications Ensue, 6 June 2006. http://complicationsensue.blogspot. com/2006/06/tom-fontana-part-six.html.

———. Telephone interview with Elijah Siegler. 8 March 2007.

Ford, James E. "*Battlestar Galactica* and Mormon Theology." *Journal of Popular Culture* (Fall 1983): 83–87.

Foucault, Michel. *Discipline and Punish: The Birth of the Prison*. Translated by Alan Sheridan. New York: Random House, 1977.

———. *The History of Sexuality: An Introduction*. Vol. 1. New York: Vintage, 1980.

Fox, Matthew. Interview. *Honolulu Star-Bulletin*, 22 August 2005.

Frankenberg, Ruth, ed. *Displacing Whiteness: Essays in Social and Cultural Criticism*. Durham: Duke University Press, 1998.

Frankenberg, Ruth. *White Women, Race Matters: The Social Construction of Whiteness.* Minneapolis: University of Minnesota Press, 1993.

Franklin, Nancy. "Dead in the Water." On Television. *New Yorker,* 25 June 2007. http://www.newyorker.com/arts/critics/television/20 07/06/25/070625crte_television_franklin.

Gabler, Neal. *Life the Movie: How Entertainment Conquered Reality.* New York: Alfred A. Knopf, 1998.

Gahr, Evan. "Religion on TV Doesn't Have a Prayer." *American Enterprise* 8 (1997): 58–59.

Gartner, Tzvi. "Problems of a Forced Get." *Journal of Halakhah and Contemporary Society* 9 (1985): 118–142.

Giggie, John, and Diane Winston, eds. *Faith in the Market: Religion and the Rise of Urban Commercial Culture.* New Brunswick, N.J.: Rutgers University Press, 2002.

Gildemeister, Christopher. *Faith in a Box: Entertainment Television and Religion 2005–2006.* Parents' Television Council, 2006. http://www. parentstv.org/PTC/publications/reports/religionstudy06/main. asp.

Gillman, Neil. *Sacred Fragments: Recovering Theology for the Modern Jew.* Philadelphia: Jewish Publication Society, 1990.

Gilmore, Ruth Wilson. *Golden Gulag: Prisons, Surplus, Crisis, and Opposition in Globalizing California.* Berkeley: University of California Press, 2007.

Gitlin, T. *Media Unlimited: How the Torrent of Images and Sounds Overwhelms Our Lives.* New York: Metropolitan, 2001.

Gladstone, Brooke. "God No!" On the Media, National Public Radio, 15 December 2006. http://www.onthemedia.org/transcripts/2006/ 12/15/01.

Godzilla. Directed by Roland Emmerich. New York: TriStar Pictures, 1998.

Goldberg, J. J. *Jewish Power: Inside the American Jewish Establishment.* Reading, Mass.: Addison-Wesley, 1996.

Goldman, Eric. "IGN Exclusive Interview: *The Wire's* David Simon," 27 October 2006. http://tv.ign.com/articles/742/742350p1.html.

Gompertz, Ron. *Chrismukkah: Everything You Need to Know to Celebrate the Hybrid Holiday.* New York: Stewart, Tabori & Chang, 2006.

Gray, Herman. *Watching Race: Television and the Struggle for "Blackness."* Minneapolis: University of Minnesota Press, 1995.

Gray, Jonathan, Cornel Sandvoss, and C. Lee Harrington, eds. *Fandom: Identities and Communities in a Mediated World.* New York: New York University Press, 2007.

Greenberg, Karen J., and Joshua L. Dratel, eds. *The Torture Papers: The Road to Abu Ghraib.* New York: Cambridge University Press, 2005.

Greene, Richard, and Peter Vernezze, eds. The Sopranos *and Philosophy: I Kill Therefore I Am.* Peru, Ill.: Open Court, 2004.

Griffin, Cynthia E., and George H. Hill. "History of Blacks on Television." In *Blacks on Television: A Selectively Annotated Bibliography,* edited by George H. Hill and Sylvia Saverson Hill. Metuchen, N.J.: The Scarecrow Press, 1985.

Griffiths, David J. *Introduction to Quantum Mechanics.* 2nd ed. New York: Prentice Hall, 2004.

Grimes, Ronald. *Symbol and Conquest: Public Ritual and Drama in Santa Fe, New Mexico.* Ithaca: Cornell University Press, 1976.

————. "Jede Menge heiße Mädels in tollen Country-50's-Outfits." Interview with Musicbeat.de. 18 July 2004, http://www.musicbeat. de/starbeat/interviews/04/ groovecoverage.php.

Gwenllian-Jones, Sara, and Roberta E. Pearson, eds. *Cult Television.* Minneapolis: University of Minnesota Press, 2004.

Ha, Louisa, and Sylvia M. Chan-Olmstead. "Cross-Media Use in Electronic Media: The Role of Cable Television Web Sites in Cable Television Network Branding and Viewership." *Journal of Broadcasting and Electronic Media* (December 2004). http://goliath.ecnext.com/ coms2/gi_0199-3626626/Cross-media-use-in-electronic.html.

Habermas, Jürgen. "Religion in the Public Sphere." *European Journal of Philosophy* 14, no. 1 (2006): 1–25.

Hall, Barbara. Guest lecture for Religion, Media, and Hollywood, University of Southern California. http://uscmediareligion.org/ ?theClassroom.

Hall, David D., ed. *Lived Religion in America: Toward a History of Practice.* Princeton: Princeton University Press, 1997.

Hanson, Marcus Lee. "The Third Generation in America" (Originally titled "The Problem of the Third Generation Immigrant," 1938). *Commentary* 14 (1952): 495.

Harding, Susan Friend. *The Book of Jerry Falwell: Fundamentalist Language and Politics.* Princeton: Princeton University Press, 2000.

Harrington, Michael. *The Other America: Poverty in the United States.* Reprint. New York: Scribner's, 1997.

Hassett, Maurice M. "Martyr." *The Catholic Encyclopedia.* Vol. 9. New York: Robert Appleton, 1910. http://www.newadvent.org/cathen/ 09736b.htm.

Haught, Nancy. "A True Believer in The West Wing." *Atlanta Journal-Constitution,* 31 March 2001. http://b4a.healthyinterest.net/news/ archives/2001/03/a_true_believer.html.

Havrilesky, Heather. "I Like to Watch: Dreamscape Architecture." *Salon,* 24 May 2004. http://dir.salon.com/story/ent/tv/review/2004/05/ 24/i_like/index.html.

————. "The Man behind *Deadwood*." *Salon*, 5 March 2005. http://dir. salon.com/story/ent/feature/2005/03/05/milch/index.html.

————. "Must-Repent TV." *Salon*. 2005. http://dir.salon.com/story/ ent/tv/review/2005/04/13/revelations/index.html.

Heffernan, Greg. "Martin Sheen: Catholic President on Prime Time." *St. Anthony Messenger*, May 2000. http://www.americancatholic.org/ messenger/May2000/feature1.asp.

Hendershot, Heather. "Lessons from the Undead: How Film and TV Zombies Teach Us about War." *Flow: An On-line Journal of Television and Media Studies* 3, no. 10 (2006). http://flowtv.org/?p=214.

————. *Saturday Morning Censors: Television Regulation before the V-Chip*. Durham: Duke University Press, 1998.

Herr, Norman. "Television and Health." Internet Resources to Accompany the Sourcebook for Teaching Science. http://www.csun.edu/ science/health/docs/tv&health.html.

"*Heroes* Continues to Dominate Mondays with High Ratings." Variety. com, 10 October 2006.http://www.heroestheseries.com.

"*Heroes* Premiere Delivers NBC's Highest 18–49 Rating for Any Fall Drama Debut in Five Years." AZCentral.com, 26 September 2006. No longer available online.

Heroes. Season One DVD. New York: NBC Universal Television, 2007.

Hill, Michael E. "God Speaks, Viewers Watch." *The Washington Post*, 9 November 2003.

Hills, Matthew. *Fan Cultures*. London: Routledge, 2002.

Hitchens, Christopher. *God Is Not Great: How Religion Poisons Everything*. Toronto: Macmillan & Stewart, 2007.

Hoberman, J. "On the Jazz Singer." In *Entertaining America: Jews, Movies, and Broadcasting*, edited by J. Hoberman and Jeffrey Shandler. Princeton: Princeton University Press, 2003.

Hoey, Matt. "All Who Wander Are Not Lost." Written By, September 2006. http://www.wga.org/writtenby/writtenbysub.aspx?id= 2195.

Hollinger, David. *Postethnic America: Beyond Multiculturalism*. New York: Basic, 1995.

Hoover, Stewart. *Religion in the Media Age*. London: Routledge, 2006.

————. *Religion in the News: Faith and Journalism in American Public Discourse*. Thousand Oaks, Calif.: SAGE, 1998.

Hoover, Stewart, and Lynn Clark, eds. *Practicing Religion in the Age of Media: Explorations in Media, Religion, and Culture*. New York: Columbia University Press, 2002.

Hoover, Stewart, Lynn S. Clark, and D. F. Alters. *Media, Home, and Family*. New York: Routledge, 2004.

Hoover, Stewart, and Knut Lundby, eds. *Rethinking Media, Religion, and Culture*. Thousand Oaks, Calif.: SAGE, 1997.

Horsfield, Peter G. *Religious Television: The American Experience.* New York: Longman, 1984.

Houston, Marsha. "Why the Dialogues Are Difficult, or Fifteen Ways a Black Woman Knows a White Woman's Not Listening." In *Overcoming Racism and Sexism,* edited by L. A. Bell and D. Blumenfeld, 52–55. Lanham, Md.: Rowman & Littlefield, 1995.

Hunt, Darnell, ed. *Channeling Blackness: Studies on Television and Race in America.* New York: Oxford University Press, 2004.

Hussain, Amir. *Oil and Water: Two Faiths, One God.* Kelowna, B.C.: Copper House, 2006. `

———. "Reflections on Exile," *Amerasia Journal* 30, no. 3 (2005): 17–23.

Ignatiev, Noel, and John Garvey, eds. *Race Traitor.* New York: Routledge, 1996.

IMDb.com: Earth's Biggest Movie Database. Comments on *House M.D.* http://www.imdb.com/title/tt0412142/usercomments ?start=30.

———. Comments on *Revelations.* http://www.imdb.com/title/tt0403795/usercomments.

Inniss, Patrick. "Atheist Meets Angels in TV Land: Guess Who Wins?" *Secular Humanist Press* (Spring 2000). http://www.secularhumanism.org/library/aah/inniss_10_2.htm.

Ito, Mimi. "Networked Publics: An Introduction." In *Networked Publics,* edited by Kazys Varnelis, 1–14. Cambridge: MIT Press, 2008.

Iwamura, Jane. "The Oriental Monk in American Popular Culture." In *Religion and Popular Culture in America,* rev. ed., edited by Bruce David Forbes and Jeffrey Mahan, 25–43. Berkeley: University of California Press, 2005.

Jackson, B. S. "Agunah and the Problem of Authority: Directions for Future Research." *Melilah* 1 (2004): 1–78.

Jally, Sut, and Justin Lewis. *Enlightened Racism: The Cosby Show, Audiences, and the Myth of the American Dream.* Boulder: Westview, 1992.

James, Caryn. "To Get the Best View of Television, Try Using a Wide Lens." *The New York Times,* 1 October 2000, 219–29.

James, Edward. "Utopias and Anti-Utopias." In *The Cambridge Companion to Science Fiction,* edited by Edward James and Farah Mendlesohn, 228. Cambridge: Cambridge University Press, 2003.

Jansen, Wm. Hugh. "The Esoteric–Exoteric Factor in Folklore." In *The Study of Folklore,* edited by Alan Dundes, 43–51. Englewood Cliffs, N.J.: Prentice Hall, 1965.

Jenkins, Philip. *The New Anti-Catholicism: The Last Acceptable Prejudice.* New York: Oxford University Press, 2003.

Johanson, MaryAnn. "A Dan Brown Christ-mess." Review of *Revelations,* 19 May 2005. http://www.flickfilosopher.com/flickfilos/archive/2005/revelations.shtml.

Johnsen, Greg. "In Yemen, a Benevolent Alternative to Osama Bin Laden." Pacific News Service, 20 January 2004. http://news.ncmon-line.com/news/ view_article.html?article_id=be013890b8c48cf458 e54f95b8708629.

Johnson, Merri Lisa, ed. *Third-Wave Feminism and Television: Jane Puts It in a Box*. London: I. B. Tauris, 2007.

Johnson, Steve. "Why *The Wire* Is the Best Show on TV." *The Chicago Tribune*, 1 June 2003.

Jones, Jeffrey M. "Some Americans Reluctant to Vote for Mormon, 72-year-old Presidential Candidates," 20 February 2007. http:// www.gallup.com/poll/26611/Some-Americans-Reluctant-Vote-Mormon-72YearOld-Presidential-Candidates.aspx.

Josephus. *The Jewish War*. Newly Translated with Extensive Commentary and Archaeological Background Illustrations. Edited by Gaalya Cornfeld et al. Grand Rapids: Zondervan, 1982.

Joshel, Sandra R., Margaret Malamud, and Donald T. McGuire Jr., eds. *Imperial Projections: Ancient Rome in Modern Popular Culture*. Baltimore: The Johns Hopkins University Press, 2001.

Karim, Karim. *Islamic Peril: Media and Global Violence*. Updated edition. Montreal: Black Rose, 2003.

Karnick, S. J. "Must-Believe TV: Christianity Gets a Fair Shake." *National Review*, 21 December 2004. http://www.nationalreview. com/karnick/karnick200412210835.asp.

Kelts, Roland. *Japanamerica: How Japanese Pop Culture Has Invaded the U.S.* New York: Palgrave Macmillan, 2006.

Kendall, Frances E. "Understanding White Privilege." 2001a. http: // www.cwsworkshop.org/pdfs/WIWP2/4Underst_White_Priv.PDF.

———. *Understanding White Privilege: Creating Pathways to Authentic Relations across Race*. London: Routledge, 2001b.

Kermode, Frank. "Waiting for the End." In *Apocalypse Theory and the Ends of the World*, edited by Malcolm Bull, 250–63. Cambridge, Mass.: Blackwell, 1995.

Keveney, Bill. "Lost in *Lost.*" USATODAY.com, 10 May 2005. http:// www.usatoday.com/life/television/news/2006-05-09-lost_x.htm.

———. "Stars of South Asian Descent Are on the Ascent." USATODAY. com, 8 April 2007. http://www.usatoday.com/life/people/2007-04-08-south-asian-actors_N.htm.

Khuc, Mimi. Personal communication with Rudy V. Busto. 5 August 2007.

Kieval, Hillel J. "Pursuing the Golem of Prague: Jewish Culture and the Invention of a Tradition." *Modern Judaism* 17, no. 1 (1997): 1–20.

Kotkin, Joel. "The Diaspora May be Moving, But Isn't Going Away Anytime Soon." *Jewish Journal* (10 November 2006). http://www.

jewishjournal.com/articles/item/the_diaspora_may_be_moving_
but_it_isnt_going_away_any_time_soon_20061110/.

Kraemer, Ross Shepard, William Cassidy, and Susan Schwartz. *Religions of Star Trek*. Boulder: Westview, 2001.

Kristine, Diane. "After the Break: An Interview with *Prison Break* Creator Paul Scheuring." Personal blog, 4 June 2006. http://unifiedtheorynothingmuch.blogspot.com/2006/06/after-break-interview-with-prison.html.

Kronke, David. "'Lost' Souls." The Mayor of Television, 27 September 2006. http://www.insidesocal.com/tv/2006/09/lost_souls.html.

Kuntzman, Gersh. *Chrismukkah: The Official Guide to the World's Most Beloved Holiday*. Seattle: Sasquatch, 2006.

La Ganga, Maria L. "Mixing Religion and Politics." *Los Angeles Times*, 27 October 2006, E16.

Lane, Philip J. "The Existential Condition of Television Crime Drama." *Journal of Popular Culture* 34, no. 4 (2001): 137–52.

Langman, Peter F. *Jewish Issues in Multiculturalism: A Handbook for Educators and Clinicians*. Northvale, N.J.: Jason Aronson, 1999.

Laura Roslin Fanfic. http://lauraroslin.biggiantspaceship.com.

Laurel Leaves: A Laura Roslin and Lee Adama Website. http://laurelleaves.net/lauralee/index.html.

Lentz, Kirsten Marthe. "Quality versus Relevance: Feminism, Race, and the Politics of the Sign in 1970s Television." *Camera Obscura* 43 (2000): 45–93.

Leonard, John. "Ancient Histories." *New York*, 7 February 2000. http://nymag.com/nymetro/arts/tv/reviews/1927.

———. *Smoke and Mirrors*. New York: Free Press, 1997.

Lerner, Michael. *The Politics of Meaning*. New York: Unger, 1996.

Leung, Wendy. "'Excellence' Airs Memorial Day." AsianWeek.com, 25 May 2007. http://www.asianweek.com/2007/05/25 /'excellence'-airs-memorial-day.

Levine, Dan. "Daniel Dennett's Theory of Religion." *Tikkun* (November–December 2006): 51–53, 77–79.

Levine, Elana. *Wallowing in Sex: The New Sexual Culture of 1970s American Television*. Durham: Duke University Press, 2007.

Levinson, Paul. "*The Sopranos* End and the Closure-Junkies." Personal blog, 12 June 2007. http://paullevinson.blogspot.com/2007_06_01_archive.html.

Levi-Strauss, Claude. *Myth and Meaning*. New York: Schocken, 1979.

Lewis, C. S. *Mere Christianity: The Case for Christianity, Christian Behaviour and Beyond Personality*. Westwood, N.J.: Barbour, 1952.

Lichter, Linda S., S. Robert Lichter, and Stanley Rothman. *Watching America*. New York: Prentice Hall, 1991.

Limerick, Patricia. *The Legacy of Conquest: The Unbroken Past of the American West.* New York: W. W. Norton, 1987.

Lincoln, C. Eric, and Lawrence H. Mamiya. *The Black Church in the African American Experience.* Durham: Duke University Press, 1990.

Lipsitz, George. *The Possessive Investment of Whiteness: How White People Profit from Identity Politics.* Philadelphia: Temple University Press, 1998.

————. *Time Passages: Collective Memory and American Popular Culture.* Minneapolis: University of Minnesota Press, 1990.

Littleton, Cynthia. "*John from Cincinnati*: David Milch Speaks." On the Air, *Variety,* 25 August 2007. http://weblogs.variety.com/on_the_air/2007/08/john-from-cin-2.html.

Loh, Sandra Tsing. "The Unbearable Whiteness of Prime Time." *The New York Times,* 26 September 1999.

Longworth, James L. *TV Creators: Conversations with America's Top Producers of Television Drama.* Syracuse: Syracuse University Press, 2000.

Lott, Eric. *Love and Theft: Blackface Minstrelsy and the American Working Class.* New York: Oxford University Press, 1993.

Lotz, Amanda D. *Redesigning Women: Television after the Network Era.* Urbana: University of Illinois Press, 2006.

Lowry, Brian. "*The Wire.*" *Variety,* 7 September 2006.

Luhmann, Niklas. "Morality and Religion." In *Religion and Media (Culture Memory in the Present),* edited by Hent de Fries and Samuel Weber. Stanford: Stanford University Press, 2001.

Lynch, Christopher Owen. *Selling Catholicism: Bishop Sheen and the Power of Television.* Lexington: University Press of Kentucky, 1998.

MacDonald, J. Fred. *Blacks in White TV.* Chicago: Nelson-Hall, 1983.

Macintyre, Ben. "*The Sopranos*: Every Inch a Shakespearean Drama." *The Times* (London), 15 June 2007. http://www.times online.co.uk/tol/comment/columnists/ben_macintyre/arti cle1934775.ece.

Marcus, Lilit. "The 'Lost' Tribe." http://www.beliefnet.com/story/211/story_21132_1.html.

————. "Sayid: The Real Leader of *Lost.*" Idol Chatter. Beliefnet, 8 March 2007. http://blog.beliefnet.com/idolchatter/2007/03/sayid-real-leader-of-lost.html.

Martin, Joel W., and Conrad E. Ostwalt Jr., eds. *Screening the Sacred: Religion, Myth, and Ideology in Popular American Film.* Boulder: Westview, 1995.

Martinez, D. P., ed. *The Worlds of Japanese Popular Culture: Gender, Shifting Boundaries, and Global Cultures.* Cambridge: Cambridge University Press, 1998.

Marty, Debian. "White Antiracist Rhetoric as Apologia: Wendell Berry's Hidden Word." In Nakayama and Martin, *Whiteness,* 51–68.

Marx, Karl. *Das Kapital*. Gateway ed. Washington, D.C.: Regnery, 2000.

Massa, Mark. "'As If in Prayer': A Response to 'Catholicism in American Popular Culture.'" In *American Catholics, American Culture: Tradition and Resistance*, Vol. 2: *American Catholics in the Public Square*, edited by Margaret O'Brien Steinfels, 112–18. Lanham, Md.: Rowman & Littlefield, 2004.

Matos, Rafael. "La Razón y La Fe." Sermon, Bellerose Baptist Church, Bellerose, N.Y., 24 June 1984.

Mattern, Patty. "U Research Shows *Will & Grace* Lessened Prejudice toward Gay Men." *UMN* News, 17 May 2006. http://www1.umn.edu/umnnews/Feature_Stories/Will_and_Grace_.html.

Mattingly, Cheryl, Mary Lawlor, and Lanita Jacobs-Huey. "Narrating September 11: Race, Gender, and the Play of Cultural Identities." *American Anthropologist* 104 (2002): 743–53.

Mazur, Eric, and Kate McCarthy, eds. *God in the Details: American Religion in Popular Culture*. New York: Routledge, 2001.

McClain, Ellen Jaffe. *Embracing the Stranger: Intermarriage and the Future of the American Jewish Community*. New York: Basic, 1995.

McDermott, Jim. "American Dreams: *The West Wing* and *Commander in Chief*." *America* 194 (2006): 21–22.

McFarland, Melanie. "NBC's New Thriller *Revelations* Joins the Push for More Christianity on the Tube." *Seattle Post-Intelligencer*, 12 April 2005. http://seattlepi.nwsource.com/tv/ 219675_tv12.html.

McNiff, Eamon, and Cliff Cuomo. "David E. Kelley Likes Stirring the Pot." *Good Morning America*, 3 November 2006. http://abcnews.go.com/GMA/story?id=2625856&page=1.

Medved, Michael. *Hollywood versus America*. New York: Harper, 1993.

Mendes-Flohr, Paul. *German Jews: A Dual Identity*. New Haven: Yale University Press, 1999.

Milch, David. Deadwood: *Stories of the Black Hills*. Bloomsbury, N.Y.: Melcher Media, 2006.

———. Guest lecture for Religion, Media, and Hollywood, University of Southern California. http://uscmediareligion.org/?theClassroom.

Miles, Margaret R. *Carnal Knowing: Female Nakedness and Religious Meaning in the Christian West*. Boston: Beacon, 1989.

Miller, Donald, and John MacMurray. *To Own a Dragon: Growing up without a Father*. Colorado Springs: Navpress, 2006.

Miller, Lisa. "Islam in America: A Special Report." *Newsweek*, 30 July 2007.

Monroe, Chris. "*Revelations*: Personal interview with creator/writer David Seltzer ('The Omen') and Executive Producer Gavin Polone." 2005. Available online at http://www.christiananswers.net/spotlight/movies/2005/revelations2005-interview.html.

Montgomery, Kathryn. *Target: Prime Time; Advocacy Groups and the Struggle over Entertainment Television.* New York: Oxford University Press, 1989.

Moon, Dreama. "White Enculturation and Bourgeois Ideology: The Discursive Production of 'Good (White) Girls.'" In Nakayama and Martin, *Whiteness,* 177–97.

Moore, Frazier. "Hail to the Chief of 'The West Wing.'" *Associated Press,* 8 May 2000. http://www.westwingepguide.com/S1/Episodes/14_TTSD.html.

Moore, Ronald D. Guest lecture for Religion, Media, and Hollywood, University of Southern California. http://uscmediareligion.org/?theClassroom.

Moores, Shaun. *Interpreting Audiences: The Ethnography of Media Consumption.* Thousand Oaks, Calif.: SAGE, 1993.

Moreland, J. P. *Kingdom Triangle: Recover the Christian Mind, Renovate the Soul, Restore the Spirit's Power.* Grand Rapids: Zondervan, 2007.

Morgan, David. *The Lure of Images: A History of Religion and Visual Media in America.* New York: Routledge, 2007.

———. *The Sacred Gaze: Religious Visual Culture in Theory and Practice.* Berkeley: University of California Press, 2005.

Nakayama, Thomas K., and Robert L. Krizek. "White: A Strategic Rhetoric." *Quarterly Journal of Speech* 81, no. 3 (1995): 291–309.

Nakayama, Thomas K., and Judith N. Martin, eds. *Whiteness: The Communication of Social Identity.* London: SAGE, 1998.

National Cable and Telecommunications Association. "Statistics." http://www.ncta.com/Statistic/Statistic/Statistics.aspx.

National Endowment for the Arts. *The Arts and Civic Engagement: Involved in Arts, Involved in Life.* Washington, D.C.: GPO, 2007. http://www.arts.gov/pub/CivicEngagement.pdf.

Newcomb, Horace. "*Deadwood.*" In Edgerton and Jones, *The Essential HBO Reader,* 92–102.

Newcomb, Horace, ed. *Television: The Critical View.* New York: Oxford University Press, 2006.

Noonan, D. P. *The Passion of Fulton Sheen.* New York: Dodd, Mead, 1972.

Norman, Tony. "TV Review: *Wire* Carries Power." *Pittsburgh Post-Gazette,* 10 September 2006.

Nussbaum, Emily. "The Long Con." *New York,* 25 June 2007. http://nymag.com/news/features/ 33517.

Nyong'o, Tavia. "No Halvsies!" *American Quarterly* 59, no. 1 (2007): 459–66.

The O.C. The Complete First Season. Warner, 2004.

The O.C. The Complete Second Season. Warner, 2005.

The O.C. The Complete Third Season. Warner, 2006.

Ondaatje, Michael. *The English Patient.* Toronto: McClelland & Stewart, 1992.

Orsi, Robert Anthony. *The Madonna of 115th Street: Faith and Community in Italian Harlem, 1880–1950.* 2nd ed. New Haven: Yale University Press, 2002.

Ostwalt, Conrad E., Jr. "Vision of the End: Secular Apocalypse in Recent Hollywood Film." *Journal of Religion and Film* 2, no. 1 (1998). http://www.unomaha.edu/jrf/OstwaltC.htm.

Pearl, Jonathan, and Judith Pearl. *The Chosen Image: Television's Portrayal of Jewish Themes and Characters.* Jefferson, N.C.: McFarland, 1999.

Pestana, Carla Gardina. "Catholicism, Identity, and Ethics." In *A Sit Down with the Sopranos: Watching Italian-American Culture on TV's Most Talked-About Series,* edited by Regina Barreca, 129–48. New York: Palgrave, 2002.

Peters, F. E. *Muhammad and the Origins of Islam.* Albany: State University of New York Press, 1994.

Peterson, Paul C. "Religion in the *X-Files.*" *Journal of Media and Religion* 1, no. 3 (2002): 181–96.

Pew Forum on Religion and Public Life. "Muslim Americans: Middle Class and Mostly Mainstream." 22 May 2007. http://pewforum.org/surveys/muslim-american.

———. "Public Expresses Mixed Views of Islam, Mormonism." 25 September 2007. http://pewforum.org/surveys/religionviews07.

———. "U.S. Religious Landscape Survey." 2008. http://religions.pewforum.org/reports.

Phillips, Bruce. "Children of Intermarriage: How Jewish?" *Studies in Contemporary Jewry* 14 (1998): 86.

Poniewozik, James. "The Best Television 2002." Time. 2002. http://www.time.com/time/bestandworst/2002/tv.html.

Porter, Jennifer, and Darcee Mclaren, eds. Star Trek *and Sacred Ground: Explorations of* Star Trek, *Religion, and American Culture.* Albany: State University of New York Press, 2000.

Porter, Lynette, and David Lavery. *Unlocking the Meaning of* Lost: *An Unauthorized Guide.* 2nd ed. Napierville, Ill.: Sourcebooks, 2006.

Postman, Neil, and Steve Powers. *How to Watch TV News.* New York: Penguin, 1992.

Prévert, Jacques. "Pater Noster." In *Paroles.* Paris: Éditions Gallimard, 1949.

Primiano, Leonard Norman. "Vernacular Religion and the Search for Method in Religious Folklife." *Western Folklore* 54 (1995): 37–56.

———. "What Is Vernacular Catholicism? The 'Dignity' Example." *Acta Ethnographica Hungarica* 46, nos. 1–2 (2001): 51–58.

Prison Break. Season One. 20th Century Fox Entertainment, 2006.

Prison Break. Season Two. 20th Century Fox Entertainment, 2007.

Projansky, Sarah, and Kent A. Ono. "Strategic Whiteness as Cinematic Racial Politics." In Nakayama and Martin, *Whiteness,* 149–74.

Qureshi, Emran, and Michael A. Sells, eds. *The New Crusades: Constructing the Muslim Enemy.* New York: Columbia University Press, 2003.

Ramji, Rubina. "From Navy Seals to The Siege: Getting to Know the Muslim Terrorist, Hollywood Style." *Journal of Religion and Film* 9, no. 2 (2005). http://www.unomaha.edu/~jrf/Vol9No2/RamjiIslam.htm.

Rammairone, Nerina. "Redemption Island?" *TV Guide* (USA), 6 February 2006, 9.

Raphaelson, Samuel. *The Jazz Singer.* New York: Brentano's, 1925.

Reeves, Thomas C. *America's Bishop: The Life and Times of Fulton J. Sheen.* San Francisco: Encounter, 2001.

"Religion Newswriters Identify Year's Top Ten Religion Stories." *Religious Studies News,* May 2007, 11.

Rhodes, Lorna A. "Toward an Anthropology of Prisons." *Annual Review of Anthropology* 30 (2001): 65–83.

Rhodes, Richard. "Living with the Bomb." *National Geographic* 208, no. 2 (2005): 98–113.

Roberts, Adam. *Science Fiction.* New York: Routledge, 2000.

Rogin, Michael. *Blackface, White Noise: Jewish Immigrants in the Hollywood Melting Pot.* Berkeley: University of California Press, 1996.

Rosaldo, Renato. *Culture and Truth: The Remaking of Social Analysis.* Boston: Beacon, 1993.

Roseman, Janet Lynn. *Dance Was Her Religion: The Spiritual Choreography of Isadora Duncan, Ruth St. Denis, and Martha Graham.* Prescott, Ariz.: Hohm, 2004.

Rosenfeld, Sam. "Five Minutes with: David Simon." 6 November 2006. http://www.campusprogress.org/features/1273/five-minutes-with-david-simon.

Rosenthal, Michele. *American Protestants and TV in the 1950s: Responses to a New Medium.* Hampshire, UK: Palgrave Macmillan, 2007.

Roush, Matt. "While *Heroes* Rises, *24* Falls." Roush Review. *TV Guide,* 23 April 2007, 24.

Rushdie, Salman. *The Satanic Verses.* London: Penguin, 1988.

Ryan, Andrew. "Corridors of Power." *The Globe and Mail,* 16 December 2000. http://www.westwingepguide.com/S1/Episodes/14_TTSD.html.

Ryan, Maureen. "The Buddhism of 'Lost.'" *Chicago Tribune,* 16 February 2006. http://www.buddhistchannel.tv/index.php?id =12,2333,0,0,1,0.

————. "*The Sopranos* Is the Most Influential Television Drama Ever." Pop-Matters, 23 April 2007. http://www.popmatters.com/pm/features/article/32795/the-sopranos-is-the-most-influential-television-drama-ever.

Sacco, Joe. "Down! Up!" *Harper's Magazine*, April 2007, 47–62.

————. *Palestine.* Seattle: Fantagraphics, 2001.

————. *Safe Area Gorazde: The War in Eastern Bosnia 1992–1995.* Seattle: Fantagraphics, 2000.

Sacks, Jonathan. "What Is Faith?" Faith Lecture Series. 26 September 2000. The Web site of the Chief Rabbi. http://www.chiefrabbi.org/faith/faith.html.

Said, Edward. *Covering Islam: How the Media and the Experts Determine How We See the Rest of the World.* Updated edition. New York: Vintage, 1997.

Sandvoss, Cornel. *Fans: The Mirror of Consumption.* Cambridge, UK: Polity, 2005.

Scalese, Marc. "ER and Medical Dramas: Moments of Grace in the Midst of Chaos." In *Watching What We Watch: Prime-Time Television through the Lens of Faith,* edited by Walter T. Davis Jr., Teresa Blythe, Gary Drebelbis, Mark Scalese, S.J., Elizabeth Winans Winslea, and Donald L. Ashburn. Louisville, Ky.: Geneva, 2001.

Schement, Jorge Reina, ed. *Encyclopedia of Communication and Information.* New York: Gale Group, 2002.

Schneider, Susan Weidman. *Intermarriage: The Challenge of Living with Differences between Christians and Jews.* New York: Free Press, 1989.

Schroth, Raymond A. "*The West Wing*—A Liberal Catholic White House?" Review of *The West Wing. National Catholic Reporter.* 22 October 1999. http://natcath.org/NCR_Online/archives21999d/102299/102299m.htm.

Schweid, Eliezer. "Jewish Messianism: Metamorphosis of an Idea." *Jerusalem Quarterly* 36 (1985). http://www.members.tripod.com/alabasters_archive/Jewish_messianism.html (accessed 18 October 2006).

Sconce, Jeffrey. "*Star Trek*, Heaven's Gate, and Textual Transcendence." In Gwenllian-Jones and Pearson, *Cult Television,* 199–222.

Shaheen, Jack. *Reel Bad Arabs: How Hollywood Vilifies a People.* Brooklyn: Interlink, 2001.

————. *The TV Arab.* Bowling Green: Bowling Green State University Press, 1984.

Shales, Tom. "NBC's *Revelations*: It's a Long Way to Armageddon." *Washington Post,* 13 April 2005. http://www.washingtonpost.com/wp-dyn/articles/A48351-2005Apr12.html.

Shenk, Joshua Wolf. "An Old City Seeks a New Model." *The Nation,* 20 September 1999.

Shepard, Lucius. "XcreMENt." In *Projections: Science Fiction in Literature and Film*, edited by Lou Anders. Austin: MonkeyBrain, 2004.

Shields, Donald C., and C. Thomas Preston Jr. "Fantasy Theme Analysis in Competitive Rhetorical Criticism." *The National Forensic Journal* 3 (1985): 102–15.

Shome, Raka. "Outing Whiteness." *Critical Studies in Mass Communication* 17, no. 3 (2000): 366–71.

Siegler, Elijah. "God in the Box: Religion in Contemporary Television Cop Shows." In *God in the Details: American Religion in Popular Culture*, edited by Eric Mazur and Kate McCarthy, 199–216. New York: Routledge, 2001.

———. "A Television Auteur Confronts God: The Religious Imagination of Tom Fontana." Draft version. 2007.

Silverstone, Roger. *The Message of Television*. London: Heinemann Educational. 1981

Sim, Joe. "Tougher Than the Rest? Men in Prison." In *Just Boys Doing Business: Men, Masculinities, and Crime*, edited by Tim Newburn and Elizabeth A. Stanko, 100–117. New York: Routledge, 1994.

Singer, Mark. "The Misfit." *The New Yorker*, 23 February 2005.

Sinko, Joseph. Review of *Revelations*. 2005. http://www.christianan swers.net/spotlight/movies/2005/revelations2005.html.

Skill, Thomas, and James D. Robinson, John S. Lyons, David Larson. "The Portrayal of Religion and Spirituality on Fictional Network Television." *Review of Religious Research* 35 (1994): 251–67.

Skill, Thomas, and James D. Robinson. "The Image of Christian Leaders in Fictional Television Programs." *Sociology of Religion* 55 (1994): 75–84.

Sluyter, Dean. "Are You Willing to Get Lost?" *Tricycle: The Buddhist Magazine*. Repr. on Beliefnet. http://www.beliefnet.com/story/186/story_18617_1.html.

Smiley, Tavis. PBS interview with Masi Oka. 27 April 2007. http://www.pbs.org/kcet/tavissmiley/archive/200704/20070427_oka.html.

Smith, Joyce. "The Media Diary of an American Priest: Christian Ministry in Popular and News Media." Presentation given at the annual meeting of the Society for the Scientific Study of Religion, Houston, Texas, October 2000.

Smith, Wilfred Cantwell. *On Understanding Islam: Selected Studies*. The Hague: Mouton, 1981.

Sollers, Werner. *Beyond Ethnicity: Consent and Descent in American Culture*. New York: Oxford University Press, 1986.

Solomon, Jon. *The Ancient World in the Cinema*. South Brunswick, N.J.: A. S. Barnes, 1978.

Sontag, Susan. *Regarding the Pain of Others*. New York: Farrar, Straus & Giroux, 2003.

Staiger, Janet. *Blockbuster TV: Must-See Sitcoms in the Network Era*. New York: New York University Press, 2000.

Stanley, Alessandra. "One Last Family Gathering: You Eat, You Talk, It's Over." *The New York Times*, 11 June 2007. http://www.anytimes.com/2007/06/11/arts/television/11sopr.html?_r=1&oref=slogin.

Steinberg, Kerri. "Photography, Philanthropy, and the Politics of American Jewish Identity." Ph.D. diss., University of California, Los Angeles, 1995.

Steinberg, Leo. *The Sexuality of Christ in Renaissance Art and in Modern Oblivion*. Chicago: University of Chicago Press, 1996.

Storey, John. *Cultural Studies and the Study of Popular Culture*. 2nd ed. Athens: University of Georgia Press, 2003.

"*Studio 60* and Evangelicals Unawares." Idol Chatter. Beliefnet, 6 October 2006. http://blog.beliefnet.com/idolchatter/2006/10/studio-60-and-evangelicals-unawares.html.

Suresh, Chandra. *Activating Evolution*. n.p., 1993. http://www.activatingevolution.org/book_p2.shtml.

Surnow, Joel. Interview. *TV Guide*, 26 February 2007, 11.

Survival Instinct: William Adama and Laura Roslin Fanfiction. http://mujaji.net/adamaroslin/index.php.

Suvin, Darko. *Metamorphoses of Science Fiction: On the Poetics and History of a Literary Genre*. New Haven: Yale University Press, 1979.

"Thirty Years of America's Drug War: A Chronology." PBS *Frontline*. http://www.pbs.org/wgbh/pages/frontline/shows/drugs/cron.

Thomas, Jolyon Baraka. "Shûkyô Asobi and Miyazaki Hayao's Anime." *Nova Religio: The Journal of Alternative and Emergent Religions* 10, no. 3 (2006): 73–95.

Thomas, Pierre, Jason Ryan, Jack Date, and Theresa Cook. "U.S. Prison Population at All-Time High." *ABC News*, 27 June 2007. www.abcnews.go.com/print?id=3321586.

"Tim Kring Biography." TV.com. http://www.tv.com/tim-kring/person/22510/biography.html.

Torres, Sasha, ed. *Living Color: Race and Television in the United States*. Durham: Duke University Press, 1998.

TWIZ TV.com—Free TV Scripts Database. http://www.twiztv.com.

van Dijk, Teun Andrianus. "Discourse and the Denial of Racism." *Discourse and Society* 3, no. 1 (1992): 87–118.

Viscusi, Robert. *Buried Caesars, and Other Secrets of Italian-American Writing*. State University of New York Series in Italian/American Culture. Albany: State University of New York Press, 2006.

Wallis, Jim. *God's Politics: Why the Right Gets It Wrong and the Left Doesn't Get It.* San Francisco: Harper, 2006.

"The War on Drugs Is Lost." *National Review,* 12 February 1996.

Ware, B. L., and Wil A. Linkugel. "They Spoke in Defense of Themselves: On the General Criticism of Apologia." *Quarterly Journal of Speech* 59 (1973): 273–83.

Waxman, Chaim. *America's Jews in Transition.* Philadelphia: Temple University Press, 1983.

Waxman, Sharon. "Hollywood Pleads Its Case." *Washington Post,* 7 May 2000. http://www.westwingepguide.com/S1/Episodes/14_TTSD.html.

Weber, Bruce. "Prodigal Returns, Bearing Dialogue." *The New York Times,* 4 November 2007. http://www.nytimes.com/2007/11/04/theater/04webe.html.

Weisberg, Jacob. *"The Wire* on Fire: Analyzing the Best Show on Television." Slate, 13 September 2006. http://www.slate.com/id/2149566/.

Wheeler, Brannon, ed. *Teaching Islam.* New York: Oxford University Press, 2003.

White, Robert. "New Perspectives on Media and Culture." *Communication Research Trends* 8, no. 2 (1987): 1–16.

Wiener, Julie. "Intermarriage: The Contest." *Los Angeles Jewish Journal,* 9 May 2003.

Williams, Patricia J. "My Best White Friend: Cinderella Revisited." *Callaloo* 19 (1996): 809–13.

Williams, Peter W. "Fulton J. Sheen." In *Twentieth-Century Shapers of American Popular Religion,* edited by Charles H. Lippy, 387–93. Westport, Conn.: Greenwood, 1989.

Williams, Raymond. *The Long Revolution.* London: Chatto & Windus, 1961.

———. *Television: Technology and Cultural Form.* London: Fontana, 1974. Repr. Hanover, N.H.: Wesleyan University Press, 1992. 2nd ed. London: Routledge Classics, 2003.

Wilcox, Rhonda V. *Why Buffy Matters: The Art of Buffy the Vampire Slayer.* London: I. B. Tauris Books, 2005.

Wilson, William Julius. *The Truly Disadvantaged: The Inner City, the Underclass, and Public Policy.* Chicago: University of Chicago Press, 1987.

"The Wire: Season 4." *Metacritic.* http://www.metacritic.com/tv/shows/wireseason4?q=the%20wire.

The Wire. The Complete First Season. New York: HBO Video, 2004.

The Wire. The Complete Third Season. New York: HBO Video, 2006.

Wlodarz, Joe. "Maximum Insecurity: Genre Trouble and Closet Erotics in and out of HBO's *Oz*." *Camera Obscura* 58, no. 20 (2005): 58–105.

Wolffe, John. *Great Deaths: Grieving, Religion, and Nationhood in Victorian and Edwardian Britain*. British Academy Postdoctoral Fellowship Monograph. Oxford: Oxford University Press, 2000.

Wood, Richard. *Faith in Action: Religion, Race, and Democratic Organizing in the United States* (Chicago: University of Chicago Press, 2002).

Wuthnow, Robert. *Saving America? Faith-Based Social Services and the Future of Civil Society* (Princeton: Princeton University Press, 2004).

Wyke, Maria. *Projecting the Past: Ancient Rome, Cinema, and History*. London: Routledge, 1997.

Yadin, Yigael. *Masada: Herod's Fortress and the Zealots' Last Stand*. London: Weidenfeld & Nicolson, 1966.

Yang, Jeff. *Introduction to Eastern Standard Time: A Guide to Asian Influence on American Culture from Astro Boy to Zen Buddhism*, edited by Jeff Yang, Dina Gin et al. Boston: Houghton Mifflin, 1997.

Yee, James. *For God and Country: Faith and Patriotism under Fire*. New York: Public Affairs, 2005.

Zook, Crystal Brent. *Color by Fox: The Fox Network and the Revolution on Black Television*. New York: Oxford University Press, 1999.

Contributors

S. ELIZABETH BIRD is professor of anthropology, University of South Florida, where she researches the role of the media and popular culture in everyday life and has published more than fifty articles and chapters in that area. Her books include *For Enquiring Minds: A Cultural Study of Supermarket Tabloids* (University of Tennessee Press, 1992); *Dressing in Feathers: The Construction of the Indian in American Popular Culture* (Westview, 1996), and *The Audience in Everyday Life: Living in a Media World* (Routledge, 2003), which won the International Communication Association's Outstanding Book Award in 2004.

SHEILA BRIGGS teaches religion and gender studies at the University of Southern California. She is a feminist theologian and historian of early Christian and nineteenth-century theology. Currently she is writing a book on the moral and religious themes in *Xena Warrior Princess*.

VINCENT BROOK teaches media and cultural studies at the University of Southern California; the University of California, Los Angeles; Cal-State, Los Angeles; American Jewish University; and Pierce College. He has written numerous journal articles, anthology essays, and encyclopedia entries; authored *Something Ain't Kosher Here: The Rise of the "Jewish" Sitcom* (2003); edited *You Should See Yourself: Jewish Identity in Postmodern American Culture* (2006); and is currently writing a book about Jewish émigré film directors.

RUDY V. BUSTO is associate professor of religious studies at the University of California, Santa Barbara. He studies and teaches in the areas of race and religion in the United States, with a particular emphasis on Asian/ Pacific American and Chican@/Latin@ religious traditions. He is the author of *King Tiger: The Religious Vision of Reies López Tijerina* (University of New Mexico Press, 2005).

ANTHEA D. BUTLER is assistant professor of religion at the University of Rochester. She writes on African American religious history and gender studies, and her latest book is *Women in the Church of God in Christ: Making a Sanctified World.* Her interest in TV stems from the portrayal of gender roles and sexuality on television, and she has been involved as a "talking head" and consultant for "The American Experience" on PBS and the History Channel.

LYNN SCHOFIELD CLARK is associate professor and director of the Estlow International Center for Journalism and New Media at the University of Denver. An interpretive sociologist, her first book, F*rom Angels to Aliens: Teenagers, the Media, and the Supernatural* (Oxford University Press, 2003/2005), received the National Communication Association's Best Scholarly Book Award from the ethnography division. She is co-author of *Media, Home, and Family* (Routledge, 2004); editor of *Religion, Media, and the Marketplace* (Rutgers University Press, 2007), and co-editor of *Practicing Religion in the Age of the Media* (Columbia University Press, 2002).

MARCIA ALESAN DAWKINS is currently an assistant professor of human communication at California State University, Fullerton. Dr. Dawkins' research concerns the natures of identity and argumentation as they pertain to mediated representation as well as to personal and public values. Her book manuscript, *Things Said in Passing,* is a critical analysis of real and imagined instances of "passing" in the United States from the late nineteenth through early twenty-first centuries. She lectures nationally and internationally on this and other important issues—such as the connections among identity, music, television studies, and faith. She also currently serves on the board of directors of the Dee Ervin Foundation, which works to feed underprivileged youths in Palm Desert, California. Most recently, she was nominated to the board of advisors for Sonic Vine Media Group in Los Angeles, California and serves as a writer for their monthly magazines *The Tub* and *Artist Launch.*

CRAIG DETWEILER directs the Reel Spirituality Institute at Fuller Seminary's Brehm Center. Craig's feature documentary, *Purple State of Mind,* bridges the religious and political divide in America. His book, *Into the Dark: Seeing the Sacred in the Top Films of the 21st Century* (Baker Academic, 2008), explores the highest ranked films on the Internet Movie Database (IMDb).

HEATHER HENDERSHOT is associate professor of media studies at Queens College/City University of New York and coordinator of the Film Studies Certificate Program at the CUNY graduate center. She is editor of *Cinema Journal* and author of *Saturday Morning Censors: Television Regulation before the V-Chip* and *Shaking the World for Jesus: Media and Conservative Evangelicals*. Hendershot edited the anthology *Nickelodeon Nation: The History, Politics, and Economics of America's Only TV Channel for Kids* and is currently writing a book on Cold War right-wing broadcasting.

AMIR HUSSAIN is associate professor in the department of theological studies at Loyola Marymount University in Los Angeles, where he teaches courses on world religions. His own specialty is the study of contemporary Muslim societies in North America. He is author of *Oil and Water: Two Faiths, One God* (Northstone, 2006) and *Muslims in the 21st Century* (Longman, 2008).

LANITA JACOBS-HUEY is associate professor at the University of Southern California, with joint affiliations in the department of anthropology and the department of American studies and ethnicity. She is author of *From the Kitchen to the Parlor: Language and Becoming in African American Women's Hair Care* (Oxford, 2006). Her current research examines notions of race and authenticity in African American stand-up comedy and the experiences of African American families raising children with acquired or traumatic brain injuries.

HORACE NEWCOMB holds the Lambdin Kay Chair for the Peabody Awards in the Grady College of Journalism and Mass Communication, University of Georgia. He has written frequently about entertainment television since the 1970s. He is the author of *TV: The Most Popular Art* (Anchor, 1974) and the editor of seven editions of *Television: The Critical View* (Oxford University Press, 1976–2007). He is the editor of the *Museum of Broadcast Communications Encyclopedia of Television* (Routledge, 1997, 2004).

LEONARD NORMAN PRIMIANO is associate professor and chair of the department of religious studies at Cabrini College, Radnor, Pennsylvania, where he is also co-director of the honors program. He is currently involved in ethnographic research and writing on the living membership of Father Divine's Peace Mission Movement. He is also working on a study of Catholic paper ephemera, such as popular prints and "holy cards," and their role in the everyday lives of American Catholics.

ADELE REINHARTZ is professor in the department of classics and religious studies at the University of Ottawa in Canada. Her main areas of research are the Gospel of John, early Jewish-Christian relations, feminist criticism, and, most recently, the Bible and film. She is the author of numerous articles and several books, including *Scripture on the Silver Screen* (Westminster John Knox, 2003) and *Jesus of Hollywood* (Oxford University Press, 2007).

ELIJAH SIEGLER is assistant professor in the department of religious studies at the College of Charleston, where he teaches a variety of courses, including Asian Religions in America, Religion and Film, and Religions of China and Japan. He has published a textbook titled *New Religious Movements* (Prentice Hall, 2006) and is currently working on a book about globalized Taoism.

DIANE WINSTON holds the Knight Chair in Media and Religion at the University of Southern California's Annenberg School for Communication. She teaches in the departments of journalism, communication, and religion. She is the author of *Red-Hot and Righteous: The Urban Religion of the Salvation Army* (Harvard University Press, 1999) and co-editor of *Faith in the Market: Religion and the Rise of Urban Commercial Culture* (Rutgers University Press, 2002). Her next book explores religion, the news media, and American identity.

Index

DATE DUE

16162

Moore Reading Room
KU Religious Studies Department
109 Smith Hall
Lawrence, Kansas